GORDON WRIGHT
Professor of History, Stanford University
ADVISORY EDITOR TO DODD, MEAD & COMPANY

SEARCHING FOR MODERN TIMES

Volume II: 1650-1789

Discussion Problems and Readings

SEARCHING
FOR
MODERN
TIMES

NEW YORK 1969 TORONTO

Volume II
1650-1789

Discussion Problems and Readings
Chosen and Edited by

OREST RANUM
Columbia University

Dodd, Mead & Company

ACKNOWLEDGMENTS

8, 1: Reprinted by permission of Cambridge University Press. 8, 2: Reprinted by permission of the Clarendon Press, Oxford. 8, 3: Reprinted by permission of the Cambridge University Press. 8, 4: Reprinted by permission of Johns Hopkins University Press. 8, 5: Reprinted by permission of the Clarendon Press, Oxford. 8, 6: Reprinted by permission of St. Martin's Press, Inc., Macmillan Company of Canada, and Macmillan & Co., Ltd. 9, 1: Reprinted by permission of Routledge and Kegan Paul Ltd. 9, 2: Reprinted by permission of the Clarendon Press, Oxford. 9, 3: Reprinted by permission of the Columbia University Press. 9, 4: Reprinted by permission of Harper & Row, Publishers, Incorporated. Copyright 1940 by Harper & Row Publishers, Incorporated. 9, 5: Reprinted by permission of St. Martin's Press, Inc., Macmillan & Co., Ltd. 10, 1: Reprinted by permission of Collins Brothers and of Harper & Row, Publishers, Incorporated. Copyright © 1962 by Marie Boas. 10, 2: Reprinted by permission of Routledge & Kegan Paul Ltd. 10, 3: Reprinted by permission of the University of Chicago Press. Copyright 1955 by University of Chicago Press. 10, 4: Reprinted by permission of Longmans, Green & Co., Ltd. 10, 5: Reprinted by permission of Harper & Row, Publishers, Incorporated, and by permission of Hutchinson & Co. (Publishers) Ltd. Copyright © 1965 by Stephen Toulmin and June Goodfield. 11, 1: Reprinted by permission of Johns Hopkins University Press. 11, 2: Reprinted by permission of Cambridge University Press. 11, 3: Reprinted by permission of the author and the *Economic History Review*. 11, 4: Reprinted by permission of Longmans, Green & Co., Ltd. 12, 1: Reprinted by permission of Princeton University Press. 12, 2: Reprinted by permission of George Braziller, Inc., Jonathan Cape, Ltd. and the Estate of Alfred Cobban. Copyright © 1960 by Alfred Cobban. 12, 3: Reprinted by permission of Yale University Press. Copyright © 1932 by Yale University Press. 12, 4: Reprinted by permission of Alfred A. Knopf, Inc., and the author. © Copyright 1966 by Peter Gay. 13, 1: Reprinted by permission of the author and of the *Past and Present Society* from *Past and Present*, "The French Peasantry of the Seventeenth Century," 1956. 13, 2: Copyright © 1956 by John Harold Plumb. Reprinted by permission of the publisher, Houghton Mifflin Company, and the author. 13, 3: Reprinted by permission of Harvard University Press. Copyright, 1958, by the President and Fellows of Harvard College. 13, 4: Reprinted by permission of the Harvard University Press. Copyright, 1953, by the President and Fellows of Harvard College. 13, 5: Reprinted by permission of Manchester University Press. 14, 1: Reprinted by permission of Longmans, Green & Co. and Holt, Rinehart and Winston, Inc. Copyright © 1961 by M. S. Anderson. 14, 2: Reprinted by permission of Alfred A. Knopf, Inc. Copyright 1951 by Hajo Holborn. 14, 3: Reprinted with permission of the Macmillan Company and Hamish Hamilton, Ltd. © by Lady Namier 1962. 14, 4: Reprinted by permission of Princeton University Press. 14, 5: Reprinted by permission of Methuen & Co.

Preface

THE HISTORY of Europe from the late fifteenth to the late eighteenth century appears in many good histories as a kind of common field in which to discover the decline or rise of whatever institutions, ideas, or persons the historian happens to be writing about. The tendency to see the period as a transition between the medieval era and our own has led to many brilliant interpretations of it—or I should say, of many aspects of it—for no synthesis which treats a period as transition may give it the significance which is its own, by definition. But does that not imply that the history of early modern Europe is still unwritten? To defend such a notion would be absurd. More disquieting, and also more important, is the reflection that these three centuries may not constitute a period at all.

What makes a period in history? The facts alone do not determine whether all the things going on at any given moment belong to a precisely defined period. This becomes obvious when one says that the facts themselves are not transitional. It is the historian's attempt to order those facts and determine the significance which makes some history seem to be transitional. Sometimes historical interpretations become so fixed and accepted for certain centuries that everything which transpired before and after these centuries is seen as transition, rise and decline, birth and death, or even more simply, what is new and what is old. This has certainly been true for medieval and modern history. And consequently the later centuries of Roman history and the three centuries we are discussing here have been studied most often as periods of transition. But historical inquiry is much more than the effort to weave diffuse and incoherent facts from many centuries into one grand scheme or interpretation.

To look for what is specifically medieval or modern in "early modern history" was much more fashionable among historians a half-century ago than in our own day. And though such interpretations are often very perceptive, perhaps it is our current apathy over them or our inability to make better ones which makes the recent works on "smaller," less inclusive topics such as the Reformation, the Scientific Revolution, and the Enlightenment, for example, so suggestive, indeed very useful for grasping just what happened in a narrower span of time. These new works are certainly no less significant than those covering more centuries, movements, and cultures.

By suggesting what I think is a change of emphasis or style in studying these three centuries, I do not wish to imply that the search for what is medieval or modern about history is anachronistic, or that it should be so. No, indeed. The search goes on, though less overtly now than, say, in Huizinga's or Becker's day, but I believe historians still take a stand on what is medieval or modern about the topics which fascinate them, even if they do so unconsciously.

History is something one does, like physics. It is asking questions and searching for answers. To be a mere student of it fates one to find history dull memorization or simple problem solving. These selections were made to help young historians discover the importance of European history from the Reformation to the French Revolution. To do this I have chosen to make underlying ambiguities of periodization as apparent and obvious as possible, in the belief that the search for modern times is personally engaging and stimulating to the imagination. But these parts of books were not picked out just to depict the problems of historiography. I have tried to preserve some kind of unity and balance on the topics themselves, to make the subject at hand rather than the interpretation claim the reader's attention while searching for modern times. History without a certain kind of playfulness, imagination, and style is dead. Awareness of the issues depicted in classic interpretations, discovery of new topics and questions, knowledge of the facts, and hard work make it come alive. I have striven to keep the introductions to the selections as brief as possible, preferring to let the works speak for themselves.

I have also deliberately chosen selections from works which are generally available but inconceivably purchasable by every young historian, in the fond hope that they will be sought out, at least in some cases, and read from cover to cover. Nothing makes the reading of history easier or more rewarding than the reading of more history, though studying works of art, ways of living, and literature from a period is equally important. They are sources for history, too.

I wish to thank my wife Patricia for doing the translations which needed to be done, as well as much of the typing; my mother-in-law, Mrs. James McGroder, for helping turn Xeroxed copy into something like manuscript pages; and Gregory Knox and Nicholas Fessenden who also helped with the translations.

Philip Winsor and Mrs. Genia Graves of Dodd, Mead were helpful in the production of these volumes. They, with the editorial assistance of Frank Kirk and of Mrs. Marian B. Reiner who handled the voluminous permissions correspondence, made preparing this book a pleasure and a valuable lesson in publishing.

 OREST RANUM

Contents

8

THE TRAVAILS OF CONSTITUTIONALISM

THE STRUGGLE to preserve rights, traditions, and charters of liberty is political activity which may be defined as constitutionalism. It is also a mentality, a climate of opinion, a way of looking at politics—and often at morals and religion.

Great respect for historical arguments and reverence for things old simply because they are old is the chief characteristic of the constitutionalist mentality. There may also be a nostalgia for former times, for a "golden age" when politics lacked corruption. Consequently, Utopianism or futurism in the sense of making rational plans for an ideal society remains uncongenial to anyone with a constitutionalist mentality.

Constitutionalism, however, is more than just a defense of the status quo. After all, not in every society are there rights and liberties to be defended. Can constitutionalism be said to exist in states long under dictatorship? Where are the legal precedents so dear to the Constitutionalists to be found? In the Magna Carta and the Bill of Rights? Without the rule of law there can be no constitutionalism, at least as it is understood in Western Europe.

In the High Middle Ages constitutionalism was the predominant political mentality of Europe. With their eyes fixed on the thick carpet of rights, privileges, and customs which lay over Europe from the tenth century on, medieval guildsmen, nobles, monarchs, and peasants conceived of politics as a struggle to preserve rights, either inherited or God-given.

Absolutism, particularly in its seventeenth-century form, developed into a strong ideology opposed to this early constitutionalist environment. First the Papacy, then princes and monarchs claimed that by conquest and divine sanction monarchy was the source of law for mankind; as such the monarch stood above the law of men, bound only by the natural law of God. As an ideology, therefore, absolutism provided a basis for undermining the carpet of privileges and liberties, either individualist or corporate, which limited royal power. Representative institutions such as the Cortes in Spain, Parliament in England, or the Estates, town councils, guilds, and ecclesiastical assemblies in other European countries, either had to bend to the king's will or defend the privileges inherited from medieval times. Philosophers, poets, lawyers, and theologians wrote defenses of both positions, while judges, chancellors, and finally generals and soldiers ultimately decided which position would triumph.

By about 1689 the violence, caused in part but not completely by this ideological struggle between Absolutists and Constitutionalists, was mostly over. The positions of each had evolved in different parts of Europe according to traditions of law and religion, but generally speaking the Roman Catholic countries remained Absolutist, while those predominantly Protestant, with some exceptions, had governments which placed law and custom above royal power. In the Danubian Monarchy (Austria), Spain, France, Naples, and the Papal States monarchy triumphed; while in the United Provinces, England, Venice, and Switzerland, the Constitutionalists either survived or won. Only in Germany and Sweden did monarchy mix with Protestantism. Total victory for either side never came about in any country. Louis XIV had the Parlement of Paris to limit his power, and the English Parliament found that William III's power remained necessarily very great with respect to military affairs and diplomacy.

Constitutions, rights written down and given theoretical underpinnings with arguments from history and natural law, grew out of this constitutionalist mentality and its victory in the Protestant countries. What, then, is the relationship between what started out as defense of ancient liberties and the constitutionalism of the modern world? To put it another way, when does the English Parliament become modern: 1640, 1689, 1762, or at some still later date? Is this type of question valuable as a means for discerning changes in institutions? J. L. Motley so revered constitutionalism that he believed modern democratic government to be indebted to the defeat of the Spanish by the Dutch. This, of course, presupposes that without the Dutch experience and victory behind them, the English Constitutionalists would not have had the power to survive Charles I's attack on English liberties. Beneath this level of "if" history, however, lies the deeper question of the extent to which moral, political, and religious traditions bind the lives of succeeding generations. Constitutionalists, medieval and modern, assert that we are bound by history. Do these selections on English, Dutch, and German history tend to support their assertion?

1.

Some English judges, antiquarians, and members of Parliament in the seventeenth century earnestly believed that the Norman Conquest of 1066 had introduced tyranny into England. Had not the Conquest, they asserted, permitted the English kings (really Norman dukes) to rule as conquerors on the principle that might makes right? Had they not disregarded customary law?

From these assertions it was only a short jump to an attack upon James I and Charles I as heirs of this "Norman Tyranny." James I lectured his subjects that the king was above the law, that he, bound only by the natural laws of God, could ignore customary privileges in the name of wisdom and better justice. Thus, almost from the beginning of James's reign, constitutional questions were at the very heart of the clashes between Crown and Parliament.

J. G. A. Pocock (1924–), Professor of History at Washington University, St. Louis, examines the arguments of those who defended customary law. If Coke and his followers viewed law as already "made," what was the lawmaker's task? What was the seventeenth-century English conception of society before the Norman Conquest? Was it akin to a state of nature? Is it, in your opinion, correct to characterize a collection of ancient laws as a constitution?

J. G. A. POCOCK: The Common-law Mind*

As a key to their past the English knew of one law alone. It was possible for them to believe that, as far back as their history extended, the common law of the king's courts was the only system of law which had grown up and been of force within the realm; for the records and histories of England did not reveal that any other law had been of comparable importance. The common law was and had been the only law by which land was held and criminals deprived of life by their country, and by which consequently the greater part of men's secular rights and obligations were determined. Civil and canon law and law merchant could be regarded, especially after the Reformation, as systems borrowed from abroad and confined within limits by the common law; and, most significant of all, there were no *pays de droit écrit* in which civil law governed the main fabric of social life. Except in Ireland, Celtic law was forgotten, and local customs, like those of Kent, survived only because the king's courts recognized them. The English need not think, as the French must, that a different system of law existed alongside their ancient native custom, one which had a different origin, had been introduced into the land at a different time and had grown up along different lines. Once the French began to think historically of their written law, they were bound to make some extension of this way of thinking to their customary law as well, and this acted as a check to any tendency they may have had to represent the whole of their law as immemorial custom. But in England it was precisely this tendency which ran riot. The English supposed that the common law was the only law their land had ever known, and this by itself encouraged them to interpret the past as if it had been governed by the law of their own day; but in addition the fact that the common law was a customary law, and that lawyers defined custom in a way which heavily emphasized its immemorial character, made even more radical the English tendency to read existing law into the remote past. An inclination to do this, to interpret the past according to the ideas and institutions of the present, is probably common to all societies aware of their history; it can never be absolutely expunged from historical thought, and there have been times in the history of historiography when it has been altogether dominant. But the historical thought of seventeenth-century England is not merely an example of a universal tendency; it acquired much of its special character and its power over the English mind from the presence and nature of that uniquely English institution, the common law.

The interpretation which the English of this period made of their legal, constitutional and, consequently, national history was accordingly one which arose within the schools of the common law, spreading from them to become the general belief of the gentry they did so much to educate. As we shall see, some of its assumptions are also the basic assumptions of the common law, and there is a sense in which it is as old as that law or older. But deeply rooted though it was in medieval thought, for its formulation in the version which was to domi-

* From J. G. A. Pocock, *The Ancient Constitution and the Feudal Law* (Cambridge: Cambridge University Press, 1957), pp. 30–55.

nate the seventeenth century we should no doubt look to that recrudescence of inns-of-court and parliamentary activity, intellectual as well as practical, which marks the later Tudor period. It received its classic formulation soon after 1600 from Sir Edward Coke, who was born in 1552; but a common lawyer who was a mature man at the time of Coke's birth would not have thought quite as Coke was to do half a century later. He would have been far more aware of the civil law as a part of the English fabric, and far more open to the medieval concept of law as a thing universal, more important in its universal characteristics than in its local and municipal manifestations. His mind would probably have been less insular than Coke's, less massively convinced that English law was purely English and that the only purely English law was the common law; and his interpretation of English history would have differed accordingly. Between 1550 and 1600 there occurred a great hardening and consolidation of common-law thought, whether this arose as the common law sought to defend itself against aggressive conciliar rivals, or whether the effect of Tudor centralization was to deliver it from more rivals than it created and actually make it easier for it to regard itself as the sole and supreme system of law in England. Coke's thought does not read like that of a man on the defensive; he does not insist or argue that the common law is the only system that has ever prevailed in England, but takes it as much for granted as the air he breathes; and the assumption seems to be made no less instinctively by the other lawyers of his generation and by most of the royalists and parliamentarians of the mid-century. It is hard to believe that the common-law interpretation of history was consciously and polemically constructed; it is much easier to see it as the result of deep-seated and unconscious habits of mind; but a detailed study of Tudor common-law thought would be necessary to show how and when it came into being. All that will be attempted here is an analysis of the assumptions on which it was founded and built up in the reign of James I.

In the first decade of the new century, then, English lawyers were prepared to define common law as custom and to defend custom against written law in language which recalls certain French ideas of an earlier generation. Whether this was done as a direct reaction to the humanist and civilian criticisms described by Maitland, neither he nor Holdsworth has perhaps made absolutely clear; but whatever the cause, Sir John Davies, then Attorney-General for Ireland, in dedicating his *Irish Reports* to Lord Chancellor Ellesmere in the year 1612, stated the case for common law and custom in prose of admirable clarity, which reveals some degree of unconscious kinship with the ideas of *Anti-Tribonian*.

For the *Common Law of England* is nothing else but the *Common Custome* of the Realm: and a Custome which hath obtained the force of a Law is always said to be *Jus non scriptum:* for it cannot be made or created either by Charter, or by Parliament, which are Acts reduced to writing, and are alwaies matter of Record; but being onely matter of fact, and consisting in use and practice, it can be recorded and registered no-where but in the memory of the people.

For a Custome taketh beginning and groweth to perfection in this manner: When a reasonable act once done is found to be good and beneficiall to the people, and agreeable to their nature and disposition, then do they use it and practise it again and again, and so by often iteration and multiplication of the act it becometh a *Custome;* and being continued without interruption time out of mind, it obtaineth the force of a *Law.*

And this *Customary Law* is the most perfect and most excellent, and without comparison the best, to make and preserve a Commonwealth. For the *written Laws* which are made either by the Edicts of Princes, or by Councils of Estates, are imposed upon the Subject before any Triall or Probation made, whether the same be fit and agreeable to the nature and disposition of the people, or whether they will breed any inconvenience or no. But a *Custome* doth never become a Law to bind the people, untill it hath been tried and approved time out of mind, during all which time there did thereby arise no inconvenience: for if it had been found inconvenient at any time, it had been used no longer, but had been interrupted, and consequently it had lost the virtue and force of a Law.

Fortescue had long ago written that the laws of England must be the best in the world, because they were certainly the most ancient—older than those of Rome or Venice—and from the Romans to the Normans the rulers of the land had had ample opportunity to change them if they had not seen that they were good. But his words, important as they are in the English cult of the law's antiquity, do not of themselves imply Davies's elaborate argument from the nature of custom, which has much in common with the sixteenth-century revolt against written law. Hotman had laid it down that law must be appropriate to the nature and circumstances of the people, and had hinted that the essential character of custom was such that it must satisfy this requirement. Davies made this explicit and proceeded to praise English customary law:

so framed and fitted to the nature and disposition of this people, as we may properly say it is connatural to the Nation, so as it cannot possibly be ruled by any other Law. This Law therefore doth demonstrate the strength of wit and reason and self-sufficiency which hath been always in the People of this Land, which have made their own Laws out of their wisedome and experience, (like a silk-worm that formeth all her web out of her self onely) not begging or borrowing a form of a Commonweal, either from *Rome* or from *Greece,* as all other Nations of *Europe* have done; but having sufficient provision of law & justice within the Land, have no need *Justitiam & judicium ab alienigenis emendicare,* as King *John* wrote most nobly to Pope *Innocent* the Third. . . .

And—just as Hotman had revealed his pleasure in the unclassical terminology of French customary law—Davies wrote a defence of law French, admitting that it was a wholly artificial language which had never been spoken outside the English courts, but arguing that centuries of use had invested its words with meanings so exactly appropriate to the legal terms and ideas they were expected to convey that it could not possibly be replaced by any other language without serious loss to the law's intelligibility. The implication was that usage had made it more perfect than any mode of expression which the individual intelligence could devise. An idealization of custom was developing which would exalt its wisdom above that of the individual. The laws enacted by prince or parliament may grow obsolete, but custom must always be perfectly up-to-date, since if it had proved inadequate to the problems of the present age the people would simply have abandoned it. On the other hand, the fact that they have retained it shows that it has confronted and solved more problems over the centuries than the present age can hope to imagine. Written laws contain no more than the wisdom of one man or one generation, whereas custom in its infinite complexity contains the wisdom of many generations, who have tested it by experience, submitting it to a multitude of demands, and by retaining it have shown that it has proved equal to them all. Custom therefore embodies a wisdom greater even than the wisdom of parliament, for, says Davies, it has often happened that a statute has altered some fundamental rule of the common law and bred thereby such a multitude of inconveniences that it has had to be repealed. Last of all, custom is purely native: that the people are ruled by customary law is proof that they have evolved their own law "out of their wisedome and experience" and disdained foreign borrowings, which—as well as being open to the reproaches which may be directed against any merely enacted law—would be derogatory to the people's glory and self-sufficiency.

All these arguments, including the defence of law French, are to be met with in Coke; the preface to his *Fourth Reports,* for instance, lists many statutes which have injudiciously altered the common law and been repealed in consequence. Coke's emphasis is less upon custom, in the pure sense in which Davies uses the word, than upon the activity of the judges in constantly refining the law, declaring its principles with even greater precision and renewing it by application to the matter in hand. But the idea of judge-made law is only a sophistication and extension of the idea of custom. The law which the judges declare is unwritten and immemorial, and Coke praises it for precisely the same reasons as Davies. It embodies the wisdom of generations, as a result not of philosophical reflexion but of the accumulations and refinements of experience. This is Coke's famous concept of "artificial reason"; what speaks through the judge is the distilled knowledge of many generations of men, each decision based on the experience of those before and tested by the experience of those after, and it is wiser than any individual—even James I—can possibly be. In his much quoted burst of eloquence upon *Calvin's Case,* Coke declared:

we are but of yesterday, (and therefore had need of the wisdom of those that were before us) and had been ignorant (if we had not received light and knowledge from our forefathers) and our days upon the earth are but as a shadow in respect of the old ancient days and times past, wherein the laws have been by the wisdom of the most excellent men, in many successions of ages, by long and continual experience, (the trial of light and truth) fined and refined, which no one man, (being of so short a time) albeit he had in his head the wisdom of all the men in the world, in any one age could ever have effected or attained unto. And therefore it is *optima regula, qua nulla est verior aut firmior in jure, neminem oportet esse sapientiorem legibus:* no man ought to take it on himself to be wiser than the laws.

As will appear further when we study the thought of Sir Matthew Hale, this concept of law is essentially Burkean. There is a process by which society constantly adapts its institutions to the dictates of new situations. Institutions which have survived this process for a long time must be presumed to have solved innumerably more problems than the men of the present age can imagine, and experience indeed shows that the efforts of the living, even mustering their best wisdom for the purpose, to alter such institutions in the way that seems best to their own intelligence, have usually done more harm than good. The wisdom which they embody has accumulated to such a degree that no reflecting individual can in his lifetime come to the end of it, no matter how he calls philosophy and theoretical reason to his aid. These propositions may all be found in the writings of Coke, Davies and Hale, as well as in those of Burke. In the three former they depend unmistakably on the notion of custom, and if Burke owed any debt at all to preceding generations, the foundations of his thought were laid at the end of the sixteenth century, when the common lawyers learned to define their law as custom in opposition to written law.

But in saying this we come upon a paradox. If the idea that law is custom implies anything, it is that law is in constant change and adaptation, altered to meet each new experience in the life of the people; and it might seem that there was no theory more likely to lead to a historical conception of the nature of law. Yet the fact is that the common lawyers, holding that law was custom, came to believe that the common law, and with it the constitution, had always been exactly what they were now, that they were immemorial: not merely that they were very old, or that they were the work of remote and mythical legislators, but that they were immemorial in the precise legal sense of dating from time beyond memory—beyond, in this case, the earliest historical record that could be found. This is the doctrine or myth of the ancient constitution, which bulked so large in the political thought of the seventeenth century and furnishes this book with half its title. The present chapter and the next are devoted to studying the assumptions and the limitations of thought on which it was based.

The clue to the paradox lies in the fact that the concept of custom is ambiguous; Selden was never more suggestive than when he called the common law the English Janus. We may regard it as that which is in constant adaptation, and to do so will give rise to ideas that are unmistakably historical. But it is equally possible to regard it as that which has been retained throughout the centuries and derives its authority from its having survived unchanged all changes of circumstances; and once we begin to think of custom as unchanging, we must remember that it is also immemorial, for if it were known to be the work of some founder it would be written or statute law and not custom at all. The political thought of the age underlined this point heavily. The Middle Ages, often seeing no essential difference between written law and custom, had spoken quite happily of kings who ordained new customs and of the two or three lifetimes which qualified a law to be considered immemorial. But by Coke's time the increasing activity of a nearly sovereign monarchy had made it seem to most common lawyers that if a right was to be rooted in custom and rendered independent of the sovereign's interference it must be shown to be immemorial in the full sense of "traceable to no original act of foundation." The idea of the immemorial therefore took on an absolute colouring, which is one of the key facts in Stuart historico-political thought. It ceased to be a convenient fiction and was heatedly asserted as literal historical truth; and the more that came to be known about remote ages, the more vigorously it was insisted that the law was before Abraham.

The common law was by definition immemorial custom. For hundreds of years before Coke and Davies it had been accepted, by an assumption common in medieval thought, that English law was *jus non scriptum* and that the function of the courts was to declare the ancient custom of the realm. Even statutes could be so interpreted, and Coke eagerly takes at least the earliest of them to be declaratory judgments. Innumerable decisions were consequently on record as declaring that everything which they contained, down to the most minute and complex technicality, had formed part of the custom of England from time out of mind; or at least so the common lawyers read them to mean, and this fact is at the root of their interpretation of history. They took everything in the records of the common law to be immemorial, and they treated every piece of evidence in those records as a declaration of what was already immemorial; so that the beginning of the records of the king's courts in the twelfth century was proof, not that those courts began at that time, but of their great antiquity, and it was usual and—given the presumptions—logical to add that if the earlier records had not been lost or stolen, they would prove the existence of the courts in times earlier still. But at however remote a date the series of records had begun, the common-law mind would still have taken their beginning as proof that at that time the laws were already immemorial; since *jus non scriptum* must by definition be older than the oldest written records.

The belief in the ancient constitution therefore rested on assumptions which were fundamental to the practice of the common law, and it had very great influence in a society whose political and social thinking were so largely dominated by this one law. It cannot therefore be regarded as the creation of any single mind. But Coke did more than any other man to summarize it and make it authoritative; at the same time he reveals the patterns of thought on which it was based with the clarity of truly representative genius. His historical thought could be described as founded on the presumption that any legal judgment declaring a right immemorial is perfectly valid as a statement of history. Thus in the preface to the *Third Reports*—his first published exposition of the view that the law was immemorial and the *locus classicus* of his methods of historical reconstruction—he selects a case from the books of assize of 26 Edw. III:

it appeareth that in a writ of assise the Abbot of B[ury] claimed to have conusance of pleas and writs of assise, and other original writs out of the King's courts by prescription, time out of mind of man, in the times of St Edmund, and St Edward the Confessor, Kings of this realm before the Conquest, and shewed divers allowances thereof, and that King H.I. confirmed their usages, and that they should have conusance of pleas, so that the Justices of the one bench, or the other should not intermeddle; out of which record (being now above three hundred years past) it appeareth that the predecessors of that Abbot had time out of mind of man in those Kings' reigns, (that is whereof no man knew the contrary either out of his own memory, or by any record or other proof,) writs of assise, and other original writs out of the King's Courts.

The fact—often paralleled—that a fourteenth-century abbot had alleged that he had precedents from pre-Conquest times, should remind us of the extreme antiquity and universality of this way of pleading and thinking in English society. Coke and his contemporaries were indeed only continuing and developing a habit of mind as old as the common law itself; but now he goes on, in a way too full of antiquarian learning to be simply a continuation of medieval thought, to argue that since writs of assize have been proved immemorial and older than the Conquest, so too must be sheriffs, because the writs are directed to them; trials by the oaths of twelve men, since the writs instruct the sheriff to conduct them; the king's courts, since the writs are returnable into them; the court of chancery, since it issues the writs; and the entire science and practice of the common law, since, as Fitzherbert points out, the procedure to be followed when writs are issued provides the fundamental rules about which it is built up. Thus a judgment that one part of the law is immemorial is first taken with historical literalness that might have surprised some of the judges, and then made the basis of an argument that the whole of the law must be of equal antiquity. Coke uses a similar technique in the preface to the *Ninth Reports,* when, having proved to his satisfaction that there were parliaments before the Conquest, he proceeds to argue that there were representatives of the commons in them.

It is evident that there were tenants in ancient demesne before the Conquest; and for a certainty therein, and to know of what manors such tenants did hold, it appears by the book of Domesday, that all the tenants that did hold of any of those manors that were in the hands of King Edward, the son of King Ethelred, or of King William the Conqueror, were tenants in ancient demesne. And these tenants then had, and yet have these privileges amongst others, for that they were bound by their tenure to plow and husband, etc. the King's demesnes before and in the Conqueror's time, and therefore they were not to be returned Burgesses to serve in Parliament, to the end they might attend the King's husbandry the better.
2. They were not to be contributory to the fees to the Knights of Shires that served in Parliament: which privileges (though the cause ceaseth,) continue to this day: therefore there were Parliaments unto which the Knights and Burgesses were summoned both before and in the reign of the Conqueror.

Here it is matter of record, rather than an actual judgment, on which the case is built up; but the procedure is exactly the same. The presence of tenants in ancient demesne in Domesday Book is taken to mean that they existed before the Conquest (and therefore from time out of mind); and their exemption from parliamentary attendance at a later date still is taken to prove the existence of a parliament with commons, both at the time of Domesday and before. The fact that Coke allows the unwary reader to assume that the parliamentary exemption is in Domesday is probably not proof of disingenuousness; he would simply take it for granted that what was mentioned at a later date must have been present at an earlier.
In the preface to the *Third Reports* Coke follows up the passage already cited with further proof of the law's antiquity, drawn from early British history as it was then understood. Brutus of Troy, he said, the first king of Britain, was

reputed to have drawn up a book of laws; so had King Dunwallo Molmutius, Mercia the queen of King Gwintelin, Sigebert of East Anglia, Alfred, Edward the Elder and reputedly many others, so that there had been at least seven books of the law (two of them Dunwallo's) before the Conquest. It is of importance to the understanding of this subject to note that it was not Coke's belief in fabulous kings out of Geoffrey of Monmouth which was primarily responsible for his belief in the antiquity of the law. He had his doubts about Brutus—"I will not examine these things in a quo warranto; the ground thereof I think was best known to the authors and writers of them"—and his interpretation of the past was soon to survive unscathed the disappearance of the legendary Trojan and British kings from the stage of serious history. His references to Brutus and Dunwallo occupy second place after the proof of the law's antiquity founded on legal, not historical sources. Coke not only accepts a legal judgment dating a law from time out of mind as historically valid, but he regards such statements as better historical evidence than those made by chroniclers. Where the courts have adjudged an institution immemorial and a historian alleges that it was set up in such a king's reign, Coke leaves little doubt that we are to think the historian wrong, and he urges the historiographers of his own day to consult a lawyer before making any statement about the history of the law. He was not relying upon legendary histories, but using them to illustrate a proof that the law was immemorial which he drew from the thought of the law courts; and conversely, he was not seeking to derive the law from any mythical founder. When, with the aid of the *Mirror of Justices,* he had traced parliament back to the reign of King Arthur, he added: "Not that this court and the rest were instituted then, but that the reach of his [Horn's] treatise extendeth no higher than to write of the laws and usages of this realm continued since the reign of that king." In the same way Davies had written:

Neither could any one man ever vaunt, that, like *Minos, Solon,* or *Lycurgus,* he was the first *Lawgiver* to our Nation: for neither did the King make his own *Prerogative,* nor the Judges make the *Rules* or *Maximes* of the Law, nor the common subject prescribe and limit the *Liberties* which he injoyeth by the Law. But, as it is said of every Art or Science which is brought to perfection, *Per varios usus Artem experientia fecit;* so may it properly be said of our Law, *Per varios usus Legem experientia fecit.* Long experience, and many trials of what was best for the common good, did make the *Common Law.*

The law was immemorial and there had been no legislator. In this respect at least common-law thought was independent of fashionable classical models. Its eyes were turned inward, upon the past of its own nation which it saw as making its own laws, untouched by foreign influences, in a process without a beginning.

But if neither a putative Trojan nor a putative Arthurian origin was of much importance in this interpretation of legal history, there was one event in the English past over which the common lawyers expended floods of ink and burned much midnight oil. This was the Norman Conquest, the one great apparent breach in the continuity of the nation's history. The motives which spurred them to their unending denials that this event had caused any change in the essential character of the law were various: sheer patriotism furnished one, and Polydore Vergil, that gadfly of the older English historiography, another with his gibes at a law derived from the semi-barbarous Normans and still uttered in their jargon; while, as we shall see, once the interpretation of history became involved in the struggle of king and parliament, a powerful political motive was added to the others. But from whatever point of view it was regarded, the idea that William I had carried out a systematic importation of new law cut right across the belief in custom and the immemorial that was coming to be an integral part of English political thought, and the common lawyers set out to deny it with all the resources of their learning and ingenuity. With Coke the argument that the courts, parliament or the law are immemorial often seems to be identical with the argument that they are pre-Conquest. Once over that stumbling-block, the rest may be taken for granted; and all the subtleties of the common-law technique of reading history backwards are called into play.

But Coke's endeavours were powerfully abetted by the conduct of the Normans themselves. While the main features of common-law historiography must be deduced from habits of mind peculiar to that profession, it remains true that the feeling that all rule must be by ancient law was one of the deepest-seated preconceptions of the medieval mind. It had seemed of scarcely less importance to the Normans than it did to Coke himself to maintain that they governed England according to the *laga Edwardi,* and throughout the twelfth and thirteenth centuries a succession of political programmes had been expressed, by claimants to the throne or dissident barons, in the form of promises or demands to restore the good old law of Edward the Confessor. The story that among the Conqueror's first acts had been to codify and confirm the Confessor's law had found its way into most of the chroniclers; and not only this, but several ingenious and quite possibly sincere men had in and after the twelfth century sat down to supply the absence of any text of this law or the Conqueror's by composing the apocryphal *leges Edwardi Confessoris, Willielmi, Henrici Primi,* the chronicle of "Ingulf of Croyland" (supposed to be an eye-witness of the confirmation), and so on. The edifice had been completed by the insertion in the coronation oath—where it remained until 1688—of a promise to observe the laws of St. Edward. When the common lawyers began to write their histories, therefore, the belief that the laws of the last Anglo-Saxon king had been confirmed by the Conqueror and his Norman and Angevin successors had long been orthodox history, though the reprehensible Polydore had as usual expressed some doubts. Furthermore, William Lambarde had in his *Archaionomia* (1568)—one of the key books of the common-law interpretation—published the apocryphal *leges* in unbroken series with such genuine texts of Anglo-Saxon law as he had been able to collect. Coke, and nearly all other historians, accepted them at their own valuation; and as the authors of the *leges Confessoris* and the *leges Willielmi* (which were supposed to represent the Anglo-Saxon laws as amended by the Conqueror) had not unnaturally attributed to pre-Conquest times the feudal institutions, described in the Norman terminology of their own day and age, there was no sign in these apparently authoritative texts of any radical breach with the past at the Conquest. Coke indeed was able to make very extensive use of Lambarde's book to prove that institutions which had in fact been introduced by the Normans formed part of the immemorial law; and he employed with no less faith and frequency two other medieval apocrypha, the fourteenth-century *Modus Tenendi Parliamentum* and (with far less excuse) the lavishly fantastic *Mirror of Justices,* to attribute to the times of Alfred and Arthur the characteristic machinery of Angevin and Plantagenet monarchy. There are few pages of his *First* or *Second Institutes* on which one of these works is not cited.

The picture thus constructed of the early history of the law is summarized by Coke—speaking in this for nearly every Englishman of the seventeenth century—in the preface to the *Eighth Reports.* Explaining that he has been asked whether the chroniclers agree with him that the law is immemorial, and first carefully reminding us that the proofs drawn from the law itself stand in no need of their corroboration, Coke proceeds to narrate that William I swore to observe the ancient laws, ordered twelve men in each shire to state what they were, and summarized them, with a few emendations of his own, into a Magna Carta, the first of its kind, under the name of the "laws of King Edward." Henry I, promising at his accession to take away all evil customs, restored King Edward's laws in a purer form, and thereafter both Stephen and Henry II confirmed them anew in coronation charters. Matthew Paris says that John's charters contain little that is not in Henry II's charter or in those laws which are called King Edward's, not because the latter enacted them but because he reduced them to writing. All this, as Coke proudly points out, is extracted from medieval chroniclers; but to get its seventeenth-century flavour we have to read it in the belief that the whole apparatus of common law was immemorial. But the apocryphal *leges* and Lambarde's Anglo-Saxon dooms are not of course the common law; Coke describes them as statutes, but succeeds in some peculiar way in regarding their existence as proof of the antiquity of the unwritten law which they do not contain:

> . . . by all which it is manifest, that in effect, the very body of the common laws before the Conquest are omitted out of the fragments of such acts and ordinances as are published under the title of the Laws of King Alfred, Edward the First, Edward the Second, Ethelstane, Edward, Edgar, Etheldred, Canutus, Edward the Confessor, or of other Kings of England before the Conquest. And those few chapters of laws yet remaining, are for the most part certain acts and ordinances established by the said several Kings by assent of the Common Council of their kingdom.

The myth of the confirmations, as it may be called, culminates with Magna Carta (which Coke liked to say had been confirmed by more than thirty parliaments), and his treatment of it, both in the posthumously printed *Second Institutes* (1641) and in the Commons debates leading up to the Petition of Right, has received most attention of all his historical interpretations. It has two aspects. In the first place he links the Charter, through Stephen Langton and

Henry II, with the successive confirmations of the Confessor's law; and in the second he studies it clause by clause to prove that it enacts the main principles of common law and parliamentary liberty in his own day, so that the men of 1628 could believe that they were not only repeating the solemn act of 1215, but taking part in a recurrent drama of English history at least as old as the Conquest. This second process, by which Coke discovers the rights of parliament and property in a feudal document of the thirteenth century, was at bottom one with the greatest work of his life, the revitalization of the common law so that precedents and principles laid down by the king's courts in the attempt to govern a feudal society could be used and found apt in the freeholding and mercantile England of James I. Coke, as we shall see further in the next chapter, had no conception that in the early common law he was dealing with the law of a society organized upon feudal principles. Therefore—still on the presumption that the law declared what had been law always—he was able to identify the law of his own day with the law of the earliest records, just as he had established the doctrine that the latter contained what had been law since time out of mind before the Conquest. At this point the identification of past and present was complete, and the possibility that the idea of custom might give rise to ideas of law being in continuous development was altogether suppressed.

Such then—assuming that Coke, whose vast influence was after all partly posthumous, may be taken as a safe guide to the thought of his profession—seem to have been the main features of what may be termed the common-law interpretation of English history, the predecessor and to a large extent the parent of the more famous "Whig interpretation." It arose essentially from latent assumptions governing historical thinking, which had been planted deep in the English mind by centuries of practice of a particular form of law; but it possessed also a political aspect, the need to make a case for an "ancient constitution" against the king; and though this book is designed primarily as a study, not of the uses which were made of it in political argument, but of the historiographical conditions which made its existence possible, the former question is an inseparable part of the latter. Only a very detailed study of seventeenth-century thought could fully reveal the variety of uses to which it was put, or enable us to estimate accurately its importance as compared with other forms of political discussion. But the greatness of that importance cannot be denied. Put very briefly, what occurred was that belief in the antiquity of the common law encouraged belief in the existence of an ancient constitution, reference to which was constantly made, precedents, maxims and principles from which were constantly alleged, and which was constantly asserted to be in some way immune from the king's prerogative action; and discussion in these terms formed one of the century's chief modes of political argument. Parliamentary debates and pamphlet controversies involving the law or the constitution were almost invariably carried on either wholly or partially in terms of an appeal to the past made in this way; famous antiquaries were treated as authorities of recognized political wisdom; and nearly every thinker noted for his contribution to political theory in its usual sense—Hunton, Milton, Lilburne, Hobbes, Harrington, Filmer, Nevile, Sidney: only Locke appears to be an exception among notable writers—devoted part of his pages to discussing the antiquity of the constitution. It would be possible to construct both a history of the ways in which historical thought was used in political argument, and a study of the ways in which historical and political theory were related in the minds of the men who wrote and thought in both modes. To the typical educated Englishman of this age, it seems certain, a vitally important characteristic of the constitution was its antiquity, and to trace it in a very remote past was essential in order to establish it securely in the present. We may therefore maintain that the historical thought which lay behind this belief helped to shape the mind of the century and will consequently help us to understand it.

It must be evident in the first place that historical thinking of the kind we have seen in Coke would make it possible to claim, with sincere and entire conviction, that many of the privileges or rights which parliament, or the courts of common law under a vigorous chief justice, desired to possess in the present had been theirs in the remote past. Thought of this kind encouraged the production, from legal or chronicle sources, of evidence of action taken in very distant times, which could then be identified with contemporary conditions and claimed as a precedent. This must very largely explain the intense interest taken in the production of remote precedents during every controversy of the period before the Civil War—as for instance during the *Ship-money Case,* when evidence from the reign of Egbert was produced and examined with perfect seriousness by both sides. But it would be insufficient to explain the seventeenth-century's habit of recourse to the past merely as a search for precedents, as an eager legal antiquarianism; it was plainly much more. To claim that a precedent exists is to claim that a system of law as old as that precedent is still in force, and the arguments used in the *Ship-money Case* implied Coke's principle that the law of England was of pre-Conquest antiquity. When it was claimed that a remote precedent existed for such a right, it might very well be claimed in addition that the right was of immemorial antiquity. When Elizabeth I's parliaments began to claim rights that were in fact new, they indeed produced precedents, but they did much more. They made their claim in the form that what they desired was theirs by already existing law—the content of English law being undefined and unwritten—and it could always be claimed, in the way that we have seen, that anything which was in the existing law was immemorial. The common lawyers began to rewrite English history on parliamentary lines in the Elizabethan House of Commons—Sir John Neale comments on the process—and by the time of the Apology of 1604 the Commons were already insisting that the whole body of their privileges should be recognized as theirs by right of time immemorial. The search for precedents resulted in the building-up of a body of alleged rights and privileges that were supposed to be immemorial, and this, coupled with the general and vigorous belief that England was ruled by law and that this law was itself immemorial, resulted in turn in that most important and elusive of seventeenth-century concepts, the fundamental law. Much has been written about fundamental law by modern scholars in the light of the contrary theories of judicial review and parliamentary sovereignty, but it does not seem to have been stated in so many words that if you had asked the representative seventeenth-century Englishman the question "What is it that makes the fundamental law fundamental?" he might indeed have been embarrassed for an answer, but would probably in the end have replied: "Its antiquity, its character as the immemorial custom of England." The adjective "ancient" was used little less often than "fundamental," was frequently coupled with it and (it may be suggested) could in the majority of cases have been substituted for it without serious loss of meaning. The fundamental law or constitution was an ancient law or constitution; the concept had been built up by the search for precedents coupled with the common-law habit of mind that made it fatally easy to presume that anything which was in the common law, and which it was desired to emphasize, was immemorial.

The content of the concept differed from time to time (as also from man to man): as parliament laid claim to new powers these were represented as immemorial and included in the fundamental law, and close study would probably also reveal that as later controversies, particularly those of the mid-century, gave rise to new political ideas and principles, these also were included. It would certainly reveal that as the century progressed assertions that the law was immemorial tended to be replaced by assertions that parliament, and especially a house of commons representing the property-owners, was immemorial. One of the underlying themes in the history of seventeenth-century political thought is the trend from the claim that there is a fundamental law, with parliament as its guardian, to the claim that parliament is sovereign. Books are still being written in the attempt to decide how far this transition was carried and at what times; but it seems to be fairly well agreed that it was both incomplete and largely unrealized. Parliament claimed its increasing powers in virtue of the fundamental law; when in 1642 its claims reached such a height as to become a claim to arbitrary sovereignty, it still alleged that these were substantiated by fundamental law. The lower house's claim to be sole sovereign often took the form of a claim that it was immemorial and therefore subject to no checks. The attempt at single-chamber despotism failed, and both the Restoration and the Revolution of 1688 could be represented as efforts to restore the fundamental law, rather than to establish the sovereignty of king in parliament. The concept of fundamental law therefore did much both to cloak and to delay the transition to a full assertion of parliamentary sovereignty. Granted the importance of fundamental law, and granted also that the concept rested on Coke's concept of ancient law, we have here perhaps the true importance of common-law historical thought in the seventeenth century.

To what ultimate political principle were men appealing when they made the claim that their rights formed part of a pre-Conquest constitution? Why did they think a law's antiquity made it binding in the present? Taking Coke as representative, we have analysed the assumptions and arguments on which that claim was based, and they have been shown to rest on the basic assumption that the law declared the immemorial custom of England. It was the idea of custom which convinced men that the law was ancient; the conclusion is a tempting one that it was as custom that they thought it was still binding. Coke and still more Davies do indeed seem to have thought at bottom in just this fashion;

but does it follow that the average parliament man, barrister or pamphleteer, who made his appeal to "our ancient and fundamental laws, our ancient constitution," was knowingly and deliberately appealing to the binding force of immemorial custom, and was clear in his mind what those words meant? It seems unlikely, yet it is hard to imagine what other ultimate basis his appeal could have had. No doubt for many it was enough to declare that the laws were ancient and fundamental, without troubling to inquire why that should make them binding. Some research, it seems, might profitably be done on the place which the concept of custom occupied in seventeenth-century thought. It appears to have been far less prominent and familiar in the scholastic and academic tradition of political discourse—the political theory of the text-books —even in the schools of natural law, than it was among common lawyers. If this impression is upheld, what are we to make of it? Was there some unifying body of assumptions, or were there more ways than one to approach political problems, arising in different intellectual milieux and stressing different basic concepts? and if this was so, which was the more representative and effective in seventeenth-century England?

To ask such questions, or suggest that they might be asked, is to raise in a new form the problem of the relations between historical thought of Coke's kind and academic political theory. Was the chief justice a political thinker and, if so, in what sense? But, however such a line of inquiry might turn out, it could probably be agreed that, even if a clearly thought-out concept of custom were proved to be not specially prevalent in the seventeenth-century mind, still the concept of an ancient constitution, very prevalent indeed, rested ultimately upon the idea of custom; and that, in this sense, common-law historical thought represented a most vigorous survival of the medieval concept of custom in English political thinking. As for the men who said "this is the ancient law" without troubling to inquire on what juridical principle that law rested, they too were carrying on the tradition of many medieval minds, who lived so much surrounded by the notion of "law" that they did not find it necessary to say very clearly from what authority—other than God or nature—the law in question derived. In the common-law interpretation of history, it seems, we have a powerful stream of medieval thought flowing into the seventeenth and eighteenth centuries, its strength surviving at least until the coming of philosophical radicalism.

But the attraction which the concept of the ancient constitution possessed for lawyers and parliamentarians probably resided less in whatever ultimate principle provided its base, than in its value as a purely negative argument. For a truly immemorial constitution could not be subject to a sovereign: since a king could not be known to have founded it originally, the king now reigning could not claim to revoke rights rooted in some ancestor's will. In an age when people's minds were becoming deeply, if dimly, imbued with the fear of some sort of sovereignty or absolutism, it must have satisfied many men's minds to be able to argue that the laws of the land were so ancient as to be the product of no one's will, and to appeal to the almost universally respected doctrine that law should be above will. A later generation, we shall see, having witnessed with alarm the spectacle of a revolutionary sovereignty styling itself that of the people, and by no means anxious in consequence to derive the laws from the act of some original popular assembly, found in the ancient constitution the perfect argument for pre-Lockean Whigs; as when the Lords were told in 1688 that "the original contract between king and people" consisted in the king's undertaking to maintain laws which he certainly had not made. Once more we see how the concept of antiquity satisfied the need, still widely felt, for a rule of law which, like Magna Carta, "would have no sovereign." But it was an argument which fell far short of logical perfection. By the very vehemence with which they insisted that the laws were immemorial and not of the king's making, its champions tacitly conceded that if the laws were not immemorial they were of the king's making—since few were prepared to go to the quasi-republican length of asserting that the laws had preceded the kingly office and brought it into being—and that if they were of the king's making the reigning king was sovereign over them. These conditional propositions appear to have been accepted more or less on all sides; some few tried to find a way round them but hardly any succeeded. The notion of historical relativity—the suggestion that the law still in force might indeed have been made by a king in some high and far-off time, but in conditions so remote that neither "king" nor "law" meant what they meant at the present day, and that consequently no conclusions could be drawn as to current rights and liberties—was after all still virtually unknown. Consequently, to prove that the laws of England had originated at a time within the memory of man was to suggest the existence at that time of some human sovereign possessing the right to make law; and the heirs of that sovereign could not be denied the right to unmake all that he had made. Once men had appealed to the immemorial, the laws must be either absolutely immemorial or subject to an absolute sovereign—there seems to have been no idea of a middle way. A polemical situation could therefore arise, in which to put forward any theory as to the origin of English law at a time within recorded human history could be interpreted, and even intended, as an argument in favour of absolute monarchy. We shall see this happening in 1681. For their part, those who saw in the immemorial constitution a good argument for limiting the prerogative would sooner or later be compelled by the same logic to attribute to it an altogether fabulous antiquity, insisting that it could be traced in and before the remotest events known to contemporary historical thought, and denying, in essence, that its origins could ever be discovered by the historian.

The doctrine of antiquity was therefore most vulnerable to criticism, and some awareness of this must explain why those who believed in it were so tirelessly and monotonously insistent that the establishment of the Normans in England did not constitute a conquest. In theory, one can easily see why this should have been so. If the monarchy of England had ever been sovereign, it had been at that moment; and if Duke William, even for a single instant, had been an absolute ruler—if he had been king by *jus conquestus*—then it did not matter if he had maintained English law instead of introducing French, and it did not matter what charters and grants of liberties he had subsequently made to his new subjects; all that had been done—even to increase the sphere of freedom and law—had been done by virtue of his unfettered will, on which his grants depended and on which (transmitted to his descendants) the laws and liberties of England for ever afterwards must depend likewise. To admit a conquest was to admit an indelible stain of sovereignty upon the English constitution. A conquest was therefore not admitted in the age of Blackstone any more than in the age of Coke. William was no conqueror, said the lawyers and the antiquaries and the parliamentarians in chorus; he was a claimant to the crown under ancient law who had vindicated his claim by trial of battle with Harold, a victory which brought him no title whatever to change the laws of England. If he had done so, it was a lawless act without validity, put right within a few generations of his death by the coronation charters of his successors and by Magna Carta, which had restored and confirmed the immemorial law of the Confessor's time.

But the remarkable fact is that the contrary argument was very seldom put forward—certainly with insufficient frequency to justify the incessant refutations which appeared. A writer of 1680, William Petyt, casting about for names with which to substantiate his allegation that a conspiracy existed to establish absolute monarchy on the theoretical basis of a conqueror's right, was able to name none who had argued in this sense except "one Blackwood, a Scotchman" —and, he might have added, a good deal of a Frenchman as well—and Mr. Christopher Hill, who believes that the conquest theory was a staple argument of pre-Civil War monarchism, can add to the mention of Blackwood only some half-hearted remarks by James I and a few sentences of Laud's which appear to bear a rather different meaning. The fact seems to be that the conquest theory was no more an essential part of pro-Stuart reasoning before the Civil Wars (or indeed after them) than was absolute sovereignty. Those who supported what the Stuart kings were doing did not normally regard their ruler as a sovereign maker of law—however vigorously they might assert his prerogative—and consequently did not argue that the laws flowed from his will or that he ruled above the law as a conqueror—the two doctrines to which a theory based on historical criticism would have led. This conclusion makes it hard to explain why the opposition constantly thought it necessary to refute an argument which nobody was putting forward; but it reminds us that the belief in an immemorial law was not a party argument put forward by some clever lawyer as a means of limiting the king's prerogative: it was the nearly universal belief of Englishmen. The case for the crown was not that the king ruled as a sovereign and that there was no fundamental law, but that there was a fundamental law and that the king's prerogative formed part of it. The antiquity of the law and the denial of the Conquest are arguments scarcely less frequently or vigorously employed by crown lawyers, or at a later date by royalist pamphleteers, than by their opponents. It is too easily forgotten that there was a common-law case for the crown as well as against it, and the former case was expressed in the same language and based on the same assumptions as the latter. Consequently, the king's side was late, slow and halfhearted in developing any historical criticism of the doctrine of immemorial law. Later chapters of this book attempt to explain how they came to do so in the end; but the conclusion seems inescapable that

English historical ideas—those, that is, on the constitution and its antiquity—were not created primarily by party polemics. They were, before all else, the result of assumptions latent in the common-law mind, themselves the result of centuries of practice and experience of a purely insular form of law: the product, in short, of English history itself, reflected in the character of the country's legal structure and shaping and limiting the way in which her lawyers thought. Those who wished to change them must do more than put forward a theory of sovereignty, founded on a doctrine of conquest or on the idea that kings were older than laws; they must destroy the limitations under which English historical thinking was carried on.

2.

The constitutional arguments which divided Chief Justice Coke (1552–1634) and James I still gave English politics their character in the eighteenth century. But between Coke, the great fountain of constitutional theory, and his greatest heir, Edmund Burke (1729–97), lay a watershed, the Glorious Revolution of 1688–89. Here for once the Constitutionalists won against a monarch, James II, without having to resort to arms. The question remained: "Is the law above the king or the king above the law?" This question was decided by act of Parliament. The "fundamental liberties" of the English were guaranteed. Law itself, customary and embodied in the English people, became sovereign with the Parliament as the maker and interpreter of law.

The great Sir George Macaulay Trevelyan (1876–1962) depicted the Revolution of 1688 as the noble triumph of English liberty. In this selection he goes beyond the formal parliamentary settlements to discuss other changes which complemented the actual legislation. Trevelyan admired Parliament and, as a Whig historian, has nothing but praise for those members who engineered the Glorious Revolution; but he goes deeper than this. What kept Parliament from becoming tyrannical? It, too, might have reduced freedom. By 1700, new, often accidentally established, institutions and arrangements made the old constitutionalism the base for a workable government. Was it accidental that judges were placed "above the sphere of politics"? For Trevelyan, as for any great Whig, there is a mystery about these things.

GEORGE MACAULAY TREVELYAN: The Revolution Settlement *

The fundamental question at issue in 1688 had been this—Is the law above the King, or is the King above the law? The interest of Parliament was identified with that of the law, because, undoubtedly, Parliament could alter the law. It followed that, if law stood above the King's will, yet remained alterable by Parliament, Parliament would be the supreme power in the State.

James II attempted to make the law alterable wholesale by the King. This, if it had been permitted, must have made the King supreme over Parliament, and, in fact, a despot. The events of the winter of 1688–9 gave the victory to the opposite idea, which Chief Justice Coke and Selden had enunciated early in

* From Sir George Macaulay Trevelyan, *The English Revolution* (London, T. Butterworth, 1938), pp. 164–71.

the century, that the King was the chief servant of the law, but not its master; the executant of the law, not its source; the laws should only be alterable by Parliament—Kings, Lords and Commons together. It is this that makes the Revolution the decisive event in the history of the English Constitution. It was decisive because it was never undone, as most of the work of the Cromwellian Revolution had been undone.

It is true that the first Civil War had been fought partly on this same issue:— the Common Law in league with Parliament had, on the field of Naseby, triumphed over the King in the struggle for the supreme place in the Constitution. But the victory of Law and Parliament had, on that occasion, been won only because Puritanism, the strongest religious passion of the hour, had supplied the fighting force. And religious passion very soon confused the Constitutional issue. Puritanism burst the legal bounds and, coupled with militarism, overthrew law and Parliament as well as King. Hence the necessity of the restoration in 1660 of King, law and Parliament together, without any clear definition of their ultimate mutual relations.

Now, in this second crisis of 1688, law and Parliament had on their side not only the Puritan passion, which had greatly declined, but the whole force of Protestant-Anglicanism, which was then at its height, and the rising influence of Latitudinarian scepticism—all arrayed against the weak Roman Catholic interest to which James had attached the political fortunes of the royal cause. The ultimate victor of the seventeenth-century struggle was not Pym or Cromwell, with their Puritan ideals, but Coke and Selden with their secular idea of the supremacy of law. In 1689 the Puritans had to be content with a bare toleration. But law triumphed, and therefore the law-making Parliament triumphed finally over the King.

But the supremacy of law could not be permanently secured if the Judges who interpreted it remained dependent upon the Crown. James had dismissed the Judges who refused to interpret the law as he wished. The Revolution secured the independence of the Bench.

One of the first executive actions of William, as King charged with the administration, was to make the Judges irremovable. This he did of his own free will, without waiting for a Bill on the subject to be passed by Parliament. He gave commissions to all the Judges under the formula *quam diu se bene gesserint*—so long as they behave properly: no longer *durante beneplacito*— at the will of the King. Prior to the Revolution some Judges had sometimes held under the more secure tenure—*quam diu se bene gesserint;* but most had held *durante beneplacito,* and not a few had suffered dismissal for political reasons. Under William and under Anne the Crown could no longer dismiss Judges. It is true, therefore, to say that the great boon of the independence of the Bench was in practice secured at the Revolution. But this independence and irremovability was only put on a statutory basis when the Act of Settlement, passed in 1701, came into force on George I's accession in 1714. The Act of Settlement lays it down that—

Judges' Commissions be made *quam diu se bene gesserint* and their salaries ascertained and established, but upon the address of both Houses of Parliament it may be lawful to remove them.

This only gave statutory force to what had been the practice of William and Anne since the Revolution; but the Act of Settlement added the power of removal by address of the Houses, as a safeguard against the Judges abusing their irremovable position. Under that tenure our Judges hold office to-day.

The station of Justice outside and above the sphere of politics was very largely achieved by the irremovability of Judges. The law was made arbiter of all issues by its own legal standards, without fear of what Government could do either to Judge or to Juries. It is difficult to exaggerate the importance of this as a step towards real justice and civilization. It has not yet been taken, or else it has been abolished, in many countries abroad, where "justice" is still a part of politics and an asset of despotism. But in England the old Tudor idea of the Judges as "lions under the throne" ceased to hold good at the Revolution. Henceforth they were independent arbiters between Crown and subject, acting on standards of law and of evidence. Nor had they ceased to be agents of royal policy, merely in order to become agents of Whig or Tory faction. Judges, like other men, are no doubt often influenced by their own opinions on party questions. But they were not dependent on Whig or Tory Governments, for they could not be removed by them. Under William and Anne, it happened not infrequently that Tory Judges thwarted Whig Governments, and Whig Judges thwarted Tory Governments by their action on the Bench.

Since public justice was henceforth to be impartial and no longer a mere instrument of the Crown, the law of Treason was altered by Statute in 1695 much to the advantage of the accused. He was to have a copy of the indictment. He was to be defended by Counsel. He was enabled to compel the attendance of witnesses for the defence. An overt act of Treason had to be proved by two witnesses. Henceforth, for the first time in our history, judicial murder ceased to be an ordinary weapon of politics and government.

This improvement in the realm of political justice was part of a more general movement in the direction of humanity and of scientific justice that was slowly setting in and which culminated in the nineteenth century. In the course of the eighteenth century there grew up a comprehension of the real value of evidence, and of the valuelessness of certain types of evidence like that of the professional informer—Oates, for instance. This improvement in the intelligence and justice of the law courts was noticeable not only in trials of a political character. In cases of every kind, the rules of the law of evidence—what evidence may be received in court and what may not—were worked out by the law courts during the eighteenth century. Sir John Holt, Chief Justice of the King's Bench under William and Anne, introduced a new regime of humanity and fairness towards the accused. The days of Scroggs and Jeffreys were over.

Owing to the experience of James's tyranny, the "liberal" element in the Revolution Settlement was as much approved by the Tories as by the Whigs themselves. The reduction of the personal power of the King, the supremacy of Parliament and of law, the independence of the Judges, the security of the rights of individuals and of chartered Corporations against the encroachments of executive power were causes highly popular with the Tories of 1689. In the last years of Charles II, the Tories had, in their anger against the Whig Parliaments, spoken and acted as extreme Royalists and had made over to the King powers which they were fain to recall after their experience under James. Never again was the Tory party a Royalist party, in the sense of being a party anxious to increase the Royal prerogative, for they never again found a king entirely to their liking, till George III ascended the throne. The High Tories soon found grounds of discontent with William III, and, contrary to their expectation, with Anne after him, and still more with George I and II. And therefore, for seventy years after the Revolution, the High Tories never recovered that enthusiasm for the wearer of the Crown which they had felt in the last years of Charles II. For this reason the reduction in the power of the Crown effected at the Revolution continued to be approved by all parties in the State. And when at last in 1760 a King agreeable to Tory sentiment ascended the throne, it was too late to revive the old Prerogative. No attempt was made to resuscitate the powers of the Stuart Kings. George III, devoted to the Protestant ascendancy, was only too faithful to the letter of the Revolution Settlement. All that he attempted was, with the consent of Parliament, to recover for himself those powers which had been left to the King in person by the original Settlement of 1689, but which had been exercised by the Whig Ministers under the early Hanoverian Kings.

But although, after the Revolution, the subjects of the land had little to fear from kingly despotism, they might fear the encroachments on liberty of new masters, the Houses of Parliament and the Government of the day armed with Parliamentary support. But this danger was mitigated by the division of Parliament into Whig and Tory, wherein lay security for the freedom of the subject under the new regime. The rivalry of the two parties made it certain that the Whigs would take up the cause of anyone oppressed by a Tory Government or a Tory House of Commons, and that the Tories would champion the humblest victim of Whig tyranny. There are a hundred instances of the working of this law of political dynamics in the reigns of William and Anne, besides the well-known cases of the Kentish Petitioners, the men of Aylesbury, and Dr. Sacheverell, and the failure of the Impeachments of Somers and of Oxford. The Revolution may have made Parliament dangerously powerful but, fortunately for freedom, Parliament continued to be a body divided against itself.

And so it proved in the important matters of the freedom of the press. The right of printing and publishing matter obnoxious to the Government of the day was secured as a result of the Revolution and of the continued rivalry of Tory and Whig. Hitherto, as in other countries so in England, it had been necessary to obtain licence from the authorities before printing and publishing any book, pamphlet or newspaper. There had, of course, been secret presses, which being illegal were usually conducted by the more violent opponents of Government, often in a very scurrilous manner. But open and legitimate discussion, whether on religion or politics, had been hampered by a rigid censorship. As a consequence of the spirit of the new age ushered in by the Revolution, this form of governmental control was abolished in 1695. In that year, the same year as the improvement in the law of Treason, the annual act for the Censorship of the Press was allowed to lapse and has never since been revived.

After this great emancipation, authors and publishers still ran, as they will run, the risk of trial for sedition or for libel before a jury of their countrymen. Without that safeguard, "liberty of the Press" would become an intolerable nuisance. The abolition of the Censorship is what is meant by a "free Press." It was for that which Milton had pleaded in his *Areopagitica, or the Liberty of Unlicensed Printing.* In that magnificent pamphlet, half poetry, half politics, occurs the famous patriotic brag—"What does God but reveal himself to his servants, and, as his manner is, first to his Englishmen?" It would have pleased Milton to know that England would be, in fact, the first great country to obtain a free Press, fifty years after the appearance of his *Areopagitica.* The violence of party in his own age, with which he himself was deeply infected, rendered freedom of speech or of printing at that time impossible. "Liberty of unlicensed printing" came in, not with Pym or with Cromwell, but as an outcome of a more peaceful and conservative revolution. For the Revolution Settlement of 1689 was not the triumph of a party, but an agreement of the two chief parties to live and let live. The balance of Whig and Tory, each jealous of the other and both jealous of the Crown, served to protect the liberties of the individual Englishmen from the onslaughts of power.

3.

Liberties and privileges in the medieval sense meant guarantees *against* centralizing kings. As such they upheld special interests, whether of merchants, nobles, or any other group. In the case of the Dutch, after the Spanish threat to independence had lessened and after the power of the princes of Orange had also temporarily diminished, the Dutch central government went out of existence. Why?

Constitutionalism offered little basis for unity in a state. Liberties pertained to special groups, provinces, or towns, and not to the Dutch as a whole. Consequently, the federal government, consisting of estates representing the provinces and great cities, virtually disappeared. Local government in the extreme took over, and endless provincial rivalries and bickering rose to undermine almost every basis for cooperation. Such negativistic government permitted religious toleration, favorable economic conditions, and a stable society, but at the same time it also caused the decline of such necessary things as common defense and foreign policy. The Dutch army fell apart in the Republican Golden Age (1650–1671). There were only provincial armies, each with its own commander, budget, and strategy. Constitutionalism thus indirectly caused the Dutch to fall prey to Louis XIV in the years between 1667 and 1678.

E. H. Kossman (1922–   ), Professor of History at the University of London, analyzes the foundations for this diversity of the Dutch Republic. After going beneath constitutionalism to economic and social conditions, he concludes that the Republic was "in practice conservative." What is meant by this charge? Is it a condemnation of constitutionalism and a bow to Louis XIV? Which English political philosopher and contemporary of De Witt could be thought of as a supporter of something resembling the Dutch "limited government"?

E. H. KOSSMAN: The Dutch Republic*

By the middle of the seventeenth century the Dutch *bourgeoisie* had acquired its typical form. The families which had grown wealthy through commerce and become influential in government during the early seventeenth century constituted the oligarchy which in fact ruled the province. They provided the men who served in the urban administrations, the States, the boards of the big trading-companies, and with these functions went the exclusive right of making appointments to numerous minor offices in the towns and the country. . . .

The political structure of the Dutch Republic was cumbersome and complicated: it did in fact not constitute one republic but a federation of seven sovereign provinces, each with its special characteristics. The federal government was weak. The most important of the federal institutions was the States General to which each of the provinces sent a delegation bound to vote as instructed by its principals. Unanimity was required for the States General to take a decision committing all their members. Yet the States General, meeting daily at The Hague for some hours, had important tasks to perform. They acted as the representative of the Union, conducted foreign affairs, controlled defence and federal taxation which was apportioned among the provinces according to a fixed key, Holland paying about 58 percent. They nominated, finally, the captain-general and the admiral-general of the Union, offices usually held by the Prince of Orange. However, the States General were clearly not a sovereign body. Sovereignty resided in the States of the various provinces, the composition of which varied greatly. The States of Holland consisted of nineteen delegations each having one vote: the nobility and eighteen towns. In the States just as in the States General important decisions were normally taken unanimously: the principle of Dutch government was that none of its members could be coerced to comply with the majority. In practice a decision was reached only after long negotiations and thanks to the persuasiveness of the leading statesmen.

The centrifugal forces in the government were sometimes checked by two important officials: the Grand Pensionary and the stadholder. The Grand Pensionary was the legal adviser of the States of Holland who acted as the president of the States and of their committees, led the provincial deputation to the States General, often carried on the correspondence of the Republic with the Dutch ambassadors abroad and received their dispatches. An energetic and intelligent man who enjoyed the confidence of the urban administrations in Holland was able to wield decisive power not only in his own province but in the whole Republic. The function of stadholder was more ambiguous. The incumbent of the stadholdership of Holland was always the Prince of Orange. He was appointed by the sovereign States and was therefore in theory a provincial official just as the Grand Pensionary. But since he was always stadholder of more than one province at the same time (Holland, Zeeland, Utrecht, Overijssel and Guelderland normally nominated the Prince of Orange, Groningen and Drente,

* From E. H. Kossman, "The Dutch Republic," in *New Cambridge Modern History* (Cambridge: Cambridge University Press, 1961), V, *The Ascendancy of France, 1648–1688,* F. L. Carsten, ed., pp. 276–83.

not represented in the States General, often did so, whereas Friesland always appointed a member of the Nassau branch of the family) and acted also as captain-general and admiral-general of the Union, he quite naturally participated in the making of federal policy. The enormous prestige, moreover, of his noble birth and the popularity of his great House gave him an influence and power not defined by any constitutional laws but none the less real and important.

Throughout the first half of the century there had been tensions between the States of Holland and the stadholder. During the 1640's the ruling oligarchy of Holland had opposed the militarist and dynastic policies of Frederick Henry, captain-general and admiral-general, stadholder of all the provinces but Friesland, because they were designed to continue the war with Spain and to enhance the position of the Orange family through the marriage of Frederick Henry's son, William II, to the daughter of Charles I, Mary. Fear and anger had been aroused by Frederick Henry's wish to support the royalist cause in the Civil War. But Frederick Henry died in 1647; in 1648 the regents had their way in making peace with Spain at Münster. His son William II, however, a young and adventurous man, appointed to all his father's dignities, felt frustrated by this victory of the States and soon considered himself strong enough to challenge Holland and Amsterdam. The conflict seemed grave and dangerous. But suddenly, on 6 November 1650, he died. The Dutch statesmen found themselves in a completely new situation. William II's only child, William III, was born on 14 November; the calm of his nursery was disturbed by the vehement conflicts between his mother, Mary Stuart, and his grandmother Amelia, the widow of Frederick Henry. In most provinces the idea of appointing Friesland's stadholder to the functions of William II did not even arise; only Groningen and the territory of Drente decided to fill the vacancy in this way. Thus for the first time in the history of the Republic five of the seven provinces represented in the States General were truly republican, although in some princely palaces at The Hague a group of Calvinist predikants and anglophile nobles and adventurers kept plotting on behalf of the greatness of the Orange dynasty.

The twenty-two years of almost completely republican rule, which followed, form a very distinctive period in Dutch history. In 1651 the States of Holland tried to lay the foundation of a new form of government by summoning to The Hague the so-called Grand Assembly and by proposing to attribute to this body, which was intended to be a joint session of all the provincial States and as such the sum total of sovereignty in the federated provinces, the right to decide arbitrarily on the cardinal problems awaiting solution. In the view of Holland the States General, still largely dominated by the protégés of William II, was not the proper place for so difficult a task. But the plan failed. The deputies sent by the provinces to the Grand Assembly had no larger powers than those sent to the States General, and what was intended to be a congress of sovereigns was in reality only a congress of ambassadors. Consequently the Grand Assembly (January–August 1651) was unable to produce any constructive plan and resigned itself to much classicist and confused oratory. The only decision of importance concerned the army. More than ever before military affairs were now to be dealt with as if they depended on the sovereign will of each of the seven provinces—with the result that the army was in great danger of being split into seven provincial armies. This was a victory for extreme particularism. Thus the real importance of the Grand Assembly was that it brought to a culmination and confirmed officially a tendency that undoubtedly was one of the main features of the confederation. The United Provinces—as John de Witt said—were not a *respublica* in the singular but *respublicae* in the plural.

John de Witt, who soon became the leader of the republican party (owing to his office of Grand Pensionary to which he was appointed in 1653), exerted himself not only to defend the new stadholderless form of government but also to justify it intellectually. It was called by his adherents the System of True Liberty and de Witt availed himself of the services of excellent publicists like the brothers De la Court and of so systematic a philosopher as Spinoza. This literary activity gives the period the character of an intellectual adventure, of an attempt made by young men—de Witt himself was 27 years old in 1653— to break with a past marred by awkward compromises. Yet this rationalistic and doctrinaire aspect of the régime was but one of the elements in a very complex reality. John de Witt and his collaborators moulded into concrete form a variety of old and respectable tendencies. The dynastic policies of Frederick Henry and William II had aroused anger among the ruling classes, particularly those of Holland, because they led to adventures of incalculable consequences. The men upon whom, after the death of William II, power naturally devolved could devote themselves to the task of strengthening their own power. In principle they had always been in possession of sovereignty, but they had never fully exercised it. They immediately barred all the ways through which the authority of the stadholder had penetrated into the towns and the urban administrations. The various States decided that the annual elections of urban magistrates would in future be the affair of the towns only and in fact always be made by co-optation. All outside influence, especially that of the stadholder, who had in certain circumstances the right of selection from a number of recommended candidates, was eliminated and the power of a small group of ruling families was confirmed. This small group of ruling families formed the strongest support of de Witt's party. Not all of them were "Wittians," but the most important among them, especially in Holland and Amsterdam, considered a régime which gave them practically a monopoly of power the best régime for the time being.

The régime was, however, not merely the dictatorship of a narrow class. It was deeply rooted in the life of the whole population, not because the ruling groups shared their power with the masses of the people, but because they turned away from them and left them alone. Thus the republican régime was silently supported by the numerous religious dissenters, who needed protection against the intolerance of the Calvinist minority. It was supported by Roman Catholics and Protestant sects, by intellectuals and wide strata of the *bourgeoisie*. It did not disturb the turbulent, restless growth of numerous and very active small groups of religious innovators and considered it its sole task ingeniously to maintain the balance between extremes and to prevent excesses. The principle of toleration was utilitarian rather than founded on any philosophical principle. The regents never tired of repeating that foreign trade would inevitably be destroyed by the establishment of an exclusive Calvinist supremacy.

By the middle of the seventeenth century probably nearly half of the Dutch population (Brabant included) were still loyal to the Catholic faith. In the towns of the provinces of Holland and Utrecht numerous missionaries were allowed to carry on their partly secret activities. The majority of the rural population in these provinces was certainly Catholic: it is not surprising that Dutch civilisation continued to be permeated by Romish elements. This does not alter the fact that the situation of the Catholics continued to be precarious. The Dutch Republic was officially a Protestant State and the Catholics, though allowed to have their own religious services if they were willing to pay for the inattention of the authorities, found it increasingly difficult to keep their posts in the urban administrations. However, Calvinism was not the only alternative to Roman Catholicism. Of a total population of perhaps about two millions probably one-third belonged to orthodox Calvinism, a creed that consequently remained what it had been during the Revolt, though of course to a much lesser degree: the creed of a minority. Beside it innumerable small sects ventured to express extremely liberal interpretations of Christian dogma or even a de-Christianised religion to the point of transforming it into a general moral philosophy.

The dissenters no doubt supported the government of the tolerant regents, without being able to save it when it was fighting for its life. This would have required a solid organisation, but this they lacked. Yet the deep divisions of the Dutch people may help to explain a fact which must be regarded as one of the salient features of Dutch history in the seventeenth century: the fact that numerous changes of government took place without the violence accompanying the contemporary upheavals in France and England. It is indeed remarkable that the events of 1618–19, of 1650 and of 1672, all fundamental conflicts, did not develop into revolutions. The suppleness of the Dutch form of government and the general prosperity partly explain this; but the complex religious divisions, which made clear-cut conflicts almost impossible and in which party divisions disappeared like water in sand, certainly contributed a great deal to the fundamental weakness of all forms of government and to the ease with which one form was substituted for another.

It is difficult to understand the nature of the opposition to the domination of the regents, but some of its elements at least are clear. No imagination is needed to see that de Witt's way of eliminating the influence of the Orange family in Holland, and as far as possible also in the other provinces, excluded a compromise with the clientele of the great House. It is also clear that the Orangists wanted to continue the policies by which Frederick Henry and William II had aroused so much antagonism. A small number of Calvinist pastors continued to nurse their ideal of an anti-Spanish crusade. These men were, of course, opposed to the religious tolerance of the regents, to their Erastian principles and to their complete lack of religious dynamism. Possibly the sharp social difference between the predikants of the lower middle class and the ruling families helps to explain the conflicts. Much more important, however, was the instinctive reaction of large groups of the population to the régime of the States in times of emergency. This reaction was often fostered by political speeches and pamphlets, but more often it arose spontaneously out of economic distress and political distrust. Sharp rises in the price of rye were caused by the Anglo-Dutch wars and, coupled with unemployment and deep suspicion, they led to vehement disturbances in the towns and a fairly general outcry against a régime suspected of treachery and inefficiency.

Yet these popular movements did not grow steadily during the years until— after the first disappointments of 1653—they became sufficiently strong in 1672 to overthrow the régime. On the contrary, their vehemence diminished. A more decisive factor contributing to the fatal weakness of the System of True Liberty in 1672 was the danger of being hollowed out from the inside. Orangist regents had retained much of their influence in some towns and provinces and their position became stronger as Prince William grew older. The sharp conflicts, moreover, within the town governments, conflicts often springing from the struggle for power, selfishness and personal hatred, naturally tended to expand and to merge with extra-mural conflicts. It was easy for a regent ousted by one of de Witt's friends to call himself an Orangist and so to infuse fresh vigour into the national party strife. Modern historians have carefully studied this phenomenon in Amsterdam and there is no reason to suppose that it did not occur in other towns also.

Thus an explanation of the political struggles in the terms of social contrasts is insufficient, although undoubtedly they formed one of the numerous elements from which the great conflict sprang. Neither is it possible to link the political development with the economic situation. It is perhaps surprising that the Orangist period before 1651 witnessed a considerable expansion of the Dutch economy, and that it came to a halt under the republican régime which was so eager to defend commercial interests. It was only about 1680 that the economy began to recover, a process which continued until the death of William III. This temporary slowing down of what had been such an amazingly dynamic development was not due to any fundamental change in the structure of Dutch commerce in general or of the Amsterdam staple market in particular. It was caused by transient changes which after the middle of the century had a stagnating effect. Especially the Baltic corn trade, the "mother commerce" of the Republic, suffered a serious decline in the years between 1652 and 1680, a decline not so much to be explained by increasing competition as by some bad harvests in the area of the Vistula, by the wars, by a fall in the demand for corn in western and southern Europe, and above all by the general depression afflicting the European economy during the 1660's and 1670's. It would be a gross exaggeration to speak of a crisis of the Dutch economy. The stagnation in the expansion of some important branches of commerce was accompanied by a sharp rise in that of others. Commercial relations with Spain became very close after 1648 and led to the development of Amsterdam as a leading bullion market. The Dutch economic hegemony in Muscovy was confirmed. Industry did not seem to suffer. It was precisely during these years that Leiden, the biggest European manufacturing town after Lyon, made its greatest advance in the cloth industry, and the industry of the area of the river Zaan in North Holland increased rapidly. Yet this does not alter the fact that the general expansion of the early seventeenth century was discontinued after 1650 and that de Witt's period witnessed economic difficulties and in some fields even a mild form of recession.

Thus in all spheres of Dutch life a similar phenomenon can be observed. The top seemed to have been reached; nothing remained but to attempt to retain the things acquired. De Witt's system, however fashionable it may have been intellectually, was in practice conservative. In a supremely intelligent way his conduct of domestic as well as foreign affairs tried to freeze the situation. In fact his whole policy was a reaction to disturbing tendencies and as such, the saturation of the Republic taken into account, a defence of fundamental Dutch interests.

The two disturbing elements which threatened the system and finally wrecked it were political. They were the closely related questions of England and Orange. Neither of them could de Witt eliminate and his ability to neutralise them was limited. England was a dangerous, but not necessarily a deadly enemy during the years in which the Dutch Republic, thanks to the uncertainties of the European political scene, was able to play the part of an arbiter. When it became clear that France was out to take over the Spanish heritage—European hegemony—English foreign policy became a very great danger because it contributed to a shift in the balance of power. The Orange question also assumed frightening proportions, and by the time Prince William came of age it dominated the situation. De Witt's greatness, the greatness of the Dutch Republic, lies enclosed between Spanish and French hegemony, between the adult vigour of William II and that of William III. It fundamentally was a greatness *ad interim*.

4.

In political thought after Machiavelli, Europeans sought to discover the reasons for the decline of civic virtue as well as the principles which would justify ancient privileges. These two things are not the same; the first leads to historical inquiry and sociology, the second to philosophy and sometimes legal studies. But blended together they made the study of government a passion for the seventeenth-century Dutch philosopher Spinoza and the eighteenth-century French thinkers Montesquieu and Rousseau. Each of these men in his own way sought the reasons for the decline of civic virtue. In doing so they submitted the ancient Roman Republic and its contemporary analogue, the Venetian Republic, to most careful scrutiny.

James Davis (1931–   ), of the Department of History at the University of Pennsylvania, also asks: Why did Venice decline? His answer is novel and very provocative for the study of constitutionalism. If Venice did not decline because of the loss of Middle-Eastern trade or because of some corruption in her morals, then what happened? Davis suggests a decline in the numbers willing to devote their services to the public good. Why did the number of nobles willing to take office decline? Economic reasons? Was there a change in notions of status? Did engaging in trade and political office lose its former distinction? Why did the election of younger men signify a decline?

JAMES DAVIS: A Manpower Shortage in Government: Venice*

During the first half of the seventeenth century the Venetian ruling class began to feel the effect of what might somewhat anachronistically be called a manpower shortage. This happened because, while the number of principal government offices remained approximately the same, the number of noblemen who were willing, qualified, and able to serve had begun to decrease sharply. During the seventeenth and eighteenth centuries it became harder and harder to find men who could and would serve in the important posts: in governorships and embassies, in the busy administrative and financial committees of the Senate, and as *savi grandi,* ducal councilors, and members of the Council of Ten. This lack of qualified candidates for principal offices seems to have been one of the most serious aspects of the Venetian period of "decadence."

The lack of qualified candidates for the principal offices may have first become a matter of public concern during the 1630's. According to the author of a little treatise on the Venetian nobility written during the latter seventeenth century, there was danger during the 1630's and the early 1640's (before a large number of new families were ennobled) of having to give even the most important offices to those who did not merit them. This writer implies that the danger arose from the decline in the number of nobles, because he says that there was talk of recalling the Venetian noble families living on Crete or of granting Venetian nobility to aristocratic families living on the mainland. Giannantonio Muazzo, a well-informed Venetian nobleman who wrote at about the same time, says that "from about 1630 after the Plague, there was talk of increasing [the nobility] in some proper and decorous manner. . . ."

The shortage of able officeholders apparently was first discussed in the Great Council in 1645 when the War of Crete, fought against the Turks between that year and 1669, had just broken out. The *Collegio* proposed to sell the privileges of Venetian nobility to five families with the aim principally of building up a war chest and incidentally of compensating for the loss of the noble families which had died out. In defending the proposal, Giacomo Marcello told the Great Council that "the foundations of the government have been the number of Patricians and their unity, and our State cannot stand on few and weak supports. The [government] offices require the minds and hearts of many; and how can one select the best man, if there are few candidates from which to choose?—the selection will be a forced not a free one. Those marks of honor—the offices of the Republic—should be not so much birthrights as rewards for ability." His remarks and the preamble to

* From James Davis, *The Decline of the Venetian Nobility as a Ruling Class* (Baltimore: Johns Hopkins University Press, 1962), pp. 75–89.

the bill to accept new families make it clear that the lack of men for offices was then a well-recognized problem.

Forty years later, the shortage of men in the ruling class seems to have been considered even more serious. At least there is far more anxiety in the remarks made by Michele Foscarini in 1684 when he persuaded the Great Council to revive the sale of rights to nobility. Sad as the rapid disappearance of many noble families was, he said, "It is even more painful to consider that the distribution of offices in the Great Council may one day become completely odious; that there may be more offices than subjects; that it may not be possible to reject the poor candidates and reward the good ones; that the men who can undertake the more demanding posts of the Republic may disappear and those who replace them will not have the means to do so [properly] . . . we should not deceive ourselves; we see the beginnings already; the competition for the offices is so rare that these . . . seem to me to be almost abhorred, and men work out expedients so that they will not be elected. But the mutual need which one citizen has of his fellow is the bond which holds our society together. If this bond should loosen, those customs will change which until now have preserved an internal peace and allowed our Republic to endure longer than any other."

Lack of public spirit is often the cause of difficulty in finding men for public offices, and this may indeed have been one of the reasons for the problem in Venice. There are some indications that there was increasing political apathy in the ruling class, and it is easy to find plausible explanations for this apathy. One might be the proportional increase in the number of poorer nobles. The attention of these men was no doubt concentrated mainly on earning a living in the mediocre offices which were designed chiefly as sinecures. They would not have been interested in holding the most important posts which were not paid at all or frequently involved expenses exceeding the salaries. Poorer men would also have known that, even if they were ambitious, their lack of wealth would prevent them from reaching the more important offices because they could not afford these posts and because lack of wealth meant lack of the requisite prestige. A lack of wealth also meant that they could not afford a good education, and without such an education they would doubtless lack both the ability and the interest to take an active part in the government. In the early seventeenth century Venice established an Academy of Nobles where a small number of sons of poor nobles were educated at public expense. But one patrician observed that "when he has finished five years [there] a Student has not learned the Latin language well, and he has picked up little more than reading and writing."

The decline of commerce may have convinced many of the more influential families that they no longer had an important stake in Venetian affairs. Senate memberships ceased to offer these families opportunities to vote for their interests—and incidentally those of the state—in such matters as galley voyages, the regulation of state banks, and the public debt; it no longer provided a listening post where they could learn about political developments with interesting financial implications. Many others may have lost interest in the government as Venice fell into the ranks of lesser political powers in the years after the Italian wars of the early sixteenth century. In the East, Venice fought one debilitating war after another against the Turks; toward the West she maintained continual neutrality. According to the patrician historian Marin who wrote just after the fall of the Republic, the War of Morea, fought against the Turks at the start of the eighteenth century, resulted in a disillusionment that caused many even of the more conscientious nobles to lose interest in the government.

And then there were many pleasant distractions in seventeenth- and eighteenth-century Venice. This was the great period of cafés, gambling, pre-Lenten celebrations that lasted for months, the comedies of Goldoni, private concerts and operas, the scholarly or convivial "academies," and especially the easy, gay life in estates on the mainland. The banks of the Brenta and Terraglio rivers were lined with handsome classical and baroque villas in which the wealthier families held their almost unending house-parties. The attractions of this easy life in the country were often stronger than the feeling of duty to the state; more than once the Senate had to send out general invitations to the negligent to return to duty. "For the grave needs of the Republic," one of these began, "the zeal and love of its citizens is needed, both with unceasing attendance in the Offices and Councils and with the use of hard work and their wealth in the important external Posts. . . . The Senate . . . should not relax its efforts at all because of the changing of the season since the dangerous circumstances of the Country are not changing. . . ." All were asked "to remain in this area in the present autumn season." These reminders were sent out from time to time.

Just before the overthrow of the Republic, a Venetian nobleman, with democratic leanings and a grudge against the government, penned a sketch of the meetings of the Senate which is certainly amusing and quite possibly accurate. He said that most of the sessions consisted of a string of decrees which were read with incredible speed and listened to very little or not at all by the senators. These men spent the time strolling, or chatting about trifles, including their amours; in winter they stayed by the fire in a room next to the Senate hall. After the readings, all the decrees were voted on together and the session adjourned. When this happened quickly, all the senators were jubilant because they were relieved of the annoyance of what they called a "long *Pregadi*" (Senate session). They used to exult: "Short *Pregadi*, short *Pregadi!*," happy because they could return so much the sooner to their pleasures.

Probably then, considerable political apathy did develop during the long Venetian decline, but there is little clear evidence of it. Most of those who wrote about the patricians' lack of interest in their government did so in the latter eighteenth century. Recent studies, furthermore, have shown that even in the last two centuries of the declining Republic there were always at least a few men in the government who took a keen interest in affairs and were willing to sacrifice their time and wealth in filling important offices.

It seems to have been primarily the changes in the nobility . . . and not political apathy, that created the problem discussed by Marcello and Foscarini in the Great Council. The "manpower shortage" was caused mainly by the decline of the number of nobles and especially the number of wealthy men. No longer was there a great body of men of varying talents and experience and wealth from which to choose 100 or so of the most qualified to fill the important and demanding offices.

What happened to two families, the Basegios and Valiers, makes clear on a small scale how the economic and demographic changes affected the Venetian political scene. The Basegios are probably the best example of men whose poverty excluded them from public offices. Their poverty dated at the latest from the early fourteenth century—long before the decline of Venetian trade—when they are mentioned as one of several poor families that backed Bajamonte Tiepolo in his unsuccessful insurrection. A seventeenth century writer described the Basegios as a family that no longer had any distinction because of their poverty and because there were so few men in the "miserable" branches of the family that still survived. Certainly few and probably no members of the family reached any of the principal offices in the last three centuries of the Republic. A letter to the government from a Venetian town in Istria in 1612 gives an idea of the position to which the Basegios' poverty consigned them. According to the writers, who pleaded with the government to pay the noble governors of their city better, few nobles wanted to serve in Isola because of the very low salary. When they were governed by a gentleman "whose restricted fortunes do not permit a better post," he was often required to remain for a long period until a successor could be found. The noble then serving in Isola was one Giovanni Domenico Basegio.

The branch of the Valier family that produced two doges in the seventeenth century was probably as wealthy as the Basegios were poor. It was eventually removed from the political scene, not by poverty, but because the line died out completely. Members of this house had served the government for generations as senators, generals, members of the Council of Ten, and in other posts. Perhaps it was in order to maintain their wealth and position that the family began to restrict marriages during the sixteenth century and subsequently even to limit family size. Massimo Valier, who died in 1573, had four sons; of these, only Silvestro married. Silvestro had only one son, Bertucci, who in turn had one son named Silvestro. In each of these generations the combination of great wealth with ability permitted very useful service to Venice. The earlier Silvestro served on the Council of Ten. His son, Bertucci, was an excellent orator and an able governor and ambassador. His wealth and ability won him the position of doge in 1656. Bertucci's son, Silvestro, may have been less able than his father but he was inspired by the same zeal for public service, which in his will he says he drank with his mother's milk. On special embassies he spent huge sums of money to maintain the Venetian tradition of a public display of magnificence. Eventually he was elected doge, this being the first time a father and son had held the office in many centuries. But Silvestro had no brothers, and when he died this distinguished branch of the Valier family disappeared.

It was the loss, many times multiplied, of families such as the Basegios and Valiers, which caused a lack of nobles capable of holding important offices in the seventeenth and eighteenth centuries. It was a nagging problem, with which the ruling class was slow to come to grips.

Of all the offices in Venice, it was probably the governorships of the subject cities that felt the decline of the ruling class most acutely and obviously. Venice ruled its *Terra Ferma* in northern Italy and Dalmatia by means of noble governors who presided in the cities and outlying forts. The principal cities, such as Bergamo, Brescia, Verona, Vicenza, and Padua, were each ruled by two men. The *podestà* was responsible for judicial and general administrative matters; the *cápitano* was in charge of the area's military organization. In the lesser places the two offices were sometimes combined; sometimes the governor bore another title such as *conte, castellano,* or *provveditore.* All told, over 100 noblemen occupied these positions. The lesser governorships paid enough to offer a livelihood to poorer men. But about fifteen of the more important ones, particularly those in the five cities mentioned above, did not by any means pay enough to meet the expenses of a governor who wanted to live in the splendorous style befitting Venice. Customs which gained increasing popularity in the later centuries required him to spend huge amounts on a magnificent arrival in the city, on splendid furnishings in his residence, and on what might almost be called a court. Only rich noblemen could afford to accept the posts. But if the great expenses and the enforced sixteen-month separation from the brilliant life of Venice were undesirable features of these governorships, the offices were nevertheless important as rungs in the ladder of offices leading to the highest, most honored positions. The richer nobles, furthermore, probably felt a civic obligation to serve at least occasionally as governors. It appears that there was no great difficulty in finding men for these positions before about the middle of the sixteenth century.

As early as 1558, however, the Great Council was encountering difficulties in finding candidates for these posts. Four electors were customarily chosen by lot to propose candidates for a governorship. A law passed in 1558 was designed to force these electors to do their duty. From the wording of the text of the law it appears that the electors shirked the responsibility of proposing men for these offices because they feared to make enemies of the men they nominated. It is interesting that this difficulty in obtaining candidates for governorships appeared some years before the plague of the 1570's and before the decline in trade which began in the last decade of the century.

There was more than one cause of the difficulties which the Republic experienced in finding men who were willing and able to serve as governors. One was the magnificent style of living which the noblemen felt they had to maintain in these offices. Wealthy noble governors spent so much on their houses and public appearances in the subject cities that other nobles could not meet the standard thus established. At the end of the sixteenth century, fines were introduced for refusals to serve in important governorships; and writing about these seventy-five years later, Muazzo remarked that "the fine was born after luxury and display made these offices excessively expensive, and consequently difficult and undesirable for many men." During the seventeenth and eighteenth centuries innumerable laws were passed decreeing how a governor might live and in what ways he could spend his money. The preambles to many of them attribute reluctance to accept election to governorships to the inability of the noblemen to match the expensive standards already set.

But inability to match an inflated standard of living was not the only cause of the lack of potential governors. More basic than the rise in what had to be spent was the decline in the number of men who could afford to meet even a simpler standard. When Marcello and Foscarini, whose speeches in the Great Council are quoted in part above, linked the difficulty in finding willing candidates for offices to the disappearance of many noble families, the offices they were thinking of above all were probably the governorships. This seems likely in view of the attention which the Great Council was constantly forced to pay to election to these offices. Not only the demographic decline but the economic one as well contributed to the lack of candidates. Preambles to some of the laws dealing with governorships link the shortage of candidates to the decline of trade. In 1625 it was noted that "because of changes in the times and in commerce over a long period of years no one seeks election to several of the governorships and offices . . ." And in 1749 the Senate noted that men were "made incapable [of accepting governorships] by the doldrums into which the private economy of the families has fallen." Luxurious living had also consumed fortunes and thus reduced the number who could serve. One purpose of the general sumptuary laws passed in these centuries was to preserve family wealth so that there might continue to be some men who could serve in governorships. The preamble to a characteristic seventeenth-century sumptuary law says that among the unfortunate consequences of luxurious living there is, "above all, that because of the resultant inequality of wealth there is frequently a lack of subjects who are willing to serve, from which result the difficulties which are well known. . . ."

Men who asked for dispensations from service in governorships to which they had been elected usually pleaded the poor condition of their family finances. Frequently they pointed out that other members of their families had previously served in governorships and that this had consumed much of their wealth. Pietro Zaguri, to give an example of one who asked for such a dispensation, begged to be excused from serving as governor at Rovigo. He had, he said, three paternal aunts, six children, and five sisters who were in cloisters, all of whom depended on him for support. A daughter was about to marry, which meant great expense, and on top of all this, some land which he possessed on the mainland had suffered heavy damage from floods. He could not assume the post without a "total devastation" of his fortunes. Generally the noblemen who asked for dispensations did not mention what may have been the generic cause of their inability to serve in the costly governorships, the above-mentioned "doldrums" of so many family fortunes.

The problem of finding men for governorships seems to have become progressively more acute. Laws controlling—or trying to control—expenditures by governors had been few in the sixteenth century, but were passed in profusion during the seventeenth and early eighteenth centuries. Meanwhile the fines for refusals were raised from 500 ducats to 1,000 and then to 3,000; these were in addition to expulsion from the Senate (if the recalcitrant noble belonged to it) and banishment from the city. At the same time, men who consented to serve in some governorships were rewarded with Senate membership. None of these means produced more men of wealth, of course, but they undoubtedly made it easier to persuade or force the available men to accept election to governorships.

One harmful result of the lack of candidates for these posts was that the field of choice was severely restricted. According to the system used in these elections of governors (and some other officers) the Senate met in *scrutinio* and chose one candidate, while four nominators who had been chosen by lot in the Great Council picked four other competitors for the same post. The Great Council then voted on these nominees. According to the nobleman Pindemonte who wrote at the end of the eighteenth century, the Senate's candidate was the only one who was taken seriously; the nominations of the other four were regarded more or less as a joke. This is confirmed by records of the men who competed for offices during the Republic's last two centuries; the Senate's candidate is usually the only one who received a large number of favorable votes. To judge by the ages of men who were elected to the governorships and by the requests for dispensation from these offices, it is fairly clear that the Senate eventually was forced to choose its candidates for a governorship simply by going over lists of men who had reached the minimum age—twenty-five for most of the governorships and thirty for some—and nominating those in the group who had not served before. Among the requests for dispensations are a few from older men who asked to be excused with the promise that their sons would serve as soon as they reached the minimum age. Of course, wealth was also a consideration. Pindemonte claims that the Senate considered only the degree of wealth of possible candidates, not their personal merits. With such a limited field of choice, the election in the Great Council was what Marcello called not "free" but "forced." Presumably he meant that the Great Council was often obliged to elect a man of inferior ability. . . .

Another problem which resulted from the changes in the nobility during the "decadent" period concerns the maturity of many men who occupied government positions. The Venetians always had great respect for the wisdom which comes with age. Men were not considered suitable candidates for the dogeship until they were in their late 60's or 70's; in one sixteenth-century election, a 55 year old candidate was considered at a distinct disadvantage because of his youth. Men of 80 could be and were elected to offices, though piteous requests might gain them dispensations. A seventeenth-century writer said that at the bottom of the Golden Staircase in the Doges' Palace there were carved two small piles of fruit covered with straw. These were intended as symbols of the fact that the ambitions of the young had to be preserved until the time when they were mature enough for the various offices in the government. Noblemen were generally chosen for important posts only after they had reached their mid-30's. Minimum ages were not, however, generally stipulated by law; apparently there was no need to formalize what was generally practiced.

In the early seventeenth century it became apparent that the men who were being elected to important offices were frequently too young. This observation recurs frequently in legislation and in the writings of commentators on the Venetian scene. According to an apparently well-informed person who wrote about the Senate in 1675, it had once been customary to choose its members only from among men who had spent about 20 years in lesser posts. Therefore a senator would have been at least 45. Honors at that time, he says, were the "patrimony of the old."

By 1675, however, Senate membership and other honors went to younger men, with a consequent serious decline in the maturity and experience of the body of senators. As the legislation cited below will show, the situation was already considered serious in 1638; but another anonymous author, writing about 50 years later, looked back to the 1630's as a time when offices were still being given to fairly mature men. From the comparison that he makes between the two periods, it appears that there was a steady trend toward the election of ever younger men to offices.

5.

Though founded somewhat later, the Estates in German principalities went through developments, trials, and defeats similar to those of Spain and France. The Estates took up the cause of defending privileges, of seeking to control royal taxation, and of limiting absolute power. The princes, in turn, after first "using" the Estates to increase their power, sought to rule without them or to abolish them altogether.

F. L. Carsten (1911–   ), Masaryk Professor of Central European History at the University of London, not only recounts the constitutionalist struggles in Germany but also raises the question of the attitude of historians toward the Estates and examines the validity of the charge that they were negativistic and dominated by motives based on self-interest. Why did the Estates decline and fail to limit royal power? Did the Germans' failure to develop political theories justifying the preservation of ancient liberties contribute to the general failure of constitutionalism? On what basis does Carsten assert that constitutionalism in Germany had positive effects?

F. L. CARSTEN: **The German Estates and the Princes** *

Broadly speaking, Estates developed everywhere in Germany in the four-teenth and fifteenth centuries for two reasons. One was financial: the princes' revenues from lands, jurisdictions, tolls, mines, and other *regalia* shrank owing to wars, economic difficulties, and the declining value of money so that many lands and rights had to be pawned or sold. This, however, merely aggravated the problem, for it diminished the princes' own revenues further and further; and they were correspondingly less and less able "to live of their own." Hence

* From F. L. Carsten, *Princes and Parliaments in Germany from the Fifteenth to Eighteenth Century* (Oxford: Clarendon Press, 1959), pp. 425–44.

they had to seek the aid of their subjects and to reach an agreement with the nobility or the towns about the terms on which they would be willing to render such aid. A famous example of such an agreement concluded at a very early time was the treaty of 1283 between the margraves of Brandenburg and their vassals about the tax of the *Bede* or *precaria,* according to which the margraves sold the tax to their subjects against a fixed annual due from land and property, and promised that they would not ask them for another tax in future, unless in two definite and specified exceptional cases. Yet this was only a temporary solution, for in the course of time the new fixed due was also sold or paid off, and the princes were more than ever unable to meet their growing expenses and to pay their debts. In their own interest a more permanent arrangement was necessary. They could have continued to negotiate with individuals, with certain districts, or with certain groups, but they found it much more convenient to negotiate with "the country" as a whole; and this was the origin of the Estates as an institution, as a corporation representing the whole country. Soon they granted taxes to their prince, but only against certain concessions and on conditions which became the object of elaborate bargaining. Soon the diet became the only place where such taxes could legally be granted, or at least this was the case in the opinion of the Estates.

The other factor which created the Estates as an institution was the endless succession of internal conflicts, fratricidal wars, and partitions of territory between brothers and cousins of the ruling families which filled the fifteenth century in particular. In such conflicts and civil wars either side had to attempt to win the support of "the country" without which they were helpless. Frequently the Estates were called upon to act as arbiters, to carry through or to guarantee a treaty, a settlement, or a partition, or to provide the regency council which was to rule on behalf of an infant prince. The history of all the German principalities is full of examples of this kind. Thus the Estates acquired political influence and began to wield power. In Brandenburg their representatives were called upon in the fifteenth century to sit as judges in cases between the margraves and refractory towns which declined to pay taxes or to open their gates to the prince. In certain instances the Estates used their newly-won powers to impose a kind of tutelage on a weak ruler, or they deposed him if he broke previous undertakings and treaties. Naturally, the Estates were strongly opposed to partitions of the territory and to the continuation of internal strife, which they sought to prevent by the conclusion of "unions" among themselves, implicitly or explicitly directed at their warring princes. As a rule, a partition of a principality also resulted in a division of the Estates. It was in vain that the Estates of Jülich, Cleves, Berg, and Mark tried to preserve their hereditary union, for it aroused the enmity of their new rulers after the division of the Jülich–Cleves inheritance. Equally, the Estates of Saxony and of Hesse were divided into two corporations with the partition of the principalities in question, in 1485 and in 1567, never to be reunited. Only in Mecklenburg did the Estates succeed in maintaining their union of 1523 and in remaining one corporation when the duchy was partitioned in the early seventeenth century: a unity they preserved until 1918. The Estates were equally opposed to sales of parts of the territory or of princely domains. They thus indirectly worked for a strengthening of the principalities, and opposed the idea that the princes could treat their territories as if they were their private property and could sell lands at their pleasure.

There is little doubt that at the outset the princes found the advice of the Estates on foreign and domestic issues useful and the aid of "the country" indispensable on account of their increasing debts; while the Estates were naturally reluctant to enter any new commitments and burden themselves with new obligations. They did not want to become a part of the new state, but to maintain their autonomy and their privileges. The princes showed the same attitude towards the Empire, and the nobility of the south-west towards the principalities from which they succeeded in emancipating themselves, becoming Free Imperial Knights. It was to the advantage of the prince to have a working institution which would come to his aid in case of need, rather than to have to negotiate with individual groups. In 1517 the Elector Palatine Louis V expressly attributed the recovery and the rise of the archbishoprics of Cologne and Mainz, of the bishopric of Würzburg and the duchy of Württemberg, to the counsel and help rendered by their Estates: an example which he wanted to follow. Those summoned, however, proved much more reluctant to grant his wish. Through the diet, moreover, the prince could associate "the country" with his policy, gain its backing for new laws and decrees, for innovations in religion, for an alliance or a policy of expansion. Yet it would be going too far to say that it was the princes who forced upon their subjects a constitution based on Estates, as has been asserted. Most of them were much too weak to do so. Louis V of the Palatinate attempted to persuade his subjects to agree to the establishment of a diet, and did not succeed. The Estates did not come into being as a planned move by one side or the other, but they grew up because they fulfilled a useful purpose, exactly as did the English Parliament. One must be very careful not to transfer the later clash of interests, the conflicts of the seventeenth and eighteenth centuries, into a period where no such conflicts existed. As the "King in Parliament" was more powerful than the king alone, so the ruler "with Estates" was stronger than he was without them; for they provided him with the means to develop the machinery of government and with the money which he so urgently needed.

Finance remained the main field of the activity of the Estates. From the point of view of the prince the main, and often the only, reason for summoning a diet was that he needed money. From the point of view of the Estates the diet provided an opportunity to raise their grievances and to make their grant dependent on the fulfilment of certain conditions. As the prince and his councillors were often incapable of managing the country's finances, and as his credit usually stood very low, the Estates of many principalities took over the prince's debts, partially or totally, with the intention of gradually paying them off, which was hardly ever possible. Therefore in many principalities the control, even the actual conduct, of the financial administration, of the levying and repartitioning of taxes, of the issue of obligations and the payment of interest, passed into the hands of the Estates. They were able to borrow much larger sums at a much lower rate of interest than their bankrupt rulers; the obligations they issued were considered a safe investment. Their financial control was exercised either together with princely officials, as in Saxony, or alone, as in Bavaria, Branden-burg, and Württemberg. For this purpose the Estates employed their own officials, responsible to them or to one of their committees; while some of their own members checked the accounts, supervised the collection of taxes, received the money, &c. These functions they fulfilled efficiently and at small cost, thus providing a practical alternative to the development of a bureaucratic machine by the state. The development of this permanent machinery greatly strength-ened the Estates. It gave them practical administrative experience, and it made them more independent of the prince who was confined to the administration of his domains, tolls, and *regalia*. Taxes could be levied only with the Estates' con-sent, and this principle became the corner-stone of their liberties and their whole position; but a strong prince would at times levy taxes by decree without consulting the diet.

Using their right of raising grievances the Estates often tried to influence their prince's foreign and domestic policies, to make the conclusion of alliances and the starting of military operations dependent on their consent, to subject the composition of the princely council to their supervision, to make the appointment of officials dependent on their being natives of the principality in question, and to gain the right of being consulted in all important affairs. They were successful in pressing these demands to a varying degree, and the rights thus obtained were incorporated in their privileges, which every new ruler on his accession had to swear to observe. But again a strong prince would not necessarily consider himself bound by such promises and would tend to conduct his policy without a reference to his Estates. In the sixteenth and seventeenth centuries, however, many Estates strongly influenced the policy of their prince, prevented arbitrary actions and petty tyranny and, by their cautiousness in granting supply, avoided many an adventure in the field of foreign policy. It has been regretfully stated that this entailed the renunciation of an active foreign policy and of military power: an opinion which seems rather incon-gruous when published in the year 1955, and might have been expressed more fittingly during an earlier period of German history. Moreover, it takes no account of the realities of the sixteenth, seventeenth, and eighteenth centuries when an active foreign policy could be directed only against neighbouring princes and would have caused perpetual civil war. That warfare was not per-petual, but only intermittent, was partly the achievement of the Estates.

The Estates had no claim to participate in legislation other than money grants. But in practice draft laws and decrees were often submitted to them, whether they were concerned with codifications of the law or legal procedure, police matters, trade, the coinage, the order of succession, or the administration. Often they seized the initiative in such matters through the grievances which they raised. In one field they were most strongly interested, that of religion, in which every individual felt most intimately concerned. As the dissolution of the monasteries in many ways violated the established rights of the clergy and the nobility, the Estates considered that the new religious order and the use of the ecclesiastical revenues were matters best to be arranged by the diet. It is true that in most Protestant principalities the Reformation was introduced without any prior consultation with the Estates. Only in Brunswick was their consent obtained by the Duchess Elisabeth, acting on behalf of her minor son. In Saxony, in Württemberg, and elsewhere the Estates nevertheless strongly influenced the religious settlement. It was due to their efforts that the monastic revenues were not entirely dissipated, but partly used for pious and educational purposes. In the archbishopric of Magdeburg the Estates even obtained the grant of religious liberty in exchange for taking over some of the debts of their prince. In the duchy of Styria the Estates in the 1570's succeeded after long negotiations in gaining full religious liberty, and similar concessions were made to them in other Habsburg territories. Even in Bavaria the Estates strongly voiced their religious demands at the diet; and thanks to their efforts the chalice was for some time conceded to the laity. In the secularized duchy of Prussia the Estates emerged as the decisive power. They considered Lutheran orthodoxy and the *Corpus Doctrinae Prussicae* their most cherished privileges. They dominated the Church and the administration and made the duke completely dependent on themselves, playing him off against the king of Poland and becoming the real masters of the country. Nor did the princes of the other Lutheran principalities gain much from the Reformation and their new position as the heads of the Church, contrary to the opinion which is usually held. Through lack of funds most princes were forced to sell the church lands very quickly, and the Estates used the ever-repeated demands for money to gain new privileges and some say in church affairs. They became the real defenders of orthodox Lutheranism. With the exception of Catholic Bavaria, their position everywhere became stronger in the course of the sixteenth century.

This growing strength of the Estates rested partly on the officials employed by them and on the machinery they developed, especially on their committees. It is true that the princes preferred to negotiate with a small committee rather than with the whole diet; but the diet only met from time to time, and meanwhile some machinery was required to deal with taxation and other current financial affairs and to safeguard the Estates' rights. The princes naturally would have liked the committees to vote them taxes and thus to be spared the expense and the opposition likely to emanate from a diet, but these attempts were everywhere strongly resisted by the Estates. They insisted on preserving intact their power of the purse and refused to empower their committees to make any money grants. Only after their opposition had been broken were the Bavarian Estates persuaded to depart from this principle and thus to accelerate their own decline. Those of other principalities, such as Saxony and Württemberg, steadfastly refused to do so and thus preserved their powers.

The machinery provided by the Estates for administrative tasks was efficient and inexpensive, for the number of officials they employed was small, and many of their own members served in an honorary capacity, or for a purely nominal salary. In Bavaria they even collected the excise on wine and beer at very small cost. Knowledge of local affairs was another asset which the Estates possessed in contrast with their rulers' "foreign" officials. All the appointments, however, soon became vested in the Estates' committees which also co-opted their own new members, with or without the confirmation of the prince, so that the whole structure assumed the aspect of a narrow oligarchy dominated by some leading families. It is certainly true that the Estates—whether the Junkers of the east or the burghers of Württemberg—acted in the interests of the class which they represented, that their horizon was narrow, and that they did not stand for liberty in the modern sense of the term. Still, in defending their liberties and in raising their grievances, for example in matters of trade or against princely monopolies, they often defended the true interests of the country against the prince and his officials. In complaining about heavy labour and carrying services and the great damage caused by deer and other wild animals they championed the interests of the peasants. In opposing forcible recruiting and too heavy military burdens they prevented some of the worst excesses of petty despotism. Neither can it truly be maintained that the Estates were not willing to undertake permanent duties, nor that they were "impervious to the needs of the modern state," that the organization of the administration remained stationary where they predominated. In many principalities the Estates developed new administrative organs, especially in the field of finance. In some they introduced the first indirect taxes in place of the antiquated and less suitable direct taxes. The mixed "deputations" of Württemberg associated the Estates with the new organs of administration and thus provided a link between them and the state. Many members of the Estates served the state willingly, and their grants were often very liberal.

These remarks also show that another common criticism of the Estates is not really justified: that they did not create anything new, but had an entirely negative function. Thus Professor Hartung in his standard constitutional history of Germany wrote only a few years ago:

The Estates resisted burdens and wrongs imposed by the princes, but they created nothing new. As a rule they were satisfied if they need not pay any taxes, if the prince's officials were not permitted to penetrate into their domains and were firmly bound to observe the country's liberties. . . . Even when the Estates raised higher demands and . . . aimed at a share in the government, their aims remained more negative than positive. They wanted to limit the prince, to prevent him from taking measures which might damage their own interests. . . . They did not think of permanently influencing the government, they were the defenders of medieval autonomy. . . .

With regard to Württemberg and the policy of the dukes in the eighteenth century he goes even further and declares: "There is no doubt that this absolutist tendency, the references to the changed times, to the *salus publica,* which demanded a departure from the letter of the old treaties, were justified. . . ."

In other words, the tendency to denigrate the German Estates and to side with the princes, who tried to suppress them, persists to the present day. This tendency has always been so pronounced that fifty years ago a German historian exclaimed: "It is unjustified simply to take on all occasions the side of the absolute state against the Estates. . . ." But his voice has remained a cry in the wilderness. Recently, however, Professor Hartung has admitted that the Estates "formed, through their mere existence, a counter-weight to absolute government and therewith kept alive the idea of liberty. The liberal movement of the nine-teenth century was able to link up with this inheritance, most clearly and most directly in Württemberg. . . ." Surely, this consideration alone ought to lead to a revision of the one-sided attitude towards the Estates. It is no accident, surely, that the liberal movement of the nineteenth century was strongest in those areas of Germany where the Estates survived the period of absolute government. Not only the idea of liberty, but the principles of self-government were kept alive by the Estates, as the Freiherr vom Stein so clearly perceived in Cleves and Mark. That this tradition did not die out in Germany was due to the opposition of the Estates to petty despotism and to the preconceived uni-formity, which was the ideal of all absolute governments.

Most of the German Estates did not buttress their positions by any political theories, but merely argued their case in a matter-of-fact and practical way. They took their stand on ancient customs and privileges which they refused to modify, but had no theories on how they had come into being. Only the Estates of the duchy of Prussia developed a theoretical foundation of their rights; but as they realized themselves, theirs was a very special position. In 1663 they outlined the historical basis of their privileges in this way to the Great Elector of Brandenburg: the Teutonic Knights originally conquered the country by force of arms and therefore possessed absolute powers. They then granted various privileges to immigrating German noblemen and commoners out of their plenary powers. Later, however, the Order did not respect these privileges and its absolute government became oppressive, so that towns and country united in defence of their liberties and reached an agreement with the crown of Poland. This crown therefore bestowed upon the Prussians weighty new bene-fits and immunities which annulled the *absolutum jus* of the Order and did not preserve any of its powers and rights, so that Prussia came under the Polish kings *certis pactis* and with only those rights which were bestowed upon Poland through this spontaneous surrender. Thus the Elector, they argued, could not claim the authority which the Order had once possessed, but only that of the Polish crown, to whose position he had succeeded, and had to accept the *pacta* by which the rights of the Estates had been fixed. There could hardly be a better example of the contract theory of government than that provided by the history of the Prussian Estates.

On many occasions the Prussian Estates emphasized that their privileges were fixed once and for all and could be altered only with their consent; that they could be augmented, but not diminished without violating their consciences; that it was their duty to hand them down to their successors as they had been entrusted to them by their ancestors and by the country; that they were not entitled to dispose of them freely, but would be held responsible by God and their descendants if they broke the fundamental laws. They denied that there was a conflict of interest between the prince and the country and that they were more concerned for its welfare than for his authority, for their officials had taken an oath to him and they themselves had sworn fealty to him. All Christian rulers, they claimed, consulted their Estates. God had given the Elector so many lands and subjects that he could not possibly rule everywhere himself and had to ask advice in important matters. They were appointed by God, and their counsel could only be blessed. They had the best knowledge of local conditions and were most interested in them. Individuals could deceive and be deceived, but not the whole country. Constitutional laws were the true foundation of government and were considered by human society the very basis of the state, as they had been agreed upon when a government was first established. All princely authority rested on this principle, without which the state would collapse, and which formed the bond between the prince and his subjects. Another time the Estates declared that they were the *corpus mysticum,* the head of which was the prince, and the heart of which was the public weal. A century and a half before the Estates of Bavaria similarly referred to the *jus naturale* and the *jus gentium,* from which they derived a right of defending themselves against illegal oppression. Against the theory of the Divine Right the Estates thus put the theory of the natural law and the original contract, of their appointment by God to be their prince's councillors, of the mutual pact that existed between their prince and them. They reminded him that his powers were limited and that they were entitled to resist oppression. They showed from the example of the Teutonic Knights what was the fate of a prince who became a tyrant against whom his subjects might revolt. Yet the Estates used this right of resistance only in very exceptional cases, and hardly ever with success.

From a position of great strength which they occupied in the sixteenth century most of the German Estates declined in the seventeenth century; indeed, as we have seen, the Estates of Bavaria already in the sixteenth century. The causes of this rapid decline, especially in the later seventeenth century, have been discussed by many historians. The growth of princely power has been attributed to the adoption of primogeniture and the cessation of the many partitions, which in the fifteenth century played into the hands of the Estates. Yet the hundred and fifty years after the adoption of the *Dispositio Achillea* in Brandenburg were the period of the Estates' greatest power; and in Württemberg there followed upon the acceptance of the same principle the deposition of Duke Eberhard and the treaty of Tübingen, and then the consolidation of the Estates' influence in the second half of the sixteenth century. With the exceptions of Bavaria and Hesse, a similar consolidation occurred at that time in most other principalities. This also disposes of another argument which has often been put forward: that the growth of princely power was due to the Reformation, the new position of the Protestant prince as the *summus episcopus* of his lands, and the strength he gained through the dissolution of the monasteries. But the German princes benefited but little from the spoliation of the Church. The victory of the dukes of Bavaria over their Estates, on the other hand, was connected with the advance of the Counter-Reformation, the financial and political backing the dukes were given by the clergy, and the activities of the Jesuits in favour of the Catholic princes. So, fifty years later, were the victories of the Habsburgs over the Estates of Austria, Bohemia, Moravia, and Silesia, whose powers rivalled those of the crown in the period before the outbreak of the Thirty Years War.

The Thirty Years War certainly marked a decisive change in the fortunes of the Estates in many German territories. But, as we have seen, in Cleves and Mark, Hesse-Cassel, Saxony, and Württemberg the Estates' influence actually increased as a result of the war. Only where their leaders were Protestants, and the princes Catholics, did the military victories of the Counter-Reformation result in a defeat of the Estates and their policy of religious liberty. Elsewhere the issue was much more complex. Nor can it be maintained that after 1648 the Estates were "rotting from inside" (*innerlich morsch*), that there was no need to defeat them, that they withered away without any great effort on the part of the princes, and that sharp conflicts between prince and Estates only occurred as an exception. The preceding pages and the sharp clashes which occurred in Brandenburg and Prussia provide ample proof that this was not the case. Even in the Habsburg territories the Estates, in spite of their defeat in the Thirty Years War, showed a surprising tenacity and survived into the later eighteenth century.

As a result of the Thirty Years War and of the wars against Louis XIV standing armies came into being in many parts of Germany. As early as the eighteenth century a Württemberg historian wrote that the existence of standing armies was incompatible with the preservation of the Estates' liberties, and his opinion has been endorsed by some modern historians. This is certainly true of Brandenburg and Prussia, but not of Bavaria, where the standing army only came into being after the Estates had been defeated. Saxony and Württemberg, although they had standing armies, preserved their constitutions intact; so did the Sweden of Gustavus Adolphus. Not only the countries in the centre of Europe, but also those at its periphery, such as Sweden and England, acquired standing armies in the course of the seventeenth century and were drawn into the struggles for power, and yet their armies did not play the part which the army played in Brandenburg and Prussia.

Drawn into the struggles for power, often against their will, many German princes sought to imitate the example of the most powerful king in Europe, who possessed the largest forces and carried everything before him. Louis XIV was strong, and he was absolute, the leading protagonist of the theory of the Divine Right of Kings and of the practice of absolute government. In their endeavours to establish a standing army most princes met with the opposition of their Estates, who rightly pointed to the extreme exhaustion of the country after the ravages of the Thirty Years War and to the need of recuperation. Thus a conflict became almost inevitable. The princes could refer to the stipulations of the Imperial diet of 1654 and to the Imperial promises of 1658, which obliged the Estates of the German principalities to maintain their ruler's fortresses and garrisons and forbade them to assemble on their own initiative and to complain on these accounts to the courts of the Empire. The princes could use the perennial disunity among the Estates and play them off against each other, make concessions to one Estate to win its support in matters of taxation, as the Great Elector so successfully did in Brandenburg and Prussia. It was not so much through the establishment of the *miles perpetuus* that he defeated the Estates, but through the introduction of the urban excise, which became a permanent tax and made it unnecessary to summon any more diets, and through the simultaneous taking over of the functions of the Estates in the field of finance which were transferred to state officials. In Bavaria and in Saxony also the excise on wine and beer became a permanent tax, but it remained under the administration and control of the Estates. The Estates of Württemberg and of Saxony also granted a general excise, but always for a limited period. It was only through the combination of these two measures that the Great Elector effectively deprived the Estates of all influence. It was only through the separation of the nobility and the towns and through the imposition of entirely different systems of taxation on the two Estates that he made their reunion and the revival of their influence impossible. As the nobility of the duchy of Prussia declared in 1683, evil men had dissected the one *corpus* of the three Estates and made a torso out of it, had separated the towns from the country, and the free peasants from the nobility. The maxim of *divide et impera* was a poisonous doctrine, only used by harsh princes, but their gracious master would, they hoped, follow the opposite one: *conjunge et conservabis, et sic feliciter imperabis.* Their prince knew only too well why he spurned this advice.

It thus depended very much on the policies and the ambitions of the princes whether and to what extent they turned against their Estates. The Estates of Württemberg, as we have seen, several times were saved only by the timely death of the duke and the accession of a minor prince, or of a duke who needed their support and thus discontinued his predecessor's policy. The Hohenzollerns seem to have been much more determined than any other ruling house to deprive the Estates of all power; and the Wittelsbachs adopted a similar policy. The resistance of many Estates, when faced with a determined opponent, quickly crumbled. They seldom enjoyed popular support, but in Cleves and Mark and in the duchy of Prussia such backing strengthened them to some extent. It certainly strengthened their opposition to a prince who adhered to a different religion: in Lutheran Prussia to the Calvinist Elector of Brandenburg, in Saxony and Württemberg to Roman Catholic dukes, in Hesse-Cassel to a Calvinist land-grave. In all these instances, Lutheran Estates resisted their prince doggedly and determinedly and made it impossible for him to exercise his *jus reformandi*: another reflection on the new powers which allegedly accrued to the princes as a result of the Lutheran Reformation. In these respects as in others the differences which existed between the various principalities were very great, so that the fate of the Estates varied greatly. The example of Brandenburg and Prussia, where the Estates virtually disappeared, was followed only by some other principalities and was not typical of the Germany of the eighteenth century; but neither was that of Württemberg and of Mecklenburg where the Estates defeated their princes' efforts in the course of the eighteenth century. In the majority of the principalities the Estates survived, but in a much weakened form.

The Estates received little support from the Emperor and from the Imperial courts to which they appealed in spite of the prohibition of 1658. The Estates of Cleves and Mark and those of Jülich and Berg were left to their fate because the Emperor needed the support of their new rulers. The Wittelsbachs received valuable help from the Habsburgs in the struggles with the Estates. The Aulic

Council did not sustain the appeals from Jülich and Berg and from Bavaria in the eighteenth century. However, it backed the Estates of Mecklenburg and of Württemberg against their dukes and thus materially contributed to their victories. Without this backing, their fate might have been very different. The somewhat surprising fact emerges that the institutions of the Empire, even in the eighteenth century, possessed a vitality and an importance which made them the arbiter in a conflict between a prince and his Estates, and which gave to the Emperor the chance to intervene in the internal affairs of many a principality. But this influence was only rarely used in favour of the Estates. The power of resistance of the nobility and the towns was sapped by social and economic changes, by the price revolution, and especially by the Thirty Years War. After its end recovery took a long time, for war continued in the west, in the southeast, and in the north during the second half of the seventeenth century, and war benefited the princes and the growth of their armies. If the seventeenth century had not been so belligerent, so filled with struggles for power, the strength of the German Estates might have persisted. The power policy of the time favoured the growth of princely authority, not only in Germany. Faced with the power of Louis XIV the methods of the Estates seemed as antiquated as was the militia, which they favoured, against the might of the French army.

The struggles between princes and Estates had much in common with the conflicts between crown and Parliament, but the outcome was usually the opposite. Thanks to the prevalence of the gentry in the House of Commons and its close links with the urban merchants and lawyers, the House of Commons possessed a social homogeneity which, in Germany, only existed in Württemberg. It also existed in the diets of Poland and of Hungary, which were entirely dominated by the landed nobility. The sharp social and economic conflicts, the antagonism and the rigid separation of nobility and towns, which were so characteristic of Germany and other continental countries, did not exist in the English Parliament, partly thanks to the fact that the knights of the shire and the burgesses sat together in one house. Even the House of Lords, thanks to the specific traits of the English peerage, was not separated by a gulf from the Lower House: in many ways the interests of the nobility were identical with those of the landed gentry who dominated the Commons and whose members might be elevated to the peerage; while the younger sons of peers often sat in the Commons. The two groups were connected by many family ties and common economic interests. Their members co-operated harmoniously as Justices of the Peace and in other functions of local government, which provided a firm basis for their activities in Parliament. In practice the nobility and the gentry formed one ruling group. Some members of the House of Lords were strongly drawn towards Puritan ideas, and in the seventeenth century some worked together with Puritan members of the House of Commons in commercial and colonizing ventures. In the critical hour of the Long Parliament a minority of the peers joined hands with the majority of the Commons in united opposition to the king. In the weapon of Puritanism they possessed an ideology and an organization, a burning faith, which were entirely lacking in Germany, even where Lutheran Estates opposed a Calvinist or a Catholic prince.

No German prince carefully nurtured the Estates as Henry VIII did; no German prince deliberately increased the Estates' privileges; no German prince went out of his way to seek the Estates' support against the Pope or against foreign enemies. A leading authority on English constitutional history under the Tudors has written:

It is remarkable that in the Tudor period—the period of despotic government— there should have been steady progress in the development and definition of the privilege of Parliament. The explanation is to be found not in the strength of Parliament but in its weakness. It was the Tudor policy to rule by means of Parliament because the Tudor sovereigns were not afraid of Parliament.

In the sixteenth century the powers of many German Estates, in the fields of finance, foreign policy, and military affairs, were considerably greater than those of the English Parliament. They had their own officials and their permanent committees, functioning even when the diet was not in session and during the intervals between one diet and the next, and they dominated the financial administration of the principality. Yet they exercised no judicial functions, hence could not wield the weapon of impeachment, and their privileges were less well-defined than those of Parliament. The German princes, on the other hand, were much weaker than the Tudors, internally as well as externally, continuously threatened by other princes and by the Emperor. They could not possibly follow the same course as the Tudors and strengthen their Estates. They were afraid of them, hence they sought to curtail their powers, although in the sixteenth century they were successful in doing so only in Bavaria. The German Estates, in spite of their great powers in the financial field, only with much hesitation used the weapon of grievances before supply. They easily granted money against fair promises, without a guarantee that they would ever be fulfilled. Many princes were able to disregard solemn undertakings, to violate the Estates' privileges, to levy taxes without their consent. Hardly any Estates thought of resisting by force such infringements of the constitution; at most they would appeal to the courts of the Empire, hoping for protection by the Emperor or a foreign ruler. Perhaps it was the teaching of passive obedience by Luther and other churchmen which prevented opposition from crystallizing into resistance. Even the Estates of Württemberg did not dream of opposing the duke by force of arms. The "conspiracy" of the Bavarian noblemen against Duke Albert V was largely a fabrication of the government. Here lies one of the decisive differences between the attitude of the English Parliament and that of the German Estates.

The great struggles between Royalists and Parliamentarians found little echo in Germany. Only in the duchy of Cleves, where the Estates maintained close connexions with the States General of the United Provinces and were animated by the spirit of Calvinism, was a comparison made between the aims of the Estates and the opposition of Parliament to Charles I. It was not the Estates, however, who claimed the title of Parliamentarians, but the Electoral government which accused them of such ambitions, presumably to blacken them in the eyes of their friends among the Dutch Estates. Likewise in the duchy of Calenberg, when the Estates made difficulties about granting supply, it was the chancellor who in 1651 asserted that "the principles of the Puritans became widespread in Germany," not the Estates who claimed this relationship. In reality, however, the spirit of the Roundheads was singularly absent from seventeenth-century Germany. Perhaps some of the stronger towns, such as Königsberg or Wesel, came closest to offering armed resistance to the Great Elector of Brandenburg, who to them was a foreign prince and represented alien interests. But a show of force, the arrest of their leaders, was sufficient to reduce them to obedience. There was no London and no Paris to oppose the king, but only small, declining towns, with an anxious spirit and few resources. Königsberg might hope for help from the king of Poland, Wesel for aid from the States General, but none was rendered. The nobility was not animated by the spirit of the Fronde, nor by that of the Huguenots, but by that of loyalty to their prince whom they were eager to serve. The nobility and the towns were bitterly hostile to each other. No revolutionary movement could arise under such conditions.

Yet the German Estates fulfilled important historical functions. Their traditions remained alive, especially in the south-west of Germany. Their opposition may not have been very effective, but it existed nevertheless. They preserved the spirit of constitutional government and liberty in the age of absolute monarchy. In many principalities they showed great vitality, even in the eighteenth century. A new spirit began to permeate them with the coming of the French Revolution and the penetration of French ideas of liberty and equality. For these reasons alone the Estates deserved an honoured place in German history. They did not reach the great eminence of the English Parliament or of the Dutch Estates. But in many principalities they retained their influence much longer than the representative institutions of other European countries, especially those of France and Spain. It has been said of the Estates of Cleves and Mark that in the struggle with the Great Elector of Brandenburg they "more than once . . . stood for the principles of the modern state." This can be maintained in a more general sense and with equal justification of the Estates of Württemberg and of Saxony, of the duchy of Prussia and of other German principalities. Germany is a country of many different traditions. One of them, and not the least important, was kept alive by the strenuous opposition of the Estates to the principles of absolute government.

6.

The English government of 1689, which Trevelyan praises as permitting freedom, nevertheless bears little resemblance to democratic government as we now know it. This is the first lesson to be drawn from Sir Lewis Namier's (1888–1960) brilliant description of English political life in 1760. Where are the modern election procedures, laws against corruption, and control or even monopoly of parliamentary seats? They were not there in 1760, and this means, of course, that they were not there in 1689 either. For the uninitiated, Trevelyan's picture seems adequate because it evokes much of what we take to be our own; but then with the details and flavor given by Namier, it becomes clear that there is a gulf between the constitution after 1689 and that of contemporary Britain. Namier, who was one of Britain's leading scholars, complements Trevelyan, by making us realize the remoteness of constitutionalist politics before the changes worked in the nineteenth century.

Then does Namier go a step further? He faces squarely the charges that English politics was corrupt and undemocratic in the sense that Parliament did not represent every Englishman in the way a current democrat would wish. What is his answer? Does he, like Trevelyan, revere the "un-reformed" government of England? How does his picture of English society reinforce his generally rosy picture of things?

SIR LEWIS NAMIER: The Land as a Basis of Citizenship*

The social history of England could be written in terms of membership of the House of Commons, that peculiar club, election to which has at all times required some expression of consent on the part of the public. At no time was the House truly unrepresentative; for with us the result of elections does not primarily depend on constituencies or electorates. Live forces break through forms, and shape results to suit requirements. Were it decided that the 615 heaviest men in the country should constitute the House of Commons, the various interests and parties could be trusted to obtain their proportionate weight in it. But the idea of representation and the nature of the body politic vary from age to age, and with them varies the social structure of the House of Commons.

In its origin the House of Commons was akin to the jury, and the representative character and functions of the two were in a way cognate; from an intimate knowledge of conditions, the House declared the sense of the commonalty on questions which most patently and directly concerned them, but did not pronounce sentence and did not meddle with matters of government or "mysteries of State." Attendance at it was truly a service. But as the position and prestige of Parliament increased, and seats in the House of Commons began to be prized, it came to represent, not so much the sense of the community, as the distribution of power within it—the two developments being necessarily and inevitably correlated. The leading territorial families, and even the gentry of lesser rank, now invaded the borough representation; and the Crown attempted to secure seats in the House of Commons for its servants and dependants—if a true equation of forces was to be attained, the executive, centring in the King and as yet extraneous to the Commons, had to receive its own representation in the House. As make-weight in favour of stable government, the royal influence in elections continued to be worked after the Revolution of 1688. When the struggle commenced between George III and his grandfather's political "undertakers," an outcry was raised against "prerogative"—the term was still current by force of ideological and linguistic survival; for ideas outlive the conditions which gave them birth, and words outlast ideas. In reality, George III never left the safe ground of Parliamentary government, and merely acted the *primus inter pares,* the first among the borough-mongering, electioneering gentlemen of

* From Sir Lewis Namier, *England in the Age of the American Revolution* (London: Macmillan, 1930), pp. 3–66.

England. While the Stuarts tried to browbeat the House and circumscribe the range of its action, George III fully accepted its constitution and recognised its powers, and merely tried to work it in accordance with the customs of the time.

The demoralising influence of the eighteenth-century electoral system is obvious, and its nonsensical features are only too patent; its deeper sense and its usefulness are less apparent. The rotten boroughs were a necessary part of the eighteenth-century organisation of the British Government, while corruption in populous boroughs was the effect of citizen status in an electorate not fully awake to national interests; even so, it was a mark of English freedom and independence, for no one bribes where he can bully. Without those boroughs the House of Commons in 1761 would practically have represented one class only, the landed interest, and in the first place those independent country gentlemen who in fact supplied most of the knights of the shires; this might possibly have sufficed for a self-centred nation, never for an Empire. A careful student of Parliamentary history gives the following description of the fifteen knights of the shire who represented Devonshire between 1688 and 1761, and ten of whom belonged to three families: "Of nearly every one we might say: he belonged to a well-known Devon family; while in Parliament he made no speeches, held no office, and achieved no distinction of any sort; but whenever he is known to have recorded a vote, it was given against the government then in office." The most respectable constituencies in Great Britain returned the dullest members; they did not supply the architects and craftsmen of government and administration. The boroughs under Government management, or acquired by the Government at the time of the election, opened the gates of the House to budding statesmen and to hard-working civil servants, the permanent secretaries of Government departments (who were not as yet disqualified from sitting in it), to various law officers of the Crown, to admirals and pro-consuls; in short, to the men who had the widest and most varied experience of administrative work; while the promising young men and the "men of business" of the Opposition were similarly provided for by its borough patrons. Since 1832 the party organisations have tried to fill the place of patrons or the Government in providing for men who are required in the House but are not of sufficient fame, wealth, or popularity to secure them seats. These endeavours have not been altogether successful—in 1873 Lord Lytton wrote in a novel about a rising politician: "In the old time, before the first Reform Bill, his reputation would have secured him at once a seat in Parliament; but the ancient nurseries of statesmen are gone, and their place is not supplied." Even now the safest, richest, and therefore most independent Conservative constituencies elect mainly local worthies, while able young men have to be sent by headquarters to doubtful constituencies, dependent on financial support from the party organisation, and succumb at a landslide.

Yet another function was discharged by the corrupt and the rotten boroughs: through them the *nouveaux-riches* in every generation were able to enter the House of Commons; and this occurred with such regularity that by tracing the history of these new men one could follow the rise and fall of various branches of commerce, the development of modern finance, and the advance of capitalist organisation in industry, and measure the relative importance of the West and East Indies. Thus even a good deal of the economic and colonial history of England could be written in terms of membership of the House of Commons.

The fact that in England money was allowed to play a great part in the selection of the governing body (much greater than in Scotland and Wales) was the result and expression of the peculiar character of English society, civilian and plutocratic, though imbued with feudal habits and traditions.

England knows not democracy as a doctrine, but has always practised it as a fine art. Since the Middle Ages, no one was ever barred on grounds of class from entering the House of Commons, and in the House all Members have always sat on equal terms; as between freemen, England never knew a rigid distinction of classes. Still, there has been throughout an element of heredity in the membership of the House, largely connected with property in land, but at no time resulting in the formation of close castes; England's social structure to this day retains more traces of feudalism than that of any other country, but it has never been hierarchical. Trade was never despised, and English society has always shown respect for property and wealth. The financial expert, usually a "moneyed" man, was valued in the House, and the Treasury has for centuries held a pre-eminent position in the Government. St. Matthew vi. 21 was quoted by the English mediaeval author of the *Dialogus de Scaccario* to prove by the authority of Christ that the King's heart was, where his treasure was, in the Exchequer; and there the heart of the nation has been ever since—which accounts for the paramount importance of Budget nights and for the excellence of British public finance.

The social history of nations is largely moulded by the forms and development of their armed forces, the primary aim of national organisation being common defence. The historical development of England is based on the fact that her frontiers against Europe are drawn by Nature, and cannot be the subject of dispute; that she is a unit sufficiently small for coherent government to have been established and maintained even under very primitive conditions; that since 1066 she has never suffered serious invasion; that no big modern armies have succeeded her feudal levies; and that her senior service is the navy, with which foreign trade is closely connected. In short, a great deal of what is peculiar in English history is due to the obvious fact that Great Britain is an island.

Encroachments on frontier provinces were never possible in the case of England (the Scottish and Welsh Borders may be here left out of account); a conquest had to be complete or could not endure. Frontier encroachments are apt to produce chaos, whereas complete conquests tend to establish strong governments. In anarchical conditions those who bear arms obtain an ascendancy over the other classes, and usually form themselves into a close, dominant caste; while a strong central government, such as was established in England after 1066, was in itself a check on class privileges. Where armies serve as "expeditionary forces" militarism has little chance to permeate the life of the nation; and there is more of the knight-errant in a merchant-adventurer than in an officer of the militia.

Feudalism was a system of social organisation whereby both army service and administrative functions were bound up with the holding of land. When a change supervened in armament and methods of fighting, on the European Continent a new type of royal army took the place of feudal levies, and the administrative structure of Continental countries was adjusted to the requirements of the new military organisation. Rank and caste were not eliminated, but they were no longer bound up with property in land. An army is necessarily built up on gradations of rank, and universal military service has imbued the Continental nations with hierarchical conceptions; even posts in the civil service were in many countries assimilated to ranks in the army. Society became sharply divided into those who were trained for officers and those who could not claim commissioned rank; and "honour," implying the right to fight duels, was restricted to members of the officer-class.

If the compelling, uncompromising exigencies of military organisation are sufficient to override tradition, war is in itself revolution; it results in a destruction of existing forms, carried out by military organisations in accordance with an accepted code. Regard for property and law can hardly be maintained in war; invasion and conquest do away with prescriptive rights. The fine growth of English Conservatism is due, in a high degree, to the country having been free from the revolutionary action of war within its borders, and of militarism within its social organisation. The true Conservative is not a militarist.

Feudalism in England, divested of its military purpose, and not supplanted by any new military establishment on a national scale, survived in local government and social relations, continuing to rest on property in land; but as there was no sharp division of classes, based on the use of arms, and no subject of the King was debarred from holding land, the new civilian feudalism—a peculiarly English product—necessarily bore a plutocratic imprint. Primogeniture, feudal in origin, survived, and titles retained a territorial character, with the result that there can be but one holder of a title. This restriction has allowed more room for new creations, while the position of younger sons has similarly worked against a sharp division of classes.

The younger sons of country gentlemen, and even of peers, went into trade without thereby losing caste; the eldest son inherited the family estates, the second, third, or even fourth, were placed in the Church, in the army or navy, at the bar, or in some government office; but the next had usually to be apprenticed to a merchant, and, however great the name and wealth of the family, the boy baptised Septimus or Decimus was almost certain to be found in a counting-house; only courtesy lords were precluded by custom from entering trade. "Trade in England," wrote Defoe in 1726, "neither is or ought to be levell'd with what it is in other countries; or the tradesmen depreciated as they are abroad. . . . The word tradesman in England does not sound so harsh, as it does in other countries; and to say a gentleman-tradesman is not . . . nonsense. . . ." "Were it not for two articles, by which the numbers of the families of gentlemen are recruited . . . when sunk and decayed . . . this nation would, in a few years, have very few families of gentlemen left; or, at least, very few that had estates to support them." But "the gentry are always willing to submit to the raising their families, by what they call City fortunes," while "the rising tradesman swells into the gentry."

Trade is so far here from being inconsistent with a gentleman, that in short trade in England makes gentlemen, and has peopled this nation with gentlemen; for . . . the tradesmen's children, or at least their grand-children, come to be as good gentlemen, statesmen, Parliament-men, privy-counsellors, judges, bishops, and noblemen, as those of the highest birth and the most antient families. . . .

We see the tradesmen of England, as they grow wealthy, coming every day to the Herald's Office, to search for the coats of arms of their ancestors, in order to paint them upon their coaches, and engrave them upon their plate, embroider them upon their furniture, or carve them upon the pediments of their new houses; and how often do we see them trace the registers of their families up to the prime nobility or the most antient gentry of the Kingdom?

In this search we find them often qualified to raise new families, if they do not descend from old. . . .

The first Lord Craven, whose father had been a wholesale grocer, "being upbraided with his being of an upstart nobility, by the famous Aubrey, Earl of Oxford, who was himself of the very antient family of the Veres, Earls of Oxford," replied that he would "cap pedigrees with him"; "he read over his family thus; I am William Lord Craven, my father was Lord Mayor of London, and my grandfather was the Lord knows who. . . ."

If anyone about 1760 could be named as prototype of the country gentleman it would be the Tory squire, Sir John Hinde Cotton, M.P., of Madingley Hall, Cambridgeshire, 4th baronet. The Cottons had been settled for centuries at Madingley, and had sat in Parliament in the fourteenth and sixteenth centuries; the father of Sir John had represented the County, and so did he himself. But his paternal grandmother was Elizabeth, daughter of John Sheldon, Lord Mayor of London; and his mother, Lettice, daughter of Sir Ambrose Crowley, the famous Durham ironmaster, whose warehouse in Upper Thames Street bore the sign of the "Leathern Doublet," to commemorate the dress in which he had come to London. "No gent., nor any pretence to arms" was the description given of his Quaker father, and Ambrose Crowley himself, as Jack Anvil, transformed into Sir John Enville, appears in Addison's *Spectator* (No. 299) as the type of the self-made man, "bent upon making a family" with "a dash of good blood in their veins." Sir John Hinde Cotton married his cousin Anne, daughter of Humphrey Parsons, Lord Mayor of London, by Sarah, another daughter of Sir Ambrose Crowley; and his sister Mary married Jacob Houblon, the son of a merchant and a descendant of the *Pater Bursae Londoniensis*. Elizabeth, a third daughter of Crowley, married John, 10th Lord St. John of Bletso; one of Crowley's granddaughters married Sir William Stanhope, M.P., brother of the famous Lord Chesterfield, and another, "with a fortune of £200,000," John, 2nd Earl of Ashburnham.

Illustrations of this kind could be multiplied indefinitely, but even a dozen examples, though, in their accumulation, subconsciously reassuring to the reader, do not prove a thesis, and the subject is too vast and complex for an exhaustive statistical examination; an analysis of the House of Commons, that invaluable microcosmic picture of England, will, however, supply a certain amount of evidence.

Wealth amassed in trade was laid out in landed estates and used to secure seats in the House of Commons, for both helped to lift their holders into a higher social sphere.

A merchant may be Member of Parliament . . . and shall sit in the House of Commons, with the sons of peers. . . . This equality it is . . . which can alone preserve to commerce its honor, and inspire to those who profess it, an esteem for their condition. . . . The lords can have no contempt for the useful professions of their fellow subjects, who are their equals, when assembled to regulate the public affairs of the nation.

Naturally purchases of landed estates by men enriched in trade were most frequent in the neighbourhood of London, though the process is noticeable also round secondary centres such as Bristol, Liverpool, Norwich, or Hull, and in industrial districts, *e.g.* the wool-manufacturing counties of the West and the iron districts of the Western Midlands; "new men rooted themselves upon old acres."

As early as 1576, William Lambard wrote in his *Perambulation of Kent:*

The gentlemen be not heere (throughout) of so auncient stockes as else where, especially in the partes nearer to London, from whiche citie (as it were from a certeine riche and wealthy seedplot) courtiers, lawyers, and merchants be continually translated, and do become new plants amongst them.

And Defoe in 1728:

I dare oblige my self to name five hundred great estates, within one hundred miles of London, which within eighty years past, were the possessions of the antient English gentry, which are now bought up, and in the possession of citizens and tradesmen, purchased fairly by money raised in trade; some by merchandizing, some by shopkeeping, and some by meer manufacturing; such as clothing in particular.

In the local histories of the home counties published between 1760 and 1830, such as Lysons, Hasted, Manning and Bray, Horsfield, Dallaway, Clutterbuck, Morant, etc., one can watch this process continue and expand, though it is no longer specifically mentioned, having become obvious and ordinary. The following account appears in the genealogical volume of the *Victoria County History* dealing with *The Landed Houses of Hertfordshire:*

In some counties the origin of their modern landed houses can be traced in many cases to great local industries; Hertfordshire, rather an agricultural and residential than an industrial county, is not without its distinctive note, though this is of a different character. Banking and brewing, chiefly in London, are responsible for the rise and wealth of a quite exceptional proportion of families in this county.

To pursue this county, as an example, in the microcosmos of the House of Commons—these were the six Hertfordshire Members returned at the general election of 1761: *Hertford County:* Thomas Plumer Byde—a squire in Hertfordshire and a merchant in London, descended on both sides from families aldermanic in origin, subsequently Parliamentary; and Jacob Houblon, the owner of large landed estates, son of Charles Houblon, a Portugal merchant, by Mary, daughter of Daniel Bate, London merchant and vintner. *Hertford Town:* John Calvert, a London brewer possessed of an estate in Hertfordshire; and Timothy Caswall, an officer in the Guards, grandson of Sir George Caswall, a London banker of South Sea notoriety, nephew of John Caswall, also a London banker, and, on his mother's side, nephew of Nathaniel Brassey, another London banker, who had preceded Timothy Caswall as Member for Hertford, and had in 1761 secured his nephew's election for the borough. *St. Albans:* James West, barrister and civil servant, the Duke of Newcastle's faithful Secretary to the Treasury, of a Warwickshire family, married to Sarah, daughter and heiress of Sir James Steavens, a Bermondsey timber merchant; and George Simon, Lord Nuneham, eldest son of Simon, 1st Earl Harcourt, by Rebecca, daughter of Charles Samborne Le Bas, and granddaughter of Sir Samuel Moyer, 1st bart., a Turkey merchant.

In short, the representation of this county, even though it had neither rotten boroughs, pocket boroughs, nor boroughs under Government management, fills in the detail of the picture given above of social amalgamation between the landed nobility or gentry and those who, as a class, have to be described by a foreign term—the big *bourgeoisie.*

Trade was not despised in eighteenth-century England—it was acknowledged to be the great concern of the nation; and money was honoured, the mystic, common denominator of all values, the universal repository of as yet undetermined possibilities. But what was the position of the trader? There is no one answer to this question. A man's status in English society has always depended primarily on his own consciousness; for the English are not a methodical or logical nation—they perceive and accept facts without anxiously inquiring into their reasons or meaning. Whatever is apt to raise a man's self-consciousness— be it birth, rank, wealth, intellect, daring, or achievements—will add to his stature; but it has to be translated into the truest expression of his sub-conscious self-valuation: uncontending ease, the unbought grace of life. Classes are the more sharply marked in England because there is no single test for them, except the final, incontestable result; and there is more snobbery than in any other country, because the gate can be entered by anyone, and yet remains, for those bent on entering it, a mysterious, awe-inspiring gate. The Chinese used to ennoble a great man's ancestors; Menelaus greeted Telemachus as a son of "godborn kings," for no man who was "low born" could have been his father; and Sir James Barrie's "Admirable Crichton," when master of the lonely island, remembered that he had been "a king in Babylon." All stars appear higher to man than they are in the skies; for while the line of light curves, the human eye follows the tangent to the last short span of the distant road which the ray has traversed; the past is always seen on the line of the present. No "Admirable Crichton," Beau Nash, or Brummel is asked for his genealogical credentials; they are taken for granted (or dispensed with) even in the leisurely life of ease, where there is more scope for fastidiousness and distinctions than in the serious work of the nation. In the phylogenetic history of the Englishman the Oxford undergraduate of my own time corresponded to the eighteenth-century man, and with him nearly foremost among social qualifications was that a man should be amusing. Anyone can enter English society provided he can live, think, and feel like those who have built up its culture in their freer, easier hours.

English civilisation is essentially the work of the leisured classes. We have no word to render the German idea of *Wissenschaft,* and we restrict the term of "science" to branches in which (alas!) the necessary labour and laboratories cannot be hidden. The German prefaces his monumental work by long chapters on methodology, and hesitates ever to take down the scaffolding which he has erected, for fear people might think the building had grown by itself. We prefer to make it appear as if our ideas came to us casually—like the Empire—in a fit of absence of mind. *Literae Humaniores,* the most English of schools, goes back to the all-round man of the Renaissance. For specialisation necessarily entails distortion of mind and loss of balance, and the characteristically English attempt to appear unscientific springs from a desire to remain human. It is not true that Englishmen have little respect for mental achievements. Whereas on the Continent scholarships rank as poor relief, at Oxford or Cambridge the scholar holds a privileged position, coveted as a distinction. More intellectual work is done by aristocrats in England than anywhere else, and, in turn, scientists, doctors, historians, and poets have been made peers—to say nothing of the discipline most closely connected with the State, law, where peerages have for centuries been the regular and almost unavoidable prizes for the leaders of the profession; but no German *Gelehrter* was ever made a baron or a count. What is not valued in England is abstract knowledge as a profession, because the tradition of English civilisation is that professions should be practical and culture should be the work of the leisured classes.

The English landowners, for centuries past, have not tilled their land; they had no serfs to work it, nor did they do so with hired labour; they leased it out to small farmers. In the eighteenth century, in some Continental countries estates were measured by the number of "souls" (serfs attached to their soil), in others by the number of "smokes" (chimneys—homesteads), yet in others by their acreage; in England alone they were described in terms of their rental. The work of the owner of an English landed estate was, and remains, primarily administrative; but, though more exacting than it may seem to outsiders, it has always left the owners a fair amount of leisure for social administration and for political work, for literary and scientific pursuits, for agricultural experiments on the home farm, for "improvements" (the building of mansions, the laying out of gardens, the developing of mines and various industrial enterprises on their estates, the making of roads and canals, etc.), for outdoor sports and recreations, for social intercourse, for life in town, and for foreign travel. The one thing never mentioned in the sketch of Sir Roger de Coverley or of Squire Western is agricultural work, such as was done until recently on big estates in Central and Eastern Europe under the immediate supervision of their owners; nor is it obvious nowadays in the life of the average English country house. But primarily on the rental of England were raised her political system and lore, and her civilisation.

This civilisation is neither urban nor rural; the English ruling classes have for centuries been amphibious. In Germany there has always been a sharp division between the towns and the "land" outside; many towns for a long time preserved an independence which emphasised still more the division, but the political power in the big Germanic States was in the hands of the "agrarians," who, except for a small circle of Court aristocracy, lived on their land. In Italy during the Renaissance, the cities were dominant, and the big landowners inhabited them, as they did in ancient Greece and Rome; in some places (*e.g.* at Treviso) they were even forbidden by law to live outside the city walls. In eighteenth-century England the ruling classes lived neither in fortified castles, nor in agrarian manor-houses, nor in town palaces, but in palatial mansions planted out on their estates (the suburban system of our time is merely a replica of that amphibious life, democratised and rendered accessible to a large part of the nation). Few attempts at outside architecture have been made by the English aristocracy in their town houses; no Chatsworth, or Longleat, or Harewood was ever built in Bloomsbury, Piccadilly, or Mayfair. But in the country the atmosphere and character of town civilisation clings to their houses; they certainly are neither primitive nor rustic.

In style the English country house is not the product of the English countryside; some old Tudor or Jacobean mansions may still pass as autochthonous; the Georgian house bears witness to the classicism of the English mind; the pseudo-Gothic "castle," or a mansion Palladian in front and Gothic at the back, to a "grand tour" gone wrong. The English country house dominates its surroundings; no old forest reaches its doors, as in America; nor does it, like an Ukrainian manor-house, hide in a "yar" (cañon), from fear of the endless steppes above, and of the sharp winds which sweep them. Its civilising influence spreads over the lawns which surround it, over the turf and trees in the park; they are not much interfered with nowadays, and yet bear such a peculiarly well-groomed appearance.

But the eighteenth century, with its exuberant zeal and ingenious conceit, did not allow parks to live their own lives; the *furor hortensis,* the passion for landscape gardening, reigned supreme. Chatham on one occasion, when summoned on urgent business to London, mapped out a garden for a friend by torchlight; and Thomas Whately, M.P., Secretary to the Treasury, who had a prominent share in drafting the American Stamp Act, was best known to his own generation as the author of *Observations on Modern Gardening*—he could not leave things alone. England offers exceptional facilities for landscape gardening; no dominant natural features, "absolutely vertical" or "absolutely horizontal"—high mountains, wide plains, or great rivers—interfere with the fancies of men. Within the limited space, closed in by hills and mists, noble views can be opened up and pointed with pleasing objects. Here is the story of William Shenstone, an eighteenth-century poet, and of rural taste as then conceived:

In 1745 he took possession of his paternal estate, when his delight in rural pleasures, and his ambition of rural elegance was excited; he began from this time to point his prospects, to diversify his service, to entangle his walks, and to wind his waters; which he did with such judgement, and such fancy, as made his little domain the envy of the great and the admiration of the skilful; a place to be visited by travellers and copied by designers. . . .

He spent his estate in adorning it, and his death was probably hastened by his anxieties. He was a lamp that spent its oil in blazing.

The zeal and conceit of the upper classes of eighteenth-century England, which spent much of its best oil "in blazing," have been paid for heavily, in matters small and great; but it was thus that Englishmen learnt to leave things well alone—to refrain from drawing up elaborate, artificial, naive schemes for parks or Empires. The self-restraint and conscious rectitude of a neo-Puritanism, "undemonstrative, gentlemanlike, and reasonable," had to be superimposed on the curious, voracious, acquisitive, utterly egotistic, and amoral energy of the eighteenth century, before the Englishman could change from a rover into a ruler. The eighteenth century was the childhood of Imperial Britain.

The relations of groups of men to plots of land, of organised communities to units of territory, form the basic content of political history. The conflicting territorial claims of communities constitute the greater part of conscious international history; social stratifications and convulsions, primarily arising from the relationship of men to land, make the greater, not always fully conscious, part of the domestic history of nations—and even under urban and industrial conditions ownership of land counts for more than is usually supposed. To every man, as to Brutus, the native land is his life-giving Mother, and the State raised upon the land his law-giving Father; and the days cannot be long of a nation which fails to honour either. Only one nation has survived for two thousand years, though an orphan—my own people, the Jews. But then in the God-given Law we have enshrined the authority of a State, and in the God-promised Land the idea of a Mother-Country; through the centuries from Mount Sinai we have faced Arets Israel, our land. Take away either, and we cease to be a nation; let both live again, and we shall be ourselves once more.

When a tribe settles, membership in the tribe carries the right to a share in the land. In time the order becomes inverted: the holding of land determines a man's position in the community. There is some well-nigh mystic power in the ownership of space—for it is not the command of resources alone which makes the strength of the landowner, but that he has a place in the world which he can call his own, from which he can ward off strangers, and in which he himself is rooted—the superiority of a tree to a log. In land alone can there be real patrimony, and he who as freeman holds a share in his native land—the freeholder—is, and must be, a citizen. Wealth consists of an accumulation, or the command, of goods and chattels; the idea of inalienable property, cherished beyond its patent value, arises from the land. Throughout the centuries rich English business men have therefore aimed at acquiring landed estates and founding "county families"—they have commuted wealth into property, be it at a loss of revenue. Even the tiny garden at the back of the workman's house is a "corner of his own," for which the clean courtyard of model buildings is no compensation; and in the most reduced, impoverished form the "corner of one's own" still appeared until recently, as a qualification for full citizenship, in the latchkey franchise. It was not in rental and leisure alone that the superiority of the landed classes was grounded in eighteenth-century England, but even more in the ease of the well-balanced existence of men who had their share in the land and the State.

In the eighteenth century this connexion between ownership of land and a share in the State was acknowledged and upheld by Tories and Whigs alike. Swift claimed that "law in a free country is, or ought to be, the determination of the majority of those who have property in land," while Defoe considered that in case of a dissolution of government the power would devolve on the freeholders, "the proper owners of the country," the other inhabitants being "but sojourners, like lodgers in a house." "I make no question but property of land is the best title to government in the world." And on the very eve of the American Revolution, constitutional right, as arising from the ownership of land, was pleaded by the Continental Congress in the address *To the People of Great Britain,* voted at Philadelphia on 5 September 1774: "Are not the proprietors of the soil of Great Britain lords of their own property? Can it be taken from them without their consent? . . . Why then are the proprietors of the soil of America less lords of their property than you are of yours?"

English history, and especially English Parliamentary history, is made by families rather than by individuals; for a nation with a tradition of self-government must have thousands of dynasties, partaking of the peculiarities which in other countries belong to the royal family alone. The English political family is a compound of "blood," name, and estate, this last, as the dominions of monarchs, being the most important of the three; that is why mansions instead of families are so often the subject of monographs dealing with the history of the English upper classes. The name is a weighty symbol, but liable to variations; descent traced in the male line only, is like a river without its tributaries; the estate, with all that it implies, is, in the long run, the most potent factor in securing continuity through identification, the "taking up" of the inheritance. The owner of an ancestral estate may have far less of the "blood" than some distant relative bearing a different name, but sprung from a greater number of intermarriages between descendants of the founder of the family; still, it is he who in his thoughts and feelings most closely identifies himself, and is identified by others, with his predecessors. Primogeniture and entails psychologically help to preserve the family in that they tend to fix its position through the successive generations, and thereby favour conscious identification. . . .

There is an inherent logic in ideas and institutions, and given certain conditions, be they even only temporary or fortuitous, forms will arise which a later age may reproduce on a different, a solid and permanent, basis; a sudden influx of Arctic air early in autumn will sometimes cover stagnant pools and ponds with a thin surface of ice, long before winter may (or may not) render them suitable for skating—it possibly anticipates things to come; but this first ice is anyhow unfit to stand the test of burdens.

Under the first two kings of the Hanoverian dynasty certain forms and even principles of Cabinet government seemed to have been established. The Government was based on a party majority in the House of Commons, the King had to accept the leaders or makers of that majority, and had to act, and even think, through them—they were already conscious of knowing the King's (constitutional) mind better than he knew it himself. The contrast which the first part of the reign of George III presented to this, in appearance, advanced constitutional period, was, and usually continues to be, ascribed to his personal character and to the principles he is said to have imbibed at Leicester House; whereas the development was in reality the logical outcome of the situation. The early constitutional development under the first two Georges rested on a lop-sided basis, and its inherent weakness is apparent even at the time of the most signal success, in the crises of 1744–46, when George II failed where his grandson was yet to score a (temporary) success.

In November 1744, Lord Granville, usually considered the favourite Minister of George II, was forced to resign, and the Broadbottom Administration was formed. But the King did not give up the game, and there were "calculations of strength, and lists of persons . . . making every day . . ." Lord Chancellor Hardwicke was therefore commissioned by the rest of the Cabinet to speak to the King, and the interview, of which Hardwicke has left a record, took place on 5 January 1744/45 (O.S.):

K. I have done all you ask'd of me. I have put all power into your hands and I suppose you will make the most of it.

Ch. The disposition of places is not enough, if Your Majesty takes pains to shew the world that you disapprove of your own work.

K. My work! I was forc'd—I was threatened.

Ch. I am sorry to hear your Majesty use those expressions. I know of no force—I know of no threats. No means were used, but what have been used in all times, the humble advice of your servants, supported by such reasons as convinc'd them that the measure was necessary for your service.

K. Yes, I was told that I should be opposed.

Ch. Never by me, Sir, nor by any of my friends. How others might misrepresent us I don't pretend to know. But, whatever had been our fate, and tho' Your Majesty had determin'd on the contrary side to what you did, we would never have gone into an opposition against the necessary measures for carrying on the war and for the support of your Government and Family. . . .

.   .   .   .

Ch. . . . Your Ministers, Sir, are only your instruments of Government.

K. (smiles). Ministers are the Kings in this country.

Ch. If one person is permitted to engross the ear of the Crown, and invest himself with all its power, he will become so in effect; but that is far from being the case now, and I know no one now in Your Majesty's service that aims at it.

The King, however, remained unconvinced and did not desist from dealing with unofficial advisers; consequently on 10–11 February 1745/6, forty-five of his "servants" resigned, only to be recalled two days later, when the failure of Bath and Granville had become obvious. George II was now told that those who were "only his instruments of Government," had to be his only instruments.

That His Majesty will be pleas'd entirely to withdraw his confidence and countenance from those persons, who of late have, behind the curtain, suggested private councills, with the view of creating difficulties to his servants, who are responsible for every thing, whilst those persons are responsible for nothing.

That His Majesty will be pleas'd to demonstrate his conviction of mind that those persons have deceiv'd or misled him by representing that they had sufficient credit and interest in the nation to support and carry on the public affairs, and that he finds they are not able to do it.

[Here follow demands for the dismissal of some, and the appointment of others, including Pitt.]

That His Majesty will be pleas'd to dispose of the vacant Garters in such manner, as to strengthen, and give a public mark of his satisfaction in, his administration.

That, as to foreign affairs, His Majesty will be pleased not to require more from His servants than to support and perfect the plan, which He has already approved.

The constitutional theory underlying these articles was clearly explained in a letter in which, on 15 February 1745/6, Charles Yorke sent an account of the crisis to his brother Joseph, then on active service in Scotland—it can be taken to sum up the opinions of their father, Lord Hardwicke.

The notion of the Constitution is this, that Ministers are accountable for every act of the King's Government to the people; if that be so, they have a right to his confidence, in preference to all others; else they are answerable for measures not their own. Here is the security both of the King and of his people. The next great policy of the Constitution is this, that whatever the King does should seem to come *ex mero motu;* the result of his own wisdom and deliberate choice. This gives a grace to Government in the eyes of the people, and here is the dignity of the Monarchy.

On the surface this looks like the full doctrine of responsible Parliamentary Government; in reality it merely defines the constitutional relations between the King and the Ministers he employs, and as such prescribes no more than self-respecting statesmen might expect even under an autocratic, if civilised, system. Hardwicke was right when he told George II that Ministers were not "Kings" so long as there was no Prime Minister; for obviously there must be a supreme direction, and this, according to Hardwicke and his contemporaries, had to come from the King. It is not Parliament as such, but the system of firmly organised parties under single leadership, which precludes an active, personal participation of the King in Government. But the ideas held about 1750 concerning the position of the King in the executive, and of parties in Parliament, differed widely from our own, and the events of 1744–46 were an accident rather than the natural consequence of the constitutional ideas held at that time.

The Crown has no choice concerning the set of men to be entrusted with office when there are firmly organised parties and a clear majority; it has to summon the leaders of the majority, who otherwise, with their entire following, automatically pass into opposition. This was not so about 1750. The same letter of Charles Yorke, containing the constitutional *exposé,* in the account it gives of the conference which Hardwicke had with the King on 14 February 1746 restates once more the doctrine about the iniquitous character of a "formed opposition." Hardwicke told the King that if he could not give his full confidence to his old Ministers, he had better "pursue the new plan," and Hardwicke and his friends would continue "supporting his government in general and giving ease to it";

that for himself especially he would say that as long as he lived he would never enter into a formed opposition to any administration, that he would not undergo the slavery nor would he partake in the guilt of it.

This abhorrence of "a formed opposition" was not a hollow phrase, nor polite pretence; it fully reappears in the confidential correspondence between Newcastle, Hardwicke, and Mansfield, when their group was once more out of office. Newcastle and Hardwicke had resigned in November 1756, in consequence of the loss of Minorca, the withdrawal of Fox, and the refusal of Pitt to join them, though at that time "there was not the least diminution of the King's goodness, affection, and confidence" to them, nor "the least appearance of any loss of . . . friends in either House of Parliament." With the Devonshire-Pitt Administration, their immediate successors, they had a tacit understanding, securing the old ministers from prosecution and the new from opposition. But when the King, having dismissed Temple and Pitt, seemed to turn to Fox, at that time the political agent of the Duke of Cumberland, the position changed completely. From Fox, who had been Secretary of State when Minorca was lost, Newcastle had nothing to fear; Pitt loathed Fox, whom he described as "the *blackest* man that ever lived," while Leicester House stood in excessive fear of the Duke of Cumberland, who, with his military character, following, and associations, was distrusted and disliked by the majority both of Whigs and Tories. Lord Mansfield, though personally friendly to Fox, told George II, "there was a general apprehension that the . . . intended administration was founded in violence and would be supported by *violence."* All the materials for a successful opposition were to hand; what line was the "old corps" of Whigs to adopt?

Newcastle, "much at a loss," on 8 April 1757 applied to Hardwicke for advice, adding from himself:

I detest in general the thought of Opposition. I have detested and blamed it in *others,* and therefore shall most unwillingly come into it *myself.* But, on the other hand, if *we* support these men and measures, . . . to the publick it is the same as if we were parties to the Administration. For without *us,* this Administration at present cannot go on. . . . Might not there be a middle way . . . might we not . . . act according to events, and as particular questions arise? This I know will be difficult and possibly in no shape satisfactory to our friends, who from thence may go part to one side and part to the other.

He thus recognised that a party or political group out of office required at least as much organisation as when it had its natural rallying-point in the Government, or was doomed to disintegration. But Hardwicke replied on 9 April 1757:

For my own part, I am determin'd not to go into a *form'd general opposition*. I have seen so much of them that I am convinc'd they are the most wicked combinations, that men can enter into;—worse and more corrupt than any Administration, that I ever yet saw, and so they have appear'd in the conclusion. Therefore I see no other way at present, but to keep off from any absolute engagement with either party . . . and to oppose wrong measures, and concur in right ones, as particular questions shall arise, or be foreseen. I am sensible that this is not the political way to keep a party together, but that is not an objection against doing what I think in my own conscience to be right.

Similarly Lord Mansfield, endorsing Lord Hardwicke's opinion, most insistently warned Newcastle against trying, by the help of "Leicester House and the People," to impose himself on the King, who would then rather forgive his bitterest enemy than one whom he had trusted so long:

To mix in factious opposition, after so many years of honourable service, wou'd blast your fame and reputation for ever. Specious pretences are never wanting; but in the present distress, it is impossible for any Court, how desperate soever, to make unconstitutional attempts; if they did, every man ought to oppose such attempts. But I speak of opposition to right or indifferent measures to force a change of hands. I desire for one to subscribe to Lord Hardwicke's declaration as the sentiment of a virtuous and loyal mind, to which I will inviolably adhere. I had much rather not exist than join at this time factiously in opposition to the King, whomsoever he employs. For his sake, for the sake of his successor, for the sake of Government itself I wou'd not do it.

Upbraided in this way by both his trusted friends, Newcastle, in a letter to Hardwicke (15 April 1757) completely receded from his previous suggestion of opposition, very faint though it had been:

I . . . entirely agree with your Lordship not on any account *to enter into a formed General Opposition;* and I thought I had stated my objections to it in the strongest manner . . . the *metzo termino* flung out in my letter, I think will be (as things stand at present) the only way; Lord Dupplin made me mention the difficulty of such a conduct in a stronger light than I should otherwise have done.

In short, these men, while at times expounding what would seem the full doctrine of responsible Parliamentary government, had no conception of a party-government unconnected with the King, and hence of a constitutional Parliamentary Opposition. For the King was to them a real factor in government, and not a mere figurehead or an abstract idea; he was a god in politics, not a deity. He was the "supreme Magistrate," the fountain-head of power and honours, the permanent pivot of the Executive; and the mere conception of a "Sole Minister," a *de facto* ruler, was indignantly disclaimed by them. It was the King's business to see the government of the nation carried on, and for that purpose he had a right to choose his "instruments"; and "support of Government" was considered "a duty, while an honest man could support it." To try to impose oneself on the King by means of a systematic opposition, "to force a change of hands," was considered by them factious and dishonest, and replete with "guilt." As the actual person of the King still always stood in the very forefront of politics, all "formed opposition" was in some measure tainted with disloyalty; for obviously, a regular opposition does aim, not at giving the Executive the best advice, but at impeding its action. And, *vice versa,* because of the very real position still held by the King, every organised political party, aspiring to office, tended to gather to a Royal person: the King in being, "the King over the water," the King to come (*i.e.* the Prince of Wales), or at least a Royal Highness (*e.g.* the Duke of Cumberland).

Prestige and patronage invested the King with considerable power both in Parliament and in the constituencies, and it was Lord Granville's maxim, "Give any man the Crown on his side, and he can defy everything." In this conviction he induced George II to make the attempt of February 1746; but when faced with mass resignations, the King, as Lord Shelburne puts it in his autobiography, "did not choose to try the experiments which his Grandson is about, nor was that time by any means ripe, I believe, for them, though Lord Granville thought otherwise." Shelburne's view seems the better founded, and not by results alone. The House of Commons at that time can be roughly divided into four groups, though it is not always easy to draw the line between them: the Administration group of placemen and civil servants, of men dependent on whatever Government was in power; the Whig connexions which had hitherto supported the Government; the "flying squadron" of discontented Whigs, men who, having quarrelled with Sir Robert Walpole, the Pelhams, and "the main body," had entered the orbit of the Prince of Wales; and the Tories who, whether they had the Jacobite leanings ascribed to them or were merely men of independent character and views, anyhow were not a rock on which to build a government. The Administration group, if united with all the rest of the "old corps," offered a sufficient basis for a stable government; but otherwise support would have to be sought from the Prince of Wales since Walpole's old friends, even if successfully detached from the Pelhams, would hardly be sufficient. Rather than submit to that, George II preferred to recall the Pelhams; it was for this reason that he abandoned the experiment which his grandson was to attempt under fundamentally different conditions.

Thus in 1746 the King had to capitulate before his Ministers because his own person still stood in the centre of political controversy; what we should now call a "constitutional" surrender came as the result of a highly unconstitutional situation. The King, as his own Prime Minister, was, or deemed himself, restricted to co-operation with one set of men, and to them he lent his means for recruiting supporters. Their majority rested at least as much on the support of the Crown as on support from the "public." No one can deny the apparent resemblance of the events of 1746 with modern practice; still, of this enforced partnership in government the appearances only were constitutional in the modern sense. The moment the King ceased to deem himself restricted to one group (which intrinsically is a much more constitutional situation), the reality of "personal government" was bound to reappear. But such a return to earlier forms did not amount to a fundamental change of system, and Newcastle, Hardwicke, etc., so far from being the spiritual ancestors of the Whig Opposition of, say, 1780, were the direct forerunners of Lord North, who served his apprenticeship as the trusted young friend of Newcastle; and their own families, with a fine instinct for realities, finished by joining North, while many so-called Tories of the reign of George II became Radicals under George III (Beckford, Meredith, Dowdeswell, etc.). The system which existed under George II, when examined in its foundations, is seen to lead up directly to the experiment of the first years of George III's reign, and to the "stabilisation" under North. There was sound sense in North, Sandwich, George Germaine, etc., never themselves discarding the "denomination" of Whigs, and in the elder Pitt working with the Tories.

The coming to Court of the Old Tories on the accession of George III marked in a signal manner the extinction of even theoretical Jacobitism, and is usually given prominence in the change of scene. But was it really this official funeral of a dead creed which set the King free to assume the lead and choose his "servants"? The conflict between successive generations of the Hanoverian dynasty had for a long time played a much greater part in English (though not in Scottish) politics than the existence of a discredited rival dynasty, alien to the nation in religion and ideas. The struggle between father and son, known in ordinary families, is very much intensified in ruling dynasties, the throne affording room for one only. But in family conflicts, scapegoats are always in demand, against whom an embarrassing hatred is diverted. Parents ascribe everything which does not suit their book to the "bad influence" of undesirable friends on their presumably feeble-minded progeny; and sons in opposition to their royal fathers (as also the other "children" of the King, his subjects) knew the tale about "wicked advisers" long before a constitutional convention gave it official status. Thus the struggle of the heir to the throne against the monarch becomes coupled with bitter hostility against his ministers. Even in recent times such developments could be observed at some Continental Courts. The Crown Prince Rudolf of Austria, in opposition to his conservative father, the Emperor Francis Joseph I, professed liberal views, indiscreetly criticising the constitutional advisers of his father to ill-chosen confidants. Similarly, the Crown Prince Frederick of Germany, though with more intelligence and discrimination, developed an advanced liberalism in opposition to William I and Bismarck, while his own son in turn sharply opposed the politics of his parents. But having succeeded to the throne, William II, though not a Liberal, felt as irresistibly moved to dismiss Bismarck as if he had come into the views, and not merely into the place, of his father; just as George III was irresistibly moved to dismiss the Ministers of his grandfather.

With the Hanoverians the conflict between the King and the Heir-Apparent was a regular institution. George II, as Prince of Wales, stood in sharp opposition to George I and Sir Robert Walpole, whose dismissal was universally expected on his accession, and very nearly occurred. In the next reign George II and his Queen, and their son Frederick, Prince of Wales, openly proclaimed their hostility to each other—". . . whoever goes to pay their Court to their Royal Highnesses, Prince or Princess of Wales, will not be admitted to Their Majesties' presence" (official notice of 12 September 1737)—"duty on the one side" was considered "disaffection on the other." In the lifetime of Frederick, Prince of Wales, the future George III received from both his parents "treatment which went the length of the most decided contempt of him, if not aversion, setting up his brother the Duke of York's understanding and parts in opposition to his, and undervaluing everything he said or did." But after the death of Frederick in 1751, the attitude of the Princess to her eldest son changed completely, and in time he took his father's place at Leicester House and in opposition to his grandfather, George II. The usual retribution came for George III in the struggle with his eldest son, George IV, who, as Prince of Wales, closely associated with the Whig Opposition in bitter hostility to his father and his Ministers. It is this struggle of successive generations which, at a time when the King's person still stood in the forefront of politics, supplied a rallying-point to Oppositions, and which, more than Tories or Jacobites, forced George II into a partnership with the Pelham group.

There is a well-known passage in the *Diary* of Bubb Dodington, under date of 18 July 1749, describing how the Prince of Wales promised, when King, to bestow a peerage on him and make him Secretary of State—"and I give you leave to kiss my hand upon it, now, by way of acceptance." Dodington was thus received into the Shadow Cabinet by the princely leader of the Opposition to His Majesty. Born in 1691, and only about eight years younger than the King, he none the less sold "spot" (he resigned the office of Treasurer of the Navy) and bought "futures," a transaction more obviously justified in young politicians who were likely to spend the best part of their lives under the King's successor. "The Prince of Wales gains strength in Parliament in proportion as the King grows older" wrote Lord Chesterfield on 25 April 1749. The death of the Prince, in 1751, which at first disturbed actuarial calculations, in the end merely increased the tension: "The Court was old; the Ministry was old; there was a long generation between them and the heir apparent." In 1755 the Duke of Newcastle explained to the King himself that he found more difficulty "from the notion of opposition from that quarter [Leicester House], which affects particularly all the young men, than from all other causes whatever." "The influence of the young Court . . . will gather new strength every month after seventy-four" was again Chesterfield's diagnosis of the situation in 1757 (George II was born in 1683).

The situation of George III on his accession differed from that of his predecessors in that he was young and had no competing heir. The Duke of Cumberland, who previously had been looked upon, rightly or wrongly, as the incarnation of what we should call "Prussianism," and as a menace to the constitution, was soon to become the acknowledged protector of the "constitutional" Whigs —this was in accordance with the law of conflict between successive generations in the Royal Family. Still, after his recent stroke of palsy, he was a poor substitute for a Prince of Wales—he was not likely to outlive George III and all his brothers. As Hardwicke wrote to Newcastle on 18 April 1761, expressing his doubts whether Pitt and Temple would go into opposition—"There is now no *reversionary* resource. Instead of an old King, and a young successor; a young healthy King, and no successor in view."

The peculiarity of an Opposition grouped round the Prince of Wales, especially while there were no clearly defined parties, was that it could hardly expect to establish itself in office in the lifetime of the King, and that its main chance lay therefore, not in a victory in Parliament or at the polls, but in the "reversion." Dodington, in the "Memorial for the Prince," dated 12 October 1749, pointed out the mistake he made in heading an active Opposition, "carried on for the private preferment of the opposers." "Can a Prince of Wales be preferred?—He must be King; and as he can be nothing else, can such an Opposition make him so, one hour before his time?" The Prince himself "cannot act at the head of any Administration," and were the King forced to call in the leaders of the Opposition, they could not assume office, without ceasing to be followers of the Prince; "it is not your interest to drive them from you," nor theirs to give up the certainty of favour in future "for the uncertain, ill-will'd, precarious emoluments which they may snatch, in the scramble of a new Administration, forced upon the Crown." The Prince should aim at becoming "the sole object of mankind's expectation, for the redress of all the grievances they feel, and the disposition of all the future benefits they hope for"; while his followers should confine themselves to carrying, one day, his "great designs into execution." The death of George II was obviously to be "the day" for all those, whether discontented Whigs or Tories, who were ready to re-enter active politics, but who during his lifetime had to remain in the outer darkness.

As the Government party, built up by Walpole and the Pelhams, owed its large majority in the House of Commons to the patronage of the Crown, to claim, as is sometimes done, that it was incumbent on the King to accept their apparent majority as constitutionally binding on him, is to put the cart before the horse. Nor, indeed, would such a theory have been popular at the time. A system had come to be established under which the Cabinet, to carry on efficiently the King's business, had to have a majority in Parliament; but the earliest outcome of the close linking-up of Executive and Legislature was the control of "the Minister" over a House of Commons which tended to "degenerate into a little assembly, serving no other purpose than to register the arbitrary edicts of one too powerful subject," "designed," as Pitt went on to say, "to be an appendix to—I know not what—I have no name for it." Others had supplied names for it in abundance during forty years of bitter campaigns against "the Sole Minister," "the over-grown Minister," the "fellow-subject lifted above others" and made into "a kind of magistrate odious to the English Constitution, who draws everything within the vortex of his own power," "treasurer, archbishop, judge, and perpetual legislator," etc.

Still, can one wonder at people not having guessed the future of the institution of Prime Minister?—who, with the patronage of the Crown at his disposal, was almost as permanent as the King, but, having personal connexions of his own and being partly dependent on them, tended to exclude a large, perhaps the larger, part of the political nation from a constructive share in national politics. This seemed a travesty of both Royal and Parliamentary government, combining the disadvantages of both; and men naturally asked themselves whether "the management of one man in the character of Prime Minister" was not in the end "more prejudicial to a country than that of the sovereign himself"—the interests of the King appearing to them more closely identified with those of the nation, and he himself more independent of factions and confederacies of men, and therefore more impartial in judging between them. By 1760 the nation seems to have reached a state of reaction against government by Cabinet and so-called party, and with other paths as yet unexplored was inclined to revert to a rather primitive monarchical idea. A Patriot King, an independent House of Commons composed of Members "guided only by the dictates of their own judgment and conscience," the enlightened voter moved by pure reason only, were inhuman fictions, "as much creatures of imagination as griffins or dragons," but had to be tried in turn before the wisest politicians came to accept human absurdities provided they worked. But about 1760, in the thoughts of the nation, the King alone stood above the "unguarded guardians"; in the calculations of politicians he alone could give to the excluded a share or turn in the enjoyment of office—and if the old King would not do so, their hopes were pinned on his successor. That the death of the King would naturally imply changes in office had for years been well-nigh an axiom. For had Ministers, placed and maintained in office through the countenance and support of a king, been able to raise a claim to surviving him, had they thus been able to establish a quasi-mortgage on the Crown, they would indeed have been "mock monarchs," " a fourth estate, to check, to controul, to influence, nay, to enslave the other three." But when in 1770 Burke in his *Thoughts on the Cause of the Present Discontents* expatiated on the "power arising from connection"—"the great Whig connections"—as a security "for the importance of the people," he carefully refrained from stating that the main foundation of their power had been the influence of the Crown.

While the theory of the King's constitutional duty to accept and continue the Ministers of his predecessor was held by no one in 1760, not even by the Ministers themselves, peculiar circumstances at the accession of George III rendered their temporary continuance advisable, or even necessary. In March 1759, Lord Bute, the Grand Vizier of Leicester House, had affirmed that he "wished the King's life as much as any subject"; which was true, for he dreaded lest the new reign (*ego et rex meus*) should start in the midst of war, and be burdened with the responsibility for negotiating a peace which was bound to arouse much heat and opposition. The Prince of Wales explicitly stated his fears of such a contingency in a letter written *c.* 2 July 1758, and deprecating further military commitments in Germany—"if this unhappy measure should be taken we shall be drawn deeper in a Continental War than ever; and when I mount the Throne, I shall not be able to form a M[inistr]y who can have the opinion of the people." Indeed, it was suggested that "Mr. Pitt and Mr. Grenville certainly wish'd to continue the War during the King's life; that the Prince of Wales might find the nation in War; and, consequently, that they should be the more necessary"; "whilst the contrary was the wish and object of Lord Bute." When it happened as Pitt was alleged to have wished, it seemed expedient to let the late King's Ministers pursue their measures and complete their work. "If this plan can be carried into execution," wrote an impartial observer a month after the death of George II, "and all political cabal and contention removed to the less critical time of peace (for this country cannot be altogether free from political struggles), we should, in the main, be happy. . . ." And on 19 December 1760, he again expressed the hope and wish, shared by most people, that "the present Ministers" should be continued "so long as the war lasts." "When a peace is once secured 'twill be time enough to attend to the insinuations of jealousy and ambition."

This, of course, was hardly the view of the old men, who for the last ten, twenty, or thirty years had waited for the death of George II; who in 1737 had thought the King "in a languishing condition," anyhow unable to "live many years"; who in 1749 had seen Frederick, Prince of Wales, "with one foot on the throne," when in reality it was in the grave; and who now, having spent very nearly the Biblical term of years in the desert, saw the Promised Land and did not want to die the death of Moses. George III, and perhaps even Bute, might have bided their time, but not the old, ravenous, embittered men. A pamphlet, called *Seasonable Hints from an Honest Man on the present important Crisis of a new Reign, and a new Parliament*, expressed the feelings of many among them besides Lord Bath, who had inspired it. Published anonymously on 16 March 1761, it was the work of his scribe and political agent, John Douglas, D.D. (subsequently Bishop of Salisbury). High wisdom and lofty sentiments are affected, but are continually dimmed by virulent invective and bitter recriminations, till at last an irrepressible, heartfelt cry pierces through all the verbiage—about "the insatiable thirst of those who, though they have been intoxicated for years, with the most copious draughts of the cup of power, are still so unreasonable as to be craving for more, to the utter exclusion of numbers who have an equal right to taste it in their turn." In *The London Chronicle* of 9 December 1760, a naïve soul, "Solomon Sage," having, it seems, genuinely hoped for redress of grievances and "economic reform" in the new reign, complained that "we hear of no pensions suspended, nor of any sinecures abolished, or needless officers discharged." But a wiser man, "David Simple," on 16 December, gave him the clue to the situation. "We hope that the cavalry shall never any more be permitted to engage in battle, but shall be entirely reserved to hunt down old Courtiers, good or bad, seeing that we are new Courtiers. . . ." In truth, there were no principles in question—it was a charge of the new courtiers led by the disappointed, embittered failures of the previous reign, by the excluded, the prematurely dead, who now wanted to force their way back to life—Lord Bath, Henry Fox, Bubb Dodington, etc.

Politicians and their quarrels had enjoyed a peculiar longevity in the second half of George II's reign. In 1760 the same seventeenth-century men continued in the forefront of politics who had stood there about 1745. The King, born in 1683, was still on the throne; the Duke of Newcastle, born in 1693, was still electioneering, distributing jobs, holding levees, and over every trifle "flinging himself" on the advice and support of his friend Lord Hardwicke (born in 1690); the Duke of Argyll, born in 1682, continued as the uncrowned King of Scotland; Lord Ligonier, born in 1680, was Commander-in-Chief of the Army; Lord Anson, born in 1697, was First Lord of the Admiralty; Lord Bath, born in 1684, and Lord Granville, born in 1690, were still overflowing with hostility and contempt for Newcastle and Hardwicke, of whom, in their long lives, though superior in brilliancy and wit, they had never managed to get the better; and some distance behind them all (to be mentioned as type rather than as individual), Bubb Dodington, born in 1691, was still making "his ideas consonant to the opinions of those men from whom he expected emoluments." The new reign, so long awaited or apprehended, had come, and here they were still all present, "young gentlemen of seventy and upwards." They remembered William III, had been engaged in politics or professions before Queen Anne died, were elderly men at the fall of Sir Robert Walpole, and were still active in 1760. The next generation was similarly complete. There were the Duke of Cumberland, the Dukes of Bedford and Devonshire, William Pitt, Lord Temple, George Grenville, Lord Egremont, Lord Granby, Lord Sandwich, Lord Holdernesse, H. B. Legge, Lord Mansfield, Henry Fox, Charles Townshend, William Beckford, Charles Yorke, etc. In fact, only two politicians of mark had died between 1745 and 1760, Frederick, Prince of Wales, and Henry Pelham. But the death of George II on 25 October 1760 marked the first breach in this seemingly immovable array; the others, even the prominent men of the younger generation, followed rapidly. The Duke of Argyll died in 1761, Lord Anson and Lord Melcombe (Dodington) in 1762, Lord Granville and Lord Egremont in 1763, Lord Hardwicke, Lord Bath, H. B. Legge, and the Duke of Devonshire in 1764, the Duke of Cumberland in 1765, Charles Townshend in 1767, the Duke of Newcastle in 1768, Lord Ligonier, Lord Granby, William Beckford, George Grenville, and Charles Yorke in 1770, the Duke of Bedford in 1771. When Lord North became First Lord of the Treasury, of those who had been leaders in 1760 and for many years before it, hardly any were alive, and, barring Chatham and Sandwich, none were any longer active in politics. It was in these ten years, 1760–70, that the real change supervened in the political personnel as well as in political ideas.

The accession of George III did not in itself mark the advent of any new ideas, nor, except for the disturbing and ineffective person of Lord Bute, did it immediately bring forth new men. With change delayed by longevity and now once more by the war, the new reign presented the extraordinary sight, both ludicrous and disgusting, of long-repressed, and still impeded, feuds fought out between men most of whom had outlived their time—between "the dead above ground." Horace Walpole, who himself half-died with his father and felt therefore a very old man at forty-four—a detached observer of a world which did not concern him any longer—after sixteen years' absence, in March 1761 revisited Houghton. Sitting in his father's "little dressing-room," by his scrutoire, he wrote what is perhaps the deepest, most sincere, and unaffected letter in the many volumes of his correspondence. His thoughts that night wandered to the church "into which I have not yet had courage to enter," to the time when he himself would at last be buried in it, to the years when his father was alive, to the scenes he would witness the next day at Lynn, where he was to be re-elected to George III's first Parliament—and he wrote about Sir Robert Walpole and those who had outlasted him: "There lies he who founded its [Houghton's] greatness, to contribute to whose fall Europe was embroiled—there he sleeps in quiet and dignity, while his friend and his foe, rather his false ally and real enemy, Newcastle and Bath, are exhausting the dregs of their pitiful lives in squabbles and pamphlets!"

Whatever the ingratitude of monarchs may be, they cannot practise it with the anonymous irresponsibility of assemblies or nations. George III could not discard those who had maintained the House of Hanover on the throne, nor the Emperor William II dismiss the man who had made the Hohenzollern Empire, with the same ease with which France dropped Clemenceau after the victory was won. Nor can monarchs talk about their "father complex" as voters do about the "swing of the pendulum," though probably the two have much in common (electorates at general elections can realise the child's dream to wash, with an enormous sponge, the face of an indignant and protesting nurse).

Monarchs feel constrained to give reasons; they plead, therefore, that there had been presumption on the part of the old retainer, and argue that in reality he had been an overbearing master who had kept the poor old grandpapa in bondage. It was inconvenient for the new Court (as later on it would have been for Burke and other opposition writers and orators) to admit that Newcastle had been only the faithful servant and political manager of George II. The would-be heirs and successors of the old Minister worked up lurking suspicions and provided the necessary arguments. Thus Dodington, in December 1760, implored Bute "to recover monarchy from the inveterate usurpation of oligarchy," and sent him some lines, which were not to be seen by anybody, "unless his lordship has a mind to make the King or the Princess [of Wales] laugh":

> Quoth Newcastle to Pitt, 'tis in vain to dispute;
> > If we'd quarrel in private, we must make room for Bute.
> Quoth Pitt to his Grace, to bring that about,
> > I fear, my dear lord, you or I must turn out.
> Not at all, quoth the Duke, I meant no such thing,
> > To make room for us all, we must turn out the King.
> If that's all your scheme, quoth the Earl, by my troth,
> > I shall stick by my master, and turn ye out Both.

Next, Lord Bath, through his agent Douglas, supplied the King and the public with very full and serious *Hints* about past "iniquities" and the changes which were required. A knot of Ministers should no longer be allowed "to grasp universal influence in domestic business" and dictate whom the King should employ, and their "factious connections and confederations" should be broken up. The King should show "that we have a monarch on the throne, who, knowing that he reigns in the hearts of a united people is determined not to resign himself to the insolent pretensions of any confederacy of Ministers," and that he will not "content himself with the shadow of royalty, while a set of undertakers for his business intercept his immediate communication with his people, and make use of the legal prerogatives of their master, to establish the illegal claims of factious oligarchy." "Can there be the least doubt that the nation, in general, would list itself on his side . . . when the competition is not between prerogative and liberty, but between the King and Ministers. . . .?" If the King decides to do his own business, "the over-grown Minister . . . will soon find that his supposed friends were only the friends of his power, and will continue firm to him no longer than while he has possession of the means of gratifying them. In the age we live in, there are but few retainers of a Court so little attentive to their interest as to forget that the Crown is permanent and administrations temporary." Indeed, a singularly accurate forecast of things to come.

Sir Robert Walpole had a policy and used the royal patronage to secure it; under Henry Pelham there was less policy and more patronage; with the Duke of Newcastle a policy was hardly traceable; nor did much real opposition remain—the number of "Whigs" was continually growing, and the difficulty of Administration was merely "to find pasture enough for the beasts that they must feed." This the Duke of Newcastle made the task of his life, leaving the work of Government to stronger men, after 1757 to Pitt, who, in his own words, had been "called to invigorate Government, and to overrule the influences of feeble and shortsighted men." In his own thinking Newcastle was primarily the servant of George II, whose reign he had to make "easy," and the chief of a "connection" of men, for whom he had to provide. As he himself put it in a memorandum of 10 August 1761 his tenure of office was "for the service of those friends, in whose cause I am, and have ever been, embarked"; and a week later, when discussing resignation, he wrote to Hardwicke: "There is one thing, I own, which does, and will affect me extremely; and that is the only one. There are some particular friends of mine, both in Church and State, whom I shall be most sorry to leave without prospect of assistance or advancement. . . ." Pitt rightly remarked about him that he had "two points only in view, viz., the disposal of employments and the confidence of the King." In neither of these did Pitt mean to give him any disturbance; for he "was not ambitious. He was modest or proud, which you would. He had taken another turn. He would not be Disposing Minister, if he could." The reason which Pitt gave for remaining in office, was "the service of the public." He was the "Minister of measures," while Newcastle was the "Minister of numbers."

By 1760 Pitt, through his conduct of the war, had earned a well-deserved, nation-wide popularity, a fact which was frankly, and even generously, acknowledged by Newcastle. Thus he recorded in his notes on 4 September 1759: "Mr. Pitt—More popular every day than ever; even in the country and with the Old Whigs"; and in a letter of 27 November 1759 he wrote about Pitt to Granby: "He is a man. A man of great merit, weight and consequence. It is for the service of the publick to be well with him; to aid and assist him." Meantime Newcastle's own thankless task of "Disposing Minister" had raised against him a host of enemies among those who, while not anxious to do real work or bear heavy responsibilities, felt equal to the distributing or accepting of places, sinecures, and pensions; and Pitt did not show as much understanding for his difficulties as Newcastle showed for Pitt's greatness. It is characteristic of the situation in 1760 that in the numerous attacks against the "confederacy of Ministers" criticisms of policy seldom occur, but complaints are continually raised against the monopolising of patronage—this being the subject of paramount interest to the crowds which did not live for, but by, politics. Newcastle was the butt of that peculiar opposition, and in the picture they drew of him, the weak, old, ill-used man grew into a Herod because of the starved ambitions and avidities for which he had failed to find room on the pastures of Government favour.

9

THE EXTENSION OF
STATE BUREAUCRACY

THE FRENCH word *bureau* may be translated into at least two different though related words in English. It can mean office, or it can just as well mean desk. Together, office and desk evoke a special sort of place. Desk-filled offices are for preparing reports, keeping records, writing letters. Someone is in charge. He may be called a bureaucrat.

The office desk is specially designed; it has "in" and "out" file boxes, rubber stamps, and registers on the top. The person sitting at it asks and answers questions or gives out blank forms to be completed and filed. The whole conveys an atmosphere. Is there a portrait of a man or woman on the wall, or a flag? Does the person portrayed wear a uniform, a judicial robe, or a business suit? The climate of the office immediately conveys a sense of the political climate of a country, or of the relations between governed and governors.

Bureaucracy is the exercise of political power by someone in the name of someone else. The bureaucrat as an individual issues no orders in his own name; he is powerless without the authority of the state behind him. Like a soldier in an army, he has his orders and a commanding officer; any good or ill resulting from his action hurts or benefits the state alone.

In the most general sense, then, bureaucracy is as old as government itself. The most primitive societies, either as a body or through their chiefs, choose individuals to aid in the task of ruling. But is not such a definition of bureaucracy so vague as to be meaningless? It implies that all who act in the name of the sovereign are bureaucrats. A general and a postal clerk certainly are two different things, we assert. But are they?

Bureaucracy in European states, or at least secular bureaucracy, began as little more than estate management in feudal times. A lord needed special servants to help collect revenues, keep accounts, and write his letters, for as often as not he was unable to write. Vis-à-vis the lord's vassals and peasants, this servant acted as a bureaucrat when he gave orders in the lord's name. Their servants were empowered to do more and more, as some lords became *real* kings and as feudal monarchy developed.

By the seventeenth century every European state had elaborate civil and military bureaucracies. Chains of command, subdivisions of authority, and regional jurisdictions had been refined to the point that the European population felt the weight of centralized government, at least on matters of justice and taxes.

What effects did the development of these bureaucracies have in the different states of Europe? Did the increase of royal power, say in Spain and France, impart a more authoritarian character to their bureaucracies? The bureaucracies developed differently in every state. Local conditions, religion, social values, and individual initiative all shaped the behavior of the "servants of the state." A Dutch tax official in 1650 bore very little resemblance to his Spanish counterpart, owing to the differences in the character of government in the two countries.

In the seventeenth century "Big" government got under way. In France alone there were three times as many bureaucrats in 1700 as in 1600. In Prussia and Russia bureaucrats representing the state appeared where none had been before. Centralized bureaucracy grew everywhere at the expense of local government. Then in England, with its tradition of being "little governed," the intervention of the state into private affairs under Anne was much greater than it had been under Elizabeth.

Why did kings and parliaments seek to intervene increasingly in affairs which had formerly been purely local? Was this steady extension of authority a conscious aim on their part? Bureaucracy may be self-perpetuating, even parasitic, in the sense that it grows on its own. How often did bureaucrats ignore orders from Paris, Berlin, or London to go on doing as they saw fit, increasing their own power at the same time?

1.

After giving his definition of bureaucracy, G. E. Aylmer (1926–   ) of the University of York, England, tests it by analyzing the English administration under Charles I. Does he conclude that England in the 1640's did in fact have a bureaucracy? In the English Revolution was the protest against the King's servants, his bureaucrats, or against his councilors and himself?

Aylmer compares the development of bureaucracy in England and France and stresses the way in which the "constitutional conflict" helped turn royal servants into bureaucrats serving the public. What conjectures does he make to defend this point?

The conclusion is highly suggestive of different criteria for determining the character or existence of bureaucracy. Is it possible to have a bureaucracy whose members do not slip into sycophancy of conduct and the use of "bureaucratese" language in their written reports? Is it not somehow in the nature of bureaucracy to subordinate initiative and style to a common norm established through either force or example by those higher up "the ladder"? Where in the era of Charles I are the forms to be filled out, rubber stamps, duplicate and triplicate copies, and file numbers?

G. E. AYLMER: The King's Servants*

For historians (the same may not be true for political scientists) it is probably most sensible to think of "bureaucracy" as referring to certain methods of administration. These must include, at a minimum, professionalism, regular hierarchy, division into departments, and heavy reliance on written records. Granted that bureaucracy, or a bureaucratic form of government, is found to

* From G. E. Aylmer, *The King's Servants, The Civil Service of Charles I, 1625–1642,* (London, Routledge and Kegan Paul Ltd., 1961), pp. 459–69.

exist in a given instance, this does not preclude us from asking questions about its alleged defects: routine, inflexibility, procrastination, extreme conservatism, and even petty tyranny. Nor are we thereby prevented from considering it in relation to the social structure of a particular country in a given epoch, and to the distribution of power in that society. . . .

By these criteria, bureaucracy certainly existed in Caroline [Charles I] England. But this needs to be qualified in two important respects. First, the bureaucracy, or the bureaucratic government, was so small that it may thereby have failed to operate in the manner which this definition normally entails. The Privy Council and its clerical staff, the Secretaries of State and theirs were such factotums, ranging over such a multitude of questions, great and small, of such extraordinarily varied character, that this was no ordinary bureaucratic government as we know it: specialized, elaborate, and professional. Second, this bureaucracy had some other very un-modern characteristics, which serve to invalidate most analogies or comparisons with more recent bureaucracies. Many junior officials, although they were in the King's service, were appointed not by the King, or by the Crown in a more impersonal sense, but by senior officials (acting as individuals), councillors, or courtiers. Many subordinates in the central courts and departments, including some important personal assistants, were not in the King's service at all, but were the private employees of other officials. The granting of reversions, the tenure of offices for life, and the general tendency to regard positions under the Crown as property rights belonging to their holders further limited the Crown's freedom of appointment and promotion. These factors also limited its ability to regulate or abolish existing offices and to set up new ones. The ways in which officers were paid meant that financially they dealt direct with other office-holders and with members of the public; they were not effectively dependent on their own head of department, on the Exchequer (that is the King's financial advisers), or on the Crown itself. Only quite a small fraction of the office-holders were in practice full-time professional civil servants. Most were also landed gentlemen, practising lawyers, or (in a few cases) actively engaged in commerce. Nor did the thought of the age have any concept of "civil servants" as an occupational classification, least of all as a class of people disqualified from taking part in politics. This was partly because the modern distinction, nowadays perhaps itself carried too far, between politics and administration was almost wholly absent.

Much of this would be true of most, if not all, pre-nineteenth-century bureaucracies. It would be easy, by employing too rigorous a definition, to conclude that, save in very rare and exceptional instances, bureaucracy had never existed before 1800. True, bureaucracy, as we know it, scarcely had existed, but to say on this account that it had not existed at all would be to show a shockingly parochial and unhistorical outlook.

With its elaborate and highly formalized procedure, the copiousness of its written records, the jealousies of its departmental divisions, its hierarchy, and its specialization, English central government had been thoroughly bureaucratic for a very long time. It is reasonable to date English bureaucracy from the "administrative revolution" of the twelfth century, And even this is to regard

Domesday Book, that stupendous bureaucratic achievement, as a flash in the pan. Another decisive shift, away from bureaucracy within the framework of household government and towards departmental "out of court" bureaucracy, occurred in the Tudor period. All ages are "ages of transition" but the tempo of change varies greatly from one age to another. This is as true in administration as in all other aspects of human life.

It remains to be considered how far the Caroline bureaucracy was bureaucratic in the sense meant by many social scientists and by almost all modern political commentators. That the officials themselves constituted *the* ruling class of early Stuart England need only be suggested to be seen to be ridiculous. Most of the middling and almost all the upper officials belonged to the armigerous landowning class; if there was *a* "ruling class," this was it, and they formed part of it.

But they formed part of it with a difference. It is not necessary to interpret the Civil War as a conflict between the "Ins" and "Outs" to recognize that the interests and outlook of the office-holders were not in all respects identical with those of the "mere" gentry, who did not hold office or reside in the capital; nor the interests and outlook of the "mere" office-holders in turn identical with those of the office-holding landed gentry. One reason why the English central officials exercised less political influence than their French counterparts was because they were even further from constituting a definable, homogeneous class or social group. True, when the French bureaucracy did make its bid for national leadership, in the *Fronde,* it failed lamentably. Even so, the attempt was made, and some degree of internal solidarity mustered in making it. In England no such bid was made, and never could have been: the question did not arise.

So much for the Caroline bureaucracy as a ruling class, or as an influence within the ruling class. As an instrument of royal power, of would-be absolutism, its effectiveness is harder to estimate. Under the so-called "eleven years tyranny," the personal government of Charles I, England was probably as "well governed" as any country in Europe then could be without revolutionary social and political changes. To those at the receiving end central administration no doubt often appeared capricious and interfering; the financial needs alike of the Crown and of its servants were constantly felt. Yet within the limits set by its own requirements and by the general climate of opinion, the Crown was genuinely solicitous for the welfare of the people. By modern standards the rights and liberties of the subject were narrowly limited and ill defined. Yet there were safeguards against the abuse of executive power. For all that has recently been suggested to the contrary, even in the 1620's–30's an Englishman was better protected against arbitrary action by the Crown or its agents than were most of his European contemporaries of comparable wealth and social standing.

Government interference in business, in agriculture, trade, industry, building, and mining was a widespread grievance under Charles I. But it was a grievance against the policy of the Crown, especially its many fiscal expedients. Individual officials had to enforce the regulations and controls, some of which undoubtedly restricted economic enterprise. And some officials certainly behaved high-handedly, like "jacks in office." But there is very little, if any, evidence that the officials as such, the bureaucracy, were felt to be encroaching on the freedom of the people, stifling creative activity, or swathing the nation in red tape. The nearest one gets to such a feeling is in the tone of resentment adopted by some "mere" gentry against the court and the government. There is Sir Anthony Weldon's complaint that the Messengers of the Chamber

were countenanced in their abuse, and insultings over the Gentry (when in their Clutches): and to such a strange passe were disorders come unto [*sic*], that every Lacquey of these great Lords might give a Check-Mate to any Gentleman, yea, to any Country Nobleman, that was not in the Court favour.

But Weldon had himself been expelled from office and from the Court in 1617; he comes in the category of embittered ex-office-holders, of gamekeepers turned poachers. As for the Messengers, there seem to be as many stories of their being insulted and even maltreated as of their behaving high-handedly or committing abuses.

Most of the complaints about royal officials relate to their exactions. The payment of officers in fees and gratuities constantly invited, and often almost compelled abuse. The Crown was at least aware of this, and in respect of fees did try to do something about it. Nor did all officers take, or attempt to take, excessive fees and gratuities. Most of them, we may infer, took what they felt was owing them, that is as much as they decently could; but only a minority were deliberate systematic extortioners.

It is impossible to tell how many instances there were of "bureaucracy" in the bad sense. These are things of which written record is unlikely to have survived. Some kinds of officials were definitely unpopular, such as the Purveyors and the Saltpetremen. But this was usually because of the nature of their duties, which virtually compelled them to act high-handedly and interferingly. If retrospective evidence is allowed, the radical protest literature (pamphlets, etc.) of the 1640's certainly contains many demands for administrative, and more particularly for legal reforms. But apart from the question of fees, it does not contain a great deal in the way of attacks on officials as such. Exceptions must of course be made for the religious extremists who regarded all temporal government as the work of the beast, soon to be swept away, and for the Diggers, and perhaps some of the Levellers, who saw existing officials merely as instruments of class rule and perpetuators of social injustice. It would be unhistorical to expect to find the modern kind of grievances against bureaucracy, when in its modern form bureaucracy itself can scarcely be found.

To assess the place in history of Charles I's officials it is necessary to re-emphasize that they were still his servants, and not those of the Crown or the Public. True, some distinction can be drawn between the household staff and those holding positions in the law courts and the departments. But it is hard to know how much to make of this. As early as the thirteenth and fourteenth centuries there was some distinction between *familiares* and office-holders in the "out-of-court" institutions. The great change, for the most part still to come, was in men's ideas about the state.

Fundamental changes in mental attitude, especially in people's tacit un-spoken assumptions about the nature of God and man, of society and the world, are usually slow to take general effect. Such was the case with the change from the Ptolemaic to the Copernican and then to the Newtonian idea of the physical universe. But once they have come about, such changes are often remarkably complete. The new attitude seems so obvious, its premises so sure, that it is hard for people of later generations to think back and imagine the circumstances of a time when their own attitude was unknown, or was the prerogative of a few isolated individuals. In the early seventeenth century it was gradually becoming possible for men to think of loyalty to the state, to the "common weal" or the public good, as something which might in certain circumstances be different from service to the King. Pym and the other parliamentarians in the Civil War claimed that they were not fighting against the King, but to rescue him from evil counsellors by whom he was being led astray. They either thought it impolitic, or else could not bring themselves, to deny the proposition that "The King can do no wrong." This reluctance to blame the King personally, to oppose him directly had a very different significance then from that which it was to acquire in the nineteenth and twentieth centuries. It reflected not the non-political role of the sovereign, but the religious basis of monarchy and the deep-seated contemporary horror of treason and rebellion. Even if Pym and his supporters in parliament did not subscribe to all this themselves, they certainly knew how powerful a hold it still had in the country at large. In 1642–3, even in 1644–5, republicanism was no more than "a little cloud . . . like a man's hand." And even in the years of victory, 1649–60, it failed to strike deep or widespread roots as a mental attitude among the people.

It is easy to repeat that all royal officials still were, and felt themselves to be the King's servants, much harder to estimate the actual degree of royal authority and control over them. How far was the King in fact master in his own house and his own government? The King and his ministers were aware of certain faults in the administrative system; so too were some of the officials themselves. And genuine attempts were made to remedy several of these faults. It would be completely wrong to picture the Caroline régime as drifting frivolously to disaster, blissfully unaware of its own shortcomings. Yet little was achieved. Why was this?

The King and his councillors were unaware of what appear to us as some of the most profound defects. They seem to have been unable to grasp that it is sometimes an economy to pay people more. It could be said that this was part of a wider failure to see the need to turn royal officials into salaried public servants. But this brings us back to the question of mental attitude. Salaried the officials might perhaps have been; public servants, before the Crown had itself been to a greater extent depersonalized and the King in some degree de-politicized, they hardly could be.

In other cases the Crown had some idea of what was needed, but lacked either the will or the authority to put such measures into effect. This was true of thoroughgoing economical reform in the household, and of the fee problem in the law and revenue courts.

There were also legal limits to what the Crown could do. In James I's reign responsible men had got up in the Commons and said that the fees of Exchequer officials were their "freehold," and could not be touched without all property being threatened. Parliament, it is true, was not the same as the courts. But even the court cases brought against office-holders show the weaknesses in the Crown's position. In 1618–19 the Lord Treasurer had been dismissed for gross corruption, but his subordinate, the Auditor of the Receipt, had only been suspended, and had to be bullied and cajoled into resigning. The great Lionel Cranfield was easily removed from the Treasury and the Wards, but his mediocre brother Randall's tenure as Master of the Mint proved considerably harder to terminate. In the 1630's, for the four or five officers who were tried, found guilty of exactions, and deprived of their positions, there were several times as many who compounded, and kept their offices with substantially the same fees as before.

Officers who had committed venial rather than mortal crimes could choose to bargain with the Crown, or in the last resort to stand their trial. Some did better, others worse, than those who submitted to the King's mercy, but at least there was room for manœuvre. Life tenure and the concept of office as a "right" were the holders' main defences. But, of course, if an entire patent could be voided, or revoked on sound legal grounds, it availed an officer nothing that one of its clauses granted him tenure for life. Hence the importance of the decision given by the Judges of King's Bench in 1637, which seems to have widened the grounds on which a patent could be voided. It is not clear how far this judgment actually became an effective precedent.

It is difficult to say exactly how much the King could touch officers' rights by issuing proclamations or by other executive orders. In theory he could not over-ride statute or go against the common law. In practice his ability to alter the law by pressure on the judges was one of the main constitutional issues of 1603–42. None of the three classic cases (Bate's in 1606, the "Five Knights'" in 1627, and Hampden's in 1637) concerned office-holders' rights. But if the King could get the law altered concerning taxation, then clearly—with the judges' help—he could also get it changed as it related to office-holding. Moreover, apart from their privileges, officers' liabilities were involved when they allowed themselves to be the instruments of illegal action, for example in collecting unparliamentary taxes (Impositions after 1606; or, a clearer instance, Tonnage and Poundage after 1626). Some customs officers indeed discovered to their cost that royal proclamations and commissions under the Great Seal not only did not change the law but did not always protect those who broke it.

By statute the King in Parliament could alter any right or privilege of any office-holder. Legally there was no impediment to the statutory abolition of the Pipe and the Remembrancers' Offices, to the institution of a fee "pool," and to the putting of all Crown servants onto fixed stipends. The limit here was set by political practicability, not by what was legally possible; ultimately it was determined by what was—given all the circumstances of the age—even think-able.

If the Stuarts had been victorious, and if an absolute monarchy of the French type had been established in England, the modernization of English govern-ment would have taken place in an utterly different political, legal, and social context. As it was, the gradual decline of royal power from the sixteenth to the nineteenth century to a large extent preceded the birth of the modern Civil Service. The outcome of the seventeenth-century constitutional conflict helped to determine the context within which the modern roles of both the Crown and the Civil Service have evolved. It may seem perverse to argue at one and the same time that his servants could not become "public" officials while the King still ruled as well as reigned, and that an "enlightened" absolutism might have initiated administrative reforms akin to those which were only fully achieved in the nineteenth century. There is force in this objection. But the answer to it may lie in suggesting some distinction between personal monarchy and absolutism. The governments of the eighteenth-century "despots" were more bureaucratic, more departmentalized, than the government of Charles I. In this respect enlightened absolutism was a stage nearer to modern autocracy, where the ruler indisputably "rules" but where the officials are no longer his personal or household servants.

In England the political victory of oligarchy appears to have had the effect of consolidating the "old administrative system" and possibly of prolonging its existence. The eighteenth-century constitution and the unreformed Civil Service were in turn undermined by new forces. New demands were made on the state, and new standards expected from its servants, particularly from the 1780's on. Extra-parliamentary public opinion, above all the voice of the greatly expanded urban middle class, made itself increasingly heard. Finally the Crown became depersonalized; executive power passed from the monarch and his (or her) chosen advisers to a cabinet selected on a "party" basis. The seeds of the nine-teenth-century reforms in administration might have been sown by Strafford, or equally well by the Barebones Parliament. What had been prevented from coming about under the rule of King and oligarchy was later to accompany the establishment of the Crown's new position, the emergence of cabinet and parties, and the rise of public opinion.

All this is to assume that the social structure of the country and the balance of political power in it were decisive in determining the limits within which the administrative system developed. Such an assumption is not necessarily correct. Unless the underlying causes in history are believed to be exclusively of one kind (for instance economic and technological, or mental and spiritual), there is no logical reason why institutions of government and systems of office-holding should not have important economic, social, political, and even cultural in-fluences. The question is how far, in practice, government (including of course the officials taking part in it) does exercise a major influence on how people live and think. And this includes the further question of how far such influence as it does appear to have represents anything more than an indirect effect of other non-administrative factors, which have—at a stage further back in the causal chain—helped to determine the system of government and the kind of people participating in it.

For England in the years 1625 to 1642 the conclusion is inescapable. It is surely beyond debate, that the growth of government and the rise of bureaucracy are major themes in modern history. But to contend that a particular phase in this process, or the political and social tensions which arose from it, provided the key to English seventeenth-century history would be to make oneself the victim of a sociological theory. And to maintain such a view would in the last resort be to go in the face of both the evidence and common sense.

The reader's as well as the author's own temperament and preferences will help to form our final picture of Charles I's Civil Service. We may think of Edward Nicholas, a worthy servant of "Thorough," working tirelessly to administer the entire Ship Money project for a nominal stipend of only £200 a year, over and above all his routine work for the Admiralty Commissioners and odd jobs for the Privy Council. Or we may think of Sir Robert Pye together with the Prest and Revenue Auditors working overtime to provide the Treasury Commissioners with an unusually detailed statement of the Crown's financial position. On the other hand we may think of the Clerk of the Ordnance being found making a bonfire of departmental records in order to escape the scrutiny of an investigating commission. We may think of the officers of the Household systematically cheating the Crown for forty years by means of a transparent and shameless accounting device. Or we may think of those who waxed rich on the fruits of extortion from the public. Yet there must have been many more officials who fell between the extremes of laxity and conscientiousness. Many, perhaps most of them, must have worked moderately hard, with fair efficiency, sticking mainly to precedent and routine, with reasonable loyalty to the Crown, and profiting only modestly out of their positions. If such "typical" civil servants of Charles I seem to have got buried in lists and tables, it is simply because evidence of a personal nature is so much likelier to have survived about those who were for one reason or another "untypical." But of their existence there can be no reasonable doubt.

In one respect typical and untypical are happily alike. The English language had reached that point in its development where almost anyone who wrote naturally—and not sycophantically or for conscious literary effect—wrote well. Even the most humdrum administrative details, the pettiest personal concerns, come alive in seventeenth-century English prose. If administrative history is sometimes said to be dull, this may sometimes be because the people involved in it were themselves dull. Whatever the truth of this for other epochs, no such extenuating plea can be entered here.

2.

Was Cardinal Richelieu a bureaucrat? Our first reaction is to say, of course not. He virtually ruled France. And yet, rich and powerful as he was, Richelieu could exercise very little power in his own name. The character of monarchy—in this case the French monarchy—vested all power in the king.

Without the support of Louis XIII, Richelieu could have accomplished nothing.

Here your author-editor attempts to describe Richelieu's basis of power. First by gaining the favor of Louis XIII, and then by coming to control all the important offices of state, Richelieu finally could exercise power.

How would you describe the personal relationships between Louis XIII and his ministers? How may these ministers, particularly Bullion, his Superintendent of Finance, have influenced the course of bureaucratic development in France? The relations between Richelieu and the other ministers were "friendly," but in what way?

OREST RANUM: The Creatures of Richelieu*

A study of the last years of the reign of Louis XIII reveals a paradox: at a time when French political philosophers and jurists were proclaiming absolutism, there was an absence of absolutist ideology or doctrine in the correspondence and working papers of the king and his ministers. But the paradox is more apparent than real. The idea that the king was the source of all political power and justice was clearly implicit on all occasions when decisions were communicated, whether between ministers or to the lower branches of the administration. All political action was in the king's name, either through institutions such as the Parlement, whose powers had been delegated to them by the Crown long before, or, more directly by the king and his ministers *vis-à-vis* the rest of the administration.

Within the framework of the *Conseil du roi* the principal minister and other councillors made decisions which were transmitted to the realm in the king's name. The traditional phrase, *par le roi en son conseil,* was not just a legal fiction. The centuries of political centralization in the person of the king, a phenomenon much older than absolutism as expressed in the seventeenth century, made commands in the king's name the only effective political power in the realm.

The same was true of relations between the ministers. Commands and political decisions were made for the *service du roi,* a phrase which Richelieu and the creatures used constantly. Often references to the king were simply automatic, but even so they reflected the nature of monarchy and maintained even the most powerful ministers in a juridical framework which gave the king unlimited powers over his ministers if he desired to use them. Richelieu made daily requests to ministers in the name of the king; and when they were to come to a political decision themselves, either Louis or the cardinal gave them permission to do so. Richelieu wrote to Chancellor Séguier: "You will send to us, if you please, with diligence the necessary powers and orders to execute the decisions which you judge that the king must make on such a subject. . . ." A reference to the king was not a mere formality; it properly expressed the nature of the government and was a political necessity.

* From Orest Ranum, *Richelieu and the Councillors of Louis XIII* (Oxford, Clarendon Press, 1963), pp. 10–26.

Often mere references to the king by ministers, or even traditional formulas, were ineffective against rebellious subjects or institutions. The presence of the king, or direct orders from him with his signature boldly visible and his seal affixed, were the only effective instruments of the government. The ministers therefore did not have political identity in themselves; on both the personal and institutional levels their orders were frequently brushed aside. Dupuy, in his letter to Chancellor Séguier, accepted the decision of the ministers, but waited for a royal letter before taking action.

On the institutional level, the position of the minister was also dependent upon the king. When Louis was away from Paris he was obliged to send letters to enforce obedience of the sovereign courts and to make them execute the orders of his ministers, even though they had acted in his name *en conseil.* At a time when new troops were badly needed, Louis wrote to First President Nicolay of the *Chambre des comptes:*

And I wish to have raised as soon as possible up to eight or ten thousand foot soldiers [in Paris] as well as in the *élection* of that city, and in the neighbouring ones; and because I expect much from the affection of my principal servants in this affair and especially from you, I am writing you this letter to invite you and exhort you as much as I am able, to contribute everything which depends on you for the progress of this levy, addressing orders especially to Monsieur the Chancellor and to the Sieur Bouthillier, Superintendent of my finances, who will make my intentions known to you. . . .

The ministers of Louis XIII did not possess delegated powers in the broad sense, merely rights and traditions which permitted them to act only in limited spheres. As the source of all power, Louis was often compelled to write letters requesting royal officials to execute the orders of his ministers.

In times of severe crisis or revolt, or when the realm was threatened with invasion, not even royal letters, much less the actions of the ministers in the *conseil,* would bring the king's subjects to obey. Only the presence of the king with military force could do so. Louis XIII, many times in his long life as king, was compelled to go to provinces or towns to quell revolts or to force a parlement to register the edicts of his ministers. Even ecclesiastical assemblies were subject to strict surveillance by the Crown. In 1635 Bullion advised Richelieu that the forthcoming Assembly of the Clergy should be held close to the king. He knew all too well the stormy sessions which inevitably occurred between ecclesiastics and royal officials as they determined the size of the "contribution" of the clergy. As a result, the power of the king alone was legally observable not only in the realm—the exterior administration outside of the king and his council—but within the council as well. The legal fiction that only the king made political decisions was guaranteed and made effective by old customs which bound the ministers as well as the lower branches of the administration.

Beyond the framework of councils and offices there was a mixture of purely administrative and personal factors which gave the government of Louis XIII its character and determined how it functioned. Traditionally, the king's ministers had formed parties which tended to counterbalance each other in importance and power; but after the Day of the Dupes, the death of Effiat, and the disgrace of Châteauneuf in 1633, Richelieu dominated all of the ministers. From the exterior they seemed to function independently of each other and in direct relationship with the king. With Richelieu as principal minister this was not so. A hierarchy within the ministry, based upon personalities and consequent favouritism, determined the importance of the minister.

This hierarchy, with Richelieu at the top, changed the traditional importance of the officers. As chancellor, Séguier probably enjoyed greater prestige but less real influence in the government than two of the secretaries of state, who held offices which, as will be noted later, had very humble beginnings. Under these circumstances the favour of the king still remained very important, but it was not so decisive as favour with the cardinal. Chavigny openly wrote to a friend that he was out of favour with Louis XIII, but since he was in favour with Richelieu he was sure that his position in the government was safe.

Louis was confronted with a unified ministry as a result of his affection for and confidence in Richelieu and of the consequent acceptance of the latter's creatures. He continued to support the cardinal and to grant him ever greater powers. The king rarely commented on the powers of his ministers, but in the Vendôme affair, where the brother of the king was accused of plotting against Richelieu, Louis explained his support for the principal minister. In the council which had been united to judge Vendôme, Louis said:

Messieurs, it is Monsieur the Cardinal who requests me to pardon Monsieur de Vendôme; that is not my opinion. I owe protection to those who serve me with affection and fidelity, as does Monsieur the Cardinal; and if I am not careful to have the plots made against his person punished, it will be difficult to find ministers to watch over my affairs with the courage and fidelity that he does.

The personality of the king was in itself the principal reason for the hierarchical relationships between the ministers. Louis was a conscientious worker at affairs of state; he was intelligent and had a marked ability for knowing and respecting the rights of his subjects. Although the government of France was significantly modified during his reign, which meant that a multiplicity of ancient rights, both corporal and personal, were trampled on by the Crown, the king was in no way a political reformer. Louis consented to these changes only when necessity required it. During the crucial years of the war from 1635 to 1640, when the old sovereign courts and minor venal officers protested so violently against the massive creations of new offices, Louis probably remained reticent and accepted such changes only when his ministers offered no other means of increasing the royal revenues. Louis XIII merited his sobriquet "the Just," partly because of the long list of executions which took place during his reign, and also because of his carefulness and respect for the rights of his subjects.

The king's views were made known to his ministers. Louis seems to have had an excellent mind for the details of government. He took special interest in the armies; no detail of provision, troop-raising and payments, or officer appointments was too small for him to consider. The king became angry and sullen whenever he discovered that his ministers, including Richelieu, had planned or executed something without consulting him. This caused an instantaneous reaction among the ministers, who never forgot that in earlier times Louis had brutally disgraced ministers. Claude le Bouthillier wrote to Richelieu:

His Majesty was surprised when the marshal informed him that the infantry had been reduced to eighty in accordance with an order that [the marshal] says he saw signed by Monsieur de Bullion. As a result, I bore the brunt of a little [of the king's] anger; but after having explained that, in spite of that resolution, Monsieur de Bullion had left funds . . . His Majesty calmed down and only commanded me to send in any case an ordonnance stating that the troops be paid according to the number present. . . .

The *mauvaises humeurs* of the king were the cause of much anxiety on the part of the ministers, including Richelieu; and his desire to review every detail obliged the ministers to prepare dispatches carefully. Louis's real interest in government, even down to the little details, was overlooked by Avenel when he observed that Richelieu requested the king to fix the price of army bread at a moment when the cardinal was enjoying the "fullness of absolute power." While the presentation of such details might seem absurd to present-day ad-ministrators, nothing could be more misleading. Louis took the *métier du roi* very seriously, and insisted on being informed of everything.

In the complex problems of government, where goals and political policies were defined, Louis's role is more difficult to determine. Little is known about this aspect for either Louis or Richelieu, because their thoughts and actions, as indicated in their correspondence, do not clearly delineate their political person-alities. The great affairs of state were usually discussed, and decisions were reached in the *Conseil d'en haut* in the presence of the king, Richelieu, Bullion, Séguier, Chavigny, and Sublet de Noyers. No minutes were taken, and to our knowledge not even a detailed description of one of these sessions is extant.

In correspondence with his ministers, Louis appears as the reviewer of policies. He did this very carefully. Claude le Bouthillier wrote to Richelieu:

I saw by a letter of Monsieur de Noyers to Monsieur the Chancellor that the King was displeased that we created [the office] of provosts generals for the prov-inces *en son conseil* without talking about it to His Majesty. His Eminence will remember, if it please him, that I gave myself the honour of talking to him about it. . . .

When Louis was displeased, the creatures quickly sought cover under the protection of Richelieu, but as this incident clearly indicates, speaking to the cardinal alone about a political decision was insufficient unless Richelieu in turn presented it to the king.

The letters from Richelieu to Louis—where problems and solutions are briefly explained in forms of alternatives so that the king could simply scribble *bon* or *il le fault* in the margin—do not help to determine Louis's initiative in government, for they generally concern only the decisions of daily government routine.

The king was always sensitive when he felt improperly informed by his ministers. He and his ministers were anxious to read dispatches newly arrived from foreign capitals or battlefields. When Richelieu or the particular secretary of state to whom a dispatch was addressed was not present when it arrived, Louis complained. Occasionally he opened such dispatches himself, to the dismay and terror of the secretaries, for they often carried on private correspondence and exchanged court gossip with other royal servants. The importance of letters in the ministry of Louis XIII cannot be over-estimated.

In an age without modern communications, and when customs and exigencies of government often separated the king from his ministers, the letter, its presentation, form, and content all had great significance. The formalities were long and complicated, and tremendously important.

The relative informality of Richelieu's letters to Louis, and vice versa, remains the most convincing proof of the affection and mutual respect which existed between the two men. Louis was often subject to fits of ill temper, moments of severe psychological depression; and frequently his attitude or even his decision on a policy was determined or greatly modified by his mood of the moment. Louis's correspondence was controlled by Chavigny, and to a lesser extent by Sublet de Noyers. It was their task to present Richelieu's letters to the king at the times when they were most likely to be well received. Chavigny wrote to Richelieu: "I showed [the letter] to the King in my accustomed fashion . . . ," indicating that he had perhaps developed a system to assure Richelieu that his letters would be favourably received by the king. In a period of difficulty, when the cardinal was not even sure of Louis's favour, Chavigny, after reporting that the king was in a bad mood, wrote: "I did not believe that I should show the letter of His Eminence [Richelieu] to the King until I am able to determine better in what disposition his thoughts are. . . ."

After 1630 the whole ministry of Louis XIII depended upon Richelieu's personal favour with the king. The cardinal might never have so cleverly dominated the entire government of France if he had not ensured his good relations with Louis through his creatures. The ministers of Louis XIII were in a direct relationship with the king, but they were not free to advise and act as they wished. The personality of Cardinal Richelieu, with his great personal favor, stood between them and the king. Through Richelieu's influence Louis XIII had appointed the other ministers; through Richelieu's favour they remained in office. When Louis was offended at something that Richelieu or the creatures had done, the cardinal appealed to him as an old and faithful servant and begged forgiveness, yet at the same time he would give the king a verbal spanking. The personality of the king, his health and moods, enabled Richelieu to establish this intermediary position between the ministry as a whole and the king.

If Louis was primarily the reviewer of policy, Richelieu was both the formulator and co-ordinator of it. When differences of views arose between the other ministers, it was Richelieu, not the king, who took the initiative in making the final decision. Louis was then informed, was asked to give his opinion, and the policy was approved or modified according to the king's pleasure; but in most cases the divergence of views between the councillor-ministers was settled before the measure was presented to him.

The hierarchical relationship and subservient position of the other ministers is clearly observable in other ways, and Louis's own actions and statements in regard to his ministers are most indicative. The king made a practice of holding Richelieu responsible for the actions of the other ministers; when one of them displeased him, he wrote to Richelieu, instead of to the offending minister, about it.

I gave all the orders for the levying of the six regiments and also for the two new ones and for the whole cavalry. I am writing to you in anger after a commissioner named Renart cut down all the old regiments by 400 men . . . all done under the orders of Monsieur de Bullion without [his] having spoken to me about it. It is indeed strange that they give such orders without my knowing it. . . . Excuse me if I am speaking to you angrily; it is simply that these things happen often.

Likewise, when the creatures did something that pleased Louis, he informed Richelieu of his approval. Louis fully understood the relationship between Richelieu and the other ministers, and he acted accordingly. On one occasion he criticized the treasurers and army munitioners, and the cardinal refused to accept the censure for what had been done by someone else.

The relationship between the king and the cardinal, as well as their health, was of the utmost importance to the creatures. The constant references to their health were not simply phrases of courtesy or friendly concern, but political realities.

Only in the king's relationship with Bullion, Superintendent of Finance, was Richelieu's middle position modified. This crafty old minister, who enjoyed much prestige and affection with Louis, did not hesitate to appeal directly to the king when a policy proposed by Richelieu seemed not to be in the best interests of the Crown. His power to control the purse strings was particularly great, and he enjoyed more independence than the other ministers, especially when the financial pinch of war brought France to the brink of bankruptcy.

Even so, both Louis and Richelieu evaded onerous and, if we are to believe Bullion, impossible tasks involving the search for money to pay for the war. Louis probably did not understand the complex financial problems of his government; in his correspondence with the superintendents, there were demands for money without any suggestion about where it was to be found.

Instead of addressing his money requests to the superintendents, Louis often wrote to Richelieu, giving him the task of extracting money from them. Indeed, he sometimes made decisions involving considerable sums of money without taking cognizance of the financial condition of the realm. At the same time, he knew full well that even Richelieu, no matter how devoted the superintendents were to him, also had difficulty in enforcing his decisions. The cardinal was sometimes obliged to solicit the king's aid in compelling the superintendents to carry out policies made by Louis and himself. When the superintendents were particularly difficult, Louis talked with them personally. Yet Louis, who probably did not understand the problems fully, requested Richelieu to instruct him on what to say to Bullion about his own finances. The old superintendent did not fear the jealousy of the cardinal when they failed to agree. He wrote to Louis in a frank, fatherly way to give his views on financial policies, but at the same time he included a good word for the cardinal. When Richelieu feared that Bullion would oppose or hinder a policy, he presented it directly to the king. Chavigny once wrote to the cardinal, after remarking that Louis had accepted Richelieu's suggestions: "It is true, Monseigneur, that it was much more convenient to have the affair accepted that way than if Monsieur de Bullion had proposed it with some preambles." The hierarchical relationship was thus maintained, although to a lesser degree than with the other ministers. Richelieu stood supreme above the others, instructing them and limiting their direct initiative with the king.

Louis's freedom to act as he pleased, while theoretically very great, was broadly limited in two ways: the first was institutional and traditional, the second personal. Louis's actions were limited by the traditional rights of his subjects, both individual and institutional; personally, his own initiative was somewhat circumscribed by Richelieu and his creatures. They controlled his correspondence, surrounded him, and sheltered him from other would-be favourites and courtiers opposed to Richelieu and his policies. They exiled the king's favourites who did not remain faithful to the cardinal, and in part even controlled the king's excursions. Letters which might upset the king were kept from him by Sublet de Noyers and Chavigny, and ambassadors complained about the tight circle of ministers around the king, which made it difficult to gain audiences with him.

Chavigny sometimes had difficulty in managing Louis, especially when he tried to persuade the king to accept a policy which he did not favour. At the same time, the *mauvaises humeurs* of the king were enough to make all the ministers tremble; even Richelieu, when Louis was angry, tip-toed softly under cover of total obeisance.

Louis depended on the creatures to explain to the cardinal not only governmental actions but also the king's views on problems, men, and suggestions made by Richelieu. The king's decisions were often transmitted verbally by the creatures, leaving Richelieu to see to their execution, a practice which, if not observed closely, leads to the old and incorrect interpretation that political decisions were made and executed solely by Richelieu. Co-operation between the secretaries, the chancellor, the superintendents, and finally the principal minister, was a necessity in the period of severe administrative crisis which began with open war in 1635. In this period Richelieu forged a ministry relatively free from intrigue and competition between the ministers; it was their dependence on him for favour which rendered them docile. At his death, jealousy and suspicion soon destroyed the cohesion that he had created among the ministers, resulting is disgrace for all of them in the early years of the minority of Louis XIV.

Under Richelieu a secretary could explain to his colleagues how he had fared with Louis, and together they harmonized their efforts to eliminate royal bad humour, and communicated the king's orders to each other for the benefit of the group. They also informed each other when the king was to be given some specific information from their departments. When Louis wanted to communicate with Richelieu on various affairs of state, he requested a secretary of state to come and see him in order to transmit what he had to say to the cardinal. The king had confidence in the men who managed his government. Richelieu and the other ministers were aware of political policies directed by the king, including the secret details.

As to Richelieu's general political relationships with his creatures, he possessed broader powers than they, though no new title was given to institutionalize them; in fact, they needed no institutionalization, for they were based upon the great favour and support of the king, as reflected in the confusion of the roles of king and principal minister in the last years of the reign. These broad powers enabled Richelieu to dominate and direct the whole government.

Richelieu did not hesitate to reprimand his underlings or to insult them with his sarcasm. Yet at the same time he showered them with gifts, political favours, and personal affection. The loss of the cardinal's favour meant disgrace; the threat hung like a pall over all the ministers, obliging them to be obedient and obsequious. At the same time, all knew that the political existence of the entire ministry depended upon the favour of Louis for Richelieu; the king guarded his supreme powers jealously, and Richelieu acted independently only when expressly authorized by Louis to do so.

Richelieu relied heavily on these officers for information and administrative details. He had confidence in them; when he was preparing for war he nervously sent the secretary of state for war a request for a statement of the condition and strength of the army. Their advice was sought, and after humbly apologizing, they gave it quite freely to Richelieu. Even Bullion, the minister second only to Richelieu in prestige and power in the government of Louis XIII, made it a practice to begin with a long apology, which nevertheless did not hide his differences of opinion from the cardinal. In this way the cardinal was able to keep abreast of governmental problems, to make decisions quickly, and with the support of the other ministers to present a unified policy to Louis XIII in the *conseil*. Although his knowledge of detail was vast, he was not an administrative superman.

Haste and efficiency were essential to seventeenth-century government; some of Richelieu's most bitter comments to his creatures concerned their failure to act quickly and forcefully. The ministers worked all hours of the day and night, and travelled almost constantly about the realm. Louis himself insisted on action, and sometimes while on a campaign he took very bad lodgings in his haste to get on with the war. As with the king, the ministers often carried verbal orders from Richelieu to each other to save time and to ensure secrecy. Intrigue against Richelieu by courtiers and would-be parties was constant, but the cardinal's confidence in the other ministers was absolute. Through his influence with the king, the cardinal had made them ministers, not because of their administrative efficiency, nor for that matter because of their knowledge of foreign affairs, finance, or the army, but because affection and fidelity were the chief personal and political pre-requisites which determined the very nature of government in the last years of Louis XIII.

How did Richelieu personally envisage his position within the ministry? In his own correspondence with the ministers he made very few comments on his role as he saw it. Once he wrote to Chavigny: "However, I will leave all the necessary orders at Amiens in fulfilment of my *charge* which, as you know, is none other than solicitor of diligence. . . ." It was much more than this. Without creating new offices or institutions, Richelieu acquired certain powers reserved only for the king. The force of his personality, first on the king and next on the ministers whom he selected, was responsible for the nature of the central government in the last years of Louis XIII.

3.

That the rebellions and civil wars against royal power occurring in the 1640's actually caused royal power to increase throughout Europe, strains our sense of neatness in history. John B. Wolf (1907–   ), Professor of History at the University of Illinois at Chicago Circle, argues that this is exactly what happened in the mid-seventeenth century. Violence and civil war strengthened governments, particularly in England and France.

Cromwell's "New Model" army and Louis XIV's crack *Maison du Roi* gave the state power unequaled since Roman times. These armies were neither feudal nor mercenary; they were standing, disciplined, and zealous. These fighting machines required drastic changes in the governments if they were to be kept paid, clothed, armed, and fed. Wolf links the rise of modern bureaucracies to their development.

Once these armies established peace and security at home, they could be used to attack neighboring states. England disbanded the "New Model"; Louis XIV sent his armies abroad to add territory to France and to bring home prestige and booty. His decision forced other European states to equip themselves with large standing armies and, in turn, to establish bureaucracies to administer and supply them. Without Louis' wars would Prussia and the Danubian Monarchy (Austria), for example, have set up centralized bureaucracies?

JOHN B. WOLF: Warfare and the Rise of Bureaucracy*

In the first two-thirds of the seventeenth century civil rebellions and international conflict created a *mêlée* in which statesmen could develop a program of action only with great difficulty. In the latter part of the century, when civil rebellion was discouraged by the disparity between the forces available to rebels and those at the disposal of the king, programs based on dynastic and states' interests were able to become the creative forces in international affairs. France under Louis XIV compelled political change and improvisation by attempting

* From John B. Wolf, "The Emergence of the European States-System," *Chapters in Western Civilization,* third ed. (New York, Columbia University Press, 1961), pp. 415–31; 411–14.

to assume the hegemony of the European world that had fallen from the hands of the Spanish Hapsburgs. Out of the effort to prevent the French king from becoming master of Europe, there emerged the institution of the balance of power, or, as it was later to be called, the Concert of Europe, by which the European community adjusted its interests. This new institution was not to become an orderly way of managing the affairs of the continent, but it was the only system that the political and cultural pluralism of Western society would tolerate, and since that pluralism, with its concomitant tensions, may well be of great importance in the subsequent civilization of the West, the system of balance of power by which it expressed itself assumes considerable importance.

Louis XIV never intended to impose the balance of power upon Europe, and he never understood his historic role in the formation of the European community. He had been brought up to believe that he must achieve his *gloire,* that is to say, that he must fulfill his destiny; Mazarin had often impressed upon him that he had both the possibility of greatness and the responsibility to achieve it. It is therefore not surprising that, when Mazarin died leaving Louis to manage his own affairs, the young king inaugurated a period of intense activity. Cooperating with the advisors that he had inherited from the cardinal, Louis struck out in all directions to make his government strong and his reign notable; reforms in the army, in the administration of justice, in the organization of economic life followed one another with rapid succession. This was the period when the basic ordinances for the organization of the bureaucracies in France were promulgated; during the rest of the reign there were to be many edicts concerning governmental organization, but they were usually merely modifications of the earlier ordinances. Since France was the most populous and perhaps the richest of the kingdoms of Europe, this burst of energy was quickly transformed into real power. The army that Richelieu had started became, under Louvois, the foremost military instrument in Europe and at the same time, with Colbert attending to commerce, colonies, and finance, the king's treasury became the most prosperous on the continent. Louis did not need to build the great colonnade of the Louvre to prove to Europe that his reign was starting auspiciously; perceptive men understood that money and soldiers augured an era of French hegemony.

Since Louis and his whole generation were brought up during wars and taught that they in turn would wage wars, it was to be expected that the young French king would use these military resources, and since his government was now in full command of the kingdom, their use would unquestionably be applied beyond the frontiers. As he explained to his son in his *Mémoires,* he was confronted with the choice of making war on England as an ally of the Dutch or upon Spain to secure his wife's inheritance; as he tells it the problem was just that simple! In another place he adds that as soon as there was talk of war, his "court was flooded with gentlemen demanding employment." In other words the moral and political climate not only implied that the king would use the force that he had, but also encouraged him to do so.

Actually, of course, Louis' decisions to make war were not as haphazard as they seem in his *Mémoires;* Louis' foreign policy continued the traditional aims of establishing the hegemony of the French Bourbon family and humbling the Hapsburgs in Spain and Austria. The marriage policies of the preceding half century had brought two Spanish princesses to France, one to be the mother, the other the wife of Louis XIV, and the provisions of the marriage contracts were such that the Bourbons might expect to inherit the thrones of Spain in default of the Hapsburg male line. The death of Louis' father-in-law, Philip IV, produced a situation in Spain that made this prospect more than a mere hope, for the sickly child king, Charles II, was the last Spanish Hapsburg male heir. For the last thirty-five years of the seventeenth century this poor creature, unable to produce an heir, occupied the throne while Europe plotted or feared the division of his crowns. While the throne in Madrid was obviously the prize sought by French diplomacy, there was also a more limited traditional goal, namely the annexation of the Spanish Netherlands. These territories were of great strategic and economic importance to France. The acquisition of the throne in Madrid with its overseas lands upon which the sun never set, and the annexation of the Netherlands on the northeastern frontier were constant territorial goals of French policy throughout the reign of Louis XIV. Naturally these ambitions aroused the fears and hostility of other powers in Europe.

The Spanish empire was not the only moribund empire in 1660; the Holy Roman Empire of the German nation was in an even more dilapidated state. French ambitions in the Empire were less well defined than those directed toward the throne of Spain, and yet from the time of Mazarin until the sensational rise in power of the Danubian monarchy under Leopold I in the late 1680s, French statesmen toyed with the idea of placing a Bourbon prince upon the throne of the Empire. And throughout the reign of Louis XIV, French policy was directed toward a division of central and eastern Europe so that the Bourbons rather than the Austrian Hapsburgs could control the development of political affairs.

Although the drive of France to the hegemony of Europe was unquestionably of paramount importance in affecting high politics in the latter seventeenth century, there were other important forces at work. In the southeast of Europe, in the Ottoman Empire, the reforming viziers of the mid-seventeenth century understood that the Turkish state had either to expand militarily or collapse, for its political life was predicated upon continuing conquest. The long naval war with Venice, the war with Persia, and the drive up the Danube, were all part of an effort to give vitality to an empire that was largely no more than an army of occupation in a conquered country. Actually, as the century was to prove, the Ottoman Empire was as moribund as the Spanish, but when Kara Mustapha appeared before Vienna with 200,000 men in 1683, this was not easy to see.

Also of great significance in the politics of the latter seventeenth century were the economic monopolies of the United Netherlands. The Dutch managed to make their market the center for much of the international trade of the day. In Amsterdam one bought French wine, Swedish iron and copper, English tin, German linen and wheat, Spanish cork; indeed almost all the products of international commerce. Traders from all Europe brought or sent their goods to the United Netherlands and exchanged them there for the goods of other nations. The Dutch grew rich as merchant middlemen, as shippers, as bankers and insurance brokers, and as finishers and graders of the raw materials that came into their hands. They also drew upon themselves the envy and dislike of merchants elsewhere, and of statesmen who regarded the Dutch market as a legitimate prey for their own predatory economic policies. The Dutch and the English fought two short wars over problems connected with trade; the English Navigation Acts attempted to supplant the Dutch multilateral trade with unilateral trade between England and the other commercial states. Both Colbert and Louis XIV regarded the Dutch market with jealous eyes; the Dutch war of 1672 may not have been primarily caused by economic rivalry, but the hostility that grew out of commercial competition created an atmo- sphere of Franco-Dutch antagonism.

In general we can say of the sources of conflict that in the late seventeenth century dynastic and states' interests combined to take the place that religion, feudal liberties, and the problems of the crumbling Spanish hegemony of Philip II had played in the first part of the century. Fortifications, tariffs, alliances and subsidies, and the hopes and fears of French Bourbon and Austrian Hapsburg princes about the many territories of the Spanish crown all com- bined to provide stuff for war.

However, these wars created something beyond and outside any of these things. The primary fact that emerged from the epoch of war was that Europe learned to check the overpowering force of the French monarchy by developing coalitions. These coalitions, in turn, became the basis of the political mech- anism, "the balance of power." When in the opening years of the eighteenth century, Peter I brought Russia into the orbit of the West under circumstances that drew the Slavic state into the system of military balances, the "constitution" with which Europe governed itself from about 1700 to 1914 was already launched upon its career. The emergence of this states-system was to provide one of the most significant themes in the history of European civilization for the next two centuries.

In the early years of his reign, Louis XIV started on his quest for greatness. He sent an expedition against the Algerian pirates, another against the Turks who were invading the Danube basin, and also gave halfhearted aid to the Dutch in their trade war with England. None of these adventures could bring notable advantages to his house. With the death of Philip IV in 1665, however, the French found a suitable pretext for action. There was no question about the rights of the sickly child, Charles II, to the throne in Madrid, but French lawyers insisted that provincial legal codes in the Spanish Netherlands justified the French king's demand that his wife and son, as heirs of Philip IV, should receive those territories. The lawyer's brief that was presented to the Spanish, as well as the other courts of Europe, to establish this claim was a formidable document, but no one was deceived: the argument was useless unless backed by arms. The

French invasion of the Spanish Netherlands in 1667 to establish Marie Thérèse's rights has been called the War of the Devolution: the legal rights that Louis pretended to defend were the "rights of devolution."

While the Spanish government at Madrid and at Brussels rejected completely the French claims, they were in no position to stop the French armies. However there were other people in Europe who had reason to object to the French annexation of the Spanish Netherlands: the Dutch politicians in the United Netherlands were the first of these for they had long since reached the conclusion that a weak Spain would be a safer neighbor than a strong France. From the time of the battle of Rocroi (1643), this conviction had been an important aspect of Dutch policy. The English, too, were easily persuaded that they would greatly prefer to have the Scheldt River in the hands of a weak Spanish government; military opinion held that an attack on England from the continent could be best launched from this point, and Englishmen not only believed this but acted upon it for the next three hundred years. Thus, in face of the French menace to their real or imagined interests, the Dutch and the English composed their own differences with the Peace of Breda (1667), and formed an alliance to check French aggression. They were able to associate Sweden with this alliance, and then offered, with thinly veiled threats, to arbitrate the Franco-Spanish conflict.

Somehow this intervention had not been foreseen in Paris; in any case Louis was unready to engage in a war both with Spain and with the newly formed triple alliance, and so the offer was accepted. The treaty that was written at Aix-la-Chapelle (1668), however, was in no way a solution of any problem; France, in effect, was left in possession of the territories that her armies had taken. This meant that the French king was given cities like Audenarde as enclaves in the Spanish Netherlands which were an obvious invitation to soldiers and bureaucrats to try to join these islands to the rest of France by securing the territory that separated them. Nor were Marie Thérèse's rights clearly settled; the peace simply ended the war leaving the bulk of the Spanish Netherlands still in the hands of Spain. The only thing that men did learn was that a coalition of military powers could indeed check the aggressive action of one power, even if that power were France. The shortness of the conflict did not raise the second question, namely: how does a coalition of powers hold together in the face of their divergent interests?

The importance of this second question was not lost on France. It was obvious that the Dutch were the heart of the opposition to French control of the Spanish Netherlands, and that their power would have to be broken before Louis could realize his ambitions in these provinces. This was most irritating to the young French king. It seemed to him that the Dutch were ingrates who had forgotten that without France they probably could never have won their independence; but what could be expected from men with bourgeois origins and revolutionary and republican traditions? He did not forget that his own ancestors (Charles V and Philip II) had once ruled these lands by divine right. Would it be possible to break up the alliance that these Dutchmen had called into being, and then remove Dutch opposition to Bourbon "legitimate" ambitions by force? This was the big question. Louis tried to answer it by creating his own coalition against the Dutch. This effort provoked the same question: How was France to maintain a coalition in face of the divergent interests of her allies?

On paper Louis' coalition against the Dutch was a formidable one. He detached Sweden from the hostile alliance by a mixture of bribery of the members of the regency government and a guarantee of a subsidy for the Swedish crown. The German princes whom Mazarin had combined in an alliance to assure the treaties of Westphalia and French influence in Germany were mobilized by subsidies to support a French war against the Dutch; even the elector of Brandenburg accepted French money and presumably French advice. Emperor Leopold of Austria was isolated from his Spanish relatives and the United Netherlands by a treaty that agreed upon a division of the Spanish empire between his family and the French Bourbons; the first of the many "partition treaties" that attempted to solve the thorny problem of the Spanish territories. Finally, the English king, Charles II, made a secret alliance, negotiated in part by his sister, who was also Louis' sister-in-law; by this treaty Charles agreed to join his naval forces in the war that was to destroy once and for all Dutch military and commercial power. If one merely looks at the treaties, the coalition was a work of art designed for the destruction of the Dutch by neighbors who had suffered from Dutch military, and even more, from Dutch commercial power: all of Louis' "friends" had good reason to hate the Dutch for their republicanism, their commercial monopolies, their egoistic economic regulations, and their political and naval arrogance. However if one looks below the surface of the treaties it becomes clear that the coalition was unstable; it overlooked the fact that with the removal of the United Netherlands from its military-commercial prominence, Europe would have to face a tremendously increased Bourbon power, and even French subsidies could not sweeten this fact.

While his diplomacy forged the coalition, Louis' soldiers and bureaucrats prepared the military forces for the destruction of the United Netherlands. Europe had not seen an army of this kind since the days of the Caesars; the French had organized a military establishment that seemed to be a crushing force, and Louis gave the command of his army (since he did not really command it himself) into the hands of two of the finest generals of the era: Turenne and Condé. Here was an interesting juxtaposition of the new and the old: the army was organized and controlled by royal bureaucrats from the king's war ministry; it was commanded, however, by a prince of the blood and by a descendant of one of the oldest and most powerful feudal families of France. Before the war was over there was considerable friction between the king's bureaucrats and his soldiers, but at the opening of the campaign, inspired by the vigorous leadership of the young king, this war machine was a formidable force. Like the coalition, it seemed to be a complete answer to Dutch objections to French ambitions in the Netherlands.

The war that followed in 1672 has been called "the Dutch War." Louis' armies marched up a corridor in northwest Germany provided by his Rhineland allies and attacked the Dutch from the rear. At the same time the Anglo-French naval forces swept through the Channel in an effort to clear the seas of Dutch ships. With such force thrown in the fray, the campaign of 1672 should have been a *blitzkrieg* crushing all opposition. But seventeenth-century transportation was difficult; armies had to march to their destination and their supplies and equipment had to follow them over bad roads and slow river transport. Furthermore, soldiers, attuned to siege warfare, were unwilling to press past a hostile fortification that might menace their rear. Thus the summer campaign was slowed by dozens of sieges and difficult transportation. This gave the Dutch time to cut the dykes and inundate a large part of the land over which the French army had to pass if it were to strike the heart of the United Netherlands. In ordering *Te Deums* to be sung in the churches of France to celebrate the capture of city after city, Louis and his advisors seemed to miss the fact that their war could not succeed if the French army failed to overrun the entire Netherlands; they thought that the Dutch, as "reasonable men," would recognize the futility of further resistance and accept their terms. Exactly the opposite happened.

The French terms were so crushing that the Dutch decided to fight to the last rather than accept them. A revolution in Amsterdam placed Prince William of Orange and his faction in control, and he immediately set out to defend what was left of his land and to try to find allies. This task was lightened by the impression that Louis' army and his conditions for peace made upon Europe. Men who a few years before had heard so much about German, French, or Bohemian "liberties" now could well wonder what was to happen to European "liberties" after a French victory. The Spanish government in Brussels rightly understood that once France ruled the United Provinces, the Spanish Netherlands would soon thereafter also be governed from Paris. Frederick William of Brandenburg, seeing his Rhineland holdings overrun by French troops, also concluded that French subsidies might not be worth their cost, and Emperor Leopold came to understand that his house and the Empire were both endangered by the rising French threat. Finally even Charles II was forced by the English Parliament to withdraw from the French alliance. In 1673 the French position in the Rhine valley was "exposed"; by 1675 Louis was forced to give up all the conquests of the first year of the war and to confine his military operations to territory closer to the frontiers of France in the Spanish Netherlands, Alsace, and Franche-Comté. In the place of a French coalition against the Dutch there had emerged a coalition against France; only the regency government in Sweden held firm to its French alliance, an act for which it was to suffer cruelly at the hands of the Brandenburg-Prussian armies.

The new anti-French coalition, however, was not organized so that a unified war effort could be achieved; each of the allies was primarily interested in problems close to home, and no leader emerged with enough prestige to make them work closely together. The Dutch worried away at the French fortresses in the lower Rhineland; Frederick William attacked the Swedish positions in Pomerania; Emperor Leopold's armies operated in Alsace; and the Spanish were unable to do more than weakly defend themselves in the Netherlands and on their own frontiers. Thus while the coalition gave Louis considerable trouble, it was unable to bring effective force to bear upon him. Indeed, even though he was obliged to withdraw his forces from their exposed position in the lower Rhine, every year Louis won "victories" in the Netherlands, in Alsace, and in Franche-Comté that could be celebrated by more *Te Deums* in Paris. Nonetheless, the coalition was obviously giving France considerable trouble; indeed by 1676 it was clear that French arms probably would not be able to impose peace upon their enemies; the coalition, even without centralized direction, seemed about to force a stalemate.

The military thinking of the period was in part responsible for the fact that neither side could win a decision. Armies were too difficult to raise to be risked in a battle unless the outcome were almost certain; both soldiers and statesmen preferred the slower and safer war of sieges, of position, of maneuver. Field armies might operate within a few miles of each other all summer, occasionally exchanging blows when small reconnaissance parties ran into each other, but never risking a field battle. Strong places were besieged and stormed in violent, bloody actions; but these were limited conflicts both in the objectives and in the number of men committed. Louis liked to conduct a siege, but he, like the majority of his contemporaries, was afraid of an infantry battle by which the war could be won—or lost—in an afternoon. Thus this "Dutch War," which had become a general war, drew itself out monotonously, costing ever larger and larger sums of money, and disturbing the peace and commerce of a large part of western Europe. The French fiscal machine seemed better able to sustain the expense, but by 1677 both France and her enemies were strained by the effort to a point where all wanted peace.

The war ended in 1678. Louis' armies made a surprise raid into the Spanish Netherlands and captured Ghent; this was too close to the heart of the United Netherlands for comfort. At the same time Charles II, pressed by the English Parliament to join the coalition against France, offered a "mediation" that was at the same time a threat that the English navy would reenter the war, this time on the side of the Dutch. And in Spain the war was creating both political and fiscal chaos to the point where peace was imperative. A Dutch embassy visited Louis' camp in the Spanish Netherlands. They were perfectly willing to see France annex the Spanish province of Franche-Comté, far from their own frontiers, providing that their own territory remained inviolate and that the French would agree to a commercial treaty. Spain could not object, the emperor and the Brandenburgers were unable to carry on without the Dutch, and Charles II in England was anxious to avoid military involvement. In 1679, by the treaties of Nymwegen, western Europe again was at peace, or so it seemed.

Although Louis had not achieved the objectives he had in mind when the war began, nonetheless, the war and the treaty of Nymwegen were imposing evidence of French power. None knew this better than the elector of Brandenburg: he was forced to return his conquests to the Swedish monarchy, even though his armies had been victorious, simply because the French king demanded it. Europe was quick to understand the basis of Louis' power: it was his army, the bureaucratic machine that supported and directed that army, and finally the French economy, organized and directed by the government. Four years after the treaty of Nymwegen, when the opportunity opened for the reconquest of Hungary, a pamphlet written by one of Leopold's councillors appeared in Vienna explaining that the Danubian Hapsburg state could become a power like France by the conquest and organization of Hungary provided that a bureaucratic machine emerged to govern the Hapsburg lands. This was the pattern of Europe after the Dutch war: European political society was committed to establishing and maintaining standing armies and navies on a scale undreamed of a generation earlier.

France again took the lead. The Dutch war convinced Louis that he needed a powerful navy as well as an army; under Colbert's guidance the small French naval establishment expanded into a force equal to the combined navies of England and the United Netherlands. New "ships of the line" mounting 120 guns set new standards for naval construction, just as the new equipment that Louvois was developing for the French army was setting new standards for land armaments. The France that could find the money for these military expenditures was also building the great palace of Versailles as a proper setting for her great king and his effective government; the challenge to Europe could only be met by imitating the governmental machinery that made it possible. The bureaucratic, military, police state that was emerging in France was thus the "wave of the future."

Nor was this French challenge merely a gesture that could be accepted or ignored, for French policy following the treaties of Nymwegen proved that the peace was only a truce. On the advice of his foreign minister, Louis set up courts in the borderlands between France and the German states to which he gave the task of "discovering" exactly what territory had been ceded by the treaties of Westphalia and Nymwegen. Seventeenth-century treaties, rather than drawing frontier lines, spoke of "provinces and their dependencies." Such phrasing was an opportunity for exploitation, for "dependencies" could be interpreted to include all sorts of things. Of course the French "Courts of Reunion" quickly found that much of the territory adjacent to lands already occupied by virtue of the treaties of Westphalia and Nymwegen also belonged to the French king, whereupon the French army immediately carried out the decision of the court by invading the disputed territory. The emperor of Austria, several German princes, and the kings of both Sweden and Spain lost lands by "court order" in which the French king acted as plaintiff, judge, and executor. Anti-French pamphleteers could not determine where this forward march would stop: France was annexing more territory in time of peace than she had gained by war. Leagues, or at least plans for leagues against France began to preoccupy the courts of Europe.

But one did not attack the king of France without preparation. His army was the finest in Europe, his navy was the largest on the seas. His bombardment of the Barbary coastal towns of North Africa and of Genoa as punishment for displeasing him was evidence of the terror that he could create; his magnificence in the new palace at Versailles was a picture of imposing grandeur that could not be overlooked. Before making war on France, the rest of Europe had to look to its resources.

At this juncture, central Europe was forced to meet attack from the east as well as French encroachment in the west. The French annexed the imperial city of Strasbourg and the city of Casale in Italy in 1681; the next year military preparations in the Ottoman Empire and agreements between the sultan and the Hungarian and Transylvanian enemies of the Hapsburgs clearly indicated that it would be folly to make war on France until the back door of the Hapsburg Danubian monarchy were closed. Negotiations attempted in Constantinople demonstrated that the grand vizier, Kara Mustapha, had no intention of being put off from his project to invade and subjugate central Europe. The Turks, with the assurance of the French ambassador that no French troops would assist the emperor, were sure that Leopold of Austria would be helpless before a determined assault. In the summer of 1683 an Ottoman army of some 200,000 men marched up the Danube valley, brushed aside the imperial forces that tried to stem the advance, and laid siege to the city of Vienna. In 1683 Leopold thus could not check the French encroachments in the Rhineland; he had too much to attend to in his own capital.

Louis XIV then earned for himself the title "the most Christian Turk in Versailles" for he saw this turn of events as an opportunity to force the emperor and the king of Spain to recognize the annexations of his Courts of Reunion. While the Turks ringed Vienna, French armies invaded the Spanish Netherlands, subjected some of the cities to systematic bombardments, and formally laid siege to Luxemburg. Peace, Louis insisted, could be had between the emperor and France, if the emperor would only agree to recognize France's "legitimate" territorial claims; according to Louis, the emperor, not France, was preventing Germany from defending itself against the Turks. Fortunately for Leopold, a combined German-Polish army broke the Turkish siege of Vienna, and sent Kara Mustapha's armies down the Danube in precipitous flight, leaving the Germans with the problem of deciding whether it would be more profitable to make war against France or against the Turks; obviously there could be no question of war against both at the same time. Under pressure from his German allies, and the urging of his own soldiers and bureaucrats, Leopold decided to make a truce with France. Louis was willing to sign a truce that would guarantee his Rhineland acquisitions for twenty years.

The war in Hungary became the center of European attention. Pope Innocent XI made it into a Christian crusade, attracting money and volunteers from all Catholic Europe. The emperor, the Republic of Venice, the king of Poland and the tsar of Russia joined in a "holy" alliance against the enemies of the cross. This was Russia's first intervention in European politics, but her war efforts amounted to practically nothing. However, both the emperor's armies and those of Venice won striking victories. The Turkish forces were driven out of Hungary, out of Transylvania, and by 1688 the imperial armies were hammering at Belgrade. At the same time the Venetians landed in the Morea (the Peloponnesus), swept the tip of Greece free of Turkish soldiers, and captured Athens. The French ambassador at Constantinople wrote alarming letters to his king telling of the disorder in the Turkish armies and finances, of the disasters that overtook their every effort, and of the expectation that Leopold would soon be in Constantinople dictating terms. Nor was it merely that the Turks were being defeated. In Hungary a new imperial army was emerging with new military techniques: the pikemen, who had been so necessary to protect the musketmen from cavalry, were replaced by musketmen with bayonets, and the volley firing that Gustavus Adolphus had first introduced on the battlefield more than a half century earlier began to come into its own. To cap it all, a revolution in the kingdom of Hungary made its crown hereditary in the house of Hapsburg, suppressed the right of rebellion theretofore enjoyed by the Hungarian nobles, created a Hungarian chancellory manned by bureaucrats at Vienna, and crowned Archduke Joseph, Leopold's son, as king. The Danubian monarchy of the Hungarian, Bohemian, and German lands was emerging as a formidable military force.

While these events were changing the political face of eastern and central Europe, another series of events in England also unleashed a revolution that was to create a new military power in the west. Upon the death of Charles II (1685) his brother James II mounted the English throne. The Test Act that had forced James to give up control of the English navy because he was a Roman Catholic did not keep him from the throne. Anglican advocates of the divine right of kings reasoned that since James' heirs, Princess Mary and Princess Anne, were both Protestants and married to Protestants there was no real danger to religion if this Catholic prince became king. James, however, felt the urgency of his position: he began systematically to staff the army and the administration with Catholics for whom he waived the disabilities of the Test Act; he introduced Catholic teachers into Oxford University; he tried to force the Anglican clergy to accept his actions; and finally his wife gave birth to a son. Protestants might call the baby an impostor, Catholics might regard him as a miracle, but everyone understood that with a Catholic heir, James might rig elections to Parliament, legalize all his actions, and bring England back into the fold of the Roman Church. These events came to a climax in 1688 about the same time that the imperial siege of Belgrade, the pleas by the Ottoman government for peace, and the election of Archduke Joseph to both the crown of Hungary and the dignity king of the Romans (successor to his father as Holy Roman Emperor) all indicated that central Europe had a new political order.

These movements in the east and the west were closely followed by all of Europe. In the Netherlands, Prince William of Orange, who was both Stadtholder of the United Netherlands and husband of King James' daughter Mary, kept in close touch with the Whig politicians in England. These men were staunch Protestants, and more important, they had developed a political theory that insisted upon the primacy of the law over the king and were quite willing to invite William to bring an army to England to force James II to do their bidding. However, as long as French armies were within reach of the Netherlands, William could not move to support James' enemies in England. Louis, on the other hand, concentrated most of his attention upon central Europe. If the Turks should be forced out of the war, if Leopold actually could mobilize the resources of Hungary and Bohemia and his German lands, then the hegemony of France and with it his newly won "rights" in the Rhineland as well as his claims to the Spanish inheritance might well be in jeopardy. As for the prospects of a civil war in England, Louis reasoned that such a conflict might actually help his cause for he believed that the Protestant and Catholic factions were about equal in strength and therefore a civil war would be a long drawn out action that would remove England from the political arena for some time.

France's decision set all Europe in motion. With an army and a navy second to none, Louis believed that he could check the onward imperial march, keep the Turks in the war, and guarantee his own position in the Rhineland; he invaded Germany in 1688. This invasion in the West heartened the Turks in the East to stay in the war and allowed William of Orange to transfer part of his army to England since the Netherlands were no longer in danger of a French attack. Within a few months of the French declaration of war, James II was deposed, William and Mary crowned king and queen in England, and a coalition composed of the Holy Roman Emperor, all of the German princes, the United Netherlands, England, and Spain emerged to challenge France. The "holy war" in the East thus merged into a war, fought all over Europe as well as in the new European dependencies beyond the seas. In the traditional histories of Europe, this war is variously called: the War of the League of Augsburg, the War of the Palatinate, the Anglo-Dutch Trade War against France, and, of course, in its central European phase, the Holy War. This confusion of titles further warrants the use of a more exact title: the First World War, 1683–1699.

This war produced revolutionary changes in the European political and military order. The conflict itself was familiar: sieges, maneuvers, an occasional field battle that failed to force a decision. But behind this façade of war of position, a new military structure was under construction. The pikemen disappeared entirely; in their place were infantry armed with flintlock muskets that could fire more rapidly than the cumbersome weapons of earlier periods. These were also elongated by a "ring" bayonet so that cavalry could not win an easy decision by shock action. The infantry were supported by the artillery and engineers who were assuming the status of soldiers rather than working men. The number of field pieces as well as their increasing effectiveness were to redeem the promise that Gustavus Adolphus' guns had made a half century or more earlier. The cavalry too were changing. Gone was most of the personal armor for the cavalry were now mounted on lighter horses and armed with horse pistols and heavy sabers for shock attack.

These soldiers were clothed, fed, and supplied by the king's commissaries and commanded by men who obeyed the king's war minister. This latter fact was not always a happy circumstance for daring generals sometimes found themselves held in leash by conservative civilian commissars and officials. Indeed, the full significance of this infantry that could learn to keep up a continuous volley of fire, artillery that could dominate a section of the battlefield, and cavalry that could be massed for rapid assault did not become apparent for a generation, until Eugene of Savoy, Marlborough, and Villars demonstrated in the War of the Spanish Succession what could be done by a decisive field battle. Nonetheless, the seed time for the new military order was this first world war that began in 1683.

With the rise of professional armies under royal control numbering hundreds of thousands of men, the problem of providing money for their maintenance grew apace. Louis once remarked that victory would be assured to the side that had a gold coin after its opponent had used his last one, and indeed this was almost what happened. All the protagonists in this new war attempted to find financial expedients that would fill the treasury. On the continent the age old methods of sale of offices, forced loans, borrowing against future taxes, and utmost expansion of existing taxes were used, but there was still a gap between income and expenses. One thing always accompanied the rise in income; an increase in the bureaucratic personnel needed to collect and administer the revenues; the armies and the machinery of government expanded together.

Only in England did a good policy emerge that provided the money needed to fight the war. The English revolution of 1688 that placed William and Mary on the throne established the principle that Parliament was supreme in the land. Parliament accepted the responsibility for finding the money needed to support England's war efforts and to subsidize England's allies. The important thing was that Parliament could and did tax for the war effort on a scale that no monarch had ever been able to achieve. Under the new political order of the revolution of 1688 the king's treasury officials explained their financial needs to the members of Parliament, who in turn provided funds that were required. This relationship between the representatives of the people who would pay the tax and the government officials who collected and spent it was England's secret weapon in the war. The other English institution that emerged with help to fight the war was the Bank of England. While Parliament might vote the money, the Bank, by developing credit facilities, provided the cash needed to pay soldiers and allies. Ultimately England's great contribution to the developing structure of the European states was this mechanism by which revenue could be raised and organized to mobilize the military potential of the society.

This first world war, like the so-called "Dutch war," was a coalition effort against France, but this time the fact that William of Orange was both king of England and Stadtholder in the United Netherlands, and that the majority of the German princes were paid subsidies by either England or the United Netherlands, gave a measure of unity to the effort unknown in the earlier wars. The emperor, the duke of Savoy, and the king of Spain did not coordinate their actions completely with the powers under William's direction, but the coalition did operate together more or less as a unit. The greatest difficulty with the coalition was its lack of a first class military leader until it found one in Eugene of Savoy at the very end of the war in the operations in the Danube basin. Louis XIV was unable to take advantage of this weakness of the coalition largely because the French also lacked imaginative leaders: only Marshal Luxembourg was willing to risk a serious field battle; the rest of Louis' general officers, like himself, preferred the "safe" warfare of sieges and maneuvers. This war of attrition accentuated the problems of finance and military administration. The war drew itself out year after year with neither side able to win, and both sides mired in economic disorder.

By 1695 the economic situation in France, aggravated by several years of bad harvest, reached a point where peace was necessary. Peace could only be achieved by surrendering some of the French conquests and recognizing limits to French ambitions, and, above all, only if the coalition could be broken. Savoy was the weak link in the chain of Louis' enemies: by offering her duke the whole of French gains in Italy since the days of Richelieu, Louis persuaded him to sign a treaty of peace (Peace of Turin, 1696) that would allow the French army in Italy to be moved to the Netherlands or to Germany. This started an avalanche of negotiation resulting in the treaties of Ryswick (1697). Louis' letters to his ambassador in Constantinople reveal his embarrassment in these negotiations. He had used every stratagem to keep the Turks from making peace only himself to desert the common cause when he received terms that he could accept. At Ryswick France was able to keep most of the annexations of the Courts of Reunion, but the treaties not only established the limits of French expansion but also imposed upon Louis recognition of the results of the revolution of 1688 in England. Two years later at Karlowitz (1699), the Ottoman Empire made peace with the emperor, Venice, Russia, and Poland. The Turks paid the big price of defeat: they ceded Hungary and Transylvania to the emperor, the Morea to Venice, and frontier territories to both Poland and Russia.

The peace treaties of 1696–99 were not important merely because of the territorial changes or even because the French king was forced to recognize limits to his ambitions; much more significant was the implicit recognition that two new great military powers had come into existence: England and the Danubian monarchy. Three decades earlier neither of these states alone or jointly could measure up to France, but by the end of the seventeenth century they had become effective counterweights to French power. By learning something of the art of organizing a coalition through the experience of war, they were on the way to the creation of a new European system. . . .

The central institution necessary for the creation of police power in the seventeenth century was the new army. If we look forward to the end of the century it becomes clear that the new military institutions were, in effect, a re-introduction of the principle of the Roman legions. The new army was a standing army, maintained in peace as well as in war; it was an army clothed, armed, and cared for by the king's war office. After seeing how dangerous a Wallenstein, or a Condé, or a Bernard could be when they commanded soldiers loyal only to themselves, it was clear that some other form of military organization was imperative. As one might expect, rather than create entirely new military institutions, what was done was to take the armies of the mercenary captains and place them under the king's war ministry. The army still remained mercenary; it was largely commanded by adventurers and its ranks were filled by rabble, social misfits, and others wishing for one reason or another to avoid civilian life. But one striking difference was that both the officers and the men now looked to the king's treasury for their pay and to the king's favor for their advancement; and both could be subjected to the king's discipline.

This raises an interesting question. Since the new army presupposes that the king's financial resources will be equal to the task of supporting it, does this not mean that the new army did not appear until the economy of Europe could provide the taxation necessary for this task? No simple answer will be satisfactory for while it is clear that Europe's economy had to be equal to the task, it is also clear that the people who supplied the money had to be willing to see their money used for military purposes. Furthermore, as Sombart, the economic historian, has pointed out cogently, the very existence of the standing army itself helped create the wealth needed to support it; the army became the first "mass market" and as such acted as a dynamic force in the economy of Europe.

What stands out incontestably is that the new standing armies were a creative force in the development of the bureaucratic institutions of the modern state. The armies and navies required the raising of theretofore unheard of sums of money and the administration of large enterprises: thus the number of officers needed for the treasury and war ministry grew enormously. Like the armies that they served these new bureaucratic machines were not created *de novo*, but developed out of the previous governmental machinery. In the Germanies the men who formerly administered the prince's household affairs and his agricultural enterprises, the officers of the *Kammer,* emerged as the officials in charge of revenues used by the army; in France the secretaries of state grew into ministers of the king in charge of the bureaus that administered war, finance, foreign affairs, and the household. The rapid increase of business in each of these areas resulted in an increase of personnel and a rise in the prestige of·the functions of government.

The importance of these emerging institutions can be measured by the changes that they wrought in the role of the king. At the opening of the seventeenth century, the king was still a relatively free agent, supervising with the aid of a few councillors, the business of his state, and holding in his own hands most of the information needed to manage his affairs. By the end of the century the king had become the head of a bureaucratic machine that was absolutely necessary because of the magnitude of the task of government; he had to rely upon his subordinates both for suggestions about policy and for the execution of his program. In effect he had become the first servant of the state machinery which now guided his actions along with those of the rest of his government. Louis XIV found this development completed in his own lifetime. When he took over the government of his kingdom in 1661, the whole administration of the country had to pass through his hands; by the time he died in 1715 the bureaucracy governed the kingdom, leaving to him the task of reviewing key aspects of policy that the ministers felt should be referred to him.

The interests of royal policy were also modified by the fiscal demands of the new military institutions; if the king were to collect the money necessary to support his army and navy, his subjects must be rich enough to supply him with that money. Even in the Middle Ages princes had made regulations concerning commerce and manufacturing, but in retrospect their action seems haphazard or at least inconclusive. By the seventeenth century, however, the situation was ripe for government to act effectively upon the economy. It is no accident that this is the period when that body of politico-economic thought that we variously call "Mercantilism," "Kammeralism," "Colbertism" appeared on the European scene. These economic doctrines were not innovations but rather elaborations of economic practices that were rooted in medieval legislation. In their simplest forms they proposed to regulate commerce in such a way that there would always be a balance of payments due the kingdom which would be made in gold or silver. These metals were universally valuable, they were necessary for the payment of soldiers, they were important for the king's treasury. This simple "bullion" theory was very popular in the sixteenth century when men were trying to understand what was really happening to the treasure that came to Europe from the Spanish New World. One thing was evident: those countries that could sell more than they bought in the markets of the world were able to import treasure, and this became an article of faith for some of the "economists." This sort of thinking could be duplicated in the medieval town's legislation as well as in the measures taken by medieval kings.

By the mid-seventeenth century, however, the "bullion" theory of political economy was undergoing radical revision or at least elaboration. It was becoming more and more clear that wealth was connected with the internal prosperity of the kingdom ("creation of plenty" as the men of the day expressed it), and therefore that the political-economic policy must concern itself with such things as roads, the establishment of new industries, and the organization of old industries, the attraction of skilled workers to the kingdom, and other such projects. The men who urged these policies were either officials or advisors of princes, and practically all of them were of bourgeois origin. They proposed measures intended to make the kingdom rich by encouraging the growth of industry, the expansion of agriculture, and the extension of commercial activity. Their programs were not intended primarily to increase the comfort and wealth of the king's subjects; what was wanted was an increase in wealth so that the king could secure more revenue from his taxes! These royal advisors were first of all state builders; they wished to control and channel the development of economic life to make their prince's government strong, that is to increase his military establishments. Their programs sometimes resulted in considerable economic advancement for the community, sometimes in meddlesome interference with the affairs of businessmen, but always they caused an increase in the number of officials in the employ of the government, and a complication of the problems of domestic and international politics.

The growth of the bureaus concerned with the collection of money and the administration of the military installations was paralleled by the development of ministries concerned with foreign affairs. At the opening of the seventeenth century it was uncommon for a prince to maintain a permanent ambassador at the court of another monarch. When there was business to conduct, a special emissary was delegated for the mission, and he returned as soon as the task was completed. The organization of foreign affairs, too, was simple to the extreme; there were no specialized foreign offices with archives and personnel since the work was largely done by the king's council and a secretary. In the course of the century, however, the practice of establishing permanent embassies in the important courts of Europe became common, and bureaus of foreign affairs presided over by a minister became the rule. Even by the end of the century not all foreign correspondence was channeled through one minister alone; nonetheless, the fact that the foreign minister ruled a bureau commanding the services of translators, code officials, and other men with special information about the problems of foreign countries tended toward that goal. The fuller development of the diplomatic corps and the ministries of foreign affairs was to be the work of the eighteenth century, but by 1700 the characteristic forms for the diplomacy of the European states-system had already clearly appeared.

4.

Prussia was the miracle state of the seventeenth and eighteenth centuries. Starting from nothing, it alone among the "underdeveloped" countries of northern Europe rose on its own initiative to become a powerful state. In 1640 Prussia did not exist. It was only a collection of divided, poor, agrarian territories lacking both cities and the rudiments of central government. In 1740 Prussia stood unified on the threshold of great-power status. How did this miracle occur?

Hohenzollern leadership explains much, of course, but Prussia also demonstrated what an efficient bureaucracy could do. Professor Walter Dorn (1894–1960) calls the Prussian bureaucrats the "galley slaves of the state." Having no powers of initiative, commanded to obey, and watched with suspicion, the Prussian bureaucrats worked a miracle.

What social and economic conditions in Prussia permitted the rise of such a peculiarly military bureaucracy? How did Prussia's army and bureaucracy become two parts of the same thing? What weaknesses were gradually built into the system, after the perfect efficiency of Frederick the Great?

WALTER DORN: The Prussian Bureaucracy*

The unique role of Prussia among the states of Europe lay not so much in its peculiar mixture of despotism and feudalism, but in the fact that it accomplished the impossible. A small, poor, still half-feudal and notoriously underpopulated country that was neither a geographic nor racial unit, with a retarded middle class that suffered from both lack of enterprise and capital, Prussia was suddenly thrust into the position of a European power. After his Silesian Wars it was no longer possible for Frederick to retreat from this European position. His only alternative to destruction by stronger neighbors was to mobilize the resources necessary to support his ever growing army, without which his European influence was utterly negligible, by means of superior organization and an unprecedented degree of social discipline. Whatever the cost, the experiment proved successful. In 1750 Prussia was the only larger continental state which

* From Walter Dorn, *Competition for Empire, 1740–1763* (New York: Harper & Brothers, 1940), pp. 52–62.

managed not only to balance its budget but to produce a steady surplus of income over expenditures. This was not due to an equitable distribution of financial burdens among the various classes of Prussian society nor to an intelligent system of taxation. In these matters Prussia was not more advanced than other continental states. The Prussian peasant, who paid about forty percent of his net income to the state and owed often unlimited services to his feudal lord, had no advantage over the Austrian or French peasant. What made the difference between Prussia and other continental states was the moral force that emanated from the greatest of the Hohenzollern and the superb quality of the Prussian bureaucracy, one of the first great modern civil service systems of Europe.

The principle, *le roi fait tout,* elsewhere an empty symbolic formula which concealed a government by bureaucrats, was an accurate description of the Prussian administrative process. The unity of leadership, the clocklike precision and co-ordination of central government agencies which Prussia possessed to a superior degree, are not to be found in Prussian institutions, but in the person of the monarch. King Frederick was literally the only central co-ordinating organ of the monarchy, and the peculiar scaffolding of the Prussian bureaucratic mechanism—the central General Directory, the provincial chambers, the local commissaries and the *Landräte*—becomes intelligible only when it is understood that the king alone came into daily and continuous contact with all the branches of government and administration. The excellence of the system consisted in the combination of a single person with the wide knowledge of large affairs which is gained only by diversified action, and the specialized skill of individual bureaucrats. The king alone formulated policy and laid down directives; the ministers were not, as in France, the vehicles of opinions and programs, but royal clerks, the *Bedienten* of His Prussian Majesty. There was a foreign office, the *Cabinetsministerium,* with two ministers, but since Frederick carried on his foreign policy by means of a direct personal correspondence with every Prussian ambassador abroad, these ministers might or might not know what the foreign policy of the king actually was. It will be pointed out in a later chapter that Frederick performed all the functions of a modern general staff of the army. But this applied also to his conduct of domestic affairs. From the day when he withdrew entire departments and whole provinces from the jurisdiction of the General Directory, only the king possessed complete information of the total financial resources of the kingdom and of the way in which money was disbursed. Convinced that foreign policy, military affairs, economic policy and finance were closely interdependent upon one another, he made himself the actual master of every department of government. Only in this way did he believe himself to be in a position to set up and pursue a consistent and rational system of politics which, he once said, must spring from a single rapid intelligence like Newton's law of gravity. It was impossible to carry the principle of autocracy to a greater extreme.

Such a personal autocracy may well appear to be a contradiction in terms in a modern bureaucratic state with its persistent urge to expand the area and intensity of its activities. Even for a man of large intellect and consummate ability like Frederick, ruling over a relatively simple and undifferentiated society such as that of Prussia, the problem presented almost insuperable difficulties. Frederick kept insisting that all impulses must proceed from him alone and yet he had to deal with a trained bureaucracy whose specialized functions and mastery of detail gave them the same kind of advantage over the king which the modern expert has over the dilettante legislator. A perpetual silent competition between the monarch and his bureaucracy for initiative was inevitable. This was not in itself an evil; in fact, it made the Prussian administrative process all the more precise and effective.

But how did the king maintain his ascendancy? First, by withdrawing himself from personal contact with his officials and negotiating with them only in writing from his Potsdam residence. Sitting in Berlin, the ministers prepared all the materials. From there they sent him their statistical reports, memorials and recommendations, and he replied by means of "cabinet orders" expedited through his private secretary Eichel, a mysterious personage, who was incorruptible and invisible to anyone but the monarch himself. The great merit of the system was the rapidity with which all public business was dispatched. Since everything was done by letter and the king's mind worked with extraordinary speed, there was no reason for delay. Nowhere in the entire Prussian bureaucratic system was there such impeccable order as in the cabinet of the king. Just as each hour of the day, each week and month, so the entire year was arranged in such a manner that no business crowded on the heels of another. A calendar on the king's table indicated not only the duties of each day and week, but reminded him when all outstanding reports, replies and other matters were due. Any official who addressed himself to the king could expect an immediate answer. The military precision of the king's life in Potsdam, where he had neither wife nor family, neither court nor French court etiquette, where he never observed a religious holiday and was never distracted by undesired interruptions, was conducive to hard work. He was the essence of practicality and good sense and he knew his kingdom like an open page. If Frederick can be said to have possessed a *faculté maitresse,* it was his moral energy and his unremitting application to work. When he called himself the first servant of the state, it was no empty phrase. What Prussia lacked in *force intrinsèque,* as he called it, was to be supplied by the moral drive of the monarch and his bureaucracy.

Frederick regarded his civil servants with an ineradicable distrust. Proceeding on the assumption that no official, however honest, was incorruptible, he provided some control device for every task which he committed to him. Dependent, as he was, upon written reports, he was forever suspecting his officials of bureaucratic inertia, of a propensity to interpret royal orders generously enough to suit the circumstances or their private convenience, of deceiving him, of deceiving him often, as he once admitted, with the best intentions. The means he employed to guarantee the honesty and integrity of his civil service may not meet the approval of a modern efficiency expert, but it cannot be denied that they were remarkably effective. At strategic points throughout the entire system, from the General Directory down to the local commissary, he placed a special royal agent, called the *Fiscal,* a curious combination of a royal scrutineer or spy and a modern prosecuting attorney, to guarantee the execution of royal orders and to report every suspicion of irregularity directly to the king. Wherever there was a responsible civil servant there was also the watchful eye of the *Fiscal* to pursue him in every official act. Although instances of actual corruption were rare, summary dismissals, whether for incompetence or negligence, were frequent. The Prussian civil servant was the galley slave of the state; he was utterly without legal rights and, unlike the Prussian citizen, could be sent to the Spandau prison without a trial. To control his ministers, the king regularly corresponded with their subordinates or with the presidents of the provincial chambers; and to assure himself of the veracity of the latter he dealt with individual members of these provincial bodies. Every year between May and August he journeyed through the provinces of his kingdom, examining his officials and interviewing private citizens, personally inspecting local conditions and consulting with burgomasters, merchants and manufacturers. In this way he tapped extraordinary sources of information which, besides the normal channels of reporting, acquainted him with everything he seriously wanted to know. Now and then he might be the dupe of bureaucratic hoodwinking, but the lynx-eyed vigilance of the king sooner or later discovered almost everything.

From what has already been said it is apparent that what distinguished the Prussian from the French bureaucracy was greater centralization and uniformity, a more effective subordination, a severe military discipline and a more precise system of accountability. To this must be added an important difference in recruiting the bureaucratic personnel. While in France offices were purchased or inherited, in Prussia the merit system had already become the fixed and universal rule for admitting candidates to public office, a rule that was not relaxed even in the case of an aspirant of noble extraction. The ability to pass several examinations was the only portal to the Prussian civil service and most officials had previously attended one or more of the Prussian universities, where in addition to jurisprudence they studied cameralism, a synthetic branch of academic studies which embraced government finance, agriculture and public administration. But the Prussian monarchs never regarded a university education as the final solution of the problem of training an efficient civil servant. It was a universal practice for every candidate, before presenting himself for his final examination, to spend one or two years on a royal farm to familiarize himself with the practical details of agriculture and the management of the royal domains. This experience brought the future official into personal contact with some of the most important problems of the Prussian monarchy: enlightened agricultural methods, the financial problems involved in drawing up a contract for leasing the royal domains, which amounted to one fourth of all the arable land of Prussia, and the realities of the lord-serf relationship. In France civil servants were for the most part jurists, in Prussia they were practical economists.

It was a matter of vast importance for the future of the Prussian monarchy that it developed a modern civil service before it produced a class of enterprising capitalists. The merit system had the effect of attracting and absorbing into the service of the monarchy the most industrious and intelligent elements of the population. Frederick encouraged the sons of his officials to follow in the footsteps of their fathers, a fact which could not fail to enhance the homogeneity and *esprit de corps* of the service. Since noble and bourgeois officials faced each other in the General Directory and the provincial chambers in approximately equal numbers, the Prussian bureaucracy was not the special instrument of a particular social class, although it is true that nobles occupied most of the higher positions. The devotion to the commonweal with which Frederick succeeded in impregnating his officials won for them the respect and confidence of all classes of Prussian society, and the deep-seated suspicion and distrust between the public and the "bureaucracy," which is so conspicuous in Anglo-Saxon countries, never arose in Prussia.

Whereas in the French system all authority was vested in the single, responsible, ministerial *chef de ressort* with a wide berth for individual initiative, the Prussian system was calculated to eliminate all personal influence whatsoever, first by binding the individual official to a collective board, then by subjecting both, the individual and the board, to an authoritative bureaucratic *règlement* which minutely prescribed every detail of the service. Not only were there no Prussian equivalents for the French functional ministries in 1740, but the four ministers of the supreme Prussian administrative authority, the General Directory, exercised identical functions, each in his special group of provinces, in such a manner that all four shared a collective responsibility for decisions in all four territorial departments. The General Directory was indubitably the weakest cog in the Prussian bureaucratic mechanism. This was in some measure due to its lumbering procedure. But it was chiefly due to the fact that Frederick incorporated with it two functional ministries of the French type, one for commerce in 1741 and one for the army in 1746, which were ill-adapted to the general scheme of the collective solidarity of the General Directory. When in 1742 Frederick established another special ministry for Silesia, which had no connection with the General Directory at all, autocracy became an absolute necessity of the system.

This lack of unity among the central institutions would have been disastrous to the efficiency of the Prussian bureaucracy had it not been for the industry of the king on the one hand and the energy and dependability of the fifteen provincial chambers (*Kriegs-und Domänen Kammern*) on the other. These provincial chambers were the vital centers of the bureaucracy. They were the classic workshops of the Prussian mercantilist state, through which the inhabitants of Prussia were galvanized into an active, thrifty people—the most highly disciplined people of modern Europe. Impatient of the obstructionist delays of the General Directory, Frederick negotiated with these provincial chambers directly, over the heads of the central authorities, issuing orders and receiving reports of which the General Directory might or might not be informed. Though sharply subordinated to the General Directory, the provincial chambers in this way acquired a certain discretionary authority which enabled them to defend their provinces against the exacting demands of the central government. An excellent opportunity for this presented itself when, beginning with 1748, Frederick annually convoked all the presidents of these provincial chambers in Berlin to discuss common measures for the prosperity of the kingdom.

The provincial chambers were pre-eminently financial organs, and their pivotal function was the prompt and accurate collection of the budgetary income. There was, however, a distinct advantage in the circumstance that the fiscalism which they represented was combined with a responsibility for the economic welfare of their provinces. They stimulated enterprise among the people, reclaimed sandy wastes, drained swamps, and made internal colonization one of their major activities. They inspected the private husbandry of peasants and the countinghouses of merchants and made indolence and shiftlessness a public offense. Their members journeyed through England and Holland to study improved agricultural and commercial methods, went out in search of markets for Prussian manufacturers, and superintended the fairs of the larger cities. There was not a phase of urban or rural life that escaped their regulating ordinances. Their ultimate aim was always to achieve that substantial "plus" in revenues which the king never ceased to demand from them and which he regarded as the only compelling proof of their efficiency.

In keeping with the collective principle, the provincial chamber was a body in which one official controlled another and all must answer for the actions of each individual member. Although each one of the fifteen or twenty members had his allotted duties, nothing was done save by common deliberation and decision. This made the grosser forms of corruption, errors of inadvertence or ignorance difficult, if not impossible. But their procedure was cumbersome and slow. The numerous control devices, the countless bureaucratic formalities commonly known as red tape, the exaggerated prominence given to the written documents which they produced in appalling quantities, slowed down the speed of the administrative process. The heroic efforts to simplify this process and to reduce the number of written documents, which run through the middle decades of the century, were only partially successful. But if their slow motions often exasperated the impatient Frederick, it should be stated that they were punctiliously exact in the impersonal application of the directives given to them from above.

The distinct and separate systems of taxation which prevailed in the towns and rural districts of Prussia required two different sets of local authorities. The local commissary or *Steuerrat,* a traveling official who supervised from six to ten towns, was a far more formidable officer than the rural *Landrat,* although both labored under the direction and scrutiny of the provincial chamber. The office of the local commissary was one of the key positions in the entire bureaucratic hierarchy. He was the executive organ of royal absolutism in the municipalities of Prussia and, with the local *gendarmerie* at his disposal, he possessed enormous executive powers. To achieve the prompt and effective execution of royal orders he might even call upon the local military commandant. Military execution by Prussian grenadiers, it should not be forgotten, always remained the *ultima ratio* of Prussian administration. The redoubtable, paternalistic tutelage of the local commissaries deprived Prussian municipalities of every vestige of local autonomy. The commissaries managed towns as though they were an integral part of the royal domains. They determined municipal budgets, fixed the local price of food and other commodities, enforced the mercantilist industrial and commercial legislation, regulated the guilds and adapted them to the needs of capitalistic enterprise, and saw to it that the local military garrison was properly billeted. Doubtless they conferred numerous blessings upon Prussian towns by guaranteeing religious toleration and freedom of thought, by improving urban sanitation, by providing the population with apothecaries and physicians, and by promoting vaccination. If Prussia did not remain a purely agricultural country but developed a commerce and industry, which, though not great, were sufficient to supply its own needs, this was largely due to the local commissaries and their superiors. Yet the exaggerated thrift of Prussian administration rested heavily on these cities; every *groschen* that was not indispensable for urgent municipal needs was syphoned from the urban treasuries to meet the larger needs of the Prussian state.

Compared with the local commissary, the *Landrat* could hardly be classified as a bureaucratic official. Always a nobleman and the owner of a landed estate, he was as often elected by the local nobility as appointed by the king, though he, too, had to pass an examination in cameralism. As the executive organ of the provincial chamber he was charged with publishing royal edicts, regulating military conscription, exercising rural police power and enforcing laws designed to protect the peasant against exploitation by his noble landlord. Representing the interests of the landowning nobility, the office of the *Landrat* lacked a bureaucratic edge. The actual unit of local government in Prussia was in reality the nobleman's patrimonial estate. The Prussian junker exercised all the vital functions of local government on his private estate, including the lower forms of justice and police power. He also collected the taxes from his peasants and supplied the army with recruits. So long as the Prussian landlord did not undermine the capacity of his peasants to discharge their fiscal and military obligations to the state, flagrantly abuse his peasants or reduce the total number of peasant holdings, he was relatively free from bureaucratic interference. Since Frederick lacked the financial resources to pay for local government authorities, he had no choice but to employ the unremunerated public service of the nobility in this capacity. In his special sphere the Prussian landlord exercised functions not unlike those of the English justices of the peace.

The boundless industry of Frederick the Great for the moment concealed the structural flaws in the Prussian bureaucracy. Even his own genius did not extend to the realm of public finance. He left unaltered the faulty excise tax, which proved to be a dead weight on Prussian commerce. He did not revise the antiquated *Kataster* or assessment rolls which served as the basis for the tax on the peasantry. For reasons best known to himself he made no effort to tax the landed nobility of the central provinces as he did those of Silesia and East Prussia. Yet despite its defective structure and its outmoded system of taxation, the management of public finance was easily the most brilliant achievement of the Prussian bureaucracy. By means of its effective system of accounting, its close-fisted parsimony, its unsparing severity against every extravagance with public funds, the Prussian civil service succeeded in making the most of the slender financial resources of Prussia. These resources supported Prussia's European position, the army and the bureaucratic machine, and enabled the king to sustain three wars in two decades without contracting a public debt worth mentioning. It is no explanation to say that in the Seven Years' War he received British subsidies; they were a mere pittance beside what he actually spent. Nor is it an explanation to say that Frederick cut his policy to suit his financial cloth. In view of the steady expansion of the army the contrary is rather the case.

In this Prussia, devoid of wealth and prosperity, the burdens and obligations of the masses stood in inverse proportion to their economic circumstances. Indeed, it was from the very poverty of its inhabitants that the Prussian state drew its greatest strength. The proud junker, living on an estate too diminutive for a decent standard of life, was constrained to seek public employment, notwithstanding the forbidding severity of its discipline. The ambitious bourgeois intellectual discovered in the Prussian civil service his best, indeed his only, opportunity for advancement. It was not wealth but connection with the army and civil service that guaranteed social position. It was the general poverty that produced the unprecedented concentration of resources, the furor, as Mirabeau was later to call it, of regulating and regimenting every aspect of public and private life, the one-sided emphasis on Spartan virtues and social discipline, in a word, what we generally call Prussianism. It is unthinkable that this Prussianism could ever have sprung from the soil of free, wealthy, parliamentary England. In England the island, as it were, replaced the state; in Prussia the state of the old regime attained its maximum expansion. While England was becoming constantly more individualistic, Prussia remained a collectivist state in which the individual was expected to sacrifice himself for the whole. The only freedom for the eighteenth-century Prussian was the *libertas oboedientiae* —the freedom to obey.

5.

The picture of Russia which one of imperial Russia's greatest historians, Vasily D. Klyuchevsky (1841–1911), draws is one of rough-and-tumble government. There seems to have been little planning and not much understanding that reforms, to be effective, must be coherent, clearly defined, and adjusted to existing political conditions.

Did Peter the Great grasp the meaning of the state, that is, in a seventeenth-century western European sense of the term? What purposes did he have in mind for bureaucracy? Does Klyuchevsky substantiate Wolf's assertion that war and the need for standing armies determined the course of bureaucratic change?

VASILY D. KLYUCHEVSKY: Peter the Great*

Of all Peter's reforms, the reform of the administration has been particularly admired. This, indeed, is the most striking aspect of his work; but far too much emphasis has been laid on the administrative institutions as they finally ap-

* From Vasily D. Klyuchevsky, *Peter the Great* (New York: St. Martin's Press, 1958), pp. 181–206.

peared at the end of Peter's reign, and not enough on their slow and difficult evolution. The chief object of the administrative reform was to create conditions favourable to the success of the other reforms; but it was not until the military and financial reforms had been introduced that the administration itself was suitably reorganised. There is therefore a discrepancy between the object of the administrative reform and its timing; and we must see how the progress of reform was affected by this discrepancy. The usual features of the Petrine reforms, their lack of coherence and general plan, their dependence on ever-changing conditions and demands, make a study of the administrative changes particularly difficult. If we take them in their chronological order we are likely to lose sight of their relations with the rest of Peter's reforms, while if we take them systematically we are likely to see in them a cohesion and unity which for a long time they did not have. It will therefore be better, in the interests of learning, to pass haphazardly from one part of the administration to another, than to follow our own inclination and try to be systematic. Our impressions will be confused, but we will be able to correct this at the end by looking over the subject once again, and following methodically the administrative divisions between central and local government, and the further subdivisions as prescribed by constitutional law. The course of events, moreover, allows us to begin properly with the central administration.

For nearly twenty years, from the fall of the Tsarevna Sophia until the Provincial Reform of 1708, there was no radical change in either central or local organisation. The twenty years were difficult years in which very drastic steps were taken to equip the country for war, and to improve the organisation of industry and finance. At the centre of the administration was the Boyar Duma whose sessions the Tsar sometimes attended. Here the only innovation was that the boyars were no longer to "deliberate alone," but to "join in Council." Some of the ancient Muscovite prikazes were amalgamated, others were divided, they were generally given new names, and new prikazes were created, modelled on the old, to deal with new affairs: the Preobrazhensky Prikaz dealt with the guards and the secret police, the Admiralty Prikaz dealt with the fleet, and the Military-Naval Prikaz dealt with foreign mercenary seamen. Attitudes, not new perhaps, but animated by a new force, pervaded the archaic administrative bodies. A result of the struggles between the Court parties led by the different Tsarevnas, the internecine feuds of the military classes, the struggles of the impoverished nobility with the parvenus, and the conflict between the traditional and the Western political tendencies, was that power came to depend on the peculiar position of individuals, to the detriment of the proper institutions of government. During the regency of the Tsaritsa Natalia, for example, her brother Leo, a nonentity who was nonetheless the head of the Possolsky Prikaz, was put in charge of all ministers but two. The exceptions were Streshnev, Minister of War and Internal Affairs, and Prince Boris Golitsyn who, as head of the Prikaz of Kazan, "ruled absolutely" over the Volga region, and according to Prince Kurakin, was responsible for its utter ruin. Moreover when the favourites were in power, the boyars in the Duma "were only spectators." Thus in 1697, when Peter was preparing to go abroad, all boyars and heads of Prikazes were ordered to wait upon the head of the Preobrazhensky Prikaz,

Prince Romodanovsky, and to "hold council with him at his request." Prince Kurakin commented that he was "an evil tyrant, drunk most of the time," and Kurbatov that "though a man of bad judgment he was all-powerful in his ruling." Prince Romodanovsky was, in fact, endowed with extraordinary powers: he was made head of the Cabinet, and even President of the Duma although, as a mere "stolnik" his rank did not permit him to sit in it. The ancient legislative formula "the sovereign has ordered, the boyars decreed" could have been replaced by "Streshnev (or Prince Romodanovsky) has ordered and the boyars remain silent." Another change, dictated by necessity, altered the activities of the Boyar Duma itself.

Faced with so many new expenses, Peter wanted to know how much money was held by the Prikazes. In 1699 he therefore re-established the Prikaz of Accounts, or "Privy Chancellery," which was to control all state finance. To the Prikaz of Accounts all other Prikazes had to submit weekly and yearly statements of receipts and expenditure, reports on their staff, buildings, etc., from which it prepared its complete statement of the accounts. . . .

All these changes were gradually altering the composition, jurisdiction, and character of the Boyar Duma itself. From time immemorial it had consisted of men of rank, but, on the decline of their power, it ceased to be the council of the boyars. It was changed into a council of limited size which was no longer recruited simply by birth, and which exercised different functions. It invariably worked with the Tsar, and under his presidency, at its legislative functions. With the Tsar frequently abroad, however, it had to deal with the current business put before it by the Prikazes and the detail and execution of Peter's hasty suggestions on internal administration; it therefore became an administrative body. Moreover Peter insisted that when he was away the council should act independently, without waiting for his opinion. So long as the Duma and the Tsar acted together, it had not been necessary to separate the responsibilities of each; the new independence of the former required some definition of its responsibilities. In 1707 Peter ordered the Boyar Duma to keep minutes of its meetings which were to be signed by all members, and confirmed his order with the words "no resolution is to be taken without this, so that the stupidity of each shall be evident," which hardly shows much respect for the councillors he had called upon to handle such important business. The evolution of the Prikaz of Accounts into a department under the Boyar Duma, and the change of that body, which now had a negligible boyar element, into a deliberative and executive council of ministers responsible for the economic problems of the war, gave a clear indication of the direction of administrative reform, the object of which would plainly be to look after the regular army and navy by looking after the Treasury.

The first step in this direction was the attempt to use local autonomy for fiscal purposes. In the seventeenth century, at the request of the local communities, the function of the *voevodas,* who had become too tyrannical, were sometimes transferred to the *gubnye starosty*[1] who were elected by the local nobility. According to Tatishchev's evidence, it was because the district *voevodas*

---

[1] Elders.

"thieved daringly" that it was decided in the reign of Tsar Theodore to allow the nobility to elect *voevodas* in the pious hope that they would be able to control the rapacity of the local officials who were supposed to keep order. What actually happened, however, was that the responsibility for collecting the Streltsy tax and the indirect taxes was transferred past the *voevodas* to the elected *starosty* who were responsible to their electors, in an attempt to protect the taxes from the ravages of the *voevodas*.

The ukaze of January 30th, 1699, went even further: in view of the prejudices of the *veovodas* and the hardships they imposed on the traders and industrialists of the capital, the latter were to be allowed to elect annually from among themselves "Burmisters,"[2] "as many good and honest men as they wish," who were not only to administer the collection of taxes, but also to try civil and commercial cases. Other towns, associations of "black-ploughing" peasants, and of court peasants were told by ukaze that they could free themselves from the offences and bribes of the *voevodas,* who were no longer to be in control, and, "if they so wish," their own elected officials would collect the taxes and try cases, provided that they paid double the tax assessment. It can be deduced from the above, therefore, that, as far as the taxpayer was concerned, there was not much to choose between the *voevoda* and the government. The ukaze now proposed that the provincial tax-paying associations rid themselves of these secondary monarchs by paying double the tax assessment, in exactly the same way that with the introduction of the *zemstvo* institutions under Tsar Ivan, the taxpayers could get out of the clutches of the *kormlenshchiki* by paying a special State tax. In a century and a half, therefore, the government had not produced any new ideas in administrative reform. The new gift, with its conditional clause, seemed a very expensive one to the taxpayers; only eleven cities out of seventy accepted, and the remainder replied that they would not pay at twice the rate, and that they did not have anybody whom they could appoint as *burmister*. Some even said that they were satisfied with their "honest" *voevodas* and officials! As a result the government dropped the double assessment, and made the election of a *burmister* compulsory. Indeed it seems from some ukazes that the autonomy of the towns was more important to the government than it was to the towns. The *voevodas* by their "waywardness and unjust exactions" were responsible for the large arrears in Treasury receipts, and it was to be hoped that the use of unpaid and responsible *burmisters* would result in an improvement. The reform of 1699 clearly reflects one of the many symptoms of the malady which, for centuries, had afflicted Russian administration. This malady was represented by the perpetual struggle between government and institutions whose quality the government was unable to improve. Thus the *voevodas,* having lost their judicial and administrative power over the commercial and industrial communities of the towns, and over the free rural populations, had only the men of service and their peasants to administer, and in the northern regions of Russia, where these social classes were non-existent, the office of *voevoda* disappeared completely.

2 "Burmister" was a corruption of burgomeister. Peter frequently used German names for his newly invented offices.

The government, however, still found it necessary to use noble associations to check the rapacity of the surviving *voevodas*. An ukaze of March 10th, 1702, abolished the *gubnye starosty,* elective officials chosen by the local nobility to enforce the law. The government, however, did not want the local nobility to remain inactive in local government, and the ukaze continued: "the *voevodas* together with the nobles, *pomeshchiks* and *votchiniks,* and good and knowledgable people, who are to be elected by the *pomeshchiks* and *votchiniks* of the towns, are to govern the towns," and two to four men were to be elected from each district. Having granted the commercial and industrial population of the towns the right to participate in a representative collegiate administration, the logical sequence of events would have been for the government to widen the system to include the rural land-owning class who, by virtue of the ukazes of 1699, were still governed by the *voevodas.* But unfortunately administrative logic broke down completely, and failed to grasp what was going on. When the regular army was created, the old Muscovite district associations of noblemen, which were based on the territorial organisation of their detachments in the militia, were dissolved. All noblemen capable of performing military duties were dragged from their native districts, and sent to join the new regular regiments which were stationed in remote areas. The only noblemen to remain were those who had been retired due to their unfitness for service, and the shirkers who had gone to earth. There was not much hope for the establishment of rural self-government if it was to depend on the invalids and the shirkers who were, in any case, liable to the loss of their civil rights. The whole problem had been dealt with very superficially, as the documents on the *voevoda* associates published by M. Bogoslovsky show. The rural associations of the nobility, or rather their remains, displayed almost complete indifference to the right conferred upon them, and only in a few places were councils elected for the *voevodas* to consult. Elections were therefore replaced by direct nominations either from the capital or by the *voevoda*—who was supposed to be controlled by his nominees. Not unnaturally, the *voevoda* quarrelled with his council, and after eight or nine years this odd reforming experiment destroyed itself by its own futility.

More important and more successful were the changes in the financial organisation of the commercial and industrial classes of the towns. The tax-paying associations of the towns had been linked only to the Prikazes in Moscow; since their liberation from the rule of the *voevodas,* the towns paid their indirect taxes to the Prikaz of the Great Treasury (Bolshoi Kazni), and their direct "Streletsky" tax to the Streletsky Prikaz. Now, however, the government wanted to place the wealthy merchants of Moscow in positions of authority over all the towns, and use them as its financial general staff. Thus in 1681 a commission of wealthy Moscow merchants was charged with settling the rate at which the towns of different means were to contribute to the Streletsky tax. The reform of 1699 turned this commission into a permanent institution, and the ukaze of January 30th, 1699, provided that, for taxation purposes, the urban offices and their elected *burmisters* were to be subordinated to the *Burmisterskaya Palata* or *Ratusha,* which consisted of the *burmisters* elected by the wealthy merchants of Moscow. Local *burmisters'* offices were to be accountable to the *Ratusha* for revenue received from customs dues and the tax on inns, and were also to send it all the revenue they had collected from other taxes. In this way the *Ratusha* in Moscow became the central office for the political organisation and taxation of the merchant and industrialist class. By-passing all the other departments, it presented its reports directly to the Tsar and in time became a sort of Ministry of Towns and Urban Taxation. A number of taxes, including the Streletsky tax, the Inns tax, and the Customs tax, together yielding more than one million roubles, which had previously been collected by thirteen Moscow Prikazes, were now transferred to the *Ratusha*.

In 1701, when the actual receipts proved larger than the estimated amount, the taxes paid into the *Ratusha* came to 1.3 million roubles, which was more than one-third—nearly a half in fact—of the total estimated tax receipts for that year. The *Ratusha's* revenue went to maintain the army. Its activities were considerably extended when Kurbatov, the projector, was appointed as inspector of its administration, and he became the President of the Council of Moscow Burmisters. Originally a household serf, Kurbatov showed anything but a servile attitude on his appointment; on the contrary, finding himself surrounded by bribery and corruption, which had increased out of all proportion during Peter's frequent absences, he waged a constant and remorseless war in the interests of the state. Every letter he wrote to the Tsar contained a complaint against embezzlement, or a denunciation of some highly placed thief. He reported that in Moscow and in other towns large sums were abstracted from taxes which had already been collected, that the *Ratusha's* clerks were robbers in the grand scale, and that the elected *burmisters* were no better. 40,000 roubles were stolen in Yaroslav, and 90,000 in Pskov. Naryshkin was sent to expose them but he was bribed, and protected the thieves. In his reports to the Tsar, Kurbatov castigated men of the highest rank, such as Prince Romodanovsky, one of the worst offenders; the only exception was his own patron, Prince Menshikov, who was the biggest swindler of all. Kurbatov asked the Tsar for absolute authority, and the power to sentence the embezzlers to death, in order to root out the evil. He wrote that he had increased the *Ratusha's* revenues by hundreds of thousands of roubles, and that they now amounted to almost 1.5 million roubles. Yet in spite of this success, the *Ratusha* barely managed to cover the military expenditure, and the Provincial reform put an end to Kurbatov's financial activities, and indeed to the *Ratusha* itself.

The Provincial reform came about as a consequence of Peter's own activities, which were stimulated by internal and external events connected, directly or indirectly, with the war. Previous Tsars had remained in the capital, except for the rare occasions when they went on a pilgrimage or on campaign, and the administration of the country had been highly centralised. Direct and indirect taxes, collected throughout the country, were sent through the *voevodas* to the capital, where they were distributed among the Moscow Prikazes who used most of the money themselves, returning only a small proportion to the provinces to pay the salaries of the provincial men-of-service and meet other local expenses. Peter completely overturned this antiquated and rigidly centralised system. First of all he freed himself from the capital and travelled, visiting the most distant parts of Russia, and causing turmoil wherever he went either by his own furious activity or by the risings it provoked. At the end of a frontier campaign in some distant Province, Peter did not leave it in peace; on the contrary, he at once urged it to some new and arduous enterprise. After the first Azov campaign, for instance, Peter started to build a fleet at Voronezh. A number of towns in the Don basin were ascribed to the Admiralty Department at Voronezh, and thousands of men were driven in to forced labour, while the taxes collected in the region were diverted at once to this undertaking instead of being sent to the Prikazes in Moscow. Similarly, after the fall of Azov, the labour and taxes of other towns were used to build a port at Taganrog. After the conquest of Ingria, on another frontier, the same thing happened with the building of St. Petersburg and the Olonetz shipyards in which the Baltic Fleet was built. In 1705 there was a revolt in Astrakhan directed against Peter's innovations; in order to pacify and reorganise the region, its taxes were transferred from the control of the central departments to the regional authorities who were to use the money for local needs. The same thing happened at Smolensk and Kiev when King Augustus was forced to make peace with Charles XII, and sign the Altranstaedt Agreement of 1706, as a result of which Charles, who had occupied Poland, threatened Peter's flank. All these events showed that it would be better for the taxes to go directly to the regional administration instead of indirectly through the Prikazes in Moscow, where the funds melted away. They also led to an increase in the powers of the regional administrators, who were given the new title of *gubernator* although the region they administered was not yet called a *guberniya*—a Province. What had already been done made it easier to carry out these changes. A number of departments in Moscow were concerned in the financial, and even in some of the military, affairs of vast regions such as Kazan, Siberia, Smolensk, and Malorossia. It was now only necessary to send the head of the relevant department to the area under its control, and to bring him into closer contact with the people, to make his task a great deal easier.

The real need for decentralisation was made more obvious by the situation Peter found himself in after the war. He appreciated that his preoccupation with diplomatic and military affairs, and his continual movement, made it impossible for him to give sufficient attention to internal affairs, and that he would therefore be a bad administrator. He wrote to Kurbatov, justifying the Provincial system, that "It is difficult for a man to understand everything, and govern from a distance." He did not believe that the central departments and the *Ratusha* were capable of producing enough money to cover his military expenditure, but he thought that if he appointed powerful vice-regents to vast areas, they would be able to find the money. Peter was the sort of man who placed more reliance on men than on institutions; hence his plan to make specific areas pay for the army, and indeed his military budget was planned with this in mind. Peter had great difficulty in understanding the advantages of centralised government and the single Exchequer which Kurbatov had discussed with him, for he shared the prevailing opinion that every item of expenditure had to be linked to its own special source of income. Later on, when explaining the purpose of the Provincial Reform, he wrote that he had made the Provinces share between them military and other expenses, so that "everybody should know from where the required receipts were coming." It was this idea which was the basis for the division of Russia into Provinces in 1708.

The reform was initiated by a typically short and obscure ukaze of December 18th, 1707, which put many towns under the jurisdiction of Provincial centres such as Kiev and Smolensk. The following year, after many alterations, the boyars of the Privy Chancellery divided three hundred and forty one towns between the eight enormous new Provinces of Moscow, Ingermanland (later called St. Petersburg), Kiev, Smolensk, Archangel, Kazan, Azov, and Siberia. In 1711 the Province of Voronezh was constituted from the group of towns which had been assigned to help with the naval construction programme at Voronezh. This brought the total to nine Provinces, which happened to be the same number of territorial divisions which had been planned in the reign of Tsar Theodore. The coincidence of number, and, perhaps, the general idea of a single military and administrative territorial unit, are the only features the two ideas had in common. The territorial configuration of the Provinces corresponded neither to the Theodorian plan nor to the territorial arrangements of the regional departments in Moscow. In some cases whole territories were incorporated into a Province, in others a territory was divided among several Provinces. In the fixing of boundaries the distances and communications between the towns and the Provincial centres were taken into account. Thus all the towns lying on the nine main roads leading out of Moscow, the roads to Novgorod, Kolomna, Kashira, etc., were included in the Province of Moscow. The influential men such as Prince Menshikov, Streshnev, and Apraxin, who knew they were to be governors, were not indifferent to the administrative rearrangements on which their interests depended. When the boundaries had been settled, the army had to be divided among the Provinces for maintenance and, so that each Province would know the size of its share, total military expenditure had to be divided up likewise.

The main purpose of the reform was to put the responsibility for the maintenance of the army on this territorial basis. The Privy Chancellery and the nominated governors worked together on this problem, which was also discussed during sessions of the Duma, and at meetings of the governors. Discussions went on until 1712, when it was decided that it was possible to put the new administrative machinery into operation. Four years of hard preparatory work were spent on the reform, but even so errors were made: thanks to its inaccurate knowledge, the Privy Chancellery, which was the co-ordinating authority, overlooked nineteen of the regiments when it was allocating them among the Provinces. After Poltava, Peter himself thought not only of dividing the maintenance costs of his regiments among the Provinces; he thought that the war was nearly over, while in fact, it was to last for another eleven years.

The Provincial reform added an extra layer of officials to the local administration. In 1715 the establishment consisted, besides junior officials, of a governor, a vice-governor who either assisted his superior or governed part of the

Province himself, a "landrichter" who was an official in charge of the administration of justice, and an "ober-proviant" and "proviantmeister" who were in charge of grain collection. The governor, moreover, was not to be the highest authority in the Province. Although the experiment of persuading Provincial associations of nobles to take an interest in local administration by electing some of their number to supervise the *voevodas* had proved a complete failure, Peter now repeated this experiment on an even wider basis. An ukaze of April 24th, 1713, provided for the creation of boards of landraty of eight to twelve men according to the size of the Province, who were to take their decisions by a majority vote, and with whom the governors were obliged to consult. The governor was to have two votes, and be not the "chief of this 'consilium' but its chairman." The landraty were chosen by the Senate from two lists of candidates drawn up by the governors, and were, in fact, modelled on the landraty of the Baltic provinces of Sweden conquered by Peter. Later on, however, no doubt realising the drawbacks of nominating councillors recommended by the governors, Peter changed his mind, and on January 20th, 1714, ordered "the nobility to choose the landraty in every town or district." But the Senate never gave effect to this order, and continued to choose the candidates from the governor's lists. In 1716 Peter changed his mind again, and instructed the Senate to choose landraty from officers retired due to age or wounds. Thus the landraty were not elected representatives of the Provincial nobility nominated to assist the governors, but officials whose powers derived from the Senate and the governor himself. By the time of this ukaze, however, the functions of the landraty had already altered completely from those of the original plan. The episode of the *voevodas* and their council had been repeated.

The Provinces into which Peter divided the country were so vast that each included several of the Provinces into which it was divided in the late nineteenth century. Thus the Province of Moscow in Peter's time included the whole, or parts, of the late nineteenth-century Province of Moscow, as well as its surrounding Provinces of Tula, Vladimir, Yaroslav, and Kostroma. These enormous Provinces were subdivided into districts which were comparatively small, and there were in consequence so many of them in each Province that the administration had to group the districts and organise another administrative unit between Province and district. This grouping of districts into *Provintsii* or sub-provinces, which started in 1711, was not done uniformly but only for particular and local reasons. In the Province of Moscow, for instance, most of the districts were grouped into eight sub-provinces.

A third sub-division, however, was still to be added. There were great disparities in the wealth, and above all in the number, of taxable households in the different Provinces. There were, for instance, 246,000 households in the Province of Moscow and only 42,000 in the Province of Azov. Peter, who liked simple mathematical schemes, wanted to reduce the variations between the Provinces to a single financial denominator, but thought the calculation household by household would be too laborious. He therefore invented a large accounting unit called *dolia,* which for no apparent reason he fixed at 5,536 households, and took the total number of households to be 812,000, a completely arbitrary figure, supposedly taken from the census returns for 1678. The contribution of each Province to the expenses of the government was to depend on the number of *dolia* in it. Peter then turned the *dolia* into an administrative unit by dividing into *dolia* not only the households on the financial register, but also the Provinces themselves, and put the landraty to run the *dolias*. We have already mentioned that the experiment of administration by *voevodas* and councils elected by the provincial nobility had failed. With the Provincial reform of 1711, however, the *voevodas* who had survived the reform of 1699 had been fully reinstated with wide financial and legal powers not only over the rural population but also over the trading communities of their districts, and with the new name of "kommendant." It is difficult to ascertain whether the suppression of urban self-government was accomplished by order from above, or by custom and usage below. As we have seen, the districts had been grouped into sub-provinces, which were administered by *ober-kommendants* to whom the *kommendants* had been subordinated.

The ukaze of January 28th, 1715, however, suppressed the territorial divisions into districts and sub-provinces and the *ober-kommendants* and the *kommendants*. It provided instead for the division of Provinces into *dolia* which were to be administered by landraty vested with fiscal, police, and judicial powers, which, however, were limited to the rural population, for the ukaze denied the landraty any jurisdiction whatever over the trading community. This ukaze effected a complete change in the provincial administration of the country when it abolished the old unit of the district. In defiance of history and geography, but in the name of arithmetic, the *dolia* of the landraty sometimes coincided with the old districts, sometimes combined several of them, and sometimes divided them. Moreover it proved impossible to divide each Province into a series of squares each containing 5,536 households, so the ukaze left the governors free to increase or decrease the size of the *dolia* "as it shall prove convenient, having regard to distances." Sometimes, therefore, a *dolia* would consist of 8,000 households, while its neighbour would have only half as many, and evidently the number in a *dolia* could differ very widely from the average. Yet it was by the number of its *dolia* that a Province's contribution to state expenses was fixed, and the number of *dolia* was determined quite haphazardly "according to the governor's judgement," so that complete nonsense was made of Peter's *dolia* mathematics. The number of landraty had to be increased: in the Province of Moscow, for instance, when the number of *dolia* had been calculated, it was found that forty-four landraty were required instead of the original thirteen.

The ukaze of 1715 also abolished the governor's council of landraty which had been the central administrative body of the Province. But, having sent the landraty to administer the *dolia,* the ukaze then showed that the government was frightened of leaving the governor without supervision. It provided that two landraty at a time should do a two-month tour of duty with the governor, and that, at the end of every year, the landraty were to meet in the Provincial capital to settle their accounts and take their decisions on all the business under their jurisdiction in plenary assembly. Not unnaturally this procedure created an ambiguity in the relationship between the governor and the landraty: as administrators of parts of the Province the landraty were the governor's subordinates, while as members of the council of landraty they were his equals. As the governor was the viceroy of the Province, however, the former relationship predominated. He treated the landraty "as if he were their overlord, and not their president"; he ordered them about, commanded their presence out of town, and, despite the law, even arrested them. These hasty institutional changes completely upset discipline in the civil service: to the excesses of power subordinates replied with disobedience. The landraty had barely taken over the administration of their *dolia* when, towards the end of 1715, they were instructed to carry out a new census. This extra task, on top of all their other administrative work, naturally slowed down everything. The census dragged on through 1716 and 1717, while the Senate and the Tsar did their utmost to speed it up. The landraty were ordered to report to St. Petersburg with the registers towards the end of 1717, but only a few appeared in 1718. One landraty was sent fifteen ukazes but never appeared. Then it was ordered that the recalcitrants were to be sent to St. Petersburg in chains, and the order sent after one of them provided not only for his arrest if he refused to go but also for the seizure of his household. He refused to go and threatened to beat anyone who tried to take them.

Peter's legislation for Provincial reforms showed neither forethought nor wisdom. The aim of the reform was purely fiscal. The Provincial institutions had a repulsive characteristic: they were presses to squeeze money out of the taxpayer, and were concerned less and less with the well-being of the people. Meanwhile the Treasury's requirements kept on increasing, and the governors were incapable of satisfying them. In 1715 the fleet cost nearly twice as much as in 1711. Ships of the line in the Baltic Fleet were afraid to put to sea for lack of equipment. Regiments did not receive their pay in time and turned into bands of marauders. Ambassadors received no money and were unable to maintain themselves or to pay the necessary bribes. Peter harassed his officials with "cruel ukazes," said his sluggish governors were "like crabs," and threatened that "he would reason with them with his hands, and not with words." The Senate was ordered not to "spare from fines" the governors who were unable to extract new taxes "without overburdening the people." The landraty who had not sent the taxes they had collected to the capital were to refund their annual salary of 120 roubles. The Provincial Commissaries, who were no more than intermediaries between the Senate and the governors, and who were innocent as far as any tax deficit was concerned, were beaten twice a week, the usual way of forcibly recovering a debt. No other means of encouragement were found than beatings and fines! Some governors, zealous in the Treasury's interests, tried everything. Apraxin, governor of Kazan, and brother to the General-Admiral, invented new taxes for his reports, and once made Peter a present of 120,000 roubles from the imaginary proceeds; to cover it he then put the most incredible pressure on the ignorant non-Russians of his Province, by forcing them, amongst other things, to buy Treasury tobacco at 2 roubles a pound which gave him a profit of 150,000 roubles. Unfortunately this enterprise turned out to be extremely expensive; the oppressed non-Russians left the Province *en masse*—there were more than 33,000 families—and so deprived the Treasury of a yearly sum amounting to more than three times the profits which Apraxin had hoped to collect from these people. Every conceivable measure was taken to make up the loss: expenditure was cut, and extraordinary temporary taxes were imposed, one of which, however, only yielded one-third of the estimated amount, a sure sign that there was nothing left to collect.

In 1708 Peter foresaw another deficit, and, having no faith in the antiquated system of Prikazes, tried to find a solution in a decentralised administration by transferring the financial departments from Moscow to the Provinces. This was unsuccessful, and he then had to consider returning the departments to the capital, justifying the fable about musicians!

Under Peter the Boyar Duma had acquired certain powers which were subsequently transferred to the institution which replaced it. The Senate had originally been intended only as a provisional institution, as were the committees of the Duma which, due to Peter's long and frequent absences, began to look somewhat permanent. On February 22nd, 1711, the eve of his departure to the Turkish campaign, Peter published a short ukaze: "We appoint the governing Senate to administer in our absence." Another ukaze was phrased in a different way: "Having to absent ourselves frequently during the wars, we appoint the Senate as ruler." Thus the Senate's right to administer was only to be of a temporary nature; after all, Peter, unlike Charles XII, did not intend to be always absent. The ukaze also lists the nine senators, nearly as many as the effective members of the once populous Boyar Duma. Three members of the Boyar Duma were appointed to the Senate: Count Mussin-Pushkin, Streshnev, and Plemmyannikov. An ukaze of March 2nd, 1711, defined the Senate's duties: it was to have complete control over the judiciary and over government expenditure, and it was to be responsible for the sources of revenue and a host of other commissions dealing with the enrolment of young noblemen and boyars' retainers into the officer reserve, the examination of government goods, trade, and bills of exchange. Its responsibilities and powers were defined in another ukaze which proclaimed that all persons and institutions were, under pain of death, to obey the Senate as they would the Tsar. No complaint of senatorial maladministration was to be made before the Tsar returned from abroad, when the Senate would have to account to him for its actions. In 1717 Peter reproved the Senate from abroad for its administrative irregularities "which I cannot supervise because I am so far away, and so occupied with this grievous war"; he urged the senators to be more vigilant "for you have nothing else to do except govern, and if you do not do this conscientiously, you will answer to God, and will not escape justice here below." Sometimes Peter made the senators come to him, in Reval or St. Petersburg, to report "on what has been done, what has not been done, and the reasons for it."

None of the old Boyar Duma's legislative functions seem to have been included in the Senate's original commission; it was not, any more than was the Council of Ministers, the Sovereign's Council of State. It was an executive institution responsible for the administration of current government business, and for special commissions entrusted to it by the absent Tsar; in fact it was a council brought together "to take his Majesty's place." Moreover the Senate had nothing to do with either foreign affairs or the prosecution of the war. The Senate inherited two subsidiary institutions from the Council of Ministers: the *Rasspravnaya Palata,* or Chamber of Justice, which was a special judicial section, and the *Blizhnaya Kantselyariya,* or Privy Chancellery, which was to help the Senate with the accounts and the control of receipts and expenditure. As the temporary headquarters on the Neva became the capital of the empire, and Alexander Menshikov, senior sergeant in the Preobrazhensky Regiment, became Duke of Izhera and "sovereign in his own domain," as Prince Kurakin put it, so did the temporary commission with which the Senate was endowed gradually become permanent.

The formation and development of the Senate is closely associated with the Provincial Reform of 1708. Moreover it was this reform that had undermined the administration of the central departments and thrown them into confusion. Some of the central departments, such as those responsible for Siberia and Kazan, were abolished, and the Provinces of Siberia and Kazan were made responsible for their own administration. Others of the central departments were reduced to the status of offices of the Province of Moscow, like the *Ratusha* which became simply the Moscow municipal council. The organisation of the country was rather strange: there were eight vast regions, the governments of which were in no way co-ordinated in the capital. Indeed a capital did not even exist, for Moscow had stopped being one, and St. Petersburg had not yet taken its place. In the place of an established geographical centre the country had to manage with a peripatetic headquarters—the location of the Tsar. The Council of Ministers only met casually, and its composition was quite fortuitous, in spite of the ukaze which clearly provided for its composition and duties. A register for 1705 shows that there were thirty-eight councillors, boyars, *okolnichy,* and *dumnie dvoriane.* Yet when immediate and decisive action was required because Charles XII, by an unexpected forced march from Poland, had cut the communications of the army at Grodno, there were only two ministers, *dumnie lyudi,* in Moscow with the Tsar; the remainder were away travelling "on service."

Only departments concerned with requisitions and expenditure remained in Moscow, i.e., War, Artillery, the Admiralty, and Ambassadors. Thus control of expenditure was concentrated in the capital, and receipts were collected by the Provincial administrations, but Moscow no longer enjoyed the presence of a superior institution responsible either for the ultimate disposition of the receipts or for the supervision of the recipients—in other words, there was no government. Peter was preoccupied with military and diplomatic problems, and seemingly failed to notice that, having created eight Provinces, he had in fact only set up eight departments to recruit and maintain the army in its struggle against a dangerous enemy; he had left the state without a centralised administration, and himself without anybody to interpret and execute his sovereign will. The ministers in the Privy Chancellery could not play the part since they had neither the necessary authority nor were in permanent session; they were concerned with other business, and were obliged to sign the minutes of their meetings so that their "stupidities" would be evident to all. At this stage Peter did not require a legislative or consultative State Council, but a simple administrative council. He needed a few intelligent men who could discover, in the laconic, cryptic, hastily written ukazes he sent them, the ideas that he wished them to embody in their ukazes, and put them into effect. In other words what was needed was a council with enough power to be feared, and with a sufficient sense of responsibility not to be without fear itself. The intention (if one admits that any intention existed at all when the Senate was created) was that, in the eyes of the people, it should be the Tsar's *alter ego,* but that it should always be sensible of the *quos ego* of the Tsar above it. Decisions in the Senate were taken on a unanimous vote, and, to avoid unanimous decisions being extorted by personal pressure, none of Peter's principal collaborators, such as Menshikov, Apraxin, Sheremetiev, or Chancellor Golovkin, were included in the Senate. These "supreme lords," "principals" as they are called by the ukaze, Peter's closest collaborators in military and diplomatic affairs over which the Senate had no authority, were likewise beyond the Senate's authority and could, indeed, send it "ukazes by order of his Majesty." At the same time, however, Peter informed Menshikov that even he, Duke of Izhera, was obliged, like other governors, to obey the Senate. Thus there were two governments acting in conflict, one sometimes subordinate to the other, and sometimes independent. The political thinkers of the period can only have accepted this situation because they either had not time to think about it or could not think out logically what was implied. Most of the Senators, such as Samarin, military Treasurer, and Prince Gregory Volkonsky, Quartermaster-General, were second-rate administrators, although they understood the Senate's main business—problems of military supply, etc.—no worse than any of the "principals," and were certainly incapable of stealing as much as Menshikov. If Senator Prince Michael Dolgoruky could not write, then Menshikov was not much better, as he had difficulty in forming the letters of his name.

As we have seen above, two conditions, the decay of the old Boyar Duma, and the Tsar's continual absence, were responsible for the creation of the Senate, first as a temporary institution, and then as a permanent one with its authority, composition, and importance defined. The first condition, the disappearance of the central administrative body, meant that a supreme governing institution with a clearly defined commission and *permanent* members was required to concentrate exclusively on the business assigned to it. The second condition was responsible for the creation of an institution which would enforce laws and supervise other departments, but which had no consultative standing or legislative authority, and could be called on to account for the use it made of its very temporary powers.

Peter created the Senate so that it might supervise the whole administrative system, and this, at the beginning at any rate, was to be its most important function. The Privy Chancellery and the Senate were to be jointly responsible for keeping the public accounts. One of the Senate's first acts was to set up an organ of control. An ukaze of March 5th, 1711, directed the Senate to appoint an intelligent and good man, whatever his social standing, as *ober-fiscal,* to supervise secretly the administration of public affairs, and to collect information concerning inequitable judicial decisions, "misappropriation of public funds, and other matters." The *ober-fiscal* was to indict the offender, whatever his rank, before the Senate. If he secured a conviction he was entitled to half the fine the Senate imposed, but, if the charges were dismissed, no blame was to attach to him, and, according to the ukaze, those who "held resentment against him" were to suffer "cruel punishment and confiscation of property." The *ober-fiscal* acted in conjunction with a network of fiscals spread throughout all the districts and administrative departments. Since the ukaze specified that each town had to have one or two fiscals attached to it, and since there were then about three hundred and forty towns in the country, there must have been no fewer than five hundred such informers spread through the Provincial and urban administration. Later on the system became even more complicated: the fleet, for instance, had its own team of fiscals and its *ober-fiscal.* The irresponsible and arbitrary power of these officials soon led to abuse. *Ober-fiscal* Nesterov denounced all malefactors, including his immediate superiors the Senators (those guardians of justice), and even accused Prince Jacob Dolgoruky, whose integrity was proverbial, and Prince Gagarin, Governor of Siberia, whom he succeeded in sending to the gallows. In the end, Nesterov, champion of justice, was himself accused of accepting bribes, found guilty, and broken on the wheel.

10

A NEW SCIENCE

WHAT IS science? It is a way of knowing, a method or approach for learning about things. Physical objects of every sort provide the subject matter, or things to be known, in science, but as such they are not science. There is nothing "scientific" about the object itself, a rock or an atom. Only man's way of looking at and knowing about these physical objects can be science.

An analogy with history may help to clarify the point that science is a way of knowing. The *fact* that Americans signed a declaration of independence in 1776 is not in itself history. As *fact* it is to be studied, explained, and compared to other *facts;* similarly, a scientist considers a rock or atom. Nothing comes of historical facts or physical objects without investigation, research, and discovery. And like historians, scientists discover objects, or facts about objects, and then interpret them and place them in a context of other facts, ideas, or mathematical formulas. Then they can describe and place facts or phenomena in relationship to other facts and phenomena. Both science and history, then, are ways of knowing.

The history *of* science consists of the study of how men in the past have known about—perceived, described, and evaluated—physical objects. There is change here, often radical change, from period to period. These changes in science are connected to the history of thought. Because science is human activity and a way of knowing, it is affected by changes in theories of knowledge, art, myths, and mathematics. No scientist ever looks at physical objects except through the lens of human experience, emotions, and preconceptions. Science is also affected by war, business, and religion, again depending on the particular influences on a person at a particular time. The scientist, obviously, is as much a person as any historian. He therefore belongs to his times in that he at least partly adopts the assumptions, modes of thought, and taste predominant in his age.

In the sixteenth and seventeenth centuries dramatic changes occurred in science. This was almost predictable for historians of ideas, because of the changes going on in other human activities. Was there a scientific revolution? Not in the sense that scientists overnight rejected medieval and ancient science to make an entirely new one. But changes did take place. Remembering that science is a *way of knowing,* we must credit Galileo and Vesalius, rather than Copernicus, with laying the foundations for a new science. Sometimes the aims in pursuit of which scientists made their observations more precise, as in the case of Kepler, remained clouded with old superstitions. But what of the results? This paradox of differences between aims and results should not surprise historians, who often set out to answer one question and end up working on quite a different one.

Is it accidental that in the same period of history when scientists began striving urgently to "correct old errors," humanists were striving to know the meanings of words in context, in some ancient text? In the sixteenth and seventeenth centuries there was also a rush to establish the correct dates of reigns of kings and of other historical events. Did medieval men have a sense of time which lent itself to scientific and historical investigation?

1.

The study of the human body attracted medieval scholars, but their knowledge of it did not surpass that of the ancient Greeks. So it was with medieval science; interesting, lofty speculation, but ultimately only derivative and insignificant. In 1500 it was still the ancients, not medieval scientists, who offered superior theoretical and descriptive treatises on natural phenomena.

Anatomy and astronomy became the first sciences in a vaguely modern way, chiefly because they were the first to dissociate themselves, although very slowly, from theology, magic, and the aura of the ancients. By 1550, mainly in the works of Vesalius and Copernicus, both anatomy and astronomy had gained new foundations for further speculation and research. Anatomy and astronomy were at the critical point on their way to surpassing the achievement of the ancient scientists; henceforth scientists in increasing numbers would make them into clearly defined disciplines.

The lines between medieval and modern are not so neatly drawn in Vesalius himself, but in his work there is a self-awareness (like Ghiberti's) and a passionate desire to improve on Galen, the greatest ancient anatomist. Marie Boas (1919–   ) of the University of London, wife of Professor A. R. Hall, describes Vesalius' achievement as part of a general change in Western thought. Had conceptions of human nature changed? Did humanism and the studies of Renaissance painters and sculptors influence anatomical study? Vesalius' debt to Galen remained very great, but the important thing was his refusal to be intimidated or overpowered by Galen's achievement. Why did he desire to be more precise, thorough, and methodical than any previous anatomist?

MARIE BOAS: The Frame of Man and Its Ills *

Anatomical study has one application for the man of science who loves knowledge for its own sake, another for him who values it only to demonstrate that Nature does nothing in vain, a third for one who provides himself from anatomy with data for investigating a function, physical or mental, and yet another for the practitioner who has to remove splinters and missiles efficiently, to excise parts properly, or to treat ulcers, fistulae and abscesses.

In 1542 Andreas Vesalius (1514–64) wrote with characteristic Renaissance smugness that "those who are now dedicated to the ancient study of medicine, almost restored to its pristine splendour in many schools, are beginning to learn to their satisfaction how little and how feebly men have laboured in the field of Anatomy from the time of Galen to the present day." It was his own belief that

* From Marie Boas, *The Scientific Renaissance, 1450–1630* (New York: Harper and Row, 1962), pp. 129–52.

his great treatise *On the Fabric of the Human Body* (1543) was the first real step forward from Galen, no small boast in view of the high esteem in which Vesalius, like his contemporaries, held the great Greek physician of the second century A.D. Modern criticism has tended to agree with Vesalius in thinking both that a revival of anatomy was a necessary preliminary to the improvement of medicine, and that the work of Vesalius himself is a landmark in that revival. The hazards of a date—1543—have brought together two diverse figures, Vesalius and Copernicus, who shared a respect for the ancients and a desire to raise modern science at least to the level of ancient science.

Progress in anatomy before the sixteenth century is as mysteriously slow as its development after 1500 is startlingly rapid. One cannot say that it was because anatomy was a forbidden subject, for the old myth that human dissection was prohibited throughout the Middle Ages has long since been dispelled. It is true that Islamic writers laid little stress on anatomy, in spite of their knowledge of the magnificent work of Galen in this field; they emphasised rather the identification of disease and the compounding of drugs, and this bent was transmitted to Western Europe through the writings of Avicenna (979–1037). The Moslem lack of interest in anatomy seems to have stemmed from religious prohibition; but there was no such prohibition by the Church in Christian Europe.[1] Indeed, it appears that distaste for opening the human body after death was a relatively late development (perhaps even appearing after the revival of anatomy), for a fifteenth-century Florentine physician, Antonio Benivieni, habitually performed post-mortem examinations and commented with surprise when, after he had treated an obscure but interesting incurable disease, the man's "relations refused through some superstition or other" to allow him to open the body and investigate the cause of death. Post-mortems were frequently performed in the fourteenth century, both privately and publicly, and members of the university faculties were commonly called in as consultants in legal cases when it was desirable to ascertain if death were due to natural or unnatural causes. (One wonders how they were able to decide.)

Nevertheless, anatomy as such was little practised. One obvious reason was the lack of a guide. Surprisingly, Galen's anatomical treatises escaped the first great wave of translation in the twelfth and thirteenth centuries, when so much of his purely medical work was translated. All that was available of his brilliant anatomical investigations was a short treatise called *De Juvamentis Membrorum* (*On the Functions of the Members*), a truncated version of his physiological treatise *On the Use of the Parts*. It was a highly abbreviated paraphrase of little more than half of the original, dealing cursorily with the function of the limbs and digestive organs, and retaining Arabic nomenclature. This could suggest a reason for studying the body, and provide a list of the principal organs, but it was of little help in directing men to a clear picture of the correct approach to anatomy. There was thus little to stimulate investigation, and even

---

[1] What the Church did forbid was the boiling up of bodies to produce skeletons. The edict (1300) was the result of what threatened to become an over-popular practice because of the desire of rich Crusaders and pilgrims to have their bones laid to rest at home. The edict was responsible for the many subterfuges such as robbing gallows and charnel houses to which later anatomists resorted in order to acquire bones when bodies were readily available for dissection.

less to help if investigation was attempted. In fact, medical men at first found they had quite enough to do in mastering the immense mass of material presented to them in books. Besides, they not unnaturally tended to accept the Moslem view, that medicine should deal with disease and its causes rather than try to fathom the structure of man. Even the surgeon had little need to know anything more than surface anatomy and the articulation of the limbs, the latter useful in case of dislocations.

The first step towards a rediscovery of human anatomy was a revival of interest: the first indication that this had taken place is the appearance of an *Anatomy* by Mondino di Luzzi, written in 1316. Mondino (*c.* 1275–1326), a professor at Bologna, was perhaps influenced by the animal dissection undertaken at Salerno in the previous century, perhaps by the growing demands of the surgeons, certainly by his reading of Galen's *De Juvamentis* mentioned in the proemium. Judging by the use which Mondino made of *De Juvamentis,* it was only imperfectly Latinised, for Mondino's terms are nearly all Arabic in origin: he was, in fact, one of those Arabicised physicians whom the poet Petrarch was to attack so vehemently in the next generation. Mondino's approach was simple: without preamble, he plunged into a brief and crude description of the parts of the body, beginning with those of the abdominal cavity and proceeding via the thorax to the head and extremities. This order became traditional in anatomical study, partly from the example of Mondino, partly from the need to examine first the parts most subject to decay. Mondino's intention does not seem to have been to write a detailed textbook, but rather to provide a rough outline of procedure for dissectors; here there are no precise directions to follow in dissecting, and no attempt at exact nomenclature. Mondino has clearly dissected a body in the way he describes, but he could not, even if he had wished to do so, delineate the position and nature of every organ. Yet the work is thoroughly professional, and Mondino is not wholly subservient to his authorities.

Because of its succinctness and utility, Mondino's *Anatomy* became the standard textbook of the medical schools; for about this time most universities incorporated into their statutes the provision that all medical students should see one or even two anatomies (always and naturally performed in the winter); and these same statutes usually specify Mondino as a text. Indeed there was no other; and references to Galen are more usually to the supplementary text of *De Juvamentis.* This remained true for another century, even though Niccolo da Reggio in 1322, six years after Mondino had finished his *Anatomy,* completed a translation of Galen's *On the Use of the Parts,* a book which Mondino would certainly have used had it been available to him. In fact, Galen was relatively neglected, because Mondino had replaced him.

By 1400, anatomical dissections were established as a regular part of the curriculum in most medical schools,[2] and a standard procedure had been

[2] Some universities were slower: Tübingen only introduced anatomical studies in 1485, and the statutes stipulated that dissections were to be conducted every three or four years! Even in 1538, when the use of Mondino was forbidden, they were still infrequent. But the Tübingen medical faculty achieved little fame—the better faculties were much more insistent on dissections.

developed. The cadaver was laid on a table, around which the students clustered closely; the actual dissection was performed by a demonstrator (often a surgeon) while the professor on his high lecture platform read the prescribed text which was Mondino or sometimes, later, Galen's *Use of the Parts*. . . . Presumably students were also able to attend post-mortem dissections when their own professors were engaged for the purpose, and the records indicate that these were fairly frequent. (One can perhaps account for the seemingly exaggerated claims of later anatomists as to the number of bodies they dissected by assuming that they lump true dissections and post-mortems together.) The printing-press helped to establish Mondino's as the official text; the first printed edition appeared in 1476, after which there were at least eight more editions in the fifteenth century, and over twenty in the sixteenth. At the same time, commentaries on Mondino were naturally being produced by the professors who lectured on anatomy, and it was in the form of commentaries on Mondino, rather than on Galen, that new anatomical treatises were presented. Of these a typical example is that of Alessandro Achillini (1463–1512), who was alternately a professor of philosophy and of medicine: his *Anatomical Annotations* (published posthumously in 1520) reveal that his lectures did not go much beyond Mondino. Yet he, like Mondino, clearly had performed dissections, and tradition assigns to him a number of minor anatomical discoveries. Achillini's work is mainly of interest in showing how anatomical study and original anatomical investigation was slowly taking root among professors of medicine.

In the early years of the sixteenth century anatomy was undoubtedly regarded as far more important than had been the case before, and anatomical studies were pursued with great vigour, and in a new way. The chief stimulus in this direction came, rather improbably, from humanism which, soon after denouncing the Arabic tradition represented by Mondino, made available the superior Greek tradition of Galen. Just as fifteenth-century astronomy rebelled against mediaeval texts and tried to return to the pure fount of Greek tradition with an intensive study of the works of Ptolemy, so in anatomy and medicine there was an attempt to restore medicine by a reconsideration of the works of Galen. First, naturally, came new editions of the texts known to the Middle Ages; among the more famous new translations are those by Thomas Linacre (?1460–1524), humanist, physician and founder of the College of Physicians, who concerned himself with medical texts as well as with Galen's great physiological treatise *On the Natural Faculties* (1523). The most influential of Galen's works in the early years of the sixteenth century was *On the Use of the Parts,* available by 1500 in a number of versions direct from the Greek, which set the style for having a discussion of the function of each organ in conjunction with anatomical dissection. It had a further curious advantage in having been unknown to Mondino, which gave it extra prestige in the anti-mediaeval and anti-Arabic climate of the period. Every attempt was made to get these Galenic works into the hands of medical students: thus in 1528 there was published in Paris a series of four handy texts in pocket size, including *On the Use of the Parts* (in the fourteenth-century translation of Niccolo da Reggio), *On the Motion of Muscles* (newly translated) and Linacre's five-year-old version of the

Natural Faculties. The rise in importance of the medical school of the University of Paris dates from the renewed interest in Galen indicated by these publications and by the activities of the Paris faculty. It was Johannes Guinther of Andernach (1487–1574) (in spite of his name, a professor at Paris) who first published a Latin translation of a newly discovered and most important Galenic text, *On Anatomical Procedures (De Anatomicis Administrationibus,* 1531). Guinther was a medical humanist, rather than a practising anatomist, but his contributions to the advance of anatomy are none the less great, and in spite of the later criticism of his pupil Vesalius, Guinther did perform anatomical dissections, as well as make translations. Vesalius as a student assisted Guinther in preparing the professor's own textbook, *Anatomical Institutions according to the opinion of Galen for Students of Medicine* (1536).

The real worship of Galen begins with the rediscovery of the *Anatomical Procedures,* and its commentary by Guinther. (His Latin version of 1531 was followed in 1538 by a Greek text, prepared for the press by a group of scholars which included the botanist Fuchs. There were many editions of both the Latin and the Greek versions through the course of the sixteenth century.) It was a Galenic treatise wholly new to the Renaissance, whose superiority to Mondino, and even to the commentators on Mondino, was conspicuous. Its immediate impact is clearly indicated in the rearrangement of procedure that was now adopted. Galen had begun, not with the viscera like Mondino, but with the skeleton, for, as he insisted, "as poles to tents and walls to houses, so are bones to living creatures, for other features naturally take form from them and change with them." This was a much needed injunction, for the skeleton was poorly known. Here too Galen indicated clearly the nature of his anatomical material; lamenting the impossibility of studying human anatomy at Rome, he explained why he had chosen apes and other animals, while insisting that one should procure human cadavers whenever possible. (Unfortunately, this warning was not always heeded.) After the bones, Galen proceeded to the study of the muscles of the arms, hands and legs, followed by the nerves, veins and arteries of the same limbs; then the muscles of the head. Only then did he proceed to the internal organs of the body, which he classed by function—alimentary, respiratory (including the heart) and the brain. This is a totally different method of procedure from that of Mondino, both in the order in which the organs are treated and the manner in which they are discussed; the immediate influence of the work is indicated by those treatises (including that of Vesalius) which follow the Galenic procedure.

When one considers both the novelty and the intrinsic value of the Galenic texts, it is not surprising that sixteenth-century anatomists eagerly seized upon them, at the same time denouncing the established tradition of the medical schools, and those in particular who claimed that Mondino and his fifteenth- and sixteenth-century commentators were preferable to Galen. Galen's work was really so immeasurably superior to what had been done in the intervening period that admiration and adulation was inevitable and desirable. For until anatomists learned what Galen had to teach there was little chance they would ever learn more about anatomy than he had known. It is not surprising that adulation sometimes turned into worship, and the conviction that Galen could do no wrong; nor that the critics who opposed Galen because they believed that mediaeval anatomists were better became confused with those who, following Galen's precepts, and exploring the problems of human anatomy, found that Galen erred. So John Caius was content to devote a major part of his life to the editing of Galen's works, and regarded dissent from Galen as an indication of academic flightiness and irresponsibility. He found Galen a perfectly adequate guide when he lectured on anatomy to surgeons, and thought others should do so too.

The astonishing thing is that contemporary with the rise of Galen worship there actually were anatomists bent on following Galen's example and admonitions, who did dissect with a fresh eye (even though the other was usually fixed on the text of the *Anatomical Procedures*). Galen certainly would have envied those, like Vesalius, who had access to human cadavers, and would have had only scorn for the fact that such men, with advantages he himself lacked, were often reluctant to accept the evidence of their own eyes, and preferred to believe that Galen was describing human anatomy when, as he himself had carefully pointed out, he knew only animal anatomy. But what scientific apprentice has not, many times since the sixteenth century, preferred to trust the authoritative text rather than his own unskilled eyes? It took time to create an independent school of anatomy, even as it takes time to make an individual anatomist. And in spite of the comparative abundance of human dissection material, it was not quite as abundant as anatomists boastfully made out; much preliminary dissection was performed on animals, and the lessons of this early training often persisted in spite of later experience.

At about the same time that humanism was influencing anatomy through the rediscovery of Galen, artistic circles were influencing anatomy in quite a different way. Every studio manifested an interest in surface and muscle anatomy as part of the attempt at naturalistic portraiture. The greatest exemplar of this tradition is Leonardo da Vinci (1452–1519), but he was merely the best of a large group which includes Dürer and Michelangelo, as well as many lesser artists, some of whom turned their hands to anatomical illustration. Leonardo was introduced to anatomy in the studio of Verrocchio (1435–88) who insisted that his pupils learn anatomy thoroughly: he taught them to observe surface anatomy, and also had them study flayed bodies, so that they could learn enough about the play of muscles to represent them accurately in action. Artists of the late fifteenth century commonly tried their hands at the dissection of human and animal subjects in pursuit of artistic anatomy; they could also attend anatomy demonstrations, either the public dissections which took place every winter in Italian universities, or the private lessons which were also widely available.

The earliest anatomical drawings of Leonardo, made about 1497–9, show only slight knowledge of dissection, though already profound understanding of surface anatomy. He began about this time to plan a great book *On the Human Figure,* intended to portray living, artistic anatomy rather than structural and physiological anatomy. Soon after 1503, however, Leonardo's approach began to change. First, he had access to more dissecting material (though never, apparently, to as much as he claimed). Then, perhaps about 1506, he read Galen's *On the Use of the Parts,* which stimulated him to further studies on bones and muscles, taught him much about anatomical fact and procedure, and interested him in physiological functioning. (He is often as scathing about the statements of Mondino as any medical humanist.) It is to this period that his greatest work belongs, much of it based upon the centenarian whose superficial anatomy he studied during visits to the hospital, and whose body he later dissected and compared with that of a seven-month foetus. Side by side with his studies on man were studies on animals: partly because, with Galen, he assumed that animal and human anatomy was basically identical, and partly from the demands of art. Leonardo studied the anatomy of the horse for the great projected equestrian statue of Ludovico Sforza, and he was as interested in the proportions of animals as in those of human bodies.

Some of Leonardo's work is extraordinary: with the advantage of an eye trained to observation he saw as clearly as any professional anatomist the correct relationships and forms of bones, muscles and organs, and his mechanical ability suggested to him a number of ingenious techniques for studying individual organs. Some of his work is poor: he either had not really observed what he drew, or had observed it wrongly. But the whole—and the level of his competence is generally high—is transformed and illuminated by the drawings which fill every page of his notes, for Leonardo was a peerless anatomical illustrator. He had, of course, the great advantage of being both observer and draughtsman. There is almost no page of his manuscript notebooks which is not a thing of beauty in its own right, and in all that he did, Leonardo looked for the hidden beauty which he believed to lie behind all (or almost all) the body's frame and structure. Leonardo stands in a class by himself: a great artist, he made of his anatomy a work of art.

Leonardo stands apart for another reason: he worked in secret and published nothing. He was known to be working on anatomy and a few artists saw some of his illustrations. In fact, his influence may have been real on anatomical illustration, though his influence on anatomy was nil. Anatomical illustration developed amazingly during the first years of the sixteenth century, to such an extent, indeed, that it is tempting to judge the worth of every work chiefly by its illustrations. This would surely be wrong. Whether the illustrations have independent artistic merit is really irrelevant to their purpose; there was as much luck as judgement involved in whether an anatomist could secure the services of a good artist or not. Even the accuracy of the drawings may reflect the artist rather than the anatomist, for, as in the case of herbals, it is not at all clear how closely anatomists were able to work with their artists. Anatomical illustration appears rather suddenly in the early sixteenth century, for though the first books on anatomy are illustrated, there are no anatomical drawings. Usually the illustrations are of dissection scenes or of surgical operations, though there were also the "wound men" indicating the probable location of difficult sword cuts, and the crude figures indicating the astrological significance of various regions of the body. The attractively illustrated *Anatomical Bundle*

(*Fasciculo di Medicinae,* 1493), which includes the text of Mondino, has an interesting seated female figure with the body opened to show the reproductive organs; though the drawing is naturalistic the anatomy emphatically is not.

The first anatomist to take advantage of the possibilities of anatomical illustration was Berengario da Carpi (*c.* 1460–*c.* 1530), who was associated with the University of Bologna which had a good anatomical tradition. Berengario published a commentary on Mondino in 1521, followed in 1522 by a short book with a long title: *A Short but very Clear and Fruitful Introduction to the Anatomy of the Human Body, Published by Request of his Students,* and both books were illustrated with true anatomical drawings. The second work contains a number of plates designed to illustrate the muscles: the artist gives a spirited view, rendering the scene arresting by drawing the body with normal facial expression, the figure in each case cheerfully holding back flaps of skin to display muscular structure. This method of demonstrating living anatomy was further developed later to give complete "muscle men" and skeletons. The figures in Berengario are all set in a bare landscape, which developed into the almost blighted and ruined background of the figures in the illustrations to the works of Vesalius, the climax of anatomical illustration in this genre.

Anatomical illustration was undoubtedly valuable, especially in the absence of a competent technical vocabulary. And it produced some wonderful picture-books. But it also had its disadvantages. Most noticeable is that it tended to draw attention away from the text, which it did not necessarily represent accurately. This was particularly undesirable in books like those of Vesalius which are more than a mere outline of anatomy. In the sixteenth century, some anatomists complained that illustrations even drew students away from dissection; having a picture, they felt less necessity to observe for themselves. As Vesalius put it, "I am convinced that it is very hard—nay, futile and impossible—to obtain real anatomical or therapeutic knowledge from mere figures or formulae, though no one will deny them to be capital aids to memory."

This difficulty still exists, especially when appraising the work of sixteenth-century anatomists: in looking at the pictures one is all too apt to forget the text, which is a far better measure of scientific achievement. And the text by itself is always interesting. Every anatomist of the period shares a certain common attitude. Thus each declares that anatomy needs clarification, because the professors are such blockheads; and each claims to have learned this need through his own dissection of innumerable cadavers. Equally, each betrays the fact that his anatomical investigations were in reality based on relatively few cadavers, supplemented by autopsies on the one hand, and numerous animal dissections on the other. This last fact explains many anomalies. It has always been a puzzle to understand why sixteenth-century anatomists "saw" in the human body what Galen described for animals, and it has been assumed that they were wilfully blind or stupid. Aside from the fact that it is often quite easy to "see" what a textbook or manual says should be seen, very often sixteenth-century anatomists used the same animal material as Galen, partly because it was readily available, partly because it did more closely resemble what Galen described. Hence the "five-lobed" liver, found in dogs and apes but not in man, yet commonly shown in anatomical illustrations including the early drawings of Vesalius. Hence, too, the insistence that the *rete mirabile* was present in man, though it was known to be difficult to detect in a body long dead.[3] Hence, too, the universal habit of representing the right kidney as higher than the left, though in man it is lower: clearly the ideas of most anatomists (even of Leonardo and Vesalius) were so firmly fixed by early dissection of animals that they never rearranged their vision when they dissected man, an indication of how difficult it may be even for practised eyes to see aright.

Beginning about 1520 there was a great rush of anatomical works, one after the other, of various degrees of originality. All are, naturally, more or less influenced by Galen, either physiologically or anatomically. Each of these books has its own merits and its own discoveries; all together represent the "new anatomy." It is difficult to distinguish them chronologically for books were often years in preparation; one of the distinctions of Vesalius was the way in which he rushed into print. Among the earliest of the new kind of anatomical treatise are those of Berengario da Carpi: the *Commentary on Mondino,* and the *Brief Introduction.* As befitted a commentator, Berengario organised his work on lines laid down by his authority, but his was immeasurably superior to Mondino's. He explained his position in the dedication:

There are many books which discuss anatomy, but they are not well arranged for the reader's comfort. The authors seem to have borrowed fables from other volumes instead of writing genuine anatomy. For this reason there are few or none at all who now understand the purpose of this necessary and important art. .

And he proved his own understanding by demonstrating his own achievements in actual dissection. He studied "the reader's comfort" too; for, in contrast to Mondino, Berengario was clear, direct, careful to explain both the names and positions of organs, indicating how they were to be handled for the most effective dissection, what precautions were necessary. Reading his account, anyone would feel almost capable of picking up a dissecting knife and going to work. Berengario was not startlingly original, but he did observe with a fair degree of accuracy. He was amusingly contemptuous of the "common opinion" that the *rete mirabile* is found in man, for "I have never seen this net, and I believe that nature does not accomplish by many means that which she can accomplish by few means": since it is not necessary, there is no need to imagine it. There are many other anatomical works in this period which have merit: the *Introduction to Anatomy* of Niccolo Massa (1536); *On the Dissection of the Parts of the Human Body,* by the French printer Charles Estienne (published in 1545, though begun about 1530; Estienne (1504–1564) ingeniously provided illustrations by taking figures from contemporary artists and having

[3] The *rete mirabile* is a network of vessels at the base of the brain, found in cattle but not in man. The difficulties connected with it are indicated by the comment of Niccolo Massa (*c.* 1489–1569) in his *Introduction to Anatomy* (1536): "some dare to say that this rete is a figment of Galen . . . but I myself have often seen the rete, and have demonstrated it to the bystanders so that no one could possibly deny it, though sometimes I have found it very small." Vesalius used to keep the head of an ox or lamb handy when dissecting a human head, in order to demonstrate the *rete* plainly.

anatomical details inserted); the *Anatomy of Mondino* by Johannes Dryander (1541); each introduced some new names and new facts worthy of note. But none is significantly superior to any other.

It is the distinction of Vesalius to have produced a work far superior to all others, anatomically, pictorially and physiologically, so far superior as almost to eclipse the work of his contemporaries. Vesalius had certain advantages, especially that of having been educated into the new anatomy. Born in 1514, he studied first at Louvain, where he learned Latin and Greek, absorbed the humanist love of languages, and found pleasure in dissecting animals. In 1533 he went to Paris for formal medical training; though he stayed only three years, and though he was later to characterise his teachers as ignorant of practical anatomy, in fact the years at Paris formed his anatomical outlook. Here, under Guinther of Andernach, he was introduced to Galen's *Anatomical Procedures;* he assisted Guinther in the preparation of his *Anatomical Institutes;* and he was profoundly influenced by the tremendous interest in Galen displayed by the medical faculty and the printers of Paris. The scorn that he later heaped on his teachers is at least partly a measure of how much they taught him: for they and Galen combined to teach him to approach anatomy, not as a textbook subject, but as a subject for research. The value of seeing for oneself, the intimate connection between anatomy and physiology—these were Galenic precepts, and Vesalius followed the path his education fitted him to follow, though he left his teachers far behind.

Vesalius left Paris for Louvain in 1536 when war forced the closing of the medical school; for a year he lectured and demonstrated with *éclat,* published his thesis, and then departed for Italy. Here, at Padua, he secured his M.D. and immediately, in spite of his youth, appointment as Lecturer in Surgery. He lectured on anatomy and as a result of his first experiences published the six sheets known as the *Tabulae sex* in 1538. These are large, perhaps so that they could be pinned on a wall, and combine illustration and text on each sheet. Characteristically, the first sheet carries a dedication which explains that it was at the demand of the students and other professors that Vesalius produced this work. The first three sheets (with drawings by Vesalius himself) represent the liver and associated blood vessels, together with the male and female reproductive organs, the venous system and the arterial system; the drawings are adequate but contain traditional errors with respect to the shape of the liver and uterus, and the relative positions of right and left kidney. The last three sheets, drawn by Jan Stephen van Calcar (a pupil of Titian) represent the three aspects of the skeleton, in living posture, with a text naming the bones. These sheets seem to have started a fashion, and after their appearance many anatomical sheets were produced for student use.

For the next few years Vesalius lectured and dissected furiously, until he felt satisfied that he had solved the major problems in anatomy and was competent to present the results of his work to the public. He presented his achievements not in one book, but in two, both published in 1543: *On the Fabric of the Human Body (De Humani Corporis Fabrica)* and a brief handbook, about the size of Berengario's, the *Epitome.* This is a fantastic achievement in the time available, the more so as Vesalius was in this period concerned with editing Guinther's *Anatomical Institutes* and contributing to the 1541 Latin edition of Galen (the Giunta edition). In 1543 Vesalius left Padua for Basle, to see his books through the press; when copies were available, he took them to the Emperor's court in Germany, hoping to secure a court position. He was successful; after his appointment as Imperial Physician to Charles V, Vesalius had little time for dissection, and his anatomical activity nearly ceased, though the second edition of the *Fabrica* in 1555 includes a fair amount of revised material. This second edition immediately preceded his appointment as physician to Philip II of Spain, just as the first had preceded his appointment as physician to Charles V. He appears to have been less successful in Spain than he was in Germany and the Low Countries, and about 1562 he gave up his post; his activities are then obscure, but he died on a pilgrimage in 1564, intending to return to teaching at Padua.

What makes the *Fabrica* superior to all other anatomical books of the period (apart from its dramatic and artistic illustrations) is its plan and its scope. As the title indicates, it is more than an account of structural anatomy; its size shows at once that it is no mere handbook. The influence of Galen was still strong on Vesalius: the content of the sections follows the plan of Galen, not of Mondino; and Vesalius included in the last book many of the vivisection experiments described earlier by Galen on the effect of cutting and tying various nerves. The first book treats the skeleton; the second, myology, carefully showing all the muscles and their relations; the third and fourth books the venous, arterial and nervous systems; the fifth and sixth the organs of the abdominal and thoracic cavities and the brain.

Vesalius was in part writing an anti-Galenic polemic; at least he was ever eager to attack the Galenists, even his own masters. He enjoyed disagreeing with Galen, as when he argued that the vena cava has its origin in the heart, not the liver, an argument he pursued in some detail. But in fact he could not have written his great work without Galen; there is a real sense in which Vesalius began with Galen rather than the human body, in the same way in which Copernicus began with Ptolemy rather than with the physical world. Neither Copernicus nor Vesalius was any the less original for that. Vesalius kept one eye on Galen, but the other was quick to look for possible discovery: for no anatomist of the sixteenth century felt that he had really established himself as an independent worker unless he found something that had escaped Galen, which he was the first to discover. Vesalius is no exception. Nor was he an exception in persisting in error in spite of many dissections "with his own hand." (His insistence that the right kidney is higher than the left is a case in point.) Vesalius was exceptional in the amount of new material that he saw, and in his detailed and lively comments. It is almost a pity that the illustrations are so fine, for they are not as accurate as the text. Occasionally the figures include both animal and human anatomy telescoped together, not, generally, through confusion, but because Vesalius was, in the text, discussing comparative anatomy, and permitted the artist to make a combined figure, either for simplicity or to save his time.

Perhaps the most striking aspect of Vesalius' work is the pains he took to deal with the relation between individual organs and the body as a whole. What starts as a complete skeleton ends as a few bones; what starts as a flayed (but active) human figure displaying its surface muscles is dissected layer by layer until only a few individual muscles are left; the bodily cavity is considered as a whole before its individual parts are discussed. This is different from the standard method of procedure as much as the aim of the book is different: for Vesalius was not writing an elementary text and handbook, but a great monograph designed as a replacement for Galen.

Not unnaturally, Vesalius was as much concerned with the use of the parts of the body as with their structure, with physiology as well as anatomy; indeed he made, like Galen, little distinction between the two. Structure is, where possible, related to function; thus Vesalius considers very carefully the difference in fibre structure between veins and muscles as these are related to their action and purpose. The main function of the veins is to serve the body in conveying nourishment, so their structure is adapted for this purpose:

Nature gave straight fibres to the vein; by means of these it draws blood into its cavity. Then since it has to propel the blood into the next part of the vein, as though through a water-course, she gave it transverse fibres. Lest the whole blood should be taken at once into the next part of the vein from the first without any pause, and be propelled, she also wrapped the body of the vein with oblique fibres.

For, "The Creator of all things instituted the veins for the prime reason that they may carry the blood to the individual parts of the body, and be just like canals or channels, from which all parts suck their food."

Following normal Galenic physiology (all he knew) Vesalius assumed that the veins take their origin from the liver (a belief presumably engendered by the striking size of the vena cava) and that their function is to carry the nutritive blood to various parts of the body, while at the same time removing waste products. Similarly, the arteries are presumed to distribute the vital spirit to all parts of the body. Very noticeable is the strongly mechanical concept of bodily function: for attraction and repulsion represent inhalation and expulsion, and the whole venous system is compared to a water supply, an analogy that was to serve Harvey in good stead seventy-five years later. The insistence upon the importance of fibre structure (especially detailed in the discussion of the lungs, in Book VI) was to be maintained continuously after Vesalius, and became emphatically mechanistic in eighteenth-century physiology.

Nutrition Vesalius discussed at great length in connection with the anatomy of the abdominal cavity. He had nothing very original to say, but he expressed clearly the common conclusions of sixteenth-century anatomists and of Galen:

Thus food and drink are taken from the mouth through the stomach into the belly, as into a certain common workshop or storehouse, that squeezes everything enclosed within it, mixes it and concocts it, and protrudes what is concocted into the intestine. Thence, the branches of the vena porta suck away what is best of that concocted juice, and most suitable for making blood, together with the moister remnant of this concoction, carrying it to the hollow of the liver. . . . However, the liver, after admitting the thick juice and fluid, adds an embellishment to it necessary for the production of perfect blood. It expels a double waste, that is, the yellow bile, the lighter and more tenuous waste, then the atrabilious or muddy juice, thick and earthy. . . . But the blood is led through the vena cava propagated in a very numerous series of branches to the parts of the body: and what in it is similar and appropriate to the individual parts they attract to themselves, assimilate, and place in position. What is superfluous and what waste arises in this concoction they exclude from themselves through their own ducts.

To Vesalius, as to Galen, the arterial system was both less important and less interesting than the venous system. The venous system derived its importance both from its responsibility for nutrition, and from the necessity of knowing the exact position of each vein for successful phlebotomy. Besides, the structure of the arterial system was less controversial than that of the venous system, though there were plenty of questions to ask about the structure of the heart, from which the arterial system arose:

The dissension among medical men and philosophers concerning the great artery is much less than that about the origins of the veins and nerves. For Hippocrates, Plato, Aristotle and Galen lay down that the heart is the fount and origin of the arteries, as is reasonable . . . But if philosophers and leading physicians have decided that the heart is the fount of the arteries, nevertheless they do differ not a little about the sinus of the heart from which the great artery springs, since some contend that it arises from the middle sinus of the heart, others from the left one. But as this controversy turns rather upon the ventricles and sinuses of the heart, than upon the origin of the artery, and since there are only two ventricles in the heart, we shall confirm the origin of the great artery in the grander left sinus of the heart.

A more difficult problem was the question of the nature of the septum, the thick wall dividing the right side of the heart from the left. The surface of the septum is covered with little pits which Galen, not unreasonably, concluded to be very small pores; he therefore assumed that they existed to allow a small amount of blood to percolate from the right side of the heart to the left. The importance of this became greater in the sixteenth century as the interest in detailed physiology increased. Vesalius was predisposed to accept the idea that these pits went through the septum, though after careful examination he could not detect any passage. He could only conclude that there was no certainty in this matter:

Conspicuous as these pits are, none (as far as can be detected by the senses) permeate from the right ventricle into the left through the septum between the ventricles; nor did any passages, even the most obscure, appear to my eyes, by which the septum would be made pervious, although these are described by the professors of dissection because they have a most strong persuasion that the blood is carried from the right ventricle to the left. Whence also it is (as I shall advise more plainly elsewhere) I am not a little doubtful of the heart's action in this respect.

Inevitably, having considered the structure of the heart, Vesalius next considered "the function and use of the heart and of its parts so far described and the reason for their structure." This seems natural, but there was a problem troubling Vesalius: if one considers the natural faculties of the heart and lungs one must become involved in the theological question of the nature of the soul. But, properly speaking, Vesalius argued, this is medical as well as theological, and is, therefore, a fit topic for a work on anatomy:

Furthermore, lest I should here meet with any charge of heresy, I shall straightway abstain from this discussion about the species of the soul, and of their seats. For today, and particularly among our countrymen (Italians) you may find many judges of our most true religion, who if they hear anyone murmur something about the opinions on the soul of Plato, or of Aristotle and his interpreters, or of Galen (perhaps because we are dealing with the dissection of the body, and ought to examine things of this kind at the beginning) they straight away imagine he's wandering from the faith, and having I don't know what doubts about the immortality of the soul. Not bothering about that, doctors must (if they don't wish to approach the art rashly, nor to prescribe and apply remedies for ailing members improperly) consider those faculties that govern us, how many kinds of them there are, and what is the character by which each is known, and in what member of the animal the individual ones are constituted, and what medication they receive. And especially, besides all this, (if our minds can attain it) what is the substance and essence of the soul.

Having thus proclaimed his right to discuss such sensitive questions, Vesalius proceeded to a detailed discussion of the functions of the heart and certain associated functions of the liver and brain. He concluded that:

Just as the substance of the heart is endowed with the force of the vital soul, and the unique flesh of the liver with the faculty of the natural soul, in order that the liver may make the thicker blood and natural spirit and the heart may make the blood which rushes through the body with the vital spirit, and thus these organs may bring materials to all parts of the body through channels reserved for them, so ... the brain ... prepares the animal spirit.

This is perhaps a rather lamely orthodox result of his bold proclamation of the rights of free medical inquiry, for it was a conclusion to which Galenists could readily subscribe, but at least Vesalius had the advantage of proclaiming his independence, however little use he made of it.

The work of Vesalius is so imposing—partly because it so often transcends anatomy—that the work of his contemporaries appears somewhat tame by comparison. But he was a member of a fertile and original generation, and when he left Padua the university found no difficulty in finding worthy successors, for there were many Italian anatomists, each of whom made his own contributions.

2.

For centuries the Church had combated magic, chiefly because of its theological implications, but also because of its assertions about the nature of the universe and the powers of man. Through the ancient texts on magic, men were encouraged to "operate" or grasp the world by the use of forces beyond the reach of any man not using magic.

In the fifteenth century the study of magic became fashionable among the brightest young scholars. They considered it part of philosophy and theology, but superior in wisdom. Every effort was made to procure texts of the ancient philosopher-magicians, and to produce good editions and translations of them.

Astrology, philosophy, astronomy, music, magic, and theology as yet had no distinct boundaries separating one from the other; in the strictest sense they were all considered sciences (*scientia*) or knowledge. Some scholars and humanists sought in them a unity that was divine and transcendent. Just as a new science in the sixteenth century began to appear, magic became more respectable and was deemed a serious subject for speculation and research.

Frances Yates (1899–) of the Warburg Institute, University of London, explores the connections between magic and modern science. Her work demonstrates that science was a part of the general history of thought and culture. That science owes a debt to ancient magic is not proved by Miss Yates, but it is clearly a possibility.

What led Copernicus to speculate that the sun, not the earth, is the center of the cosmos? Miss Yates charts an almost mystical path between Renaissance science, which was influenced by magic, and modern science, which was not. The religious implications remained, however, as the scientists themselves admit. Even Descartes, who seems so coldly rational in his *Discourse,* may have found creativity as much a religious experience as anything else.

FRANCES YATES: **Renaissance Magic and Science** *

The cult of the *prisca theologia*[1] laid a greatly increased emphasis on the sun, and two of the *prisci thealogi* in Ficino's lists had taught that the earth moves. These were Pythagoras and Philolaus; the latter had published the astronomical views of the Pythagorean school, which were that the earth, sun, and other bodies revolve around a central fire. The cult of Hermes Trismegistus also tended to suggest a different position for the sun to that which it held in the Chaldean-Ptolemaic system, universally accepted in the Middle Ages. The Egyptian order of the planets was different from the Chaldean order, for the Egyptians put the sun just above the moon, and below the other five planets, not in the middle of the seven. The difference between the two systems was emphasised by Macrobius—a Platonist much studied in the Middle Ages and Renaissance—who pointed out that the Egyptian order, in which the sun is much nearer to the earth, was the one which Plato accepted. Ficino in his *De sole* mentions the Egyptian order, soon afterwards remarking that the sun has been put nearer to the earth than the firmament by Providence in order to warm it with *spiritus* and *ignis*. The Egyptian position of the sun, only just above the moon which is the channel of all astral influences, would better suit Ficino's sun-centred *spiritus* magic than the Chaldean order. However, there is no evidence that he rejected the latter; both here and in other passages he accepts it.

* From Frances Yates, *Giordano Bruno and the Hermetic Tradition* (Chicago: University of Chicago Press, 1964), pp. 151–56, 432–37, 447–53.
[1] pristine theology

Unquestioning belief in the Ptolemaic position of the sun was nevertheless somewhat shaken by the *prisci theologi,* but more important than this in fixing attention on the sun was the immense religious importance attached to it by the earliest (so Ficino believed) of the *prisci theologi,* Hermes Trismegistus, the Egyptian Moses. The sun, of course, is always a religious symbol and has always been so used in Christianity; but in some passages in the Hermetic writings the sun is called the demiurge, the "second god." In the *Asclepius,* Hermes says:

The sun illuminates the other stars not so much by the power of its light, as by its divinity and holiness, and you should hold him, O Asclepius, to be the second god, governing all things and spreading his light on all the living beings of the world, both those which have a soul and those which have not. (*Ipse enim sol non tam magnitudine luminis quam diuinitate et sanctitate ceteras stellas inluminat. secundum etenim deum hunc crede, o Asclepi, omnia gubernantem omniaque mundana inlustrantem animalia, siue animantia, siue inaminantia.*)

There are also passages on the divinity of the sun in *Corpus Hermeticum* V and X, and above all, in XVI (though the last-named sixteenth treatise did not influence Ficino since it was not in his manuscript; it was published, in Lazzarelli's translation, by Symphorien Champier in 1507). The admired Egyptian religion included sun-worship, and the sun is among the list of the gods of the Egyptians given in the *Asclepius.*

These Egypto-Hermetic sun-teachings undoubtedly influenced Ficino's sun-magic, and they connected philosophically with Plato on the sun as the intelligible splendour, or chief image of the ideas, and religiously with the Pseudo-Dionysian light symbolism. All these influences can be perceived, working together, in Ficino's *De sole* and *De lumine.* As we have tried to outline in previous chapters, the concentration on the sun in the astral magic, led upwards through the Christian Neoplatonism of Pseudo-Dionysius to the supreme *Lux Dei,* and in this way the sun very nearly is for Ficino what it is for Hermes or for the Emperor Julian, the "second god," or the visible god in the Neoplatonic series.

The *De revolutionibus orbium caelestium* of Nicholas Copernicus was written between 1507 and 1530, and published in 1543. It was not by magic that Copernicus reached his epoch-making hypothesis of the revolution of the earth round the sun, but by a great achievement in pure mathematical calculation. He introduces his discovery to the reader as a kind of act of contemplation of the world as a revelation of God, or as what many philosophers have called the visible god. It is, in short, in the atmosphere of the religion of the world that the Copernican revolution is introduced. Nor does Copernicus fail to adduce the authority of *prisci theologi* (though he does not actually use this expression), amongst them Pythagoras and Philolaus to support the hypothesis of earth-movement. And at the crucial moment, just after the diagram showing the new sun-centred system, comes a reference to Hermes Trismegistus on the sun:

In medio vero omnium residet sol. Quis enim in hoc pulcherrimo templo lampadem hanc in alio vel meliori loco poneret, quam unde totum simul possit illuminare?

Siquidem non inepte quidam lucernam mundi, alii mentem, alii rectorem vocant. Trimegistus [sic] visibilem deum.[2]

There are perhaps echoes of Cicero's words for the sun in that famous Dream, on which Macrobius commented, in this passage, but the main echo is surely of the words of Hermes Trismegistus in the *Asclepius,* which we have quoted above.

The teleological framework in which Copernicus presents his discovery has long been recognised, but it is still not generally realised that this framework was the contemporary one. Copernicus is not living within the world-view of Thomas Aquinas but within that of the new Neoplatonism, of the *prisci theologi* with Hermes Trismegistus at their head, of Ficino. One can say, either that the intense emphasis on the sun in this new world-view was the emotional driving force which induced Copernicus to undertake his mathematical calculations on the hypothesis that the sun is indeed at the centre of the planetary system; or that he wished to make his discovery acceptable by presenting it within the framework of this new attitude. Perhaps both explanations would be true, or some of each.

At any rate, Copernicus' discovery came out with the blessing of Hermes Trismegistus upon its head, with a quotation from that famous work in which Hermes describes the sun-worship of the Egyptians in their magical religion.

A recently discovered text tells us that Giordano Bruno, when advocating Copernicanism at Oxford, did this in a context of quotations from Ficino's *De vita coelitus comparanda.* This famous philosopher of the Renaissance thus saw the Copernican sun in some close relationship to Ficinian sun magic. . . . Bruno was an intense religious Hermetist, a believer in the magical religion of the Egyptians as described in the *Asclepius,* the imminent return of which he prophesied in England, taking the Copernican sun as a portent in the sky of this imminent return. He patronises Copernicus for having understood his theory only as a mathematician, whereas he (Bruno) has seen its more profound religious and magical meanings . . . because Bruno's use of Copernicanism shows most strikingly how shifting and uncertain were the borders between genuine science and Hermetism in the Renaissance. Copernicus, though not uninfluenced by Hermetic mysticism about the sun, is completely free of Hermetism in his mathematics. Bruno pushes Copernicus' scientific work back into a prescientific stage, back into Hermetism, interpreting the Copernican diagram as a hieroglyph of divine mysteries.

This chapter has only hinted in a partial and fragmentary way, and with but a few examples, at a theme which I believe may be of absolutely basic importance for the history of thought—namely, Renaissance magic as a factor in bringing about fundamental changes in the human outlook.

The Greeks with their first class mathematical and scientific brains made many discoveries in mechanics and other applied sciences but they never took

---

[2] Truly the sun rests in the center of all things. For who would put the splendor in this most beautiful shrine into another or better place—than where it can light everywhere at the same time? Some wisely call this lamp of the world the conscience, and others the guide. And Trismegistus calls it the visible god.

whole-heartedly, with all their powers, the momentous step which western man took at the beginning of the modern period of crossing the bridge between the theoretical and the practical, of going all out to apply knowledge to produce operations. Why was this? It was basically a matter of the will. Fundamentally, the Greeks did not *want* to operate. They regarded operations as base and mechanical, a degeneration from the only occupation worthy of the dignity of man, pure rational and philosophical speculation. The Middle Ages carried on this attitude in the form that theology is the crown of philosophy and the true end of man is contemplation; any wish to operate can only be inspired by the devil. Quite apart from the question of whether Renaissance magic could, or could not, lead on to genuinely scientific procedures, the real function of the Renaissance Magus in relation to the modern period (or so I see it) is that he changed the will. It was now dignified and important for man to operate; it was also religious and not contrary to the will of God that man, the great miracle, should exert his powers. It was this basic psychological reorientation towards a direction of the will which was neither Greek nor mediaeval in spirit, which made all the difference.

What were the emotional sources of the new attitude? They lie, it may be suggested, in the religious excitement caused by the rediscovery of the *Hermetica,* and their attendant Magia; in the overwhelming emotions aroused by Cabala and its magico-religious techniques. It is magic as an aid to gnosis which begins to turn the will in the new direction.

And even the impulse towards the breaking down of the old cosmology with heliocentricity may have as the emotional impulse towards the new vision of the sun the Hermetic impulse towards the world, interpreted first as magic by Ficino, emerging as science in Copernicus, reverting to gnostic religiosity in Bruno. As we shall see later, Bruno's further leap out from his Copernicanism into an infinite universe peopled with innumerable worlds certainly had behind it, as its emotional driving power, the Hermetic impulse.

Thus "Hermes Trismegistus" and the Neoplatonism and Cabalism associated with him, may have played during his period of glorious ascendance over the mind of western man a strangely important rôle in the shaping of human destiny.

The attack on Renaissance magic, with its associated so-called Neoplatonism and its animistic philosophies of nature was led in France in the early seventeenth century by "le bon père" Marin Mersenne, of the Order of the Minimes. Mersenne, a most devout Christian and an eager scientific enquirer, friend of Descartes and of Gassendi, admirer of Galileo, played an important part in encouraging the new movement, by putting enquirers into touch with others working on similar lines through his vast correspondence with all the savants of Europe. As Lenoble has succinctly pointed out, the issue was not seen by those, like Mersenne, who were actively engaged in the conflict, as solely an issue between the new philosophical and scientific attitudes and the old scholastic tradition. Descartes broke the Aristotelian physics finally, but he also despised, ignored, brushed aside, Renaissance naturalism which he saw to be more incompatible with his own views, in spite of an apparent resemblance in the anti-Aristotelianism of some Renaissance thinkers. And for Mersenne the chief enemy, both of orthodox Christianity and of true science, was Renaissance naturalism with all its associated magics. He therefore devoted his energies to dethroning the Renaissance Magus from his seat and to attacking the efflorescence of base magics of all kinds which the long prevalent Hermetism and Cabalism had brought in their train.

In the opening years of that momentous seventeenth century, every kind of magic and occultism was rampant. The authorities were deeply alarmed. In France, hundreds of sorcerers were being burned ever year, which, as Lenoble has said, is an indication not only of the prevalence of magic but of belief in its powers. There can be little doubt that the esoteric and demon-ridden atmosphere of this period was the final outcome—as it were, the decadence—of the revaluation of magic ultimately deriving from Ficino and Pico and which, extravagantly continued by such descendants of theirs as Cornelius Agrippa, had received support from the animistic interpretations of nature of the Renaissance philosophers. As Koyré has said, "Pour les gens du XVIe et du XVIIe siècle tout est naturel et rien n'est impossible, parce que tout est compris en fonction de la magie et la nature elle-même n'est qu'une magie avec un Dieu magicien suprême"[3] It was into such a world as this that Mersenne and Descartes were born, and Mersenne saw it as his mission to fight it with every weapon he possessed. The scientific weapons were not, as yet, very strong. We are inclined to forget, dazzled as we are by the immense advance in the acquisition of exact scientific knowledge made in the course of this century, how little there was of it at the start, and how slight was the armour with which Mersenne advanced to attack the prevailing magical view of nature as the only scientific explanation of its phenomena.

Mersenne's *Quaestiones in Genesim* (1623) is an awkward book to grasp, not only because of its immense length, but also because the contents seem confusingly arranged. The sections, which are of extremely uneven length, are headed by verses from the first three chapters of *Genesis,* and indeed the book, as its title shows, is intended to be a commentary on *Genesis,* the general purpose of which is not easily seized by the reader as he makes his way through what seems like a collection of treatises on a highly miscellaneous variety of subjects. Lenoble has, however, well seen what may be the principle of unity in the work. He regards it as mainly directed against all magical and divinatory arts, against Cabalists and occultists of all kinds, against naturalist and animistic philosophers whom Mersenne suspects in general of being either atheists or deists. In other words, the Bible text is being used as a canvas for Mersenne's *summa* against Renaissance magic, its whole way of thinking, and all its off-shoots in the vast contemporary dissemination of magical practices. It is also, suggests Lenoble, a *summa* of Mersenne's own scientific interests, his studies in music, mathematics, physics, astronomy and the like. Thus, within the frame-

---

[3] For the men of the sixteenth and seventeenth century everything is natural and nothing is impossible, because everything is understood in terms of magic and nature herself is merely magic with God as the supreme magician.

work of the Mosaic account of creation, Mersenne is both driving out the old magical way of approaching nature, and also bringing in the new way, the coming way of science and genuine mathematics.

From the vast mass of material in this most important book, which lies between the Renaissance and the modern world, only a few points can be selected. Mersenne is extremely well-informed about the Renaissance magic which he so much detests; probably he made a good deal of use of Del Rio's book against magic which he several times mentions. On Ficino he is very clear-sighted. Ficino does not speak as a Catholic when, in the book *De vita coelitus comparanda,* he affirms that images and characters have power on all inferior things, which Catholics deny. In another part of the book, where he gives a long and extremely knowledgeable account of the properties of stones and of magic images, he sees the connection which has been made in Renaissance Platonism between magic images of the stars and Platonic ideas:

Sunt qui ad Platonis ideas recurrant, quae praesint lapidibus, adeout quilibet suam habet ideam, a qua vim & energiam suam accipiat; vel cum Hermete, & Astronomis ad stellas, & imagines coeli (recurrant).[4]

Here he uncovers the magical core of Ficinian Platonism, its confusion of the ideas with magic images and with Hermetism. To attribute such powers to such images seems to him merely insane.

Verum nemo sanae mentis dixerit illas imagines vim habere, ut constellationes magis influant.[5]

Mersenne is a modern; he has crossed the watershed and is on the same side of it as we are; belief in the power of magic images of the stars seems to him quite mad. A drawing by Mantegna, he thinks, is of more value than all the images of the necromancers. He does not condemn such images because he is afraid of their power but because they are meaningless. Mersenne, who completely discards astrology, naturally also discards astral magic, the miraculous virtue of plants, stones, images, and the whole apparatus upon which *magia naturalis* rested.

He condemns the doctrine of the *anima mundi* or at least the extravagant extension of this indulged in by the Renaissance naturalists who affirm that the world lives, breathes, even thinks. Once again he has detected here the magical core in Renaissance Platonism, for this universal animism in nature was the basis for the operations of the Magus, and the *spiritus mundi* was the vehicle which he used.

Concerning the Cabala, Mersenne would admit an orthodox Cabala, concerned with mystical interpretation of Scripture. But Cabalist magic he, naturally, whole-heartedly condemns, and the whole system of Cabalist angelology and its connections with cosmology.

---

[4] There are those who have recourse to the archetypes of Plato, which precede the concrete to the degree to which each has its idea; from which its strength and efficiency derive; or who have recourse with Hermes and the astronomers to the stars and heavenly images.

[5] Indeed, no one of a healthy mind would say that those images have the power to flow into the constellations by magic.

In the course of this energetic clearance, which demolishes the Hermetist-Cabalist basis of Renaissance magic, Mersenne mentions and condemns all the chief propagators of these views, Ficino, Pico della Mirandola and their successors; he is naturally most severe against arch-magicians, such as Cornelius Agrippa or Trithemius. Against Francesco Giorgi, one of the most celebrated of Hermetic-Cabalists and author of the influential *Harmonia Mundi* he has many passages, and he also devoted another book specifically to refuting him. Patrizi's theory of light comes under review and is condemned. Bruno and Campanella are attacked, the former briefly (Mersenne's main attacks on Bruno come in other books), the latter in long passages. In short Mersenne's vast *Genesis* commentary contains within its covers penetrating critical analyses of almost every aspect of the way of thinking which we have been studying in this book. The life-blood of the Renaissance Magus drains away under this onslaught; his most cherished theories, illusions, and delusions are turning into so much useless lumber in the cold clear light of the new age.

But we have not yet mentioned the chief game which Mersenne is hunting. The dead and gone Hermetist-Cabalists were not so dangerous and abhorrent to him as the living one, Robert Fludd. There can be little doubt that Fludd in whom Mersenne saw, and rightly, a contemporary who was deliberately reviving and re-enforcing with all his power the world view of the Renaissance Magus which Mersenne was bent on destroying, was really the latter's main target. Fludd's works, and particularly his *Utriusque cosmi . . . historia,* were the immediate irritant which precipitated the whole vast counter-flood (if this bad pun may be permitted) of the *Quaestiones in Genesim.* And if we think of how Fludd constantly and for ever quotes Ficino's *Pimander,* equating this with the Mosaic account of creation, we begin to see how Mersenne has planned his book as a reply to that; and we perceive another unifying, guiding principle in his *Genesis* commentary, besides those to which Lenoble has pointed. For Mersenne's own commentary, on its theological side, uses only the Fathers and accredited doctors of the Church. It is not as a Hermetist-Cabalist like Fludd that Mersenne approaches *Genesis,* but as an orthodox Catholic. He is using orthodox *Genesis* commentary as the framework for his attack on Fludd's Hermetist-Cabalist commentary, and on all that had been built on to the Hermes-Moses equation from Pico della Mirandola onwards. Thus, it may be suggested, the true unifying principle of Mersenne's work is Moses, an orthodox Moses, who, turning his face against magic, ushers in the new science.

Mersenne does not often mention Hermes Trismegistus; and when he quotes from the *Hermetica* it is always in Greek, never in Ficino's Latin translation. But he fully realised how basic was Hermes for Fludd and for the whole tradition from whence Fludd derived. The macrocosm-microcosm theory of Fludd's "two worlds" cannot be proved, says Mersenne, because the "Egyptians" teach that man contains the world and because "Mercurius" (also meant by "the Egyptians") calls man a great miracle and like to God. . . .

The seventeenth century is the creative period of modern science, and the Fludd controversies come at the crucial moment when the new turn begins to be made, when the mechanical philosophy of nature provided the hypothesis and the development of mathematics provided the tool for the first decisive victory of man over nature. For "the whole magnificent movement of modern science is essentially of a piece; the later biological and sociological branches took over their basic postulates from the earlier victorious mechanics."

With the history of genuine science leading up to Galileo's mechanics this book has had nothing whatever to do. That story belongs to the history of science proper, to Duhem's researches which demonstrated the advances made during the Middle Ages, and which were gathered up and continued in the Aristotelian school of Padua, to the Renaissance revival of Greek mathematics, to the intensive development of mathematical studies generally on which an influence of Neoplatonism is acknowledged. The phenomenon of Galileo derives from the continuous development in Middle Ages and Renaissance of the rational tradition of Greek science, and it is for this that Mersenne stands as he beats off the terrible magicians.

The history of science can explain and follow the various stages leading to the emergence of modern science in the seventeenth century, but it does not explain *why* this happened at this time, why there was this intense new interest in the world of nature and its workings. Historians of science are aware of a gap here. "For if one thing has at least now grown clear it is that the emergence of modern science was a very complicated affair, and involved a great variety of factors." "In its initial stages, the Scientific Revolution came about rather by a systematic change in intellectual outlook, than by an increase in technical equipment. Why such a revolution in methods of thought should have taken place is obscure." One writer has suggested that what is needed is "historical studies aiming to ferret out the fundamental motives and other human factors involved" behind the scientific movement.

It is here, as a historical study, and particularly as a historical study of motives, that the present book may have a contribution to make towards elucidating these problems. It is a movement of the will which really originates an intellectual movement. A new centre of interest arises, surrounded by an emotional excitement; the mind turns whither the will has directed it, and new attitudes, new discoveries follow. Behind the emergence of modern science there was a new direction of the will towards the world, its marvels, and mysterious workings, a new longing and determination to understand those workings and to operate with them.

Whence and how had this new direction arisen? One answer to that question suggested by this book is "Hermes Trismegistus." And under that name I include the Hermetic core of Ficinian Neoplatonism; Pico's momentous association of Hermetism with Cabalism; the direction of attention towards the sun as the source of mystico-magical power; the magical animation throughout nature which the Magus seeks to tap and to operate with; the concentration on number as a road into nature's secrets; the philosophy, present in both a magical textbook like *Picatrix* and in the philosophical Hermetic writings, that the All is One, and that the operator can rely on the universal validity of the procedures which he uses; finally, and this is in some ways the most important point, those curious historical errors by which "Hermes Trismegistus" was Christianised, so that it was lawful for a religious Hermetist to speculate on the world in his company, to study the mysteries of creation with his assistance, and even (though not all were willing to stretch the point thus far) to operate with the world forces in magic.

The reign of "Hermes Trismegistus" can be exactly dated. It begins in the late fifteenth century when Ficino translates the newly discovered *Corpus Hermeticum.* It ends in the early seventeenth century when Casaubon exposes him. Within the period of his reign the new world views, the new attitudes, the new motives which were to lead to the emergence of modern science made their appearance.

The procedures with which the Magus attempted to operate have nothing to do with genuine science. The question is, did they stimulate the will towards genuine science and its operations? In an earlier chapter in this book I suggested that they did, giving as an example John Dee, who on one level of his mind is a genuine mathematician, in the line leading to the scientific advances, and on another level is attempting to summon angels with practical Cabala. Much more detailed "ferreting out" of the motives behind the work of Renaissance scientists is needed before more positive statements can be made as to the influence upon them of the dominant Hermetic-Cabalist tradition. In his re-examination of the sources of Leonardo da Vinci, E. Garin has drawn attention to Leonardo's mention of "Ermete Filosofo" and to the resemblance of some of Leonardo's doctrines to Ficinian Hermetism. Might it not have been within the outlook of a Magus that a personality like Leonardo was able to co-ordinate his mathematical and mechanical studies with his work as an artist?

Taking a very long view down the avenues of time a beautiful and coherent line of development suggests itself—perhaps too beautiful and coherent to be quite true. The late antique world, unable to carry Greek science forward any further, turned to the religious cult of the world and its accompanying occultisms and magics of which the writings of "Hermes Trismegistus" are an expression. The appearance of the Magus as an ideal at this time was, as Festugière has said, a retreat from reason into the occult. The same writer compares the appearance of the Magus ideal in the Renaissance as similarly a retreat from the intense rationalism of mediaeval scholasticism. In the long mediaeval centuries, both in the West and in the Arabic world, the traditions of rational Greek science had made progress. Hence, it is now suggested, when "Hermes Trismegistus" and all that he stood for is rediscovered in the Renaissance, the return to the occult this time stimulates the genuine science.

The emerging modern science is still clothed in what might be described as a Hermetic atmosphere. Francis Bacon's *New Atlantis* is perhaps not a very good example to take since Bacon's former position as Father of Experimental Science is now weakened. Nevertheless, the *New Atlantis* is a scientist's Paradise where every kind of discovery and invention is put to the service of the happy people. It is ruled by an Order or Society called "Salomon's House" dedicated to the study of the Works and Creatures of God. The Father of Salomon's House rides in the great procession on a chariot on which there is "a sun of gold, radiant upon the top, in the midst." Whether or not there is any real connection between the *New Atlantis* and the *City of the Sun,* those two Utopias come out of the same stream, and the stream is Hermetic, or Hermetic-Cabalist.

The Hermetic impulse as a motive force behind imaginative formulation of a new cosmology is exemplified by Giordano Bruno. From the new approach to him put forward in this book, Bruno once more swings into place as an important landmark in the history of thought, not for the old wrong reasons but for the new right ones.

Ever since Domenico Berti revived him as the hero who died rather than renounce his scientific conviction of the truth of the Copernican theory, the martyr for modern science, the philosopher who broke with mediaeval Aristotelianism and ushered in the modern world, Bruno has been in a false position. The popular view of Bruno is still roughly as just stated. If I have not finally proved its falsity, I have written this book in vain.

For what is the truth? Bruno was an out-and-out magician, an "Egyptian" and Hermetist of the deepest dye, for whom the Copernican heliocentricity heralded the return of magical religion, who in his dispute with the Oxford doctors associated Copernicanism with the magic of Ficino's *De vita coelitus comparanda*, for whom the Copernican diagram was a hieroglyph of the divine, who defended earth-movement with Hermetic arguments concerning the magical life in all nature, whose aim was to achieve Hermetic gnosis, to reflect the world in the *mens* by magical means, including the stamping of magic images of the stars on memory, and so to become a great Magus and miracle-working religious leader. Sweeping away the theological superstructure which the Christian Hermetists had evolved, using Cabala only as subsidiary to Magia, Bruno is a pure naturalist whose religion is the natural religion of the pseudo-Egyptian Hermetic *Asclepius*. Bruno's world view shows what could be evolved out of an extension and intensification of the Hermetic impulse towards the world. Through a Hermetic interpretation of Copernicus and Lucretius, Bruno arrives at his astonishing vision of an infinite extension of the divine as reflected in nature. The earth moves because it is alive around a sun of Egyptian magic; the planets as living stars perform their courses with her; innumerable other worlds, moving and alive like great animals, people an infinite universe.

Drained of its animism, with the laws of inertia and gravity substituted for the psychic life of nature as the principle of movement, understood objectively instead of subjectively, Bruno's universe would turn into something like the mechanical universe of Isaac Newton, marvellously moving forever under its own laws placed in it by a God who is not a magician but a mechanic and a mathematician. The very fact that Bruno's Hermetic and magical world has been mistaken for so long as the world of an advanced thinker, heralding the new cosmology which was to be the outcome of the scientific revolution, is in itself proof of the contention that "Hermes Trismegistus" played some part in preparing for that revolution. The philosophy of Giordano Bruno, instead of being studied as has been done in the past in isolation from its true historical context, can now be examined by historians of thought as a remarkably complete example of a Hermetic world view in the immediately pre-scientific age.

"Hermes Trismegistus" had to be cast off to free the seventeenth century for its advance, and his dating by Casaubon came at the right moment when his work was done. Nevertheless, the history of the emergence of modern science is incomplete without the history of that from which it emerged; Mersenne's reaction cannot be understood without understanding of what he was reacting from; the swing of the pendulum back towards rationalism needs to be seen in the context of the Renaissance revival of the occult.

Moreover, the mechanistic world view established by the seventeenth-century revolution has been in its turn superseded by the amazing latest developments of scientific knowledge. It may be illuminating to view the scientific revolution as in two phases, the first phase consisting of an animistic universe operated by magic, the second phase of a mathematical universe operated by mechanics. An enquiry into both phases, and their interactions, may be a more fruitful line of historical approach to the problems raised by the science of to-day than the line which concentrates only on the seventeenth-century triumph. Is not all science a gnosis, an insight into the nature of the All, which proceeds by successive revelations?

In that interesting human document, Baillet's life of Descartes, we read how the young philosopher, ardently seeking for truth, fell into a kind of enthusiasm "qui disposa de telle manière son esprit . . . qu'il le mit en état de reçevoir les impressions des songes et des visions."[6] It was November 10th, 1619, and he lay down to rest "tout rempli de son enthousiasme, & tout occupé de la pensée d'avoir trouvé ce jour-la les fondemens de la science admirable."[7] In the night he had three consecutive dreams which seemed to him to have come down from on high. We are completely in the atmosphere of the Hermetic trance, of that sleep of the senses in which truth is revealed. The atmosphere is maintained on the following pages which tell of how Descartes heard of the "Frères de la Rose Croix" who were said to be in possession of a "véritable science." He tried to learn more of them and their secret, but could find out nothing about them, though, on his return to Paris from Germany in 1623 he was suspected of having joined the Rosicrucian brotherhood. This was not true, but it became clear that such a brotherhood was not entirely imaginary because "several Germans and also the Englishman, Robert Fludd, have written in their favour." The atmosphere in which Descartes is casting about for truth is the atmosphere of the great controversy about Fludd and the Rosicrucians.

At about this time, says Baillet, Descartes had almost given up his favourite study of mathematics and geometry which seemed to him to have no certainty.

Il ne trouvoit rien effectivement qui lui parût moins solide que de s'occuper de nombres tout simples, & de figures imaginaires . . . sans porter sa vuë au delà. Il y voioit même quelque chose de plus qu'inutile; & il croyoit qu'il étoit dangereux de s'appliquer trop sérieusement à ces démonstrations superficielles, que l'industrie & l'expérience fournissent moins souvent que le hazard: & qui sont plutôt du ressort des yeux & de l'imagination que de celui de l'entendement.[8]

[6] . . . which disposed his spirit in such a manner . . . that it put him in a state to receive the impressions of dreams and visions.

[7] . . . completely filled with his enthusiasm and completely occupied with the thought of having found the principles of the admirable science on that day.

[8] Essentially, he found nothing which appeared to him less solid than working with ordinary numbers and imaginary figures without looking beyond them. He even saw something here more than useless, and he believed that it was dangerous to work too seriously on those superficial demonstrations which are less often a result of industry and experimentation than of chance; and which belong rather to the sphere of the eyes and the imagination than to that of the understanding.

This might well be a description of the Fludd type of Hermetic diagram. It will not do for Descartes, who was looking for a "Science générale" which might be called "Mathesis, ou Mathématique universelle." His vision confirmed him in the conviction that mathematics was the sole key to the secrets of nature, and shortly afterwards he invented "a new and most fruitful tool, analytical geometry."

The Cartesian mathesis was a vision of genuine mathematics as the clue to the universe and led to the discovery of a genuinely scientific tool for investigations. A transition has been made to an epoch in which what is still a Hermetic, almost a "Rosicrucian," impulse towards the world results in valid scientific intuitions. But may not the intensive Hermetic training of the imagination towards the world have prepared the way for Descartes to cross that inner frontier?

3.

Most scientists of the sixteenth and seventeenth centuries were, in some sense, Christian believers. Many, including Copernicus, Galileo, and Descartes, were raised in the Roman Catholic faith. This Church and its Protestant counterparts assumed the ominous duty of investigating and rooting out heresy. This was a difficult task indeed, because the boundaries between doctrines and heresy were shifting and ill-defined.

That priests might investigate scientific works for heresy seems strange to us, but this practice was so old and acceptable to scientists that Galileo's famous trial by the Inquisition in 1633 actually shocked contemporaries less than we would suspect.

Professor Giorgio de Santillana (1902–   ) of the Massachusetts Institute of Technology re-creates the trial by relying on the court records. Of what was Galileo accused? What is the difference between conjecture and opinion? Is the Church portrayed as unified and monolithic?

Is there evidence here to suggest that Galileo consciously tested or even flouted the Inquisition? Note Inchofer's assertion that Galileo supports the Pythagoreans and Copernicans. Pythagoras was dear to the cult of the *prisca theologia*. In what way might authoritarian attitudes have stifled scientific inquiry? The Inquisitors objected to Galileo's brashness in attacking Aristotle and Ptolemy. Why?

GIORGIO DE SANTILLANA: The Crime of Galileo*

On the twelfth of April, 1633, the first hearing took place before the Commissary-General of the Inquisition and his assistants. The Commissary's name was Father Vincenzo Maculano, or Macolani, da Firenzuola, which caused him to be currently called "Father Firenzuola" from the name of his home town. We know very little of this man whose career was to lead him later to the purple. He was, like all Inquisitors, a Dominican friar, but he had been singled out by the Pope (at least according to the talk of the town) not so much for his theo-

* From Giorgio de Santillana, *The Crime of Galileo* (Chicago: University of Chicago Press, 1955), pp. 237–57.

logical zeal as for the technical and administrative capacities he had shown in supervising the fortification of Castel Sant'Angelo. Urban VIII was no fanatic, and he liked to have humanists and executives in his entourage.

Galileo had officially surrendered to the Holy Office on that morning, for it was a standing rule that the accused were to be held imprisoned and in strict seclusion until the end of the trial. Out of consideration for his state of health and also for the Grand Duke's prestige, he was exceptionally allowed quarters in the Inquisition building itself, which was located close to the Vatican.

According to procedure, the defendant was put under oath and asked whether he knew or conjectured why he had been summoned. He answered that he supposed it was on account of his last book. He was shown the book and identified it as his. They then passed on to the events of 1616. He said that he came to Rome in that year, and *of his own accord,* he specified, in order to know what opinion it was proper to hold in the matter of the Copernican hypothesis and to be sure of not holding any but holy and Catholic views. These were soft words, but he had been advised to keep to the safe and submissive side. He was then asked about the conferences he had had with several prelates prior to the decree, and he explained that they had been due to the desire of those prelates to be instructed about Copernicus' book, which was difficult for laymen to understand. He could be glad now of his precaution to have put his arguments down in writing. The Inquisitor then asked what happened next.

A.: Respecting the controversy which had arisen on the aforesaid opinion that the Sun is stationary and that the Earth moves, it was decided by the Holy Congregation of the Index that such an opinion, considered as an established fact, contradicted Holy Scripture and was only admissible as a conjecture [*ex suppositione*], as it was held by Copernicus [*sic*].

Q.: Was this decision then communicated to him, and by whom?

A.: This decision of the Holy Congregation of the Index was made known to me by Cardinal Bellarmine.

Q.: Let him state what Cardinal Bellarmine told him about said decision, and whether he said anything else on the subject, and what.

A.: The Lord Cardinal Bellarmine signified to me that the aforesaid opinion of Copernicus might be held as a conjecture, as it had been held by Copernicus, and His Eminence was aware that, like Copernicus, I only held that opinion as a conjecture, which is evident from an answer of the same Lord Cardinal to a letter of Father Paolo Antonio Foscarini, provincial of the Carmelites, of which I have a copy, and in which these words occur: "It appears to me that Your Reverence and Signor Galileo act wisely in contenting yourselves with speaking *ex suppositione* and not with certainty." This letter of the Cardinal is dated April 12, 1615. It means, in other words, that that opinion, taken absolutely, must not be either held or defended.

This was neat. It was surely not the time to try to correct their obstinate preconceptions about Copernicus, if those preconceptions could be turned to some use. But Galileo was now requested to state what had been decreed in February, 1616, and communicated to him.

A.: In the month of February, 1616, the Lord Cardinal Bellarmine told me that, as the opinion of Copernicus, if adopted absolutely, was contrary to Holy Scripture, it must neither be held nor defended but that it could be taken and used hypothetically. In accordance with this I possess a certificate of Cardinal Bellarmine, given on May 26, 1616, in which he says that the Copernican opinion may neither be held nor defended, as it is opposed to Holy Scripture, of which certificate I herewith submit a copy.

Q.: When the above communication was made to him, were any other persons present, and who?

We can see Galileo suddenly getting suspicious. This was the first intimation that something more might have taken place on that day, for Riccardi, Serristori, and the Pope himself had mentioned only Bellarmine, and he was confident he knew exactly what Bellarmine had said. But Bellarmine had been dead these thirteen years, and he had only this piece of paper. He tries to be careful.

A.: When the Lord Cardinal made known to me what I have reported about the Copernican views, some Dominican Fathers were present, but I did not know them and have never seen them since.

Q.: Was any other command [*precetto*] communicated to him on this subject, in the presence of those Fathers, by them or anyone else, and what?

At this point the old man is becoming frankly scared. The Commissary is looking at a document in front of him; Galileo has no idea what the document may contain, and this is the mysterious Inquisition. He is afraid of falling into a trap; he is afraid of contradicting openly. We see thoughts racing through his mind. Was Bellarmine's *precetto* something else, juridically, than what he thought it to be? He must have gone over it with Niccolini and his canonist friends. Could the whole decree be construed as a disguised bill of attainder? Had some words escaped his memory that made it a special command *ad personam?* Did anyone else make a move on that day? Could the presence of those Dominicans have meant something?

A.: I remember that the transaction took place as follows: The Lord Cardinal Bellarmine sent for me one morning and told me certain particulars which I had rather reserve for the ear of His Holiness before I communicate them to others. But the end of it was that he told me that the Copernican opinion, being contradictory to Holy Scripture, must not be held or defended. It has escaped my memory whether those Dominican Fathers were present before or whether they came afterward; neither do I remember whether they were present when the Lord Cardinal told me the said opinion was not to be held. It may be that a command [*precetto*] was issued to me that I should not hold or defend the opinion in question, but I do not remember it, for it is several years ago.

Q.: If what was then said and enjoined upon him as a *precetto* were read aloud to him, would he remember it?

A.: I do not remember that anything else was said, nor do I know that I should remember what was said to me, even if it were read to me. I say freely what I do remember, because I do not think that I have in any way disobeyed the *precetto,* that is, have not by any means held or defended the said opinion that the Earth moves and that the Sun is stationary.

The Inquisitor now tells Galileo that the command which was issued to him before witnesses contained: *"that he must neither hold, defend, nor teach that opinion in any way whatsoever."* Will he please to say whether he remembers in what way and by whom this was intimated to him.

A.: I do not remember that the command was intimated to me by anybody but by the Cardinal verbally; and I remember that the command was "not to hold or defend." It may be that "and not to teach" was also there. I do not remember it, neither the clause "in any way whatsoever" [*quovis modo*], but it may be that it was; for I thought no more about it or took any pains to impress the words on my memory, as a few months later I received the certificate now produced, of the said Lord Cardinal Bellarmine, of May 26, in which the order [*ordine*] given me, *not to hold or defend* that opinion, is expressly to be found. The two other clauses of the said command which have just been made known to me, namely, *not to teach* and *in any way,* I have not retained in my memory, I suppose because they are not mentioned in the said certificate, on which I have relied, and which I have kept as a reminder.

Q.: After the aforesaid *precetto* was issued to him, did he receive any permission to write the book that he has acknowledged was his?

The old man has stood his ground desperately, but he is obviously terrified. He has thought it better to concede that the notification in audience may have been some kind of command. He no longer knows where he stands, and this is no time to cite the Pope's ill-advised encouragements or to implicate the authorities. It might all fall back on his head. The only thing is to duck.

A.: I did not ask permission to write the book, because I did not consider that in writing it I was acting contrary to, far less disobeying, the command not to hold, defend, or teach that opinion.

[There follows a factual account of the negotiations concerning the printing.]

Q.: When asking permission to print the book, did he tell the Master of the Palace about the *precetto* which had been issued to him?

A.: I did not happen to discuss that command with the Master of the Palace when I asked for the imprimatur, for I did not think it necessary to say anything, because I had no doubts about it; for I have neither maintained nor defended in that book the opinion that the Earth moves and that the Sun is stationary but have rather demonstrated the opposite of the Copernican opinion and shown that the arguments of Copernicus are weak and not conclusive.

With this the first hearing was concluded. The very last statement is a poor job, for Simplicio's peroration could by no manner of means be construed as a "proof"; but by then Galileo was more dead than alive. His name below the proceedings is signed with a shaking hand. It cannot be said, however, that he lost his presence of mind. The statement that he had not told Riccardi about the *precetto* because he did not think it necessary may sound embarrassingly like Junior not telling Nurse what Mummy had told him to tell her, but it is not so at all. If we accept Galileo's undeviating position, that Bellarmine had simply notified him of the imminent decree, it would have sounded rather silly on his part to go and solemnly remind Riccardi that he hoped he knew a decree had been issued in 1616. Riccardi would have answered jokingly: "I trust this is what your conversations with His Holiness have been about, or else what are we doing here?"

It was quite another matter if there had been a formal injunction of the Inquisition in 1616 not to teach, defend, *or in any way discuss* the theory, for that involved a suspicion of heresy, or at least resistance, and would require an elaborate rehabilitation before the author could write again. And surely, even then, the Pope was at fault, for he should have known; the instructions of February 25, as we have seen . . . prescribed, in case of recalcitrance, an injunction, and even arrest, and the report of Bellarmine on March 3 should have reflected those events. It actually did not, and that is the important point. So the Pope could not know. It was Galileo, he said, who should have come and told all in due obedience. Now he was under the odium of "having been found out."

All this is ridiculous and pitiful, of course. It was no time to be playing at Nurse and Mummy. A great and rigid authoritarian administration with a thought police which is supposed to know all should at least keep its records straight. Before granting permission to write the book, the Pope should either have remembered or have had his memory refreshed, or someone from the Inquisition might have told him. Worse: as a party to the secret deliberations of the Congregation of 1616, the Pope could not possibly have forgotten, if the injunction really took place, that he and the other members had been secretly directed to handle Galileo as a dangerous character; yet he had publicly favored and encouraged him in 1624, and now he was acting injured innocence, because there was no mention of an injunction in the *Decreta.*

About all of this Galileo was still in the dark. So far as he knew, all might have been in order, some kind of injunction might have been mysteriously made out in due form, and he might have been hanging himself by obstinately refusing to admit it. Yet he felt it safest to cling to what he knew. He remembered nothing else; he had never acknowledged anything else, except a simple notification not to hold or defend.

The Inquisitor had been dragging him along on an equivocal term. When he said *precetto,* he implied from the start a personal prohibition. . . . For Galileo, it meant only the notification from the Cardinal. It is the text of that notification that seems to him to be challenged, until the Inquisitor asks insistently whether he remembers being addressed by anyone else. But he does not go beyond that, and down to the very end—that is, until the sentence—Galileo is never told that it *was* someone else and that it was the Commissary-General of the time. Hence his answer has to remain correspondingly indefinite. Was this done so he should not be able to deny explicitly that the Commissary had ever spoken? Was it in order to create the equivocation so cleverly exploited in the summary, as we shall see later? Was it because it was a principle never to disclose the charges? In any case, it is only when he understands that he is really being asked about a "command" that he replies anxiously: "It may be that a command was enjoined on me, but I do not remember." From that moment, he is on his guard. He is obviously trying to remember whether anyone said anything that he had better admit. He does not have a lawyer who could ask what kind of injunction they are talking about. But, as the Inquisitor returns five times to the question of who had addressed him and tries to draw him out in various ways, Galileo answers again and again: "No one except Bellarmine."

In so doing, he has foiled the whole maneuver. For it had been clearly the Inquisition's intention to extract out of him, were it in a moment of bewilderment or fright, the admission that there *had* been a special command by the Commissary enjoined on that day. Such an admission in a signed protocol would have been a substitute for all the irregularities of the injunction. From that moment, the document of 1616 would have become fully legal. As it was, instead, Galileo had re-established consistently the fact that Bellarmine had informed him only of the contents of the coming decree; and thus the text of the decree remained the only legal directive to be considered both by him and by the censor. The injunction, on the other hand, if assumed valid, would have been a directive to the censor to suppress all and any writings of *this* particular person in the matter of Copernicus, or to prosecute them if published.

Where Galileo instead had walked into the delayed-action trap in his very attempt to play safe was in the last statement in his interrogation. To say that he had demonstrated the opposite of the Copernican opinion sounded very much like an attempt to fool the judges. It is not impossible that he should have reserved just such a line of argument, relying on some geometrical legerdemain and on his persuasive capacity. To say, however, that this was "why" he had not told about the notification made it worse. Like so many prisoners under questioning, he was protesting too much. It worked to his undoing, for five days after the audience the results of the official examination of the text came in, and they were not such as to make his plea look good. Three Counselors of the Inquisition, Augustinus Oregius (the Pope's theologian), Melchior Inchofer, and Zacharias Pasqualigo, delivered their reports, which came to the same conclusion: The author had not only "discussed" the forbidden view; he had maintained and taught and defended it, and there was a "vehement suspicion" that he was inclined to it and even held it to this day. Inchofer and Pasqualigo gave a long list of passages which could leave no doubt. On the whole, their quotations were correct, in that they were faithful to the sense.

We shall summarize Inchofer's seven-page report, which is the most explicit.

1. The accused does teach, for, as St. Augustine says, what is teaching except to communicate knowledge? Now Galileo certainly does so and has done so since his pamphlet on the sunspots. It is of a teacher to hand on to his disciples first those precepts of a science which are easiest and clearest, so as to enlist their interest, and to present the science as a new one, which attracts curious minds wondrously. Moreover, defendant makes it appear as though a number of effects which have been already truly and authoritatively explained otherwise could be solved only by the motion of the Earth.

2. He does defend. One may be said to defend an opinion even if he does not refute the contrary one; all the more, then, if he tries to destroy that utterly. In law this is called an impugnation.—Copernicus only proposed a more convenient

method for computations [this interpretation is, as usual, due to Osiander's Preface], whereas Galileo tries to confirm and establish it as a doctrine and with new reasons, which is twice to defend.—Because, if the intention had been disputation and intellectual exercise, he would not so proudly and arrogantly traduce and ridicule Aristotle, Ptolemy, and all the truths he will not acknowledge. And, if he does so in writing, there is no doubt he must have done it much more in conversation.

3. He does hold. He does so on two counts, through necessary conclusions and also through his assertiveness, for we need not consider valid the occasional pretended protestations that he interposes in order not to appear to go against the decree. As for the reasons given in his Preface, it is certainly not the "mutterings against Church Consultors" which could have moved a serious man to undertake such a work; and I did not come across a single publication of ultramontane authors in which this matter of the decree is as much as mentioned, not to speak of the Consultors. It is sure that of Catholics no one would have dared. And then, if this was the motive, why did he not undertake really to defend the decree and the Holy Congregation? But this is so far from his thoughts that he goes on to arm the Copernican opinion with new arguments that no ultramontane ever suggested, and he does so in Italian, surely not the language best suited for the needs of ultramontane or other scholarship but the one most indicated to bring over to his side the ignorant vulgar among whom errors most easily take hold.

4. The author claims to discuss a mathematical hypothesis, but he gives it physical reality, which mathematicians never do. Moreover, if defendant had not adhered firmly to the Copernican opinion and believed it physically true, he would not have fought for it with such asperity, nor would he have written the *Letter to the Grand Duchess,* nor would he have held up to ridicule those who maintain the accepted opinion, and as if they were dumb mooncalves [*hebetes et pene stolidos*] described them as hardly deserving to be called human beings.

Indeed, if he had attacked some individual thinker for his inadequate arguments in favor of the stability of the Earth, we might still put a favorable construction on his text; but, as he holds all to be mental pygmies [*homunciones*] who are not Pythagorean or Copernican, it is clear enough what he has in mind, especially as he praises by contrast William Gilbert, a perverse heretic and a quibbling and quarrelsome defender [*rixosum et cavillosum patronum*] of this opinion.

This last sentence affords a rewarding glimpse into the ways of thought of the thought police. The good Jesuit never stops to consider whether the magnetic phenomena discovered by Gilbert might not be highly relevant, as in fact they are, to a discussion of physical principles. For him, the only point is that Gilbert is a perverse heretic, and hence guilt by association is established. "Quibbling" and "quarrelsome" are hardly apt descriptions of Gilbert's scientific style; they are stock adjectives from Inchofer's Scholastic equipment, roughly equivalent to the present-day "subversive."

But if, intellectually, this expert is the *homuncio* whom Galileo had sized up well in advance, he is otherwise shrewd and competent enough. He pins down the quarry. His report in its relentless animus is well worthy of the hand that wrote the *Tractatus syllepticus.* The defendant is shown to have transgressed not only the questionable injunction but Bellarmine's direct notification "not to hold or defend."

One cannot but wonder what had happened to the previous deliberations hinted at by Monsignor Serristori: "All points have been allowed to drop, except one." Such helpful hints could have come only from the Commissary's office, and Galileo had seized on them for guidance in preparing his defense. The injunction alone provided a legal point, and Niccolini could confirm it, for Galileo knew himself triply protected against a trial of mere intention: by the Pope's authorization, by the explicit instructions to the licensers, and by the license itself. The first day of the questioning had not belied it, for the Commissary had insisted on nothing but the injunction. Hence Galileo had understood this to be still the dangerous point and felt that he was easing the task for any leniently disposed judge by making a stand on the injunction and by abounding otherwise in the sense of pious conformism. And, now that the reports had come in, it turned out that he had only been making a noose to hang himself.

Does this again imply Machiavellian duplicity on the part of the authorities? We have tried to show in the previous chapter what the situation seems to have been. The search for the point of indictment had led to a long-drawn-out fumble between different conceptions; and, as the first scene comes to a close, we see those conceptions embodied in two factions which are still far from agreeing on a common line. The Dominicans of the Inquisition, no longer the ruthless ones of a generation before, were still trying to handle the affair on a restrictive legalistic basis; but they had against them the will of the Pope and the plans of a curial group allied with the Jesuits, of whom men like Inchofer were the spearhead, who were pressing for judicial slaughter. The hints dropped by the officials, which were intended to help Galileo, had led him astray. The Jesuit faction had outmaneuvered its opponents and sprung its trap.

This was in truth legal "railroading," as we have said, for in those times it was well understood that a man could go quite far in playing "double truth" and yet stay within judicial orthodoxy, as long as he covered himself with explicit clauses of submission—and an official license. At most he could have been asked to rewrite in a "problematic" form. One-half of the existing literature could otherwise have been condemned by such methods.

We must insist on this point, because Inchofer's report may look to the modern reader more objective than it really is. To demonstrate that Galileo considered the Copernican argument as convincing for human reason was to hit him below the belt, for that was exactly what he had been supposed to do under the Master of the Palace's written instructions of July 19, 1631: "Signor Galilei will have to add as a peroration the reasons from divine omnipotence dictated to him by Our Lord's Holiness, which must quiet the mind, even if there were no way out of the Pythagorean arguments [*ancorchè da gl'argomenti Pitagorici non se ne potesse uscire*]." That was why the Preliminary Commission, although summoned by the Pope in his anger, had found itself compelled to conclude lamely: "The faults that we have found might be corrected, if the book is deemed worth publishing." How little, how miserably little, correction could entail technically is shown by what happened more than a century later, in 1744.

In that year a Pope of great sense, Benedict XIV (still affectionately known in Italy as "Papa Lambertini"), gave permission to print a revised edition of the *Dialogue,* although Galileo and Copernicanism itself were and remained under condemnation. Now in this "revised" edition *not one word* of the text has been altered, and only a few marginal headings expunged or modified by the insertion of an *if* which makes them into "probable" statements. Such was, and had always been, the formal meaning of the command not to "hold" an opinion. It had a mile-long jurisprudence behind it. Galileo had some right (if the story is true) to challenge the cardinals on the day of his sentence to show him what could be wrong with his book. But the Consultors' report had driven him to break on the rock that he had tried to avoid by steering the discussion around to real issues. As he lay there, day after day, in the building of the Inquisition, racked with acute sciatic pains and intestinal trouble, for all that he had fine rooms and Niccolini's own majordomo to attend him, he might as well have been confined like anyone else in the dark holds of the Castle.

Weeks passed, and nothing happened. The judges were deliberating. The Inquisition was always slow. But in this case we can guess why it was being slow. The Inquisitors had a clear case already, and they did not know what to do with it. In the exploratory phase they had been worried about the rather shaky personal injunction which was the keystone of the case as it had been handed to them. Now they could feel they had gotten past that, for the defendant's denials, in the light of the Consultors' report, made as clear an incrimination as anyone could need to put the machinery into gear—if this was what was really wanted. The Inquisition had been built into a dreadful apparatus in order to make terrifying examples whenever needed, so that no one should feel secure. Once the procedure had been turned on, a man was virtually at their mercy. This time they had been requested by the Pope to oblige with a political performance and a "limited example." It would be like administering a shampoo with a Bessemer converter. Some of the judges at least were balking at this point—perhaps even, at last, the Pope himself.

We know this from what followed, which does credit to all concerned. Cardinal Francesco Barberini, who was himself one of the ten judges, had put discreet pressure on the Commissary to find a way out. One day the Commissary walked into Galileo's room and sat down with him. It was Ivanov coming to Rubashov. The story is told in a letter written to the Cardinal, which was unearthed by Pieralisi in 1833:

In compliance with the commands of His Holiness, I yesterday informed the Most Eminent Lords of the Holy Congregation of Galileo's case, the position of which I briefly reported. Their Eminences approved of what has been done thus far and took into consideration, on the other hand, various difficulties with regard to the manner of pursuing the case and of bringing it to an end. More especially as Galileo has in his examination denied what is plainly evident from the book written by him, since in consequence of this denial there would result the necessity for greater rigor of procedure and less regard to the other considerations belonging to this business. Finally, I suggested a course, namely, that the Holy Congregation should grant me permission to treat extrajudicially with Galileo, in order to render him sensible of his error and bring him, if he recognizes it, to a confession of the same. This proposal appeared at first sight too bold, not much hope being entertained of accomplishing this object by merely adopting the method of argument with him; but, upon my indicating the grounds upon which I had made the suggestion, permission was granted me. That no time might be lost, I entered into discourse with Galileo yesterday afternoon, and after many and many arguments and rejoinders had passed between us, by God's grace, I attained my object, for I brought him to a full sense of his error, so that he clearly recognized that he had erred and had gone too far in his book. And to all this he gave expression in words of much feeling, like one who experienced great consolation in the recognition of his error, and he was also willing to confess it judicially. He requested, however, a little time in order to consider the form in which he might most fittingly make the confession, which, as far as its substance is concerned, will, I hope, follow in the manner indicated.

I have thought it my duty at once to acquaint your Eminence with this matter, having communicated it to no one else; for I trust that His Holiness and your Eminence will be satisfied that in this way the affair is being brought to such a point that it may soon be settled without difficulty. The court will maintain its reputation; it will be possible to deal leniently with the culprit; and, whatever the decision arrived at, he will recognize the favor shown him, with all the other consequences of satisfaction herein desired. Today I think of examining him in order to obtain the said confession; and having, as I hope, received it, it will only remain to me further to question him with regard to his intention and to receive his defense plea; that done, he might have [his] house assigned to him as a prison, as hinted to me by your Eminence, to whom I offer my most humble reverence.

Your Eminence's most humble and
most obedient servant,
FRA VINC°. DA FIRENZUOLA

ROME, April 28, 1633

One wonders what the initial conversation between the two may have been like. It makes one regret that the tape recorder was not in existence; for, this once at least, it was Galileo who had something on the Commissary. He had received in October a letter in which Castelli reported a meeting with Firenzuola, whom he had known for a long time, he said, as a competent military engineer and "a decent person." Castelli had gone to Firenzuola when the first trouble was stirring and, as between monks, had talked to him as vividly and "heretically" as he knew how. "I told him I had no scruple in holding firmly that the Earth moves and that the Sun stands still and that I saw no reason for prohibiting the *Dialogue*. The Father told me that he was of the same opinion and that these questions should not be determined with the use of the authority of Holy Writ. He even told me he intended to write on the subject and would show it to me."

Thus, Galileo knew that the reluctant dragon who had been ordered to devour him held really the same opinion that he did; and there must have been much curious sparring between the two on the lofty subject of theological interpretation. After "many and many arguments and rejoinders," the Commissary must have felt that he was getting nowhere and told him the facts bluntly, somewhat like this:

"My dear Signor Galileo, you do not seem to realize your position. You insist on talking about your text, while I have not asked you about it. You still want us to believe both the rightness of your thought and the purity of your intention, allowing at most that you misunderstood the instructions. You think you can make a stand on Bellarmine's certificate. But the Holy Office cannot be defied like that. It is desired from high quarters, as you realize, that we should make an example, and we are going to. The question is: How far do you want to push us?

"You may quote the licenses again. You may try to allege that the injunction we have was—shall we say—well, lacked your signature. You are going to say that you were encouraged by high quarters to discuss the doctrine and that one cannot discuss it without teaching the contents. But don't you see that in that case you compel us to go into your motives? Don't tell me that your intention is not in question. It is. And I am very much afraid that it might come out, God forbid, that you were, and are, a Copernican. Please—you are not talking to Firenzuola now; you are talking to the Commissary. That you held, as I was saying, the opinion all along and that you do even now—with dissimulation and pertinacity in the face of your inquirers—hold it. I might just as well tell you that this is the way it looks, now that the experts' report upon your book has come in. This would be quite enough in itself. For Cardinal Bellarmine left you in no doubt about the Church's intentions; you promised to obey and then chose to disregard them. You did try to outwit us and affirm your will, which has become contradictory to that of the Church on theological matters. May I add that you further used the freedom you had been given to slip in a couple of propositions which directly deny the transcendence of the Divine Mind. You know what that is called, don't you? A real procedure *de vehementi*, once started, cannot be so easily checked. We shall have to go through the routine of rigorous questioning, by regrettable means if necessary, and the admission will come out. After that there is only our mercy, which means perpetual incarceration in the prisons of the Holy Office. Nobody wants that.

"If you would only understand, you ought to see that a plea of disobedience is still your best bet. Admit it. Plead forgetfulness, complacency, pride, vanity, conceit—choose your own out of the catalogue of venial sins—and we shall have no need for inquiring further. You will get off with a light spanking, and everybody, please believe me, will be much the happier."

Whatever the words, this was the gist of it, as is clearly indicated in the letter, and it was well said. It was the stroke of lightning that rent the veil of Galileo's obsolete Renaissance convictions. He had been introduced to the modern state.

When he was called in two days later, April 30, he was asked whether he had anything to say. He spoke as follows:

In the course of some days' continuous and attentive reflection on the interrogations put to me on the twelfth of the present month, and in particular as to whether, sixteen years ago, an injunction was intimated to me by order of the Holy Office, forbidding me to hold, defend, or teach "in any manner" the opinion that had just been condemned—of the motion of the Earth and the stability of the Sun—it occurred to me to reperuse my printed *Dialogue,* which for three years I had not seen, in order carefully to note whether, contrary to my most sincere intention, there had, by inadvertence, fallen from my pen anything from which a reader or the authorities might infer not only some taint of disobedience on my part but also other particulars which might induce the belief that I had contravened the orders of the Holy Church.

Being, by the kind permission of the authorities, at liberty to send about my servant, I succeeded in procuring a copy of my book, and, having procured it, I applied myself with the utmost diligence to its perusal and to a most minute consideration thereof. And as, owing to my not having seen it for so long, it presented itself to me, as it were, like a new writing and by another author, I freely confess that in several places it seemed to me set forth in such a form that a reader ignorant of my real purpose might have had reason to suppose that the arguments brought on the false side, and which it was my intention to confute, were so expressed as to be calculated rather to compel conviction by their cogency than to be easy of solution.

Two arguments there are in particular—the one taken from the solar spots, the other from the ebb and flow of the tide—which in truth come to the ear of the reader with far greater show of force and power than ought to have been imparted to them by one who regarded them as inconclusive and who intended to refute them, as indeed I truly and sincerely held and do hold them to be inconclusive and admitting of refutation. And, as an excuse to myself for having fallen into an error so foreign to my intention, not contenting myself entirely with saying that, when a man recites the arguments of the opposite side with the object of refuting them, he should, especially if writing in the form of dialogue, state these in their strictest form and should not cloak them to the disadvantage of his opponent—not contenting myself, I say, with this excuse, I resorted to that of the natural complacency which every man feels with regard to his own subtleties and in showing himself more skilful than the generality of men in devising, even in favor of false propositions, ingenious and plausible arguments. With all this, although with Cicero "avidior sim gloriae quam sat est,"[1] if I had now to set forth the same reasonings, without doubt I should so weaken them that they should not be able to make an apparent show of that force of which they are really and essentially devoid. My error, then, has been—and I confess it—one of vainglorious ambition and of pure ignorance and inadvertence.

This is what it occurs to me to say with reference to this particular and which suggested itself to me during the reperusal of my book.

After this declaration, the defendant was dismissed; but he came back after a moment (*post paullulum*), asking to be allowed to make a supplementary statement:

And in confirmation of my assertion that I have not held and do not hold as true the opinion which has been condemned, of the motion of the Earth and stability of the Sun—if there shall be granted to me, as I desire, means and time to make a clearer demonstration thereof, I am ready to do so; and there is a most favorable opportunity for this, seeing that in the work already published the interlocutors agree to meet again after a certain time to discuss several distinct problems of

---

[1] I may be more greedy of fame than is necessary. [Corruption of "sum avidor etiam, quam satis est, gloriae": Cic. Fam. 9.14.2]

Nature not connected with the matter discoursed of at their meetings. As this affords me an opportunity of adding one or two other "days," I promise to resume the arguments already brought in favor of the said opinion, which is false and has been condemned, and to confute them in such most effectual manner as by the blessing of God may be supplied to me. I pray, therefore, this holy Tribunal to aid me in this good resolution and to enable me to put it in effect.

By enlisting the co-operation of Galileo, the Commissary had obtained the admission he needed, and with it he had regained the initiative over his opponents.

Historians have wept unrestrained tears over this final self-degradation of the great man. Nothing apparently would have satisfied them except his being roasted at the stake in Campo di Fiori, as Bruno had been thirty-three years before. In fact, it was a rational move, and it would have obtained for Galileo all that he really wanted—the circulation of the *Dialogue*. No doubt it was bitter to him. He skipped it in his first statement and then drove himself back to say it. He knew he had to say it. It was what Niccolini had advised, much earlier in the game, and what he suggested again now. In an age which laid so much more weight than ours on formalities, everyone knew the difference between due form and intention. Kepler himself, the blameless and fearless Kepler, had thought well in 1619 to send to his bookseller in Italy a letter to be shown to the authorities, so they would not prohibit his *Harmonice mundi.* Although a fervid Protestant, he avowed himself to be "a son of the Church" and added: "As much as I have been able to understand of the Catholic doctrine I not only submit to but indorse it with my reason, and I have tried to show it in several passages of this work." The censor must have raised his eyebrows in wonderment over such a peculiar "son of the Church," but what Kepler lacked was only practice in the proper language. Anyway, on the Index forthwith did he go.

Moralist historians do not seem to notice that their perspective is that of believers in another religion. They would have Galileo behave like Jerome of Prague or like a prophet of Bruno's strange un-Christian God. They forget that he was a member of the Apostolic Roman communion and had to submit in some way. Quite apart from the personal inconvenience of being burned at the stake, it would have been a sin of diabolical pride on his part to push the Vicar of Christ into committing a crime.

He had gambled and lost. He was not a religious visionary being asked to renounce his vision. He was an intelligent man who had taken heavy risks to force an issue and to change a policy for the good of his Faith. He had been snubbed; he had nothing to do but to pay the price and go home. The scientific truth would be able to take care of itself.

He had realized at last that the authorities were not interested in truth but only in authority. They did not expect him to change his mind. They wanted, most illegally, to kill it; and he was going to consider his own interests henceforth.

4.

A clear indication that a new science had developed by about 1670 is the changed character of scientific controversy. Scholars had quarreled and sought to refute each other for centuries, and they went on doing so, but a new kind of controversy arose in the Age of Newton. Instead of refuting each other, scientists quarreled over who had *first* discovered or formulated an achievement which in itself was accepted by most scientists. In mathematics and astronomy scientists seemed to be making the same discoveries in many parts of Europe. Newton had several famous and bitter quarrels with other philosopher-scientists, including Leibniz, over the question of who had first developed the calculus. The calculus as such was scarcely challenged by leading scientists; the problem was who had discovered it first.

This changed character of controversy could only come about after a significant, coherent explanation of phenomena had been made and published. In the seventeenth century, discoveries, particularly in physics and astronomy, had a cumulative, "snowball" effect. The achievements of one generation of scientists led to the advances of those of later generations. A community of scientists, which was international but supported by governments, worked on essentially the same problems. In this atmosphere, then, it might be fair to assert that "it was only a matter of time" until further discoveries would be made. The emphasis on discovering slowly changed to refining and adding to already accepted knowledge or theory.

Professor A. R. Hall (1920–) of the Imperial College of Science, University of London, summarizes the elements of a new physics which Newton synthesized and surpassed. What was Newton's conception of science? How could Newton's achievements serve as a model for further scientific achievement in a way that Galileo's could not? Is Newton's conception of God traditional?

A. R. HALL: The Principate of Newton*

Clearly no one invented the theory of gravitational attraction; it grew through many diverse stages. And clearly also the genesis of the theory of *universal* gravitation is found in Kepler. Newton's hasty calculation of 1666, his later theory of the moon, and his theory of the tides, are all embryonically sketched in [Kepler's] *Astronomia Nova*. But the attraction was still specific, applicable only to heavy, earthy matter; Kepler himself did not go so far as to suppose that the sun and planets were also mutually attracting masses, or that the dynamical balance he indicated as retaining the earth and moon in their orbits with respect to each other also preserved the stability of the planetary orbits with respect to the sun. He failed, as Copernicus, Gilbert and Galileo failed, to see the full power of gravitational attraction as a cosmological concept.

* From A. R. Hall, *The Scientific Revolution, 1500–1800, the Formation of the Modern Scientific Attitude* (London: Longmans, 1954), pp. 263–74.

Nevertheless, Kepler's idea that the satellite revolving round a central body is maintained in its path by two forces, one of which is an attraction towards the central body, although applied only to the earth-moon system, holds the key to all that followed and to the *Principia* itself. Galileo, like Copernicus, had believed the planetary revolutions to be "natural," i.e. inertial; the celestial bodies were subject to no forces. Kepler, however, believed that the motive force of the universe resided in the sun which, rotating upon its own axis, "emits from itself through the extent of the Universe an immaterial image [species] of its body, analogous to the immaterial image [species] of its light, which image is itself rotated also like a most swift whirlpool and carries round with itself the bodies of the planets." Each planet, moreover, was endowed with its own "soul" which influenced its motions. Such notions confused the dynamical elements of the situation for Kepler—since the sun's force operated tangentially upon the planet, he did not imagine that a centripetal force was necessary to retain it in the orbit. In the singular case of the earth and moon, it was necessary for him to suppose that the "animal or other equivalent force" of the moon was sufficient to overcome the attraction towards the earth which would have distorted its path. This physical, attractive property of heavy matter could not as yet be made the basis of the stability of the celestial system; rather it was a disturbing feature which the cosmological properties of the heavenly bodies had to overcome.

With Descartes the position was altogether reversed. He knew that bodies in free motion move in straight lines. He knew that his planets, swirled like Kepler's in a solar vortex, would if unconstrained travel in straight lines outside its limits. He knew, therefore, that some centripetal force must bend these straight lines into the closed curves of the orbits. Rejecting Kepler's mysterious attraction, he supposed this force to be provided by the varying density of the solar vortex, which resisted the planets' natural tendency to recede towards its periphery.

After the publication of Descartes' *Principia Philosophiæ* (1644) which for the first time applied the law of inertia systematically to the planetary motions, the elements of the problem of universal gravitation were completely assembled. The essential step was to replace Descartes' conception of the nature of the centripetal force required to hold the universe together by the Keplerian idea of attraction, with the sun taken as the central body. Kepler's problem could now be approached from a completely fresh aspect: knowing that the moon must be, as it were, chained to the earth to prevent it flying off into space, might not this bond be that "corporeal affection between cognate bodies towards their union" described by Kepler? Three men, all about the year 1665, formulated this question in similar terms, and attempted to answer it: Alphonso Borelli, Robert Hooke and Isaac Newton.

Borelli, who was a member of the Accademia del Cimento, tried to find in Kepler's ideas the basis for a complete mathematico-mechanical system of the universe. He regarded the light-rays radiating from the sun as levers pressing upon the planets, revolving because the sun revolved, and able to exert a pressure because they were themselves material emanations. He explained that the least force would impart some motion to the greatest mass, and that therefore (in the absence of resistance) the planets would move with a speed proportionate to the force impressed. This, like Kepler, he supposed to become more feeble as the distance from the sun was greater, so that the outer planets would move more slowly than the inner. Instructed by Descartes, Borelli knew that under such circumstances a centripetal force was necessary to maintain the planets in their orbits, but he carefully avoided speaking of this as an *attraction* since the word was banned from the phraseology of mechanism. Nor did he identify this force with that which in the earth is called gravity. Instead, he postulated that all satellites in the celestial machine had a natural tendency or appetite to approach the central body about which they revolve—thus the planets sought the sun—an appetite constant at all distances, and not at all affecting the central body itself. The stability of the planet in its orbit was therefore conditioned by the perfect balance of the centrifugal and centripetal forces to which it was subject, and this he was able to illustrate experimentally; but Borelli was further required to explain why these orbits are elliptical, not circular. The answer is highly ingenious: Borelli imagined that each planet was created *outside* its circular orbit. In this position the excess of centripetal over centrifugal force would urge the planet to its proper distance from the sun, but the momentum acquired would carry it beyond, to a point *inside* the circular orbit. Here the centrifugal would exceed the centripetal force, and the planet would again be pressed outwards, and again carried by momentum to its former station. Then the cycle would be repeated. Thus the ellipse was a result of a slow oscillation about a stable position—a circle round the central body—compared by Borelli to the oscillation of a pendulum, to and fro, passing through a stable position at the perpendicular. This hypothesis was in accord with the observed fact that the velocity of the planet is greatest at its nearest approach to the sun.

Borelli's theory, an amalgamation of those of Kepler and Descartes, in regarding the planets as impelled by a sort of vortex centred upon the sun conceived of the universe as a driven, not a free-spinning, machine. To it the law of inertia could not be directly applied—hence Borelli's confusion concerning force and momentum. Both Hooke and Newton took two more important steps: they assumed that the planetary motions were purely inertial—the universe was a great top—and that there was a universal, mutual attraction between masses of matter. Newton, moreover, remedying the mistakes in the principles of dynamics which permeate Borelli's treatise, effected a meticulous analysis of the forces which the latter (and Hooke) had described so loosely.

There is ample evidence that by 1685 Robert Hooke had a very complete picture of a mechanical system of the universe founded on universal gravitation. In the early days of the Royal Society he performed unsuccessful experiments to discover whether gravity varies above and below the earth's surface. In *Micrographia* (1665) he conjectured that the moon might have a "gravitating principle" like the earth. In a discourse read to the Royal Society in 1666 Hooke improved on Borelli with the supposition that a "direct motion" might be inflected into a curve by "an attractive property of the body placed at the centre." Like earlier writers he compared this centripetal attraction to the tension in the string of a conical pendulum, which retains the bob in its circular path. In 1678 he wrote: "I suppose the gravitating power of the Sun in the center of this part of the Heaven in which we are, hath an attractive power upon all the planets, . . . and that those again have a respect answerable." This is the first enunciation of the true theory of universal gravitation—of gravity as a universal principle that binds all the bodies of the solar system together. The same force whereby the heavenly bodies "attract their own parts, and keep them from flying from them," also attracts "all the other celestial bodies within the sphere of this activity." It is this force which, in the sun, bends the rectilinear motions of the planets into closed curves. And this force is "the more powerful in operating, by how much nearer the body wrought upon is" to the attracting body.

These ideas, Hooke claimed, he had expounded as early as 1670. But it was not until 1679 that he hit upon a hypothesis to describe the rate at which the gravitational attraction should decrease with distance. In that year he renewed his correspondence with Newton, discussing an experiment to detect the earth's rotation through the deviation of falling bodies. This in turn led to a debate on the nature of the curve which a heavy body would describe if it were supposed to be able to fall freely towards the centre of the earth, during which (in a letter to Newton dated 6 January 1680) Hooke stated the proposition that the force of gravity is inversely proportional to the square of the distance, measured from the centre of the gravitating mass.[1] He was convinced that this "inverse square law" of attraction, combined with the ideas he had already sketched out, would be sufficient to explain all the planetary motions.

Hooke's scientific intuition was certainly brilliant. Of all the early Fellows of the Royal Society, in a generation richly endowed with genius, his was the mind most spontaneously, and sanely, imaginative; schemes for new experiments and observations occurred to him so readily that each day was divided between a multiplicity of investigations; physiology, microscopy, astronomy, chemistry, mechanics, optics, were each in rapid succession subjects for his insight and ingenuity. No topic could ever be broached without Hooke rising to make a number of pertinent points and to suggest fruitful methods of inquiry. With regard to celestial mechanics, Hooke's conception was as far-reaching as Newton's; but it was not prior and it was not proven. The publication of the *Principia,* accompanied by Hooke's charge of plagiary against Newton, inflamed the suspicion between the two men into outraged anger. Both suffered from a touchy pride; neither would recognize the true merits of the other. In Newton's eyes, Hooke grasped after other men's achievements, having merely patched together some notions borrowed from Kepler, Borelli and Huygens. To Hooke,

---

[1] Hooke thought that this same law would apply to the force of gravity below the earth's surface. Newton later proved (*Principia,* Bk. I, Prop. LXXIII) that within a sphere the centripetal force is inversely proportional to the distance from the centre, not to the square of the distance. Ismael Bouillau, in *Astronomia Philolaica* (1645), had argued that the intensity of Kepler's "moving virtue" resident in the sun would decrease, like that of light, as $\frac{1}{d^2}$. Therefore, he said, since the velocities of the planets are not in this proportion to their distances from the sun, they could not be impelled by such a force emanating from it.

Newton had merely turned into mathematical symbols ideas that he had himself already expressed without attracting notice or reward. He was ever unwilling to admit the supreme advantage that Newton held over himself, of being mathematician enough to demonstrate as a theory, confirmed by observation, that which Hooke himself had only been able to assert as a hypothesis. In fact the different status which attaches to a scientific *theory* and a scientific *hypothesis*— a difference which Newton emphasized more than once—was something to which Hooke proved himself insensitive by a number of episodes in his career. As Newton pointed out, Hooke did not invent the theory of attractive forces, as such; and after Huygens' theorems on the centrifugal acceleration of rotating masses had been published, the inverse square law could easily be deduced. Granting the highest merit to Hooke's scientific intuition, it is quite clear from certain confusions inherent in the development of his hypothesis between 1666 and 1685 that his mastery of the principles of dynamics was never completely confident, and that his thought was never safeguarded by the precision of mathematical analysis.

Newton complained, in a letter to Halley at the time when Hooke was voicing his protests before the Royal Society, that the latter wished to assign to him the status of a mathematical drudge and claim for himself the sole invention of a new system of celestial mechanics. The truth is far otherwise. By 1666 Newton was already able to calculate centrifugal accelerations. This calculation, applied to Kepler's laws, gave him the inverse square law of attraction.[2] If the earth's gravitational attaction was assumed to act upon the moon, he computed that in accordance with this law, at the distance of the moon from the earth this centripetal force would be "pretty nearly" equal to the centrifugal force created by the moon's own revolution about the earth. Gravity would be precisely the chain required to bind the moon in its orbit.[3] But such a calculation was not strictly appropriate: for a planet's (and the moon's) orbit is not circular but elliptical, with the central body (sun or earth) at one focus of the ellipse. Moreover, in calculating the distances and relative forces, Newton had proceeded as though the earth and moon were points, that is, reckoned that if the force of gravity at the surface of the earth was $\frac{g}{1}$, then at the moon it was $\frac{g}{(60)^2}$. He had not *proved* that the external gravitational attraction of a sphere could be computed as though its mass were concentrated in a point at the centre. The

---

[2] In a circle of radius r, if T is the time taken by a body to complete one revolution, the centripetal force required to hold it in its path is $F = \frac{kr}{T^2}$. But according to Kepler's Third Law, in the solar system $T^2 = k'r^3$. Substituting, $F = \frac{kr}{k'r^3}$ whence, omitting the constants, F is proportional to $\frac{1}{r^2}$.

[3] Newton's calculation in 1666 did not give a perfect confirmation of the inverse square law, because the value he took for the earth's radius (and hence the distance of the moon from the earth) was too small. It used to be supposed that this discrepancy induced him to lay the matter aside. The view given below is now generally accepted.

difficulties involved in perfecting the hypothesis upon which his first casual trial was founded were mainly mathematical, and at this time beyond Newton's skill. So great were they that Halley was astonished to learn (in 1684) that Newton had overcome them; had proved, in fact, that the path followed by a body, moving obliquely in relation to a second which exerts a centripetal force upon it, must correspond to one of the conic sections.

In 1666, therefore, Newton was not satisfied that the inverse square law represented more than an approximation to the truth. Impressed by the mathematical difficulties involved, he laid the hypothesis aside. For about thirteen years (1666–79) there is not the least evidence that he paid any attention to dynamics, universal gravitation or celestial mechanics. Optics, mathematics, alchemy and perhaps already theology, filled his mind. So much, at least, Newton owed to Hooke: that he was compelled to return to his former hypothesis. Even when driven, by Hooke's unwelcome letters, to review the mystery of gravity, he was guilty of blunders and misapprehensions. Even when, pricked by Hooke's corrections, he had solved the problem of the inverse square law and the elliptical orbit, Newton once more set his success to cool for a further five years. Only Halley's visit to Cambridge in 1684, and the warmth of his admiration and offers of assistance, set the *Principia* in train.

The book is often described as though its sole function was to establish what has been called the Newtonian system of the universe. That it did so is, indeed, its main historical importance; the Third Book and the *System of the World*, in which Newton set himself directly to this task, are likely to be read with far greater interest than the earlier sections. But Newton's influence on subsequent science, in this work alone, penetrated to a far greater depth. He defined mass and the laws of motion. He gave to science formal concepts of space and time which needed no revision for two centuries. He expounded—and exemplified— a "method of philosophizing" that is still regarded as a valid model. He virtually created theoretical physics as a mathematical science in the form which it preserved to the end of the last century. For Newton, the mathematical principles in nature were not merely evidenced by the elementary dynamics of Galileo, or even by his own majestic computations relating to the planetary motions, but were to be traced in the whole field of experimental physics and —more conjecturally—in the phenomena of light, in the constitution of matter and the operations of chemistry. Outside physics, Newton's work was never finished—it could not be finished—and his ideas remained half-formed. The *Principia,* however, is a treatise on physics almost as much as it is a treatise on celestial mechanics; and in some sections Newton made meticulous use of the quantitative experimental method. The theorems and experiments on the vibrations of pendulums in resisting media, on the free fall of bodies and the trajectory of projectiles in the same, are not perhaps of great intrinsic interest, as certainly they were of no practical importance, nor closely relevant to the motions of the planets; but it is not impossible to understand why Newton concerned himself with them. For, firstly, such problems were close to the heart of seventeenth-century physics, in a tradition which Newton himself brought to a climax. And secondly, they served to prove his point that the principles of nature are mathematical; that with number and measure science could reach beyond the uncontrolled imagination of a Descartes, or even the idealism of a Galileo. In Newton's eyes, scientific comprehension was not limited to vague qualitative theories on the one hand, or definite statements about a state of affairs much simpler than that which is actually experienced on the other; it could proceed, by due techniques, to definite ideas about all that is physical, down to the properties of each constituent corpuscle. To illustrate this conception of science is the purpose of the *Principia*.

Otherwise, both logically and emotionally, the framework of celestial mechanics would have been without foundation. Here Newton and Descartes were more alike than the crude antithesis of their cosmologies would allow. Descartes had proceeded, in the *Principles of Philosophy,* from his clear ideas of what must be, through the laws of motion and the properties of moving bodies, to his celestial mechanism. Newton likewise: developing his mathematical method from the definitions and the laws of motion, through the long analyses of the motions of bodies in many different circumstances until he could discern in the heavenly motions special cases of those principles of motion that he had already elucidated. Newton perceived, as Descartes had done, as Huygens did when he all but abandoned Descartes, that a theory which attributed the most noble and enduring phenomena in nature to the play of mechanical forces could not stand on a handful of assumptions, two or three happy computations and the vague, undemonstrative, mechanistic philosophy that had become fashionable. Like Descartes, but with an infinitely more subtle logic, with all the rigour of mathematics and with cautious appeal to observation and experiment, Newton displayed the whole science of matter-in-motion before he turned to the solar system specifically. An unfinished treatise, *De Motu Corporum,* preceded the *Principia;* the study of a particle in motion must precede that of a circling planet. And if Newton found it necessary to investigate the solid of least resistance, or the flow of liquids, it was to prove the universality of that science of moving particles that he proposed to apply, not to a minute part, but to the whole of man's physical environment. The *Principia,* in fact, does not expound a particular scientific theory to account for the motions of the heavens: it develops a theory of physical nature which embraces these phenomena, and all phenomena of matter-in-motion, within its compass.

As such it was, of course, a mechanistic theory. No other was, or is, conceivable within the range of physics. Not that Newton excluded God from the universe:

This most beautiful system of the sun, planets, and comets, could only proceed from the counsel and dominion of an intelligent and powerful Being. . . . He endures forever, and is everywhere present; and by existing always and everywhere, he constitutes duration and space.

God was for Newton the Final Cause of things, but, excellent and laborious theologian as he was, he made no confusion between physics and theology. That Newton seemed, by the theory of universal gravitation, to contravene the principles of mechanism, was due to misapprehension. Though certain phrases in the *Principia* might seem to indicate the contrary, he did not believe that gravity was an innate property of matter, nor that two masses could attract each other at a distance without having any mechanical relationship. To Bentley Newton wrote:

It is inconceivable that inanimate brute matter should, without the mediation of something else, which is not material, operate upon and affect other matter without mutual contact. . . . That gravity should be innate, inherent, and essential to matter, so that one body may act upon another at a distance through a vacuum, without the mediation of anything else, by and through which their action and force may be conveyed from one to another, is to me so great an absurdity that I believe no man who has in philosophical matters a competent faculty of thinking, can ever fall into it.

He added to the second edition of the *Principia* a brief statement that by *attraction* he meant only to describe the tendency of bodies to approach each other, no matter what the cause. As to the probable nature of this cause, he professed himself ignorant. It was sufficient to infer that the phenomenon existed and was universal; like Galileo, Newton regarded the effect as established if it could be described, though the cause were hidden. To suppose that particles or masses exert a gravitational attraction was not, therefore, in Newton's language to postulate an occult quality in matter but to describe a fact— a fact that was to be demonstrated in the laboratory by Henry Cavendish seventy years after Newton's death. Nor did Newton believe that the celestial spaces across which the sun's attraction holds the planets in their orbits were necessarily empty of all matter.

His refusal to ascribe a cause or mechanism to universal gravitation was indeed one of Newton's principal advantages in celestial mechanics. He was free, as the Cartesians were not, simply to state and analyse the observable facts, and the inferences necessarily drawn from them. He did not seek to construct a model which would be rendered clumsy and contradictory by the very attempt to explain everything in nature by corpuscular mechanisms.

Hypotheses [wrote Newton], whether metaphysical or physical, whether of occult qualities or mechanical, have no place in experimental philosophy. . . .[4] And to us it is enough that gravity does really exist, and act according to laws which we have explained, and abundantly serves to account for all the motions of the celestial bodies, and of our sea.

The concluding paragraph of this *General Scholium* indicated a possible solution of many "occult" mysteries, fully in the seventeenth-century mechanical tradition. For,

We might add something concerning a most subtle spirit which pervades and lies hid in all gross bodies; by the force and action of which spirit the particles of bodies attract one another at near distances, and cohere, if contiguous; and electric

---

[4] Newton, of course, did not mean that tentative hypotheses have no use in an investigation; he framed many such himself. He meant that an unconfirmed and undemonstrated hypothesis should not be taught as an adequate theory.

bodies operate to greater distances . . .; and light is emitted, reflected, inflected, and heats bodies; and all sensation is excited, and the members of animal bodies move at the command of the will. . . .

Newton's imagination was not less generous than that of Descartes, though less dogmatic. He was as fully convinced of the existence of an *æther*, the residuum of the major secrets of nature, as Descartes or any nineteenth-century physicist. Further hints were to be given years later in the *Queries* appended to the *Opticks*, but Newton did not know how these things could be investigated, much less proved.

Nevertheless, his attitude (less plain certainly in the first edition of the *Principia* than it has since become) was widely misunderstood. Newtonian empiricism was rapidly accepted by his own countrymen: probably no scientist has received a more immediate, or a warmer, acclaim from the intellectuals as well as the professed scientists of his race. Abroad it was distrusted. Neither Huygens nor Leibniz (who set the tone for many lesser men) could stomach the downright statement of Proposition VII, Book III.[5] Attempts to reconcile the Cartesian mechanical theory of celestial vortices with Newtonian mathematical laws were prolonged into the mid-eighteenth century. Not until fifty years after the publication of the *Principia* did Voltaire's proclamation of his admiration for the profound English geniuses, Newton and Locke, begin to win adherents. The essential truth, that Newton and Descartes shared the same idea of nature, was thus long obscured; and Newton has perhaps been too often praised for being other than he was. The idol of perfection who was endowed by the nineteenth century with every attribute of scientific insight and vigour, with abhorrence of hypothesis and mystery, with serene temper and conventional religion, was not the genuine Newton. It is perhaps paradoxical—but not unjust—that his greatest successor was to arise not from the crowd of reverend English gentlemen who were to claim Newton as their own, but in the person of the sceptical French mathematician, the Marquis de Laplace, whose *Mécanique Céleste* (1799–1825) extended in time the laws that Newton had traced in space.

5.

The ancient Greeks had asked questions about the age of the world and the universe, but their answers came to nothing for modern man. Yet it was this question along with a curiosity about minerals which became the basis of the science of geology. There were few hints in the ancient texts, and no achievement such as Galen's in anatomy, for example, to stimulate speculation and research in geology.

In these circumstances is it surprising that geology developed much later than physics, the biological sciences, and chemistry? Not until after 1750 had a perspective on the age of the world appeared which would provide a basis for geology. The Judeo-Christian conceptions of the creation of the universe

5 "That there is a power of gravity pertaining to all bodies, proportional to the several quantities of matter which they contain."

and its supposed short life also blinded scientists so that they did not speculate on the age of the universe. Indeed, mountains, valleys, and oceans were
thought to have existed unchanged since the creation as told in the Bible.

Stephen Toulmin (1922–   ) of Brandeis University and June Goodfield
(1927–   ), his wife, recount the early history of scientific research on the age
of the earth. Were there any connections between developments in geology
and those in physics? What had undermined the Renaissance conception of
Nature? How is geology both science and history?

STEPHEN TOULMIN AND JUNE GOODFIELD: The Earth Acquires a History*

During the second half of the eighteenth century, philosophical debate had
shown the possibility of replacing the static Renaissance view of Nature by a
dynamic, developmental one. But philosophy alone could not dispatch the older
time-scale finally: for that, an alternative numerical chronology had to be
worked out from the evidence of scientific observation. Now it was up to the
natural scientists to carry this possibility into effect, and to demonstrate how the
natural world could have acquired its present form through the lapse of time.
So, by A.D. 1800, geologists and zoologists were once again attacking the fundamental questions posed originally by Anaximander and his fellow-Ionians, at
Miletos some 2300 years before. In the event, the first branch of natural science
to become genuinely historical was geology: the crucial battle between scrip-
tural chronology, based on human traditions, and natural chronology, based on
"the testimony of things," was fought out over the history of the Earth. If our
ideas about the past are now no longer restricted within the time-barrier of
earlier ages, this is due above all to the patience, industry and originality of
those men who, between 1750 and 1850, created a new and vastly extended
time-scale, anchored in the rock strata and fossils of the Earth's crust.

This is not to say that the *motives* of the first modern geologists were universally, or even predominantly, historical ones. To begin with, many of them
were concerned only to study the present make-up of the Earth's crust, classify
the different rocks, and see whether any consistent order could be found in the
strata of different countries and regions; and often enough the reasons for their
interest in such questions were practical ones—for geology has always been
largely an applied science, allied to mining and metallurgy. The historical
significance of their new knowledge dawned on them only gradually. Initially,
they scarcely recognized that the Earth had a history at all: at any rate, anything
more than was contained within the story of the Creation and the Deluge. But,
even before 1800, discoveries were accumulating which, on the older view, were
frank anomalies. Some of these, like the fossil marine shells found in inland
rocks, had been known since the classical era: others, like the extinct volcanoes
of the French *Massif Central,* were now recognized for the first time. Either way,
these anomalies served as pin-pricks to men's confidence in the Creation-story

* From Stephen Toulmin and June Goodfield, *The Discovery of Time* (New York: Harper
and Row, 1965), pp. 141–52.

and the accepted time-scale. Unless those were called in question, it was equally embarrassing to explain the geological origin of the anomalous formations, or to dismiss them as incomprehensible survivals from the original Creation. Once the fact of geological change had been admitted, questions about the temporal sequence of these changes were inescapable: what agencies were responsible, whether they were the same as those now acting, how long they had taken to produce their visible effects. In their turn, these historical questions led to further research, and so to more discoveries, which rebounded once again on inherited ideas and assumptions. So observation and theory snowballed, and a brand-new temporal framework was gradually forced on men.

During the hundred years of this progressive erosion and resynthesis, men lived with uncertainties as profound, and dilemmas as agonizing, as those provoked earlier by Copernicus' reforms in astronomy. In some ways, the situation was even more difficult. The new geology could never hope to achieve the kind of mathematical certainty which Newton's theories stamped upon the new astronomy: like a successful piece of criminal detection, it carried conviction only through the cumulative weight of circumstantial evidence. And, as in the Copernican revolution, though the outlines of the new system were discerned early, it superseded the older one only when it had been worked out in detail and established unanswerably. In such an intellectual situation, this type of pattern is probably inevitable. Where the issues are so profound, it is not enough to throw doubt on older ideas. An alternative account must be presented which is equally complete and more convincing; and, until this is done, men cannot be blamed for being tenacious of long-cherished traditions. . . .

By 1750, men were beginning to recognize that the present face of the world might carry enduring traces dating from much earlier, even prehuman times; and that, if only we could interpret them, these traces would provide evidence about the past as direct and reliable as any human tradition. But the problem of interpretation was still as much of a challenge as ever. Human records might be corrupt, and so untrustworthy, but at any rate they were "testimony" in the literal sense of the term: that is, undisguised assertions about the past. Rock-strata or fossils provided "testimony" only in a transferred sense: their present forms served as clues to events in former epochs only for men whose scientific principles gave them a basis for interpretation. The question was still, as it had always been, "What kind of principles can justify retrospective inferences, and so provide an intellectual bridge back to the past?"

The men who now attacked this question relied on two main lines of argument, one broader, the other narrower. Some attempted to fit geology into Newton's all-embracing framework of physical laws. Given the properties and dimensions of the planet on which we live, what (they asked) do the principles of Newtonian physics imply about its earlier history? Others proceeded in a more piecemeal way. By studying in detail the structure of the Earth's surface, they hoped to reconstruct the successive stages by which the Earth acquired its present form. If each different type of rock or fossil could be persuaded to tell its own story, these separate testimonies should combine to give a consistent account of the Earth's development. Later, a third line of argument was added, based on biological principles rather than physical ones, and the intellectual claims of the modern, extended time-scale were finally established by the resultant interweaving of geological considerations with evolutionary ones.

The first excursion into the physical history of the Earth to result in serious numerical estimates of past time was published in the 1770s by that striking, prolific and courageous figure, Georges Louis Leclerc, Comte de Buffon. Buffon had no hesitations. He never doubted that the Earth had in fact a long history, nor that the task of reconstructing it was within the capacities of the human reason, and his overall programme of enquiries has outlived all his detailed arguments. For he analysed with great elegance the scientific problems which the "time-barrier" posed for natural historians, and he established convincingly that, even on the most restrictive assumptions, a geological history based on the established principles of physics would extend the scale of our chronology to 168,000 years, at the very least. (His own private estimate was nearer half a million years.)

Like Aristotle and Linnaeus, Buffon was less an individual scientist than a committee, and his library was the centre for a wide circle of correspondents. His *Natural History* was a life-work: the first three volumes were published in 1749, and the series was not complete when he died in 1788, just before the French Revolution. Buffon had aimed to produce a scientific encyclopaedia dealing in succession with the planetary system, the Earth, the human race and the different kingdoms of living creatures: at the time of his death, his published volumes had got as far as the birds, and he was in the middle of cataloguing the fishes. Described so baldly, his achievement may sound pedestrian, but in fact he saw this multitudinous mass of detail in relation to a wider—and an original —scheme of ideas. Furthermore, his books contain long and penetrating digressions about scientific theory and method, and so read at times like a scientific *Tristram Shandy:* any curious and intriguing fact of nature (say, the sterility of mules) is liable to be an occasion for a far-ranging theoretical argument. Still, behind these apparent irrelevancies, there is an underlying system. His books cover some forty years of a busy career, and these theoretical asides show his point of view developing from decade to decade, in the light of new discoveries and controversies.

Buffon's conception of *Histoire Naturelle* embraced what we are here calling the history of Nature. His early hypothesis about the origin of the Solar System was intended to be the opening instalment of a story which would cover cosmological, geological and zoological development. These plans were, however, frustrated by the theologians of the Sorbonne, and he was compelled to issue a formal retraction. For the next twenty-five years Buffon kept his unorthodox speculations to himself, but by 1774 he felt sufficiently secure to return to the dangerous topics. In his *Introduction to the History of Minerals,* he described a comprehensive series of experiments on the rates at which spheres of different sizes and substances cooled down; and in a long appendix he calculated the times needed for the different planets and their satellites to cool from a white heat to an inhabitable temperature. He wrote without apology, just as though his *Theory of the Earth* had never been condemned. His purpose was concealed partly by the laboriousness of his arithmetic, partly by a mollifying heading (*partie hypothétique*). Reassured by the reception of this *Introduction* he followed it in 1778 with a fuller account of the successive *Epochs of Nature* through which the Earth had presumably developed.

The fundamental problem for the history of Nature has never been more clearly formulated than it was in his opening words:

Just as in civil history we consult warrants, study medallions, and decipher ancient inscriptions, in order to determine the epochs of the human revolutions and fix the dates of moral events, so in natural history one must dig through the archives of the world, extract ancient relics from the bowels of the earth, gather together their fragments, and assemble again in a single body of proofs all those indications of the physical changes which can carry us back to the different Ages of Nature. This is the only way of fixing certain points in the immensity of space, and of placing a number of milestones on the eternal path of time.

The past is like distance: our view of it would shrink and even be lost entirely, if history and chronology had not marked the darkest points by beacons and torches. Yet despite these lights of written tradition, let us go back a few centuries, and how uncertain are our facts! How confused are the causes of events! And what profound darkness enshrouds the periods before that tradition! Besides, it tells us only about the deeds of a few nations, i.e. the doings of a very small part of mankind: the rest of the human race is as nothing, either for us or for posterity. Thus civil history, bounded on one side by the darkness of a period not far distant from our own, embraces in the other direction only those small areas of the Earth which have been occupied in succession by peoples mindful of their own tradition. Natural history, on the other hand, embraces in its scope all regions of space and all periods equally, and has no limits other than those of the universe.

However unchanging Nature might appear to human eyes, the Earth's present state was without question very different from its original one; and, during the intervening period, it must have passed through several other phases, occupying longer or shorter times. These periods he called *epochs,* and the problem was to reconstruct them, using evidence of three different kinds:

The surface of the Earth has taken different forms in succession; even the heavens have changed, and all the objects in the physical world are, like those of the moral world, caught up in a continual process of successive variations . . .

But so as to pierce the night of past time—to recognize by a study of existing objects the former existence of those which have been destroyed, and work our way back to this historic truth of buried facts by the force of existing facts alone; so as to judge (in short) not merely the recent past, but also the more remote, on the basis of the present alone . . . we shall employ three prime resources: (i) those facts which can take us back to the origin of Nature; (ii) those relics which must be regarded as evidence of earlier eras; (iii) those traditions which can give us some idea about subsequent eras—after which we shall attempt to link them all together by comparisons, so as to form a single chain descending from the zenith of the scale of time down to ourselves.

By "facts," he meant those physical properties on which he founded his arguments about the cooling of the planets; by "relics," he meant such things as fossils, shells and mammoth-bones; and, by referring also to "traditions," he hoped to forestall the inevitable religious opposition—attempting to harmonize his scientific ideas with the Old Testament, by judiciously reinterpreting the opening chapters of *Genesis*. The *Book of Genesis* (he argued) had not been written for scientists, but for the unlearned. The Days of Creation could not have been "days" such as we know now—of twenty-four hours each—since the very succession of day and night was established only on the third "day," after the creation of the Sun. Rather, we should read the Biblical word "days" as referring to periods of indefinite length, about whose exact duration Moses had not committed himself. In this way we could rescue *Genesis* from all danger of contradicting the facts of Nature and the conclusions of reason.

With this preamble, Buffon launched into an account of the geological epochs corresponding to the seven Days of Creation. These epochs had lengths ranging from 3000 to 35,000 years: in all, the Earth's history had by now occupied some 75,000 years, and a further 93,000 remained before life would be extinguished by cold. For the first epoch, he revived his theory about a near-collision between the Sun and a passing comet; in the second, he supposed the Earth to have solidified, with the greater part of the fusible rocks on the surface; during the third, all the continents were covered with water; fourthly, the oceans withdrew, and volcanoes built up the land; during the fifth epoch, tropical animals were spread across the whole Earth; in the sixth, the different continents separated; and finally, in the seventh and last epoch, one reached the period of Man's existence.

Taken separately, none of Buffon's chief steps was entirely new. Descartes had spoken of the planets as having formed out of incandescent stars, Leibniz had developed this idea further in his *Protogea,* and even Newton had used the same idea to explain the flattening of the Earth at the Poles. (This was the result of centrifugal action while the planet was still hot and plastic.) The idea of interpreting the Days of Creation as geological epochs had been hinted at in the 1690s, during the discussion prompted by Burnet's *Sacred History of the Earth.* Again, Benoit de Maillet's posthumous dialogue, *Telliamed,* had foreshadowed Buffon's extension of the time-scale: the "Indian sage" into whose mouth de Maillet put his own original speculations had insisted that we should not "fix a beginning to that which perhaps never had one. Let us not measure the past duration of the world by that of our own years." Finally, Buffon's experiments on cooling were consciously modelled on those by which Newton had established the basic laws governing the rate at which bodies lose heat. In fact, Newton had gone so far as to enquire, in an incidental note, how long it would take for an iron sphere the size of the Earth to cool down from red heat, and had arrived at an answer comparable to Buffon's—*viz.*: 50,000 years. For once, Newton's calculations led to a result that he could not square with his religious convictions, and he unhesitatingly rejected it: there must be something wrong with his calculation—perhaps his assumption that a large sphere would cool very much more slowly than a small one—and he added: "I should be glad that the true ratio was investigated by experiments."

What distinguished Buffon's *Epochs of Nature* was the cumulative weight of his whole argument. He drew together into a unified whole half a dozen ideas which had previously been thrown out independently. Furthermore, he patiently settled down to work out, in numerical terms, the actual periods of time demanded by a physical theory of the Earth's development. To summarize his 1774 figures for the Earth's cooling:

If we suppose, as all the phenomena seem to indicate, that the earth was once in a state of liquefaction caused by fire, our experiments then prove that, if the globe was entirely made of iron or of ferrous matter, it would have solidified as far as the centre only after 4,026 years, cooled to a point at which it could be touched without burning after 46,991 years; and that it would not have cooled to the present temperature until after 100,696 years. But since the earth, so far as we know it, seems to be made up of fusible and calcareous materials which cool in a shorter time than ferrous materials, it is necessary, so as to get as close as possible to the truth, to allow for the respective times of cooling of these different materials, such as we have found them to be in our experiments . . . [So] one finds that the terrestrial globe will have solidified to the centre in 2,905 years approximately, cooled to the point at which one could touch it in 33,911 years approximately, and to the present temperature in 74,047 years approximately.

This last figure he adjusted to 74,832 years, to allow for the effects of the Sun's radiant heat. Using similar arguments, he worked out how long all the different planets and their satellites must have taken to reach habitable temperatures.

These calculations may have been over-simplified, but they were a beginning. Newton could not explain how the globe became habitable after no more than a few centuries, as the Biblical time-scale required. Buffon replied that it could not possibly have done so, short of an arbitrary and unreasonable supernatural intervention. No doubt his own figures were far greater than those commonly believed to possess Biblical authority, but one must not fly in the face of reason. Men were no longer intimidated by the vast distances of Space, nor did they find it difficult to imagine (e.g.) one hundred thousand pounds in money; why, then, should their minds recoil from the idea of seventy or a hundred thousand *years?* In fact, the figures he calculated were the absolute minimum required for the formation of the Earth; and, if they were hard to grasp, we must simply remind ourselves that

there is no difference [in authority] between the truths that God has revealed [in scripture], and those which He has permitted us to discover by observation and enquiry.

In one respect, Buffon remained a typical eighteenth-century natural philosopher. For all the modernity of his tone and his arguments, he took it for granted that "whatever can exist, does exist": it was enough to calculate when each of the bodies in the solar system would reach a temperature capable of supporting life, and thereupon life had presumably appeared. Like Fontenelle before him, he treated the plurality of worlds as implying a plurality of *inhabited* worlds:

(i) Organized nature as we know it, is not yet born on Jupiter, whose heat is still too great today for one to touch its surface, and it will only be in 40,791 years [i.e. 115,623–74,832] that living creatures will be able to subsist there, but thereafter once established they would last 367,498 years on that large planet;

(ii) living nature, as we know it, has been extinct on the fifth satellite of Saturn for the last 27,274 years; on Mars, for the last 14,506 years, and on the Moon for the last 2,318 years; [etc. etc.] . . .

[Hence my belief in] the real existence of organized and sensible beings on all the bodies of the solar system, and the more-than-likely existence of the same beings on all the other bodies making up the systems of other suns, so augmenting and multiplying almost to infinity the extent of living Nature, and at the same time raising the greatest of all monuments to the glory of the Creator.

By our standards, of course, Buffon's calculations had given the Earth not too long, but far too short a life. Where did his physics go astray? He acknowledged that the present temperature of any planet or satellite must be determined by two separate factors—the radiant heat falling on ,it from the Sun, and the residual heat remaining from its original molten state—and he did his best to estimate the relative contributions of these two factors. In the 1770s the laws of normal cooling were well established, but radiant heat was little understood: Buffon mistakenly decided that the effects of solar radiation were of secondary importance as compared with the Earth's residual heat. He would have reached a more accurate result if he had assumed the exact reverse. The present temperature of a planet or satellite depends almost entirely on the amount of incoming solar radiation: to a first approximation, one can neglect the heat coming from the interior of the planet itself. This fact became evident soon after 1800, when physicists began to study radiant heat seriously, and within forty years of their original publication Buffon's calculations were completely undercut by the new ones of Fourier.

Scientifically, then, Buffon's pioneer attempt to estimate the age of the Earth by appeal to physical principles had been a failure. His religious compromise, equally, had satisfied none of the parties affected. So, in retrospect, the *Epochs of Nature* may seem at best a magnificent ruin. Yet, this verdict would be unjust. Buffon's figures were wrong; but his was the voice of the future, and—above all—his books were very widely read. Moreover, his calculations had proved the essential point: that the time-barrier could be breached. By invoking the laws governing familiar physical processes, such as cooling, one might infer the former state of things from the present face of Nature, and determine the dates of physical events far earlier than the first human records. If Buffon had lived to see the next fifty years of geology, he would have been well content, for by the 1820s literal-minded fundamentalism was in full retreat, and the defenders of orthodoxy were thankful to take refuge in his own interpretation of the Days of Creation. The details of his argument could go overboard: he had made the points that mattered. As things turned out, Buffon's own theories about the age of the Earth made little immediate contribution to geology proper, and the cosmological approach to the subject soon went out of fashion. For his was a speculative and roundabout way of arguing, in which the history of the Earth was deduced indirectly from a general theory of the planetary system, rather than being pieced together directly from the actual evidence of geological exploration. The results might carry a certain abstract conviction to Newtonian natural philosophers, but they had no great relevance to the experience of practical men, and they were not easily reconciled with the ideas such men inherited from their predecessors. Indeed, as we shall see later, until well into the twentieth century certain glaring discrepancies remained between physical cosmology on the one hand, and zoology and geology on the other.

Meanwhile, however, other men were scrutinizing the Earth's surface directly, and beginning to enquire about the agencies that had shaped it into its present form. At first—as we said—they were not moved by historical curiosity: they were concerned merely to map the rock-strata found in the Earth's crust at different places, and to discover whether there was any common sequence in the formations overlaying one another in different countries and regions. It was some time before the discovery of a widespread *geographical* order in the nature of the crust came to be recognized as evidence of a *temporal* order in the processes by which the rocks had come into existence—instead of being accepted unquestioningly as the pattern imposed at the original Creation. And it took most of a century for geologists to establish what agencies had been involved in these processes of formation, to discover how one might compare the ages of strata geographically distant from one another, and to build up a consistent history of the Earth's crust from the evidence of its present form and fossil content.

To begin with, there were two chief centres of geological research, one in Germany, the other in France. Ever since mediaeval times, German craftsmen had been building up a tradition of mineralogy and mining, and this practical aspect marked the first German contributions to the new science. Anyone with first-hand experience of mining technique knew something about the stratification of rock-layers, and much was done to lay the foundations for geology by simply describing and naming the different types of rock and rock-strata. The chief leader in this work was the Saxon geologist, A. G. Werner. Like Boerhaave, Werner was one of the supreme scientific teachers, who made his mark primarily by stimulating the interest of his students; and as with that other great teacher, Linnaeus, the men who learned from him were won over by his intimate and detailed mastery over his subject-matter, rather than because of his theoretical penetration. In geology as much as in zoology and botany, what the eighteenth century demanded was a comprehensive and orderly classification, together with a precise nomenclature. These Werner provided: he classified the superimposed rock-strata into four or five main types, and several dozen subdivisions—ranging from granite and gneiss, in which fossils were never found, up through the various fossil-bearing strata to the sands, clays and volcanic lava of the surface layers—and he saw that the superposition of layers must have a historical significance also, the fossil-bearing rocks being younger than the granite, and the superficial rocks being the most recent of all.

In France, meanwhile, other historical clues were coming to light. In 1751, J. E. Guettard stopped at Montélimar on his way back from a journey throughout southern Italy. His attention was caught by the fact that the paving of the streets was of a type of stone—hexagonal basalt—strikingly like some which he had seen in the volcanic regions around Vesuvius, and that the milestones and even some of the local buildings were also made of volcanic-looking stone. He enquired where this stone had come from, and was directed into the mountains west of the Rhône. Here he found a region of steep river valleys, containing dramatic cliffs of basalt "organ-pipes," and leading to a central plateau dominated by a range of conical peaks. One of these mountains was the Puy de Dôme, the site of Pascal's experiments on atmospheric pressure. In the neighbouring village of Volvic, men had been quarrying a durable black stone for centuries. It had been used to build the cathedral at Clermont Ferrand, and is still used for milestones on French roads to this day. Until Guettard arrived, however, the quarries of Volvic and the neighbouring peaks had kept their most important secret, which could be discerned only by men who looked at them with the right questions in mind. As Guettard immediately realized, the surrounding mountain peaks were the cones of extinct volcanoes, and the paths of their ancient lava-streams could be clearly seen in the surrounding countryside. One had only to strip off the surface disguise of top-soil and vegetation, and the whole region was recognizable as a vast area shaped by volcanic action.

Like the first deciphering of a hitherto-unintelligible script, Guettard's discovery precipitated a chain of others. Once the first step was taken, everything else fell neatly into place. During the decades that followed, similar regions of extinct volcanoes were recognized in a dozen parts of the world, many of them associated with the hexagonal basalt characteristic of Giants' Causeways. Yet the puzzle remained: if the time-span of the world was really less than 6000 years, how could such violent volcanic action have gone on unrecorded? It seemed impossible that all these formidable eruptions could have taken place during the short span of time before the earliest human records. Faced with evidence such as this men were gradually driven towards the conclusion which they had so long resisted: that the present phase in the Earth's history was only the most recent in a series of prolonged epochs, and that the face of the globe had changed radically from age to age.

11

COMMERCIAL CAPITALISM
AND SOCIAL CHANGE

IN 1789 EUROPEAN economic life was somewhat less agrarian and the population less land bound than it had been in 1500. But how great or extensive were these economic and social changes, and what was their impact on society? Even more important, how can these changes be defined, and how do we explain them?

The countries on the North Atlantic coast, with the exception of Spain and Scandinavia, underwent the greatest changes. The fact that the west of France witnessed a greater economic expansion than her eastern portion tempts us to assert that Atlantic trade including the colonial trade, more than anything else, changed the European economy.

On the other hand, if we look at Europe as a whole, the striking feature is continuity, not change. Eastern Europe remained a vast area of fields and peasants with very little manufacturing or commercial activity. Southern Italy, southern France, and Spain remained virtually unchanged over three and even more centuries.

A third observation is that some of the areas where urban-commercial centers had flourished in medieval times declined after about 1550. The city states of northern and central Italy, with their tremendous head start in the techniques of using capital and in industrial-commercial organization, actually declined. Why was it not the first area to witness an industrial revolution? The decline seems to have been uneven but nonetheless steady; as the Levantine trade dwindled, Venetian merchants became gentleman-farmers. Economic growth was also uneven in the Netherlands, that other major medieval trade center. Flanders suffered a setback in the seventeenth century when Amsterdam replaced Antwerp as the commercial capital of Western Europe. During that century a prodigious economic expansion gave the Dutch the highest per capita living standard in Europe; but, as formerly in Italy, the high rate of growth was not sustained. This unevenness of development, this lack of continuity between early starts toward urban-commercial economies, and the final outcome—modern economic life—raises difficult questions for historians.

And what about the social effects of the continuity of agrarian life? The social changes on the land—for example, the subjection of Eastern European peasants into serfdom—had consequences as great as, if not greater than, those social changes occurring on the Atlantic coast as a result of commercial capitalism.

The horizon of perhaps 90 per cent of Europeans in 1789 differed very little from that of their medieval ancestors. The same villages, fields, vineyards, forests, olive groves, and pastures met their eye. And do we speak of manorialism as an eighteenth-century phenomenon? Of course not. But this does not mean that it did not exist. Again, to characterize change is a question of emphasis and significance. Most economic historians who interpret this period tend, at least until recently, to stress the changes, which were the first signs of modern economic life, rather than the continuity.

In 1789 only a tiny portion, less than 1 per cent, of the European land mass was covered by towns and all-weather roads or canals; barely five cities could boast of being populous enough to cover areas having a diameter of more than three miles. Only London and Paris had populations greater than half a million; these two cities, if combined, would not have been significantly larger than Minneapolis and St. Paul, Minnesota, today.

Peasants and farmers living near towns felt urban influences in a way not unlike those of medieval times. "Putting out" still supplemented incomes from small gardens yielding tiny crops, and the urban market also affected the type and price of those crops; but apart from these traditional influences and perhaps a greater amount of "enclosing" in England, the character of life changed little.

Where, then, were the changes, and why did they occur? Economists since laissez-faire theorists like Smith and Ricardo have been asserting that capital is the single most important element in the transformation of an agrarian society into a commercial and industrial one. There are other factors too, of course, but savings or some form of wealth which can be invested in ships and goods is indispensable.

How is capital acquired? This question has preoccupied economists; historians, and rightly so, have been preoccupied with what a society *does* with it once it is acquired. To answer the question of how capital was utilized, historians examine the patterns of expenditure made by various social groups. They must give evidence and precise data to back up vague generalizations. For example, noblemen supposedly spent more on clothes, paintings, and houses than they invested in commerce. Historians must test such an assertion by analyzing the evidence for different countries and historical periods. How did the nobles' capital investment affect the balance between agrarian and urban economies? It is equally necessary to determine who is a nobleman.

The patterns of investment by merchants are not as simple to perceive as might be supposed. Not all their wealth went into profit-seeking. They bought far more land, bonds, houses, and works of art than was once thought. Here, as with every other social group, national and regional differences make it impossible to generalize for all of Europe. Even so, in seeking the origins of modern economies, it is essential to attempt to find a pattern connecting the utilization of capital with social change.

1.

Miss Violet Barbour (1884–   ), Emeritus Professor of History at Vassar College, defines the mentality and interests of the great Dutch merchants of the seventeenth century.

Miss Barbour argues that the Dutch, with the exception of trading in actions, or stocks, failed to develop new techniques for investing or accumulating capital. Their trade was extensive—the world was their market—yet no spectacular innovations led to sustained growth. Surely it was not for lack of capital. What political developments, such as the rise of France under Louis XIV, may have curtailed economic growth in the United Provinces? Miss Barbour hints at other explanations, chiefly social ones, which also may tell why an industrial revolution did not occur in the Netherlands in the seventeenth century. Then, too, the emphasis on commerce with far-off places, rather than on trade and manufacture at home, may have, as in the case of Venice, led to a dead end or to a new kind of imperialism.

VIOLET BARBOUR: Characteristics of Amsterdam Capitalism*

The cosmopolitan spirit and geographical dispersion of certain merchant families whose business headquarters were in Amsterdam, interestingly foreshadowed the international histories of later capitalist families. The international capitalist from his earliest to his latest appearance has generally been, where business was concerned, a Man without a Country, and the seventeenth-century Amsterdammer, though by no means a man without a city, was strikingly uninhibited by abstract considerations of patriotism or by theories of economic nationalism. One can understand why this was so. In the historic past the loyalty of Netherlanders had centered more strongly in province or town than in such widespread and remote-seeming sovereignties as Burgundy, the Empire, or "the Spains"; and in the seventeenth century these local loyalties were still stronger than any as yet commanded by the loose confederation of the United Provinces. But in this century of warring religious convictions, many successful merchant dynasties of Amsterdam had, in coming there, sacrificed their allegiances to native towns and provinces on the altar of conscience. Their first loyalty was to creed. For economic nationalism the country was too small and too poor in natural resources. Though complaints were occasionally voiced that Hollanders were too greedy for riches to put their money into trade, industry, or land, and therefore invested their funds in foreign countries, it is probable that trade, industry and agriculture got all the capital they could use with prospect of profit.

The extraordinarily dense population of Holland, which amazed foreign visitors, lived by trade and activities stemming from trade, and could not long forego intercourse with any trading country, whether friend or foe. Trade with the enemy must contribute to war with the enemy. Why make a present of that trade to Hamburg or England? The great profits to be derived from contraband trade lent cogency to this argument. During the war with Spain Amsterdam merchants had not only traded with the enemy—that was common enough— but had invested in Dunkirk privateers which preyed on Dutch shipping. Laurens de Geer, Swedish subject yet burgher of Amsterdam, was suspected of selling munitions to England during the first Anglo-Dutch war. In 1659, a year when both the Dutch navy and the merchant fleet were in great need of tar, the brothers Trip declined to sell their holdings of that indispensable com-

* From Violet Barbour, *Capitalism in Amsterdam in the Seventeenth Century* (Baltimore: Johns Hopkins University Press, 1950), pp. 130–42.

modity except at monopoly prices, and in the meantime were shipping out consignments of tar, some of which may have reached the enemy. As we have seen, the contract to exploit the republic's dependence on Swedish munitions was signed on the eve of the second war with England. Amsterdam did not refrain from providing cordage and sailcloth for the English navy during the English wars. The terrible famine which struck at defeated France in 1709, was relieved by a fleet of Dutch grain-carriers from the Baltic, in which some principal merchants of Amsterdam were said to be interested. Financing the enemy was easier than trade with the enemy, movements of credit and even of coin being more difficult to trace than movements of ships. Credits necessary to keep the French armies on foot were remitted from Amsterdam by exchange on Geneva, thence to Lyon, and so to Paris. Specie consignments were made to bankers in the Spanish Netherlands, thence to find their way into the towns recently annexed by France.

Amsterdam was incurably cooperative towards foreign companies, including those founded to supplant the Dutch in important branches of their trade. In successive French attempts to open a trade to the East Indies, Dutchmen had some part, and Amsterdam was somewhere in the background. Thus in the East India Company projected by Gérard de Roy, who had made a voyage or voyages to the East, presumably in one of the expeditions sent out from Amsterdam by the *vóórcompagniën,* moving spirits were Balthasar de Moucheron of Middelburg, Pieter Lintgens, a Hollander, and Isaac Le Maire, ex-Antwerpenaar settled in Amsterdam, who had subscribed f. 60,000 to the stock of the United East India Company of 1602, but had later been expelled from that company. We have met him before as speculator in the company's actions. In the grand but still-born project of Richelieu for a general company for trade and colonization, we find the Hollander Nicolas Witte. A French plan to initiate trade with China was set on foot in 1660. The principal ship of the contemplated flotilla, the *St. Louis,* was built and equipped in Amsterdam and, as De Witt wrote: "Apparently the first move in this matter came from here, and for the most part it was inhabitants of Holland who were concerned in it, the shipmaster and almost all of the principal officers of this ship being Hollanders." Colbert's East India Company, founded in 1664, attracted a number of secessionists from the Dutch company, chief among them François Caron, who had occupied a position of trust in the service of the United East India Company in Japan, and now organized and shared in the direction of the first French expedition to the Indies. This fleet was in part outfitted in the Netherlands, and the Amsterdam house of Coymans acted as agent for the French company.

When the first joint-stock of the English East India Company was afoot in 1614, we find an Amsterdammer, Pieter Hoote, knocking at the door. He had lived some thirteen years in the Indies in the service of the Dutch company, and now agreed to adventure £4,000 in the English company's stock, besides £400 for his freedom and the broke.

The first Danish East India Company, erected in 1616, was launched by two Hollanders, Jan de Willem and Herman Rosenkrantz. Both were domiciled in

Copenhagen, but De Willem had a brother in Amsterdam, like himself immersed in Danish affairs. In 1621 the ubiquitous Isaac Le Maire was contemplating entering this company with his Amsterdam associates. The first expedition was ably and vigorously directed by Marcelis de Boshauer who, in the employ of the Dutch company, had shown greater enterprise in the penetration of Ceylon than the directors were prepared to approve. Though De Boshauer died on this voyage, the company seized Tranquebar, and thereafter from time to time sent out small trading ventures to the East, usually with Dutch masters, Dutch pilots, and some Dutch and Hamburg capital engaged. By the middle of the century the company was deeply in debt and had ceased to trade, but in 1670 it was reorganized, again with Dutch participation. This time direction was in the hands of Ernst and Jan van Hoogenhoeck, the former of whom had long served the Dutch company in Japan. The three shipmasters who went out with the first expedition in 1674 had also been employed by the United East India Company, and had taken service with the Danish organization because the latter permitted them to do some trading for themselves, which was strictly prohibited by the Dutch company. Initial success was followed by disaster in 1677 when a large and richly laden ship, the *Oldenburgh,* at the beginning of her voyage to India was lost with all save four of her complement of about 200 men, among them Jan van Hoogenhoeck, several members of his family, and many Hollanders who were going out as assistants, bookkeepers, and merchants in the service of the Danish company.

Netherlanders who were not of Amsterdam, but whose knowledge of the East India trade was probably picked up in that city, are found laying plans for an East Indian trade from Tuscany in 1608, from Scotland in 1622, and from Brandenburg in 1681.

West India (or Guinea or African) companies launched in several countries had a leaven of Dutch enterprise, and a suspicion, or more than that, of Dutch capital. Thus the Danish West India Company organized by Jan de Willem and his Amsterdam friends in 1625, was prepared to send out its first expedition without any participation by Danish capital. A Swedish African Company was chartered in 1649 by the enterprise of Louis de Geer who, with the cooperation of Amsterdam, found five-sixths of the capital. Direction of the company was placed in the hands of Laurens de Geer, who managed his father's business interests in Amsterdam. International competition for the lion's share of the slave trade was intensified by the versatility of one Hendrik Caerloff, a native of Rostock, it is believed, who from serving the Dutch West India Company as *commies-fiscaal* in Guinea, was won over to the Swedish company by Laurens de Geer. When the De Geer heirs lost control of the company to Swedish stockholders in 1657, Caerloff organized in Amsterdam and with the cooperation of several highly-placed citizens, an African Company of Glückstadt, nominally Danish, for which two obliging Hamburgers supplied a façade. Its trading, however, was managed by Caerloff and other former agents of the Dutch company. An intercompany war for possession of forts and lodges on the slave coast ensued, in which Negro tribes were encouraged to participate, and the recently founded Royal African Company of England found good fishing in troubled waters. Caerloff, it is interesting to note, changed allegiance again, and is last heard of in the service of the French West India Company. We need not follow the territorial claims of the companies into the realm of diplomacy, where they were eventually settled.

A Brandenburg African Company had been originally projected by Aernoult Gijsels van Lier, a native of Gelders, who had been governor of Amboyna under the Dutch company. Nothing came of this tentative, but in 1680 the subject was resumed by Benjamin Raulé of a Flemish family settled in Middelburg, where this particular scion became a prosperous merchant and official of the city, with an account in the bank of Amsterdam. In 1675 he is found sending out privateers under the flag of Brandenburg to capture Dutch ships carrying Swedish trade. Five years later he had risen to be economic adviser and minister of marine to the Elector of Brandenburg, and promoter of a company to open trade with Guinea and Angola. This company was ostensibly of Königsberg, but capital, ships, shipmasters and factors were of Zeeland and Holland.

The spacious and idealistic plans of Willem Usselincx, one of the many ex-Antwerpenaars resident in Amsterdam, for the colonization of the New World as a new world, found no sympathetic hearing in realistic Amsterdam, and the West India Company was modelled fairly closely after the East India Company. Disillusioned, Usselincx went off to Sweden, where he obtained a charter for his Söderkompanie, but the project got no further. It remained for two practical Amsterdammers, Samuel Blommaert and Peter Minuit, to screen out the idealism and make a business proposition of the Söderkompanie. The former was a merchant who by trade or investment had become interested in Sweden, and had proffered economic advice to Chancellor Oxenstierna. Minuit, a native of Wesel long resident in Amsterdam, had served the West India Company as governor of New Amsterdam. Together they entered Usselincx's hitherto inactive company, Minuit bringing with him several of his fellow officials of the West India Company. In all, Amsterdam supplied one-half of the capital of f. 24,000 which launched the colony of New Sweden. The brief initial success of this enterprise, followed by the snuffing out of the infant Swedish settlement on the Delaware river by the Dutch company, need not be retold here.

Although several of the projects we have been reviewing were matters of common knowledge in Amsterdam, little effort was made to bring offenders to book even when a legal monopoly was violated. In the tangled episode of the rivalry of Dutch-sponsored "Danish" and "Swedish" companies with the West India Company for primacy in the slave trade, the fact emerged that Isaac Coymans, a wealthy merchant of Amsterdam who had twice represented the West India Company in Africa, had been detected in correspondence of a treasonable nature with the "Danish" company; had even incited it to stir up Negro tribes to attack the Dutch factories on the coast of Guinea. The revelation not unnaturally made a noise in the city, and Coymans was at first proceeded against with exemplary severity, but in the end he was let off rather easily. As we have seen, De Witt condemned promotion by Amsterdammers of French plans to enter the Far Eastern trade, and the States General made the futile gesture of banning investment in foreign companies. In 1668 De Groot, Dutch ambassador at Stockholm, wrote his mind on this subject with reference to Swedish companies, "being convinced that all the misfortune which our countrymen encounter here and elsewhere, is set on foot and organized by Netherlanders who have settled here, and are the greatest stockholders and directors in the companies which are adjudged so injurious to the commerce of the inhabitants of our country." But no genuine effort was made to check this expatriation of capital and enterprise. Had it been made, and made so effectively as to check the free outflow of capital to foreign countries, it must have resulted in an evasive exodus of that capital, and so in an earlier termination of the city's primacy as money market of Europe than actually occurred. On the contrary the States General showed a tender concern for the property rights and economic interests of its subjects and ex-subjects in foreign lands, and often interceded with the governments of those countries in their behalf.

Much of the eagerness to get into foreign East-Indian and African companies may be ascribed to resentment of those excluded from all but the meagerest share in the trade of three continents by the charters of the two India companies. Some of it sprang from impatience and frustration within the companies at the narrow conservatism, inertia, and dog-in-the-manger attitude of the directors. The East India Company's policy of scarcity, or "keeping the market hungry," was unquestionably a brake on expansion of the Eastern trade. It is noteworthy that certain owners of herring-busses of Rotterdam expressed a willingness to remove to Denmark provided they might be permitted to enter the Danish East India Company. Usselincx declared in 1645 that if the East India Company's charter were renewed in its existing form, many experienced Dutch merchants would emigrate to places where they might be free to engage in trade to the Far East. When, in the depths of the republic's misfortunes in 1672, English agents attempted to persuade the provinces of Holland and Zeeland to put themselves under the king of England's protection, certain "chief men of Rotterdam and Dort" were willing to negotiate "if they were but sure of a certain share in the trade of the [English] East India Company."

It would be idle to speculate on the results to the republic, to Europe, and to the world, if the energy, ambition, and capital resources expended by Netherlanders in other countries of Europe had been directed towards overseas settlement. Voices were not lacking to urge a more statesmanlike and far-sighted colonial policy on the States General than that pursued by the India companies. Jan Pietersz. Coen, distinguished governor-general of the East India Company's possessions, had stressed in a memorandum of 1623, the arguments of overpopulation and excess of investment capital. The proposals of Johan Maurits of Nassau for the colonization of Brazil and opening of the trade thither not only to Dutchmen but to foreigners, met with obstruction from the West India Company similar to that which Coen's ideas encountered from the East India Company. When Brazil had been lost to the feeble Portuguese power, La Court pointed out that "by an open Trade, and consequently well settled Colonies, we should not only, with small Charge, have easily defended those vast Lands of Brazil, Guiney, Angola, St. Thomas &c. against all foreign Power, but . . . have been able to carry on a very great Trade with our own Nation, without fear that any foreign Potentate should seize our Ships, Goods, or Debts, to which those Hollanders that trade only in Europe are continually exposed." He claimed that, contrary to received opinion, Netherlanders made better colonists than any other nation. "And those that doubt hereof, let them please to observe, that the Hollanders . . . even under Foreign Princes, have made very many new Colonies, namely in Lyfland, Prussia, Brandenburgh, Pomerania, Denmark, Sleswick, France, England, Flanders, &c. And moreover, have not only manured unfruitful unplanted Lands, but also undertaken the chargeable and hazardous task of draining of Fenlands." Views such as these received small attention in Amsterdam, where the great merchant houses preferred an empire of trade, snug monopolies, and the expectation of quick profits to the unpredictable, un-collectible returns from colonization. In 1661, when peace with Portugal and abandonment of Brazil were being discussed, the English resident, after men-tioning the opposition of Zeeland to peace, partly on the score of the interest of its inhabitants in Brazil, but even more because its privateers were doing well in the matter of Portuguese prizes, analyzed the attitude of Holland thus:

Holland on the other hand considers that it would be too costly a worke to goe about the regaining Brazeile by force, especiallye considering that the King of England is like to bee soe well enclyned towards Portugall, and besides that if they had Brazeile, they knowe not how to gett people to plant it, and therefore that it is better for them to make Peace and content themselves with Trafficque thither, besides the Holland East Indye Company have ever bin in an ill understanding with the Holland West Indy Companye, and doe not desire they should gett up again, yet on the other hand they would keepe off the Peace a while, at least in relation to the East Indyes, and to that effecte gave in a request yesterday to the States of Holland representing that they had bin at the expence of 85. Tunns of Gold, and desireing that such a time might bee sett for that Peace its takeing place in the East Indyes, as that they might not loose the benefitt of this years Equipage.

There is no reason to suppose that a poll of merchant opinion in Amsterdam at this time would have favored more enlightened or more broadly national views.

As one reviews the unfolding capitalism of Amsterdam, it is evident that its strength lay in extension and intensification, not in experiment or innovation. The most familiar type of business organization in the city was the oldest of all such organizations, the family partnership or company. Business connections were quite commonly cemented and invested with relative permanence by inter-marriages within the families concerned. Marriages of convenience among the patrician families of Amsterdam were not less common than among the English gentry or the French aristocracy. Great fortunes, it has been noted, were gen-erally built up by continuous efforts of successive generations within families. To this continuity the education of women in business made striking contribu-tion. Most of the women who made names for themselves in business were widows carrying on their husbands' affairs until their sons should come of age, and not seldom continuing in partnership with them afterwards. Thus of ten women trading to the Mediterranean in 1646–1647, all but one were widows. One should not think of them, however, as merely conserving and transmitting inherited wealth. Certain of them—the Widow Deutz, the Widow Thibaut, the Widow Rogge—displayed acumen and capacity in their affairs.

There was another aspect of the continuity of Dutch business houses which English and French observers stressed, and perhaps overstressed. Though capital went into land and industry at home and abroad, as we have seen; went into *rentebrieven* and company stocks; went into the acquisition of public office and expense incidental thereto; into fine houses and luxurious living; it was surplus capital in excess of that needed for trade, shipping, and other forms of commercial investment. "The Dutch maister us in Trade," said Josiah Child. "Wee always begin young men heere, there it holds from generation to generation." And Jacques Savary wrote gloomily:

From the moment that a merchant in France has acquired great wealth in trade, his children, far from following him in this profession, on the contrary enter public office . . . whereas in Holland the children of merchants ordinarily follow the profession and the trade of their fathers, ally themselves with other merchant families, and give such considerable sums to their children when they marry that one of these will have greater wealth when he begins trading on his own, than the richest merchant of France will have when he stops trading to establish his family in other professions: therefore, since money is not withdrawn from trade, but continues in it constantly from father to son, and from family to family as a result of the alliances which merchants make with one another, individual Dutch merchants can more easily undertake the Northern and Muscovy trades than individual French merchants can undertake them.

A very common form of business cooperation in seventeenth century Holland, common elsewhere in Europe and probably of mediaeval origin, was known as *rederij.* This was a highly flexible type of joint enterprise by which capitals large and small were combined for a purpose limited as to scope or as to time. A group of *reders* might join in building, buying, chartering, or freighting a ship, or might make a collective venture in a fishing or trading voyage. They might take shares, as we find them doing in the Zaan villages, in a mill, a train-cookery, a lighter, an anchor-smithy, a rope-walk, a lime-kiln, or a starch factory. An interesting joint enterprise of this nature was the construction and operation of the Zaandam *overtoom,* an ingenious mechanism by which ships were hauled over the bar separating the upper from the lower basin of the Zaan. There were sixty-four shares in this utility. Whether these humble forms of combination were as common in Amsterdam as in the Zaan industries, cannot be answered with certainty. We hear of *rederij* in building and freighting ships, in whaling expeditions, and in the Norway timber trade, but not in the variety of small enterprises for which it was utilized in the Zaan villages.

For the instruction of French merchants Savary described the various types of companies common in his time, concluding with the *sociétés anonymes* frequently formed by Dutch merchants and factors trading in France. These were not the limited liability companies to which the name *sociétés anonymes* was later to be applied, but secret and temporary combinations of buyers or sellers of some particular commodity or group of commodities in a particular market, with the object of influencing prices; in other words, merchant rings whose members ostensibly traded as individuals, but were actually in agreement on price strategy. We have noticed that similar groups to control trading in certain commodities were formed in Amsterdam from time to time. Though not peculiar to that city, they were probably more common in that greatest of markets than elsewhere in Europe.

There was indeed no institution nor any practice common in Amsterdam's business in this century—the trading in actions excepted—which had not been earlier known and used in the Italian cities, or Lyon, or Augsburg, or Antwerp: bourse, joint-stock company, cartel, banking and exchange, brokerage and insurance. Amsterdam gave these more precise formulation, greater flexibility and extension, and used them effectively over a wider field. Europe learned much from her, but her golden age was rather the climax of a period of transition than the beginning of a new economic era.

2.

Modern economic theory has no medieval heritage. Medieval thinkers had ideas about economic life and what it should be, but, strictly speaking, they did not theorize about or attempt to explain economic phenomena. To theorize is to search for relationships, formulas, and causes and effects. In economics, to theorize is to speculate on the relationships between productivity, wealth, consumption, trade, and the impact of fiscal and monetary policies on a state economy. The first to do this kind of theorizing were the so-called mercantilists of the early seventeenth century. For medieval thinkers, ideas about the economy were rather more a part of ethics than an attempt to explain phenomena in the world. Mercantilist theorists established the rudiments of what would become a science of economy.

Mercantilist theories developed in about 1600 for three reasons. The first was that gold and silver imported from America led such scholars as the Polish astronomer Copernicus, the French philosopher Bodin, and the Spanish political philosopher Mariana to speculate on the effects of these imports on prices in Europe. They might never have sought answers to this question if, even with the influx of precious metals, civil war and a severe depression had not caused misery and famine in many parts of Europe. The second reason was a change in the attitudes of governments. Kings and their ministers sought more than ever before to stimulate the economic life of their kingdoms, partly out of a desire to secure their thrones against rebellion, and partly out of a sense of Christian duty. Another reason was the rise of a new science. Whatever the phenomena of the physical world, scholars turned to attempts at cataloging and defining them, or theorized on their origins. Is it merely coincidental that economic theory was born in that age of tremendous discoveries in astronomy, anatomy, and political theory? No theorist rose to make economics a science as did Hobbes in political theory, but even so, the beginnings of economics date from his lifetime.

The accumulation of capital, self-sufficiency, hard work, and the founding of new "manufactures" became the principal tenets of the early mercantilists. Vague, unsystematic, and greatly influenced by national traditions, the first economic theorists—including Bodin, Mariana, and their seventeenth-century followers, Laffemas and Mun—arrived at similar definitions of an aspect of human existence and attempted to explain conditions affecting entire countries. Their specific suggestions often influenced public policy.

The question of the extent to which mercantilist theories, as implemented by public policy, actually influenced economic behavior has largely been ignored by historians. For France, where mercantilist theories had the greatest influence, at least until 1770, little is known of their impact through royal policy. The companies founded by Henry IV and Louis XIV have been studied in some detail, but virtually nothing is known about the bigger questions of the influence of mercantilist theories on tariff policies and the consequent influence of the tariff policies on the economy.

Only for England under James I and his son Charles is there a history of the relationships between these vague theories and public policy. Professor B. E. Supple rightly asserts that it is of little use to concentrate on the interminable, repetitive laws and edicts. Rather it is the study of economic conditions and of the general aims of royal officials which provides the background for a study of the influence of economic theory. What social conditions stimulated royal officials to intervene in the English economy? Does Supple assert that "encouraging or enforcing the circulation of capital" was in fact applied mercantilist theory? Professor Supple (1930–   ) teaches at the University of Sussex, England.

B. E. SUPPLE: The Government and the Economy*

The leading proponents of the existence of a mercantile system—however much they disagreed on its content, its theoretical validity, or its practical usefulness—combined in attributing to government policy in the sixteenth and seventeenth centuries an overall and integrated content based upon conscious thought and primarily directed towards the creation of some ideal economic or political society. On this view, specific government actions were very much parts of a whole, and aimed at more than the solution of short-term problems or the effecting of partial changes in economic structures. Adam Smith, for instance, in his biting attack on mercantilism, held it to be founded on a basically invalid principle which identified national wealth with treasure and which guided official action towards the unbounded accumulation of money by manipulation of the balance of trade. By the German historical economists of the late nineteenth century, mercantilism was gratefully and approvingly reinterpreted in political terms: as a centralized policy directed towards the building of national states and the concentration of national power. In this century Eli Heckscher found in the mercantile system concepts of unification, national power, protection, money, and society; these he systematized and, measuring them against the tenets of *laissez faire,* found wanting. Whatever the particular emphasis, however, traditional views of mercantilism as a system of policy have held it to be rooted in consciously articulated doctrine, with the result that a significant number of official economic measures over an extended period of time could be seen as component parts of a larger plan. Further, on this view, it is normally

* From B. E. Supple, *Commercial Crisis and Change in England* (Cambridge: Cambridge University Press, 1959), pp. 225–53.

held that the mercantilist doctrines were propounded with more reference to an ideal economic or political state than to the prevailing economic conditions. Most extreme of all, Heckscher denied any possible influence of economic environment on government policy. To all these views we can reasonably take exception on the basis of the processes already described.

Nearly every detailed study of particular aspects of economic policy in the sixteenth and seventeenth centuries has, inevitably, been forced to deal with the economic environment within which that policy has been shaped, and it has been the rule rather than the exception that the conclusions of such studies point to a crucial relationship between actual events and government actions. It will be the argument here that "mercantilist" doctrine was not the spontaneous product of an ideal of society nor is it evidence of the momentum of medieval concepts. Instead, officials in the early seventeenth century had in mind quite unexceptionable ends whose simplicity contrasts sharply with those so often attributed to "mercantilism."

On the whole, Tudor and Stuart governments directed their regulatory efforts to the maintenance of social order, public peace, national security and the achievement of economic prosperity—simply defined. Certain policies had obviously strategic roots. They were directed towards the encouragement of shipping, of the provision of naval supplies, armaments and necessary foodstuffs. These doctrines and actions do not need investigation here: the prevailing international political climate was one of warfare and it was therefore only natural that some attention should be given to the military and civil preparation for such an environment. And particular variations in the frequency, nature and sincerity of policy measures are to be explained only in terms of the personalities and politics involved, the dangers threatening, and the funds available. We can also exclude from consideration another aspect of policy: that whose *raison d'être* was a prohibition of some form of economic activity merely in order to derive an income from licensing exceptions to it. Indeed, the altruistic light in which we shall view attempts at economic regulation did not distinguish all government activity at the time. The policies which provoked the maximum public criticism were precisely those which reflected the worst features of the Stuart Court: plagued by impecunious parasites and desperately anxious for new sources of income and new possibilities of corruption. Thus industrial intervention was only too frequently the result of attempts to satisfy the greed of the hanger-on at Westminster or the extreme financial needs of government itself. The patents and monopolies, the cloaking of selfish aims beneath verbose platitudes, were an integral part of the fabric of Stuart government. And the fate of many seemingly sincere policies was to degenerate into inefficient taxes on enterprise: taxes which rarely reached the royal coffers. This is a feature of policy with which we shall not be concerned. It is with other aspects of official action that we shall deal; with the more purely economic measures and with those adopted in some way to preserve order or maintain the social fabric.

The outstanding feature of such policies, it will be argued, was that their timing and content were explained above all by the context within which they were promulgated and the urgency with which economic problems were brought to the government's attention. An understanding of the economy and the nature of its day-to-day workings is essential to an understanding of economic policy. From this point of view it is far from a useful procedure to cloak generations of policy under one term, and the methodological concepts of those historians who believed in a "mercantilist system" are decidedly not the most useful tools for appraising official action. Instead, even at the risk of economic determinism, we must conclude that while economic conditions shaped the course of economic doctrine and regulation, it was the more violent short-run variations in the economic environment which best explain the dynamic components of policy. On this basis the continuous recurrence of various *motifs* in official action (for instance, bullion laws, wage-regulation, plans for exchange control, and anxiety concerning the balance of trade) is evidence not so much of a continuity of ideas *per se* but of a not surprising recurrence of short-term situations, and specifically depressions, within the framework of an economy whose essential characteristics were slow to change.

Even more than this: economic policy was attuned most exactly to *downswings* in economic activity, and there is hardly an important government measure during the period—with the obvious exception of the strategic policies and the strange Cockayne plan—which was not stimulated by the urgent demands of a period of short-term (if recurrent) dislocation. In the words of a critic of Heckscher's views of mercantilism, "I have long felt that a graph showing business fluctuations should be a compulsory frontispiece for every historical study of commercial policy. . . . The relationship between depression on the one hand, and discontent, drastic demands, concessions to the vociferous, and great changes in policy, on the other hand, is intimate." This lesson, it is hoped, has already been made apparent in the foregoing chapters: the most powerful type of stimulus to the formulation and application of a body of government policy—however we baptize it—was precisely the sort of economic fluctuation which has been the subject of this book. And the inevitable result was that the emphasis of this policy was defensive. . . .

Although there was no such thing as a mercantilist *system* of economic regulation, it is possible to distinguish, at a less complex level, some common attributes of policy during the early seventeenth century. But, as might be expected, these spring less from a continuity of administrative outlook than from the nature of the economic environment within which men thought out their actions. For, given the general economic structure at the time, men fashioned policy under the sharp stimulus of short-run dislocation in the hope of reducing the harmful effects of the type of disturbance which was likely to arise in such an economy. In the last resort, as we shall see, the mass of official regulations aimed at alleviating those situations from which food riots might result. Thus the maintenance of public order was among the primary ends of government action. Since the commercial disturbances which threatened public order were comparable in the effects they had, it is not surprising that the official reaction to them should itself display some continuity over the years. There was, in addition, another feature which distinguished official action at the time, and it is possible that herein lies the real distinction between mercantilism and *laissez faire:* policy was formulated with a specific and unquestioned assumption as to the necessary role of the government in the economy. With this assumption we may usefully start our analysis of economic regulation during the period.

More than most other periods of English economic history the sixteenth and seventeenth centuries illustrate the acceptance of government participation in and regulation of economic affairs. Official willingness to shape economic and social institutions and the course of economic change has rarely been greater, the framework of laws and administrative edicts propounded as a result has rarely been more complex, and this was more than matched by an almost universal faith on the part of contemporaries that this arrangement, rather than the free play of market forces, was the natural order of things. The validity which was imputed to the government's far-reaching role was little affected by the constant demonstration of its failure to do what it proposed to do, or its success in aggravating the very problems which it had set out to solve! Of course, there were always those who argued that some aspect of the economy— usually one in which they themselves were busy seeking a profit—would be better off without regulation, or with a laxer system of official controls. But such pragmatic approaches were rarely couched in terms of a general principle, and were virtually never based on a broad theoretical foundation. Views as heretical as those of Adam Smith would have received short shrift from the economic orthodoxies of the seventeenth century. Whatever the level of inspired inefficiency with which government policy was applied to the intransigent facts, no one thought to question in any serious way the government's right, whether by prerogative or parliamentary approval, to extend its influence over everyday life. Nor was there any real opposition to the view that disaster would attend any experiment by which the government abstained entirely from participation in economic affairs.

The actual formulation of policy during the early seventeenth century was principally the responsibility of the Privy Council. True, the House of Commons was always a sounding board for possible government action, and its members, representative of widely diverse economic interests and areas, were never loath to give their opinions on the state of the economy or to attempt to advance relevant legislation. In addition there were some not unimportant instances when Parliament took the initiative in framing, or breaking down, a particular code of commercial regulations. Important in these respects were the 1604 debates on free trade, the 1606 Act ensuring an unregulated trade to France, Spain and Portugal, the urgent considerations of 1621, and the pressure then and in 1624 which produced a significant liberalization of the organization of the trade to Germany and the Low Countries. But in the main, and not least because of the discontinuity of parliamentary sessions, government policy in the period was determined, enforced or delegated by the Privy Council.

One other reason why the legislature took second place to the executive in this matter lay in the fact that, given the contemporary reaction to economic crisis, except in relation to the potentialities of an unregulated trade, there was relatively little scope for fresh economic legislation. On the whole, the tendencies of policy, even in the face of a continually changing commercial scene, could ideally be satisfied by the selective application of existing laws. In other words, there was no great demand for institutional revolutions. For the men concerned with government, regulation was best carried on by the administrative organ: it was the council's responsibility to emphasize those aspects of the inherited framework of statutes which it imagined best fitted the needs of the economy. If, for example, the desire was to prevent the export of money then contemporary policy-formulation demanded no more than could be satisfied by the prevailing penal statutes against the shipment of coin or by the unquestioned right of the executive to manipulate Mint prices. If anxiety was expressed concerning the low quality of English textiles, then the requisite regulatory laws were on the statute books and it was open to non-parliamentary powers to set up commissions to investigate, or corporations to control, the processes of manufacture. In questions of poor-relief, of anti-unemployment policies, of wage regulation and industrial codes, and of monetary affairs the power and prerogative of the Privy Council were, in theory at least, sufficient unto the day.

It was, then, the council which attempted to enforce old laws, promulgated new proclamations, took far-reaching administrative action, issued commissions for a host of purposes, and acted as the energizing force for local authorities whose all-important task it was to administer the day-to-day requirements of policy. The political configurations which went far to explain the position of the Commons need not be considered here. But it is abundantly clear that parliamentary supremacy might have made little difference to economic regulation. The principal exception in this respect is probably in the field of the award of privileged areas of trade and strict rights of self-government to London mercantile companies—the economic interests in Parliament consistently displayed the strongest suspicion of these metropolitan cartels. Yet even on this point the council, although in the long run content to maintain the fabric of regulation, frequently demonstrated that it was not irrevocably committed to the concept of regulated commerce, and in 1621 and 1624, when the parliamentary pressure groups succeeded in throwing open large portions of the Merchant Adventurers' trade, this step was taken with the not unwilling concurrence of the Privy Council. In most other matters, however, it is doubtful if there existed even the possibility of a cleavage on matters of economic regulation in the face of commercial crises. Commons' debates and suggestions arising from economic troubles display no great deviation from those which came before the privy councillors. This was true with respect to currency problems, unemployment measures, poor law enforcement, the regulation of the cloth industry, and the attitude towards sharing the burden of depression between labour and capital or industry and trade. The real break between Parliament and Crown came on matters remote from the critical attributes of the commercial fluctuations which intermittently disturbed sectors of the English economy. It was reserved for questions of politics and religion, and in so far as it concerned economic matters, it dealt in the main with taxation, patents and agriculture, and with questions of principle as to *who* should determine the national destiny, and by what authority.

As far as possible the Privy Council attempted to give direct attention to important matters: it was rarely reluctant to exhort local officials to positive action in any matter which it felt to be important, or to call to account those who too blatantly went against its will. But as the burden of necessary work accumulated it was only to be expected that there should be some delegation of the responsibility for sifting and evaluating evidence, and even for some decision-making. The result was an informal and ever-changing structure of committees and commissions. As exemplified already, the investigating committees might be completely independent groups representing one particular viewpoint; for example, the merchant committees that investigated projects for currency enhancement in 1618 and 1620, or the special committees appointed in 1622 to appraise the collapse of the exchange rates. On the other hand, these committees might be quasi-official bodies, whose task it was to present a balanced view of a particular problem and suggest remedies for it. The outstanding example here was the group that considered all aspects of the commercial depression in 1622. One result of the deliberations of this committee was the appointment of a more permanent commission, and in this sort of appointment we can see another fundamental development of policy delegation.

There were clearly many matters that the council wished to control but which might evade its own oversight by reason of the pressure of work or the need for its members to be in London. In these circumstances it could at best issue a commission for the specific task in mind, and delegate administration to a chosen body of men. Thus in 1631, at a time of widespread poverty and famine, a general commission was set up to enforce relief measures throughout the country, and in the early 1630's a commission was active in the western counties "for reformation of the abuses in clothmaking." It was, however, in the autumn of 1622 that the most significant departure took place. As a consequence of the prevailing depression and the recommendations of the investigating committee earlier in the year, a large commission was appointed to investigate and oversee most crucial questions of commercial and industrial policy. In effect this move amounted to the delegation of an enormous area of economic supervision, and subsequent commercial and industrial controversies frequently came before the commission directly. Thus, the critical debates on the mechanism of the exchanges were held under its auspices in 1622 and 1623. In this respect the great depression of the early 1620's, which did so much to shape economic thought and policy, served to mark a turning point in the evolution of government institutions. For the body appointed in 1622 was revivified in 1625 and in its operations and scope one can detect the origins of the later Board of Trade.

The thesis has already been proposed that the most significant aspects of government policy during the early seventeenth century are best explained in terms of an attempted defence against the vagaries of economic dislocation. Governments reacted to the intermittent commercial crises which afflicted the economy in a manner primarily calculated to alleviate the worst effects of depression or to alter the arrangements of factors of production so that another crisis would be less harsh. Only rarely was there any attempt to propound policies primarily designed to get to the roots of potential dislocation.

The most critical element of instability as far as the government was concerned was the possibility of chronic unemployment. And it has already been indicated that in this last respect the textile industry played an almost unique role at this time. Thus variations in the effective demand for cloth were the principal causes of outbreaks of unemployment for people who might, at such times, find few alternative sources of income. England, like the neighbouring lands, was a poor nation whose population lived, for the main part, close to a subsistence level. Even when he was employed, the average textile worker had little enough income to buy his basic necessities, quite apart from any possibility of his saving enough to establish a buffer between slump and starvation. Consequently, the unemployed weaver was even less tender than the underprivileged farm labourer of the rights of property or the king's peace, and when—as was normally the case—the looms stopped in areas where cloth manufacturing was a concentrated industry, the result might not be far from anarchy. The potential barriers between unalleviated unemployment and a dangerous outburst of rioting were only two (if we exclude the possibility of superhuman patience in the face of starvation): social welfare measures, which served to redistribute income by means of poor-relief, and the exercise of an efficient police power. In both respects Stuart England was poorly equipped to meet the urgent problems of a depressed area; any except the slightest disruption could pose alarming threats to social peace. The poor-law will be dealt with below, but in general it was true that the paucity of resources, the inefficiencies of local administration, and the opposition of local propertied interests to the necessary taxation, hamstrung all but the most determined efforts to organize relief. On the other hand, a ramshackle administrative system, poor communications, and financial stringency kept everyday police powers close to the ludicrous—Dogberry and his men were no more than the inspired exaggeration of a cruel truth which lasted well beyond Shakespeare's time. Clearly, no Stuart government could look with equanimity on the possibility of a declining cloth market putting local resources and aptitudes to the test. If one had to choose, it would be fear of the bread riot rather than adherence to a medieval philosophy of social harmony which went furthest to explain measures directed at the maintenance of economic peace and stability in local communities.

Since the prevention of social unrest by the maintenance of employment in textiles was a major aim of policy, governments were clearly forced to consider the relationship between commercial crises and the structure of the cloth industry. Indeed, in the sixteenth century such considerations, as has already been intimated, led to the emergence of a school of thought that was opposed to industrial development in textiles precisely because it felt the price—measured in intermittent bouts of chronic unemployment—was too high. To quote Lord Burghley's words again: "it is to be thought that the diminution of clothing in this realm were profitable to the same . . . first, for that thereby the tillage of the realm is notoriously decayed. . . . Secondly, for that the people that depend upon making of cloth are of worse condition to be quietly governed than the husbandmen."

Although such views were not confined to any one brief period of time, it is abundantly clear that they derived their strength from appraisals of specific depressions in the course of the mid-sixteenth century. They were the horrified reactions, of men who appreciated only too bitterly the danger of tumultuous poverty, to the intrusion of a complicated and unstable industrial development into an agrarian economy. And they were embodied in a framework of regulation whose aim was, in part, "the diminution of clothing in this realm." The Cloth Acts of the mid-sixteenth century, and even the Statute of Artificers, were directed towards the restraint of unbridled industrial expansion in order to guard against the impact of potential contractions in demand. Laws were passed which aimed at the maintenance of quality in English woollens, which confined the manufacture of cloth to those who had served an apprenticeship of seven years in the industry (although this requirement was subsequently relaxed for towns and cities), and which limited the number of looms and apprentices which even a qualified rural manufacturer might employ. And the great Statute of 1563, by its apprenticeship, wage and labour-contract clauses "made illegal that mobility of labour without which rapid industrialization and spectacular commercial expansion are impossible." Behind this series of enactments lay not a medieval ideal of a stable agrarian society but the reality of a disastrous slump. The significance as well as the timing of some of the outstanding sixteenth-century measures of economic regulation are explained by the prevailing economic environment.

But, although anxiety on the score of dangerously concentrated pockets of industry was still evident in the early seventeenth century, by that time, as far as official doctrine was concerned, all thoughts of unduly restraining the processes of industrialization had disappeared. As previously mentioned, men's attention now increasingly turned to the possibilities of expansion rather than contraction. England's industrial destiny, as much as it was then apparent, was the accepted starting point for policy discussions. And this change in outlook had a twofold origin. First, market forces were doing more than the Elizabethan government ever could to prevent the undue expansion of the traditional broadcloth industry. Second, the beginnings of a new international economic order were affording opportunities of commercial diversification into textile innovations, new markets and new trades. Rather than concentrating on preventing factors of production from entering a burgeoning old-drapery industry, the government now attempted to facilitate their entry into fields of endeavour which compensated for industrial decline in the traditional manufacture. The new "economic gospel" banished thoughts of a primarily agrarian society. Government planning was too busy investigating the potentialities of new demand.

Nevertheless, the problem of critical fluctuations in the demand for textiles remained a pressing one. And, correspondingly, the government now felt its task to be not to reduce the relative importance of the industrial sector of the economy but positively to buttress that sector against the vicissitude of market forces. Yet there was little sign that those in office had sufficient analytic skill or the effective power to countervail directly the principal causes of decline in the overseas demand for English cloth. For example, in the early 1620's there was virtually no appreciation, in government circles, of the essential relationship between currency manipulations abroad and declining cloth output at home. And even if the connexion had been proved beyond all question it is doubtful— to judge by the passivity in the face of pressure on other grounds to manipulate the English coinage—if a policy of devaluation, in order to increase demand for exports, could have been effected. In any case, in so far as the principal causes of abrupt depressions in English industry derived from the European scene, the government was normally powerless to prevent them. It is true enough that there were attempts to counter European developments—e.g. the frequently reiterated prohibition of the export of raw materials to feed the growing continental industry—and that at each fresh crisis there was a frenzied effort to get to its root causes. But the fact remains that nearly every onslaught of depression caught the government unawares and ran its course independently of official action.

Clearly, therefore, it was not unreasonable that the government should devote its principal attention to those phases of economic dislocation where its authority could be most directly exercised and where, to unsophisticated eyes, it seemed easiest to alleviate the rigours of a slump. Hence the council, unable effectively to alter the forces which reduced the overseas demand for English cloth, concentrated its efforts on the intermediate demand exerted by exporting merchants, on the possibilities of owners of capital assuming more of the financial burden of a slump, and on measures of poor relief. From this willingness to manipulate economic structures in order to maintain employment, either in anticipation or, more often, in the face of a depression, there sprang some of the most representative of contemporary policies.

At times of extreme crisis the Privy Council might seriously discuss, as it did in 1616, the possibility of enforcing the participation in trade of non-mercantile capital in order to take unsold stocks off clothiers' hands. But in the main, official attention was confined to merchants. In attempting, with varying degrees of success, to find some means of persuading traders to continue buying cloth at a time when they claimed that they were unable profitably to sell it abroad, the council found itself in a hornets' nest of controversial issues. Questions of immediate significance concerned the organization of trade in regulated companies as against more freedom to individual merchants to choose the time and destination of their shipments; the supply and turnover of mercantile capital; the clash of economic interest between industrial entrepreneurs and merchant exporters; and the extent to which different economic groups should bear or transfer the brunt of the effects of industrial deflation. Such matters in the main were not discussed with grandiose "mercantilist" concepts of society in mind, but on the basis of an urgent quest for measures to relieve short-term exigencies. Although special interests—such as the outport merchants who pleaded for free trade in 1604, or the Staplers who perpetually tilted at the Merchant Adventurers' privileges—rarely ceased their quest for a favourable re-alignment of policy, it is evident that on the whole the government was willing to envisage the most extreme experiments only at times of the most extreme economic fluctuation.

The initial government reaction to almost every outbreak of unemployment in cloth manufacturing was to call before the council the merchants or representatives of the companies normally concerned with the export of the relevant textiles. This was as true of crises provoked by an experiment in commercial organization such as that of 1614–17 as it was of the industrial depressions resulting from the sudden collapse of European markets. Thus the Merchant Adventurers came before the privy councillors in 1620 when reports of unemployment flowed in from the broadcloth industry of the West, and English and foreign merchants exporting to France were interviewed in 1629 when depression settled on the East Anglian new drapery manufacture. In nearly every case the council demanded from the merchants an explanation of their failure to maintain purchases and ordered or exhorted them, sometimes on the direct promise of government action to improve the situation, to recommence their buying.

To such requests that they assume more of the burden of a depression, either by bearing the cost of unsold stocks or running the likely risk of falling prices, the traders might well answer that their capital was exhausted or tied up in existing stocks of their own, or that the market was so bad that they could see no reason in such a procedure. As with the Adventurers in April 1622, they might be pushed to the point of at least claiming that they would withdraw from their trade, never to return, rather than be forced to continue to do business unprofitably in order to satisfy the clothing counties. The Privy Council, on its side, might threaten to withdraw the privileges of the company and throw the trade open to all comers if its request was not complied with. Thus early in 1622—even while debates were proceeding which gave them an increased control of Baltic imports—members of the Eastland Company exporting cloth through the Sound were told that if they did not maintain their purchases of East Anglian textiles their trade would be thrown open to the manufacturers who had such a "great quantity of cloths lying upon their hands." Indeed, some Suffolk clothiers used this instance as a defence against subsequent charges of having traded in the privileged areas. In cases like this it was not so much that the government felt that a regulated company was positively hindering trade recovery: such threats were used as incentives to merchants to assume costs which the council felt they ought to bear in order to guard against the greater dangers of chronic unemployment. The best illustration of this tendency was the assumption by the government of its right to enforce a quota system by which individual merchants were obliged to purchase stipulated amounts of cloth. This happened with the Cockayne adventurers in 1616, and with the Merchant Adventurers, who were otherwise threatened with disenfranchisement, in February 1622, and with the merchants dealing in new draperies in 1629. At the root of such a development in government policy lay an attitude to property which would be almost unthinkable in the twentieth century. For it assumed that the government might exercise direct command over the distribution of private traders' capital with no regard for compensation and no possibility of alternative uses.

The companies' trading policies could also be manipulated in another direction by forcing merchants to ship goods at a time when they were reluctant to do so on non-economic grounds. Thus, the Adventurers in 1627 were trying to bring pressure to bear on the Dutch by abstaining from shipments to the United Provinces. The council, in its anxiety to preserve industrial peace, was forced to order the company to send off its convoys notwithstanding the demands of private economic policy.

There was, however, a limit to the extent to which the merchant groupings could be bullied into adopting policies repugnant to their members. The threat to throw open a trade might not always be matched by the availability of alternative supplies of trading capital. If a trade were opened to the generality, and if the established merchants then withdrew from active business, the likelihood was that there would not be sufficient entrepreneurial skill or working capital to maintain commerce even at the low level which had originally occasioned the pressure on the existing traders. The primary example of this had occurred during the Cockayne experiment, which had been effectively sabotaged by the refusal of leading Merchant Adventurers to participate. And in the previous reign, when, in response to a slump, Blackwell Hall had been opened to all in 1587 and the Adventurers had refused to co-operate, the lesson had been that the remedy was worse than the disease: the company was speedily reinstated. Yet whatever the final outcome of such policies, the government more often than not put its own estimation of social peace higher than its regard for commercial property.

The official attitude towards industrial capital was no less marked by a solicitous regard for the maintenance of employment in the textile areas. Of course, clothiers could always claim with some justice that all their capital was tied up in unsold stocks so that, without help from mercantile capital, it was absolutely impossible for them to maintain production. This was, for instance, the almost unanimous complaint of manufacturers in 1622, and was the argument put forward by Surrey clothiers in 1630. Nevertheless, there were times when the Privy Council was as firm with clothiers as it was with merchants: commanding them, on the threat of extreme displeasure or the promise of government efforts to stimulate mercantile purchases, to continue to provide work for their employees. This attitude, as well as that towards overseas traders, is best exemplified by the letter which was sent to the J.P.s of the ten leading clothing counties in 1622, in the course of which entrepreneurs were treated to a disquisition on the duties as well as the rights of industrial and commercial enterprise:

as upon calling of the merchants here before us and due examination of the state of their trade at this present, we have taken order in the behalf of the clothier for the taking off (as far as may be) of such cloth as now lieth upon the clothiers . . . so we do hereby require you to call before you such clothiers as you shall think fitting and to deal effectually with them for the employment of such weavers, spinners, and other persons as are now out of work . . . so may we not induce that the clothiers in that or any other county should at their pleasure and without giving knowledge thereof unto this Board dismiss their workfolks, who, being many in

number and most of them of the poorer sort, are in such cases likely by their clamour
to disturb the quiet and government of those parts where they live . . . wherein if
any clothier shall after sufficient warning refuse or neglect to appear before you or
otherwise shall obstinately deny to yield to such overtures in this case as shall be
reasonable and just, you shall take good bonds of them for refusing to appear before
us and immediately certify their names unto this Board. [A general rule for wool-
growers, merchants and clothiers is that] whosoever had a part of the gain in profitable times since his Majesty's happy reign must now in the decay of trade (till that
may be remedied) bear a part of the public loss as may best conduce to the good
of the public and the maintenance of the general trade.

The government's main aim in all of this was to keep the wheels of industry
turning by encouraging or enforcing the circulation of capital. Hence there
might even be successful attempts to protect debtors who were temporarily
short of funds where those debtors were manufacturers whose businesses might
otherwise cease. This happened in the early 1620's when the council used its
powers to protect insolvent clothiers in Suffolk and Devon.

Such direct interferences with the processes of private business and the flows
of private capital were not the only reflection of government anxiety concerning
the disastrous repercussions of large-scale unemployment. Intermittent depression time and again had forced men to question the wisdom of prevailing modes
of trade organization. And an economic crisis was in almost every case the cue
for bitter discussion on the rival economic virtues of a regulated as against a
free trade. In the main the government was concerned to investigate the repercussions of different trading arrangements on the effective demand for English
cloth and therefore on the state of public order. Parallel with this tendency,
and, for obvious reasons, much more continuous than the anxiety of privy councillors on the subject, was the opposition of important groups in the Commons
to any company which tended to concentrate trade in London to the detriment
of the provincial ports or whose control of the timing of and destination of
exports militated against the provincial merchant with his small stock of capital
and his need for a rapid turnover. Nevertheless, the free trade movement in the
Commons, which was almost directly representative of the outports, had little
hope of shaping policy unless the executive concurred. And the only time at
which there was a possibility of such concurrence normally came during a
slump. Thus, the outstanding example of a variation in a government policy
during the period came as a result of the crisis of the early 1620's.

The Merchant Adventurers, who normally handled almost three-quarters of
London textile exports, came under severe criticism as a result of the depression,
as did most of the mercantile cartels. Parliamentary pressure, with the connivance of the council and the reluctant acquiescence of the company itself,
secured an important liberalization of trading arrangements: the council clearly
anticipated—or hoped—that the unsold stocks of manufacturers might be disposed of more easily if more merchants were allowed to participate in the trade.
Consequently, in a drastic policy-change of 1621 and 1624, membership in the
Merchant Adventurers was thrown open, all non-members were allowed to
trade in kersies, dozens and new draperies, and, in addition, provincial mer-

chants were given permission to export coloured cloths to the company's privileged areas. Practical expediency had at last rendered effective the traditional jealousies of provincial merchants; although ten years later the Privy Council revoked this freedom, in response to another period of poor trade and without the benefit of parliamentary advice or the stimulus of parliamentary harrying, at the request of the company, and committed itself once again to the concept of a strictly regulated trade.

It was, however, not only at times of economic depression that the government was called upon to adjudicate the controversy between supporters and opponents of a regulated trade. Provincial merchants and interlopers, who could not or would not keep to company rules regarding shipments, were permanently opposed to this method of organization. Clothiers, on the other hand, would normally be unconcerned with such matters while demand and prices held up; only during a crisis would they tend to demand more buyers. Finally, there were those who sincerely felt that it would be to England's economic benefit to dispense with trade regulation. And as the realization spread that English textiles could best subsist in a competitive world by competitive pricing, so this last viewpoint increased in importance. All critical arguments emphasized that the original basis of company organization—the limitation of competition between English exporters, the attempts to create a seller's market abroad—was not suited to a continued and prosperous demand for the products of England's export industries. Commercial expansion, critics argued, could be the welcome result of a destruction of corporate monopolies and a liberalization of the conditions of trade. The defenders of the regulated companies, on the other hand, usually claimed that the organizations benefited the nation as a whole by successfully maintaining export prices, by keeping the costs of imports low, by defeating the attempts of aliens to arrange commerce to England's disadvantage, and by generally supporting industry at a prosperous level and stimulating high-quality production. However, in addition to these arguments on principle, the companies were frequently forced to state their case on a specific issue. When answering the bitter attacks during a depression, adherents of a regulated trade indicated the poor trading conditions already existing as a strong reason against allowing more merchants into the trade. More consumers rather than more dealers would be the answer to the depression, they said: "what needs that [more exporters] when there are already ten times as many Merchant Adventurers as the quantity of the trade will employ?" "To add more persons to be Merchant Adventurers, is to put more sheep into one and the same pasture, which is to starve them all."

Since a free trade was the exception in the significant commercial areas during the sixteenth and seventeenth centuries, it would be undeniably true to say that in the last resort the government favoured the system of company regulation. But this was principally because it was an arrangement which men in power considered best suited to the prevailing conditions. Of course, this might merely mean that a privileged company was one of the best means of securing to government officials non-salaried incomes which a more circumspect age had labelled bribes. But on the whole, it could be argued that such an organization fulfilled various important functions: it acted as a quasi-official protective and representative agent abroad, much as later consuls did; it was a strategic source of royal loans and a convenient site for discontinuous taxation; its control of trade facilitated the collection of customs; it was, in the bellicose conditions of the time, a useful agent for the organization of convoys and the protection of shipping; and, in a period which, to a considerable extent, still viewed trade as an extension of warfare by which one country's gain was another's loss, a strong company was held to be the best means of ensuring England's interest against the European countries, of maintaining export prices and reducing import prices, and of carrying on that extensive economic war of ban and counter-ban, which passed for peaceful commerce at the time.

There are also examples of official protection to company trading which stem directly from an employment policy—although they bear the superficial marks of being concerned solely with private or strategic interests. Outstanding in this respect was the order of 1622 which confirmed the Eastland Company's monopoly of Baltic imports. At first glance this appears as a forerunner of the Navigation Acts in so far as they aimed at stimulating English shipping and countering the mercantile strength of the Dutch. But closer investigation has shown that in fact the order was a direct response to the complaints of the company that competition (from the Dutch) in imports was seriously reducing the capacity of English exporters to buy up the products of the depressed East Anglian cloth industry. It was hoped that by ensuring Englishmen the control of their returns from the Baltic, the export of cloth would be stimulated at a time of slump.

There was yet another reason why, over the long run, the privileges of the leading companies were very little impaired. This derived from a practical factor already mentioned: the nature and sources of the risk capital available for investment in specific lines of commerce. As in the case of its ability to bring pressure to bear on merchants to buy up stocks, the council was limited in its attempts to experiment with the structure of trade by reason of the danger of alienating the existing participants. In 1614–17, for instance, it was found that the abstention of the leading Adventurers, with their capital, had reduced the trade to northern Europe to near chaos. In the subsequent words of the company: "ignorant, weak newcomers . . . with all the spurs that were almost weekly put into them by the complaints of the clothiers . . . and by their orders enforcing the particular brethren to buy up the cloth . . . yet were not able to buy up the cloth or maintain the markets in any good measure." To throw open the trade, on the pretext of expanding demand, with no assurance that company members would remain active, might only aggravate the slump. There were obvious economic limitations to a policy which contradicted the expectations of private capital.

In fact, in nearly every severe crisis the government found that its powers to affect demand were exhausted at an early stage. But even before this point had been reached it was the general practice to bolster these attempts to maintain private industrial activity with other measures, which tried much more directly to alleviate distress at the local level. Indeed, it was for just such a purpose that the Elizabethan Poor Law had been designed, and the government was never reluctant to use its powers in the cause of protecting living standards by the enforcement of general poor relief, price control, and minimum wage supports. The practices of Stuart officialdom in this regard, however much they reflected a sophisticated social conscience, were marked by a practical expediency. For they were an integral part of the overall effort to keep the populace in a quiescent frame of mind. Clearly, this aim would be strongest when the council was trying to dispense with parliamentary aids to government and therefore desired to offset any distress which might lead to an irresistible popular demand to recall Parliament. It is this which explains the reputation of the personal government with regard to the efficiency of its central administration. And to judge by the experience of the years after 1628, official attempts at poor relief were as sincere and wholehearted as was then humanly possible.

The narrative sections of the earlier chapters of this book have already illustrated how it was in the face of textile depression that the government attempted to secure a more than normally efficient enforcement of the requirements of the Elizabethan Poor Law. This applied as much to the provisions for "setting the poor on work" with capital derived from local taxation, as it did to those which aimed at more direct relief. Thus in the early 1620's the Privy Council exerted considerable effort in exhortations to J.P.s in the western counties to enforce the Poor Law, "because we have been informed of diverse tumultuous assemblies and riots in some of those western parts occasioned partly through want of employment for the poorer sort by the decay of clothing." The situation seems to have been even more urgent after 1628, and the closest attention was given to problems of poor relief in East Anglia, which ultimately led to the issue of a special commission in 1631. It was, indeed, at the latter time, in the textile-producing counties, that the principal efforts were made, and most success attained, in easing the burden of the slump for the distressed weavers and spinners and their families. The depressed years after 1628, in their effects upon the stimulation of poor relief by the central government, were a fitting prelude to the period of Caroline paternalism.

In conjunction with these moves to redistribute income to the benefit of the poor, a slump which coincided with a bad harvest would normally provoke far-reaching government efforts to facilitate the supply of food and lower the price of bread. At times this might be almost impossible. But, given the normally poor system of transportation and distribution, there was often scope for price reduction through an easing of the processes of immediate supply of grain and an elimination of its more frivolous uses. On this basis the government moved not so much with some ideal of a consumer society in mind, as with a positive fear of starvation and the unrest which accompanied it. And it was in just such a context that the anti-middleman policy, which has been held to be a marked feature of internal trade regulation, was bolstered and applied. The roots of such a policy lay in the fear of the effects of the high price of necessities upon economic and social well-being, and a depression was most likely to bring this fear into the open. Thus during the crises of the early 1620's and the early 1630's the government moved as firmly as it could to control the supply of grain, eliminate speculators and hoarders, avoid unnecessary processing of barley, and bring down the current price of bread. By January 1631 the Book of Orders, which outlined the requisite regulations, was issued on a permanent basis.

Finally, in the way of direct local efforts to improve the lot of the poverty-stricken textile workers, it was natural that the government should now and then feel stirred to interfere in the free play of market forces which, no matter what their beauty or inevitability, were combining to reduce real wages. Government wage policies in the sixteenth and seventeenth centuries were ambivalent. On the one hand, the Statute of Artificers and many local wage assessments aimed at a ceiling for wages which might limit industrial mobility and/or keep down industrial costs. On the other hand, there were times when the short-run effects of fluctuations in demand and supply put a pressure on wages sufficient to threaten social disturbance. In these latter circumstances the official reaction was to intervene in order to establish minimum rates of pay at least at subsistence level. Examples of this occurred in 1603–4, when statutory power was given to the assessment of minimum wages; in 1629, when Essex J.P.s were ordered to maintain the wages of employees in the bay-making industry; in 1630 and 1631 generally throughout East Anglia; and in 1636, again in Essex.

The lesson was obvious: industrial no less than commercial regulation had to be an essential attribute of a government policy whose primary aim was the continuity of employment. With respect to the textile industry government policy, no less than in regard to the commercial structure, illustrates a search for stability which should be distinguished from the sixteenth-century emphasis on the passive ideal of an agrarian society. The prevailing fear was of unemployment or excessively low standards of living, and any move which might guard against such eventualities was favourably considered. It was for this reason that frequently there were conscious attempts *not* to enforce aspects of the Elizabethan code of industrial regulation. This applied, for instance, to the legal requirements of a seven-year apprenticeship before practising the trade of cloth-making. For by the early seventeenth century there were sufficient un-apprenticed weavers, clothiers and the like to make the enforcement of such a provision a dangerous prelude to unemployment for a host of textile workers. The same principle—that a conflict between the law and the desire to maintain employment should more frequently be decided in favour of the latter—was applied in the case of laws or proposed edicts towards the improvement of the quality of English textiles.

The recurrent campaigns against false manufacture can themselves be seen as integral parts of a policy designed to increase the demand for English cloth: certainly this was the burden of most complaints by merchants at times of depression. It was felt that if the quality could be improved then cloth would secure a better sale abroad. Consequently there were intermittent attempts throughout the period to enforce the laws designed for this purpose. But the fact, not entirely appreciated at the time, that low-quality manufacture was more often a sign of cost-reducing measures than a proof of original sin, meant that a strict application of the law, by increasing costs, might put the marginal operator out of business. And when the realization came that this was more than just a remote possibility, the government was forced to compromise with its legalistic principles. This happened, for example, in the 1630's when strong efforts to experiment with the arrangements for textile production in the West were abandoned as it came to be recognized that an elimination of the notorious gig mills or of the specialist market spinner, whatever their effects on quality, would only serve to provoke a crisis of unemployment.

Hence the government's approach to the industrial structure of the old draperies was determined in the last resort by a desire to guard against those periods of distress and tumult, fear of which in the sixteenth century had produced legislation designed to restrict industrialization. However, by the early seventeenth century the primary emphasis had been concentrated on at least sustaining the level of employment, and possibly increasing it. There was no thought of enforcing any policy which, no matter what its effect over a long period of time, might throw people out of work in the short run. However, there was no way of telling which way the government might act with these feelings in mind. Thus in 1615 and 1616 there was a renewed campaign against that bane of the sixteenth-century humanist, the middleman. Out of the controversy which accompanied the stoppage of trade consequent upon the Cockayne project emerged a theory that the price of English wool was too high. As was normal in such circumstances, it was widely felt that elimination or control of the despicable wool brogger would go far to reduce prices, and therefore make English textiles more competitive in European markets. As a result, an extensive survey of the mechanism of the internal wool trade in 1615 and 1616 was followed by orders designed to restrict the activities of wool broggers in all areas except those where small-scale producers of new draperies were dependent on middlemen the year round. On the other hand, the crisis of the early 1620's saw an attempt to raise the price of wool by a repeal of the 1552 statute against wool middlemen (21 Jac. I, c. 28). And modern research has indicated that industrial regulation, in all the variety inherited from the sixteenth century, was not, by the early seventeenth, considered to be anything more than peripheral to the central concerns of government. As far as positive industrial policy went, it concentrated on the problems which most immediately might effect the peace and livelihood of local communities.

It is possibly this which goes furthest to explain a new aspect of industrial policy: one which reflected the expanding possibilities of a more diversified economy and, ultimately, the economic reality of a decline in the traditional textile manufacture. Government intervention turned in the direction of industrial expansion.

As far as the government itself was concerned this was the real motive behind the Cockayne experiment. The adventurers themselves . . . far from embodying a sincere desire to create a large-scale finishing industry, concentrated their efforts largely on the hope of forcing the old company to share its profitable privileges with respect to unfinished broadcloth. But for the privy councillors the project, quite apart from the bribes which they received, provided an opportunity of satisfying what has subsequently been thought of as typically "mercantilist" desire: to increase the value of exports and raise the level of employment. This, they hoped, might be done by converting the preponderant export of white broadcloth into the sale of dyed and dressed textiles, with a consequent increase in values and the growth of a domestic finishing industry capable of beating the Dutch out of the market. The experiment was a dismal failure. Its main interest from the point of view of government policy, however, resides in the fact that such a horrendous and arbitrary alteration of the established structure of commerce should have taken place when, far from there existing the urgent environment of a slump, the woollen trade to northern Europe was at the height of its prosperity. Whatever the other reasons for this departure, it is clear that the council was only finally persuaded to support the project, against its better judgement, by pressure from the Throne and extreme duplicity on the part of the projectors. It needed the exercise of extraordinary power to instigate an extraordinary experiment.

Less extraordinary, although in final effect they were much less important than Alderman Cockayne's plans, were those projects, favourably considered or even stimulated by the central government, for a different type of industrial expansion. In the main, government officials did little more than look with benign satisfaction on the developments which were beginning to make their mark in the early seventeenth century. But in some areas more positive steps were taken in an effort to promote economic growth.

In its efforts to encourage the influx of new capital into old industries (e.g. the manufacture of soap, salt and starch) or to stimulate in new ways such pursuits as fishing or the manufacture of new draperies, it was natural that the government should envisage an adaptation of the traditional corporate and gild organizations. The result was a series of unsuccessful experiments in economic development, whose structure ranged from an industrial monopoly to a network of regional joint-stock organizations, and whose aim was more often the establishment than the regulation of a particular industry. With respect to the new draperies there were two main efforts to set up a system of quasi-public corporations, the second of which emerged from the confusions of the crisis of the early 1620's. These bodies were to be based on county administrative units and in part integrated with the poor-law system. They were intended to stimulate, and also exert quality control over, a growth in the new manufacture. In the end, these plans, like all the others, came to nothing. Their failure has been attributed to a fatal rigidity in the gild system itself and to the lustiness of new competition: the powers of the corporations, it has been said, bore no relation to the problems they had to solve. In the main, therefore, the government was forced to let the principal elements in economic growth go their own way, and in the event it was even found impossible to regulate the quality of the new manufacture. Once more the government was forced back to a short-term approach to economic regulation. This was even more evident, to take another example, in its relationship with the monetary system.

The concern to alleviate dislocation which directly or indirectly shaped almost every important measure of industrial and commercial policy during the period, was an equally marked feature of the official attitude to the national and international currency system. As has already been abundantly shown, the economic fluctuations which so shook the economy of the early seventeenth century were to a significant degree intermingled with the general repercussions of an unstable monetary system. At one level variations in the prices of gold and silver provoked abrupt shifts in the flow of commodities, the balance of trade, and industrial prosperity. More basically, such variations stimulated even more violent ebbs and flows of bullion and ready money. It was therefore quite natural that so much government time and energy, in the line of economic policy, was devoted to questions of coinage valuations and monetary supplies. From this background . . . there emerged the framework of official discussion and activity so familiar to historians of "mercantilist policy."

There is no further need to outline the details of proposed and accepted policy which demonstrate, beyond all doubt, that the stimulus to government action lay immediately in the desire for an adequate supply of money in the kingdom—and that this found its origin in the painful experiences of intermittent monetary shortage. The role of liquid capital as a stimulant to continuous, diversified productive effort and the importance of a steady supply of cash in an underdeveloped economy deprived of the benefits of a sophisticated banking structure and widely circulating fiduciary instruments, do not need re-emphasis either. Threats to the monetary supply struck at the basis of an enormous range of internal economic activity, and, therefore, the *defensive* note which runs through other aspects of policy was more than ever evident in the official approach to monetary affairs.

It is not too difficult to recognize, in government attitudes and actions, widespread feelings concerning the wisdom of accumulating treasure and the economic and strategic strength which, it was felt, England might derive from such a process. These concepts, indeed, viewed by Adam Smith as a systematization of thought and policy, were those which he identified with mercantilism and ridiculed so ably on theoretical grounds. But it has already been argued in these pages that it would be misleading to attempt to understand policy solely in terms of a spontaneous regard for the unlimited acquisition of treasure. In any case, it is likely that such views envisaged the inflow of bullion not so much as an augmentation of monetary supplies—which would be inflationary and self-defeating—but as an increase in the supply of capital, to be absorbed into an expanding economic system. But quite apart from such arguments, the fact remains that it is possible to see every policy measure in the light of the prevailing economic conditions which posed direct and indirect threats to England's monetary supplies and forced the government on to the defensive and into policy discussions primarily intended to reduce an outflow rather than augment an inflow of money. This was equally true, although in each case little positive action resulted from them, of all considerations of monetary policy: the proposed enforcement of statutes prohibiting the export of coin and commanding the "employment" of the proceeds of imports by aliens; the plans for government monopolies of money-changing and exchange transactions; the projects for currency manipulation and export- and import-control. In the event the government was forced to leave the determination of bullion flows to market forces operating within the framework of established mint prices, supplemented by the intermittent enforcement of pre-existing laws. And, not surprisingly, the criterion used to defeat great plans for monetary experiments was comparable to that which occasioned the initial discussions: the reverence for economic stability. In the last resort the government concluded, or was reluctantly persuaded, that the cost of projects to maintain monetary supplies—measured in economic dislocation at other points—was too great to justify experiment. At all points the delicacy of the economic and social mechanism was appreciated as perhaps the most important consideration in shaping policy.

We have seen that government action in the early seventeenth century was marked by a search for stability: by a valid fear of unemployment and economic instability. Contrasted with the sixteenth century, which had the same ends in view, the period under discussion demonstrated that industrial restrictions were not the only possible outcome of such an attitude. The aim was, instead, to protect England against the harsher repercussions of economic fluctuation without regressing in terms of the industrial and commercial structure. And the urgency of this aim explains the assumption that, in its cause, the rights of private property and of established organizations could be abrogated without further thought. In its fear of the bread riot the government, short of shattering the very bases of society, was willing to entertain virtually any idea. Indeed, among the primary motives of the quest for expansion and diversification, which was a feature of long-term developments, was a desire to compensate for the decline in the traditional industry and provide outlets for unemployed factors of production. This last attitude ultimately shaded imperceptibly into a new appraisal of the role and value of competition for English trade and industry. It served to set the stage for those revolutions in policy and more especially in outlook which became so evident in the generations after the Restoration.

Thus the setting within which it is absolutely necessary to study the formulation of government economic policy is that which has been the general subject-matter of this book. Policy and intermittent trade crisis are historically inseparable. This is true to the extent that we can never consider in isolation those elements of official policy which so many students of the period have called "mercantilist." The desire to prevent or alleviate undue commercial fluctuation is surely not a remarkable or exceptional administrative viewpoint. Yet it is the only element which really binds together generations of policy; and reasonably consistent and pragmatic responses to consistent fluctuation in an economic environment whose basic elements were slow to change hardly merit treatment as a full-blown system. Disparate official measures were not meaningful and complementary parts of any "plan" greater than a pressing need to maintain the economy on at least an even keel. In any case, few statesmen had the inclination or the ability to formulate an ideal image of economic society and the policy which would bring it into being.

However, few processes could be more misleading than to measure the extent of the Stuart government's economic participation by the number and range of the laws in existence, by edicts promulgated, or by the formal exhortations to action which proceeded, with such monotonous regularity, from the Privy Council. Historians by now are quick to appreciate that a plethora of regulations may well be, by the very frequency of the latter, a better indication of what was *not* done than of what was. For we are dealing with an age in which the formal ability to articulate policy had developed well beyond the administrative capacity to enforce it: an England all of whose economic regulations were fully in force would have been unrecognizable as well as unthinkable.

This inability to shape the larger economic developments closer to the government's heart's desire went along with a relative failure to alleviate more directly the impact of depression. The government failed to control, as far as England was concerned, the international flows of bullion. It was unable to come effectively to grips with the principal causes of commercial fluctuations and its attempts to sustain demand by pressure on English capital had obvious limits beyond which they could not go. The grand design for finishing cloth was a dismal holocaust of official expectations. The most that industrial policy could do was to abstain from those measures of interference (for example the enforcement of quality requirements) which might have provoked further unemployment. The dynamic elements in economic development during the early seventeenth century were moulded by market forces, and the government's relation to the economy—although its extent was admittedly wide—was effectively confined to sustaining some of the commercial and industrial organizations destined, in the long run, to survive or perish more by dint of their economic usefulness. The period, as far as the government was concerned, was marked by no revolution in the institutional framework within which economic fluctuations and developments took place. There is nothing to compare with the sixteenth-century economic statutes or the eighteenth-century Enclosure Acts. Adherents of government action must have derived most satisfaction from an appreciation of the direct relief organized and stimulated by the central government. The poor laws and the regulations for grain markets, although they were to some extent hamstrung by an impecunious and ramshackle administrative structure, were frequently marked by a sincerity and doggedness of purpose which served as a peripheral defence for some communities during the starvation-ridden horrors of a seventeenth-century slump.

These concluding remarks are not intended to be either a proof of the inevitability of governmental inefficiency or a further indication of the poverty of talent under the first two Stuarts. In large part the absence of any wholesale social engineering reflects the government situation during a period in which administrative structures were too weak to carry into effect the tasks which might have been entrusted to them. Yet the absence of any real tendency in this direction also needs explanation. Even the relaxations of trade regulations in 1621 and 1624, which might be taken as evidence of a less conservative approach to commercial problems, ultimately, by the tentative nature of their application and the relative speed of their revocation, only serve to underline the fact that the time was one which was far less "heroic" in its approach to commercial problems than, for instance, the mid-sixteenth century. To some extent this may have been due to a distinct decline in the standards of administrative ability under the first two Stuarts. Men of vision and executive power were markedly absent from most of the deliberations on commercial affairs at the time, while James's most important contribution merely led to the disasters of the cloth-finishing project and Charles's attempts at direct economic interference too often produced only extreme mercantile insecurity. But quite apart from the low calibre of men of affairs the official approach to trade and industry primarily derived its character from the fact that the early seventeenth century marked one of the many transitions in English economic life. It bridged a gap between an England whose typical statutory products were the Cloth Acts of the 1550's and one whose significant legal expressions lay in the Navigation Laws. Operating when the established framework of industrial England was no longer seriously questioned and before the new developments had become sufficiently important to be candidates for significant legal buttressing, the administrators of the first forty years of the seventeenth century were in no position, and did not possess a sufficiently forthright philosophy, to attempt to interfere spontaneously and effectively in the course of economic events.

It was for this sort of reason that the government's main problems were those of day-to-day administration. And in this respect, although part of its emphasis was novel, it added little to the inherited official tools of policy. This was perhaps more because the sixteenth century had exhausted the possibilities of administrative enactment, than because the seventeenth was particularly unimaginative. That most of the official efforts positively to participate in the economy were failures is no reason to ignore the implications of government policy. For policy and official discussions were directly involved with economic change, and an appreciation of them, while it demonstrates their specific inability to direct the course or guard against the consequences of change, can tell us a great deal about the obdurate economic facts with which they so unsuccessfully tried to deal.

3.

In seventeenth-century France earning money by trade or business was considered socially degrading by the nobility. R. B. Grassby (1935–   ), Fellow of Jesus College, Oxford, explains the social origins of this prejudice against trade.

So long as commerce and industry were viewed as degrading, the patterns of capital investment would inevitably be influenced by hunger for prestige as much as by desire for profit. Miss Barbour has noted that Dutch merchants had observed the propensity of their French counterparts to get out of business as soon as they could afford to do so. By buying offices, fine town houses, estates, even fiefs, *bourgeois gentilshommes* employed their capital to abandon commerce.

Under these conditions, then, it was not the availability of capital or even the amount of it which influenced economic development. The flight of capital from commercial and industrial enterprises was recognized by ministers of Louis XIV, including Colbert, but their efforts at making business honorable failed. Why? What attracted French capital? From the patterns of the utilization of capital, can you deduce which industries developed the most rapidly in France? Luxury goods, of course. What else? Here, as elsewhere, social changes were linked to the utilization of capital; but, in the case of France, did these changes shake the traditional structure of society?

R. B. GRASSBY: Social Status and Commercial Enterprise under Louis XIV*

In Restoration England, the distinction between wealth and honour was a subject for comedy and malicious conversation, but ridicule could not permanently impair the prestige of the successful merchant, nor gossip degrade the legal status of a peer in trade. Across the channel, however, the distinction was taken more seriously. The rank and file of the French *noblesse,* those families which neither attended the Court nor sat in the *Parlements,* chose to perpetuate a scale of values and a system of rewards reminiscent of the Heroic Age. To them the *raison d'être* of the merchant was the acquisition of material wealth, his dominant motive personal gain. For his base and calculating virtues a fortune was ample recompense. Social prestige, on the other hand, should be reserved for those who displayed valour or piety, and who devoted themselves without remuneration or distraction to serve the community on the battlefield and in the chancel.

This artificial distinction sprang from the prejudices and fears of noble families, who saw their social position threatened by the wealth of the *Tiers État.* It had no basis in fact. Demographic and economic forces had transformed beyond recognition that legendary feudal *noblesse* which survived in the law books, and the status and prestige of the *noblesse* had survived, not through military prowess or public service, but because of the wealth and privileges inherited from the past. So long as this wealth remained intact, the purchase of nobility by wealthy *roturiers* was gloomily accepted as unpleasant, but inevitable. But by the accession of Louis XIV, a redistribution of the increasing wealth of France had accelerated this natural process, and the consequent confusion in the social hierarchy had converted acceptance into hostility. As economic conditions enriched the merchant interest, and impoverished those *gentilshommes champêtres* deprived of the pensions of the Court and the sinecures of the Church, so the survival of the rural *noblesse* seemed to depend on a rigid distinction between wealth and honour. As the methods of translating money into social status were facilitated and augmented by an impoverished and calculating Crown, so determined efforts were made to draw a more distinct line between the *noblesse* and the *Tiers État.* Birth was no longer a practical criterion of nobility, because few *gentilshommes* had ancient or impeccable pedigrees, and the traditional hallmarks of nobility—the possession of fiefs, exemption from the *taille,* and an extravagant *mode de vie*—were easily accessible to wealthy *roturiers.* So the provincial *noblesse* revived in the early seventeenth century the ancient, but dormant, custom of derogation, and declared the status of nobility incompatible with trade. An act of self-sacrifice, the voluntary rejection of business was expected to separate the sheep from the goats, and by renouncing the only means of restoring their economic position the rural families hoped to avert their annihilation as a class. This did not discourage the ambitious merchant. By service to the Crown, by marriage, and by the

* From R. B. Grassby, "Social Status and Commercial Enterprise under Louis XIV," *Economic History Review,* 1961, pp. 19–38.

purchase of noble fiefs or legal offices, he continued to acquire both the form and substance of hereditary nobility. Indeed the attitude of the *noblesse* merely encouraged this process, for the lower the status of trade the more imperative it was for the socially conscious merchant to enter the *noblesse*. But it did separate the business from the social world.

This schism constituted a severe impediment to the development of French trade. The driving force of vanity was divorced from and opposed to the creative energy of the acquisitive instinct. Where they could be combined, in the acquisition of the financial privileges of nobility, it was to the detriment of trade. Because nobility was now defined in terms of exclusion from trade, it was impossible for the merchant to revert to trade without endangering his expensively acquired dignity. The prejudice against trade immobilized therefore the capital and energies, not only of the *ancienne noblesse* but also of newly ennobled merchants who, to preserve their status, invested their commercial profits in office, land and government bonds, and lived as *rentiers*. Only those who could not afford nobility remained in trade, and they were the least well equipped to replace their more successful predecessors. The economic significance of this loss of capital and experience can be exaggerated. Some of this capital did return to trade through the medium of government investment, and withdrawal from trade by the third generation of a business family was common even in commercially advanced countries like England. Nor can the slow rate of economic growth in France be explained simply by reference to the structure of French society. That is to ignore the influence of geography and opportunity, the movements of population and prices, and the other objective factors that limit the role of incentive in economic development. Nevertheless, it is clear that social attitudes did create an important obstacle to French commercial expansion, and it is both appropriate and useful to ask why these attitudes persisted, what attempts were made to change them, and why they were unsuccessful.

The contempt of Frenchmen for trade had not escaped the attention of contemporary observers. Dazzled by the brilliant expansion of English and Dutch trade, French commentators throughout the seventeenth century had sought the elusive key which would explain why France, with her favourable geographical position, her great natural resources, and her reserve of skilled and industrious manpower, had failed to emulate her political and religious rivals. Foremost among the explanations ranked the divorce of wealth from honour. Not all writers went as far as the author who believed that "wealth is no more sought for its own sake: it is principally desired because it can lead to honour." But throughout the profuse economic literature of the period can be detected a conviction that the desire for riches was not the only incentive to trade, and that the desire for social status should be turned to productive use. Many a pamphleteer writing about bullion or a reckoner compiling tables of compound interest felt it necessary to point out the attitude of indifference towards business, and the prejudices which alienated both the *noblesse* and the merchant interest from commerce. The discussion normally centred on the sale of office, a practice attacked from its inception, but seen increasingly as a sponge absorbing the energies of the business world. This stream of comment was swollen by much repetition and imitation. Many authors were propagandists or patriots, hired to defend a private interest or eager to whip up nationalist feeling, and others through missionary zeal could not resist extravagant overstatements of their case. But a few examples from the more intelligent and original thinkers will show not only that the problem had received thorough analysis, but also that practical solutions had been devised.

At the core of the problem was seen the prejudice against trade. If commerce was considered an honourable profession the problem would disappear, because the *noblesse* would no longer fear absorption by an inferior class, and merchants would not have to abandon trade to win social respect. The obvious solution seemed therefore to elevate the status of business as a profession, and many pamphleteers charged themselves with this very task. To balance the traditional scale of values, they advanced two lines of argument, that commerce could not be ignored because it played an indispensable rôle in national life, and that it could not be scorned because it embraced both the objectives and qualities characteristic of the *noblesse*. The utility of trade in its material aspects did not require elaboration, but the extent of its influence and benefits needed further clarification. This work was best and most fully done by three well-known writers of the early seventeenth century—the irrepressible Huguenot adviser of Henry IV, Bartholomew de Laffemas, the Huguenot rebel and dramatist Antoine de Montchrétien, and the historian, polemicist and monk Jean Eon. Laffemas abandoned the blank verse and musical scores characteristic of his early pamphlets, and vividly contrasted the limited function of the static privileged orders with the productive function and international renown of merchants, who bridged great oceans and on their letters of credit raised great fortunes. Eon, in his classic work *Le Commerce Honorable,* rounded off the pioneer work of Montchrétien. He invoked the imagery and philosophy of pagan Antiquity, the wishes of the Almighty and the historical examples of primitive Israel and contemporary Europe, to show that trade was not the preserve of grasping and petty usurers, but the source of social stability, national prosperity, political power, and civilized life. He argued that overseas trade brought prosperity not only to individual merchants, but to all members of society. It provided money for the needs of government and war, markets for the agricultural produce of the landowners, employment for the younger sons of the *noblesse,* new endowments for the Church and learning, litigation for the lawyers, work for the artisans and relief for the poor.

Utility however was not enough. To place commerce on an equal footing with the more traditional occupations required a purification of the acquisitive instinct, an appeal to those qualities most admired by the *noblesse*. Consequently emphasis was placed on the glory, rather than the material benefits, which resulted from trade, its aggressive instead of its sober qualities. Many pamphleteers were unashamed patriots who believed, not without justification, that the world's resources were finite, and who therefore envisaged trade as a continuous war on the prosperity of other states. There were a few men who thought that God had distributed natural resources unequally over the world to encourage peace and brotherhood. But most contemporaries were convinced that trade was not to be shared but conquered and defended, and in this belief they approached the military and spiritual objectives of feudal society. The predatory instincts of the *noblesse* could easily be identified with the conquest of markets, with territorial colonization, with the gamble of speculative investment, and with privateering, in an age when piracy was often indistinguishable from honest trade. To these elements of risk and adventure could be added the prospect of missionary work in overseas lands, the conversion of the heathen, and a crusade against the prosperous heretics of the world. These arguments had been developed by Eon, a disciple of *la gloire* and quick to notice that the military and naval power, developed under pressure of war, could further and protect French shipping and interests in time of peace. But the best example of this type of propaganda is the treatise, commissioned by Colbert and written by the *académicien* Charpentier, to attract investors to the revived *Compagnie des Indes Orientales.* The flamboyant preamble to this treatise exploited the glamour of the Orient, the brilliant successes of the Dutch and Portuguese, and the infinite glory of a commercial Empire conquered from the enemies of France by the bravery of the *noblesse* and the energy and intelligence of the *Tiers État.* Hard work and thrift might be the founding virtues of successful business, but honour could only derive from a display of courage and devotion.

By these arguments contemporary writers hoped to discredit the false antithesis between trade and the functions characteristic of a feudal hierarchy. They realized however that more direct action was necessary to remove the fears as well as the prejudices of the *noblesse* and merchants. The *noblesse* should be protected against loss of status should they enter trade, and some means should be found to honour merchants without forcing them to buy office and to leave business. The pamphleteers had provided a reasoned basis for the fusion of the two classes; it was the task of the Crown, as head of the social order, to translate their policies into reality. The various measures proposed do not need individual citation. Many were quickly stereotyped and others, like proposals to convert the conspicuous consumption of the Court into commercial capital, have only a bizarre significance. It will suffice to record the views of three important writers —the astonishingly precocious Louis Turquet de Mayerne, the humane Cassandra from Blésois, Du Noyer, and the spokesman of the urban nobility of Marseille, the priest Marchetti. In his *Monarchie Aristodémocratique,* written at the end of the sixteenth century, Mayerne argued not only that the *noblesse* was entitled to trade, but that this was the only occupation which could justify their privileges, and that merchants should by virtue of their productive function rise automatically to the *noblesse.* Mayerne, who had made a fortune in business and had married his granddaughter into the *noblesse,* possessed a clearer conception of a business aristocracy than any other French writer of the period. His main ideas were echoed however by Du Noyer, who criticized the parasitic court *noblesse* and the imitative merchant, and who wanted to force the *noblesse* to invest in trade, and to ennoble merchants who invested in shipping on condition that they remained in business. A different approach was made by Marchetti, writing to protect the *noblesse commerçante* of Marseille from a governmental inquiry into usurpations of nobility. Diverted occasionally by the necessity of pleasing the royal commissioners, he yet produced a coherent scheme for maintaining the social status of both the nobles and merchants actively engaged in trade. Most of these scattered proposals were eventually codified by Jacques Savary, himself a descendant of a noble line which had reverted to commerce in the fifteenth century, a man who knew the risks of investment in office, and a member of the commercial aristocracy of Paris, the *corps de merciers*. The best known and most widely read pamphleteer of the century, Savary did not make any original contribution to the literature of the period, but as the person employed by Colbert to help draft a new commercial Code, his words had great authority and a receptive audience. In his *Parfait Négociant* he transmitted both his own experience and the best ideas of previous writers to those with the power and inclination to reform.

Not all pamphlets enjoyed serious consideration, and many may have shared the fate of one anonymous treatise upon whose pages its purchaser composed amorous verse. But the Crown, to which advice was generally directed, was both sensitive to such literature and a great publisher of this sort of material. It needed little persuasion to accept the importance of trade, and the utility and honour of commerce had been a commonplace of royal preambles since the fifteenth century. Eager to extend its authority over the total resources and population of France, the monarchy had from its earliest struggle for centralization encouraged the growth of trade, both to increase the resources available for government and war, and to maintain a level of prosperity without which the stability and security of the state could not be preserved. The social impediments to trade, outlined by professional observers and confirmed by the reports of its own officials, were therefore a source of much concern. This is indicated by the interest taken in the problem by the two greatest royal ministers of the century —Richelieu and Colbert. The Cardinal, who had personally experienced the poverty of the *hobereaux* and whose grasp of the importance of economic power pervades his *Testament Politique,* expressed a desire to attract the *noblesse* into trade, and to "suppress offices firmly, and give value to traffic and rank to merchants." He created on paper a hereditary Catholic order of knighthood, drawn from the wealthier merchants as well as from the two privileged orders, with the express duty of extending French trade and Catholicism overseas. The more pragmatic *fonctionnaire* Colbert, descended from businessmen who had won social status, also wanted to utilize all social classes to further French trade, and tried to persuade his royal master to elevate the status of commerce by showing his personal approval of businessmen.

The result was that many of the measures proposed by the pamphleteers for the *noblesse* and the merchants were put into effect. The safeguards against derogation, enjoyed by nobles residing in commercial and banking centres like Marseille and Lyon, were confirmed, and investors were attracted to the companies launched by the Crown for overseas commerce and colonization by provisos protecting them from derogation in the charters of foundation. No effort was spared to force the *noblesse* to invest in the *Compagnie des Indes* in

1664, including personal pressure at Court and a careful tuning of the pulpits, and further protection from derogation was afforded by the sale of "lettres de réhabilitation." An even more direct challenge to the binding force of local custom came from royal edicts. The precocious Louis XI had projected an ordinance opening trade "by sea, land and inland waterways" to the *noblesse,* but his contemporaries and immediate successors disapproved, and when the *Ordonnance* of Orléans in 1560 codified former legislation and custom concerning derogation, it withdrew the financial privileges of the *noblesse commerçante.* It was not until 1628 that article 452 of the *Code Michau,* under the inspiration of Richelieu, publicly declared overseas trade compatible with nobility. This article represented the limit of royal intervention up to 1701. Colbert's edict of August 1669 did maintain in an enthusiastic preamble that "there is no means more innocent and legitimate to acquire wealth than trade," but it did little more than confirm the existing law. In 1701 the protection against derogation, accorded by the Crown, was still limited to overseas and wholesale trade.

Similar encouragement had been offered to merchants. The Crown recognized the nobility conferred by high municipal office, as at Nantes and Toulouse, and offered nobility to *roturiers* who invested in the commercial companies or in colonial enterprises. Twelve of the associates of the *Compagnie de la Nouvelle France* were, for example, not only granted titles of nobility, but also exempted from the terms of an edict directing the payment of *taille* by nobles of less than twenty years standing. The *Code Michau* conferred the privileges of nobility upon those who maintained a merchant ship of two or three hundred tons for five years, and upon *"marchands-grossiers"* who had become *échevins, consuls,* or *gardes* of their corporations. A more effective measure was the granting of individual letters patent. Louis XI had conferred nobility— though not exemption from the *taille*—upon successful merchants, and his impecunious successors periodically put up letters patent for sale. The financial origin of many of these grants rendered them insecure, because the Crown was always tempted to revoke and resell them, but they were eagerly sought as the most impressive *entrée* to nobility. Only wholesale, colonial, and overseas merchants were, however, eligible for this distinction, and except in financial emergencies the Crown limited these grants to those who armed ships against its enemies, and did not grant them wholesale to the merchant interest.

The limited efforts of the Crown did not make much impression. The *noblesse* was not indifferent to the advantages of trade. Indeed the supreme rôle of commerce had been a familiar feature of the *Cahiers* of the *États-Generaux* since the fifteenth century. The joint *Cahier* of the Three Estates in 1484 described trade as a necessary and useful means of creating abundance, and in 1560 and 1614 the need for government intervention and protection was strongly urged. The *Assemblée des Notables* in 1627 endorsed the opinion of the *Garde des Sceaux,* that trade was a source of both prosperity and honour, and that the *noblesse* should be permitted to participate. The *grande noblesse* had always possessed widespread economic interests, and the rural *gentilshommes* had engaged even in the retail trade by letting their nobility lie "dormant" while they mended their fortunes. But the fear of social absorption, expressed in the attempts of the *noblesse* in the sixteenth century to enforce sumptuary legislation, had by the middle of the seventeenth century driven the *noblesse* away from trade back to the land. Brittany, formerly the scene of the most active participation by the *noblesse* in trade, rigidly enforced the exclusion of nobles from commerce, and even the "mystery" of glassmaking, the one trade permitted for artistic reasons by immemorial custom to the *gentilshommes,* was not widely practised. As the custom of derogation grew more binding, and when after 1665 the Crown appointed commissions to enquire into usurpations of nobility, the *noblesse* were reluctant to risk participation in business, because loss of rank also entailed loss of the financial privileges without which they felt their economic position would be intolerable. The *grande noblesse* continued to dabble in speculation and to glean the financial pickings of the Court, but the rank and file of the *noblesse,* so far as can be ascertained, vegetated on the land and remained on the perimeter of trade and industry. As the *noblesse* refused to become a *noblesse commerçante,* so the merchant interest continued to play the *bourgeois gentilhomme.* Refused the opportunity of buying patents of nobility, compatible with trade, the wealthy merchant continued to seek his social salvation by the purchase of offices which could not be combined with business. Government action had therefore been both half-hearted in application and limited in effect, and contemporary writers had reason to complain that the glowing promises of royal preambles had not been fulfilled.

This situation might have continued unchanged but for the pressure of economic difficulties at the end of the seventeenth century. The successors of Colbert, although they followed his precepts devoutly, could not cope with the extraordinary cost and injuries of the Nine Years' War, and by 1700, although the peace brought some relief, the economic position of France was far from satisfactory. At a time when the treaties of Ryswick constituted a check to the political ambitions and international prestige of France, the *mémoires* of the *Intendants* indicated economic stagnation. In contrast, the heretical limited monarchies of England and Holland were humiliating examples of prosperity and *grandeur.* As an instrument to reverse this situation and restore French trade, the Crown decided in 1700 to revive the *Conseil de Commerce* used in the past by Laffemas, Fouquet, and Colbert. This was the advisory board of Colbert's *Conseil* pruned of its administrative functions and the royal presence. It gave full regional representation to the merchant interest of France for the first time, by summoning deputies from the chief commercial towns, and as their first task it instructed the deputies to present individual *mémoires* on the state of trade in general. Intended as a symbol of royal determination to help French trade in every possible way, the *Conseil* marked a co-operative effort by both the leading merchants and government officials to cure the evils of the French economy. From this burst of energy was to come the final attempt to solve the dichotomy between commerce and social status.

Submitted during the winter of 1700 the reports of the deputies of the *Conseil,* although they embraced every aspect of economic life, brought the social question to the fore. Many deputies doubtless spoke to justify and defend, as well as to explain, and often expressed their personal opinions rather than the views of the towns they represented. Although they all had experience of business, they had normally retired before their election and now possessed private political interests in addition to the commercial interests of their home towns. But their conclusions, arrived at by independent observation and thought, proved to be remarkably similar, and taken together give an authoritative picture of France. Much time was devoted to an attack on *"Colbertisme"* as applied by Colbert's successors—the monopoly of the royal companies, the impediments of tariffs and taxation, the restriction of trade by unnecessary regulation. But they also restated in classic form the social reasons envisaged by earlier writers for French backwardness. All but two of the deputies emphasized that the profit motive must be reinforced by social recognition for merchants.

At the core of the problem they placed the fact that prestige remained identified with political and military splendour. The deputy of Bayone contrasted republics like Holland, where prestige was unceremoniously sacrificed to profit, with monarchies like France whose "genius prefers glory and the profession of arms . . . which had prevented serious attention being paid to commerce, which had never been regarded as a serious business." It was considered essential to reverse this order of priorities, to treat the pursuit of wealth as an end in itself, and not merely as a means to the traditional end of military glory. Du Hallay, the brilliant deputy of Nantes, hoped that the bellicose instincts of France were satisfied by the late wars, that now she would acquire the "commercial spirit" necessary to snatch commercial supremacy from the English and the Dutch.

French merchants, they complained, were always in the pillory. According to the deputy of La Rochelle, the most eminent merchants—even those who had become *juge-consuls*—were "no more respected than the common people"; the ignorant prejudice against trade remained so strong, added the deputy of Dunkirk, that the *noblesse* remained reluctant to enter commerce. Indeed, such was the scorn of the *officiers* and *fermiers,* remarked Du Hallay, that a dowry of 10,000 *livres* could not guarantee the daughters of merchants a socially advantageous marriage, and civic distinctions were conditional upon leaving trade. A major difficulty was the ambiguity of the term *"marchand."* The greatest merchant bore the same title as his tailor, and was associated in popular imagination with the fraudulent pedlar and the hated shopkeeper. To make it worse, pointed out the deputy of Bayonne, the only Frenchmen who did make commerce "so to speak the sole subject of their attention" were those excluded by their religious faith from all other professions, and they were now excluded from France. Reluctant martyrs for commercial progress, successful merchants abandoned trade as soon as they could afford to purchase the respect which accompanied the ownership of land or office. To the deputies this was both justified and inevitable. Had not Mésnager, the deputy of Rouen, left trade ten years earlier to become *"secrétaire du roi,"* and did not Héron, the deputy of La Rochelle, devote his time and salary, in later years, not to service in the *Conseil,* but to litigation over a similar office? The blame, if any, the deputies of Lyon and Lille emphasized, was due to the endless creation and sale of posts, to which undue social superiority was attached.

Whatever the explanation, the effect was rightly considered harmful. Not only, said the deputy of Lille, did these posts "divert the minds of the people from the attention that they should pay to trade," but merchants borrowed so heavily to purchase them that "reasons of interest, more pressing than those of honour scarcely allow them to fill their posts with dignity." Even worse was the effect on capital accumulation and commercial efficiency of this flight from commerce. The techniques of business could not be acquired in a moment, and only rigorous training of the new generation of merchants by the old could produce skilled personnel. But, said Du Hallay, "our young men prefer to study French airs, and to acquire polish, rather than to apply themselves to serious matters," and daily bankruptcies were evidence of amateurs without capital or experience. This was not the whole story. The deputy and former mayor of St-Malo pointed out that in his port everybody lived by trade, and merchants sent their children overseas to gain experience; yet trade was depressed. Nevertheless the basic problem remained. The humiliation to which merchants were reduced by French society was starving French commerce of incentives, capital and skill, and thereby contributing towards economic decay.

The solutions that the deputies advised were as familiar as their analysis. The prejudice against trade must be forcibly attacked, and various devices employed to break down the barriers between the *noblesse* and the commercial world. The right to trade without derogation should be confirmed by the Crown and extended, many deputies thought, to the *noblesse de la robe* and to include both apprenticeship and wholesale business within France. Municipal posts and consular judicatures could be confined to merchants, and their holders put on equal footing with the *avocats* and *officiers*. But the central solution offered was to grant "some marks of honour" to those who would excel at commercial enterprise. When debating a project to create provincial counterparts of the *Conseil de Commerce* in the provinces, the deputies had firmly rejected a proposal to convert them into commercial equivalents of the *Parlements,* by making the posts in these *Chambres de Commerce* noble and hereditary. But most of them did want to create an active commercial nobility, and recommended the granting of nobility to families which had remained from three to four generations in trade, and to those who would serve as deputies in the *Chambres de Commerce* once they were established. Distinction *vis-à-vis* the other orders of society necessitated distinctions within the commercial world. The majority agreed with the deputy of La Rochelle, that all those engaged in wholesale and overseas commerce should be distinguished from other *"marchands"* by the title *"négociant,"* and that only those enrolled as *négociants* should enjoy the privileges and honours previously suggested. The solution seemed at hand; only a warning from Du Hallay about the complexity of the problem and the technical difficulties of the solution gave any indication of the trials to come.

On the strength of these *mémoires* the commissioners of the *Conseil* ordered the deputies to co-ordinate their proposals, and after two weeks of discussion and revision the deputies produced a joint report. This incorporated their original suggestions safeguarding the privileges, exemptions, and precedence of the *noblesse commerçante,* but was chiefly concerned with elaborating their proposals to honour merchants. To clarify the distinction between *"négociants"* and *"marchands,"* they differentiated wholesale commerce from retailing by the size, weight, and value of merchandise involved. When a *"marchand"* wished to become a *"négociant,"* he would apply to his local *Chambre de Commerce* or consular jurisdiction with proof of his change to wholesaling; if he reverted to retailing, he would be permanently excluded from his title, usurpation of which would entail heavy fines. Similar but lower fines faced *artisans* or *ouvriers* who called themselves *"marchands."* Certain privileges, exemptions, and rights of precedence were proposed for *"négociants,"* immediately forfeited however if they went bankrupt. They would enjoy the right to hold posts as high as *Trésorier de France* and to trade freely without the obligation to enter a *corps de marchands* or to justify apprenticeship. They would be exempt from *ban* and *arrière ban* if they owned noble land, and from billeting, watch, and guard, if and when they held office as *juge-consuls;* and they would take precedence immediately after the *officiers* of the *Présidiaux.* But the crowning proposal was the prospect of nobility. Letters of nobility would be offered to the fourth generation of families which had an honourable and continuous tradition of wholesale commerce; to ensure proof of this ancestry, merchants would in future enrol their names at the consular jurisdictions. For their own efforts the deputies requested the title of *conseiller du roi.*

Copies of this *mémoire* were now sent to those towns which sent deputies to the *Conseil.* Several towns were slow to return their comments, and others had nothing to say. But the remaining replies, in their detail and comprehensiveness, constitute a poll of commercial opinion unparalleled since Colbert's quest for capital for the *Compagnie des Indes.* Coming as they did from every important commercial centre in the provinces, they give substance to the elaborate guess-work by which the attitudes of the merchant interest are normally deduced, and reflect the regional variations and vested interests which dominated French trade. The deputies had sought a legislative formula applicable to, and in the best interests of, the whole body of French merchants. But relations between the *noblesse* and the towns varied from region to region, and even the outward forms of social status were not uniform throughout France. Consequently their formula could not meet every need and created severe problems of administration. These technical difficulties were fostered and enlarged by the predominance of powerful local interests. The commercial towns were divided not only by distance and geography, but also by historical development and private interests. Certain towns enjoyed special privileges and consideration, such as the monopoly of certain types and areas of trade, and they competed with each other for prosperity and influence. It was natural, therefore, that they should regard the proposals of the deputies not from the standpoint of the merchant interest as a whole, but from the benefits and disadvantages which would accrue to their own town and region. The Basque town of Bayonne, declining without sympathy or attention, sought direct assistance, and wished "that a more effective method could be found to induce merchants to remain in their profession." The Channel port of St-Malo was only concerned to confirm her right to confine municipal posts to merchants. The comments of the towns do more than illustrate the technical difficulties of enforcing the plans of the deputies; they indicate the provincialism and lack of unity among French merchants, which augured ill for the success of reform.

Much time was spent on the proposal to attract the *noblesse* into trade. The difficulties of adaptation were quickly spotted. Marseille pointed out that humility was a necessary quality in an apprentice, and Bordeaux that the landed property of the *noblesse* could not easily be converted into movable capital. These doubts do however suggest a reluctance to face competition from a *noblesse commerçante,* and the proposal by Nantes, to compel a long apprenticeship for new recruits to business, probably had the profits of the older hands in mind. Similar fears arose from the proposal to distinguish wholesaling from retailing. The arguments over definition indicate how important retailing was as a source of capital, and all the towns agreed with Bordeaux that a rigid distinction would be harmful, that "to elevate wholesaling it did not seem necessary to degrade retailing." Nantes, where several civic dignitaries were retailers, argued that it would suffice to enforce a distinction between *"marchands"* and *"artisans,"* and to oblige *"marchands"* to hyphenate to their title the name of their particular trade. Lyon proposed as an alternative the broad and innocuous definition of wholesaling established in a legal case at Lyon in 1667, in which some local merchants had successfully defended their nobility against imputations of retailing.

Opinions varied on the efficacy of the proposal to ennoble the fourth generation of merchants. Fabre, when he reported to the *Chambre de Commerce* of Marseille, said that he had advised nobility for the third generation, since by the fourth "a child, who had inherited a considerable fortune from his father would not take advantage (of this proposal) there being other and shorter channels to nobility." That ancient and venerable assembly thought that this argument would apply even to the third generation, and that compulsory enrolment would prejudice other methods of access to polite society. Nor would the prospect of nobility be a great incentive in Provence, Languedoc and Dauphiné, since in those provinces the *taille* was *réelle* and nobility had less financial significance. This view was not shared by towns of more recent growth. Nantes urged the sale of letters of nobility at regular intervals to merchants, on condition that they remained in trade. Rouen suggested that they should be given and not sold. Despite the narrow outlook of the towns, it is clear that they supported the project in principle, provided that in practice it did not impinge on any of their cherished immunities and prerogatives.

Objections on principle came from an anonymous *mémoire* which restated the classic defence of the *noblesse,* the distinction between wealth and honour. Although, it argued, merchants played an important rôle in society, yet "it must be recognised that the wealth which is created by their efforts, enriches them first." The *noblesse,* on the other hand, had sacrificed their private interests and fortunes to devote themselves to public service, and were therefore entitled to the compensation of honour and privileges. The emigration of merchants from commerce was not serious, because it served to redistribute wealth and to give opportunities for others to rise through business. Moreover, to prevent the buying of office, it was only necessary to exclude merchants from official posts until three years after they had wound up their businesses. Ennoblement would solve little, since experience proved that merchants who acquired nobility quickly severed and denied any connexion with trade. The author was willing to permit some reforms, including a distinction between ordinary wholesale merchants and those who rose to municipal office or seats in the *Chambres de Commerce*. But he emphasized the basic distinction between trade and honour.

Opposition was not confined to the merchants and the *noblesse*. It now came from the representatives of the Crown, the commissioners in the *Conseil de Commerce*. The proposals of the deputies, modified in the light of the comments by the towns, were submitted to the commissioners for their decision. A preliminary draft of their intentions revealed a marked change of emphasis. The commissioners approved the clauses protecting the *noblesse* from derogation, and even extended this protection to guarantee succession to landed property by a noble in business. But the proposals to honour merchants were drastically pruned. The distinction between *"négociants"* and *"marchands,"* and all claims to privilege, exemption and precedence by the merchants and deputies were erased. The definition of wholesale trade was considered "too abbreviated," and the proposal to ennoble the fourth generation was supplanted by the noncommittal statement that the King would grant honours to merchants at his pleasure. Finally in September, when the commissioners moved to Fontainebleau with the Court, they prepared, after private discussion, a rough draft of a royal declaration which they forwarded to the deputies at Paris for their comments.

Less severe than the first reaction to the deputies' proposals, the rough draft still dropped ten of the original twenty-one clauses, and only added a preamble. The *noblesse de la robe* were specifically excluded from trade, but the commissioners approved the apprenticeship of younger sons of the *noblesse d'épée,* if undergone overseas, and even permission to engage in retailing. They took as their definition of wholesale trade an elaborated version of the judgement at Lyon in 1667, and opened municipal posts to merchants who came within this definition, all existing statutes notwithstanding. They retained the proposal to institute compulsory enrolment of wholesale merchants, but left the prospect of nobility for eminent merchants vague. In sharp contrast was the benign and complimentary preamble. The Crown, this declared, had always protected commerce as an essential resource of the state, had "always regarded wholesale trade as an honourable profession . . . which had even led it on several occasions to grant letters of nobility to some of the principal merchants, to bear witness to the esteem with which those who distinguished themselves in that profession were regarded." Since the King had discovered that merchants ennobled in this way were excluded by social pressure from trade, and since he was eager to retain merchants and their children in commerce, he had decided to scotch any current misconceptions by public confirmation of his sentiments.

This rough draft was discussed by the deputies in a private session. The preamble evoked no comment, but they objected to the exclusion of "magistrates and other *Gens de Robe*" from commerce, a proposal which would isolate those merchants who had become office holders. The prohibition of apprenticeship within France was treated as prejudicial to the poorer *noblesse,* who could not afford to send their children overseas, and the proposed permission for the *noblesse* to become retailers was considered prejudicial to merchants. They stood by their original definition of wholesaling, and wanted to abolish all the restrictive regulations of the *corps de marchands,* thus enabling both the *noblesse* and overseas merchants to trade freely within France with foreign merchandise. Nor were the retailers forgotten. Even if they were to be denied equal footing with the *avocats* and *médecins,* they should still be permitted to hold municipal office. Greatest criticism was levelled however against the emasculation of their proposal to ennoble merchants. What had been intended as a permanent incentive to future merchants, they remonstrated, had now been reduced to a hatful of rewards, for careless distribution among those who had already succeeded in commerce.

On 30 December 1701, a Declaration was despatched to the *Parlement* of Paris and other courts for registration. This was the rough draft of the commissioners couched in the plural of Majesty. The only criticism accepted from the deputies was that attacking permission for the *noblesse* to become retailers. All the other articles survived their opposition. The Edict of 1669 was officially confirmed and extended to wholesale and overland trade, but apprenticeship was not mentioned and the *noblesse de la robe* was specifically excluded. Retailers were still excluded from municipal office, and only members of the *noblesse* were freed from the regulations of the *corps de marchands.* A slightly elaborated version of the judgement of 1667 was formally accepted as a definition of wholesale commerce. Some clauses from the original *mémoire* were preserved intact. Certain posts were open to wholesale merchants without obligation to leave trade or to obtain *lettres de comptabilité,* and compulsory enrolment and forfeiture for bankruptcy remained. But the key proposal of ennoblement was left obscure: the King would grant honours at his pleasure.

The Declaration was more than a confirmation of the Edict of 1669, and did provide a partial remedy for the social problem. Wholesale trade within France was permitted by law to the *noblesse* for the first time, a right extended on request in March 1702 to subsidiary manufactures. Many merchants were ennobled as promised, notably deputies like Fénellon and Du Hallay, who retired with honour from the debate, and many others purchased letters of nobility from a government struggling to finance the War of Spanish Succession. For merchants like Pierre Colomès, who had acquired nobility through municipal office, the Declaration was a godsend. It decided the case which he had been fighting against the commissioners into usurpations of nobility for nearly a decade, and enabled him to bring up his children in trade as he desired. For those who, throughout the century, had advocated a social hierarchy based on commerce, it was nevertheless a defeat; the Crown had effectively rejected the programme of parity between the *noblesse* and the merchant interest. The issue was re-opened in 1757 and 1767 by the next generation of literary reformers, but no further legislative action was taken, and the decision of 1701 survived until the Revolution. It is significant that when, in December 1701, the deputies had to defend themselves against charges of incompetence, they did not mention the project to honour commerce in their list of achievements.

It is tempting to dismiss these abortive attempts to create a business aristocracy as utopian. Plausible arguments can be advanced to suggest that the ideas, developed by economic writers and accepted by the commercial advisers of the Crown, were incapable of realization because they contradicted the fundamental interests of the *noblesse* and the merchant interest. On this premise, the prejudice against trade persisted because it embodied rational economic and social interests, against which the Crown was powerless to legislate. In fact the reverse was true. The benefits to the *noblesse* and merchants, which the pamphleteers and deputies had seen in the destruction of the false antithesis between land and trade, were real enough. The only victim of such a change would be the Crown, whose representatives had been responsible for emasculating the project of 1701. In the last analysis, the distinction between social status and trade was maintained by the prejudices of the *noblesse* and merchants, and by the personal interests of the monarchy.

At first glance, nevertheless, the charge of impracticability seems to carry weight. If it was poverty which forced the *noblesse* into trade, how could they raise the capital necessary to start a business? Moreover what training had they received for the skilled and exacting techniques of commerce? Even if they could surmount the initial difficulties of transition, they risked losing their social status and the financial privileges so essential to their economic survival. Were they likely to endanger their certain immunity from taxation for the unknown profits that lay in trade? It appeared more prudent to develop their own land commercially, and not to rely on royal protection against derogation, which might be withdrawn in financial emergencies by the Crown. Furthermore, by entering trade they surrendered the last justification for their financial privileges. The duties of military service and local government, in return for which their rights of immunity had originally been granted, had been rendered obsolete by a professional army and royal centralization of the administration, and only their exclusion from profit-making occupations could forestall public condemnation. It was a vicious circle from which the project to honour trade was no escape.

Similar arguments could be used to show that the merchants had nothing to gain. Was the creation of a rigid commercial caste any solution to the inclination of heirs to business fortunes to enjoy a comfortable life of security and honour? How could the Crown prevent the prodigal son from squandering his father's capital, or the aged merchant from buying an office on which to retire? If office and *rentes* provided both a more secure and a more profitable source of income, nothing but iron regulations could keep capital in trade, which the failures of the great companies and the danger of war had made a very risky source of investment. Quite apart from the technical difficulties of administering the proposals, the interests of most merchants seemed well served by the *status quo*.

It is important however to distinguish between real and apparent interests. The hard fact remains, that under prevailing circumstances both the *noblesse* and the merchants were sacrificing a potential source of income to enjoy social respect. On the other hand, by combining their capital and resources to exploit business opportunities to the full, and by making their wealth and the scale of their activities the criteria for social distinction, they could preserve both wealth and honour. There was no guarantee of profits from trade, and in the process of fusion many would fall by the wayside, but this was happening in any case and at least this new policy offered the prospect of recovery. The financial privileges of the *noblesse* could not preserve them from bankruptcy, and younger sons could be apprenticed and enter trade without a heavy capital outlay. The poorer members of the *noblesse* could provide the manpower, their richer counterparts the capital. Similarly, although the sons of merchants could not be forced to follow in their fathers' footsteps, and while investment in land and office would continue to offer economic and social advantages, it was possible to establish greater fluidity between land and trade. The income from office and *rentes* was by no means secure from speculation, inflation, and repudiation, and many of the offices held by merchants were little more than clerkships. If the barriers between land and trade could be broken down, at least land, office and trade would present competitive fields of investment, between which capital could be easily transferred as needed.

Honour would also be satisfied. So long as the acknowledged symbols and trappings of social status—titles and privileges—were open for sale, little would be gained by trying to distinguish wealth from honour. Furthermore a new justification for social privilege was needed. For the *noblesse* to define their status in terms of unproductivity, and to risk bankruptcy to justify their privileges, was both absurd and dangerous. It brought values into contempt and failed in its intention to discourage merchants from entering the *noblesse*. On the other hand, by granting nobility simply to the rich and successful, irrespective of function, social distinction would be both enhanced by a smaller élite, and anchored to some productive function. The successful exploitation of both land and trade could then serve as the theoretical justification for the privileges and status of their beneficiaries, and the problem of derogation would disappear. Moreover an aristocracy of this type, linked by intermarriage and founded on wealth, would enjoy the political influence without which prestige had a hollow ring.

Both the economic and social interests of the *noblesse* would consequently be preserved by the creation of a *noblesse commerçante*. Some were unable to see this, and did oppose the project on grounds of interest. But the main opposition of the *noblesse* derived from an innate prejudice against trade, which rejected any association with merchants, even in a directorial capacity, and made the co-operative plan for a business aristocracy unworkable. The *Parlement* of Brittany rejected the Declaration of 1701, as being incompatible with the *Coutumes de Bretagne* and the status and duties of the *noblesse*. In Chateaubriand's famous phrase, the age of predominance and privilege had given way to an age of vanities. The reasons for the survival of this prejudice, even when it conflicted with the real interests of the *noblesse,* are by no means clear. Many arguments were advanced to defend this attitude, notably the political stability, self-sufficiency and military strength of a society based on land, the suspicion that money was made at the expense of others, and the belief that business was incompatible with the demands of morality and civilized life. These arguments were as well-worn as the prejudices they defended, and were presented without reference to the actual state of affairs. There was visible and concrete evidence to show that a commercial state could fight great wars and preserve national independence, that capital created employment, and that commercial wealth could be the basis of a leisured class. The explanation behind this sentimental ruralism and fear of change might be that both agriculture and industry, in which the *noblesse* were less reluctant to engage, are productive occupations, while trade and finance are from a layman's point of view merely concerned with exchange. But whatever the reasons, the fact was that these prejudices were much stronger than the more rational arguments advanced by the pamphleteers. Even the efforts by the deputies to use retailing as a scapegoat for the prejudice against commerce could not break down the reluctance of the *noblesse* to fuse with the merchant interest.

Merchants did not share the same prejudices, but neither did they have sufficient faith in the importance of their own profession to obviate the need to seek social respect in the ranks of the *noblesse.* Commerce was still a function, not a profession. Self-respect had not yet supplanted the need for the respect of others; respectability had not replaced honour, and the self-made man could not stand on his own feet. This lack of self-confidence shows that the commercial world still lacked an ideology independent of traditional values, the coherence of a separate class. It had a well-developed hierarchy—a political élite, the *corps de merciers,* and an administrative élite, the *noblesse de la cloche.* But it was difficult to maintain even the basic distinction between wholesalers and retailers, and there was little interest in founding commercial dynasties on the Dutch model. This lack of unity is not surprising, when the disunity of economic life in France is considered. Different regions and towns had developed independently, and local rivalries and jealousies were rampant. There was no dominant commercial centre around which a merchant class could develop, and no system of political representation to bring local interests together. The major fault lay however in the restricted horizon of the merchants themselves. Colbert's impression of French merchants as selfish, narrow-minded individuals, indifferent to public needs and concerned only with preserving their own interests, was not too exaggerated. They were not interested in increasing national prosperity, and bitterly opposed the Huguenots and alien merchants, whose productivity created serious competition. They were reluctant to gain social prestige at the price of economic competition from the *noblesse,* and even when the government took the initiative they were loth to follow. Their ambitions were therefore those of the conservative *rentier* rather than the speculative entrepreneur—the respectability and safe, if modest, income of a small office. So limited and dependent an attitude could not compete with the traditional values of the *noblesse.* Consequently French merchants accepted the social system as it stood, and sought recognition on its terms. So long as they could buy the profitable immunities of the old order and the prestige that accompanied land and office, there was no pressure to develop a different social hierarchy or to join forces with the *noblesse* in business. Against such opposition the proposals of the deputies could make no headway. They had tried to give commerce the outward forms of nobility, but commercial organization was not amenable to the rules of social precedence. Reform had to come from the bottom as well as from the top, and the merchant preferred to exploit rather than to change the structure of society.

The guarantor of this social system was however the King, and the monarchy was in the strongest position to reform. Nobility on one definition was simply recognition by the Crown, and by throwing the weight of royal prestige and authority into the scales, the prejudices and preferences of the *noblesse* and merchants could have been overcome. Why therefore did the Crown withdraw from a policy created by its own initiative? Although the noblesse had received more thorough protection from derogation, the monarchy refused to exploit its power of ennoblement on behalf of merchants, and rejected the project of a business aristocracy. This was partly because Louis XIV did not want to change the structure of society, partly because he could not afford such a change. Although the Crown was the representative of national interests, *vis-à-vis* the interests of local pressure groups, matters of state were inextricably bound up with the person of the monarch and the interests of the dynasty. The proposal to equate commerce with social status, though in the overall interests of the kingdom, was a danger to these private interests.

Fundamentally Louis XIV yearned for the glory of territorial expansion and military power, and preferred the social class most closely associated with these ends. Sometimes these ambitions could be identified with economic interests—the defence of French trade against the English or the attack on Dutch commerce—and Louis never forgot that the financial burden of his military ambitions could only be borne by a prosperous society, and by ruthless exploitation of the social system for financial ends. Consequently the Crown provided the resources, energy and initiative lacking among French merchants to extend, plan, and regulate French trade, and fought tariff and trade wars with economic weapons. The King had assumed responsibility for national welfare, and sought if possible to achieve both plenty and power. But in a crisis, when commercial interests conflicted with the demands of war, ends were distinguished from means and profit was sacrificed to prestige and order. Despite the unparalleled economic supervision of his reign, Louis' heart still cherished the ideals of the *noblesse.*

This was not however just a vague preference. *A noblesse commerçante,* as Montesquieu later pointed out in the *Esprit des Lois,* was incompatible with the real interests of the monarchy. The Crown had appealed to the *Tiers État* in its struggle to emasculate the military *noblesse,* and had supported merchants against the hostility of the *noblesse.* But it would also support the *noblesse* against the pretensions of merchants, because the claim to prestige by business was, in the long run, more dangerous to royal supremacy than the old social power of the *noblesse*. The royal prerogative of raising to the nobility was more than a backstairs source of income; it was a political weapon that had to be used with care and not too often. The monarchy had by the reign of Louis XIV broken the military power of the *noblesse,* and channelled their surplus energy into foreign wars. By the timeless principle of divide and rule, by distinguishing between *grandeur* and *pouvoir,* it had created a situation in which the *noblesse* was compensated by social supremacy and privilege for the political power which the Crown exercised through its own instruments, the *Intendants.* This internal balance of power would be upset by any fusion between rank and wealth, by a *noblesse* enjoying independent and hereditary wealth, acting in accord with a merchant aristocracy enjoying independent and hereditary prestige. On the other hand, by selling offices, the monarchy not only raised the money needed for its wars, and the pensions of the court; it put the merchants who became office holders in a position of dependence. Thus, although eager to expand trade, and to increase the wealth upon which external glory and internal solvency ultimately depended, the crown would not eliminate the buying of office by direct ennoblement on a large scale. The preambles to royal edicts show the policy which was dictated by the interests of the *noblesse* and the merchants; their clauses reveal the private political interests of the Crown. The merchant could not find his place in the sun, because he might eclipse the *Roi Soleil.*

The divorce of wealth from honour was therefore a question not only of prestige but also of power. Just as an equitable system of taxation would increase demand for political representation, so a fluid social system would release energies dangerous to royal power. It has become fashionable to soften the contrast between absolute monarchy in France and the mixed constitutions of England and the United Provinces, to emphasize the great efforts made by French Kings to develop French trade. But the failure of the attempt to equate social status with trade suggests that absolute monarchy was only superficially compatible with commercial enterprise. If the French Crown was responsive to the needs of its commercial subjects, it could afford to ignore them, whereas it could not afford to abandon the social *status quo.* The author of a *mémoire* in 1701 was not far from the truth, when he remarked that honour for trade was all very well in republican states, where merchants ruled, but France was a monarchy.

4.

The term capitalism was abused by historians and social scientists of the 1920's and 1930's. The favorite term for describing economic practices and institutions that seemed "modern," capitalism almost ceased to have a meaning because it was so ill-defined.

By World War II capitalism as a term was no longer used by careful historians, though it still reigned supreme in the textbooks. Professor George V. Taylor (1919–   ) of the University of North Carolina has revived the term. His definition of capitalism is both general and specific. On the one hand, capitalism for him implies financial activity, or the investment of large quantities of money. Traditional so far, and dangerously vague as well; but Taylor then adds four adjectives, which define what he asserts are four really different kinds of capitalism. As you learn the specific characteristics of merchant, court, industrial, and real-property capitalism, do you discern neat borders between them? Taylor's definitions offer many advantages over the old-type, monolithic definition of capitalism. However, do Taylor's definitions permit historians to determine who were the capitalists in the *Ancien Régime?* If capitalism was indeed pluralistic, not monolithic, is it possible to envisage any pattern of social change resulting from the investments of large sums of money?

GEORGE V. TAYLOR: Types of Capitalism in Eighteenth-Century France*

The question of whether capitalism existed under the old regime and in what sense depends upon how the term is defined. Our modern notion of capitalism is inapplicable because it designates a system of factories, railways, and finance that became socially important in France only forty years after the old regime had collapsed. No doubt the technological and entrepreneurial antecedents of such a system existed before the Revolution, but they differed from their derivatives and belonged to an economic order that merits a different appreciation from that, say, of Marx's time. French business and family papers now accessible and studies written on the basis of them make this clear. As long as our documentation consisted mainly of government documents, business and finance were interpreted "from the outside," inference was substituted for data, and nineteenth-century realities were read back into the institutions of the old regime. But with the materials now at hand we see how poorly the ordinary concept of capitalism agrees with the patterns of the old order and how misleading it is to use the economic patterns of the nineteenth century as conceptual tools for analysing the society and politics of the eighteenth.

If the word capitalism must be applied to the prerevolutionary economy we should acknowledge that the new materials and studies indicate four spheres of action for exploiting substantial wealth for profit—or, in other words, four types of capitalism. Each differed from the others in the kinds of wealth exploited. Each had its distinctive historical roots. Each was a self-consistent and fairly discrete category of economic activity. Together they comprised a "preindustrial" or "pre-modern" economic order closer to that of the sixteenth century than to that of the Second Empire. The first was what Marx, Sombart, and Sée have called merchant capitalism, the traditional pattern of post-Renaissance commerce, consisting of trade, banking, and domestic manufacture. The second was finance, or court capitalism—the exploitation by individuals and syndicates of government farms, state loans, and joint-stock flotations and speculation. The third was an embryonic form of industrial capitalism, represented not so much by factories, of which there were few, but by mines and primitive metallurgical

* From George V. Taylor, "Types of Capitalism in Eighteenth-Century France," *English Historical Review,* 1964, pp. 478–97.

industries, largely in noble hands and located in agrarian settings. The fourth was a capitalism of real property practised by proprietors and rentiers who exploited rural and urban land and sometimes invested in private loans and long-term public securities.

This way of viewing the prerevolutionary economy suggests a pluralistic pattern rather than a cohesive and unitary one. Men of the eighteenth century had no sense of a developing integration of action and interests, of the subsuming of agriculture, trade, and finance under industrial structures. The economy they knew was disparate, and it would have been unnatural for them to call it by a single name or identify it with a single concept. Accordingly, they appear not to have used the word *capitalisme,* for they knew nothing that needed such a name. To them a *capitaliste* was a person from whom a loan or deposit could be obtained or who would discount commercial paper, not a founder of companies or mobilizer of investment funds. *Capitale* (or *capitaux*) meant ordinarily net worth and sometimes a quantity of investment funds, but as far as we can see was never used to suggest an economic interest or social force. In forming concepts of capitalism appropriate to the old regime we are making definitions and distinctions unknown to the period but acceptable, we believe, to anyone who had lived and worked within it because they seem to agree with the economic realities of the time.

In this paper we wish to characterize the first three of these early forms of capitalism and give examples that will render them more meaningful and concrete. Although the fourth, which may be called proprietary capitalism, has never been an object of our research, it is known to us through incidental encounters wherein merchants and bankers are seen owning land or accepting deposits from rentiers and nobles. Briefly, it centred in the ownership of urban and rural land and the reinvestment of profits and rent derived from its exploitation. In an economy that remained basically agricultural the passion for owning land was remarkable. Nobles and roturiers exploited estates and farms, either directly or through agents; or they rented out small holdings, fields, or gardens to money tenants or *métayers.* They bought and sold real estate, developed it, and invested surplus funds in mortgage loans, personal loans, royal or provincial *rentes,* grain stocks, or interest-bearing deposits with notaries or merchants. Forster in his study of the Toulouse nobility presents a revealing picture of nobles as rentiers, carefully managing their capital, shrewdly profiting from all kinds of operations in land and private loans. In all the urban and rural centres there were well-to-do commoners who imitated this noble mode of using wealth, and in the electoral documents of 1789 they were called "bourgeois" or "bourgeois living nobly on their revenues" and met in assemblies separate from those of business and the professions. This kind of capitalism deserves much more recognition and study than it has received; unfortunately, we are in no position to develop the topic here.

The merchant capitalism of the old regime was carried on within an economic and social community called *le négoce.* Wholesalers, commission and maritime merchants, bankers, and merchant manufacturers were called *négo-*

ciants. In the social structures of the towns they rivalled the bourgeois and professional people and were sharply distinguished from the craftsmen and shopkeepers of the guilds, who occupied a lower status. In most cities they constituted a separate corps organized around a chamber of commerce, or a general assembly of commerce, or the consular court. Their profession imposed upon them standardized practices and techniques, and from these they acquired a vocabulary, outlook, and set of values that set them apart from other orders and bound them in a common bond of understanding.

Businesses were conducted from *comptoirs* staffed with partners and clerks. The *comptoir* was a place of work and negotiation, furnished with plain counters, writing tables, stools, and the massive journals and ledgers appropriate to operations. It was not only a headquarters but a school in which young merchants learned to keep accounts, write letters, record and evaluate the inventory, calculate exchange rates, and negotiate with salesmen and customers. This training was arduous and ill-paid. It had a textbook literature, written by merchants, that taught arithmetic, commercial techniques, and business law, preached the morality of prudence, hard work, loyalty, and thrift, and described the main channels of production, trade, and credit. There was a standard epistolary style, the *style marchand* or *commerçant,* terse, explicit, and deliberately prosaic, and filled with symbols and abbreviations that sometimes constitute an impenetrable code. Merchants also had their own jurisprudence and courts of first instance in which elected merchants adjudicated business quarrels and tried to prevent cases from being appealed to regular courts, where the legal profession could prolong them to its profit. In all these ways the vocation of the *négociants* made them a national and international community, conscious of a common way of life, with their minds and personalities adjusted to a profession that demanded unremitting attention and commitment to prescribed attitudes and codes of conduct.

Until the end of the old regime a single entrepreneurial form, the partnership, met all the needs of merchant capitalism. To judge from the agreements we have read it resembled its twentieth-century counterpart. Agreements ran for three to ten years, mostly for six. At expiration they were renewed, cancelled, or renewed with alterations (as by taking in new partners, dropping out old ones, increasing the capital). The result was a constant flux of enterprises and turnover of partners that fixed the continuity of business history in persons and families rather than firms. Silent partners with restricted management rights or none at all were admitted as *associés commanditaires* with limited liability, while the other partners, the *commandités,* were responsible to the extent not only of their investments but also of their personal wealth. Such companies, called *sociétés en commandite,* enlisted capital from nobles, rentiers, cautious relatives, retired merchants, and even other partnerships to an extent that for the simple partnership (the *société générale*) would have been impossible.

The distinctive feature of the eighteenth-century French partnership was its lack of fixed assets and investments. Rarely, if at all, did a firm own real estate; it rented the *comptoir* and warehouse, and often the partners, clerks, and servants lived in the rented building. Even in maritime commerce merchants avoided fixed investments. Every voyage was a joint venture. The *armateur* invited his friends and correspondents to subscribe for shares, and with the money paid in he bought the ship, the supplies, and the cargo. At the end of the voyage the ship was sold, and the loss or gain from this transaction entered into the profit and loss of the voyage. In merchant manufacturing some entrepreneurs owned machines and others did not, but in any case the looms, spinning wheels, and jennies were simple and inexpensive, being made almost entirely of wood. In the silk industry at Lyon, for example, the master craftsmen worked on piece-work rates for the master merchants and *négociants,* and it was the craftsmen who owned the looms and other necessary equipment. It is the nearly total absence of fixed assets that explains why in eighteenth-century books of account and accounting treatises the concept of depreciation costs and reserves was unknown. In the annual inventories of Lyon partnerships the *ustencilles du magasin* or *du commerce* or *de fabrique* figured for petty amounts and often were omitted from the ledgers and statements. This lack of fixed investment made it possible to operate large businesses on minimal capital and avoid reliance on joint-stock forms of organization, which in the world of merchant capitalism were unknown.

With astonishing flexibility the partnership lent itself to co-operative and interlocking relationships and vertical and horizontal combinations. The ordinary co-operative relationship was that of the joint venture. Houses in different cities set up operations on joint account (*compte en partage*) or half-shares (*compte à demi*); one house produced or bought the merchandise and shipped it to the other house, which sold it. On the seller's books the supplier received interest on his credit balance, and at the end of the operation, which might run profitably for years, the account was closed with a division of the earnings. In organizing a maritime voyage *armateurs* enlisted as many as sixty participants in the venture, some being correspondent houses and bankers, others being professional persons, nobles, or rentiers. It was also common for a partnership to invest capital in other firms, becoming a partner in its own right, sometimes a simple partner and sometimes a partner *en commandite.* By this means a house could establish branches and affiliates in distant cities or in allied lines of activity.

In order to show how readily partnerships invested in one another we present some details from a statement filed in 1795 by Braun, Bergasse frères of Lyon. This was a large house with important international contacts and specialized in banking, shipping, and the commission business. It participated in maritime voyages and invested in four affiliates, and these investments and participations represented thirty per cent of resources. We have consolidated the asset side of the statement to show this.

Large partnerships could operate on little capital. Since there was no public reporting of statements and accounts except after failure, merchants easily overextended themselves and thereby endangered their creditors. The partnership agreements specified the original capital contributions and were filed in the consular courts, where prospective creditors could consult them, but there was nothing to prevent partners from reducing their capital by borrowing through withdrawals charged to their current accounts, which could be in debit balance. When the firm needed more working capital partners threw in additional funds

Assets

		Livres tournois
Cash, drafts, accounts receivable, merchandise		2,366,120
Martin Salavy & Cie., Marseille, interest in a voyage		20,000
"Delaville of Nantes for our Interest in Lost Slave-Traders"		4,832
Roulage de Strasbourg (a transport company), Capital Account		30,000
Henry & Louis Bergasse frères, Marseille		
Capital Account	40,000	
Participation Account	34,322	
	———	74,322
Pierre Olivier Veyrin Lieutaud & Cie., Lyon		
Capital Account	30,000	
Obligatory Current Account	70,000	
Participation Account	60,265	160,265
Louis Simond & Cie., New York	———	
Capital Account	50,000	
Obligatory Current Account	100,000	
Free Current Account	551,700	
	———	701,700
Fixed Assets (Furniture and Warehouse Equipment)		800
Total Assets		3,358,039

that were credited to their current accounts at interest, and when their personal resources were exhausted they called upon other sources of support. Well established and stable firms accepted time deposits from relatives, friends, and bankers. These deposits ran for fixed periods—three months, six months, or a year—at negotiated rates of interest, and in function correspond to the time deposits of modern savings banks. The depositors received interest, the merchants used the funds as working capital. For example, in the statement of B. Camel père et fils, iron merchants (Lyon, 1795), the deposits came to fifty-seven per cent of the liabilities and capital combined. The depositors included B. Camel père (no longer a partner), one Lecoq of Clermont, the Widow Willermoz of Lyon, Gros & Dubost, the guardians of the Maiden Audibert, and thirty-five other partnerships and bourgeois.

Under merchant capitalism credit was prodigiously expansible. Merchants gave and received credit on open account and took interest on their credit balances. They paid their accounts in drafts (*lettres de change*) that did the work of the modern bank cheque and circulated in enormous volume. The draft was not only a means of payment but also an instrument of credit and object of speculation. Most drafts were payable at stipulated future times. If the holder wished to realize the draft before maturity he could discount it with a banker or send it to a correspondent for credit to his account. The draft was also the normal mode of the banker's loan. Having obtained a banker's permission, a merchant would draw a ninety-day draft against him, get his acceptance, and endorse the instrument to his creditors, who would discount it if they did not wish to hold it until maturity. On or before payment date the drawer (borrower) would send the banker some "provision" for paying the draft; the "provision" might consist of new drafts on some other banker or merchant, and anyone who had the confidence of many correspondents could maintain what was called a "circulation" of considerable size. As long as he could go on writing new drafts to cover old ones he enjoyed a highly expanded working capital, but it was a game that could easily get out of hand. Whenever money was scarce and sales and payments slow imprudent merchants multiplied their drafts beyond safe limits, and when their credit was exhausted they failed, taking some of their creditors down with them. Since the failure of one merchant usually precipitated that of others, crises took shape as failures spread from house to house and city to city. At Paris during the seventeen-eighties speculators sustained their operations by drawing continuously on bankers. They were accused, perhaps justly, of having driven the interest rate above ten per cent, and their overextension frightened the government and the provincial merchants.

To understand the varied uses of the *lettre de change* is to understand the commercial banking system of the old regime. According to the definitions of the time, banking was nothing more nor less than the commerce in drafts, and all substantial merchants were drawn into it. Those with correspondents in major payment centres sold drafts on those centres to fellow-townsmen who needed them, or bought drafts on those centres from fellow-townsmen who had to get rid of them, and for these services they charged commissions of from one-half to two per cent. Since at every place the commercial paper on another city, foreign or domestic, was in more or less demand, there was a price or rate (*cours*) for each type of paper bought and sold, and by exploiting the differences in these rates a merchant could dispose of his paper at a profit or hold in expectation of a better future rate. Although the discounts and premiums were small, a large volume of transactions yielded considerable gains. The accounts of such a merchant with correspondents who used him as a banker are similar to accounts in modern banks. Proceeds of drafts that customers deposited for discount or collection became credit balances against which the customers drew drafts with which they paid their creditors. He who bought and sold drafts became of necessity what we should call a banker.

This is to say that in merchant capitalism banking was inseparable from trade. All merchants of any importance accepted deposits and bought and sold drafts, and many permitted their correspondents to draw upon them without having credit balances. Those well known for providing these services were called *banquiers,* but it was only at Paris and in a few houses that bankers divorced themselves entirely from commerce. This admixture of banking and trade explains why the sources of bank credit escape attention. The flow of money and credit was broadly diffused in the commercial and industrial sector, and the wealth of bourgeois and even noble families was directly available to partnerships. Given this diffusion of the banking functions—loans, discounts, and the machinery of payments—it was impossible for bankers to centralize credit as they now do in corporate banking structures, investment trusts, insurance companies, and mutual funds, or to exercise a preponderant influence over investment decisions.

The court capitalism of the old regime was centred in Paris, and its operations were those from which merchant capitalism was excluded or which it preferred to avoid. Paris was the focus of government and the social elite. Revenues flowed in from the treasurers, farmers-general, and receivers-general of finance in the provinces. Nobles at Paris and Versailles borrowed heavily; because they were "slow pay," the business people to whom they owed money were also chronic borrowers. The state was a notorious consumer of credit and contracted with private bankers to merchandise public loans in France, Switzerland, and the Netherlands. It appointed bankers to serve as bankers to the court or treasurers of ministries and elevated a banker, Necker, to the highest ministerial office. The court granted charters for privileged joint-stock enterprises like the Indies Company, the Discount Bank, the Paris Water Company, and the three insurance companies founded in 1786–8 by Panchaud and Clavière, and the battles between the speculative cliques that established these companies were settled in the King's Council, where influence and intrigue were the standard weapons. During the seventeen-eighties transactions in government loans and joint-stock shares developed into a dangerous boom. Nobles, financiers, bankers, and professional speculators brought the government into questionable speculative operations and used their influence to procure official decisions that raised or depressed prices or released speculators from disadvantageous future commitments. Without the royal court and the opportunities to which it held the key, Parisian finance and speculation on the scale on which it was practised would have been inconceivable, and for that reason we may call it a court capitalism, like that which in the Renaissance enriched several banking dynasties and in the seventeenth century created the chartered trading monopolies hated by the bankers and merchants of the French ports.

Another good reason for calling the Parisian capitalism of the old regime a court capitalism was the largely aristocratic complexion of the personnel. When in 1794 thirty-one members of the General Farm were tried before the Revolutionary Tribunal twenty-six of them were listed as "ex-nobles," and two others were described as onetime secretaries of the king, meaning that they held an honorary office that conferred hereditary nobility. All owed their financial appointments to patrons at court and shared their profits with their benefactors or with persons designated by their benefactors, as a result of which the king was in the Company for the equivalent of a full share and his sisters for the equivalent of a half. When the farmer-general Nicolas Deville submitted a declaration for the forced loan of the Year II he listed as an asset a half-share in the Company, but against this asset he listed advances from the vicomte and vicomtesse de Vergennes, then living at "Sarrelibre." His investment in the Company consisted of 438,000 livres furnished by the vicomte, 300,000 livres constituting the dowry of the vicomtesse, and only 42,000 of his own. Like certain other members of the Farm, he was a "front man" (*personne interposée*) for a noble family or a court interest. In a recent study the families of the farmers-general are presented as a self-contained social group well on the way to the exclusive, hereditary, and aristocratic status that characterized the nobility of the robe. For the most part their personal fortunes seem not to have been derived from commerce and industry.

The sector of court capitalism enlisted many non-nobles and raised some of them to noble status. Laborde, a Bayonne merchant with important Spanish contacts, became a protégé of Choiseul and, according to the testament he wrote for his son, was virtually compelled to become a farmer-general and a noble. In Laborde, just as in Magon de la Balue, another banker to the court, we have a conjuncture of trade, banking, foreign and colonial commerce, government finance, and ennoblement. Something of the same blend appears in Simon-Emmanuel Le Normand, banker and financier, son of a French merchant established in Spain. Le Normand failed in 1792, and the statement he furnished his creditors showed assets of more than thirteen million livres, including bad and doubtful accounts of six million and a deficit from profit and loss of nearly a million. He had two French estates, held shares in the Spanish Company of the Philippines, invested in *rentes viagères* and maritime voyages, and had an interest in his family's mercantile house at Cadiz. His creditors included his mother, the investors in the Canal of Murcia, Magon de la Balue, merchants and bankers of Paris, Amsterdam, Cadiz, Rotterdam, Lisbon, London, and the French port cities, and the holders of more than three million livres in drafts for which in one way or another he was liable. During 1783–6 he was an administrator of the Discount Bank and in 1787 and 1789 receiver general of finance for the *généralité* of Tours. Here was a man who took his profits where he found them, whether in the capitalism of the court or of the mercantile world. The totals shown on his balance sheet are more than three times as large as those of any financial statement we have seen issuing from the commercial houses of Lyon and Bordeaux.

At Paris big bankers and speculators (*agioteurs*) of noble and non-noble origins exploited court influence for profit. The annuity loans (*emprunts viagers*) by which Necker financed the American War gave investors incredible returns, and Calonne, for lack of an alternative, continued to create them. Favoured banking houses got blocs of new issues at par or less and sold them at premiums in France and in foreign centres like Amsterdam, Geneva, and Genoa. The joint-stock companies that the government chartered after 1777 had more value as speculative schemes and investment trusts than as enterprises. The Discount Bank, for example, rediscounted drafts at four per cent, but Parisian speculators and bankers monopolized its facilities and after 1786 merchants had trouble getting accommodation. The trading record of the New Indies Company (1785) was poor and one of its historians has concluded that the directors were more interested in personal profit or stock-jobbing than in developing Asiatic commerce. The Fire Insurance Company and Life Insurance Company that Clavière founded in 1787 and 1788 were accumulations of capital that the directors invested in real estate and ten per cent royal annuity loans, and there is little indication that either of them sold much insurance. In obtaining a charter to form the Life Insurance Company, Clavière and his backers carried their fight against Panchaud, chieftain of a rival speculative circle, to the king's council, where they won by promising to use part of the capital to purchase the Parisian properties of the Choiseul family. The attempt of the abbé d'Espagnac and the notary Baroud to corner the market in Indies Company shares in 1787 was made possible by Calonne, who furnished a speculative syndicate with government funds so that, by buying in the market, they could stabilize stock prices. All these examples indicate that the most spectacular operations of old regime capitalism were made possible by royal finance and political manipulation rather than industrial or maritime enterprise.

Between court and merchant capitalism there were obviously points of contact. Clavière, for example, was the son of a Genevan textile merchant and had learned business in his father's *comptoir*. Parisian bankers like Haller, Girardot, Mallet frères, Huber, and most of the others had made their capital in trade. Delessert and Grenus were recent arrivals from Lyon, where they continued to maintain offices under the direction of their partners. The Lecouteulx family kept its main house at Rouen and its branch at Cadiz, where the young men were trained, and had a bank at Paris. All these bankers continued to maintain accounts with merchants while dealing in government loans and joint-stock shares and loaned to speculators on margin. They moved in two spheres. But in spite of the space we have given them here they were exceptional. The great mass of merchants had to put their capital into inventories and accounts rather than *rentes* and shares, as their statements show, and this created a natural disjunction of interest between them and the Parisians. In general they distrusted the financiers, whom they considered court favourites and parasites, and the speculators, whom they thought dangerous and immoral. They believed, perhaps correctly, that capitalism at Paris weakened public credit, milked the royal treasury, raised the interest rate, and threatened the entire business world with a credit crisis and chain reactions of bankruptcies. By interest and preference they kept aloof from the world of finance and *agiotage*.

The distinctive feature of industrial capitalism is to require large fixed investments in land, plant, machinery, patents, or concessions. For years an enterprise may have to live on its capital, which is consumed in development costs or construction and expansion of plant, and occasionally the proprietors have to furnish supplementary subscriptions or obtain new capital through reorganizations and mergers. In a report of 1850 the Anzin Company estimated that the first commercial shipment of coal taken from its mines in 1735 had cost four million livres in preparatory works and operations.

In such a situation the partnership proved inadequate. Rarely would the fortunes of from one to four merchants suffice. There would have to be many principals. Moreover, at law the partnership was dissolved on the death of a partner, and the kind of enterprise we are describing would need a perpetual existence. During the years of development and exploitation the families at interest needed freedom to withdraw their capital without destroying the company, and this could be arranged only by making the shares of capital transferable, a procedure which under the law of partnerships was inadmissible. The result was the improvisation of new forms of enterprise that prefigured the modern corporation, the *société par actions* and what Lévy-Bruhl has called the private company of shareholders. Both limited the liability of the investors to the sum of their investments. So new were these forms that neither had been defined at law; as economic realities they were ahead of the jurisprudence.

In the eighteenth century what Gille has called "big capitalist enterprise" was brought into being not in textile production, which accounted for from sixty to sixty-five per cent of French industrial activity, but in mines, metallurgical industries, canals, and chemical plants. The textile factory, as the English had developed it, was nearly unknown. The future revolutionary Roland, an inspector of manufactures at Rouen, Amiens, and Lyon, knew the word *usine* and defined it in the seventeen-eighties as an "immense workshop of which the heavy machines are, commonly, powered by water," but all the French examples he gave were in iron or copper, and in his three authoritative volumes of 1784–90 on manufactures not one of the textile establishments he described met his definition. This and much other evidence confirms that the French textile industry was organized almost exclusively on the putting-out basis. The unit of production was the craftsman's workshop or the villager's cottage. Sometimes these establishments sold directly to the markets, sometimes they were organized into *fabriques* and *manufactures* by merchants who might or might not furnish the machinery, which, being made of wood, was simple and inexpensive. At any rate, it was an industry dominated by merchants and in all its characteristics fell within the sphere of merchant capitalism.

The true factories of the old regime have often been listed, but always the same ones are named: Réveillon's paper enterprise in Paris, the royal tapestry works at Aubusson and Felletin and the porcelain works at Sèvres, calico plants employing large cylinders for printing cotton, like those of Oberkampf at Jouy, "Milord" Périer at Vizille, and Johannot at Wesserling. In England the first textile factories were mills for spinning cotton thread. Called into being by the development of Arkwright's water-frame, these establishments multiplied rapidly during 1771–80, and by 1790, according to the French intendant of commerce Tolozan, England had two hundred of them, equipped with seven to eight thousand "Arkwright machines." At this same time, according to Schmidt, who thoroughly searched the administrative reports in the series F^{12} of the Archives Nationales, France could have had no more than eight, all consisting of English equipment or machines copied from English equipment, installed and even operated by British mechanics and workers. During 1790–2 several others were established. One of them was the spinning-mill of Boyer-Fonfrède at Toulouse. Founded in 1791, it exploited English machines, child labour, and confiscated church property. But since our purpose is to establish the extent of French industrial capitalism at the beginning of the Revolution we have no interest in those built after 1789. At the end of the old regime a census of genuine textile factories in France would comprise eight *filatures de coton* and less than twenty well equipped calico works, and in the total industrial activity of France their output would have amounted to very little.

The reason that the number of factories has been exaggerated is the ambiguity of the words *fabrique, fabricant, manufacture,* and *manufacturier.* According to Roland, a *fabricant* personally supervised the work of his employees, while a *manufacturier* employed overseers; a *fabrique* involved a small number of operations and a restricted variety of products, while a *manufacture* combined all or nearly all the necessary processes and produced a large variety of products; both words could mean all the workshops (*ateliers*) under the control of a person or all the workshops of a town or region. A *fabrique,* therefore, would consist of one or more workshops and a *manufacture* several workshops, workhouses (*ouvroirs*), or other installations, but neither necessarily implied the existence of a factory.

It was "heavy industry" that produced true anticipations of industrial capitalism. Even here the record is far from clear. Most of the iron enterprises were country forges employing from six to twenty workers, shifted from place to place as the local wood supply gave out, but a few of them were truly large-scale affairs, permanently located, with large fixed investments in land, buildings, and machines. One of the striking features of mining and metallurgical enterprises is the important role played by noble investors and directors. This noble leadership and participation arose naturally because the land for mining coal and metallic ores, the wood used for fuel, the sand for making glass, and other raw materials were mainly in aristocratic hands. Rising prices and the increasing competition for social display drove the owners to exploit these resources. And so during 1763–76 the marquis de Mirabeau formed a *société par actions* to mine lead at Glanges in the Limousin. The shareholders were three dukes, five marquises, four counts and countesses, and a baron. In 1773 the marquis de Trainel formed the mining company of Aniche. Among the proprietors named in the *contrat de société* ten and probably more were nobles and commanded at least twenty-eight per cent of the profits. In the minutes of the Bureau of Commerce for the seventeen-eighties we read of the glass-making projects of the duc de Bouillon and the duc d'Orleans, the forges of the comte de Buffon, and the porcelain works of the comte d'Artois. The comte de Custine had a pottery works in Lorraine and in 1788 had to discharge from three to four hundred workers. Calonne, the controller-general, bought a metal factory in Artois which his subordinates had urged the king to purchase because it produced naval equipment. The baron d'Allarde exploited a mine on his estates and under the Empire became a forge-master. The comte de Broglie had a steel forge at Ruffec, and the king had a porcelain factory at Sèvres. Baron Frédéric de Dietrich, assisted by his father-in-law, the banker Hermani, made of the properties left to him in Alsace a veritable metallurgical empire. These examples could be multiplied many times. The predominance of nobles in these industrial ventures is too regular a pattern to be dismissed as a series of exceptions. Among 601 forge-masters of determinable status listed in the royal investigations of 1771 and

1788, Gille has identified 55 members of the clergy, 305 nobles, and only 241 members of the third estate, so that almost exactly sixty per cent of these proprietors came from the privileged orders. It was the rural location of the resources, along with ownership of land and investment capital, that gave French aristocrats a commanding place in the emergent world of industrial capitalism, and French industrial capitalism may well be considered in part as an offshoot of the older proprietary capitalism.

The ordinary form for organizing large mining and metallurgical enterprises was the private society of shareholders. "Very restricted," observed Rouff, "stamped with aristocracy, it carried a certain rigidity of statutes and deliberately kept apart from its operations and its profits the public at large." For example, the *contrat de société* of the Anzin Company (1757) discloses a merger of three mining enterprises. There are twenty-four shares. The principal director, the prince de Croy, has three and his old partners another. Eight shares go to the marquis de Cernay and his associates. Five and three quarter shares belong to the vicomte Désandrouin and three and three quarters to the noble heirs of a *conseiller au parlement* named Taffin. The two remaining shares are split among four persons, including the dame Reboul and the children of a M. Cordier. If one of these investors wished to sell his interest the company had the right to buy it for a sum equal to that offered by an outsider, so that ownership rights were not freely negotiable as they would have been in a *société par actions* like Le Creusot.

During the French Revolution and the decades that followed many salient features of the old French economy waned or disappeared. The entrepreneurial participation of nobles in commerce and heavy industry was reduced by revolutionary expropriations that deprived them of investments in companies and control over resource-bearing land. Even those who recovered property or benefited from the indemnity of 1825 seldom resumed their positions as mercantile or industrial entrepreneurs, for often during their absence or concealment their companies were liquidated or their interests acquired by others. Embittered by the Revolution, the aristocracy adopted a new *hidalgoisme,* much more intense than the old, which insisted upon a complete separation of gentility and trade. This new alienation of nobles from business, an economic consequence of political events, simplified the social distribution of ownership in commercial and industrial capitalism, so that as heavy industry emerged the earlier entrepreneurial role of the nobles was effaced or forgotten, and what had promised to be a joint participation of nobles and roturiers in industrial development was largely aborted.

As the nineteenth century wore on there were other changes, subtle but infinitely important. The three forms of capitalism described in these pages, fairly disjunct under the old regime, tended to fuse as investment banking grew and joint-stock practices burgeoned. Because the Revolution had abolished corporate social structures, the self-contained and fairly exclusive character of merchant capitalism deteriorated, and although merchants continued to find unity under the chambers of commerce they never completely recovered that esprit de corps which under the old regime had made their attitudes, habits, and traditions fairly uniform and curbed diversification. Factories appeared and increased in size and number. Slowly the putting-out industries were overshadowed, and the domination of industry by merchants declined, In other words, as industrial capitalism matured the patterns of the old economy dissolved. Everyone knows this. It is implicit in the whole concept of economic change. What we have emphasized here is that this happened after the Revolution, not before, and that anyone who attempts to relate revolutionary thought and action to an economic base should begin with a realistic appreciation of the pluralism and prematurity of old regime capitalism. He should take it, in other words, for what it was and not for what it was to become.

12

THE ENLIGHTENMENT

THE THINKERS of the Enlightenment were the first to claim that their own thought and culture were modern. They used the term modern itself, applying it discriminately to works and acts they believed to be different from and superior to those of the past.

This claim to modernity could only have been made by thinkers who felt themselves cut off from medieval and even from seventeenth-century rationalistic philosophy and culture. Voltaire, in his *Century of Louis XIV* (1751), analyzed what was really recent history with the same detachment as Montesquieu in his essay on the decline of the Roman Empire (1734). The Philosophes' detachment and sense of anachronism, of past, present, and future, gave them a self-awareness in history which their Renaissance predecessors lacked.

In 1784 the German philosopher, Immanuel Kant, boldly recapitulated the Philosophes' program in a kind of manifesto entitled *What Is Enlightenment?* Kant's aim was to increase the sense of self-awareness and difference from the thought and times of the immediate past. Through knowledge, he asserted, an explicit and increasing awareness of human nature, society, and the universe would lead man to free himself from his two worst enemies, ignorance and superstition. "Dare to Know" was Kant's motto for turning an enlightened age into an Age of Enlightenment.

During the Philosophes' own lifetime the term enlightenment took on the special significance it still bears. *Siècle des Lumières, Aufklärung,* and Enlightenment became labels for a program and fixed the Philosophes' place in history. Like the man who chooses his own epitaph, the Philosophes self-consciously labeled themselves and their movement, again partly out of the desire to stand out and be recognized as the first moderns.

Of course claiming to be modern in no way demonstrates that the Philosophes were in fact modern. Historians have tested this claim and, after arguing over such things as the significance or meaning of originality, have reached little agreement on a definition of the meaning of modern.

But for all the Philosophes' claims and self-awareness, the meaning and significance of the Enlightenment are still disputed. Historians, by emphasizing one particular aspect of learning, such as philosophy or science, while ignoring others, have depicted the Enlightenment as many different things. In addition, great confusion over the meaning of important terms, such as reason and nature, has led historians to make different, quite contradictory interpretations of eighteenth-century thought. The coherence, or lack of it, in this thought has often been debated; and the fact that the Philosophes themselves did not agree has been used to support the argument that their thought did not present a systematic program.

In the following selections sympathy for the Enlightenment, not hostility to it, gives a similar tone to each analysis. But beneath the surface lie differences of emphasis and interpretation. Can you find various definitions of modernity in these selections?

A word about the anti-Enlightenment historians: Their interest is rather narrowly focused on the problems of the origins of totalitarianism and modern-day conservatism, or of the place and meaning of Rousseau and Burke in Western thought. The variety and richness of interpretation is less here, perhaps because the *parti pris* is greater.

1.

Ernst Cassirer (1874–1945) must not be thought of as a historian, but as a philosopher who wrote, among other things, history. Though one of the greatest philosophers of the twentieth century, Cassirer did not restrict himself to philosophy, for he saw no boundaries between his own creative work and the understanding of past intellectual development. Without an understanding of and explanation for intellectual development since Ancient Greece, Cassirer believed it would be impossible to do philosophy. His theory of the relationship between past and present ideas is expressed in his historical works. "For we see again and again that the divergence of the paths followed by the intellect in its attempt to encompass all of reality is merely apparent. If these paths viewed objectively seem to diverge, their divergence is, nevertheless, no mere dispersion." Cassirer asserts that in the eighteenth century this unity of effort to "encompass all of reality" was called reason.

Cassirer's *Philosophy of the Enlightenment* may be considered a historical work because it is an explanation of a critical moment in Western thought. Not an account or a description, this explanation of what happened is at once historical and philosophical.

How does Cassirer differentiate the achievement of seventeenth-century thinkers from that of the Philosophes? How does he define the "modern analytical spirit"?

ERNST CASSIRER: The Mind of the Enlightenment*

D'Alembert begins his essay on the *Elements of Philosophy* with a general portrait of the mind of the mid-eighteenth century. He prefaces his portrait with the observation that in the intellectual life of the last three hundred years the mid-century mark has consistently been an important turning-point. The Renaissance commences in the middle of the fifteenth century; the Reformation reaches its climax in the middle of the sixteenth century; and in the middle of the seventeenth century the Cartesian philosophy triumphantly alters the entire world picture. Can an analogous movement be observed in the eighteenth century? If so, how can its direction and general tendency be characterized? Pursuing this thought further, d'Alembert writes:

* From Ernst Cassirer, *The Philosophy of the Enlightenment,* translated by F. C. A. Koelln and J. P. Pettegrove (Princeton: Princeton University Press, 1951), pp. 3–27.

"If one examines carefully the mid-point of the century in which we live, the events which excite us or at any rate occupy our minds, our customs, our achievements, and even our diversions, it is difficult not to see that in some respects a very remarkable change in our ideas is taking place, a change whose rapidity seems to promise an even greater transformation to come. Time alone will tell what will be the goal, the nature, and the limits of this revolution whose shortcomings and merits will be better known to posterity than to us. . . . Our century is called, accordingly, the century of philosophy par excellence. . . . If one considers without bias the present state of our knowledge, one cannot deny that philosophy among us has shown progress. Natural science from day to day accumulates new riches. Geometry, by extending its limits, has borne its torch into the regions of physical science which lay nearest at hand. The true system of the world has been recognized, developed, and perfected. . . . In short, from the earth to Saturn, from the history of the heavens to that of insects, natural philosophy has been revolutionized; and nearly all other fields of knowledge have assumed new forms. . . .

"The study of nature seems in itself to be cold and dull because the satisfaction derived from it consists in a uniform, continued, and uninterrupted feeling, and its pleasures, to be intense, must be intermittent and spasmodic. . . . Nevertheless, the discovery and application of a new method of philosophizing, the kind of enthusiasm which accompanies discoveries, a certain exaltation of ideas which the spectacle of the universe produces in us—all these causes have brought about a lively fermentation of minds. Spreading through nature in all directions like a river which has burst its dams, this fermentation has swept with a sort of violence everything along with it which stood in its way. . . . Thus, from the principles of the secular sciences to the foundations of religious revelation, from metaphysics to matters of taste, from music to morals, from the scholastic disputes of theologians to matters of trade, from the laws of princes to those of peoples, from natural law to the arbitrary laws of nations . . . everything has been discussed and analyzed, or at least mentioned. The fruit or sequel of this general effervescence of minds has been to cast new light on some matters and new shadows on others, just as the effect of the ebb and flow of the tides is to leave some things on the shore and to wash others away."

These are the words of one of the most important scholars of the age and of one of its intellectual spokesmen. Hence they represent a direct expression of the nature and trend of contemporary intellectual life. The age of d'Alembert feels itself impelled by a mighty movement, but it refuses to abandon itself to this force. It wants to know the whence and whither, the origin and the goal, of its impulsion. For this age, knowledge of its own activity, intellectual self-examination, and foresight are the proper function and essential task of thought. Thought not only seeks new, hitherto unknown goals but it wants to know where it is going and to determine for itself the direction of its journey. It encounters the world with fresh joy and the courage of discovery, daily expecting new revelations. Yet its thirst for knowledge and intellectual curiosity are directed not only toward the external world; the thought of this age is even more passionately impelled by that other question of the nature and potentiality of thought itself. Time and again thought returns to its point of departure from its various journeys of exploration intended to broaden the horizon of objective reality. Pope gave brief and pregnant expression to this deep-seated feeling of the age in the line: "The proper study of mankind is man." The age senses that a new force is at work within it; but it is even more fascinated by the activity of this force than by the creations brought forth by that activity. It rejoices not only in results, but it inquires into, and attempts to explain, the form of the process leading to these results. The problem of intellectual "progress" throughout the eighteenth century appears in this light. Perhaps no other century is so completely permeated by the idea of intellectual progress as that of the Enlightenment. But we mistake the essence of this conception, if we understand it merely in a quantitative sense as an extension of knowledge indefinitely. A qualitative determination always accompanies quantitative expansion; and an increasingly pronounced return to the characteristic center of knowledge corresponds to the extension of inquiry beyond the periphery of knowledge. One seeks multiplicity in order to be sure of unity; one accepts the breadth of knowledge in the sure anticipation that this breadth does not impede the intellect, but that, on the contrary, it leads the intellect back to, and concentrates it in, itself. For we see again and again that the divergence of the paths followed by the intellect in its attempt to encompass all of reality is merely apparent. If these paths viewed objectively seem to diverge, their divergence is, nevertheless, no mere dispersion. All the various energies of the mind are, rather, held together in a common center of force. Variety and diversity of shapes are simply the full unfolding of an essentially homogeneous formative power. When the eighteenth century wants to characterize this power in a single word, it calls it "reason." "Reason" becomes the unifying and central point of this century, expressing all that it longs and strives for, and all that it achieves. But the historian of the eighteenth century would be guilty of error and hasty judgment if he were satisfied with this characterization and thought it a safe point of departure. For where the century itself sees an end, the historian finds merely a starting-point for his investigation; where the century seems to find an answer, the historian sees his real problem. The eighteenth century is imbued with a belief in the unity and immutability of reason. Reason is the same for all thinking subjects, all nations, all epochs, and all cultures. From the changeability of religious creeds, of moral maxims and convictions, of theoretical opinions and judgments, a firm and lasting element can be extracted which is permanent in itself, and which in this identity and permanence expresses the real essence of reason. For us the word "reason" has long since lost its unequivocal simplicity even if we are in essential agreement with the basic aims of the philosophy of the Enlightenment. We can scarcely use this word any longer without being conscious of its history; and time and again we see how great a change of meaning the term has undergone. This circumstance constantly reminds us how little meaning the terms "reason" and "rationalism" still retain, even in the sense of purely historical characteristics. The general concept is vague, and it becomes clear and distinct only when the right "differentia specifica" is added. Where are we to look for this specific difference in the eighteenth century? If it liked to call itself a "century of reason," a "philosophic century," wherein lies the characteristic and distinguishing feature of this designation? In what sense is the word "philosophy" used here? What are its special tasks, and what means are at its disposal for accomplishing these tasks in order to place the doctrines of the world and of man on a firm foundation?

If we compare the answers of the eighteenth century to these questions with the answers prevailing at the time when that century began its intellectual labors, we arrive at a negative distinction. The seventeenth century had seen the real task of philosophy in the construction of the philosophical "system." Truly "philosophical" knowledge had seemed attainable only when thought, starting from a highest being and from a highest, intuitively grasped certainty, succeeded in spreading the light of this certainty over all derived being and all derived knowledge. This was done by the method of proof and rigorous inference, which added other propositions to the first original certainty and in this way pieced out and linked together the whole chain of possible knowledge. No link of this chain could be removed from the whole; none was explicable by itself. The only real explanation possible consisted in its "derivation," in the strict, systematic deduction by which any link might be traced back to the source of being and certainty, by which its distance from this source might be determined, and by which the number of intermediate links separating a given link from this source might be specified. The eighteenth century abandons this kind of deduction and proof. It no longer vies with Descartes and Malebranche, with Leibniz and Spinoza for the prize of systematic rigor and completeness. It seeks another concept of truth and philosophy whose function is to extend the boundaries of both and make them more elastic, concrete, and vital. The Enlightenment does not take the ideal of this mode of thinking from the philosophical doctrines of the past; on the contrary, it constructs its ideal according to the model and pattern of contemporary natural science.

The attempt to solve the central problem of philosophic method involves recourse to Newton's "Rules of Philosophizing" rather than to Descartes' *Discourse on Method,* with the result that philosophy presently takes an entirely new direction. For Newton's method is not that of pure deduction, but that of analysis. He does not begin by setting up certain principles, certain general concepts and axioms, in order, by virtue of abstract inferences, to pave the way to the knowledge of the particular, the "factual." Newton's approach moves in just the opposite direction. His phenomena are the data of experience; his principles are the goal of his investigation. If the latter are first according to nature ($\pi\rho\delta\tau\epsilon\rho\sigma\nu\ \tau\hat{\eta}\ \phi\acute{\upsilon}\sigma\epsilon\iota$), then the former must always be first to us ($\pi\rho\delta\tau\epsilon\rho\sigma\nu\ \pi\rho\delta\varsigma$ $\dot{\eta}\mu\hat{\alpha}\varsigma$). Hence the true method of physics can never consist in proceeding from any arbitrary *a priori* starting-point, from a hypothesis, and in completely developing the logical conclusions implicit in it. For such hypotheses can be invented and modified as desired; logically, any one of them is as valid as any other. We can progress from this logical indifference to the truth and precision of physical science only by applying the measuring stick elsewhere. A scientific abstraction or "definition" cannot serve as a really unambiguous starting-point, for such a starting-point can only be obtained from experience and observation.

This does not mean that Newton and his disciples and followers saw a cleavage between experience and thinking, that is, between the realm of bare fact and that of pure thought. No such conflicting modes of validity, no such dualism between "relations of ideas" and "matters of fact" as we find in Hume's *Enquiry concerning Human Understanding,* is to be found among the Newtonian thinkers. For the goal and basic presupposition of Newtonian research is universal order and law in the material world. Such regularity means that facts as such are not mere matter, they are not a jumble of discrete elements; on the contrary, facts exhibit an all-pervasive form. This form appears in mathematical determinations and in arrangements according to measure and number. But such arrangements cannot be foreseen in the mere concept; they must rather be shown to exist in the facts themselves. The procedure is thus not from concepts and axioms to phenomena, but vice versa. Observation produces the datum of science; the principle and law are the object of the investigation.

This new methodological order characterizes all eighteenth century thought. The value of system, the *"esprit systématique,"* is neither underestimated nor neglected; but it is sharply distinguished from the love of system for its own sake, the *"esprit de système."* The whole theory of knowledge of the eighteenth century strives to confirm this distinction. D'Alembert in his "Preliminary Discourse" to the French *Encyclopedia* makes this distinction the central point of his argument, and Condillac in his *Treatise on Systems* gives it explicit form and justification. Condillac tries to subject the great systems of the seventeenth century to the test of historical criticism. He tries to show that each of them failed because, instead of sticking to the facts and developing its concepts from them, it raised some individual concept to the status of a dogma. In opposition to the "spirit of systems" a new alliance is now called for between the "positive" and the "rational" spirit. The positive and the rational are never in conflict, but their true synthesis can only be achieved by the right sort of mediation. One should not seek order, law, and "reason" as a rule that may be grasped and expressed prior to the phenomena, as their *a priori;* one should rather discover such regularity in the phenomena themselves, as the form of their immanent connection. Nor should one attempt to anticipate from the outset such "reason" in the form of a closed system; one should rather permit this reason to unfold gradually, with ever increasing clarity and perfection, as knowledge of the facts progresses. The new logic that is now sought in the conviction that it is everywhere present on the path of knowledge is neither the logic of the scholastic nor of the purely mathematical concept; it is rather the "logic of facts." The mind must abandon itself to the abundance of phenomena and gauge itself constantly by them. For it may be sure that it will not get lost, but that instead it will find here its own real truth and standard. Only in this way can the genuine correlation of subject and object, of truth and reality, be achieved; only so can the correspondence between these concepts, which is the condition of all scientific knowledge, be brought about.

From the actual course of scientific thinking since its revival in modern times the Enlightenment derives its concrete, self-evident proof that this synthesis of the "positive" and the "rational" is not a mere postulate, but that the goal set up is attainable and the ideal fully realizable. In the progress of natural science and the various phases it has gone through, the philosophy of the Enlightenment believes it can, as it were, tangibly grasp its ideal. For here it can follow step by step the triumphal march of the modern analytical spirit. It had been this spirit that in the course of barely a century and a half had conquered all reality, and that now seemed finally to have accomplished its great task of reducing the multiplicity of natural phenomena to a single universal rule. And this cosmological formula, as contained in Newton's general law of attraction, was not found by accident, nor as the result of sporadic experimentation; its discovery shows the rigorous application of scientific method. Newton finished what Kepler and Galileo had begun. All three names signify not only great scientific personalities, but they have also become symbols and milestones of scientific knowledge and thought. . . .

The philosophy of the eighteenth century takes up this particular case, the methodological pattern of Newton's physics, though it immediately begins to generalize. It is not content to look upon analysis as the great intellectual tool of mathematico-physical knowledge; eighteenth century thought sees analysis rather as the necessary and indispensable instrument of all thinking in general. This view triumphs in the middle of the century. However much individual thinkers and schools differ in their results, they agree in this epistemological premise. Voltaire's *Treatise on Metaphysics,* d'Alembert's *Preliminary Discourse,* and Kant's *Inquiry concerning the Principles of Natural Theology and Morality* all concur on this point. All these works represent the true method of metaphysics as in fundamental agreement with the method which Newton, with such fruitful results, introduced into natural science. Voltaire says that man, if he presumes to see into the life of things and know them as they really are in themselves, immediately becomes aware of the limits of his faculties; he finds himself in the position of a blind man who must judge the nature of color. But analysis is the staff which a benevolent nature has placed in the blind man's hands. Equipped with this instrument he can feel his way forward among appearances, discovering their sequence and arrangement; and this is all he needs for his intellectual orientation to life and knowledge. "We must never make hypotheses; we must never say: Let us begin by inventing principles according to which we attempt to explain everything. We should say rather: Let us make an exact analysis of things. . . . When we cannot utilize the compass of mathematics or the torch of experience and physics, it is certain that we cannot take a single step forward." But provided with such instruments as these, we can and should venture upon the high seas of knowledge. We must, of course, abandon all hope of ever wresting from things their ultimate mystery, of ever penetrating to the absolute being of matter or of the human soul. If, however, we refer to empirical law and order, the "inner core of nature" proves by no means inaccessible. In this realm we can establish ourselves and proceed in every direction. The power of reason does not consist in enabling us to transcend the empirical world but rather in teaching us to feel at home in it. Here again is evident a characteristic change of meaning in the concept of reason as compared with seventeenth century usage. In the great metaphysical systems of that century—

those of Descartes and Malebranche, of Spinoza and Leibniz—reason is the realm of the "eternal verities," of those truths held in common by the human and the divine mind. What we know through reason, we therefore behold "in God." Every act of reason means participation in the divine nature; it gives access to the intelligible world. The eighteenth century takes reason in a different and more modest sense. It is no longer the sum total of "innate ideas" given prior to all experience, which reveal the absolute essence of things. Reason is now looked upon rather as an acquisition than as a heritage. It is not the treasury of the mind in which the truth like a minted coin lies stored; it is rather the original intellectual force which guides the discovery and determination of truth. This determination is the seed and the indispensable presupposition of all real certainty. The whole eighteenth century understands reason in this sense; not as a sound body of knowledge, principles, and truths, but as a kind of energy, a force which is fully comprehensible only in its agency and effects. What reason is, and what it can do, can never be known by its results but only by its function. And its most important function consists in its power to bind and to dissolve. It dissolves everything merely factual, all simple data of experience, and everything believed on the evidence of revelation, tradition and authority; and it does not rest content until it has analyzed all these things into their simplest component parts and into their last elements of belief and opinion. Following this work of dissolution begins the work of construction. Reason cannot stop with the dispersed parts; it has to build from them a new structure, a true whole. But since reason creates this whole and fits the parts together according to its own rule, it gains complete knowledge of the structure of its product. Reason understands this structure because it can reproduce it in its totality and in the ordered sequence of its individual elements. Only in this twofold intellectual movement can the concept of reason be fully characterized, namely, as a concept of agency, not of being.

This conviction gains a foothold in the most varied fields of eighteenth century culture. Lessing's famous saying that the real power of reason is to be found not in the possession but in the acquisition of truth has its parallels everywhere in the intellectual history of the eighteenth century. Montesquieu attempts to give a theoretical justification for the presence in the human soul of an innate thirst for knowledge, an insatiable intellectual curiosity, which never allows us to be satisfied with any conception we have arrived at, but drives us on from idea to idea. "Our soul is made for thinking, that is, for perceiving," said Montesquieu; "but such a being must have curiosity, for just as all things form a chain in which every idea precedes one idea and follows another, so one cannot want to see the one without desiring to see the other." The lust for knowledge, the *libido sciendi,* which theological dogmatism had outlawed and branded as intellectual pride, is now called a necessary quality of the soul as such and restored to its original rights. The defense, reinforcement, and consolidation of this way of thinking is the cardinal aim of eighteenth century culture; and in this mode of thinking, not in the mere acquisition and extension of specific information, the century sees its major task. This fundamental tendency can also be traced unambiguously in the *Encyclopedia,* which became the arsenal of all such information. Diderot himself, originator of the *Encyclopedia,* states that its purpose is not only to supply a certain body of knowledge but also to bring about a change in the mode of thinking—*pour changer la façon commune de penser.* Consciousness of this task affects all the minds of the age and gives rise to a new sense of inner tension. Even the calmest and most discreet thinkers, the real "scientists," are swayed by this movement. They do not dare as yet to specify its final aim; but they cannot escape its force, and they think they feel in this trend the rise of a new future for mankind. "I do not think that I have too good an idea of my century," writes Duclos in his *Thoughts on the Customs of this Century,* "but it seems to me there is a certain universal fermentation whose progress one could direct or hasten by the proper education." For one does not want simply to catch the contagion of the time and to be driven blindly on by whatever forces it may contain. One wants to understand these forces and control them in the light of such understanding. One does not care merely to dive into the eddies and whirlpools of the new thoughts; one prefers to seize the helm of the intellect and to guide its course toward definite goals.

The first step which the eighteenth century took in this direction was to seek a clear line of demarcation between the mathematical and the philosophical spirit. Here was a difficult and intrinsically dialectic task, for two different and apparently contradictory claims were to be equally satisfied. The bond between mathematics and philosophy could not be severed, or even loosened, for mathematics was the "pride of human reason," its touchstone and real guarantee. Yet it became increasingly clear that there was also a certain limitation inherent in this self-contained power of mathematics; that mathematics to be sure formed the prototype of reason, and yet it could not with respect to content completely survey and exhaust reason. A strange process of thinking now develops which seems to be motivated by diametrically opposed forces. Philosophical thinking tries at the same time to separate itself from, and to hold fast to, mathematics; it seeks to free itself from the authority of mathematics, and yet in so doing not to contest or violate this authority but rather to justify it from a new angle. In both its efforts it is successful; for pure analysis is recognized in its essential meaning as the basis for mathematical thinking in the modern era; and yet at the same time, precisely because of its universal function, such analysis is extended beyond the limits of the purely mathematical, beyond quantity and number. The beginnings of this trend are already discernible in the seventeenth century. Pascal's work *Of the Geometric Spirit* seriously attempts to draw a clear and distinct line between mathematical science and philosophy. He contrasts the "geometric spirit" with the "subtle spirit" (*esprit fin*) and tries to show how they differ both in structure and in function. But this sharp line of demarcation is soon obliterated. "The geometric spirit," says, for instance, Fontenelle in the preface to his work *On the Usefulness of Mathematics and Physics,* "is not so exclusively bound to geometry that it could not be separated from it and applied to other fields. A work on ethics, politics, criticism, or even eloquence, other things being equal, is merely so much more beautiful and perfect if it is written in the geometric spirit." The eighteenth century grapples with this problem and decides that, as long as it is understood as the spirit of pure analysis, the "geometric spirit" is absolutely unlimited in its application and by no means bound to any particular field of knowledge.

Proof of this thesis is sought in two different directions. Analysis, whose force had hitherto been tried only in the realm of number and quantity, is now applied, on the one hand, to psychological and, on the other, to sociological problems. In both cases it is a matter of showing that here too new vistas open up, and that a new field of knowledge of the highest importance becomes accessible to reason as soon as reason learns to subject this field to its special method of analytic dissection and synthetic reconstruction. But psychological reality, concretely given and immediately experienced, seems to elude any such attempt. It appears to us in unlimited abundance and infinite variety; no element, no form, of psychological experience is like any other, and no content ever recurs in the same way. In the flux of psychological events no two waves exhibit the same form; each wave emerges, as it were, out of nothingness, and threatens to disappear into nothingness again. Yet, according to the prevailing view of psychology in the eighteenth century, this complete diversity, this heterogeneity and fluidity, of psychological content is illusory. Closer inspection reveals the solid ground and the permanent elements underlying the almost unlimited mutability of psychological phenomena. It is the task of science to discover those elements which escape immediate experience, and to present them clearly and individually. In psychological events there is no diversity and no heterogeneity which cannot be reduced to a sum of individual parts; there is no becoming which is not founded in constant being. If we trace psychological forms to their sources and origins, we always find such unity and relative simplicity. In this conviction eighteenth century psychology goes one step beyond its guide and master, Locke. Locke had been content to indicate two major sources of psychological phenomena; in addition to "sensation" Locke recognizes "reflection" as an independent and irreducible form of psychological experience. But his pupils and followers attempt in various ways to eliminate this dualism and to arrive at a strictly monistic foundation of psychology. Berkeley and Hume combine "sensation" and "reflection" in the expression "perception," and they try to show that this expression exhausts both our internal and external experience, the data of nature and those of our own mind. Condillac considers his real merit and his advance beyond Locke to be that, while retaining Locke's general method, he extended it into a new field of psychological facts. Locke's analytical art is effective in the dissection of ideas, but it goes no farther. It shows how every idea, be it ever so complex, is composed of the materials of sensation or reflection, and how these materials must be fitted together in order to produce the various forms of psychological phenomena. But, as Condillac points out, Locke stops with his analysis of psychological forms. He limits his investigation to these forms but does not extend it to the whole realm of psychological events and activity, or to their origin. Here then is a province for research hitherto scarcely touched and of untold riches. In Locke the different classes of psychological activity were left alone, as original and irreducible wholes like the simple data of sense, the data of sight, hearing, touch, motion, taste, and smell. Observing, comparing, distinguishing, combining, desiring, and willing are looked upon by Locke as

individual independent acts existing only in immediate experience and not reducible to anything else. But this view robs the whole method of derivation of
its real fruits. For psychological being remains an irreducible manifold which
can be described in its particular forms but can no longer be explained and
derived from simple original qualities. If such derivation is to be taken seriously,
then the maxim which Locke applied to the realm of ideas must be applied to
all operations of the mind. It must also be shown that the apparent immediacy
of these ideas is an illusion which does not withstand scientific analysis. Individual acts of the mind, when analyzed, are in no sense original, but rather
derivative and mediate. In order to understand their structure and true nature,
one must examine their genesis; one must observe how, from the simple sense
data which it receives, the mind gradually acquires the capacity to focus its attention on them, to compare and distinguish, to separate and combine them.
Such is the task of Condillac's *Treatise on Sensation*. Here the analytical method
seems to celebrate a new triumph in the scientific explanation of the corporeal
world, a triumph not inferior to its performances in the realm of natural science.
The material and mental spheres are now, as it were, reduced to a common denominator; they are composed of the same elements and are combined according to the same laws.

But in addition to these two spheres of reality there is a third which, similarly,
must not be accepted as consisting of simple sense data, but which must be
traced to its origins. For we can only succeed in reducing this reality to the rule
of law and reason by an inquiry into its sources. The third sphere of reality is
that which we find in the structure of the state and of society. Man is born into
this world; he neither creates nor shapes it, but finds it ready-made about him;
and he is expected to adapt himself to the existing order. But here too passive
acceptance and obedience have their limits. As soon as the power of thought
awakens in man, it advances irresistibly against this form of reality, summoning
it before the tribunal of thought and challenging its legal titles to truth and
validity. And society must submit to being treated like physical reality under
investigation. Analysis into component parts begins once more, and the general
will of the state is treated as if it were composed of the wills of individuals and
had come into being as a result of the union of these wills. Only by virtue of this
basic supposition can we make a "body" of the state and subject it to that
method which had proved its fruitfulness in the discovery of universal law in
the physical world. Hobbes had already done this. The fundamental principle
of his political theory, that the state is a "body," means just this: that the same
process of thought which guides us to an exact insight into the nature of physical body is also applicable without reservation to the state. Hobbes's assertion
that thinking in general is "calculation" and that all calculation is either addition or subtraction also holds for all political thinking. Such thinking too must
sever the bond which unites the individual wills, in order to join them again by
virtue of its own special method. Thus Hobbes resolves the "civil state" into the
"natural state"; and in thought he dissolves all bonds of individual wills only to
find their complete antagonism, the "war of all against all," remaining. But
from this very negation is derived the positive content of the law of the land in

its unconditional and unlimited validity. The emergence of the will of the state from the form of the covenant is set forth because this will can only be known by, and founded in, the covenant. Here is the bond which connects Hobbes's doctrine of nature with his doctrine of the state. These doctrines are different applications of Hobbes's logical basic assumption, according to which the human mind really only understands that which it can construct from the original elements. Every true formulation of a concept, every complete definition, must therefore start from this point; it can only be a "causal" definition. Philosophy as a whole is understood as the sum total of such causal definitions; it is simply the complete knowledge of effects from their causes, of derivative results from the totality of their antecedents and conditions.

The eighteenth century doctrine of the state and society only rarely accepted without reservations the content of Hobbes's teaching, but the form in which Hobbes embodied this content exerted a powerful and lasting influence. Eighteenth century political thought is based on that theory of the contract whose underlying assumptions are derived from ancient and medieval thought, but it develops and transforms these assumptions in a manner characteristic of the influence exerted by the modern scientific view of the world. In this field too the analytic and synthetic method is henceforth victorious. Sociology is modeled on physics and analytical psychology. Its method, states Condillac in his *Treatise on Systems,* consists in teaching us to recognize in society an "artificial body" composed of parts exerting a reciprocal influence on one another. This body as a whole must be so shaped that no individual class of citizens by their special prerogatives shall disturb the equilibrium and harmony of the whole, that on the contrary all special interests shall contribute and be subordinated to the welfare of the whole. This formulation in a certain sense transforms the problem of sociology and politics into a problem in statics. Montesquieu's *Spirit of the Laws* looks upon this same transformation as its highest task. The aim of Montesquieu's work is not simply to describe the forms and types of state constitutions —despotism, constitutional monarchy, and the republican constitution—and to present them empirically, it is also to construct them from the forces of which they are composed. Knowledge of these forces is necessary if they are to be put to their proper use, if we are to show how they can be employed in the making of a state constitution which realizes the demand of the greatest possible freedom. Such freedom, as Montesquieu tries to show, is possible only when every individual force is limited and restrained by a counterforce. Montesquieu's famous doctrine of the "division of powers" is nothing but the consistent development and the concrete application of this basic principle. It seeks to transform that unstable equilibrium which exists in, and is characteristic of, imperfect forms of the state into a static equilibrium; it attempts further to show what ties must exist between individual forces in order that none shall gain the ascendancy over any other, but that all, by counterbalancing one another, shall permit the widest possible margin for freedom. The ideal which Montesquieu portrays in his theory of the state is thus the ideal of a "mixed government," in which, as a safeguard against a relapse into despotism, the form of the mixture is so wisely and cautiously selected that the exertion of a force in one direction immediately releases a counterforce, and hence automatically restores the desired equilibrium. By this approach Montesquieu believes he can fit the great variety and diversity of the existing forms of the state into one sound intellectual structure within which they can be controlled. Such a basic arrangement and foundation is Montesquieu's primary aim. "I have established principles," he points out in the preface to the *Spirit of the Laws,* "and I have observed how individual cases, as if by themselves, yielded to these principles, and I have seen that the histories of all nations are but sequences, and that each individual law is connected with another law or depends on a more general law."

The method of reason is thus exactly the same in this branch of knowledge as it is in natural science and psychology. It consists in starting with solid facts based on observation, but not in remaining within the bounds of bare facts. The mere togetherness of the facts must be transformed into a conjuncture; the initial mere co-existence of the data must upon closer inspection reveal an interdependence; and the form of an aggregate must become that of a system. To be sure, the facts cannot simply be coerced into a system; such form must arise from the facts themselves. The principles, which are to be sought everywhere, and without which no sound knowledge is possible in any field, are not arbitrarily chosen points of departure in thinking, applied by force to concrete experience which is so altered as to suit them; they are rather the general conditions to which a complete analysis of the given facts themselves must lead. The path of thought then, in physics as in psychology and politics, leads from the particular to the general; but not even this progression would be possible unless every particular as such were already subordinated to a universal rule, unless from the first the general were contained, so to speak embodied, in the particular. The concept of the "principle" in itself excludes that absolute character which it asserted in the great metaphysical systems of the seventeenth century. It resigns itself to a relative validity; it now pretends only to mark a provisional farthest point at which the progress of thought has arrived—with the reservation that thought can also abandon and supersede it. According to this relativity, the scientific principle is dependent on the status and form of knowledge, so that one and the same proposition can appear in one science as a principle and in another as a deduced corollary. "Hence we conclude that the point at which the investigation of the principles of a science must stop is determined by the nature of the science itself, that is to say, by the point of view from which the particular science approaches its object. . . . I admit that in this case the principles from which we proceed are themselves perhaps scarcely more than very remote derivations from the true principles which are unknown to us, and that, accordingly, they would perhaps merit rather the name of conclusions than that of principles. But it is not necessary that these conclusions be principles in themselves; it suffices that they be such for us." Such a relativity does not imply any skeptical perils in itself; it is, on the contrary, merely the expression of the fact that reason in its steady progress knows no hard and fast barriers, but that every apparent goal attained by reason is but a fresh starting-point.

Thus it is evident that, if we compare the thought of the eighteenth century with that of the seventeenth, there is no real chasm anywhere separating the two periods. The new ideal of knowledge develops steadily and consistently from the presuppositions which the logic and theory of knowledge of the seventeenth century—especially in the works of Descartes and Leibniz—had established. The difference in the mode of thinking does not mean a radical transformation; it amounts merely to a shifting of emphasis. This emphasis is constantly moving from the general to the particular, from principles to phenomena. But the basic assumption remains; that is the assumption that between the two realms of thought there is no opposition, but rather complete correlation—except for Hume's skepticism which offers an entirely different approach. The self-confidence of reason is nowhere shaken. The rationalistic postulate of unity dominates the minds of this age. The concept of unity and that of science are mutually dependent. "All sciences put together," says d'Alembert repeating the opening sentences of Descartes' *Rules for the Conduct of the Understanding,* "are nothing but human intelligence, which always remains one and the same, and is always identical with itself, however different the objects may be to which it is applied." The seventeenth century owed its inner solidarity, particularly as exemplified in French classical culture, to the consistency and rigor with which it clung to this postulate of unity and extended its application to all the spheres of knowledge and living. This postulate prevailed not only in science, but in religion, politics and literature as well. "One king, one law, one faith"—such was the motto of the epoch. With the advent of the eighteenth century the absolutism of the unity principle seems to lose its grip and to accept some limitations and concessions. But these modifications do not touch the core of the thought itself. For the function of unification continues to be recognized as the basic role of reason. Rational order and control of the data of experience are not possible without strict unification. To "know" a manifold of experience is to place its component parts in such a relationship to one another that, starting from a given point, we can run through them according to a constant and general rule. This form of discursive understanding had been established by Descartes as the fundamental norm of mathematical knowledge. Every mathematical operation, according to Descartes, aims in the last analysis to determine the proportion between an unknown quantity and other known quantities. And this proportion can only be strictly determined when the unknown and the known participate in a "common nature." Both elements, the unknown and the known, must be reducible to quantity and as such they must be derivable from the repetition of one and the same numerical unit. Thus the discursive form of knowledge always resembles a reduction; it proceeds from the complex to the simple, from apparent diversity to its basic identity. Eighteenth century thought holds firmly to this fundamental method, and attempts to apply it to broader and broader fields of knowledge. The very concept of "calculus" thus loses its exclusively mathematical meaning. It is not merely applicable to quantities and numbers; from the realm of quantities it invades the realm of pure qualities. For qualities too may be placed in such a relationship to one another that they are derivable from one another in a strict order. Whenever this is possible, the determination of the general laws of this order enables us to gain a clear view of the whole field of their validity. The concept of "calculus," therefore, is co-extensive with that of science itself; and it is applicable wherever the conditions of a manifold of experience can be reduced to certain fundamental relations and thus completely determined. Condillac, who first clearly formulated this general scientific concept in his essay *The Language of Calculus,* attempted in his psychology to give a characteristic sample and a fruitful application of the concept. For Condillac, who supports the Cartesian concept of the immateriality and spirituality of the soul, there can be no doubt that a direct mathematical treatment of psychological experience is impossible. For such a direct application of the concepts of quantity is valid only where the object itself consists of parts and can be constructed from these parts; and this can take place only in the realm of corporeal substance, which is defined as pure extension, but not in the realm of thinking "indivisible" substance. However, this fundamental and unalterable opposition between body and soul is no insurmountable barrier for the pure function of analytical knowledge. This function ignores material differences for, by virtue of the purity of its form and the formal nature of its operation, it is bound by no presuppositions regarding content. Even if psychological experience cannot like corporeal experience be divided into parts, yet in thought it can be analyzed into its constitutive elements. To this end it is only necessary that the apparent diversity of such experience be resolved by showing that it is a continuous development from a common source of all psychological phenomena. As proof, Condillac introduces the famous illustration which he places at the center of his psychology. Assuming a marble statue, he describes how it progressively comes to life and acquires an increasingly rich spiritual content because the individual senses engrave their special qualities on the marble. Condillac tries to show that the continuous series of "impressions" and the temporal order in which they are produced are sufficient to build up the totality of psychological experience and to produce it in all its wealth and subtle shadings. If we succeed in producing psychological experience in this manner, we have at the same time reduced it to the quantitative concept. Now everything that we call psychological reality and that we experience as such proves to be fundamentally a mere repetition and transformation of a certain basic quality which is contained in the simplest sense perception. Sense perception forms the borderline between the marble as dead matter and a living being endowed with a soul. But once this borderline has been passed, there is no need of any further assumptions or of any essentially new creations. What we commonly regard as the "higher" powers of the mind, contrasting these powers with sensation, is in reality only a transformation of the basic element of sense perception. All thinking and judging, all desiring and willing, all powers of the imagination and all artistic creation, qualitatively considered, add nothing new, nothing essentially different to this fundamental element. The mind neither creates nor invents; it repeats and constructs. But in this repetition it can exhibit almost inexhaustible powers. It extends the visible universe beyond all bounds; it traverses the infinity of space and time; and yet it is unceasingly engaged in the production of ever new shapes within itself. But throughout its activities the mind is concerned only with itself and its "simple ideas." These constitute the solid ground on which the entire edifice constructed by the mind, both in its "external" and in its "internal" aspects, rests—and from which the mind can never depart.

Condillac's attempt to show that all psychological reality is a transformation, a metamorphosis, of simple sense perception is continued by Helvetius in his book *On the Mind* (*De l'Esprit*). The influence which this weak and unoriginal work exerted on the philosophical literature of the eighteenth century is explicable in that the epoch found here a basic element of its thought expressed with pregnant clarity, and indeed with an exaggeration which parodies this thought. In Helvetius's exaggeration the methodological limitation and danger of this mode of thinking is clearly presented. The limitation consists in a leveling process which threatens to deny the living wealth of human consciousness and to look upon it merely as a disguise. Analytical thinking removes this disguise from psychological phenomena; it exposes them, and in so doing reveals their naked sameness rather than their apparent diversity and inner differentiation. Differences in form as well as in value vanish and prove to be delusions. As a result, there is no longer a "top" and "bottom" or a "higher" and a "lower" in the realm of psychological phenomena. Everything is on the same plane—equal in value and in validity. Helvetius develops this line of thought especially in the field of ethics. His main intention was to sweep away all those artificial differentiations which convention had erected and was trying hard to maintain. Wherever traditional ethics spoke of a special class of "moral" sensations, wherever it thought it found in man an original "feeling of sympathy" which rules over and restrains his sensual and egotistical appetites, Helvetius tries to show how poorly such a hypothesis corresponds to the simple reality of human feeling and action. Whoever approaches this reality without prejudice will find none of that apparent dualism. He will find everywhere and always the same absolutely uniform motivation. He will see that all those qualities which we refer to as unselfishness, magnanimity, and self-sacrifice are different only in name, not in reality, from the elementary impulses of human nature, from the "lower" appetites and passions. No moral greatness rises above this plane. For no matter how high the aims of the will may be, no matter what supernatural values and supersensible goals it may imagine, it remains nonetheless confined within the narrow circle of egotism, ambition, and vanity. Society does not achieve the suppression of these elemental impulses, but only their sublimation; and in so far as society understands its own function, this is all it can ever expect or ask of the individual. Consideration of the theoretical world should be guided by the same viewpoint. According to Helvetius there are neither fundamental gradations in the scale of ethical values nor radical gradations of theoretical form. On the contrary, all such distinctions boil down to the same undifferentiated mass of sensation. The so-called faculties of judgment and cognition, imagination and memory, and understanding and reason, are by no means specific original powers of the soul. Here again we have been subject to the same delusion. We think we have transcended the sphere of sense perception when we have only slightly modified its appearance. The criticism which explains away this modification also applies to theoretical distinctions. All operations of the mind can be reduced to judgment, and judgment consists only in grasping similarities and differences between individual ideas. But the recognition of similarity and difference presupposes an original act of awareness which is analogous to, or indeed identical with, the perception of a sense quality. "I judge or I perceive that of two objects the one I call 'fathom' makes a different impression on me from the one I call 'foot,' and that the color I call 'red' affects my eyes differently from the color I call 'yellow.' Hence I conclude that in such a case to judge is simply to perceive." Here, as one sees, both the edifice of ethical values and the logically graded structure of knowledge are demolished. Both structures are, as it were, razed to the ground because it is thought that the only unshakable foundation of knowledge lies in sensation.

It would be erroneous to consider the fundamental viewpoint represented by Helvetius as typical of the content of the philosophy of the Enlightenment, as has often been done; and it is equally erroneous to regard it as typical of the thought of the French Encyclopaedists. For the sharpest criticism of Helvetius's work was exercised by precisely this school of thought; and this criticism originated among the best minds in French philosophical literature, as, for instance, Turgot and Diderot. But one thing is undeniable, namely, that in Helvetius as well as in Condillac a certain methodology appears, a methodology characteristic of and decisive for the entire eighteenth century. Here was a form of thinking whose positive achievement and immanent limitations, whose triumphs and defeats, were so to speak predetermined.

2.

In what ways were the Philosophes enemies of Christianity? The awareness of the alternatives between Christian and pagan preoccupied much of their thinking not only about religion but about ethics and psychology as well. Professor Alfred Cobban (1901–1968), of the University of London, describes the impact of paganism on ethical thought. What is meant by the "argument from design"? Were the Philosophes more preoccupied with the problem of good and evil than with the existence of God? Note how Cobban refutes the charge that the Philosophes somehow failed because they gave "no final answer to the problem of morality."

Despite the fact that the Philosophes clearly did not agree on the questions of the nature or existence of God, can you discern any common assumptions or themes in their works? What had happened to the promise of life after death?

ALFRED COBBAN: The Problem of Good and Evil*

It would not be entirely fanciful to describe the seventeenth and eighteenth centuries as a second age of the sophists. At the time their intellectual achievements must have seemed similarly destructive to those who clung to any of the various orthodoxies. Religious faith was the principal victim of the new ideas, and the undermining of religion had far-reaching results, for the whole existing

---

* From Alfred Cobban, *In Search of Humanity* (New York: Braziller, 1960), pp. 75–89.

pattern of political and moral behaviour seemed to be based on religion, and to survive only by virtue of the religious sanction. Morality was equated with the commands of God. What was good in politics and morals was so because such was the teaching of religious authority. With the loss of this, an alternative source had to be found. This is why, as in the ancient world, the decline of religious faith was accompanied by the rise of moral philosophy, and of course in other periods the inverse process can be seen. Never perhaps has there been any century so intensely concerned with the problem of social morality as the sceptical and infidel eighteenth century.

The trend had set in strongly even earlier. In the sixteenth century humanist writers had brought Epicurean ideas back into currency, and these were to form one important strand in the growth of a new pattern of moral speculation. By the first half of the seventeenth century there was a fairly pronounced current of hedonistic thought. Pierre Gassendi (1542–1655), a French cleric, theologian, philosopher and mathematician, might be mentioned in many different connections, and particularly as a critic of Aristotle and advocate of experiment. He opposed the views of Descartes, and anticipated Locke in proclaiming "Nihil in intellectu quod non prius fuerit in sensu." Like many others his scientific thinking was strongly influenced by Lucretius, whose *De Natura Rerum* went through some thirty editions between the *editio princeps* of 1473 and 1600. Gassendi did not make any important contributions to science, but he is significant as the author of a life of Epicurus, in which he defended Epicurean doctrines, proclaimed that virtue and pleasure are not opposites, and declared that the end of life is happiness.

A more systematic hedonistic morality appeared in the *Leviathan,* where Hobbes stated unequivocally:

Whatsoever is the object of any man's appetite or desire, that is it which he for his part calleth *good;* and the object of his hate and aversion, *evil* . . . there being nothing simply and absolutely so; nor any common rule of good and evil, to be taken from the nature of the objects themselves.

Locke put equally plainly the principle that the terms good and evil are to be used only with reference to pleasure and pain. For him, happiness, pleasure and good were equated. He held also that moral truths possess the same certainty as mathematical and are similarly capable of demonstration, though he did not demonstrate any.

The search for moral principles independent of religion was now well started, but there was one preliminary question to be answered—it had been implicitly posed by the extremer libertines—whether and why there was such a thing as morality at all. If there were good and evil in the world, and the good was preferable to the evil, why was this so? God could not be left out of this argument: it was still felt by all except a very few advanced thinkers that he was necessary as a basis for morality. The problem therefore was that of justifying belief in the existence of a deity in the absence of religious faith. As has been suggested above, science, which had largely caused the difficulty, seemed to offer the solution.

The wonders of nature were called in as evidence of the existence of God. A host of books elaborated on this theme. Their titles tell us really all we need to know about them—Burnet's *Sacred Theory of the Earth,* Clarke's *Demonstration of the Being and Attributes of God,* John Ray's *Wisdom of God in the Creation, La vérité de la religion chrétienne démonstrée par l'ordre géométrique, The Christian Philosopher: a Collection of the best discoveries in Nature, with religious improvements, L'existence de Dieu démonstrée par les merveilles de la Nature, Théologie des insectes,* and so on. *Le spectacle de la nature* (1732–50) by the abbé Pluche, which passed through many editions, was the most successful of all the zoological theologies. Pluche wrote: "The Prospect of Nature then is a kind of vulgar Theology . . . The whole world is one great Picture, in which are displayed the Perfections of God." Or again: "Providence has formed some Animals to live with Man, and be serviceable to him; and has created others to people Woods and Deserts, animate every Part of Nature, and chastise Mortals when they grow impious and abandoned."

The intellectual level of Pluche, it will be seen, was not a high one. The mathematician Maupertuis satirized the argument from design by reference to those who found God in the folds of the skin of a rhinoceros, because the animal's hide being so hard it would not be able to move without these folds. Conyers Middleton was more savage:

As to the other part of the Cavil, that *God does nothing in vain;* you answer; that the *Foreskin was not made in vain;* that in *ordinary cases it was better to have it on, than off; but for extraordinary,* it was wisely contrived, that there might be *something to spare, something to cut off as occasion should require:* A most *admirable Solution;* which amounts just to this; that had not *God wisely provided it,* he could never have order'd it to be *cut off.*

A frontal attack on the whole argument from design was made by the French writer Formey in his *Examen de la preuve qu'on tire des fins de la nature pour établir l'existence de Dieu.* And in such an iconoclast as the abbé Meslier it is inverted and the defects of the human organism used to prove either the wickedness or the non-existence of God.

From the religious point of view the argument from design was a dangerous way of demonstrating the existence and the goodness of God, and thus providing a moral foundation for the universe. Glorifying God in nature was only a step from glorifying nature. This step was taken by Locke's pupil, one of the most influential, if not profoundest, moralists of the eighteenth century, the third Earl of Shaftesbury. "O glorious nature!" he exclaims, "Supremely fair and sovereignly good! all-loving and all-lovely, all divine! . . . O mighty Nature! wise substitute of Providence," etc., etc. This comes a little unexpectedly from the author of *A letter concerning Enthusiasm,* but the merits or demerits of enthusiasm depended on what one was enthusiastic about. Religious enthusiasm, Shaftesbury thought, could have undesirable consequences—there was some historical justification for this view. On the other hand nature was a harmless object of adoration. Nature, Shaftesbury held, is good. Evils only appear as such because we cannot see the whole. It follows that man as part of nature is also good. Supernatural influences are hence not needed to make him moral, and in fact the belief in them is destructive of real virtue. True religion is based on nature, virtue consists in following nature, and beauty and goodness are ultimately the same. Whereas morals had been for Locke demonstrative, comparable to a geometrical theorem, for Shaftesbury they are "as natural to us as natural affection itself"; because there is a "natural moral sense." The importance of the step that Shaftesbury took should not be underestimated. "Delight in beholding torments, and in viewing distress, calamity, blood, massacre and destruction," he wrote, "can now be condemned as unnatural." Nature can thus take the place of God as the basis of morality. Moreover, by means of the moral sense the chief difficulty in hedonistic morals is solved, for it identifies self-love and social good: "Thus the wisdom of what rules, and is first and Chief in Nature, has made it to be according to the private interest and good of everyone, to work towards the general good."

The optimistic view of the world and man represented by Shaftesbury's moral theory was put into elegant verse by Pope in his *Essay on Man* (1732–4), which rejected, denied, and ruled out as irrelevant or misunderstood, all considerations that might seem to contradict the optimistic faith:

> All Nature is but Art, unknown to thee;
> All Chance, Direction, which thou canst not see;
> All Discord, Harmony not understood;
> All partial Evil, universal Good;
> And, spite of Pride, in erring Reason's spite,
> One truth is clear, *Whatever is, is right.*

This was good orthodox theology for the time. Pope might have found it in Archbishop King's *De Origine mali,* printed in Latin in 1702 and translated into English in 1731, just before the publication of his *Essay.*

The older idea of the Chain of Being, which joined all existences in a divinely planned hierarchy, and in which the lower subserved the ends of the higher, contributed to the same stream of thought. The true philosopher is one who is—

> Slave to no sect, who takes no private road,
> But looks thro' Nature up to Nature's God,
> Pursues that chain which links th'immense design,
> Joins Heav'n, and earth, and mortal, and divine.

Universal harmony also solves the problem of the conflict of individual interest and social morality:

> Thus God and Nature link'd the gen'ral frame,
> And bade Self-love and Social be the same.

But it would be unfair to Pope to represent him with these quotations alone. The laureate of optimism was too good a poet not to be capable of better poetry and more pessimistic sentiments, though they are less relevant to our theme. In the same poem, but in a different mood he sees man—

> Plac'd on this isthmus of a middle state,
> A being darkly wise and rudely great:
>
> .   .   .   .   .
>
> Sole judge of Truth, in endless Error hurl'd;
> The glory, jest, and riddle of the world!

As the shadows darken, Pope finds it difficult to keep his courage up the whole time. Philosophers could do that better than poets, but even they only so long as they continued their whistling in the dark. A poet could not but touch reality:

> Behold the child, by Nature's kindly law,
> Pleas'd with a rattle, tickled with a straw:
> Some livelier plaything gives his youth delight,
> A little louder, but as empty quite:
> Scarfs, garters, gold, amuse his riper stage,
> And beads and pray'r-books are the toys of age:
> Pleas'd with this bauble still, as that before;
> Till tir'd he sleeps, and life's poor play is o'er.

Pope's optimism declines into a quiet melancholy. Other eighteenth-century moralists faced the problem of suffering and evil more seriously. It weighed heavily on the minds of men like Swift and Voltaire and Dr Johnson. The problem of evil was not a new one: it had been coped with, after a fashion, by the religious thought of the past, with the aid of the Devil, Original Sin and a future state of rewards and punishments. Unfortunately in enlightened thought these were all discredited. Wesley's vigorous faith in the Devil and all his works came to the rescue of the common man, but the Devil's future career was destined to be on a rather lower level of society than he was accustomed to. For enlightened men, the Devil and Original Sin disappeared into the limbo of unbelief along with the serpent and the apple, Adam and Eve, and the rest of the fascinating Jewish-Christian mythology. They left a void: somebody had to be responsible for all the evil in the world; and if the Devil became a myth, and man was naturally good, who remained but God? This was a terrifying thought. If God were the author of evil, how could he function as the sanction for morality? And how could a perfect being be responsible for evil? Or if he were not responsible for it, what had happened to his omnipotence? These questions were easier to pose than to answer.

One way of dealing, after a fashion, with the dilemma appeared in 1705, in a little anonymous verse pamphlet of twenty-six pages and costing sixpence. It was called *The Grumbling Hive: or Knaves Turned Honest.* Enlarged and re-published in 1714 as Mandeville's *Fable of the Bees,* with the sub-title "Private Vices—Public Benefits," it had many subsequent enlargements and additions until it had swollen to the size of two volumes. Mandeville's theme is well known. He draws a picture of a prosperous and happy but far from moral hive, in which all the little bees, each pursuing his (or her) own selfish and amoral interest, gather honey while they may and so contribute to the general weal. However, a few ruthless moralists are not content with this condition and fill the

air with their complaints about the prevailing vice. Jove, tired of their importunities, at last "rid the bawling hive of fraud." What happens? Industry weak-
ens, trade decays, all the professions fall out of employment, population declines, foreign enemies and rivals triumph, and finally a pathetic remnant of
the once great and flourishing community takes refuge in a hollow tree. The
moral is drawn in Mandeville's own words:

> Then leave complaints: Fools only strive
> To make a great an honest hive.
> T'enjoy the World's Conveniences,
> Be fam'd in War, yet live in Ease,
> Without great Vices, is a vain
> Eutopia seated in the Brain!
>
> .   .   .   .   .
>
> Bare Vertue can't make Nations live
> In Splendour; they, that would revive
> A Golden Age, must be as free
> For Acorns, as for Honesty.

Mandeville, writes Leslie Stephen, "puts in its most offensive form the dogma
that what we call virtue is but selfishness masquerading." But his views should
not be written off merely as witticisms. Montesquieu wrote "I would willingly
enter into the ideas of the author of the *Fable of the Bees.*"

The same strain appears in the *Beggar's Opera* (1728) of John Gay, whose
rogues and whores play out, on a sordid stage and in tattered finery, the tragi-
comedy that their betters enact in Court and Parliament. In France, *Gil Blas*
(1715) teaches the same lesson. It must not be supposed that the cynical phase
in literature necessarily reflected any general deterioration in conduct. It was
rather a reflection of the growth of scepticism about traditional moral principles; but a more philosophical treatment of the problem of evil was also
needed.

Among those who attempted this was Soame Jenyns, in *A Free Enquiry into
the Nature and Origin of Evil* (1757). He began with what was by now the
general assumption, of which he provides one of the most striking statements in
eighteenth-century literature, that good is the same as happiness, and evil as
unhappiness:

To say truth, Happiness is the only thing of real value in existence; neither riches,
nor power, nor wisdom, nor learning, nor strength, nor beauty, nor virtue, nor
religion, nor even life itself, being of any importance but as they contribute to its
production. All these are in themselves neither Good nor Evil; Happiness alone is
their great end, and they desirable only as they tend to promote it.

Morality he defines, logically, as the pursuit of happiness, though he adds to
it, as a kind of bonus, the virtue acquired by obeying the decrees of religion.
Jenyns, however, does not put us off with the superficial optimism of a Shaftesbury or Pope. He recognizes as a fact the existence of evil on an extensive scale.

He has been blamed for this instead of being praised for his intellectual honesty; but this is because, as well as accepting it, he tries to fit it into the eighteenth-century pattern of a rational world, presided over by a benevolent deity. His explanation is that even God cannot create good without evil. For Jenyns, necessary evil takes the place of Original Sin; and with the aid of the old "Chain of Being" idea he revives, in an extreme form, the view that partial evils contribute to greater good. But because Jenyns did not pretend that the evils were other than they were, the result seemed to some of his contemporaries peculiarly shocking. He writes, in the strain of Mandeville: "Luxury maintains its thousands, and Vanity its ten thousands . . . and thus private vices become publick benefits by the force only of accidental circumstances." This seems comparatively harmless, but he also says:

Poverty . . . is what all could not possibly have been exempted from . . . ; for had all been rich, none could have submitted to the commands of another, or the necessary drudgeries of life; thence all governments must have been dissolved, arts neglected, and lands uncultivated, and so an universal penury have overwhelmed all, instead of now and then pinching a few.

This was the kind of explanation that stood in the way of any attempt at amelioration of human conditions. There is no reason to believe that Soame Jenyns was other than an humane man, but he has to argue that ignorance being the opiate of the poor, they should not be deprived of it by "an ill-judged and improper education." Or even that "There is something in the abstract nature of pain conducive to pleasure; [so] that the sufferings of individuals are absolutely necessary to universal happiness." The goodness of nature begins to be almost as mysterious as the way in which God moves to perform his wonders. Ruthlessly optimistic to the last, Soame Jenyns speculates that the sufferings of the lower forms of creation may subserve, and therefore be justified by, the happiness of the higher. Perhaps even the evils with which the face of man is disfigured, he suggests, may contribute to the pleasure of higher beings.

This aroused the indignation of Dr Johnson, who knew from personal experience, better than Jenyns, what these sufferings were. In a review he let fly with Johnsonian wrath:

Many a merry bout have these frolic beings at the vicissitudes of an ague, and good sport it is to see a man tumble with an epilepsy, and revive and tumble again, and all this he knows not why. As they are wiser and more powerful than we, they have more exquisite diversions, for we have no way of procuring any sport so brisk and so lasting, as the paroxysms of the gout and stone, which undoubtedly must make high mirth, especially if the play be a little diversified with the blunders and puzzles of the blind and deaf.

The difference between Soame Jenyns and Dr Johnson does not lie in the inhumanity of the one and the humanity of the other, but in the fact that the former was still trying to maintain the optimistic world-view of Pope's *Essay on Man,* and to integrate the facts of evil that he recognized into the picture; while the latter had abandoned the attempt to build a theoretical system that would justify the nature of things. Dr Johnson fell back, in *Rasselas,* on a stoical acceptance of the misfortunes of life. What else can be said of a tale that begins:

Ye who listen with credulity to the whispers of fancy, and pursue with eagerness the phantoms of hope; who expect that age will perform the promises of youth, and that the deficiencies of the present day will be supplied by the morrow; attend to the history of Rasselas, prince of Abyssinia.

And ends: "Of these wishes that they had formed they well knew that none could be obtained."

The pessimism of Dr Johnson does not belong to the story of the Enlightenment; but equally its moral theory does not end with the blind optimism of Shaftesbury or the optimism *malgré tout* of Jenyns. This kind of optimism was only a phase, mainly confined to England, and not a lasting one even there. Dr Johnson himself noticed the parallel between his own story *Rasselas* and Voltaire's *Candide,* which was published almost at the same time. There is no reason to believe that Dr Johnson, poverty-stricken, ugly and ailing, had ever shared the world-view of the *Essay on Man;* but Voltaire, as a young writer enjoying premature and astonishing success, with the world at his feet, had admired the honeyed verse of Pope and condemned the tragic vision of Pascal. In the *Lettres philosophiques* he wrote: "I dare to take the side of humanity against this sublime misanthrope; I dare to assert that we are neither as wicked nor as unhappy as he says."

The young Voltaire hymned the praise of luxury and proclaimed "le paradis terrestre est où je suis," or, as an earlier version put it, "le paradis terrestre est à Paris." Age and experience brought a remarkable change. The Lisbon earthquake of 1755 finally forced the problem of evil on his notice, and like Dr Johnson he found he could not pretend that evil was really good, even indirectly or in disguise. In the preface to the poem evoked by this disaster, he still praised Pope, whom, he said, he continued to admire and love; but the belief that "tout est bien" had since Pope been so perverted that it had become "an insult to the sufferings of our life." Bayle was the better guide, because he had taught men to doubt. In a spirit of Johnsonian stoicism Voltaire concludes:

> Dans une épaisse nuit cherchant à m'éclairer
> Je ne sais que souffrir, et non pas murmurer.[1]

Even the *Poème sur la loi naturelle,* which accompanied the poem on the Lisbon earthquake and was intended to rescue the deistic ideas of natural religion and universal morality, is something closer now to Pascal than to Pope:

> Dans nos jours passagers de peines, de misères,
> Enfants du même Dieu, vivons au moins en frères,
> Aidons-nous l'un et l'autre à porter nos fardeaux:
> Nous marchons tous courbés sous le poids de nos maux;

> .   .   .   .   .

[1] In a dense night seeking to find the light,
  I only know how to suffer and not complain.

Ah n'empoisonnons pas la douceur qui nous reste.
Je crois voir des forçats dans un cachot funeste,
Se pouvant secourir, l'un sur l'autre acharnés,
Combattre avec les fers dont ils sont enchainés.[2]

The last lines bring to mind the second great shock that completed the under-mining of Voltaire's optimism—the Seven Years War. The subsequent ap-pearance of *Candide* is not a chronological accident, for by now he had come to detest the optimistic world-view with its implied justification of so much suffer-ing. His long preoccupation—one might almost call it an obsession—with Leibnizian optimism comes to a head in the bitter satire he directs against Dr Pangloss, though rather than Leibniz Pangloss may have represented his egre-gious popularizer Christian Wolff, whose ideas Voltaire would have known well enough through Mme du Châtelet. Voltaire's own view is summed up when Cacambo asks, "What is optimism?" "Alas," said Candide, "it is the mania for pretending that all is well when all is ill."

He returns to the subject in the article "Tout est bien" in the *Dictionnaire philosophique,* which sums up Leibniz as teaching that this is the best of possible worlds, and one ingredient in it is necessary evil. Mock-seriously, Voltaire pre-sents various explanations of the existence of evil:—the theory he attributes to Lactantius, that evil is necessary, because without it God could not have given us good; the view of Bolingbroke, Pope and Shaftesbury that all is well, which means that all is governed by immutable laws, and particular evils add up to general good; the Manichaeist dualism, with good and evil as the two equal powers that rule the world; the box that Pandora opened; or, finally, the sug-gestion that perhaps the world was made by inferior angels and so is a sub-standard article. He ends with the conclusion that the "all is well" theory can-not but represent God as an all powerful and evil-doing ruler. The existence of evil remains inexplicable: it is something we do not understand, but "Il faut cultiver notre jardin."

The stoical resignation of a Dr Johnson or the resigned pessimism of a Vol-taire were not for the ordinary man, who was less acutely aware of the deeper issues. A subsidiary but more practical problem, that of reconciling self-interest with the utility of the public, pressed more consciously on the minds of those who continued to pursue the moral debate. One of the most influential attempts at a solution is that proffered by David Hartley in his *Observations on Man* (1749). Hartley takes his start from some suggestions that Locke had thrown out. He picks up the passing suggestion of Locke that possibly a material being

---

[2] In our fleeting days of pain, of troubles,
　Children of the same God, let us at least live as brothers,
　Let us help one another to bear our burdens:
　We are walking all bent over under the weight of our ills;

　Ah let us not poison the sweetness which we still have.
　I think I see prisoners in a grim dungeon,
　Able to help one another, [yet] they attack one another,
　Fighting with the irons which chain them.

can think and proceeds to interpret the operations of the mind in terms of material vibrations. With this beginning it is not difficult for him to look for some force which will play the part in mental activity of gravity in Newtonian physics. In place of the active function of reflection, which Locke allows to play on the simple ideas acquired by the senses, Hartley hypothesizes an entirely automatic process of association:

Any Sensations A, B, C, etc. by being associated with one another a sufficient Number of Times, get such a Power over the corresponding Ideas a, b, c, etc. that any one of the Sensations A, when impressed alone, shall be able to excite in the Mind b, c, etc. the Ideas of the rest.

Now God, who is "the Cause of all Things," has so arranged that the desire of happiness is the necessary result of the universal principle of association in the human mind; and it follows from this that the tendency of Benevolence is "to augment itself without limits" and of Malevolence to destroy itself ultimately. This, says Hartley, "appears to be a very strong Argument for the infinite Benevolence of God." From which, he concludes: "It is probable from Reason, that all Mankind will be made happy ultimately."

Religion found another solution to the dilemma in terms of utilitarianism, by bringing in the pains and pleasures of a future life to redress the balance of the present one. This "other-worldly" morality was perhaps not a new element in religious thought except in the terms in which it was stated, which were sufficiently plain. Archdeacon Paley's *Moral and Political Philosophy* (1785) was its classic statement, which Leslie Stephen has summarized rather cruelly:

Christ came to tell us that we should go to hell if our actions did not tend to promote the greatest happiness of the greatest number; and the Almighty has contrived a means for giving him satisfactory credentials. The man at whose order the clock strikes thirteen must be in the secret of the artificer, and we may trust his account of a hidden part of the machinery.

Another line of approach to the problem, which took the form of a combination of Shaftesbury's moral sense and Locke's moral newtonism, is to be found in the theory of Francis Hutcheson. God, he held, has implanted in the individual a moral sense by which he is able to see, and when he sees to desire, that which is for the common good, which Hutcheson defined, in a phrase which was to become famous when a greater thinker used it, as "the greatest happiness of the greatest number." Adam Smith's *Theory of Moral Sentiments* (1759) adopts a similar line of argument, except that without denying the moral sense, he takes ethical behaviour as the product of all the other sentiments, moderated by the operation of social sympathies. Its result is that happiness of mankind which "seems to have been the original purpose intended by the author of nature." The superficial optimism which, in Soame Jenyns, aroused the wrath of Dr Johnson, is echoed by Adam Smith. Despite the appearances of disorder in this world, "yet even here every virtue naturally meets with its proper reward." It is true that wealth is unequally distributed, but as a result of the expenditure of the rich:

They are led by an invisible hand to make nearly the same distribution of the necessaries of life which would have been made had the earth been divided into equal portions among all its inhabitants.

By now, however, the eighteenth century had doubtless had enough of this kind of thing. It was becoming clear that the debate in England was petering out, and it might be thought that all that could be said on these lines had already been said, almost ad nauseam; but in fact a major contribution to ethical thought has still to be mentioned. The work of most lasting value in the field of moral philosophy published in the eighteenth century was that of Richard Price in his *Review of the Principal Questions and Difficulties in Morals.* Price set the whole discussion of the moral sense on a sounder basis by refusing to go behind the fact of the moral judgment. We know, he declared in effect, that we do make moral judgments continually. "To *behold* virtue," he declares, "is to *admire* her . . . to *perceive vice* is the very same as to *blame.*" This is to say that morality is intuitive: it is derived from an inner sense. At the same time, he does not yield up moral behaviour to the uncontrolled sway of some hypothesized and vague moral emotion. The application of these intuitive judgments, the assessment of their relevance when, as is often the case, more than one comes into play or their transference into action is not clear, calls for the employment of, and indeed control by, reason.

Price's theory of intuitive ethics is the most logical statement of one trend in eighteenth-century ethical thought. The stricter utilitarian view, on the other side, was to culminate in Bentham. Neither remained quite independent of, or uninfluenced by, the other; and the combination of the two was perhaps more fruitful than either would have been by itself.

In France the debate had followed rather different lines, as may be seen by a glance at the treatment of the question of morality in the *Encyclopédie.* The basic moral problem which appears in its pages is whether there is a natural morality, preceding society and the institution of laws, or whether all ideas of morality are the product of society. Excluding a religious basis for morality or any innate moral ideas, and seeing man as a part of nature, Diderot and his collaborators gave an affirmative answer to the first question. It followed that it should be possible to discover the nature of the necessary moral rules from a study of the facts. Natural morality should be scientific, positive and sociological. In practice the Encyclopaedists' line of inquiry was nothing of the sort. They made no serious attempt at an empirical inquiry. The mass of information that existed on the social customs of the various peoples of the world they largely ignored. Anything that they could not understand was dismissed as a product of human folly or roguery, probably of priestcraft. The Cartesian faith in first principles, and their own preconceived notions, were too strong for them. Their belief in a natural morality was a belief in a theoretical pattern, of universal validity, which merely needed to be discovered to be applied. Diderot himself saw better than many modern thinkers the difficulty of the attempt to derive a moral theory from the fantastic varieties of human behaviour, which seemed to lead to the conclusion that there was scarcely any supposed vice that was not a virtue somewhere.

The *philosophes* are not necessarily to be criticized for their failure to build up a scheme of morality on the shifting and contradictory bases of the facts of differing societies. If they looked to the physical and psychological needs of man to provide a system of morals, the result was hardly more encouraging; societies were so rarely natural, and universal, unchanging human nature could seldom be detected in actual customs. Thus they fell back on speculation. Their discussion of the origin of moral sentiments was hypothetical rather than historical or practical. Some sought to discover by psychological analysis how morality *must have* originated. Others, like de Jaucourt, clung to the traditional moral ideas of the Natural Law school of thought. Under the influence of Cartesianism they all tended to believe that what was clear, simple and universal was true, in morals as in mathematics. They were, indeed, trying to achieve the deductive system of morals that Locke had proclaimed, and were no more successful than he was in giving it a positive content.

Utilitarians, like Helvétius and d'Holbach, and intuitionists like Rousseau, were to carry on the debate, within the limits of their systems, more profitably. Diderot, combining both tendencies, and adding a special insight of his own, summed up the contributions and contradictions of a century in his writings. These later developments remain to be discussed, but already it will be evident that eighteenth-century thinkers gave no final answer to the problem of morality, any more than they had to the problem of evil. They are not to be criticized too severely for this failure. It can hardly be claimed that their successors have answered the questions that the eighteenth century had at least the credit of raising, or that later generations deserve higher praise for abandoning a debate of which the greatest merit lay simply in the fact that it was carried on with such sincerity and intensity. If a serious debate over moral problems, as distinguished from an unquestioning acceptance of views established by tradition or authority, is any test of morality, then the age of the Enlightenment was the most moral of all ages.

3.

Carl Becker's (1873–1945) works and his teaching at Cornell University earned for him the honor of being one of the country's first great historians. Neither narrowly preoccupied by national history—but at home with it— nor overly eager to compete with European historians, Becker's achievement became unique because of this detachment, breadth of vision, and sheer intelligence.

In a brilliant and influential essay Becker challenged the Philosophes' claim to modernity. He does not deny this claim or refute the assertions of previous historians who had accepted it. Rather, he argues that the Philosophes' debt to medieval thought was greater than they knew or wanted to recognize.

CARL BECKER: The Heavenly City of the Eighteenth-Century Philosophers*

We are accustomed to think of the eighteenth century as essentially modern in its temper. Certainly, the *Philosophes* themselves made a great point of having renounced the superstition and hocus-pocus of medieval Christian thought, and we have usually been willing to take them at their word. Surely, we say, the eighteenth century was preëminently the age of reason, surely the *Philosophes* were a skeptical lot, atheists in effect if not by profession, addicted to science and the scientific method, always out to crush the infamous, valiant defenders of liberty, equality, fraternity, freedom of speech, and what you will. All very true. And yet I think the *Philosophes* were nearer the Middle Ages, less emancipated from the preconceptions of medieval Christian thought, than they quite realized or we have commonly supposed. If we have done them more (or is it less?) than justice in giving them a good modern character, the reason is that they speak a familiar language. We read Voltaire more readily than Dante, and follow an argument by Hume more easily than one by Thomas Aquinas. But I think our appreciation is of the surface more than of the fundamentals of their thought. We agree with them more readily when they are witty and cynical than when they are wholly serious. Their negations rather than their affirmations enable us to treat them as kindred spirits.

But, if we examine the foundations of their faith, we find that at every turn the *Philosophes* betray their debt to medieval thought without being aware of it. They denounced Christian philosophy, but rather too much, after the manner of those who are but half emancipated from the "superstitions" they scorn. They had put off the fear of God, but maintained a respectful attitude toward the Deity. They ridiculed the idea that the universe had been created in six days, but still believed it to be a beautifully articulated machine designed by the Supreme Being according to a rational plan as an abiding place for mankind. The Garden of Eden was for them a myth, no doubt, but they looked enviously back to the golden age of Roman virtue, or across the waters to the unspoiled innocence of an Arcadian civilization that flourished in Pennsylvania. They renounced the authority of church and Bible, but exhibited a naïve faith in the authority of nature and reason. They scorned metaphysics, but were proud to be called philosophers. They dismantled heaven, somewhat prematurely it seems, since they retained their faith in the immortality of the soul. They courageously discussed atheism, but not before the servants. They defended toleration valiantly, but could with difficulty tolerate priests. They denied that miracles ever happened, but believed in the perfectibility of the human race. We feel that these Philosophers were at once too credulous and too skeptical. They were the victims of common sense. In spite of their rationalism and their humane sympathies, in spite of their aversion to hocus-pocus and enthusiasm and dim perspectives, in spite of their eager skepticism, their engaging cynicism, their brave youthful blasphemies and talk of hanging the last king in the entrails of the

* From Carl Becker, *The Heavenly City of the Eighteenth-Century Philosophers* (New Haven: Yale University Press, 1932), pp. 29–31; 47–69.

last priest—in spite of all of it, there is more of Christian philosophy in the writings of the *Philosophes* than has yet been dreamt of in our histories. . . .

If we would discover the little backstairs door that for any age serves as the secret entranceway to knowledge, we will do well to look for certain unobtrusive words with uncertain meanings that are permitted to slip off the tongue or the pen without fear and without research; words which, having from constant repetition lost their metaphorical significance, are unconsciously mistaken for objective realities. In the thirteenth century the key words would no doubt be God, sin, grace, salvation, heaven, and the like; in the nineteenth century, matter, fact, matter-of-fact, evolution, progress; in the twentieth century, relativity, process, adjustment, function, complex. In the eighteenth century the words without which no enlightened person could reach a restful conclusion were nature, natural law, first cause, reason, sentiment, humanity, perfectibility (these last three being necessary only for the more tender-minded, perhaps).

In each age these magic words have their entrances and their exits. And how unobtrusively they come in and go out! We should scarcely be aware either of their approach or their departure, except for a slight feeling of discomfort, a shy self-consciousness in the use of them. The word "progress" has long been in good standing, but just now we are beginning to feel, in introducing it into the highest circles, the need of easing it in with quotation marks, that conventional apology that will save all our faces. Words of more ancient lineage trouble us more. Did not President Wilson, during the war, embarrass us not a little by appearing in public on such familiar terms with "humanity," by the frank avowal of his love for "mankind"? As for God, sin, grace, salvation—the introduction of these ghosts from the dead past we regard as inexcusable, so completely do their unfamiliar presences put us out of countenance, so effectively do they, even under the most favorable circumstances, cramp our style.

In the eighteenth century these grand magisterial words, although still to be seen, were already going out of fashion, at least in high intellectual society. It is true that theologians still made much of them, but even they felt called upon to offer a rational apology for doing so. Bishop Butler's famous *Analogy of Religion, Natural and Revealed* (1737) was only one, although one of the most elaborate and painstaking, of many exercises of this kind. But for the sophisticated, men of letters and men of the world, these masterful words were regarded with distaste. Unable to pronounce them without discomfort, enlightened "men of parts" commonly employed substitutes or euphemisms with less explicit, less compromising implications. The picture of salvation in the Heavenly City they toned down to a vague impressionistic image of a "future state," "immortality of the soul," or a more generalized earthly and social *félicité* or *perfectibilité du genre humain.* Grace was translated into virtue, virtue with a certain classical implication in the meaning—*ce fonds de rectitude et de bonté morale, qui est la base de la vertu,* as Marmontel defined it. To be esteemed a "man of virtue" was both sufficient and efficacious, and likely to give one, without any painful searchings of the heart, the assurance of being in a state of social justification, or even, if the esteem were general enough, of complete sanctification. I suppose that Hume and Franklin, when they were in France, for example, must have had this assurance as fully as any saint of the church ever did.

With the Heavenly City thus shifted to earthly foundations, and the business of justification transferred from divine to human hands, it was inevitable that God should be differently conceived and more indifferently felt. Not that he could be (except by a few unnaturally hardened souls) dispensed with altogether. Most eighteenth-century minds were too accustomed to a stable society with fixed ranks, too habituated to an orderly code of manners and a highly conventionalized art, to be at all happy in a disordered universe. It seemed safer, therefore, even for the enlightened ones, to retain God, or some plausible substitute, as a kind of dialectical guaranty that all was well in the most comfortable of common-sense worlds. But, obviously, the Creator as a mere first premise no longer needed those rich and all too human qualities of God the Father. Having performed his essential function of creation, it was proper for him to withdraw from the affairs of men into the shadowy places where absolute being dwells. Thus withdrawn, he ceased to be personal and inconvenient. No longer demanding propitiatory sacrifices, he could be regarded merely as that Omniscience or Beneficence which men of sense could serenely contemplate with respect untempered with fear or adoration. Yet, even men of sense needed some word for this necessary thing, some suitable substitute for God the Father. Supreme Being? Author of the Universe? Great Contriver? Prime Mover? First Cause? Surely, any of these would serve. We know at least, to our great discomfort, that all of them were freely used.

It would have been impossible, would it not, for the *Philosophes* to have thus complacently permitted God the Father to fade away into the thin abstraction of a First Cause unless they were prepared to dispense with his revelation to men—the revelation through Holy Writ and Holy Church. This was, indeed, the whole point of their high, offensive gesture. Renunciation of the traditional revelation was the very condition of being truly enlightened; for to be truly enlightened was to see the light in all its fulness, and the light in its fulness revealed two very simple and obvious facts. One of these contained the sum of those negations which we understand so well—the fact that the supposed revelation of God's purposes through Holy Writ and Holy Church was a fraud, or at best an illusion born of ignorance, perpetrated, or at least maintained, by the priests in order to accentuate the fears of mankind, and so hold it in subjection. The other fact contained the sum of those affirmations which we understand less easily—that God had revealed his purpose to men in a far more simple and natural, a far less mysterious and recondite way, through his works. To be enlightened was to understand this double truth, that it was not in Holy Writ, but in the great book of nature, open for all mankind to read, that the laws of God had been recorded. This is the new revelation, and thus at last we enter the secret door to knowledge. This open book of nature was what Jean Jacques Rousseau and his philosophical colleagues went in search of when they wished to know what God had said to them.

Nature and natural law—what magic these words held for the philosophical century! Enter that country by any door you like, you are at once aware of its pervasive power. I have but just quoted, in another connection, extracts from the writings of Hume, Voltaire, Rousseau, Volney: in each of them nature takes without question the position customarily reserved for the guest of honor. To find a proper title for this lecture I had only to think of the Declaration of Independence—"to assume, among the powers of the earth, the separate and equal station, to which the laws of nature and of nature's God entitle them." Turn to the French counterpart of the Declaration, and you will find that "the aim of every political association is the preservation of the natural and impre-scriptible rights of man." Search the writings of the new economists and you will find them demanding the abolition of artificial restrictions on trade and industry in order that men may be free to follow the natural law of self-interest. Look into the wilderness of forgotten books and pamphlets dealing with religion and morality: interminable arguments, clashing opinions, different and seemingly irreconcilable conclusions you will find, and yet strangely enough controver-sialists of every party unite in calling upon nature as the sovereign arbiter of all their quarrels. The Christian Bishop Butler affirms with confidence that "the whole analogy of nature . . . most fully shews that there is nothing incredible in the general [Christian] doctrine of religion, that God will reward and punish men for their actions hereafter." The deist Voltaire, rejecting the Christian doc-trine of religion, asserts with equal dogmatism that "natural law . . . which nature teaches all men" is that "upon which all religion is founded." The atheist Holbach, rejecting all religion, nevertheless holds that "the morality suitable to man should be founded on the nature of man." Christian, deist, atheist—all acknowledge the authority of the book of nature; if they differ it is only as to the scope of its authority, as to whether it merely confirms or entirely supplants the authority of the old revelation. In the eighteenth-century climate of opinion, whatever question you seek to answer, nature is the test, the standard: the ideas, the customs, the institutions of men, if ever they are to attain perfec-tion, must obviously be in accord with those laws which "nature reveals at all times, to all men."

Not that the concepts of nature and natural law were new in the world. Aristotle justified slavery on the ground that it was in accord with nature. The stoic emperor, Marcus Aurelius, understood that "nothing is evil which is ac-cording to Nature." Roman jurists endeavored to reconcile positive law with the law of nature and right reason. Thomas Aquinas knew that the "participa-tion of the eternal law in the rational creature is called the natural law." Accord-ing to Calvin, "Natural equity . . . demands that princes be armed . . . to defend the subjects committed to their care whenever they are hostilely assailed." Robert Barclay, the Quaker, tells us that "this forcing of men's con-sciences is contrary . . . to the very *law of nature.*" Vittoria, a Dominican pro-fessor, defined the law of nations as "that which natural reason establishes between all nations." Suarez, the Jesuit philosopher, thought that the "natural light of intelligence, spontaneously pronouncing on that which should be done, may be called the natural law." Grotius founded civil and international society on human nature, which is the "mother of . . . natural law." English Levelers in the seventeenth century founded their revolt on the "laws of God and nature." Hobbes defended, and Locke refuted, the doctrine of despotic power on the same high ground. Montaigne, who welcomed and relished every idea that ever was, felt it not reasonable that "art should gain the pre-eminence of our great and powerful mother nature." And, finally, not to try your patience further, Pascal was familiar enough with nature and all her ways to pronounce a final judgment. "But what is nature? Why is custom not natural? I much fear that this nature is itself only a first custom, as custom is second nature."

Not the exclusive possession of the eighteenth century, this "ideal image" of nature; no, but after all a different, a more substantial image arises to charm that century. In earlier centuries the ideal image of nature was, as one may say, too ghostly ever to be mistaken for nature herself. Nature herself had hitherto seemed to common sense intractable, even mysterious and dangerous, at best inharmonious to man. Men therefore desired some authoritative assurance that there was no need to be apprehensive; and this assurance came from theologians and philosophers who argued that, since God is goodness and reason, his creation must somehow be, even if not evidently so to finite minds, good and reasonable. Design in nature was thus derived *a priori* from the character which the Creator was assumed to have; and natural law, so far from being associated with the observed behavior of physical phenomena, was no more than a conceptual universe above and outside the real one, a logical construction dwelling in the mind of God and dimly reflected in the minds of philosophers.

Once safely within the eighteenth century we cease to be haunted by this ghostly ideal image. The ideal image is still with us, but it has taken on a more familiar and substantial body. No one ever looked more attentively at the eighteenth-century image of nature than Hume, who knew better than anyone else that it was an illusion; and for that very reason there is no better description of it than that which he put into the mouth of Cleanthes, one of the characters in his *Dialogues Concerning Natural Religion.* In defense of natural religion, Cleanthes says:

Look around the world: contemplate the whole and every part of it: You will find it to be nothing but one great machine, subdivided into an infinite number of lesser machines, which again admit of subdivisions, to a degree beyond what human senses and faculties can trace and explain. All these various machines, and even their most minute parts, are adjusted to each other with an accuracy, which ravishes into admiration all men, who have ever contemplated them. The curious adapting of means to ends, throughout all nature, resembles exactly, though it much exceeds, the productions of human . . . intelligence. Since therefore the effects resemble each other, we are led to infer . . . that the causes also resemble; and that the Author of Nature is somewhat similar to the mind of man; though possessed of much larger faculties, proportioned to the grandeur of the work, which he has executed.

The passage is significant in two respects. We note at once that the logical process has been reversed. Cleanthes does not conclude that nature *must* be rational because God *is* eternal reason; he concludes that God *must* be an engineer because nature *is* a machine. From this reversal of the logical process it follows that natural law is identified with the actual behavior of nature. What ravishes Cleanthes into admiration is not the exceeding beauty of a logical concept of the world, but the exceeding intricacy and delicate adjustment of the world itself. For him nature is not a logical concept, but a substantial reality; and natural law, instead of being a construction of deductive logic, is the observed harmonious behavior of material objects.

This transformation of the ideal image of nature was the result, as everyone knows, of the scientific discoveries of the seventeenth century. Galileo observed that the pendulum behaved in a certain manner, and then formulated the law of the pendulum in terms of mathematics. Newton did not doubt that the heavens declare the glory of God; but he was concerned to find out, by looking through a telescope and doing a sum in mathematics, precisely how they managed it. He discovered that every particle of matter, whether in the heavens or elsewhere, behaved as if it attracted every other particle with a force proportional to the product of the masses and inversely proportional to the square of the distance. This was a new kind of "law of nature." Formerly, as the editor of the second edition of the *Principia* tells us, philosophers were "employed in giving names to things, and not in searching into things themselves." Newton himself noted the difference by saying: "These Principles I consider not as occult Qualities, supposed to result from the specific Forms of Things, but as general Laws of Nature, by which the Things themselves are form'd." This was the new way to knowledge opened up by "natural philosophy": to "search into Things themselves," and then to formulate the "general Laws of Nature by which the Things themselves are form'd."

Certainly, this new philosophy ravished the eighteenth century into admiration; and not the least astonishing thing about it was the commonplace methods employed to discover such marvelous truths. That Newton discovered the nature of light seemed even less significant to his contemporaries than that he did so by playing with a prism. It was as if nature had for the first time been brought close to men, close enough to be tangible and clearly visible in all its wonderful details. Nature, it seemed, was, after all, just the common things that common men observed and handled every day, and natural law only the uniform way these things behaved. Steam bubbling from the spout of a kettle, smoke whisking up a chimney, morning mist lifting from meadows—here was nature all about, moving in ways not mysterious her wonders to perform; and revealing, to the eyes of common men, no less than to the learned, those laws that imposed on all things their reasonable and beneficent, even if curious and intricate, commands.

When philosophy became a matter of handling test tubes instead of dialectics everyone could be, in the measure of his intelligence and interest, a philosopher. As Goethe tells us:

Many a one became convinced that nature had endowed him with as great a portion of good and straightforward sense as, perchance, he required to form such a clear notion of objects that he could manage them and turn them to his own profit, and that of others, without laboriously troubling himself about the most universal problems. . . . Men made the trial, opened their eyes, looked straight before them, observant, industrious, active. . . .

. . . every one was now entitled, not only to philosophize, but also by degrees to consider himself a philosopher. Philosophy, therefore, was more or less sound and practised common sense, which ventured to enter upon the universal, and to decide upon inner and outer experiences. . . . and thus at last philosophers were found in all of the faculties, nay, in all classes and trades.

"Until philosophers become kings, . . . cities will not cease from ill," said Plato; but philosophy is perhaps in an even better way to exert influence (whether for good or ill) when common men become philosophers. The reason is that common men take up philosophy, if at all, not as an exercise in dialectic, but as something that holds for them the assurance of a better way of life. They are apt, therefore, to associate any philosophy that interests them with the name of some great man, whom they can love or hate for having given the world a new idea; and they are sure to invest the new idea with some meaning that it did not originally have. We are familiar with this procedure, having noted, during the last fifty years, the association of the "evolutionary philosophy" with the name of Darwin, and the transformation of "Darwinism" into "monkey-ism" or the "white man's burden" as the case may be—into something at all events which Darwin, simple man, would be astonished to hear of. The same thing happened in the eighteenth century. Common men associated the new philosophy with the name of Newton because it appeared that Newton, more than any other man, had banished mystery from the world by discovering a "universal law of nature," thus demonstrating, what others had only asserted, that the universe was rational and intelligible through and through, and capable, therefore, of being subdued to the uses of men.

The "Newtonian philosophy" was, accordingly, as familiar to common men in the middle eighteenth century as the "Darwinian philosophy" is in our day. "Very few people read Newton," Voltaire explained, "because it is necessary to be learned to understand him. But *everybody talks about him.*" Why, indeed, should ordinary men read Newton? They were not greatly interested in the proposition that "reaction is always equal and opposite to action." They were interested in the Newtonian philosophy, a very different thing. No need to open the *Principia* to find out what the Newtonian philosophy was—much better not, in fact. Leave that to the popularizers, who could find in the *Principia* more philosophy than common men could, very often more, I must say, than Newton himself ever did. Anyone might open, instead of the *Principia*, Benjamin Martin's *A Plain and Familiar Introduction to the Newtonian Philosophy, in Six Sections, Illustrated by Six Copper-Plates* (1751), of which there appeared in due time five editions; or James Ferguson's *Astronomy Explained upon Sir Isaac Newton's Principles, and Made Easy to Those who have not Studied Mathematics* (1756), which ran to seven editions; or Voltaire's *Éléments de la philosophie de Newton,* which could be read in English (1738) as well as in the original French; or Count Algorotti's *Il Newtonianismo per le dame,* which ran to three editions in Italian, was translated into French (1738), and into English under the title *Theory of Light and Colors* (1739); or (for those poetically inclined) J. T. Desaguliers' *The Newtonian System of the World the Best Model of Government, an Allegorical Poem* (1728).

In these books, or in others like them, common men could find the Newtonian philosophy, a philosophy which was of interest to them, not so much for the scientific discoveries it set forth as for the bearing of those discoveries upon the most fundamental of human problems—that is to say, the relation of man to nature and of both to God. What those relations were, or were taken to be, is admirably stated by Colin Maclaurin, Professor of Mathematics in the University of Edinburgh, in his book, *An Account of Sir Isaac Newton's Philosophical Discoveries,* perhaps the ablest of the popular expositions in English.

To describe the *phenomena* of nature, to explain their causes . . . and to inquire into the whole constitution of the universe, is the business of natural philosophy. A strong curiosity has prompted men in all times to study nature; every useful art has some connexion with this science; and the inexhausted beauty and variety of things makes it ever agreeable, new, and surprising.

But natural philosophy is subservient to purposes of a higher kind, and is chiefly to be valued as it lays a sure foundation for natural religion and moral philosophy; by leading us, in a satisfactory manner, to the knowledge of the Author and Governor of the universe. . . .

We are, from his works, to seek to know God, and not to pretend to mark out the scheme of his conduct, in nature, from the very deficient ideas we are able to form of that great mysterious Being. . . .

Our views of Nature, however imperfect, serve to represent to us, in the most sensible manner, that mighty power which prevails throughout, acting with a force and efficacy that appears to suffer no diminution from the greatest distances of space or intervals of time; and that wisdom which we see equally displayed in the exquisite structure and just motions of the greatest and subtilest parts. These, with perfect goodness, by which they are evidently directed, constitute the supreme object of the speculations of a philosopher; who, while he contemplates and admires so excellent a system, cannot but be himself *excited and animated to correspond with the general harmony of nature.*

The closing words of this passage may well be taken as a just expression of the prevailing state of mind about the middle of the eighteenth century. Obviously the disciples of the Newtonian philosophy had not ceased to worship. They had only given another form and a new name to the object of worship: having denatured God, they deified nature. They could, therefore, without self-consciousness, and with only a slight emendation in the sacred text, repeat the cry of the psalmist: "I will lift up mine eyes to Nature from whence cometh my help!" With eyes uplifted, contemplating and admiring so excellent a system, they were excited and animated to correspond with the general harmony.

The desire to correspond with the general harmony springs perennial in the human breast. Saints of all ages have aspired to become one with whatever gods there be. In medieval times the approved method, in Europe, was thought to be fasting and prayer, denial of the flesh, the renunciation of the natural man. "Who shall deliver me from the body of this death!" The physical dwelling place of the spirit was thought to be a disharmony, a soiled and cloying vesture of decay closing in and blinding the spirit so that, during its earthly pilgrimage, it could only with difficulty, if at all, enter into the harmony that was God. But the enlightened ones knew that it was not so. From this darkness also they had emerged into the light which enabled them to see that the natural and the spiritual man were but different manifestations of one harmonious whole.

The rationalization of this will to believe was provided by John Locke in his epoch-making book, *An Essay Concerning Human Understanding,* which became the psychological gospel of the eighteenth century. Its great service to the men of that time was to demonstrate that the mind owed nothing to inheritance, to "innate ideas"; everything to environment, to the sensations that flowed in upon it from the outer world. A modern critic assures us that the theory of innate ideas which Locke demolished was "so crude that it is difficult to suppose that any serious thinker ever held it." That may well be. Maybe serious thinkers are few, and maybe the world is ruled by crude ideas. What Locke aimed at no doubt, what the eighteenth century acclaimed him for having demolished, was the Christian doctrine of total depravity, a black, spreading cloud which for centuries had depressed the human spirit. For if, as Locke maintained, the mind at birth was devoid of implanted and ineradicable ideas and dispositions, was in fact no more than a blank white sheet of paper upon which the outer world of nature and human association was to write whatever of good or ill repute might be found recorded there, why, then, the mind of man was a record made by that outer world: jazzed and discordant now that the outer world was so; a satisfying and ordered symphony when that outer world should become, as it might, what men had conceived it ought to be. This was Locke's great title to glory, that he made it possible for the eighteenth century to believe with a clear conscience what it wanted to believe, namely, that since man and the mind of man were shaped by that nature which God had created, it was possible for men, "barely by the use of their natural faculties," to bring their ideas and their conduct, and hence the institutions by which they lived, into harmony with the universal natural order. With what simple faith the age of enlightenment welcomed this doctrine! With what sublime courage it embraced the offered opportunity to refashion the outward world of human institutions according to the laws of nature and of nature's God!

I need not say that the difficulties were great: endless difficulties in the realm of practice; one fundamental difficulty in the realm of theory. Hidden away in the elaborate structure of Locke's *Essay* was a most disconcerting corollary. It was this: if nature be the work of God, and man the product of nature, then all that man does and thinks, all that he has ever done or thought, must be natural, too, and in accord with the laws of nature and of nature's God. Pascal had long since asked the fundamental question: "Why is custom not natural?" Why, indeed! But if all is natural, then how could man and his customs ever be *out of harmony* with nature? No doubt the difficulty could be avoided by declaring that there was no disharmony.

> All are but parts of one stupendous whole,
> Whose body nature is, and God the soul;

.   .   .   .   .

> All discord, harmony not understood;
> All partial evil, universal good:
> And, spite of pride, in erring reason's spite,
> One truth is clear, *Whatever is, is right.*

But this, addressed to the intelligence, was not an answer; it was merely an avoidance, a dishonest begging of the question. To assert that all that is, is right, was to beat all meaning out of the word "right," unless indeed one were willing to hood one's eyes once more in the cloak of Christian faith. For Pope was merely repeating St. Thomas, who had written twenty volumes to reassure a world on the verge of doubt—twenty volumes to say that it was really right that things should be wrong, God only knows why.

A poet in search of peace and epigrams might be permitted to repeat the ancient theologians, but the Philosophers could not do so unless they were willing to renounce their premises or deny the evidence of common sense. The very foundation of the new philosophy was that the existence of God, if there was one, and his goodness, if goodness he could claim, must be inferred from the observable behavior of the world. Following Newton, the Philosophers had all insisted on this to the point of pedantry, and so, even, had the enlightened Christian theologians in their desperate effort to find arguments to convince doubting Thomases. How then could Philosophers say that all was somehow good in God's sight unless they could also say that there was no evil to be observed in the world of nature and man? Yet to say that there was no evil in the world—a world where Lisbon earthquakes occurred, where Bastilles functioned, where crowds still gathered to gloat over the lingering agony of men broken on the wheel—was an insult to common sense. No, whatever Locke may have done, he had done nothing to solve, even if for the unwary he had done much to obscure, the problem of evil in the world.

Before the middle of the century Hume had taken up this world-old problem, had looked at it straight, had examined it attentively round and round about; and then, in his *Dialogues Concerning Natural Religion,* with all the dialectical resources of the new philosophy, with a penetrating insight matched only by the serene urbanity with which he displayed it, had remorselessly exposed the futility of reason to establish either the existence or the goodness of God. "Epicurus's old questions are yet unanswered. Is he [God] willing to prevent evil, but not able? Then he is impotent. Is he able, but not willing? Then he is malevolent. Is he both able and willing? Whence then is evil?" In the end Hume manages to chevy Christian mystics and atheists into the same camp, since they obviously agree on the main point, that reason is totally incompetent to answer ultimate questions; and so he concludes with that masterpiece of irony: "To be a philosophical Sceptic is, in a man of letters, the first and most essential step towards being a sound, believing Christian." To read Hume's *Dialogues* after having read, with sympathetic understanding, the earnest deists and optimistic philosophers of the early century, is to experience a slight chill, a feeling of apprehension. It is as if, at high noon of the Enlightenment, at the hour of the siesta when everything seems so quiet and secure all about, one were suddenly aware of a short, sharp slipping of the foundations, a faint far-off tremor running underneath the solid ground of common sense.

There it was then—the ugly dilemma, emerging from the beautiful premises of the new philosophy: if nature is good, then there is no evil in the world; if there is evil in the world, then nature is so far not good. How will they meet it, the enlightened ones who with so much assurance and complacent wit have set out with the rule of reason to rebuild an unlovely universe according to nature's design? Will they, closing their eyes to the brute facts, maintain that there is no evil in the world? In that case there is nothing for them to set right. Or will they, keeping their eyes open, admit that there is evil in the world? In that case nature fails to provide them with any standard for setting things right. They have followed reason faithfully. Will they follow her to the end? She is pointing in two directions: back toward Christian faith; forward toward atheism. Which way will they choose? It does not really matter much, since in either case she will vanish at last, leaving them to face existence with no other support than hope, or indifference, or despair.

4.

In the first volume of *The Enlightenment: An Interpretation,* Professor Peter Gay (1923–   ) of Columbia University analyzes the impact of ancient Greek and Roman thought on Western Europe from Petrarch to Hume. This long perspective enables him to define the origins of secularism and modernity in the Renaissance, in the seventeenth century, and finally in the Enlightenment. For Gay, each of these periods played a crucial role in the development of modern conceptions of man, science, ethics, and politics.

Unlike Becker, however, he stresses the debt of Enlightenment thought to the ancient world rather than to the Middle Ages. The subtitle to his volume, *The Origins of Modern Paganism,* gives a clue to Gay's explanation of the rejection of Christianity by the Philosophes. Was this rejection complete? As in the case of all works on the Enlightenment, or for that matter of intellectual history, pay special attention to the use and analysis of crucial terms and phrases, like nature, reason, and natural law. Did Hume belong to the *Heavenly City?*

PETER GAY: **In Dubious Battle** *

The philosophes' claim to distance from their Christian world has rarely been fully honored. Instead the philosophes have been sarcastically commended for "merely" secularizing religious ideas and caricatured as medieval clerks in modern dress, ungrateful and forgetful heirs of the Christian tradition who combated the pious wish for salvation in the name of a secular salvation disguised as progress; who denied the immortality of the soul only to substitute the immortality of reputation; who laughed at religious idolatry but had their own saints—Bacon, Newton, and Locke; who excommunicated their heretics—Rousseau; and even made pilgrimages—to Ferney.

Such analogies are seductive and even telling: they draw attention to origins the philosophes did not like to remember. There was some point after all in the

* From Peter Gay, *The Enlightenment: An Interpretation* (New York: Knopf, 1966), pp. 322–27, 370–81, 404–19.

derisive observation that the Enlightenment was a derivative, vulgarized re-statement of traditional Christian values: the new philosophy a secularized faith, optimism a secularized hope, humanitarianism a secularized charity. For this much of course is true: pious Christians from Luther and Calvin down to the eloquent Arminian publicists and learned Catholic scholars of the early eighteenth century built a bridge between modern religion and modern philosophy, a bridge of reason and good sense on which Christian ideals and Christian scholarships traveled to receptive audiences in the age of the Enlightenment.

But from the vantage point of each camp the same set of facts takes on two very different shapes. What Christians saw, with some justice, as an act of imitation, the philosophes saw, with greater justice, as an act of repudiation or, at best, of exploitation. The image of a bridge is helpful but incomplete; it fails to evoke the essential hostility between eighteenth-century religion and eighteenth-century secularism: the philosophes rudely treated the Christian past rather as Voltaire treated the plays of Shakespeare—as a dunghill strewn with diamonds, crying out to be pillaged and badly needing to be cleaned out. For even when the philosophes openly sought a secular equivalent for a Christian idea, they were engaged in revolutionary activity: it makes a difference whether a man is terrified of hell or concerned for his posthumous reputation, makes God or a historical hero into a father figure, admires a universe that allows the invasions of Providence or one that persists in unalterable, lawful regularity. The origins of ideas may be a clue to their function, they do not determine it. Christianity made a substantial contribution to the philosophes' education, but of the definition of the Enlightenment it forms no part.

While the philosophes acknowledged that there were Christians who sounded like decent and sensible men, they hedged even this grudging concession with reservations: David Hume slyly suggested that the Roman Emperor Julian had conceded "the great Charity of the Christians, which they extended, he says, even sometimes to Heathens: But he asserts, like a Rogue as he is, that they borrow'd that Virtue from the writings of Homer & other heathen Poets." The clandestine anonymous pamphlet *Le militaire philosophe* made the obverse of this point a little less elegantly: "There is not a single impertinence in the most extravagant paganism which has not been faithfully copied in our Religion." While the Christians, in other words, had incorporated and intensified pagan vices, they had incorporated and debased pagan virtues. Hence the philosophes —rogues that they were—could claim that they were doing to the Christians what the Church Fathers had claimed they had done to the Greeks and Romans: they were merely taking back what had originally belonged to them.

This philosophic estimate is uncharitable, positively un-Christian; still, here as so often before, we encounter the curious duality of the Enlightenment's historical verdicts: the philosophes were ungenerous and prejudiced and still right in substance. What the philosophes took over from Christian theologians and Christian philosophers were the least distinctively Christian, the least religious, parts of their teachings—they were usually ideas that had come to the Church Fathers from the Stoics. Moreover the philosophes rarely left these semipagan borrowings untouched—as the ancient Greeks unmistakably made their own what they took from their neighbors, so the philosophes emptied what they borrowed of its religious content.

This freedom permitted the philosophes to be condescendingly tolerant of at least some Christians and to discriminate among individuals and denominations: they agreed that Christian rationalists were more sensible than Scholastics, moderate Calvinists more tolerant than Puritan enthusiasts, Protestants in general less superstitious than Catholics. These distinctions were neither fixed nor absolute: usually, and not unexpectedly, the philosophes were more indulgent with sects other than those into which they had been born. D'Alembert was delighted to find Genevan pastors sociable, intelligent, and humane; Voltaire held up the humanity of English Quakers for imitation; David Hume, who had grown up among Scottish Presbyterians, therefore enjoyed the company of cultivated French Catholics.

And just as they reluctantly recognized that the opposition had its virtues, the philosophes also recognized, quite as reluctantly, that they had a debt to the era of pagan Christianity—and not to its pagans alone. They knew that the dunghill of superstition displayed diamonds of rationality. They did well to recognize this, for their debt in fact was sizable. The culture of the sixteenth and seventeenth centuries, divided and enriched by acrimonious controversies, had thrown up rationalist versions of Protestantism and philosophical interpretations of Roman Catholicism which the philosophes could read without hostility and absorb without embarrassment, if with some rather drastic amendments. Socinians, Cambridge Platonists, advocates of a universal religion, Christian pacifists—all could be put to use. They could be exploited, of course; nothing was easier than to harness their learned and vitriolic polemics against other believers to the Enlightenment's campaign against all organized religion. But these modern Christians had other uses as well; they found their natural heirs among British deists and German Aufklärer. There were scores of theologians and scholars—most of them unknown to the Enlightenment, many of them treated with contempt, and only a few of them honored—who embodied qualities and advocated ideals echoed in the philosophes' philosophy and who had these qualities and ideals, I must emphasize, not because they were Christian Stoics or Christian Skeptics but simply because they were Christians. Much of the decency in seventeenth-century civilization, much of its intelligence and critical acumen, was exercised by Christians for Christian purposes. And it was largely these Christians who created the atmosphere of the late seventeenth and early eighteenth century into which the philosophes were born, when manners were beginning to be polished, toleration became fashionable, and pulpits filled with Latitudinarians, Arminians, and rational Catholics.

In these modern believers reason and religion were firmly yoked together. "The denial of reason in religion," Joseph Glanvill laid down late in the seventeenth century, "hath been the principal engine, that heretics and enthusiasts have used against the Faith." A little later, Swift offered his savage clinical analysis of those very enthusiasts in the name of a reasonable Christianity. The philosophes were grateful for all such opinions, even if they strove to separate the two things, reason and religion, which these Christians had tried so valiantly to keep united. They were grateful especially to Archbishop Tillotson, the most eloquent of Latitudinarians, whose optimism and reasonableness delighted his Anglican listeners and later delighted deists and skeptics. Hume used Tillotson's argument against the Real Presence, Voltaire called him the best preacher in Europe, while the deist Anthony Collins acknowledged him as the divine "whom all English free-thinkers own as their head." Meanwhile Dutch Arminians and French Jesuits offered similar doctrine on the Continent, and even the German Pietists thought it right to stress a certain worldliness in their academies: Francke's school in Halle trained its pupils not merely in true piety and the essentials of science but also in eloquence and good manners. For some Christians—all too many, the rigorists feared—the essence of Christianity was summed up, blandly, in Young's *Night Thoughts:* What is religion? the poet asks, and answers, "Religion *what?*—the Proof of Common Sense." Anthony Collins's well-known witticism against the learned Dr. Samuel Clarke—that no one had doubted the existence of God until Dr. Clarke tried to prove it— may well be extended: no one had thought that Christianity might give way to rationalism until Christians tried to prove that Christianity was reasonable.

The French philosophes and British infidels like Hume or Gibbon rejected revealed religion so vehemently and so completely that the Christian contribution to their ideas was modest and subterranean; they were usually unaware of it. It reinforced their Stoicism and contributed—when it contributed anything at all—to the general benevolent climate of opinion in which heathens could publish their polemics with relative impunity. But among the deists and even more the *Aufklärer* the Christian component was more overt and more important, and left its traces in their autobiographical utterances and theological controversies.

There are moments in intellectual history when a small change in quantity induces a change in quality, when the addition of a new shade to a seemingly continuous spectrum produces a new color. Such a moment occurred in England shortly before 1700. Locke published his *Reasonableness of Christianity* in 1695; it was followed the next year by Toland's *Christianity Not Mysterious,* and nothing could demonstrate more forcibly than these two books the strange illogic that governs the history of ideas. Toland claimed to be a disciple of Locke, and he was right; Locke repudiated Toland, and he too was right. Liberal Anglicanism and the dawning deist Enlightenment were connected by a thousand threads: both saw the universe as rational and God as beneficent, both despised enthusiasm and mysticism, both were critical of the written tradition and long catalogs of dogma. Yet they were separated by a chasm as impassable as it was narrow. In 1706 a critic charged that Locke was responsible not merely for the deism of Toland, but that of Tindal as well: *"The Reasonableness of Christianity:* and *Christianity not Mysterious,"* he wrote. "Those two Titles are different in Sound, but agree in Sense." And now "another Book is lately published, Intituled, *The Rights of the Christian Church,"* which has been "writ by a Gentleman"—that is, by Matthew Tindal—"mislead by the Principles establish'd in the *Essay of Human Understanding."* Three years later Locke's perceptive disciple Shaftesbury recognized the poignancy of the situation: "Mr. Locke," he wrote in 1709, "as much as I honour him on account of other writings (viz., on government, policy, trade, coin, education, toleration &c.), and as well as I knew him, and can answer for his sincerity as a most zealous *Christian* and believer, did, however, go in the self-same tract, and is followed by the Tindals, and all the other ingenious free authors of our time." Locke had tried to prove that Christianity was acceptable to reasonable men; Toland, that what was mysterious and miraculous about Christianity must be discarded— and in that single amendment the essence of revealed, dogmatic religion evaporated. . . .

In their earnest rancor against religion the philosophes resembled no one quite so much as Lucretius, and it was fitting that Lucretius should provide them with their favorite tag: *tantum religio potuit suadere malorum.*[1] Montesquieu quoted the line, and so did Holbach: the first generation of philosophes, like the last, was confident that it had been called by history to expose, and if possible eradicate, those evils.

That confidence, as we know, found more and more strident expression as the century went on. In the fashion of imperialists the spokesmen of the Enlightenment grew more radical and expanded their program: the more they got, the more they wanted. Polemical victories turned out to be not a reason for accommodation but for war to the end. In 1715, when Louis XIV died, the most imaginative French anticlericals confined themselves to private impiety and calls for reforms within the Church: their ideal was a kind of Anglicanism —a reasonable, respectable established church with little political power, no passion for repressing the free commerce of ideas, and no religious fervor. In 1788, when Louis XVI convoked the Estates General, the surviving philosophes were asking for complete disestablishment, a laic state. By that time, and even before, the audacious but playful blasphemies of Epicurean aristocrats had given way to the aggressive and humorless militancy of writers like Holbach and Diderot. Christianity, Diderot told his friends and family at Langres in a relatively early letter, serves its God by murder, "fire and sword in hand," and it recruits its servants—monks and nuns—from sick spirits seething with resentment. Ten years later he told Damilaville, just back from a visit to Voltaire, a fanciful and shocking fable about the origins of religion: a misanthrope, having retired to a cave to meditate vengeance on mankind, emerged to shout the word "God, God!" and from that day on, once that "abominable name" had been pronounced, men began "to argue, to hate each other, and to cut one anothers' throats." Of all the vicious institutions perpetuating that abominable name, Christianity was surely the worst, but as time went by Diderot expressed some confidence that its days might be numbered. "It is raining bombs in the house of the Lord," he told Sophie Volland in 1768; there was hope that "the great prostitute of Babylon" might soon give way to the "reign of Anti-Christ." Still, while men were living in a time heady with promise, the danger was not over:

[1] Religion can induce so much evil. [Lucr. 1.101]

Diderot feared "the last convulsive movements of a wild beast wounded unto death."

This was radical talk, but it had its parallels, if perhaps in somewhat milder tones, in other countries. In the German states the first overt though cautious defiance of orthodoxy came at the beginning of the eighteenth century, with the diffusion of historical criticism, rationalist metaphysics, and English deism. By the 1770's, when Lessing the theologian was at his most embattled, natural religion appeared as a serious competitor to Christianity, at least among intellectuals, and *Aufklärer* like Basedow and Wieland infuriated their pious contemporaries with their little didactic essays exposing superstitions and defending philosophy. In the Italian states anticlerical propaganda—which was taken by the Church, not without good grounds, as a form of anti-Christian, or at least heretical anti-Catholic, propaganda—reached heights of furious invective and was viciously repressed by the authorities. The gifted Neapolitan historian Pietro Giannone subjected the history of the Roman Church to unsparing criticism: in his vast *Istoria Civile del Regno di Napoli,* first published in 1723, he assailed the Inquisition, the wealth of the clergy, the worldliness of religious orders, the Index, the papal power of excommunication, and contrasted the corruption of the modern Church with the purity of apostolic times. He was forced into exile and led a wandering life until he was arrested in 1736 on Sardinian territory— ironically on Easter Sunday, while he was taking communion—and kept in prison until his death in 1748. In the north Beccaria warmly, if privately, applauded d'Alembert's book against the Jesuits: "The philosophers," he wrote to d'Alembert, "see the wrong the Jesuits have done purely from the side of humanity and science." Such sentiments were held only by a small minority— when Leopold of Tuscany abolished religious fraternities and closed roadside shrines, he was faced with a popular revolt—but the minority was growing in numbers and in audacity. In Britain, finally, religious criticism passed from the deists into the hands of Hume, Bentham, and other utilitarians—nearly all of them uncompromising, outspoken secularists.

While the variations among the philosophes are far from negligible, they only orchestrate a single passion that bound the little flock together, the passion to cure the spiritual malady that is religion, the germ of ignorance, barbarity, hypocrisy, filth, and the basest self-hatred. It is true that just as they disagreed on their diagnoses, the philosophes disagreed on their prescriptions for health: the atheists reduced the simple doctrines of natural religion to a mere expressive metaphor for the majesty of nature, and the skeptics doubted that the truth of natural religion could be reliably established. But both groups conceded to the deists that natural religion alone—a religion without miracles, priestly hierarchies, ritual, divine saviors, original sin, chosen people, and providential history—was tolerable and intellectually respectable. All other religions deserved to be extirpated: this was the meaning of Voltaire's slogan—which was also the slogan of the others—*Ecrasez l'infâme.*

The roots of this splenetic program are buried deeply within Christian civilization itself. It was an anticlerical program, angrily so, and skeptical, but it was more than anticlericalism or skepticism. To lampoon the clergy, to lament its corruption, its worldliness and deviations from its true vocation, had been a favorite occupation of educated and often uneducated men for centuries. Such criticism was at times the inspired lament of saintly men: through history there have been great Christians who were anticlerical and who were great Christians precisely because they were anticlerical. At other times this sort of criticism was merely scurrilous gossip, resentment against a privileged literate clerisy. But whatever it was, it was far from dangerous to religion or even to the clerical establishment: it served to discharge hostilities and occasionally induced ecclesiastics to reform themselves. In the same way skepticism about miracles or other proofs for Christianity was in itself relatively innocuous: it was confined to a narrow circle of emancipated spirits. Anticlericalism and skepticism became, as it were, political only as they joined forces with a naturalistic world view, a secular ethical system, and above all a triumphant scientific method. It was not Bayle or Erasmus singly or together but Bayle and Erasmus allied with Newton and Locke that created the atmosphere hospitable to the Enlightenment's Lucretian mission. The treason of the clerks did the rest.

The first men in modern times to set out on this mission were the English deists. Today their reputation is not high: they lie unread and are in fact for the most part unreadable. Indeed, when Burke contemptuously wrote their epitaph at the end of the eighteenth century, their vogue had long passed. But while their intellectual limitations are evident and their defeats at the hands of Bishop Butler and David Hume were devastating, their historical significance was considerable: they redrew the religious map of Europe. They were acute if not profound thinkers, equipped with a shrewd perception of their opponents' weaknesses; besides, whatever the shortcomings of their central principle—their watchmaker God who had endowed the world at the beginning of time with ethical laws that every individual can discover for himself through the use of his unaided reason—theirs was a philosophy emotionally appealing and logically persuasive. Goethe, who witnessed the deist phase of German thought, rightly suggested that in an atmosphere saturated with Newtonian science and the cult of common sense, deism was a perfectly sensible religion to adopt. The deists came at the right historic moment with the right arguments; they faded not mainly because they were bested in debate but because their teachings and their criticisms had become commonplace—that is to say, widely accepted.

The English deists were a true school of thought, a loosely joined family of intellectuals who sounded much like one another. A few among them, like Thomas Woolston, were eccentrics to the point of clinical insanity; more were rather like Anthony Collins, who was a respectable metaphysician and sober gentleman. But all of them were ruthless controversialists in an age of ruthless controversy, and while they refined their arguments as time passed, their basic position remained the same for more than half a century.

The real strength of this position, powerful enough to sting scholars like Bentley and satirists like Swift, lay in that happy conjunction of destructive and positive motives that also marks the philosophes' writings. With few exceptions, of whom Woolston was probably the most extreme, the deists never ceased to claim that their crusades against miracles or priestcraft were undertaken solely for the sake of a pure, a natural Christianity: the deist Thomas Morgan, among others, went so far as to call his doctrine a Christian deism. To be sure (and here too they anticipated the philosophes) many of the deists were prudential liars, skillful evaders of the authorities. They had some reason to be: John Toland was unwelcome in most polite society across Europe, while Thomas Woolston, unable to pay an exorbitant fine for blasphemy, died in custody. Both men were unconventional, with no capacity for self-restraint, but they were persecuted for their views, not for their character: Anglican divines as unbalanced as they continued to hold college fellowships or lucrative livings. It is true that their self-proclaimed championship of a Christianity without reve-lation was at best self-contradictory and for the most part an Aesopian subter-fuge. But whether they were prudent pagans or illogical Christians, the deists were animated not merely by spleen but by idealism as well. Like Voltaire, their most famous admirer on the continent, they destroyed in order to build.

While the deists observed a certain division of labor, they all tended to scatter their shots across the broad front of revealed religion. Each of their targets—the logic, ethics, and social consequences of Christianity—was equally inviting, but it was the first that figured in deist strategy as decisive. Christian asceticism could be discarded, Christian conduct amended, but Christianity was absolutely, certainly true, or it was false; it was divine, or it was nothing. For the believer down to the middle of the eighteenth century, probability was not enough, and when Bishop Butler argued in his refutation of deism, *The Analogy of Religion,* that Christianity, like everything else in this world, rested on proba-bilities, he was not merely cutting the ground from under deist objections, he was paying tribute to the power of the deist argument.

John Toland, Locke's unwelcome disciple, was the first to develop the logical argument fully and so persuasively that the later deists, Collins, Woolston, Tindal, Middleton, and the others, often turned to his work in search of argu-ments and proofs. Toland's *Christianity Not Mysterious* rests on a simple ra-tionalist proposition: the only religion worthy of that name is a reasonable religion. Now, in its inception Christianity had been just such a religion: "There is nothing in the Gospel contrary to reason, nor above it." This claim is reminis-cent of the Christian rationalists of the seventeenth century; Locke had argued that revelation is reason expanded, a divine support of fallible humans which, far from contradicting reason, enhances its potency and enables men to grasp the mysteries of the faith. But this resemblance is deceptive: the reasoning of Locke and Toland was more divergent than their rhetoric. For Toland "reason" meant what it meant in ordinary speech: what seems irrational to sensible, self-critical, educated men must in fact be irrational. It follows—and Toland was not afraid to draw this consequence—that since Christianity is at bottom reason-able, its proofs must be and appear to be reasonable also. The mysteries that envelop it cannot be part of the divine plan or proof of man's weak under-standing; they must be deliberate mystifications. Christianity, Toland argued, has been tampered with: without the "Pretense" of mystery, "we should never hear of the *Transubstantiation,* and other ridiculous Fables of the Church of Rome; nor of any of the *Eastern Ordures,* almost all receiv'd into this *Western*

Sink." It was a favorite polemical tactic in Protestant countries to attack all revealed religion indirectly by dwelling on the supposed absurdities of Roman
Catholicism, but this was a device that Toland disdained. He included all Trini-
tarian doctrines, the Lutheran teaching of impanation, and even Arian speculation among the Eastern Ordures: converted Jews and superstitious Gentiles had
introduced mysteries into Christian worship to its permanent damage.

From a critique of mysteries to a critique of the documents that recorded and
the clerics who retailed them was only one short step. In 1698 in his *Life of
John Milton* and a year later in *Amyntor* Toland raised doubts about the authenticity of the canonical gospels. He had already suggested in *Christianity Not
Mysterious* that the clerisy kept nonsensical mysteries alive so "that we might
constantly depend upon them for the Explication." Men are born superstitious,
or made superstitious by their nurses, and kept so by the priestly caste greedy
for power. Thus Toland combined a straightforward rationalism with a naturalistic reading of the Bible and traditional anticlericalism to repudiate all historical forms of Christianity except the primitive—and largely imaginary—teaching of the man Jesus.

Anthony Collins, unlike Toland a Lockian whom his master was glad to
acknowledge, added little to this line of reasoning: he denounces priests for
falsifying sacred documents, urges men to exercise their reason freely and repudiate improbable tales of divine intervention, maliciously calls attention to the
unending quarrels among theologians on all points, and asks that the Bible
be read as any other book—and in all this he sounds like Toland. It is only
when he considers the authority of prophecies that he strikes out on his own.

As Christian apologists had understood since the beginnings of modern criticism, the status of the Old Testament prophecies was of critical importance.
To the scandal of many pious contemporaries Locke had insisted that a good
Christian need believe only that Christ is the Jewish Messiah as foretold by the
prophets of the Old Testament. This is all he needs to believe, but he must
believe that. Collins, far from repudiating this argument, made it his own: the
proof of Christianity lies in the literal fulfillment of the prophecies; the divine
authority of the New Testament depends on the divine truths contained in the
Old. But, Collins adds, it can be shown that these prophecies did not literally
come true. What, then, remains? For centuries Christian apologists had argued
that the prophecies were fulfilled through the life of Christ in an allegorical
rather than a literal sense. But to employ the canon of allegory, Collins comments, is to open the floodgates of fancy; almost any event whatever may be said
to have been foretold in the opaque, elliptical pronouncements of the prophets.
Thus Collins's logic makes what he calls "the difficulties against Christianity"
invincible: the believer who rests his belief on the literal fulfillment of prophecies stands exposed as naïve; the believer who depends on allegory is a sophist.
Here was a simple but telling argument in an age thirsting for reliable proofs
and bewildered by the cacophony of controversy.

Collins first employed this argument in 1724, in his *Discourse of the Grounds
and Reasons of the Christian Religion;* it was taken beyond the bounds of common sense and good taste in Woolston's six *Discourses on the Miracles of Our*

Saviour, published between 1727 and 1729: the prophecies had foretold the central miracle of the Christian religion, the Incarnation, and Collins had shown these prophecies to be unintelligible or unfulfilled; Woolston now proceeded to argue with some cogency but extreme heat that Collins's critique held true of all the miracles reported in the New Testament—they are allegories, that is to say, stories. Some of them are delightful, a few point a moral, but most of them are insidious lies. The miracles supposedly performed by Jesus are ludicrous romances; the Virgin, far from being divinely pure, was human and fallible; and the Resurrection is plainly "the most notorious and monstrous Imposture, that ever was put upon mankind." Voltaire—who enjoyed Woolston's polemics, borrowed some of Woolston's arguments, but refined his language—recalled late in life that "no one before him had taken boldness and offensiveness this far. He treated the miracles and the Resurrection of our Saviour as puerile and extravagant stories. He said that when Jesus Christ converted water into wine for the guests who were already drunk, he must have been making punch." Indeed, speaking through the transparent disguise of a rabbi, Woolston offered a drastic remedy: the only consequence that sensible Christian divines could draw from a careful examination of the New Testament was to "give up their *Religion* as well as their *Church.*"

This was shocking talk, but there were other deists, notably Tindal, who came to similar conclusions in somewhat less extravagant language. In his *Christianity as Old as Creation* (published in 1730, the year that Woolston went to prison for blasphemy) Tindal combined a virulent anticlericalism and scornful skepticism of the Bible with a warm, generous confidence in the natural religion of reason, inscribed in the hearts of humanity and accessible to men of the highest as well as those of the meanest understanding. Priests, far from realizing the purposes of natural religion, have perverted it: "Priests, on the pretence of the good of the Church" work the people up "to Tumults, Mutiny, Sedition and Rebellion"; and a close look at "Ecclesiastical History" will show that the clergy have allied themselves with the secular power: "The worst of princes have been most sure of their Assistance even in carrying on the vilest Designs." Nothing but reasoning can improve reason; no man but moral man, free to criticize and exercise his mind without constraint, can discover the laws that the Divinity has laid down and is following Himself. "The primitive Christians believed, there was an exact Agreement between *Natural* and *Reveal'd* Religion; and that the Excellency of the Latter, did consist in being a Republication of the Former"—and the primitive Christians were right. Long after this kind of faith in universal rational nature and this equation of religion with morality had faded, Tindal's ideal of the autonomous man and his criticisms of revealed religions and their keepers retained their vitality for his many readers.

By the early 1730's most of the leading deists had done their work; what followed was largely the effort of epigones. Conyers Middleton's *Free Inquiry,* which put the argument against miracles on a historical basis, was a late fruit: it came out in 1748, the year David Hume entered theological controversy with his celebrated essay on miracles. Besides, Middleton's intelligent historical argumentation was as much a weapon against as a weapon for the deist cause. But while deism decorously decayed in England and theological polemicists lost readers to the novelists, it found a ready hearing on the Continent. German culture, still unformed and unsure, was particularly open to foreign influences, and many educated Germans seasoned Wolff's popular but relatively tame Christian rationalism with a vigorous dash of English deism. Christlob Mylius, the adventurous journalist who deeply impressed the young Lessing, publicly praised "the learned Toland" and the "searching Woolston." A German version of Tindal's *Christianity as Old as the Creation* became available in 1741, and other deist writings followed—some of them translated by liberal theologians like Spalding. Readers too impatient to wade through long exposition and involved argumentation turned to the popular periodicals, which were printing appreciative reviews and generous excerpts from radical English literature. The English deists came to enjoy a popularity in the German states that enraged the orthodox and alarmed the authorities.

Characteristically the man who kept the deist cause alive in Germany was Lessing, who thrived on controversy and cherished debate as the lifeblood of culture. When he published fragments from Reimarus's *Apologie,* the notorious *Wolfenbüttel Fragments,* between 1774 and 1778, he aroused a storm of protests. Each of the fragments, taken alone, was both radical and familiar, but placed together they amounted to a scandal, and the sixth fragment, which questioned the historicity of the Resurrection, called forth passionate rebuttals and plunged Lessing into the most sustained and most acrimonious dispute of his life. It kept him busy, but he must have enjoyed it, for in 1778, harassed by persistent, vociferous critics, he brought out "Vom Zwecke Jesu and seiner Jünger," the last, longest, and most inflammatory of Reimarus's fragments that Lessing was to publish. "Vom Zwecke Jesu" portrays Jesus as a traditional Jew, persuaded that he is the Jewish Messiah foretold in the Old Testament, divinely called to found an earthly kingdom: he is the charismatic national leader who cares for his people alone. At first his followers, as fanatical a group of disciples as Jesus was a leader, believed in this circumscribed mission, but after his death they universalized his program, translated the earthly into a heavenly kingdom, and revised the story of Jesus's life to fit their altered purposes. Much of the gospels, in other words, consists of tactical interpolations and downright falsifications, and thus historical Christianity is a gigantic deception. . . .

"There is only one relation to revealed truth: believing it"—thus Kierkegaard epitomized in one striking sentence the essential characteristic of the Christian, and many centuries of apologetic effort. For Hume, of course, the appropriate relation to what passed for revealed truth was not believing it, and his own critical task was to find the reasons why it was unbelievable. He was as ready as the deists and the materialists to retail stories about the crimes of priests and the follies perpetrated by superstitious men, but that was mainly for pleasure or to supply supporting evidence. In the main Hume was concerned with the logic of belief and with its causes rather than with its consequences.

The first and most controversial of Hume's dissections of religion was his essay on miracles: Samuel Johnson was justified in singling it out as Hume's most insidious production. It was also his most characteristic production—in the time and circumstances of its composition, in the manner of its final appearance, in its tone and method of argument.

Hume wrote the essay at a decisive time in his life. It was both symptom and agent of his liberation from his religious heritage, an act which, like many such acts, was an act of aggression. In the late 1730's, recovering from his nervous illness in agreeable retirement at La Flèche, as he walked, debated with the local Jesuits, and wrote his *Treatise of Human Nature,* he discovered an argument which he was confident would rob all reports of miracles of their weight. He wrote it down, cautiously showed it to a few friends, and then, after some reflection, deleted it from the *Treatise:* "I am at present castrating my work, that is, cutting off its nobler parts," he wrote in December 1737, fearful that his reasonings might give offense. He rationalized his prudence (which he himself called his "cowardice") with a characteristic excuse: "I was resolved not to be an enthusiast in philosophy, while I was blaming other enthusiasms." It was only a decade later that he felt bold enough to publish the essay as a chapter in his *Enquiry Concerning Human Understanding.*

Its placement (whether its intended placement in the *Treatise* or its final placement in the *Enquiry*) also places it in Hume's philosophy. Hume had, after all, hit upon its argument while he was reasoning his way through severely technical problems involving the meaning of causality, the evidential force of moral assertions, the relation of mathematical to factual statements. And now he incorporated the essay not into a treatise on theology but into an enquiry into the conditions of knowledge. Clearly Hume's argument on miracles was intimately associated with his epistemology; it was an indispensable part of his total world view—the critical counterpart and destructive precondition for his secular philosophy.

The essay itself exhibits this association subtly but unmistakably: it is pervaded by the attitude that marks all his work—his moderate skepticism, his confident philosophical modesty. This very modesty reinforces his strategic position: seeking to prove little, he disproves much. Hume's point is not that reports of miracles can never be sincere. It is not even—despite his own unwavering incredulity—that they can never be true. It is rather that they can never be satisfactorily demonstrated.

Hume constructs this argument through an implicit and devasting syllogism: "A wise man" proportions "his belief to the evidence," that is, he will adhere to a creed only if the evidence for it is adequate. Now, Hume claims, as far as all "popular religions" are concerned (and his phrase is a transparent euphemism for all revealed religions) we "may establish it as a maxim, that no human testimony can have such force as to prove a miracle, and make it a just foundation for any such system of religion." It follows—and Hume is delighted to draw the conclusion in a much-quoted sentence, a sentence that mimics the Christian fideist to perfection—it follows that "upon the whole, we may conclude, that the Christian Religion not only was at first attended with miracles, but even at this day cannot be believed by any reasonable person without one." The logic of belief was rocky terrain, and it had earlier been explored by the deists and by skeptics like Bayle. Just which miracles to accept was a question that had long divided Protestants from Catholics and created noisy divisions within Protestant sects and among Catholic scholars: erudite theologians had for centuries attempted to sort out the true from the spurious miracle. But all Christians, from the most emancipated to the most superstitious, had insisted on treating at least one class of miracles as a class apart: the miracles of Jesus Christ were privileged evidence, immune from criticism. Now Hume held that these reports must be judged precisely like other historical reports: they are subject to criteria of credibility. In addition to advancing this subversive idea Hume was ready to supply the criteria: "No testimony," he wrote, "is sufficient to establish a miracle, unless the testimony be of such a kind, that its falsehood would be more miraculous, than the fact, which it endeavours to establish."

It is clear that this maxim, which asks men to adopt the most naturalistic explanation compatible with the evidence, owed its persuasiveness in large part to the century in which it was conceived and the public to which it was addressed. This, after all, was the age of modern Christianity, when the natural sciences and their methods were rising in prestige and growing in popularity, and when educated Christians were expressing serious reservations about most tales of prodigies. Even Samuel Johnson subscribed to this part of Hume's case and warned against a blind, childlike credulity. This was the public Hume was trying to persuade when he defined a miracle, accurately but in shrewdly chosen words, as a "violation of the laws of nature."

Hume recognized that his syllogism, damaging as it was, did no more than to make miracles appear implausible. Therefore, to convert implausibility to impossibility—or rather (to do justice to his mocking, triumphant modesty) into extreme improbability—Hume turned to psychology and history for supporting evidence. It is a pervasive trait of human nature, he said, to seek out the unusual and to indulge the agreeable passion "of surprize and wonder": thus psychology, by uncovering an all too human propensity, yielded reasons for the popularity of miracles while it undermined their credibility. History, the temporal arena of miracles, performed the same function in Hume's argument. Critically read, history discloses that miracles have been attested by few men of "good-sense, education, and learning" and have almost all been disputed by eye-witnesses. Besides, they have usually been reported among "ignorant and barbarous nations," and they have declined, perhaps not so strangely, in our time. To the surprise of the Reverend William Adams, who had written a courteous refutation of Hume's essay—to his surprise, perhaps, but not to ours, for Hume's assault was deadly—Samuel Johnson was prepared to use all methods, elevated or mean, to discredit his formidable, seductive antagonist: "ADAMS. 'You would not jostle a chimney-sweeper.' JOHNSON. 'Yes, Sir, if it were necessary to jostle him *down*.'" Whoever might later jostle Hume down—largely by taking seriously his ironic fideism and proclaiming the continuing miracle of Christian revelation—it is safe to say that it was not Samuel Johnson.

In the essay on miracles Hume had speculated on man's passion for "surprize and wonder"; in the "Natural History of Religion" he extended his psychological epigrams into a sustained indictment. He was entering an arena crowded with philosophes, all busy seeking the reasons why men believed in supernatural beings, in the efficacy of charms, prayers, and certain ritual actions. It was, after all, obvious—pleasantly obvious, for it provided the philosophes with agreeable employment—that most men in all ages had entertained religious beliefs. To a critical age this fact required explanation.

The philosophes were here, as so often, the quick-witted and enterprising disciples of classical antiquity. Poets like Euhemerus and Lucretius, philosophers like Plato and the Stoics, had offered some startling conjectures about the origin of myths, and these were enlisted in the eighteenth century, complete with modern psychological terminology, in the indictment of Christianity. Some— the Euhemerists—had speculated that the gods had originally been powerful heroes or beneficent kings apotheosized by their worshipful admirers to serve as models for all mankind; others argued that the gods were intelligences animating, and represented by, heavenly bodies. A third school, following the Stoics, interpreted the gods as allegories, personifications of virtues, vices, and moral lessons. And finally there was the psychological theory, which explained religion as the product of men's fears and hopes, as their desire for immortality, their longing to recapture childlike innocence, their dread of the unknown.

For obvious reasons the philosophes preferred the last of these schools of thought to the others: the psychological theory alone was, as it were, denominationally neutral, as critical of Christianity as of pagan cults. This was a psychological age, an age when philosophy had turned from metaphysics to epistemology, when men's motives were being scrutinized with new vigor and new methods. And besides, this theory offered the philosophes some scientific support for their stock villains—priests, who, in league with kings, imposed fables on the credulous masses for their power and profit. This imposture was a variant of the psychological theory with a rationalist touch: it explained the enthusiasm of the many but postulated at the same time the rationality of the few through the ages. This explanation of religion did not go unchallenged; its rivals had their supporters. But, usually accompanied by the imposture theory, it held the field in the Enlightenment. It had been articulately propounded by Bayle and Fontenelle and diffused throughout Europe by their readers. For disciples of Lucretius it was wholly appropriate: it was, of all theories, the one most devastating to accepted beliefs.

Hume's "Natural History of Religion" is an elegant representative of this dominant school of thought. Its very title is provocative: to examine the "natural" history of religion is to treat the sacred as a social phenomenon like any other and to strip it of the privileged status on which its prestige depends. True, in the very first paragraph Hume disclaims any intention of questioning the foundation of religion "in reason"—that, he says, is secure and beyond cavil. He proposes to inquire solely into the "origin" of religion "in human nature." But to outraged clergymen this was a meaningless distinction, a transparent veil designed to cover—and to reveal—the most unmeasured impieties. After all, Hume had made it evident in other writings, and, subtly, in the *Natural History* itself, that he did not really believe religion to have any rational foundations at all. Besides, if religion could be traced to its origins in human nature, it was degraded into a product of fancy, a mere projection, and its claim to objective veracity was gone. Bishop Warburton, who dogged Hume for the right reasons but with inadequate weapons, detected Hume's intentions with a perception sharpened by dislike: the design of the *Natural History,* he wrote darkly, is "to establish *naturalism,* a species of atheism, instead of religion." No reader of Hume's essay will be inclined to discount Warburton's suspicion.

Warburton's anger, matched by the anger of pious readers everywhere, was easy to understand. The essay, Warburton said in exasperation, taught Bolingbroke's atheism "without Bolingbroke's abusive language." This, of course, was precisely Hume's strength: no philosophe was more skillful than he in clothing his passion against religion in the vocabulary of logic and supporting it with judicious arguments—and in the process converting that passion into science. Hume's method in the "Natural History" is therefore as remarkable and as destructive as his conclusion. In his search for the roots of religion he combines induction with deduction, information supplied by the records of the past and the reports of travelers (history and rather rudimentary anthropology) with speculative psychology. His hypothetical history of man's intellectual development is thus imaginative but not fanciful, inventive but realistic.

As Hume interpreted the evidence, man's belief in an "invisible, intelligent power" was widely diffused but by no means universal—some nations had no religion, and each religious nation differed from its neighbor in its worship and pious sentiments. It followed (and this was, for Hume, a weighty consideration) that the religious emotion was founded in deep-rooted but merely "secondary" passions: men's fundamental instincts, the instincts that call forth self-love, sexual desire, love of offspring, were so uniform that they could not possibly be responsible for a phenomenon as varied as religion. Rather, Hume argued, religion arose "from a concern with regard to the events of life, and from the incessant hopes and fears, which actuate the human mind." Confronted by a monstrous birth, the uncertainty of the seasons, by storms and a myriad of unexplained and seemingly inexplicable events, primitive man oriented himself in his world by inventing a large number of special, parochial deities: Hesiod had listed thirty thousand of them, and even they were not enough. Antiquity (Hume records in a footnote worthy of Gibbon) even produced a god of sneezing, and "the province of copulation, suitably to the importance and dignity of it, was divided among several deities." To barbarians the ordinary was extraordinary and required extraordinary explanations: "The anxious concern for happiness, the dread of future misery, the terror of death, the thirst of revenge, the appetite for food and other necessaries" create hopes and, more significantly, arouse fears, and so "men scrutinize, with a trembling curiosity, the course of future causes, and examine the various and contrary events of human life. And in this disordered scene, with eyes still more disordered and astonished, they see the first obscure traces of divinity."

The first religion of mankind, therefore, was inevitably polytheism; monotheism was a late invention, the fruit of abstract thinking. Precisely for the same reason the first gods were anthropomorphic, projections with the features and characters of men; while the theists' conception of a god liberated from his human limitations, pure, remote, and worthy to be worshipped by a rational man, was the reward of maturity and cultivation. "We may as reasonably imagine, that men inhabited palaces before huts and cottages, or studied geometry before agriculture; as assert that the Deity appeared to them a pure spirit, omniscient, omnipotent, and omnipresent, before he was apprehended to be a powerful, though limited being, with human passions and appetites, limbs and organs."

The religions prevalent in modern times were thus the offspring of a long development, a development that Hume refused to call progress. In the first place, Hume considered the evolution of belief from polytheism to rigorous monotheism as neither straightforward nor inevitable: the history of religion, in fact, was the history of "flux and reflux." Men "have a natural tendency to rise from idolatry to theism, and to sink again from theism into idolatry." Especially the "vulgar," the poor and the illiterate are incapable of the logical and ethical effort required to sustain monotheism, and they generally indulge in a covert idolatry. This is evident in all religions, but especially so in Roman Catholicism: with its saints, its Virgin Mary, its superstitious doctrine of the Real Presence—with all this, Catholicism was a polytheistic superstition masquerading as a monotheistic creed. Besides, the advantages of monotheism were doubtful: polytheism was crude in its teachings but tolerant in its practice, while monotheism, for all the nobility of its theology, easily turned to persecution to enforce its claim to a monopoly of the truth. But both had unwholesome odious social consequences: they produced degrading self-contempt or crime.

The consequence implied in Hume's sociology of religion was that all houses of faith were houses of infection and that a rational man must escape, after exposing, the squabbles of theologians. That, indeed, was Hume's celebrated conclusion, much quoted but worth quoting once again: "The whole is a riddle, an aenigma, an inexplicable mystery. Doubt, uncertainty, suspense of judgment appear the only result of our most accurate scrutiny, concerning this subject. But such is the frailty of human reason, and such the irresistible contagion of opinion, that even this deliberate doubt could scarcely be upheld; did we not enlarge our view, and opposing one species of superstition to another, set them a quarrelling; while we ourselves, during their fury and contention, happily make our escape into the calm, though obscure regions of philosophy." Thus Hume, disciple of Cicero and Bayle, having made his case, took to his heels.

What he left behind was an ambiguous legacy. In two strategically placed passages, one in the first paragraph, the other in the last section of the "Natural History," Hume professes to subscribe to the argument from design: "A purpose," he writes, "an intention, a design is evident in every thing"; and again, "the whole frame of nature bespeaks an intelligent author." These categorical pronouncements read like generous, even decisive concessions to the proponents of natural theology, whether of the Christian or the deist persuasion. But in fact Hume found these concessions easy to grant because they were empty; they were rhetorical flourishes, nothing more. Warburton, speaking for a whole school of divines who would not trust Hume in anything, found these sentences offensively tepid and suspiciously rare, and he denounced them as veils for atheism. And Voltaire, speaking for the deists, was disturbed by Hume's hypothetical history of religion: a "philosophical scholar," he wrote in his *Dictionnaire philosophique,* courteously but firmly, "one of the profoundest metaphysicians of our day offers some strong reasons for believing that polytheism was man's first religion"; but, he rejoined, "I dare think, on the contrary, that people began by acknowledging a single God, and that later human weakness led to the adoption of several." As Voltaire recognized, Hume's supposition that polytheism was the primitive religion was a threat to the deists' rather complacent epistemology, which held that man recognized by instinct, or at least with ease, the traces of God in the glorious workings of nature.

Hume's "Natural History of Religion" thus offered formidable if largely implicit objections to the deist position. They were brought into the open by Hume's *Dialogues Concerning Natural Religion,* which demolished that position completely. To be sure, the demolition was an academic affair: the *Dialogues* was not published until 1779, three years after Hume's and one year after Voltaire's death. By that time deism was no longer fashionable even among philosophes, although the argument from design persisted, a stubborn, troublesome ghost, into the nineteenth century. Hume's *Dialogues* is therefore less a lethal weapon than a death certificate.

Whatever its final cultural meaning, the *Dialogues Concerning Natural Religion* was the book that Hume cherished most. It had a poignant history, as pathetic as that of a posthumous child. Hume had largely completed the manuscript by 1751, revised it carefully, and circulated it among a few chosen friends, including Adam Smith. They urged him to suppress it, and reluctantly, comically proclaiming himself the victim of tyranny, Hume acceded. But he was too fond of the *Dialogues* to permit it to remain in permanent obscurity: in the last months of his life he took precise, almost pedantic measures to guarantee its publication after his death. His solicitude was appropriate to its object: the *Dialogues* is Hume's "Dictionnaire philosophique," the epitome of his life's work; his "Nathan der Weise," dramatizing his deepest convictions, a work of literary art impressive even to those who reject its conclusions; his "Neveu de Rameau," a conscious, free imitation of a favorite classic, Cicero's *De natura deorum,* which makes its point as forcibly by the resonances evoked by its borrowings as by its departures from the model. It is almost unique in the literature of theological disputation in its felicitous marriage of form and substance—a drama, cerebral but exciting.

Hume knew that it was a drama he was writing: in 1751 he asked a correspondent to supply him with arguments that would strengthen one of the protagonists whom, he feared, he had neglected. About ten years before, he had criticized his beloved Cicero for reserving the good speeches in his dialogues to representatives of his own point of view. This was not a mistake Hume proposed to make.

He did not make it. Hume is Philo, described in a brief prologue as the representative of "careless skepticism," but the reader may well be unaware—in fact, most readers have been unaware—of this identity. And the dialogue is a genuine confrontation of ideas; Hume gave it life, provided it with tension and verisimilitude, by having his three protagonists shift alliances in accord with the requirements of the debate and by distributing intelligent, convincing arguments among his speakers. To be sure, Demea, who stands for "rigid inflexible orthodoxy," is less important than the other two, since Philo-Hume's real antagonist is Cleanthes, a man of "accurate philosophical turn," who upholds the claims of rationalist natural religion and defends the argument from design; and it is Cleanthes, who sounds rather like Bishop Butler or like Voltaire in his constructive religious phase, on whom Hume expended his most anxious literary care. But while Demea is largely a foil, he is not a fool: his main argument for religion—man's invincible ignorance and perpetual misery—is the pious version of Hume's skepticism, and Hume must have delighted in having a "rigid" Christian pronounce his own most skeptical reservations.

Philo, however, is Hume's favorite, and Hume endows Philo's speeches with so much energy and subtlety, so much wit, that any summary must do them violence. Philo sets his antagonists against one another: he compels Cleanthes, who deduces God from the glory of the world and the possibilities of man and who draws analogies that reduce the deity to little more than human stature, to contend against Demea, who proves God's existence from man's misery and who denies that any epithet applicable to man is applicable to His august majesty. But this sort of confrontation, which suggests the inconclusiveness of all theological proofs of God, is, while cunning, also a very old technique, and consequently Philo is not content to depend on it alone. He does more: he deprecates the intuition to which Cleanthes appeals as a will-o'-the-wisp, an unreliable guide to religious truth; and he tries to demolish the popular argument from analogy. Analogy, he suggests reasonably enough, can never provide a strong proof for anything; little can be legitimately inferred from apparent, and even from real, similarities. Indeed, the particular analogy on which proponents of natural religion generally rest their case is exceptionally feeble: we may concede that a watch implies a watchmaker—and it does so only because we have no experience of a watch that was not produced by a human artificer—but this does not mean that the universe necessarily implies a creator. A watch is not unique; the universe is. Besides, the universe resembles a watch or a house far less than it does an animal or a vegetable: Philo mischievously proposes that the Creator might be a vegetable rather than a craftsman. Nor is this all: if we observe the universe without our ordinary preconceptions, we may well conclude that the intelligence that created it was little better than an amateurish bungler who, for all we know, made and discarded other worlds before he settled on this one.

Little, very little, remains of the "religious hypothesis" after this assault. No matter how rationally argued or energetically defended, it is unconvincing and probably untrue. *"To know God,"* concludes Philo, significantly quoting Seneca, *"is to worship him.* All other worship is indeed absurd, superstitious, and even impious." A reasonable man can do no more than to give a philosopher's calm recognition to the possibility that *"the cause or causes of order in the universe probably bear some remote analogy to human intelligence";* but nothing follows from that recognition except the pleasure of modest, rational assent to a sensible proposition. It warrants no belief in extraordinary tales, justifies no prayer and no church, and does not even provide guidance to conduct. For Hume religion has lost all specificity and all authority; it is no more than a dim, meaningless, and unwelcome shadow on the face of reason.

Near the end of the *Dialogues Concerning Natural Religion,* the protagonist of orthodoxy, pleased up to that moment with Philo's critique of the argument from design, suddenly wakes up to the true import of the skeptic's line of reasoning: "Hold! Hold! cried Demea: Whither does your imagination hurry you? I joined in alliance with you, in order to prove the incomprehensible nature of the divine Being, and refute the principles of Cleanthes, who would measure every thing by a human rule and standard. But I now find you running into all the topics of the greatest libertines and infidels; and betraying that holy cause, which you seemingly espoused. Are you secretly, then, a more dangerous enemy than Cleanthes himself?" Not long after this outburst Demea rather ostentatiously leaves the field, while Cleanthes and Philo—deist and skeptic, who are, significantly enough, close friends—stay to conclude the discussion.

It is a superbly dramatic and profoundly touching moment: it shows, perhaps more clearly than any other passage of his work that I know, why Hume was at the same time the most isolated and the most representative of philosophes: he was simply the purest, most modern specimen of the little flock. Demea's vehement rhetorical question is far from naïve: as we have seen over and over again, in the great combat, anti-Christian deist and secular skeptic were allies, champions of criticism in deadly combat with the mythopoeic mentality. Even the modern rationalist Christian—if that is whom Cleanthes represents—could be enlisted in the struggle against myth. But within the army of the Enlightenment it was true that Philo was indeed a more dangerous enemy to religion than Cleanthes; with all their secularism, all their incredulity, the deists retained some rhetorical and even some emotional connections with the "religious hypothesis." In Hume the last threads are torn; his philosophy embodies the dialectic of the Enlightenment at its most ruthless—it appeals to antiquity at its most disenchanted, its tension with Christianity is wholly unappeasable at all points, and it pursues modernity most courageously.

For David Hume was both courageous and modern; he understood the implications of his philosophy and did not shrink from them. He was so courageous that he did not have to insist on his courage; he followed his thinking where it led him, and he provided through his own life (and, Samuel Johnson to the contrary, in the face of death) a pagan ideal to which many aspired but which few realized. He was willing to live with uncertainty, with no supernatural justifications, no complete explanations, no promise of permanent stability, with guides of merely probable validity; and what is more, he lived in his world without complaining, a cheerful Stoic. Hume, therefore, more decisively than many of his brethren in the Enlightenment, stands at the threshold of modernity and exhibits its risks and its possibilities. Without melodrama but with the sober eloquence one would expect from an accomplished classicist, Hume makes plain that since God is silent, man is his own master: he must live in a disenchanted world, submit everything to criticism, and make his own way.

13

THE PERSISTENCE
OF FEUDAL SOCIETY

IT IS difficult to say what was any longer "feudal" about the knights, dukes, and princes of eighteenth-century nobility. Dressed in satin, their hair powdered, these overrefined nobles do not resemble their rough, bellicose, and illiterate counterparts of five hundred years earlier.

Nor do the eighteenth-century castles. Lovely gardens, large windows, and elegant interiors have nothing in common with the massive, fortified piles of medieval times. Social historians are, therefore, tempted to drop the term feudal for the eighteenth century. And yet a strong reluctance to do so persists.

What precisely is meant by the terms feudal, feudalism, and feudal society? Historians of the eighteenth century naturally turn to the specialists of medieval history, hoping to find definitions of these terms. But these specialists have proved to be of little help because their definition of feudal tends to be so narrow that it excludes everything which does not specifically relate to the military relationship between lords and vassals. These specialists see feudalism as disappearing around 1400, so their definition is of little use for historians of a later period.

The changes which took place between 1300 and 1700 were enormous, but they did not wipe out certain fundamental characteristics of economic and social life established before 1300. Did the rise of powerful monarchies with their bureaucratic machines change the character of rural life? Historians must look to the land in this still preindustrial eighteenth century to discern the persistence of what Bloch calls feudal relationships.

1.

In making surveys of their lands in the 1670's, several large abbeys near Beauvais designated their holdings as "lordships" and the peasants who constituted them and paid seigneurial dues as "vassals." Now, one suspects that the monks in the *Ancien Régime* never thought of calling on these peasant "vassals" for military service, but an aura of the feudal relationship remained.

Perhaps more important than the centuries-old terminology lay the important fact that over half the arable land in the region was owned by persons who did not farm it themselves. In one way or another, virtually every peasant was a tenant or "vassal," and the traditions, laws, and courts of the

Ancien Régime represented a monolithic kind of feudal "system" to keep them in that dependent status.

Professor Pierre Goubert (1915–   ) of the University of Paris at Nanterre, vividly recounts the critical, near-catastrophic conditions of peasant life in the Beauvais region, one of the richest agriculturally in northwestern France. His attention centers on the crucial question of who owned the land rather than on the precise problem of whether this ownership can be called feudal. Nevertheless, we see how the peasants were barraged with Church, seigneurial, and royal taxes in a way which seems to have changed very little from the fourteenth century. It would be interesting to know what percentage of the arable land in the region of Beauvais was owned by the Church and the nobility from century to century beginning in the High Middle Ages. From what social groups did abbots usually come? This "under side" of rural life in France before the Revolution explains the source of the income needed by the nobility—both ecclesiastical and lay—for a refined, courtly life in Versailles or Paris.

The peasants seem to have been almost continuously in debt. What social group profited from and hired the agents, who were usually very harsh on defaulting creditors? The bourgeoisie, of course. Why did the bourgeoisie seek to acquire peasant lands? The courts of law also seem to have been on the side of the lenders rather than on that of the defaulting peasants. Which social group controlled the courts?

PIERRE GOUBERT: The French Peasants*

I shall confine myself largely to presenting a picture of rural society as it appears in the last quarter of the seventeenth century, based on an abundance of source-material which is both detailed and (I believe) sound. I shall then attempt a brief sketch of a social evolution ranging over the whole of the seventeenth century and the early part of the eighteenth; but I fully admit that in the latter part of this project there will be an element of personal speculation, the extent of which I shall indicate as precisely as I can.

A detailed survey of 38 parishes of the *Election de Beauvais* was carried out in 1717. This survey was initiated by the government and was not peculiar to this corner of France. The intention of the *Conseil Royal du Commerce* was to consider a fresh imposition of the *taille,* the principal direct tax of the day. The division of the landed property in these 38 parishes was as follows: 22% of the land belonged to the church, 22% to the nobility, 13% to the *bourgeoisie* of Beauvais, and 43% to the peasants. The peasants owned only a very small part of the vineyards, woods, and meadows (these being, incidentally, the most profitable form of cultivation). For our present purpose the important thing to notice in this government survey is the proportion of land held by the various groups: the peasants did not own half the land they tilled; their portion did not include the best lands; further, their holdings were more widely scattered than the lands of the privileged orders.

* From Pierre Goubert, "The French Peasantry of the Seventeenth Century," *Past and Present*, 1956, pp. 56–71.

Forty years earlier a few large abbeys in the Beauvaisis had carried out a complete, careful, and accurate survey of the numerous parishes of which they held the lordship (*seigneurie*). These abbeys did not concern themselves exclusively with their own estates (*domaines*) which their tenant-farmers cultivated; they also surveyed and charted the lands of their "vassals"—the peasants who paid them seigneurial dues (and often tithes, as well, which the large abbeys had generally taken over from the parish priests.) Most of the maps made between 1670 and 1680 are accompanied by separate tables of proprietors and parcels of land. An examination of this complex of documents yields results similar to those which we have just quoted for 1717. Between 1670 and 1680 the peasants nowhere owned as much as half the land; sometimes, as in the neighbourhood of Beauvais, they owned only a quarter. In addition, at this date too, peasant-land was the most scattered and the poorest in quality.

The field-maps prepared by the abbeys have an additional advantage: they show how the lands were divided among the peasants themselves. To take a few examples—at Goincourt, of 98 peasant proprietors, 3 owned 10, 12, and 18 *hectares* respectively (a French *hectare* = nearly 2½ acres); 94 owned less than 2 *hectares*. At Espaubourg, of 148 peasant proprietors, not one held as much as 10 *hectares*, and 125 held less than 2 *hectares*. At Coudray-Saint-Germer, 106 out of 125 held less than 2 *hectares;* only one owned as much as 30 *hectares*. These examples fall in the period 1672–1680; they are all drawn from that part of the Beauvaisis which comes within the *Pays du Bray,* a region of great common pastures, where one might expect the peasants to be able to rear livestock at low cost. We shall see how far this possibility was, in fact, realized.

Two distinctive features, then, emerge. The peasants did not own half the land they cultivated, and among the peasants themselves holdings were extremely unevenly distributed. At least 80% of the peasantry of the Beauvaisis owned only tiny plots; only a small minority of them owned more than 10 *hectares* (i.e. less than 25 acres). Were we to erect a social pyramid of peasant property, it would have a very broad base and an absurdly slender apex.

As the lands of the nobles, church, and *bourgeoisie* were leased to peasants, it is clear that the latter were working that large proportion of the land of which they were not themselves the owners. It is not as easy to chart tenancy as landownership, nor as easy to compile a statistical analysis of tenants as of owners. To do so it would be necessary to assemble a wide range of documents that are, of course, scattered over a multiplicity of records and archives. Even so, the result would not correspond closely to reality. A general point does, however, emerge: the scattered parcels of land owned by the privileged orders and *bourgeoisie* were let out to small peasants, whereas the lands concentrated in large units (especially those belonging to the church) were leased *en bloc* to enterprising tenants, such as the *laboureurs-fermiers* (substantial tenant-farmers) or *receveurs de seigneurie* (receivers for the lords of the manors): the latter formed the peak of the peasant social pyramid. But as these substantial people took on lease considerable estates (estates of 80, 100, 150 *hectares,* or more), they were only to be found in the villages in ones and twos; in some villages they were not to be found at all. Therefore, a general examination of tenancy in the Beauvaisis leads to both a confirmation and a correction of the conclusions arrived at from the study of the ownership of land. It leads to a confirmation in the sense that the small leases (of 1, 2, or 3 *hectares*) go to the small proprietors, and that they remain "small men" (there are, however, a few exceptions to this rule). But it also leads to a correction, because we shall now have to place at the summit of the economic and social hierarchy of the peasants the great *fermiers-receveurs* of the nobility and clergy, and not the ordinary *laboureurs* who, as we shall see, rarely owned and exploited holdings of more than 30 *hectares.*

We shall, therefore, not be tempted to base the rest of our account on the antithesis *laboureur* (peasant)—*manouvrier* (wage-worker), which expresses almost the sum total of what is generally known about French peasant society. If this oversimplified antithesis remains roughly true, it is far from expressing the whole graded complexity of social relations in the village. It has, however, the merit of stressing the interest in social terminology which prevailed in the French countryside. Like the town-dwellers the French peasants were very conscious of titles and dignities. One has only to look through the registers of baptisms, marriages, and burials (the most abundant of all French documents of the seventeenth century), or to peruse the tax-rolls to see that Jacques Bonhomme or Pierre Durand is only too glad to assume a title to express his position in society. If he can do no better, he is merely "Jacques Bonhomme, manouvrier." If he tenderly cultivates three rows of bad vine-stock, he styles himself, "vine-grower." If, in the course of the winter, he repairs three pairs of wheels, he becomes "wheelwright." Should he sell a few sacks of wheat or a few fleeces in the neighbouring market, he proudly calls himself "merchant." Should he happen to own that great wooden instrument bound with a few pieces of iron, which in the Beauvaisis was the usual plough, and the two horses required to pull it, he becomes "laboureur." But if he holds lands of the Prince de Conti, of the nuns of the Abbaye Royale de Saint-Paul, or of Jacques-Bénigne Bossuet, Bishop of Meaux and Abbot of Saint-Lucien-les-Beauvais, Jacques Bonhomme flaunts the title of "laboureur, fermier, et receveur de Monseigneur."

In fact, the host of *manouvriers* constituted, in nearly every village, the majority—the overwhelming majority—of the inhabitants. In the Beauvaisis it was rare for a *manouvrier* to be a fully-fledged proletarian. Doubtless there existed a few wretched families, dependent more or less on begging, who eked out their lives in hovels of wood, straw, and dried mud, which could scarcely be called houses. These poor wretches appear in the tax-rolls as "propertyless," "destitute," "impotent," taxed symbolically at a farthing. Except in times of plague and famine, however, these social outcasts remain the exception.

The typical *manouvrier* owns a few acres, a cottage, and a small garden—for the *manouvriers* of the Beauvaisis were almost all very small proprietors. The garden yielded hemp, beans, cabbages, and a few apples. Their few acres produced some sacks of maslin (a mixture of wheat and rye): in short, enough to feed a family for a few months or a few weeks a year. Could the *manouvriers* count on their cattle to improve their situation? Poultry and pigs, though providing tasty dishes, are ravaging, scavenging, and marauding beasts, that compete with human beings in their greed for grain. The Beauvaisis *manouvriers* generally kept three or four hens, but rarely a pig. The regular habit of eating salt bacon and "chicken in the pot", was, to all intents and purposes, impossible for him. Could he not at least get milk from his cow, seeing that our best writers commonly speak of the cow as the "poor man's beast"? Our documents bring to light a few skinny cows: for lack of a meadow or even common pasture, young lads would drive them along the lanes and occasional thickets on the edge of the fields. But one *manouvrier* in two had no cow of his own. The real "poor man's beast" was the sheep, whose fleeces and lambs helped to pay his taxes. It fed as best it could—on the stony plots they call "riez" in Picardy; on the fallow-land four months in the year, between gleaning and the first ploughing; in winter, in the stall, grazing off its straw litter for want of real hay (for it is certain that what they called "fodder" in Picardy was straw).

It is understandable, then, that the *manouvrier* should often hire himself out to the *laboureurs* and large farmers. He was the all-round countryman who worked for others at trivial, seasonal, and occasional jobs: at haymaking, harvesting, gathering grapes, threshing, clipping hedges, sawing wood, or cleaning out ditches. The larger farms, especially in summer, had need of this cheap and abundant labour. The *manouvrier* received for his pains a bowl of soup, a jug of wine, a few ears of corn, a few pence; and often he did not actually receive any money since he was already in debt to his employer. By working for the man who had ploughed a field for him, advanced him seed, peas, or wood, the *manouvrier* paid back his creditor and might hope for new loans, new advances, new services, which might help him to get through the year.

To get through it without too much hardship and to supplement the meagre resources provided by his few acres and insufficient wages, the *manouvrier* often tried to set up as a tenant-farmer himself, or to take up some kind of subsidiary occupation, generally of a seasonal nature.

Having no horses and insufficient cattle to provide an abundance of manure, and being without capital reserves, the peasant smallholder could not be other than a small tenant-farmer. The owner of three acres, he could hardly hope to take on the cultivation of more than another three. He would find land to lease among the small plots belonging to country churches or *fabriques*—small religious institutions in the parishes. Again, he might lease a few scattered fields that a stranger to the village had inherited or a townsman had acquired from a mortgaged debtor. In any event, these snippets of land cost the *manouvrier* dear in return for a meagre, sometimes nonexistent, profit. In a bad year the rent swallowed up the yield; in a plentiful year, when the price of corn was low, the harvest represented a poor return for a heavy expenditure of toil; but at least it then helped to feed his household.

It was better, in fact, to try to take up a secondary occupation. The coopers, wheelwrights, tailors, and weavers, that one finds in such large numbers in every village, were really *manouvriers* seeking additional means of livelihood. Their village clients, however, were not sufficient to keep them in full employment: they would work at their trade from time to time, at the most favourable seasons of the year. But always they were peasants rather than artisans. Yet there is one exception—if indeed it is an exception—which is to be found in the plains of Picardy: that is the countrymen who worked wool in the south and west of Picardy, and linen in the east and north-east. On the outskirts of Beauvais a dozen villages were engaged in carding and combing the wool produced locally or imported from neighbouring districts. The carders and combers were also spinners, for they did not always leave the handling of the spinning-wheel and winder to their womenfolk. Very often, too, they prepared the serge-warp, which they sold to the manufacturers of Beauvais. Further north, towards Amiens and Abbeville, we find serge-weavers rather than carders and combers, who wove their heavy, coarse Picard cloths on crude looms—cloths ranging over every conceivable type of serge, whose names are taken from such villages as Blicourt, Aumale, and Tricot. These country weavers owned neither their raw materials nor their tools; these they hired from Amiens and Beauvais merchants, who paid them by the piece, in kind more often than in cash. Most of the villages were peopled with a host of these "sergers" and carders, and looms were more in evidence than ploughs. All these textile-workers are, of course, *manouvriers* and smallholders, who would interrupt their weaving to tend their garden of beans and their acre of maslin: in the summer they would hire themselves out for the harvest. And so, in this almost pastureless plateau of Picardy, which yielded nothing but grain, its dense population was often saved from starvation by its occupation in the various processes of woollen manufacture. So it was in the case of the *mulquiniers* who wove linen cloth in the region of Clermont, Péronne, and Saint-Quentin: these men, working in damp and gloomy cellars, were also peasants—tiny proprietors, dwarf graziers, in fact *manouvriers*.

It is clear that, generally speaking, numerous imperceptible gradations lead from the mass of *manouvriers* to the favoured, restricted group of *laboureurs*. But these shades of social distinction and transitional stages are not to be found on the plateau of Picardy. In that bleak countryside, with its monotonous type of farming, peasant society appeared only in brutal contrasts. At the social peak was the big farmer, flanked by five or six *laboureurs;* down below was the wretched mass of *manouvriers;* between them, nothing.

The southern part of the Beauvaisis, however, affords a sharp contrast. Here we find rolling pastures, reminiscent of Normandy, cut by the fertile banks of the Oise and the Thérain; its hillsides covered with vines and crowned with woods, on the borders of the Ile-de-France. The charm, freshness, and diversity of the landscape seem in themselves to give rise to a rural society in which the finer gradations and distinctions abound. Here we no longer find serge-weavers tied to town manufacturers or merchants, but one or two weavers in every village who work up, for all, the hemp which everyone grows in his garden. There are still *manouvriers,* but they often possess their own cow and half a dozen sheep, sometimes even their own sow, for here it is easier to feed livestock. These *manouvriers* are not only a little less poor, they are also far less numerous, and rarely a majority in their village. The largest proportion of the population is composed of the most "French" of all the peasants: these were not the village poor, still less were they proletarians, nor were they ever prosperous members of the community: they were gardeners rather than farmers, vine-growers rather than corn-growers: skilled enough in the use of their hands to make remarkable craftsmen, artists even, though unrecognized: intelligent and adaptable enough to vary their occupation according to the season, the year, local urban demand, or the whims and fashions emanating from "the big city," Paris, which lay ten or fifteen leagues away. These were the *airiers,* a kind of market-gardener who supplied the neighbouring markets with fresh vegetables: those of Bresles grew artichokes and asparagus for Paris; others tended high-grade apple-trees which they imported from Normandy. On the slopes overlooking the Oise and the Thérain, in the near vicinity of Beauvais, vine-growers forced, from a soil too heavy and starved of warm sunshine, a few hogsheads of dry, bitter, harsh wine that was either drunk immediately or sent north, especially to Amiens. They were makers of the *blondes* and *noires,* the names given to a species of linen-thread lace which "invaded" Paris in Louis XIV's time and, in the eighteenth century, "conquered" Spain and the West Indies. Among them, too, were the makers of fans and fancy-wear in the district of Meru, skilled in working ivory for sale to Paris dealers. Less prosperous were the *blatiers* (corn-chandlers), peasants furnished with a donkey or mule, on which they carried, one sack at a time, corn to the mills of Pontoise or flour to the bakeries of Gonesse. Or there were those who drove Norman cattle to the plains of Poissy to be fattened up before being handed over to the butchers of Paris.

Of course, all these peasants tended their gardens and a few fields, became haymakers, reapers, and threshers, and periodically hired themselves out as wage-workers pure and simple; but they refused to call themselves *manouvriers.*

Very close to these social types were the so-called *haricotiers* (kidney-bean growers), found in the district of Bray in the Oise valley and occasionally in the Soissonnais. Not that they specialized in growing kidney-beans: indeed what we now call kidney-beans were called peas in the seventeenth century. The *haricotiers* with whom I am most familiar—those of the Bray district—owned a few more acres than the ordinary *manouvrier:* they normally farmed about 20 acres, of which they owned at least half. They kept one or two cows, five or six sheep, and sometimes a mule. They sold apples, eggs, and cheese. They made vine-props and worked in wicker, flax, or wood. Yet these humble peasants rarely hired out their labour to rich farmers: their own occupations kept them too busy. Were we to adopt a modern, colloquial, yet reasonably appropriate, term, we might call them *bricoleurs* (jacks-of-all-trades).

None of these different types of peasant—*haricotiers,* craftsmen, vine-growers, corn-chandlers, gardeners—had the pretension to call themselves by the exalted title of *laboureur.*

In other provinces—in Poitou for example—there existed *laboureurs à bras,* that is *laboureurs* who did not possess a plough or a horse. In the Beauvaisis such a thing would have been impossible. In fact no social term had so clear and concise a meaning: a *laboureur* was, almost by definition, a man who owned a plough and a pair of horses. (Oxen were quite unknown, both as draught-animals and for stock-raising.) The social importance of people who possessed so precious and rare a capital may be appreciated: a simple plough-horse, fully grown and in good health, was worth at least 60 *livres.* This corresponded to the price of three fatted cows, or twenty sheep, or twenty *hectolitres* (fifty-five bushels) of corn in a good year. The *laboureur,* therefore, took a pride in ploughing, three or four times a year, his own land with his own horses. He could take on lease other lands and plough them when he wished: he could use his horses for carting manure, crops, straw, hay, wood, or wine. He would hire out his horses to the *manouvriers* and *haricotiers,* who were incapable of engaging in the humblest form of farming without the essential aid of the *laboureur's* horses. Thus the *laboureurs* became the creditors of the mass of small peasants and, when occasion demanded, their employers at low wages.

How much better the *laboureur* lived than the mass of the peasants! He ate off pewter, sometimes laid out on a table-cloth. His cupboards were stocked with pairs of sheets, towels, shirts—some of fine embroidered cloth. He had reserves of corn, peas, beans, and even a whole pig in his earthen salting-tub. His Sunday-clothes were of stout serge. To attend mass or the village ball his wife and daughters would deck themselves out in linen bodices, bright-coloured skirts and petticoats, and a small golden cross at their necks. All of which was in glaring contrast with the manner of living of the bare-footed *manouvrier,* clad in coarse hempen cloth, often without bed- or table-linen, without even a table or provisions, eating a thick soup from an earthen bowl with a wooden spoon.

But the *laboureur* is a fairly rare social specimen. At Loueuse, out of 86 householders, only 3 were *laboureurs:* in Saint-Omer en Chaussée, 10 out of 93: at Crillon, 6 out of 70: at Glatigny, 3 out of 90: at Litz, 6 out of 43: at La Houssaye, only 1 out of 46 payers of the *taille.*

Yet even within this strictly limited social class, so clearly cut off from the mass of the peasantry, there were many grades both in the size of landholding and in social position. There were genuine *laboureurs* who farmed no more than 35–40 acres and kept only three cows. Others were the owners, apart from their horses and cattle, of a mere two or three pieces of land; they farmed chiefly as tenants. Such a man might keep a fair number of pigs, perhaps 20 or more— because he had bought from the lord of the manor the *droit de glandée,* the right to graze his pigs in the lord's wood when the acorns fell. At Loueuse, in 1694, François Andrieu had the distinction of not renting any land: he farmed his own land, nearly 100 acres, with five horses and two ploughmen. This large peasant-proprietor, however, owned no more than 3 cows, 2 pigs, and 23 sheep —an indication of the small amount of livestock owned by even the largest farmers in this province at this period. In a better grazing district, Charles Bournizien of Villers-Vermont, in 1683, kept 13 cows and 85 sheep: he had a few enclosed pastures of his own, was the tenant of a noble lady, and had the use, in the Bray district, of the common pastures of his village, which, though not yielding grass of the highest quality, were extremely spacious. Bournizien and Andrieu are the most substantial *laboureurs* that I have come across in the Beauvaisis between 1670 and 1700. They both possessed the enviable privilege of never having to fear hunger and of always having a surplus of produce for sale —grain, calves, or fleeces: yet even they are not at the top of the peasant social hierarchy.

That position, without any doubt, is occupied by the big tenants and receivers of the *seigneuries.* Claude Dumesnil, tenant and receiver of the Abbaye Royale de Saint-Paul at Goincourt, worked 100 *hectares* of land, 12 *hectares* of meadow, a large vineyard, and two woods, with the aid of 12 horses, 2 carters, 2 ploughmen, and an abundant supply of seasonal workers. Tenant of the abbey lands, he also farmed the seigneurial rights, the tithes (which the Abbey had appropriated from the local priest), and the monopoly of the wine-press. For all this he paid the "Ladies of Saint-Paul" 1,200 *livres tournois* and 40 *hectolitres* of best wheat a year. He had leased out his own property (a house and a few fields) for 100 *livres*. At Goincourt he owned 25 cows, 6 sows, and 225 sheep. These are the highest figures I have come across. The seigneurial dovecot on his farm housed 160 pigeons: 180 fowl fed in his backyard: among them were a couple of dozen turkeys, and as many ducks—birds that are seldom found at all, even among the wealthiest *laboureurs*. His reserves of grain, beans, peas, liquor, and timber, were considerable: there were more than 8,000 sheaves, over 100 barrels of wine and cider, and 200 fleeces in his barn. Half the villagers of Goincourt were in his debt, and 41 families in the adjoining parishes owed him a total of 1,700 *livres*. Dumesnil lent out horses, wagons, corn, hay, timber, and even money. It was this rôle of creditor that made him a figure of economic, social, and political importance. In short, he was a power in the land. Dumesnil even owned a small library, composed of pious works and stories of travel: many a merchant in the neighbouring town possessed no more than a prayer-book.

Such persons were to be found in every parish where the *seigneur* owned a large, compact domain. They usually appear to be the tenants of bishops, canons, and large abbeys. The tenant of the Ursulines of Beauvais at Moyenneville lent money to the convent, where his two daughters were inmates. The tenant of the Benedictine monastery of Saint-Germer at Coudray-Saint-Germer had ruined the petty noblemen of the neighbourhood by lending them money at heavy rates of interest on mortgages. By the end of the seventeenth century the large *fermiers-receveurs* constituted a closed caste. They intermarried, succeeded one another from father to son, or from father to son-in-law, entered into agreements to reserve for themselves the best leases, and left no tenancies available for those outside their circle. During the Revolution they frequently bought up the lands which their old master, now expropriated, had for many years been renting to their families. Even to-day it is not uncommon to find established on former ecclesiastical lands, sold at the time of the Revolution, the descendants of the powerful receivers of the *ancien régime*. It is these receivers, placed high above the common peasant, that form the apex of the peasant hierarchy of the Beauvaisis.

A precise answer must now be attempted to the question—how many of all these peasants were able to enjoy economic independence—to feed their families from that portion of the harvest left at their disposal?

First, let us consider the most vital product of all, wheat. It represents the staple food of the people of the north and centre of France, whether in the shape of bread, soup, or gruel. M. Labrousse has shown that a daily ration of 2 to 2½ pounds of bread was essential to the maintenance of each adult, and that the value of this amount of bread represented at least half the poor man's budget. These calculations apply to the more prosperous part of the eighteenth century, from 1733 to the Revolution. There are good reasons for supposing that these figures are not high enough for the seventeenth century; nevertheless, let us accept them as a basis. The most common type of peasant household consisted of six persons—father, mother, three children, and a grandparent. Even if it included two very young children (fed from an early age on gruel and bread), it is unlikely that a family of this size consumed less than ten pounds of bread per day. To produce this amount of bread for a whole year required 18 quintals of wheat. From extensive documentary evidence it appears that the yield of the best lands in the Beauvaisis, even with the most favourable harvests, rarely exceeded 9 quintals per *hectare,* or six times the outlay of seed. In years when harvests were bad, the yield barely reached 4 quintals per *hectare.*

Yet we cannot conclude from the above that 2 *hectares* of land in good years and 4½ in bad were sufficient to feed a household of peasants. For one thing, the whole of the Beauvaisis belonged to the great region of triennial rotation: usually a field would be under wheat for only one year in three. We shall therefore need to treble the areas just quoted, which will give us a minimum of 6 *hectares* and a maximum of 13½. Secondly, we must remember that the peasant-proprietor could not possibly retain his whole crop. What deductions had first to be made from it?

In the first place, he had to deduct his future seed—one sixth of his crop, and a larger proportion in bad years. He had to pay the *taille* to the king. An average peasant—let us say a fair-sized *haricotier* or small *laboureur*—would have to pay at least 20 *livres tournois* a year, the equivalent of 4 quintals of wheat in a year when prices were low, or the output of half a *hectare* of land. He was subject to other royal taxes as well, such as the *gabelle* (salt-tax), which, though their incidence is hard to compute, amounted to at least as much as the *taille.* So the king took from our small *laboureur* the equivalent of the full yield of a *hectare* of wheat, corresponding to three *hectares* of land. The ecclesiastical tithe-owner had been the first to appear on the scene and had already carried off from six to nine in every hundred sheaves. The *seigneur,* of course, had his share as well: what he exacted varied widely from place to place. In the northern Beauvaisis, the *droits de champart* (tributes in kind) took a heavy toll: nine sheaves in every hundred on top of the tithe. A further charge was the grain paid as wages to the reapers and threshers, whose services were generally required. If we total up these various initial charges—seed, sundry expenses, royal taxes, ecclesiastical and seigneurial dues—they amount to at least half of the wheat-crop. (Similar charges also applied to spring-sown cereals, such as oats, and even to wine.) In fact, the peasant proprietor who aimed to feed his family on the produce of his land would need to grow twice the amount he required for this purpose. To run over the figures again: the peasant who aspired to a state of economic independence had to farm a minimum of 12 *hectares* (nearly 30 acres) in years of plenty, and 27 *hectares* (65 acres) in years of shortage. Thus, not a single *manouvrier,* not a single *haricotier* or average *laboureur,* could be economically independent. The large *laboureurs,* the owners of at least 27 *hectares*—considerably less than one tenth of the peasantry—alone were assured of being able to feed their families comfortably under all circumstances. Those owning less than 12 *hectares* of land could not provide from the produce of their own fields the means to feed their families: they would have to buy additional wheat—that is, sell their labour in exchange.

Leaving aside the large tenant-farmers, whose lot need arouse no pity, the position of the majority of the tenant-farmers was even more precarious. Indeed, in their case, the rent has to be added to all the other charges already mentioned. In the northern part of the Beauvaisis the rent usually amounted to 1½ quintals of wheat per *hectare*. So the annual charge of the landlord amounted to a proportion varying from one sixth to one third of the crop, according to the nature of the harvest.

In short, the small peasant who was least severely affected by the complex system of initial charges on the yearly produce was the proprietor who farmed his own land: the most severely affected was the small tenant-farmer who owned but few acres. By heavy toil, the *manouvriers, haricotiers,* and small *laboureurs* were able, in favourable years, to extract from a good deal of rented land, a fair proportion of the food required for their family's upkeep, which their own fields were unable to provide. In years of bad harvest small farms were more of a burden than a support. In no case could a holding of less than 12 *hectares* assure its occupant of the slightest trace of economic independence. As our documents amply illustrate, the great majority of peasants—three quarters or more—remained well below that level. Were they, then, condemned to suffer hunger, or even starve to death?

The answer is most definitely in the affirmative. Three facts emerge beyond dispute. In the first place, the majority of the peasants of the Beauvaisis suffered from almost continuous undernourishment. Secondly, they devoted considerable courage and imagination to attempts to procure that extra food which their own lands could not produce. Thirdly, they did not always succeed in doing so: during lean years, which were not exceptional, they had to resign themselves to dying in their thousands for lack of food.

The first fact, the most difficult to prove beyond all doubt, emerges from the study of a large number of inventories drawn up after death. The almost total absence of meat from the *manouvrier's* diet was due, as we have seen, to his lack of livestock. He hardly ever had bacon since he had not the means to feed pigs. His vegetables were those of low food value: apart from cabbages, green vegetables were little known, and certainly rarely grown, except just outside the towns. There was a general absence of fruit, except in autumn: soft fruit was scarce since it takes a long time to ripen. The wild berries picked in the hedges were mostly used in drinks; and cider-apples and pears were crushed to make weak cider, heavily diluted with water. A little fruit of better quality was sold in the town-markets: the income derived from it helped to pay the tax. On the plateau of Picardy only the wealthier *laboureurs* and the larger tenant-farmers had milk and cheese: in the pastoral district of Bray, milk was made into butter and cheese and sold to Parisians at Gournay. As for whey, we know that the great bleaching establishments of Beauvais had a considerable demand for it between March and September. What we know for certain is that the basis of the diet was formed by bread, soup, gruel, large peas (called *bizaille*), and beans—a diet both heavy and lacking in nutrition, insufficient during winter and increasingly so as spring approached, despite the seasonal addition of the first green vegetables, gathered in fields, meadows, and ditches. Nor did his pale cider or bitter, green wine (that quickly spoiled) have any nutritional, or even medicinal, value.

In our analysis of peasant society we have repeatedly stressed the incessant search for other forms of income, for piece-work and such like, that is characteristic of all the *manouvriers,* of almost all the *haricotiers,* and of most of the smaller *laboureurs.* This search, which was absolutely essential in order to feed their families, to pay the *taille,* and to survive at all, took the form of hunting for vacant leases, for wool to spin, for lace to manufacture, for wood to chop, carve, or sell, for any small job on the larger estates. If need be, should ordinary work fail, they would resort to all sorts of alternatives—picking leaves, herbs, acorns, berries, which every forest-owner forbade, royal, noble, or episcopal. The result was a considerable crop of offences against the forest-laws, not to mention breaches of the laws relating to fishing and hunting. (It is a striking fact that nearly every peasant went armed.) It was but a small step from this to a profusion of minor thefts, or even to open begging. This was a particularly distinctive feature of those dreadful years when, as the saying went, "the times were out of joint," and harvests shrank to a half, or even to a third, of their normal yield.

At such times that considerable majority of peasants whose farms were too small fell short of everything: of wheat, first of all, and then of all those subsidiary foods just mentioned, which formed part of their basic subsistence. In fact the larger *laboureurs* and farmers reduced the number of their hands and cut their wages. The weavers, too, lacked work: in times of high prices the woollen cloth bought by the poor of the Beauvaisis found no sale, and merchants, fearful of adding to the stocks already in their hands, compelled the town and country craftsmen to stop their looms. Everything fell off at the same time—crops, work in the fields, and work in industry.

Some of the peasants, normally tied to the soil, would then take to the road in search of bread. They would beg at the doors of the rich farmers and the *curés;* but even if the latter were charitably disposed they could not help everybody. They would go knocking at the gates of the wealthy abbeys, some of which would organize a free distribution of bread; but then thousands of poor wretches would appear, bringing with them the inevitable accompaniment of contagious disease. Most of the impoverished peasants would try to enter the towns, where there was always some provision of relief organized by a variety of charitable bodies. But the towns would turn away these "foreigners," by force if need be: they were already bearing the heavy burden of their own poor.

Very swiftly the weaker elements of the rural (and urban) population would begin to die off—old folk, infants, adolescents. In September or October, two months after the harvest, the names entered in the parochial burial registers would begin to mount up. There would be no fall in the mortality rate during the winter, and it would reach its peak in the spring, when dwindling stocks of food would be exhausted, and epidemics, thriving on weakened physiques, would spread among the poorer classes and, eventually, strike the rich, who, till then, had suffered nothing. At the same time there would be fewer marriages and even births would fall far below their accustomed figure: the very fertility of the population would be severely affected. In ten or twelve months—between 1661 and 1662, between 1693 and 1694, and again between 1709 and 1710—ten to fifteen per cent of the inhabitants of a village would disappear, carried off by famine or epidemic. Some townships of the Beauvaisis lost as much as a quarter of their population in this manner. The *manouvriers* were always the hardest hit, both relatively and absolutely. After such a blood-letting their followed a few years of comparatively prosperous existence: there was more work for fewer hands, there was more land to let, and the people of the countryside could breathe a little more freely, until the next disastrous harvest, which inevitably brought in its train, at least until 1740, the same or similar misfortunes.

There can be little doubt that these phenomena—and they are amply proven —express a kind of periodical disequilibrium between an irregular food-supply and a prolific population, subject to fitful and uncontrolled increase. It seems likely that they left a deeper mark on a cereal-producing region like Picardy than on a fertile and varied region such as Normandy and the Ile-de-France: and this difference suggests that small-scale farming, so roundly condemned by the Physiocrats in the eighteenth century, had certain solid advantages. Above all, we must not forget that, in those years of endurance, the memory of which remained deeply imprinted on the popular mind, the villages suffered as much or perhaps more than the towns, and that the social structure of the peasantry was then brutally laid bare: those who died in their thousands were the *manouvriers,* the small peasants who owned a few acres and a cow and could not find work to supplement their incomes.

Although every adult had had some experience of such years, these years of heavy mortality were fairly rare—not more than one in ten. During the years of respite the Beauvaisis peasants managed, in one way or another, to make a living; yet it was under a growing burden of debt.

It would require a whole volume on its own to study the question of peasant indebtedness in any detail—an important question, though little explored. Here we can only indicate its diversity, inevitability, and intensity. Every small peasant was indebted to one or more *laboureurs,* who lent him horses and working-stock, carted his produce, sold or advanced him a lamb, timber, beans, wheat. Every small peasant owed his landlord arrears of rent and for advances of seed or money. His debts to the *seigneur* were not so great; but he always owed substantial amounts to the tax-collector, since he found difficulty in having the necessary ready-cash available. Then, less onerous, but a burden nevertheless, there were his debts to the blacksmith, wheelwright, tailor, weaver, village shepherd, the religious confraternity, the schoolmaster, not to mention the innkeeper of the nearest township. Finally, there were the usual rural moneylenders—lawyers, innkeepers, large farmers, magistrates—whose activities extended over a large part of the countryside. They often acted as "covers" for the wealthy *bourgeois* of Beauvais. This type of lender was the most dangerous: he held contracts for loans drawn up by lawyers, and they always involved a mortgage on the debtor's property. When the debtor defaulted his land passed to the creditor. The courts automatically returned a verdict in favour of such transfers, all the more readily since the creditors were often themselves the judges.

2.

English historians are reluctant to label as feudal any aspect of their own eighteenth-century society. Partly because English medievalists champion the definition of feudalism which treats it narrowly as a military institution, and mostly because English historians like to stress a certain social openness and uniqueness about their aristocracy, the term feudal is never applied seriously to the Age of Walpole.

And yet there may have been something feudal about English eighteenth-century aristocracy. Owning much of the arable land, controlling judicial and political life as well as the army and navy, and living extravagantly, these nobles were not unlike their French and Spanish counterparts. Again, beneath the veil of medieval law and traditions, which deeply affected the style of life, there remained the solid power of the aristocrats who governed the country.

But instead of looking for similarities between their aristocracy and those of the Continent, English historians have tended to stress two unique aspects of the English pattern. The law of primogeniture and the participation of aristocrats in commercial life, they assert, mark the English aristocracy as distinctly different from that of the waning feudal society of France.

Professor J. H. Plumb (1911–   ) of Cambridge University mentions these traditional distinctions and hurries on to define the English aristocracy as a caste where blood ties were strong. In fact, he discerns a "general hardening of caste" in the Age of Walpole. What might have caused this?

Who was Squire Western? In France his equivalent was the *hobereau*, the poor, stupid, uncultivated nobleman who led an uncouth existence. Plumb dismisses Fielding's Western, not so much because such a person never existed, but because Macaulay had overdrawn his portrait of Western so that it might fit that of the gentry. Was there a gentry in France?

Plumb likens William III's ministers to the so-called "robber barons" of American capitalism. How did these ministers live? How did their style of life prepare them for living on familiar terms with the aristocracy of blood? Instead of stressing a kind of social openness, Plumb's eighteenth-century society is one made sordid and potentially violent by rigid class lines. Did these lines correspond to ancient feudal distinctions?

J. H. PLUMB: The Classes of Men: England*

In the early eighteenth century English politics were influenced by the smallness of the population, by the difficulty of communication and by the prevalence of disease. People were sparsely spread over the land: outside London, which contained perhaps an eighth of the population, the majority lived in tiny hamlets and small country towns no bigger than present-day villages. The squires, yeomen and the few professional men of the neighbourhood—attorneys, stew-

* From J. H. Plumb, *Sir Robert Walpole* (London: Cresset Press, 1956), pp. 3–34.

ards, doctors—came together at the markets and fairs to gossip and grumble. They saw events in personal terms; supported or opposed the election of a mayor or Member of Parliament because they supported or opposed his family. Ancient wrongs and ancient loyalties as much as conviction often led men to adopt the opprobrious title of whig or tory. Sometimes even the hatred of one part of a county for another—East and West Sussex, for example—could result in a bitter conflict of opinion. The number of men in any county with political influence being very small, they all knew each other intimately and in consequence the personal factor in politics was strengthened. Often there was a little oligarchy of power rooted in a provincial town and its neighbouring countryside, but such a group was often isolated and this consequently led to the fragmentation of politics and inhibited the effectiveness of propaganda, confining it to race meetings and quarter sessions.

These neighbourhoods—that admirable eighteenth-century term which describes exactly the basic unit of society and politics—were joined together by wide green roads which sometimes followed the straight line of an old Roman road or prehistoric trackway, but more often meandered haphazardly up hill and down dale, threading their way through the great open fields. Along them lumbered coaches, waggons and strings of pack-horses; in summer movement was easy, but for the rest of the year always difficult and often dangerous. At St Ives, wrote Celia Fiennes, "the road was so full of holes and quick sands I durst not venture" and later in her journey, on the way to Leicester, she found "very good land but very deep bad roads . . . being full of sloughs, clay deep way, that I was neer 11 hours going but 25 mile." Twice she was nearly drowned, a fate which Wesley only just escaped on the Great North Road. Travel was so difficult that business as well as social and political life was circumscribed; within a limited area there was great activity, but men hesitated to leave their "country" unless necessity impelled them. This did much to prevent the formation of closely-knit political parties at a time when the governing classes of the nation were strongly divided on fundamental principles and particular issues. The absence of parties organized on a national basis consolidated political power in the hands of those actively engaged at the centre and enabled them to take decisions without over-much consideration of public opinion. The effect was to give greater pliability to political leadership often at the expense of principle. The smallness of the population and its isolation had much to do with the intensely personal nature of English politics in the Augustan age; this is well known and hardly needs stressing, but the prevalence of disease is a factor more generally ignored or misunderstood.

The placid exteriors of Georgian houses, the well-kept lawns, the restfully contrived vistas, the distant folly and unruffled lake breed of themselves a sense of expansive well being, of *calme, luxe et volupté*. The hacking coughs, the violent fevers, bloody remedies and desperate deaths are banished and forgotten. Forgotten, too, that longing for the summer and that fear of winter which haunted men and women of those days.

"Since I wrote last to your Lordship I have been under a little severe discipline of blisters behind my ears, and other medicinal applications for a swell'd face, attended with a slight fever," wrote Sir Thomas Cave to his brother-in-law

Earl Verney. "Could I but perswade the weather to be a little on the summer establishment, I am hopes my cough would also leave me which is near of kin to the weather glass . . . Poor Peggy too has frequent returns of her illness . . . she would receive benefit too, if the old fashioned thing called summer would make its appearance."

Sir Thomas Cave's longing for the warmth of the sun is echoed in writer after writer, year in year out, for sickness had a greater hold on life than now. Walpole was frequently and violently ill and at times his career was nearly jeopardized by his prostration. Lord Egmont in 1732 thought that it was amazing that Walpole could undertake the burden of his office, considering his poor state of health throughout his life. As with illness, so with death; suddenly it would strike; every family, rich or poor, was used to its visitation. But for the death of his brother, struck down in his prime, Walpole would have entered either the Church or the Army. Within eighteen months of each other Walpole's greatest rivals—Stanhope and Sunderland—dropped dead, thereby clearing his way to power. The grip of influence, the strength of a faction could suddenly be weakened by unexpected death. As kings and ministers aged, politicians were led to gamble on their futures; speculations in mortality were made by whigs and tories, by men in and out of office, for death was a lottery, breeding anxiety, but giving an edge to appetite, heightening the light and darkening the shade of the passing years.

These are general factors touching all classes and all politicians great and small. They influenced little the distribution of political power which was controlled by wealth and birth.

Social and political life was dominated by the aristocracy. It was a small caste, closely inter-related and very conscious of its special privileges, but freer in its composition than most of the nobilities of Europe. It was saved from rigidity by two factors. The sons of peers became commoners and there were no social barriers to their economic activities in the earlier years of the century. Lord Townshend's uncle, Horatio, for example, was a City merchant. And no stigma was attached to a nobleman's marrying the wealthy daughter of a merchant; indeed such heiresses were much sought after. The great wealth of the Dukes of Bedford came in part from the wise marriage arranged for the young Marquess of Tavistock in 1695 to Elizabeth Howland, a London merchant's daughter, and granddaughter of Sir Josiah Child, the banker, and Chairman of the East India Company. By Anne's reign the Bedfords had developed wet and dry docks at Rotherhithe and the *Streatham* was trading for them with the Indies.

The broad base of the nobility's power rested on their estates which varied greatly but were mostly large. The Dukes of Newcastle owned considerable lands in thirteen counties and enjoyed a rent-roll of over thirty thousand a year. The Dukes of Bedford were equally rich; there were few acres of the Vale of Berkeley which did not belong to its Earl. Those disasters of human life to which the eighteenth century was so prone—early death and failure of heirs— tended through the close intermarriage of noble families to make these estates ever larger. But land had ceased to be the sole source of their wealth for they were quick to seize the opportunities which the growing commercial prosperity of the country afforded.

They invested in Government securities; they dabbled in the East India Companies, in building projects, in mines, in real estate, in water works, in shipping and shipbuilding. In that bustling world of aggressive commercial enterprise their money was everywhere to be found. When the Earl of Sunderland dropped dead in 1722 he had about seventy-five thousand invested in stocks and shares. Harley Street, Wimpole Street and Mortimer Street are witnesses of the land speculation and building promotion of Robert Harley, Earl of Oxford. Cavendish Square was a joint venture of Lords Dartmouth, Carnarvon, Harcourt, Bingley, Bathhurst and Castleton. The Dukes of Chandos and Devonshire with the Earl of Nottingham supported the York Building Waterworks Company against the New River Company in which the "proud" Duke of Somerset, Queen Anne's Master of the Horse, was heavily engaged. The speculations of the Duke of Chandos were astonishingly varied. He undertook large building projects in London, Bath and Bridgwater; he invested in oyster fishery, pipe clay, coal, copper and alum mines; he dabbled in land in New York State; he promoted a glass works, a soap factory and a distillery; he speculated in diamonds and silver; he invested in every stock and share that was quoted on the Exchange. He admitted having lost £700,000 of his profits in the South Sea Bubble and £125,000 in the Africa Company: his unit of investment in stocks at times was the princely sum of £50,000. True enough Chandos was something of a portent to his own generation—"a bubble to every project" as Onslow called him, but he was symptomatic of the way the aristocracy were using their wealth, and also of the methods many of them were using to make money.

Chandos had become a rich man through office; he was Paymaster-General during Marlborough's wars. This was the most lucrative place which could fall to a politician's lot, but there were many others which brought enduring wealth to their holders. Daniel Finch, second Earl of Nottingham, was Secretary of State for just over six years (March 1689–November 1693: May 1702–May 1704) and he made a clear profit of over £50,000 on the office. Smaller places brought in less but in 1726 a quarter of the active peerage held offices of administrative importance either in the Government or about the Court; most of the rest were in the hands of their dependants or relations. Land, speculation, place, these were the sources of the nobility's wealth; the variety of their economic enterprise aroused a keen interest in many aristocrats in the commercial destiny of their country and lifted their eyes beyond the confines of their own broad acres. In a similar way the active pursuit of office, both for gain and for glory, led them into the hard routine of administration as well as politics, which in its turn gave this sheltered and privileged class of men a core of social purpose.

There were very few aristocrats—perhaps never more than about a hundred and fifty really active ones, including the few Scottish noblemen who played a part in English political and social life. They were rich, and getting in general richer; they dominated the Court and the social life of London. They were educated to consider themselves a separate order of society. Such wealth, security and privilege could lead to excess, amounting at times to an open disregard for the law. In 1692 Lord Lincoln's servants battered to death a young man named Webb because he had the impertinence to laugh at his Lordship's belly. Lord Mohun made short work of a brace of men who insulted him, only to die himself in a duel with the Duke of Hamilton. Most, however, confined their excesses to the bottle, the bed and the gaming board. And, of course, there were many who lived peaceful, orderly and sober lives, devoting themselves to the business of their estates and the welfare of their dependants. Yet there were few who did not enter eagerly into the ostentatious display which had come to be regarded as a necessary aspect of aristocratic life. This usually took the form of building country palaces and adorning them with magnificent collections of furniture and pictures. The great efflorescence of aristocratic building activity in the late seventeenth and early eighteenth centuries was due, however, to deeper motives than mere display. The country house was a symbol of greatness; not only of a man but of a family and of the social and political power which it could exercise both in the neighbourhood and in the nation at large. It was also something more—the administrative centre of a large and complex economic enterprise. The thousands of acres which were farmed or let, the minerals and mines, the vast complexity of property rights, demanded a considerable staff of bailiffs, stewards and clerks. Large houses were necessary, but these were far larger than necessity demanded. It was natural that pride should breed a competitive spirit and that the nobility's growing wealth should lead to an exuberant display. Houses became ever larger; decoration richer and more ornate; furniture more expensive; pictures more costly. Millions of pounds were poured into stone and plaster to give England a magnificent architectural heritage. The old Elizabethan manor houses were torn down and replaced by the Palladian palaces which Burlington and Kent made fashionable. They needed a setting appropriate to their splendour, and the surrounding countryside was remodelled; woods, vast lakes, artificial ruins were created by men who were building not only for themselves but for eternity. At Woburn the Duke of Bedford, confident of the destiny of his house, began plantations which could only reach maturity in the days of his great-grandchildren. And George Dodington bequeathed a handsome slice of his fortune not to his heir, George Bubb, but to the house which he was building at Eastbury; his trustees were to use £1,800 per annum from his estate until this grandiose Vanbrugh palace was completed. On 6 June 1734, Sir Thomas Robinson, the garrulous son-in-law of the Earl of Carlisle, found Lord Strafford busily at work building a new home at Wentworth.

If in some things Lord Strafford's fell short of what I was told of it, I was very agreeably surprised in finding this place improved in all respects since I was last here infinitely beyond my expectations. What may properly be called the house is about the same length in front as Lord Tilney's (260 feet); that front towards the garden is entirely finished, being partly patch-work of the old house and partly a new building, and excepting a very fine library, little can be said in its praise, but when you come to the court front, amends will be sufficiently made to all lovers of architecture, and when finished 'twill be a stupendous fabric, infinitely superior to anything we have now in England; the front of the house and offices (exclusive of the stables) being a line of 606 feet built of the most beautiful hewn stone and the best masonry I ever saw; these offices on each side of the house are entirely finished. The upright of the house will be the same style as Lord Tilney's, only this portico will have 8 columns in front.

The hall will be 64 feet by 53 deep and 48 high, a prodigious room; on each side of it are three rooms, all six 24 high; two of them will be 36 feet square, two 26 in front and 38 deep, and two 24 in front and 36 deep. This whole front will contain 21 windows, 5 of which are now just covered in. The whole finishing will be entirely submitted to Lord Burlington, and I know of no subject's house in Europe [which] will have 7 such magnificent rooms so finely proportioned as these will be. This part of the house will be built entirely new from the foundations, and very conveniently disposed to lay it to the old house; and as Lord Tilney's has hitherto been thought so fine [a] house, as some people imagined would never have been excelled, I am very glad for the honour of Yorkshire to see a pile going forward here that will in every respect infinitely exceed it. The outworks are also large, and my Lord has a very fine command of wood and water; but none of the finishing strokes which give the beauty to the whole are yet completed.

The rivalry, the sense of competition, is implicit in every line of Robinson's letter. Yorkshire was to have the greatest private house in the land, perhaps the finest in Western Europe! It was an achievement and so it remains.

Such grandiose palaces demanded a style of living which the sovereign princes of Germany and Italy might have envied. Europe was ransacked for pictures and statuary; manuscripts, books, medals, exotic plants and birds, all that could give distinction or singularity were collected assiduously and regardless of expense. The extravagant Chandos maintained a superb collection of exotic birds. In his aviaries were "whistling owls and flamingos from Antigua . . . blue macaws and geese; Muscovy ducks, Virginia fowls and songbirds; a Gold Coast redbird of peculiar prettiness; Barbadoes 'Powises' and parakeets, an eagle and a crown bird." A large private orchestra, under Pepusch, provided him with music; his personal wants and those of his Duchess and children were attended by ninety-three household servants; the gardens of one of his houses, Cannons, employed nineteen gardeners. . . .

There was one other aspect of this expensive display in which the aristocracy indulged. Younger sons could be fobbed off with a career in the Army, the Church, or even in trade, but daughters had to be married high. This could not be done cheaply. His daughters' portions cost Daniel Nottingham £52,000, as much as he spent buying his estate in Rutlandshire and nearly twice as much as he spent on his house. Only the very wealthiest merchants could attempt to endow their daughters so handsomely. The effect, of course, was to bind aristocratic families in a close union of blood relationship which gave rise to a heightened sense of caste and privilege. George I's advisers wished to close the ranks of the peerage by Act of Parliament and although Walpole secured the bill's rejection the upshot was roughly the same. The Act would have allowed creations of nobility to replace extinction of title. As it happened George I and George II were so determined to protect the peerage from dilution that they ennobled very few men and the aristocracy hardly increased at all during their reigns. A highly successful lawyer, soldier or sailor might win a peerage; the politically active son of a nobleman was likely to obtain a seat in the Lords to strengthen the government, but there was little hope for anyone else unless they were prepared to spend a lifetime in politics and often a fortune as well.

This was all a part of that general hardening of caste which took place during Walpole's lifetime. The aristocracy became increasingly aware of its special privileges and powers. In 1744 the Duke of Richmond was outraged when his daughter eloped with Henry Fox, although Fox's father had been the servant of Charles II throughout his life and died immensely rich. The letters of Chesterfield and Horace Walpole create the same impression of a deepening sense of caste, isolated by its conventions from the rest of society. These attitudes were protective devices used to secure the world of privilege, both social and political, which it enjoyed. The basis of that privilege was landed wealth and the nobility were fully conscious that this was so; by devising very strict settlements they attempted to preserve their great estates from the damage which a feckless and extravagant heir could do. These settlements were hedged about with thickets of legal restrictions and by turning the head of a great estate into a tenant for life they helped to keep intact the conglomerations of wealth which the aristocracy had amassed.

And finally the aristocracy monopolized the Court. It had, of course, always done so, though in earlier centuries there were few to envy their privileged station. But riches were spreading. There were many merchants as affluent as the greatest noblemen: scores of families who had left trade for the land. Their eyes turned enviously towards the privileged world of society which Hervey and Horace Walpole have so brilliantly depicted. Few, however, were bidden into that charmed circle. And, of course, there were not many who could live as the aristocracy lived even if the privileges of birth were ignored. An outstandingly rich merchant or an occasional country gentleman of great estate might vie with the nobility's way of life but no one else. Their world became a world to adore or to hate, to emulate or to despise. This ambivalence of attitude is clearly marked in the class most closely associated with the aristocracy in their provincial domains—the gentry.

Every man now, be his fortune what it will, is to be doing something at his place, as the fashionable phrase is, and you hardly meet with anybody who, after the first compliments, does not inform you that he is in mortar and heaving of earth, the modest terms for building and gardening. One large room, a serpentine river, and a wood are become the absolute necessities of life, without which a gentleman of the smallest fortune thinks he makes no figure in his country.

Long before these words were written in the days of Walpole's father, the country gentleman had grown tired of his ancient rambling manor house. The local masons had been called in to give it a classical façade; here and there a rich squire like Sir William Fermor of Easton Neston in Northamptonshire could afford to emulate the aristocracy, demolish his old family house, and employ the most fashionable architects for his new mansion. In each county there were gentle families of ancient lineage—Rolles of Devon, Cartwrights of Northamptonshire, Musgraves of Cumberland, Napiers of Dorset, who were as rich and powerful in their neighbourhoods as many a nobleman; at times they even intermarried. The wife of Sir Roger Mostyn of Mostyn was the only daughter of the second Earl of Nottingham allowed to marry outside the peerage. On the other hand, according to family tradition, Colonel Walpole would not permit his daughter Dorothy to marry Charles, Viscount Townshend, but then the Walpoles hardly belonged to the highest circles of the country gentry.

The lesser gentry lived on a more modest scale and confined their building activities to adding a wing to the old house, putting in new sash windows, sticking on a portico—jobs done with the aid of the local stonemason, the estate carpenter and a handbook of architectural designs. In the same way their style of life was more modest. Instead of a private orchestra Walpole's father depended on the waits from King's Lynn or the wandering fiddlers from Swaffham and Thetford. His luxuries were confined to an occasional barrel of oysters, a lobster or two, a pot of coffee or dish of tea; these and the strong red Portuguese wine, were the only extravagances which distinguished his table from that of his tenant farmers. For these homespun squires visits outside their counties were rare. They were associated in their daily life with the merchants, attorneys and prosperous yeomen. With them they gathered together over their pots of ale and pipes at the fairs and markets of the little country towns. There was far less distinction of class between these groups than between the aristocracy and the squirearchy. Country gentlemen of the middling sort were prepared to marry their daughters to local families in trade or land, and even their younger sons if an heiress was available, although they would rarely consent to the eldest sons going outside their own class. Until Robert Walpole married Catherine Shorter in 1700 most male Walpoles for well over a hundred years had married into an East Anglian family of equal standing. There was hardly a squire of any importance in Norfolk to whom the Walpoles were not distantly related. As the cousinage of the aristocracy covered the whole of England in a network of blood-relationship so the counties and neighbourhoods were covered with a similar network by the squirearchy.

The gentry's wealth was based on the land. Some of their estates they farmed for themselves; the rest was let to tenants. A thrifty squire would buy a mortgage or add to his lands by direct purchase. He might spread himself in a few luxuries as did Walpole's uncle, James Hoste of Sandringham, whose wife bullied him into buying a coach, gorgeously painted with his coat of arms, with the seats especially constructed to fit her short and dumpy person. Fine clothes, London wigs and new silver plate soon followed. Or they might buy a few tenements in the nearest town. But opportunities for investing money were very limited. The major source of their income remained the land, and was subject to the vagaries which beset it—bad harvests, plagues and equally disastrous bumper crops.

Lord Stanhope of Shelford, the father of the great Earl of Chesterfield, wrote to his cousin, James Stanhope, on 17 February 1702, from Lichfield:

"As I had no occasion for the hundred pounds when some months ago you offered to pay it me back, so I now do freely tell you that at this time necessity obliges me to ask you for it. Since my Tenants never paid my rents so ill as this last half year which puts me in a streight for money to pay off my tradesmen in this little dirty town."

Later, still desperately short of money, Stanhope tried sterner measures.

"I have sent an attorney among my tenants," he told his cousin when he wrote on 10 March 1702, to thank him for sending the hundred pounds, "to force them to pay me my rents, but he finds that all their corn lyes dead upon their hands so that to seize their persons when they have no money among them will do no good."

As the eldest son of a peer, Lord Stanhope had fine prospects which were ample security to see him through his troubles. Squires of small degree were not so lucky. In January 1700, Sir William Chaytor was forced to quit his ancestral home for the Fleet, the debtors' prison, where he lived until he died seventeen years later. He found plenty of good company there. The gentry had fallen on difficult days. "Many ancient families," writes Professor Hughes, "the Blenkinsops of Bellister, the Radcliffes of Redheugh, the Riddells of Shipcote, to mention only a few, mortgaged and later sold piecemeal their ancestral lands." And behind the Jacobite rebellion of 1715 he discerns the discontented gentry poised on the precipice of bankruptcy.

Nor was this situation peculiar to Northern England. In 1736 the Rev Patrick St Clair wrote to his patron, Ashe Windham of Felbrigg: "Your old neighbour Mr Paston went off in his coach and four, on Sunday last, and absconds ever since . . . they say if he should pay all his debts honestly, he would not have above one hundred a year left, so he is not like to be able to show his head any more." St Clair's prognostication proved accurate; never again did a male Paston live in Norfolk. They were not the only ancient family to vanish. Le Gros, Palgrave, Heydon, Potts, Spelman, Gleane, ancient families all, who had lived generation after generation on their modest estates, sank into oblivion. This was not a new process; throughout the centuries, since that first great agrarian expansion of the thirteenth, landed families had risen only to fall again. For one that survived a score were destroyed, overtaken by those natural disasters which beset families—failure of heirs, wanton extravagance, reckless loyalty, sheer bad luck. But debt, the crushing, inexorable burden of debt, extinguished most. As it pressed them down, the needy gentlemen viewed with hatred the wanton luxury of the well-to-do, and envied jealously the manna which fell from the Court into favoured laps. It is not an accident that Norfolk's few Jacobites should be found amongst the needy small squires; nor that the crusted and embittered tories were to be found amongst the ranks of those whom life was dispossessing. The failure to succeed had always been hard to bear; the rebellions, revolutions and plots, which make up the narrative of seventeenth-century history, were fed by the gentry's hopeless plight. William's and Marlborough's wars piled the heavy burden of taxation on to the squires' shoulders, and men who had reviled James soon learned to hate their Protestant King. The flamboyance of the rich, merchant or nobleman, did not make the gentry's lot easier to bear. It became doubly difficult to accept the frugal life which prudence demanded if bad years were to be lived through without disaster. Nothing, however, was easier to turn into coin than land and the squires found attorneys and scriveners eager to offer mortgages, for the hunger for land of the moneyed classes was not easily assuaged.

Sir Thomas Cave of Stanford Hall in Leicestershire was very typical of country gentlemen of his day. He loved racing his horses almost as much as hunting the fox over the shires. His hospitality was open-handed and generous. He hated taxes, wars, Dutchmen, placemen, courtiers and London money-lenders. Man of action that he was he did not like to hate to little purpose; so he stood for Parliament for his county, raising the money as best he might. At thirty-nine, in 1719, Sir Thomas Cave dropped dead, leaving four young children and an estate vastly encumbered with debt. His wife had to sell everything—plate, coach-horses, hounds, her own jewels, even the one hogshead of red wine in the cellar. Most of the servants were dismissed; the great deer park was turned back into a farm; only after years of the strictest economy was the estate saved. This story could be repeated for every county in the land except that the endings might not be so happy.

The bulk of the gentry were faced with a most difficult problem. Only a lavish expenditure could bring them the style of life which they felt, rightly or wrongly, was due to their station. Only the very wealthiest of them could afford it without risking mortgage and debt. It was a dilemma from which there were few methods of escape. The most favoured was marriage to an heiress, but even this was not without its dangers. An heiress's conceptions of the appropriate style of life necessary for herself and family could fly very high; her dower was, more often than not, difficult to turn into liquid assets without mortgage, and once mortgage was incurred the old familiar story tended to be repeated again. More satisfactory was a place at Court or in the government, but a small squire had little chance of obtaining a place unless he had suitable connections. Marriage might do this for him, as it did for the Custs of Stamford who had beggared themselves trying to maintain their parliamentary influence there against the inroads of the great house of Bertie. They were saved by a stroke of luck; Sir Richard Cust married a Brownlow of Belton whose family was closely allied with the Dukes of Rutland. They were gradually weaned from their old-fashioned tory prejudices against courtiers; seats in Parliament and a steady flow of perquisites, culminating in the Speakership of the House of Commons, illustrate the wisdom of their decision, as they moved from obscurity and debt into favour and affluence.

Alliance with a great family offered the best insurance to a country gentleman. That was why the powerful Court aristocracy found it so easy to dominate their own localities, or (perhaps more accurately) so relatively easy, for there was not room for all. There were not enough scraps of patronage to go round. Men who were politically astute found little difficulty in assessing the political, social and personal value of any squire; unless he had something to offer and was willing to give unquestioning loyalty he would find entry into the caucus difficult and exclusion easy. If he happened to be related to the dominant family he might have to be accepted, but even the ties of blood were likely to prove very thin in the world of political patronage.

The whig leaders preferred to ally with the more aggressive sections of local society, with attorneys and merchants, or newly-landed families who still retained such interests, otherwise they kept close to the great landowners to whom they were related by marriage.

The small squires tended therefore to drift into the politics of resentment. Some called themselves old whig, others tory. They had their moments of hope in the reign of Queen Anne. At times they could win an election by sheer force of numbers, particularly in the county constituencies. They remained disgruntled, crotchety, drawing consolation from the vituperation which the *Craftsman* poured on Walpole and his government. They developed a venomous hatred of place-holders, pensioners and the aristocratic world of London. They looked back with longing affection to the Stuarts, and sometimes played the Jacobite, under the extravagant delusion that their plight had been better, forgetting that many of their grandfathers had talked treason with Shaftesbury and trundled James II out of the land.

The ambivalence of attitude between the aristocracy and the smaller gentry gives an edge to local politics in the early eighteenth century which otherwise they might lack. It kept alive the old struggle of whig and tory in the constituencies long after the conflict between them had become meaningless at the centre of politics. And this too must be remembered—they were far more numerous than the whig oligarchs who ruled their lives. After Walpole had brought peace to the land, the growing prosperity of the country in which they shared, tended as year followed year, to soften their asperity and bring them to a grumbling indifference. But they could never be ignored. Their representatives in Parliament, the independent country gentlemen, could act decisively in a conflict between factions. When roused to violent opposition, as they were by Excise, they could still play an effective part in general elections. In the political struggles with which this volume deals they were of far greater influence. It was on their fears and jealousies that Robert Harley played so dexterously. By their help he was able to climb to power, by their folly Bolingbroke was able to betray him. This conflict within the landowning classes sharpened the struggle for power at Westminster.

Before we leave the gentry to examine other and equally important strata in society it is necessary to dispel a myth—the attractive myth of Squire Western, that boorish, stupid, unlettered, drink-sodden oaf of good heart and no wit. A literary caricature was given historical reality by Macaulay in his Third Chapter and the country gentleman of Stuart or Hanoverian days has been a figure of fun ever since. Often, however, these small squires were men of culture and learning. There were sots among them but sots could be found at Court, in the Army, on the Bench, or in the Church. There were lechers, too, and men crazed with horses and gaming. The rest of society, high or low, were not ignorant of such vices. But the bulk were well educated. Their libraries, like Sir Pury Cust's or Walpole's father's, contained the classics—Homer, Thucydides, Plutarch, Livy, Cicero, Seneca, Virgil, Ovid, Lucretius, Pliny; plenty of history; Dugdale, Brady, Holinshed, Daniel, Raleigh; some French books, perhaps, usually Bossuet, Corneille, Racine, and Bayle's Dictionary; a book or two on architecture; a great number of law books; a little poetry, Spenser and Milton, occasionally

Dryden; a shelf of sermons and theology; a few pursued the new rationalism and purchased Bacon, Hobbes and Locke.

At every fair in East Anglia there were bookstalls, and it was not only the local parson who bought there. Political problems were then couched in historical terms. Men believed that by studying the country's past, especially its law, they could unravel those mysteries of authority and obligation which so baffled them. As the strong red wine circulated round the oaken tables the talk ran on statute law, on Norman despotism, on Witanagemot, on Adam and patriarchy. Sometimes the deeper problems of man's destiny troubled them, for the old biblical certainties were crumbling. Yet squires were not always solemn; they had their lighter side. They loved music—every village had its waits and fiddlers who wandered from country house to country house certain of a warm welcome and modest tip. They were passionately devoted to architecture and knew something of painting; most of them spent more time and money than they could afford on their gardens and trees. They studied intelligently the new forms of husbandry and made their own modest experiments. There were mindless ones amongst them who thought of nothing but horses, hounds and gun: others were equally obsessed by their pursuit of learning; but most combined a little of both, happy with a good day's hunting in the crisp autumn air but just as content to spend a raw day indoors by the huge log fire in the panelled library, reading of the iniquities of Dudley and Empson and thinking darkly of Walpole and Townshend.

There were other strains in society in the early eighteenth century which helped to sharpen political differences. The merchant class was no more harmonious than the landowners. Throughout the seventeenth century the number of merchants had been growing and so, too, had their wealth and power. The long wars with France, which had been a consequence of the revolution of 1689, had given the wealthier merchants a chance to make large fortunes and to consolidate their economic position. By the time Walpole entered politics the commercial life of London was dominated by a small group of financiers of immense wealth. These men were not only directors of the Bank of England but were also the controllers of the East India Company, the Africa Company and Levant Company. They owned blocks of London property; they dabbled in mortgages; they spread their money in land; wherever there was gain or security for money, they were investors and buyers. The extent of their wealth is undiscoverable. Sir James Bateman, one-time Governor of the Bank of England, Sub-Governor of the South Sea Company, director of the East India Company, gave his daughters £10,000 each for their portions. He bequeathed his eldest son an estate in Herefordshire, his second an estate in Kent and his youngest an estate in Essex. They were all given houses and property in London. The grandchildren were not forgotten, careful provision being made to permit them to use free of charge the slate and stone from his quarries in Durham in addition to their legacies in estates. Largesse was scattered to the poor of half-a-dozen parishes and Sir James was wise enough to make provision in his will for his executors to have a book-keeper at £50 per annum. His son acquired the social distinction which his wealth commanded. He married the daughter of Charles, Earl of Sunderland, and in 1725 became the first Viscount Bateman; true, the viscounty was only of Ireland, for George I had strong prejudices about birth, but it was sufficient to obliterate the stigma of trade. Nor was Sir James Bateman's reputation for wealth confined to London; his name was good security in Antwerp, Holland and Germany. Bateman was an extremely rich man but he was not unique. Sir Josiah Child held over £50,000 India stock in 1691, and India was only one of his many interests. Or there was Sir Robert Clayton, the scrivener, who held mortgages on the estates of half the nobility of Surrey and Sussex. He was rich enough to buy the manor of Bletchingley and with it the right to return two members of Parliament, and so rich that, although he was an intolerable nuisance as a Commissioner of Customs, he was too powerful to be dismissed.

"Besides these imputations of corruption and partiality to his old fellow servants, however unfit and disaffected they are," wrote Sir John Somers bitterly in 1694, "he does continually insist so stiffly and unreasonably against reforming any errors or abuses that are practised in the office, that it is sufficient to say a thing is an ancient custom, to ingage him blindly to espouse it, so that while he remains no reformation can be hoped for in that office."

Shrewsbury, Sunderland, Godolphin and Trenchard, in fact all of King William's leading ministers, agreed with Somers, yet much as they hated the obstinate and cantankerous old man, they dared not recommend his dismissal. They left the decision to the King. Clayton, however, had lent William III £30,000. He remained in office for a further three years, until, goaded beyond endurance, the ministers secured his dismissal. These merchants were comparable to the Carnegies, Huntingtons and Mellons of the great age of American capitalism. Like them they had their favoured charities. Edward Colston, a Bristol slave trader, besides making vast and generous endowments for schools and almshouses in his native town also left legacies to augment thirty parishes and nineteen charity schools elsewhere, but he hedged about his charities with the utmost care to prevent the possibility of any of his benevolence reaching a dissenter. Such merchants could live on a scale comparable to that of the richest members of the aristocracy. Sir Josiah Child built Wanstead House, the largest residence in England until Vanbrugh completed Castle Howard. "Some merchants," wrote César de Saussure in 1727, "are certainly far wealthier than many sovereign princes of Germany and Italy. They live in great state; their houses are richly furnished, their tables spread with delicacies." They formed an aristocracy of wealth, in many ways as narrow and as exclusive as the aristocracy of birth into which their daughters so frequently married. They were drawn to the government rather than the Court. They were willing to forgo the passions of party strife and throw in their lot with any group of politicians who could give security to an administration. Their natural allies were the courtiers who, like them, preferred to avoid extremes for the sake of stable government. They looked to Godolphin or Harley rather than to Bolingbroke or Wharton, and in Walpole they found a man entirely after their own heart—compliant, unadventurous, careful of the pence—at least in public policy if not in pursuit of his own career. England was prosperous; they were rich; plots, riots, rebellions, and in Walpole's day, even wars, were to be deplored. There was a rich cake and few of them to eat it.

Just as this great but narrow aristocracy of wealth dominated London, so smaller oligarchies dominated the commercial cities of the provinces. Bristol was controlled by its sugar and tobacco magnates and the princes of the slave trade—the Colstons, Days, Yates and Youngs. Hull was firmly in the hands of the Baltic and Dutch merchants, the Maisters, Ramsdens and St Quintins; Newcastle in the hands of the Blacketts, Liddells and Ridleys, the lords of the coal trade. King's Lynn was just as firmly under the sway of Walpole's relatives, the Turners.

King's Lynn thrived in the late seventeenth century. The draining of the fens opened up new, rich farming land whose products found their way down the Ouse. The improvements in its navigation—by 1700 barges could reach Bedford and Cambridge—made the port a convenient entry for much trade to the East Midlands. Until the 1730s when the silting of the harbour led to a sharp decline in its prosperity, King's Lynn enjoyed boom conditions in which many families made their fortunes. Coal, wine, consumption goods of all kinds were shipped through Lynn, and in exchange corn, hides, hay and some woollen goods were exported to home and foreign markets. It was in wine that the Turners had first made their money. John Turner, the son of a Norfolk attorney of modest means, founded his fortune in story-book fashion. Apprenticed to a Cambridge vintner, he married his master's widow and immediately moved to Lynn. There his brother, Charles, was already well established as an attorney. They prospered, indeed they prospered exceedingly. They became aldermen, and were mayors not once but several times. They built splendidly, fine houses for themselves and costly public buildings for the town's comfort and embellishment. In politics they were all discretion. John Turner shared the representation of Lynn with his friend, Samuel Tayler, another vintner; discreetly they avoided the perils of Exclusion politics. Together on their knees they surrendered their town's charter to James II and in return received the accolade. But this did not prevent Sir John from promptly deserting his King for William of Orange in 1689, thereby keeping his seat in Parliament and his control of the borough. As became men of wealth, the Turners planted themselves out in the country, buying estates at Warham, taking others on lease or mortgage at Crostwight and Great Dunham. Sir John, too, had the pleasure of seeing his nephew marry into one of the most important Norfolk families, the Walpoles. It was natural that so distinguished a nephew should join him in the representation of Lynn and add to the family honours by becoming a baronet. By the time he was seventy, Sir John had the satisfaction of knowing that his family had no rival in Lynn; feeling his age and knowing his place, he readily resigned his seat, as soon as it was demanded of him, to Walpole; without the Turner influence Walpole would never have enjoyed the complete security of tenure of his seat in Parliament. By wealth and by persistent attention to local politics, the Turners, in alliance with families into which they married, became as powerful and as unassailable as the Childs or Batemans in London.

"The vested interests of these families," writes their historian, "stretched like the tentacles of an octopus in, over and around the entire life of the borough in all its aspects—commerce, politics, customs, law, all fell within their compass."

These great merchants, metropolitan and provincial, acquired so much power and so much wealth, that it induced in them great caution, a desire to avoid change, and a passionate adherence to any administration which avoided risk. Subservient to authority they deplored the buccaneering spirit which had created, and was creating, that vast revolution in trade in which the strength and greatness of England lay.

Broadly speaking, these men lacked passion in politics, they were close kin to the Vicar of Bray and moved from discreet toryism to discreet whiggery as occasion demanded. For them Walpole's ministry, once established, was all excellence. It offered years of untroubled security and peace. Their contentment was disturbed only by their own colleagues.

Some merchants, some of the very richest, were not content with Walpole's world. They were restless for greater power and greater wealth. They were happy in Marlborough's war, distressed by Utrecht, and in the 'twenties and 'thirties bewildered by Walpole's forbearance to France and Spain. They were alive to the opportunities of their age. Many were truculent, courageous, aggressive men like "Diamond" Pitt, Chatham's grandfather, who defied the East India Company, damned its monopoly of trade, and made a couple of fortunes before he was thirty. The early eighteenth century offered glorious opportunities for quick wealth. England's trade had expanded with great rapidity towards the end of the seventeenth century; not only was it brisk in exports, but the favourable trade balance stimulated the home market and home industries. There were insufficient outlets for capital investment and this gave rise to extravagant projects long before the South Sea Bubble. In consequence there was money, and money to spare, for exotics, and the consumption of tea, coffee, chocolate, new muslins and calicoes from the East rose quickly. Men in commerce or industry profited most and the gentry with high taxes and insecure rents least; and it was natural that the appetite of traders and manufacturers should be whetted. The expansion of English wealth could not proceed too rapidly for them. They were impatient of any foreign policy which curbed their aggressive spirit; they hated the great chartered companies from which they were excluded; they undermined the Elizabethan legislation which protected their journeymen from exploitation. They were impatient of authority, hence their natural sympathies were whig, although they were opposed to Walpole who, they felt, betrayed their interests by the appeasement of Spain and friendship with France. Many of them, particularly provincial merchants, were drawn to those forms of protestantism which encouraged individual judgment. And amongst them, too, lingered the puritan attitude to life with its stress on plain living, thrift and hard work, for the most aggressive merchants were of the middling sort. And, as is natural with men, they were not above denouncing the morals and fashions of those from whom their wealth was derived.

We are fond of French clergymen, French goods and French fashions though mere trifles, shittlecocks and gewgaws. No inventions please us unless they be French-made, and, like their apes, we imitate their garb and their housekeeping. Their toothdrawers and their barbers are our admired surgeons. We are mad upon French music, French players, French misses, French danceing-masters, French language, French airs, French legs, French hats, French grimaces and compliments.

Barnes and his kind hated the luxury of the Court and the corruption of government, for they deplored its sophistication. They busied themselves with the morals of the poor whose discipline and capacity for honest toil meant so much to them. They concerned themselves with the social content of religion, giving warm support to all religious societies bent on the reformation of manners. Some extended their benevolence to include the support of charity schools where small boys were taught the elements of book-keeping and girls those of domestic service. Aggressive, suspicious, hard-fisted, relentless in the pursuit of wealth, they were the sinews of England's trade.

They were, of course, a large and amorphous class, lacking the unity and self-consciousness of the aristocracies of birth or wealth, or even of the gentry; thus their attitude to politics, although coherent on the broad issues, became less predictable on specific questions. As most of them were freeholders, they created the factor of uncertainty in those parliamentary elections which could not be controlled by patronage. Because they were literate and had leisure to read, they were the target for the stream of political propaganda which poured from the Press. As far as there was a public opinion, they, with the gentry, formed it. Because of the fascination of the art of patronage and political management, their significance for eighteenth-century politics has been overlooked by recent historians. Yet the struggle for their support gives life, vitality and meaning to political history of the eighteenth century.

Still nothing has been said of the mass of the population. Here again there were fine gradations of wealth and rank from the prosperous shopkeepers and craftsmen to the day labourer, from the upper servants to the casual weeders in the garden. But their lives are submerged and must be reconstructed indirectly from newspapers, police and poor-law records, wage assessments, wills and inventories, an occasional letter and even more rarely a diary or autobiography. More vividly their lean faces and hollow eyes stare at us from the savage satires of Hogarth. It was a life of great insecurity and only those who were hardworking, thrifty, cunning and lucky survived. The ease and wellbeing of the majority of working men varied in direct relation to the fluctuations of harvest and trade. Hours were long, wages far from high but food in good years was plentiful and cheap; more often than not there was an abundance of work. Even so men and women could starve to death in the very heart of London. Disease flourished in the overcrowded and insanitary conditions in which they lived; death was frequent and sudden, a common visitor to youth as well as age, and a lover of children. And yet there was an atmosphere of prosperity.

"They eat well," Defoe wrote of the mass of the population in 1728, "and they drink well; for their eating (*viz.*) of flesh meat, such as beef, mutton, bacon, etc., in proportion to their circumstances, 'tis to a fault, nay, even to profusion; as to their drink, 'tis generally stout strong beer, not to take notice of the quantity which is sometimes a little too much, or good table beer for their ordinary diet; for the rest, we see their houses and lodgings tolerably furnished, at least stuffed well with useful and necessary household goods: Even those we call poor people, journeymen, working and pains-taking people do thus; they lye warm, live in plenty, work hard, and (need) know no want."

Furthermore in London, and perhaps in Bristol and Norwich, they were exceptionally free from restraint. There was no police force in the modern sense, the power of the Church to enforce social discipline was greatly decayed. In the rural communities the authority of squire and parson was more effective. The drift to the towns was partly due to the lack of economic opportunity in the villages but it was also the air of freedom and opportunity and prosperity which lured many a young countryman to London.

Broadly speaking, the bulk of the working population was tory and was to be opposed to Walpole's government. Furthermore they were passionately interested in politics and devoured the newspapers avidly. They were tory because, although there was an opportunity to make money, the conditions of labour were hardening. Their masters, who wanted more and more goods, insisted on longer hours and did whatever they could to destroy what remained of the protective legislation and guild organization of the Tudors and Stuarts. It was natural that the journey-men, like the gentry, should look back to a world in which their position had been more secure. But some of their toryism was due to a hatred of government and authority, a dislike of restraint, and a healthy contempt for an institution which they were convinced was corrupt to the core. They relished the savage attacks on Walpole and the lampoons on the Court. It was their animosity which was to breed in Walpole a hatred of London and brought him to the decision to curb its powers. Yet, though the bulk of the population was tory, it was an old-fashioned, naïve toryism, and not in the least Jacobite.

But there was a part of the working class which was more volatile and dangerous. There was always a large number of men and women in Hanoverian England who lived on the verge of starvation, to whom unemployment meant absolute personal disaster. Their attitude to the government moved directly with the index of prices. Dear corn meant violence and rioting in which plunder was as important as their impotent protest against the hostile world. The rabble in action was a terror to all governments, and yet politicians in opposition never hesitated to provoke them. Their prejudices were deliberately exploited by Bolingbroke and others who were opposed to Walpole. But it was a dangerous weapon and on occasion the cynical use of the mob rallied responsible men to the government's support; a factor, indeed, which was to help Walpole through the dangers of many a crisis. In the countryside the abject poor could for the most part be more easily controlled. They were herded into workhouses or kept alive on a pittance from the parish rates. At times their despair drove them to riot, and mobs gathered in the countryside almost as frequently as they did in towns. On 7 June 1696, Abraham de la Pryme wrote in his diary:

This day I heard of one that is come from Lincoln, that the country people had been up about Stamford, and marched in a great company, very lively, to the house of Sir John Brownley. They brought their officers, constables, and churchwardens amongst them, and as they went along they cryd, "God bless King William, God bless King William" etc. When they were come to Sir John's, he sent his man down to see what their will was, who all answered: "God bless King William, God bless the Church of England, God bless the Parliament, and the Lords Justices, and Sir John Brownley! We are King William's true servants, God forbid that we should rebel against him, or that anything that we now do should be construed ill. We come only to his worship to bisieech him to be merciful to the poor; we and our familys being all fit to starve, not having one penny that will go," etc. Sir John hearing all this (as soon as his man) at a window where he was viewing them, sent them a bagg with fifteen pound in it of old milled money, which they received exceeding thankfully, but sayd the sum was so little, and their number and necessitys so great, that they feared it would not last long, therefore must be forced out of their necessity to come see him again, to keep themselves and their familys from starving. Then they desired a drink, and Sir John caused his doors to be set open and let them go to the cellar, where they drank God bless King William, the Church of England, and all the loyal healths that they could think on, and so went their ways.

No doubt they hoped to get more money and more drink from the neighbouring landowners. This was an astutely led mob which made full economic advantage of its implied threat of violence. Fears of destruction of their wealth often caused landowners, merchants and manufacturers to adjust wages rapidly or to display a hasty benevolence. Such victories kept alive the rural mobs and in Walpole's old age they were as common as in his youth. In the summer of 1735 the poor of Gloucestershire and Herefordshire revolted, tore down turnpikes, and threatened the countryside. The gentry assembled and made what was called "a becoming opposition," but they were too weak to win a victory and troops had to be dispatched before the countryside was pacified. Violent mobs, urban as well as rural, induced a sense of apprehension in the upper classes; the fear of anarchy put a high premium on authority and made the longing for political stability more intense. The main political effect of the restlessness of the poor was to help take off the edge of controversy amongst the property-owning classes. There were squires of Bray as well as vicars who were just as willing to give their allegiance to any power which could prove itself strong enough to maintain its authority. Fear of the consequences had a tonic effect on the national genius of compromise.

3.

Professor Hans Rosenberg (1904–   ), of the University of California at Berkeley, analyzes the social composition of the Prussian bureaucracy in the critical period of Prussia's early development as a strong state. How did Frederick William I view these officials? He enjoyed slandering and vilifying them. That manners in northern Germany were coarse and cruel might be true, but there were other reasons for treating these bureaucrats like domestic servants. The bureaucrats of Brandenburg-Prussia were not much more than servants insofar as esteem and status went. Charged with collecting taxes, keeping accounts, and doing other paperwork, they were social inferiors who were on the rise through princely favor.

Why did the Electors not turn to the nobility itself to perform these services? The nobles were more influential than the bureaucrats in the countryside. What were the attitudes of the nobility toward education?

Frederick William the Great Elector—like Louis XIV, William III, Frederick III of Denmark, Charles XI of Sweden, and Peter the Great—relied on commoners for the crucial, intimate aspects of making policy. This fact would indicate that the nobilities of Europe could still threaten or thwart royal power. Did the commoner-bureaucrats continue generation after generation to remain socially inferior? How did their rise indirectly strengthen European nobilities?

HANS ROSENBERG: The Composition of the New Bureaucratic Elite: Prussia*

Who, then, were the "new bureaucrats" who gave administrative form to the absolute monarchy and gradually reduced the old line officials to a subsidiary position? It is impossible to identify precisely the personnel of this managerial elite. Its members were hard-pressed commissars, councilors, board presidents, and ministers, who were occasionally lifted up by a word of appreciation but were, far more frequently, called by their suspicious, explosive, and exacting employers "fools, stupid devils, idiots, dogs, school boys, crooks, thieves, scoundrels, rebels, rascals."[1]

The available printed records, despite their abundance and factual richness, contain many gaps and pitfalls. The blurring of *officier* and *commissaire* status; the tenure of multiple positions by a single person, the reappearance of the same man, not always identifiable by name, in different departments; the conferment and sale of official titles unaccompanied by commissioned duty; the persistence of absentee jobs and sinecures even in the new executive service—such practices preclude exact quantitative measurement.

No less difficult is the gauging of qualitative factors, such as the determination of educational group or subgroup attributes. For instance, many civil bureaucrats who came from the native nobility had previously received a "university education." Actually, these select noble children who registered as university students, usually at the age of fourteen or fifteen, hardly went through a modest secondary school curriculum, even if they were uncommon enough to concentrate on their studies. To obtain an academic degree was such a rare oc-

---

* From Hans Rosenberg, *Bureaucracy, Aristocracy, and Autocracy, The Prussian Experience, 1660–1815* (Cambridge: Harvard University Press, 1958), pp. 57–73.

[1] Frederick William I, noted for his coarse language and merciless butchering of German grammar and spelling, added other vilifying appellations to this list, "nicknames" such as *"Erzfickfacker, Konfusrat, Galgenschelm, miserabler Schurke, Köter, Kanaille, Retinent, verfluchter Blagkscheisser,"* words which are difficult or impossible to translate into English. See *Forschungen*, XXX (1918), 43–44; *A.B.B.*, II, 130ff.; III, 164; VI, 2, 739. The Great Frederick, great also as a temperamental expert in name calling, was, like his father, not overly inclined to give a clean bill of moral health and professional fitness to the "lazy and idiotic war councilors who, unfortunately, are numerous in all boards" and only too often prove to be "vile human trash who steal like magpies." "Among one hundred war councilors ninety-nine always deserve to be hanged, for if a single honest man is among them it is much." See *A.B.B.*, VII, 563, 617; XV, 363; *Preussische Jahrbücher*, CXXX (1907), 286.

currence that it almost implied conduct unbecoming a nobleman. Less exacting methods of asserting social exclusiveness were preferred.

The prevocational training of the intellectual *haute volée* of the Junker nobility was no better. It provided highborn students of law with a smattering of the rudiments of this discipline. The "culture" produced by the lengthy "cavalier's tour" through France and Italy, and now and then also Holland and England, was no less superficial. Only too often this splendid opportunity simply took the rough edges off rustic squire scions, endowed them with snobbish manners, and taught them the courtly arts of debauchery.

Throughout the formative period of Hohenzollern absolutism from 1660 to 1740, the Prussian nobles as a group stood far below their south German and Austrian "class equals" in cultural refinement. In the straightforward judgment of Frederick William I, himself but slightly touched by Germany's ancient *Kultur,* the "vassals" of his north Rhenish principalities were "dumb oxen but as malicious as the devil"; they "drink like beasts, and this is all they know."

As a matter of fact, until the mid-eighteenth century the expansion of dynastic state service lowered the educational level of the Junkers. Since the traditional education was expensive, this deterioration was partly a consequence of the great economic depression which had been particularly persistent in Brandenburg and Pomerania. But in the long run more important was the rise of the "Royal Prussian Army" with its very modest entrance and promotion requirements for men of noble origin. After some initial hesitation, the new poor among the wellborn in the heartlands of the Hohenzollern monarchy seized the military job opportunities which gave a fresh lease on life to illiterate noble boys, landless noble bumpkins, unemployed nobles returned from service in foreign armies, and impoverished or bankrupt squires with little or no formal education.

For a quarter of a century after 1680, this social movement was checked by heavy competition. The sudden immigration of aristocratic Huguenots after the repeal of the Edict of Nantes—by 1688, 29 per cent of the "Prussian" military officers were Frenchmen—and, then, the short-lived practice of promoting numerous commoners to commissioned rank restricted the openings for the Junker nobility. Some of its members now had to be content to serve many years as simple privates or noncommissioned officers.

The turn of the tide came with "the soldiers' king." He methodically neutralized the political restlessness, allayed the fears, and reconciled most of the Junker clans to the growth of autocratic central power by inviting the noble "reserve army" to regain a secure and highly honored position in society by joining the ranks of the professional military service aristocracy.

Many of these experts in local tyranny were experienced in whipping the backs, hitting the faces, and breaking the bones of "disrespectful" and "disobedient" peasant serfs. Thus they were eminently fitted to be the drillmasters of common Prussian soldiers who, as Frederick II envisaged their proper status, should "fear their officers more than any danger to which they might be exposed." The outdoor relief provided by the rapid growth of the "all-Prussian" army reduced the pressure for positions in the civil state service, where a certain modicum of formal schooling had become almost indispensable for admission to the higher brackets.

One primary fact emerges from an examination of the credentials and social antecedents of the personnel that converted the administrative mechanism of early Prussian absolutism into a going concern. It was indeed an unusual *mélange* of individuals who managed to enter the evolving elite of "public law bureaucrats." This small band comprised a few dozen men by the end of the 1660's and a few hundred by 1740, when the total population of the Prussian monarchy amounted to two and a half million. Drawn from many walks of life, these social stragglers, when thrown together into the hierarchy of commissioned Hohenzollern servants, suddenly faced each other as professional associates in a joint enterprise. Collectively, they formed a distinct functional status group. As individuals, however, they differed sharply among themselves in class origin, educational and occupational background, personal ability and achievement, the amount and sources of income, and, consequently, also in their tastes, attitudes, loyalties, and modes of living.

Under the Elector Frederick William, the most noteworthy component of this service class, in numbers, prestige, and ease of opportunity, consisted of indigenous nobles. Prior to their appointment as councilors or commissars, these "new men" had been judges, courtiers, army officers, plain squires and agricultural entrepreneurs, or young university students. These Junker elements were joined by noble immigrants, attracted by the career prospects of the rapidly growing Hohenzollern dominions, who had previously been employed by other German potentates or by the rulers of France, Austria, and Sweden, the three countries which most influenced the early development of the institutions of Prussian absolutism.

Alongside the beneficiaries of noble pedigrees were some commoners, mostly jurists. Among the Elector's top aides were several bourgeois intellectuals, the former law professors Fuchs, Rhetz, and the Jena brothers, and the son of an obscure tax collector, Franz Meinders, a student of the classics who likewise was thoroughly familiar with the literary and learned culture of contemporary France.

The social sources for replenishing the upper layers of the administrative bureaucracy broadened under Frederick William's successor. Though he was destined to become the first Prussian king, Frederick I was anything but a monocrat. The political confusion and the unstable social relations which marked the "interregnum" from 1688 to 1713 provided an excellent opportunity for the pushing and thriving dynastic servants to learn to stand on their own feet. Unhampered by effective royal control, they filled up their swiftly growing membership mainly by coöptation. But the gates of admission were not closed to new social elements.

Little men who had started out in Prussian government employment as office clerks, tax collectors, or cashiers, men like Levin Schardius and Christian Schöning, now got their chance of being elevated to the higher ranks. No less significant was the influx of self-made merchants and business entrepreneurs. The most outstanding member of this tiny subgroup was Johann Andreas Krautt who died, in 1723, as a minister of Frederick William I and, next to his sovereign, the richest man in Berlin.

Throughout the inconclusive political interlude from 1688 to 1713, the reins of Prussian state power were held, on short tenure, by rival court cliques. The permanently organized bureaucracy acquired massive strength precisely because of the instability and growing dilettantism of political leadership at the center. This indispensable body of executive technicians was then also the guardian of continuity in administrative state activity and, hence, of institutional consolidation. Under these circumstances, the key men of the central government could be career bureaucrats such as the foreign-born and foreign-trained Baron Bodo von Knyphausen and the newly ennobled administrators Meinders, Fuchs, Luben, Krautt, and Ilgen; or they could be lowborn but exceptionally gifted and strategically placed, like the former tutor of the king, Eberhard von Danckelmann; or blue-blooded "political generals" like Barfuss, Dohna, Dönhoff, and Wartensleben; or professional civilian courtiers such as the counts Wartenberg and Wittgenstein.

Significantly enough, not even during the abortive "noble reaction" to the halfway rise of dynastic absolutism which followed Danckelmann's dismissal could the cavalier-directors of the government dispense with the services of social upstarts. They had to share influence and booty with expert members of the regular bureaucracy, with men like Fuchs, Krautt, and Ilgen, with an ex-professor, with an international merchant-banker, and with a former petty official. This situation foreshadowed the flowering of limited competition which made possible the administrative reorganization of the Prussian state under Frederick William I.

When Frederick William I ascended the throne, he found in existence a civil bureaucracy which his careless father had allowed to become a serious contender for supreme power in the dynastic state. Frederick William I, chief designer of the Prussian "style" and indefatigable champion of the garrison state, pursued a personnel policy which both restricted and widened the avenues of appointment to the upper grades of the executive hierarchy. In general, the number of jurists and of "civilian" nobles declined while the ascent of businessmen, petty officials, and noble army officers accelerated. To be sure, former judges and lawyers continued to be a substantial subgroup. Even personalities with scholarly interests, mostly men with Latinized names (Cellarius, Cortrejus, Mylius, Ursinus) were occasionally given prominent positions. Although in general Frederick William held book learning in contempt, two former university professors (Fuchs and Cocceji) managed to rise to the rank of minister. But relative to the meteoric advance of the "cameralists" and of the military elements, the jurists lost importance in a system of state management which was dominated by fiscal and military considerations. Hence many of the newly nominated councilors were businessmen, who had made a place for themselves in trade, industry, mining and, above all, large-scale farming before they became "royal servants." These men of affairs who knew how to produce, what Frederick William I admiringly called a "plus," signified the intensified drive for efficiency.

Another group of favored commoners was made up of men who were lifted by the grace of their king from positions as bureaucratic subalterns. Posts of trust and profit were occasionally accessible to former municipal officials and, more frequently, to clerks thoroughly familiar with technical detail and the routines of "red tape" who were able enough to run an office or to direct a field branch.

Among the clerical employees and petty functionaries of the Prussian government of the eighteenth century were many who were subordinates in official rank only. In fact, these inferiors surpassed many of their nominal superiors in education, vocational skills, and executive ability. Men of such caliber often did the real work for which the high-ranking officials took credit. Yet, the Prussian Old Regime, in matters of professional careermaking and advancement in social status, provided infinitely better opportunities to gifted "subalterns" than the far more restrictive personnel practices of the "progressive" nineteenth century, which made it impossible, in law and in fact, to pass from the lower to the upper grades of the civil service.

Particularly striking features of the recruitment and promotion policies under Frederick William I were the heavy influx of military bureaucrats and the curb on the career prospects for the old nobility who had no special connections and were not army officers. Both Frederick William I and Frederick II filled many of the non-noble upper positions in the civil administration with *Regiments-quartiermeister,* the successors of the old "march commissars," and with *Auditeure,* military judicial officials. These army functionaries, often men with some legal training, were professional administrators. They were not, however, "civilians in uniform," for their stiffly authoritarian mentality, their conceptions of efficiency, leadership, and obedience had been molded in close association with senior members of the army officers' corps and in the image of the grim Prussian military service regulations. For this very reason these men were transferred to permanent positions in the civil state service.

The War and Domains Board of Brandenburg, as of 1767, furnishes a representative sample of the relative position which militarized commoners and former petty officials came to occupy in the upper ranks of the bureaucracy. Of the twenty-three councilors, five had previously served as *Auditeure.* One was a former sergeant major, while five others had risen from the lower grades of the regular administrative hierarchy.

The employment of professional soldiers and ex-soldiers in the civil branches of the government also became a methodically pursued policy in the eighteenth century. This entailed a fourfold utilization of military manpower for non-military functions. In the first place, noble army officers, because they were expected to set a model for blind obedience and quick action, were transferred to ranking posts in the regular administrative service. Secondly, trusted staff officers and generals were often appointed members or chairmen of special royal committees and boards and given temporary assignments or commissions with special powers, whether only of report or of decision and executive action. These tasks frequently included the obligation to "investigate" civilian functionaries. Thirdly, the military exercised a strong influence in urban administration. Regular army officers sat on municipal committees, usually as chairmen. In garrison towns the military commander regulated the local retail trade and fixed, in coöperation with the *Steuerrat,* the prices of basic foodstuffs. Finally, numerous subordinate posts in the civil bureaucracy were set aside in place of a pension for the upkeep of uneducated noble soldiers and of nonnoble noncommissioned officers who had lost their physical fitness for active military service and who were without private income.

With the formation of large administrative and military bureaucracies, a delicate and unstable balance was struck in government employment between commoners and the heirs of superior social rank. It was generally characteristic of the rising absolute monarchies that a considerable percentage of the "new bureaucrats" was supplied by "illborn" persons and, except for France, also by foreign, in preference to native, nobles. Men of such defective background were more dependent upon, and therefore more obedient to, the royal authority.

The diverse composition of the executive elite of the Hohenzollerns reflected, in accord with this continental trend, the bewildering currents of social mobility. However, the gathering of a "Prussian" staff of professional administrators under monarchical control did not involve a sudden or radical break with the past when almost only men with long pedigrees had access to the spoils of "public service." A more flexible policy had gained ground in parochial Brandenburg during the first half of the seventeenth century. Almost all the members of the elector's privy council, founded in 1604 to circumvent the influence of Junkerdom, were either foreign noblemen or commoners. Yet it was here that the ancient *status quo* was restored on the eve of the transition to monarchical absolutism by reserving the majority of all significant government positions for native nobles. The reorganization of the privy council, in 1651, was preceded by a social purge. In 1640, the ratio of nonnobles to nobles in the council had been five to three. A decade later it was only one to five. Of the thirty-four privy councilors appointed from 1653 until 1687, only seven were commoners. Some of the latter, moreover, felt themselves suppressed and stigmatized by their ancestor-conscious colleagues. The relative position of the lowborn in the upper ranks of the General War Commissariat was stronger, if not only the War Commissars proper, but also the *commissarii loci,* the predecessors of the *Steuerräte,* are included in the reckoning. But on the whole, the founder of Prussian absolutism, because of social prejudice, personal preference, and political expediency, set aside the most distinguished civil state employments for nobles of old lineage, mostly Junkers.

Even accurate statistics can be quite deceptive. The numerical preponderance of the "blood nobility" in the councils of Elector Frederick William obscures the fact that after 1660, during the absolutist phase of his career, bureaucrats of middle class origin were his chief political advisers and diplomatic assistants. In the 1640's, a Brandenburgian Junker soldier, von Burgsdorff, had guided his young prince. In the 1650's, Count Waldeck and, then, a Pomeranian noble-man, Otto von Schwerin, served virtually as a one-man "brain trust." But after 1660 the tide turned against the increasingly anachronistic survivors of the old *Ständestaat* regime. During the 1660's, a former university professor, Friedrich Jena, was the "suggesting" deputy prime minister. When his star declined, he gave way to another commoner, Franz Meinders, who held his own for about fifteen years, until he was overshadowed by still another scheming ex-professor, Paul Fuchs.

The numerical balance between the high and lowborn in the civil bureau-cracy was reversed in the course of the first half of the eighteenth century. The political entrepreneurship of Frederick William I turned out to be a golden age for select men of common origin. He created chances for advancement un-matched in Prussian government employment until the 1920's when the Prus-sian state was a stronghold of the Social Democrats. To increase his personal power and to speed up the subjugation of the old official hierarchy; to demon-strate to the titled aristocracy that there were limits to its indispensability; to prevent a sagging of ambitions in the service of the crown, he gave qualified priority to pliable nonnobles in the civil establishments.

Thus, in filling the functionally important positions in the administrative bureaucracy, he largely relied on men who could not boast of ancestors who, even before the Hohenzollerns had settled down in eastern Germany, had been masters of the land. Frederick William I was bent on preventing monarchical absolutism from being a mockery. Like Frederick III of Denmark, Charles XI of Sweden, Louis XIV of France, and Peter of Russia, he was drawn to men he could make and unmake and, therefore, use effectively as tools in the pursuit of a policy of domesticating the native nobility. Hence the "common intruders" were called upon to keep a watchful eye on the predatory *seigneurs,* the Junker *officiers* and the squire judges in the higher courts who, in the past, had banded together in converting a large part of the dynastic patrimony into a wonderful means of making a cavalier-like living. All this, combined with the drive for the raising of professional quality, accounts for the sharply marked ascendancy of social parvenus in the civil state service from 1713 to 1740. . . .

The composition of the civil and military service elites of the Hohenzollern state was indicative of some of the major social changes which crystallized everywhere with the growth of the monarch's personal powers and of bureau-cratic organization on a large scale. Since absolute government and the expan-sion of the dynastic labor market opened up fresh sources of differentiation, the stratification of society grew more complex. By giving rise to novel segments of the governing class, absolutism disturbed and confused the old social system, built on birth and privilege, on hierarchy and hereditary estate distinctions (*ständische Gesellschaft*).

The new civil and military bureaucracies constituted professional classes of great functional and political importance. Hence they were recognized by their creator, the sovereign ruler, as superior status groups. Having like organizational status and a common way of life as "royal servants," they formed two distinct occupational estates (*Berufsstände*), an estate of administrative government officials (*Beamtenstand*) and an estate of military officers (*Offiziersstand*). These hierarchies of appointed and removable dynastic employees did not fit into the neatly defined divisions of the traditional society of northeastern Germany, the essential features of which had been the rigorous partition into hereditary estates (*Geburtsstände*), into closed, caste-like legal classes. In such a society "man was not man"; he was either superior, common, or inferior.

The nobility, being superior to all other groups in power, privilege, and prestige, had formed the First Estate (*Adelsstand*), the upper class. The commoners or burghers, i.e., the permanent town residents subject to municipal law and administration, being only "second class people" in influence and rights, had constituted the Second Estate (*Bürgerstand*), the middle class, inferior to the nobility but superior to the peasantry. At the bottom of the scale had stood the "inferiors," the Third Estate (*Bauernstand*), identical with the rural masses, mostly peasant serfs.

The formation of new upper class strata, made up of the holders of the higher positions in the civil and military bureaucracies, complicated social rankings. But their emergence also reacted on the relations between social stratification and political hierarchy. By their very existence and by virtue of the heterogeneous social antecedents of their personnel, the service estates challenged the complacent illusion that inherited superior status and ownership of a landed estate as such assured the right to rule as well as fitness for leadership and managerial ability.

Even titled aristocrats were now impelled, before they were entrusted with definite duties, to give the impression of competence. This requirement often aroused hurt feelings in the circles of the large landed proprietors, infuriated by any violation of noble privileges, especially where "places" and the "right of the native-born" were at stake.

The competitive struggle for professional advancement and individual social success among the bureaucratic partisans of absolute government gave birth to a type of functionary more opportunistic and more "rational" than the *Ständestaat officier* had been. Within the royal service careful calculation of personal chances and the adoption of rules of behavior designed to outwit and trip up rivals by shrewdness, superior performance, intrigue, or eel-like maneuvering, came to be typical ingredients of "personal ability," "special skills," and "efficiency." For the persevering climber it was not enough to learn self-discipline. He had to make a methodical attempt to appraise his professional colleagues and superiors in terms of their fluctuating "value" and the influence of their relatives, friends, and cliques. In short, he had to be a special kind of social and political arithmetician. He could not get ahead without the favor of prominent influence peddlers in the good graces of the absolute prince, the chief dispenser of power, emoluments, social prestige, and other favors.

The "new bureaucrat," as a social type, was well represented by the aides of Frederick William, the Elector, and of his immediate successor. These restless, intensely selfish men played their cards with cold-blooded efficiency. They were ardent collectors of tips, bribes, and valuable gifts. They had to be unscrupulous, ever suspicious, sharp-witted careerists to come out on top for a while in the turmoil and controversy following the harrowing decades after the Thirty Years' War. The "servants" of King Frederick William I were certainly not superior in intelligence or energy, let alone in forcefulness of personality to the early pioneers, but they had grown conscious of the burdensome proprieties of "Prussian Puritanism."

Although the nobles of descent continued to enjoy great initial advantage, their rise in the official hierarchy was often impeded or blocked by the success-ful competition of "immodest" commoners of some distinguishing personal quality. This trespassing on traditional class functions and monopolies and the ensuing rivalry between nobles and nonnobles were a notable phenomenon only in a little, though extremely important niche of the social order: in the realm of dynastic employment. Here, from the outset, a major problem presented itself, the problem of the compatibility of two coexistent, disparate social ladders of advancement.

In view of this situation, some *modus vivendi* had to be found between the antagonistic claims to social position which arose from the old, simple way of equating noble birth with superior social worth and personal excellence and the new, more individualized and more fluid practice of rating man on the basis of his vocational qualities, political utility, and official grade in the state service.

The ancient social rank order was regulated by inherited privilege, land-ownership, and genealogical considerations. The new service rank order was determined by office, function, and the will of the autocratic prince. In govern-ment employment, official position as a fountain of social esteem and self-respect competed with rank derived from exalted birth. Men of "poor extrac-tion" frequently became the supervisory or commanding officers of old-estab-lished aristocrats.

4.

The main avenue of admission for commoners into the French nobility was the purchased judicial office. Sold by the Crown, these offices, of different ranks and prices, provided an income for their purchasers and also raised their status in society.

Dean Franklin Ford (1920–   ) of Harvard University analyzes the legists' claim to noble status for officeholders and then describes how this claim became a fact. In 1700 nobles of the robe were clearly noble but were still inferior to those nobles of the sword whose families were older and more distinguished by military service. What were the characteristics of each group?

Ford hints at what would happen between 1700 and 1740 in the sentence: "All that was needed was the passage of time." What did time do? What other forces tended to foster a union of the robe and sword? Finally, note how the magistrates acquired land, learned to hunt, and actively played the part of lords in the countryside.

FRANKLIN FORD: **The Magistrate as Nobleman***

The most important single fact about the high robe's nobility in 1715 was that in legal terms there was no longer any doubt about it. Admission to the full social status of gentlemen might still be dependent on individual wealth and marriages rather than on high office alone, although even here the old sentiment that "les conseillers sont nobles et leurs petits-fils gentilshommes" was rapidly becoming meaningless, because so many eighteenth-century councilors were also grandsons of councilors. In any event, recognition of the sovereign court magistrate's nobility rested on an impressive combination of legal bases: fifteenth- and sixteenth-century precedents, pronouncements of the great jurisconsults, and, more recently, the combination of express legislation and judicial confirmation. The course of late seventeenth-century developments in this regard had already led a commentator at the end of Louis XIV's reign to write: "since that time, there is, it seems to me, no longer any excuse for confusing the magistracy with the Third Estate." At the time these words were written, a full century had passed since the Estates General of 1614, when last the high robe had figured among the commoners; the very passage of time had brought its own, in this case exalting, influence to bear in support of a group which had never for a moment relaxed its own pressure for higher honors.

Although direct written evidence of magistral nobility in the medieval period is naturally scarce, there is reason to believe that beginning in the thirteenth century at the latest, certain non-noble legists who had worked their way to the highest ranks in the king's service received royal grants of personal and in some cases hereditary noblesse. The king's informal action in conferring such dignity on an individual robin might have reflected either gratitude, the desire to provide subordinate officials with an example of loyalty's rewards, the administrative necessity of making the judges less vulnerable to the scorn of titled subjects, or a combination of all these motives. In the sixteenth century, with the progressive elaboration of legal distinctions in such works as André Tiraqueau's *Tractatus de Nobilitate* and the growing need for precise criteria in tax exemption cases, formal *lettres de noblesse* in favor of high magistrates became increasingly common. Among the papers of the Paris Cour des Aides for 1558, for example, we find letters from Henry II solemnly ennobling "nostre cher et bien amé maistre Nicole Berthe, advocat en nostre Cour de Parlement et demourant en nostre ville de Paris," as a reward for the "bons et agreables services qu'il a par cy devant faitz et fait chacun jour en son estat."

Involved in this and similar cases, however, was a degree of royal caprice, or individual payments for individual favors, which could not indefinitely be reconciled with the organizational needs of a developing government. Beginning with the reign of Henry IV, there was elaborated a complex but nonetheless relatively coherent system for determining questions of noble rank among high robe officers. The key to this system lay in gradations of dignity, that is to say,

* From Franklin Ford, *Robe and Sword* (Cambridge: Harvard University Press, 1953), pp. 59–70, 209–21.

in the differing periods of time and/or number of successive generations which a robe family must have served at a given official level before it could claim full, hereditary nobility. This conception emerges clearly, albeit in negative form, from the great *Règlement des Tailles* of 1600:

It is forbidden that any person assume the title of esquire (*écuyer*) and introduce himself into the corps of nobility, if he has not issued from a father and grandfather who have served the public in certain honorable charges from among those which, according to the laws and customs (*moeurs*) of the kingdom, are capable of initiating nobility.

This, however, was obviously too vague to provide the sort of sharply defined standards needed in cases of dispute. Furthermore the reference to existing "laws and customs of the kingdom" indicated a more or less submerged body of jurisprudence which, along with Henry IV's edict itself, called for the regularizing efforts of contemporary theorists.

Of the latter, I shall here cite only the two most important, partly because they were to become the decisive authorities for later reference, partly because their views reflect not only scholarly care but also a broad acquaintance with how the courts were actually ruling and on what grounds. The first, Jean Bacquet, in his *Droit d'anoblissement,* begins with a distinction between "nobles de race" and "nobles par benefice du Prince," then goes on to classify the latter according to several sub-categories, beginning with those ennobled by letters patent and arriving thereafter at "Estats, Dignitez & Offices." He lists the maîtres des requêtes, the officers of the parlements, chambres des comptes, cours des aides, and the trésoriers généraux de France as functionaries ennobled by their offices. But only at the third generation in such functions can a family be said to have acquired hereditary nobility, or so Bacquet interprets recent decisions by the Paris Cour des Aides in tax cases. This was the principle to which the legists had assigned one of their cherished phrases from Roman law: "Patre et avo consulibus."

Much more complete than Bacquet was Charles Loyseau, whose *Cinq livres du droit des offices* (Paris, 1610) and *Traité des ordres et simples dignitez* (Paris, 1613) constitute an incomparable fund of information on public functions and nobility as conceived by the early seventeenth century. One of his most important contributions was that of supplying an exact set of terms for distinguishing those functions which he believed to confer immediate, hereditary noblesse from those which carried only personal noblesse for their incumbents during the first two generations. The following officers he recognized as invested with "perfect" nobility the moment they took office: the Great Officers of the Crown (Chancellor, *Connétable, Grand Maître, Grand Chambellan, Grand Amiral, Grand Écuyer,* etc.); those of the Household (*Grand Aumônier, Grand Maître des Cérémonies, Grand Fauconnier, Grand Louvetier,* etc.); members of the Conseil Privé, and hence by extension all presidents of sovereign courts, to whom Loyseau assigns the rank of privy councilors. Also exalted by their offices but entitled to only personal nobility are, among others, the secrétaires du Roy and the councilors of sovereign courts. In the *Cinq livres,* from which the above is extracted, the doctrine of *patre et avo* is not adduced; but Loyseau employs it in his *Traité des ordres,* where he cites councilors of sovereign courts among those officers whose family nobility can become transmissible in the third generation of successive occupancy. The concept is here more precisely defined than in Bacquet; for not only does Loyseau clearly distinguish the offices requiring three generations from those of the higher class, he also cites a rule of either twenty years service or death while in office as the requirement for each generation.

It is not always easy to determine the concrete importance of the legists' theories, inasmuch as later legislation reveals considerable confusion even in official quarters about the very niceties of doctrine which had been set down with such confidence by the jurisconsults. But it would be a grave mistake to assign their writings only academic significance. Down to the end of the old monarchy, one finds them, especially Tiraqueau, Bacquet and Loyseau (as well as the later codifier, La Roque), quoted at length in judicial opinions, beside precedent-making decisions of the courts themselves. In questions of social rank, as in all else, French jurisprudence remained throughout the *ancien régime* an amalgam of Roman formulas, case law, local custom, and legislative texts as reported and expanded by authoritative interpreters.

The weight of theoretical commentaries had thus been placed behind the high robe's nobility very early in the seventeenth century. Succeeding decades saw it further buttressed by a combination of legislative and judicial recognition. In 1639, for example, a special taille law for Dauphiné endorsed the *patre et avo consulibus* rule as a test for transmissible nobility among officers of the Grenoble Parlement, Chambre des Comptes, Cour des Aides (then separate) and Bureau des Finances. It was during the first years of Louis XIV's troubled minority, however, when the Queen Regent and Mazarin were desperately bargaining for political support, that the sovereign courts received their detailed charters of nobility. Hence the 1640's and 1650's were a period of crucial importance for the background of this question.

The basic grant was embodied in an edict of July 1644, which conferred perfect nobility on all presidents, councilors, gens du roi and greffiers-en-chef of the Parlement of Paris. This was quickly followed by similar concessions to Grand Conseil officers in December of the same year and to the Paris Chambre des Comptes in January 1645. The extension of these privileges to other sovereign courts arose out of the Fronde crisis, or rather out of the efforts of Anne of Austria and her minister to liquidate it. . . .

All this detailed legislation is apt to leave a confused impression on the modern reader's mind, as indeed it often did on a seventeenth-century Frenchman's, especially after the inevitable revocations and subsequent confirmations under Louis XIV had done their baffling work. It will be noted, for example, that most of the royal declarations cited above had initially conferred perfect nobility on all specified courts in the first generation, momentarily passing over Bacquet's and Loyseau's treasured formula of *patre et avo consulibus*. A general edict of 1669 restored the third generation rule for councilors and below; but this in turn was rescinded by another edict in 1690, only to be re-established in

August 1715, so that the old requirement was technically in force, though actually seldom mentioned, during the period under examination. This sort of confusion, however, while characteristic of legislation under the *ancien régime,* should not obscure the central fact that by 1715, whatever uncertainties about technical points might arise in borderline cases, there remained no question that practically all officers of sovereign courts were, in the eyes of the law, noblemen beyond a shadow of doubt.

Official proof of this appears in the results of Louis XIV's Grande Recherche concerning fraudulent claims of rank. In Toulouse, for example, I have examined eleven cartons of *Jugements d'usurpation de noblesse* imposed by the intendant, Lamoignon de Basville, between 1697 and 1716, without finding a single case of a high robe officer thus condemned. In the parallel series of *Jugements de maintenue,* on the other hand, there are mentioned innumerable officers of the Parlement of Languedoc, the Chambre des Comptes at Montpellier and the Cour des Aides at Montauban—all confirmed in their nobility.

It is perhaps worth re-emphasizing at this point what I have already had cause to indicate: that the two thousand or more sovereign court officers in service when Louis XIV died were by no means the only functionaries who had benefited from the theoretical writings, legislation, and investigators' decisions just described. They and their predecessors had conquered the legal status of noblemen during the seventeenth century in company with the maîtres des requêtes, the presidents of bureaux des finances and their subordinate *trésoriers de France,* and the superior officers of the Châtelet at Paris. Technically, they shared their rank with the hundreds of secrétaires du roy, holders of *charges sans fonction,* whose noblesse had been established as early as 1484 in a sweeping pronouncement by Charles VIII. Finally, there was the special category of nobles de cloche or municipal officials ennobled as *maires, échevins* or *capitouls* of the *bonnes villes,* which in the eighteenth century still included Poitiers, Angoulême, St-Maixent, Tours, Toulouse, Lyon, Angers and Nantes.

Enough has been said of the sovereign courts' special rôle, however, so that it scarcely seems necessary further to justify looking more closely at their members' peculiar position in the French aristocracy. For now that they are solidly placed within the boundaries of noblesse as defined by law, there arises the problem of defining distinctive rather than common characteristics. In other words, where did the high robe of 1715 fit into the whole nobility and in what respects was it set apart?

As a nobleman, the *parlementaire* (using this term in its eighteenth-century sense to denote any sovereign court officer) enjoyed all the standard privileges. . . . In addition, however, he had special rights which he did not share with non-robe noblemen. As a royal councilor he benefited from the privilege of committimus, which empowered him to carry personal litigations either directly to a parlement or, if he was a member of the Paris Parlement, all the way to the king's own privy council—in other words, ironically enough, above the jurisdiction of his own court. Once he had served twenty years in office, he could obtain royal *lettres d'honoriat* which even after his resignation would assure him free access to the palais de justice, admission to his old court's deliberations, and retention of his professional titles and honors.

Some fiscal exemptions were so narrowly confined to the parlementaire as to appear forms of political blackmail paid by the government. He was exempt from a wide range of feudal dues collected by the crown, including the *lods et ventes* which the non-robe noble ordinarily still paid for royal permission to sell any portion of a fief. And the royal declaration of September 1723, which announced the famous tax on offices, land grants, and commercial privileges "à cause de l'Avénement du Roi à la Couronne," specifically excused all officers of the parlements, chambres des comptes, Grand Conseil, cours des aides, and cours des monnaies. From a purely fiscal point of view, it is not difficult to see why high robe office might appear attractive even to a member of the wealthier aristocracy. The parlementaires had achieved a position of special privilege within the ranks of the privilégiés themselves.

The question of the extent to which a high robe magistrate thought, looked, and acted like the typical nobleman quite naturally suggests a second question: whether or not there *was* any special manner in which a typical nobleman had to think, look, and act. Enough has been said of the internal diversity of the sprawling noble class to suggest caution in positing any "typical" characteristics, except for legal recognition as noble and a general set of prerogatives. The list of attributes which were essential parts of the concept "living nobly" is undoubtedly much shorter than some writers have assumed. It was not necessary that a family have a *devise,* such as the Beaumanoirs' "J'aime qui m'aime" or the Pontecroix' more cryptic "Naturellement," in order to qualify as gentle. Some, of course, had proudly retained medieval or at least medieval-sounding war cries, such as the Montmorency's "Dieu aide au premier baron chrétien!" or the Levis' singularly unoriginal "Dieu aide au second baron chrétien!" But a president or councilor could and generally did eschew these more bizarre vestiges of chivalry. Similarly, although he duly registered his escutcheon in the *Armorial général,* he was on solid enough ground not to feel called upon to fabricate, as did more than one enthusiastic noble de race, a fantastic genealogy to prove his descent from a Roman emperor, a Greek or Biblical hero, or a Germanic king.

No precise code of dress was at work to unify the nobility in its external aspects. The history of French sumptuary legislation is long and complex, but the very frequency of legislative enactments forbidding roturiers to use certain types of adornment (there were nine laws concerning furs, silks, laces and jewelry between 1601 and 1667) is the best possible proof of how completely they had been ignored. Nevertheless, a high robe officer stood out from the general populace by the rich materials of his dress, while the rabat at his throat, the frequent though by no means inevitable absence of a sword, and the customarily square cut of his periwig also set him apart from a *noble d'épée,* even after Louis XIV's insistence on the public wearing of robes had become a dead letter.

By 1715, as I shall have cause to note again when examining the evolution of robe families, a substantial percentage of sovereign court officers had obtained prestigious titles by the simple expedient of paying the crown to erect their greatest land holdings into baronies, counties or marquisates. Certain of the highest designations still remained closed to the robe, as to most other nobles. In 1717, for example, there were 12 princes, 53 ducs et pairs, 10 ducs *non pairs,* 11 marshals of France, and 5 cardinals, all of whom could claim titular superiority to the highest placed magistrate. But as a group the personnel of the sovereign courts stood well up in the hierarchy of designations, with their professional titles as an added element of distinction. To a proud chevalier in a truly old family these titles might not constitute perfect gentility; but even before 1715 they were already in the cask and aging. All that was needed was the passage of time.

In their choice of names as in their titles, the magistrates had by 1715 drawn closer to the rest of the noblesse; for the "de" had appeared mysteriously in scores of families. Nevertheless, the characteristic seventeenth-century preference of the robe for Biblical or Roman first names had not yet and in fact never did completely yield to the invasion of François', Philippes and Hyacinthes. In its titles and names, as in most other respects, the high magistracy bore the marks of honor equal to that of all save the highest noblesse de race; but shadings of difference had by no means wholly disappeared.

The change in the high robe's way of life, destined to bring it progressively closer to that of other aristocrats in the eighteenth century, was already adumbrated in the era of Louis XIV's passing. Already the more facile presidents, councilors, and gens du roi had begun to make their mark in salon society and to display the skill in conversation, gaming, and lovemaking which that society demanded. Even on the rougher side of noble mores certain of the younger magistrates had begun to take their place. Their participation in the dangerous pastime of dueling had already drawn an expression of Louis XIV's wrath, directed specifically against *gens de robe.* Hunting, the noble's sport par excellence, was becoming more and more accessible to magistrates as they extended their landholdings ever farther into the broad, wooded fiefs of rural France. Yet care must be taken not to read into the individual practices of certain robe nobles the one-sided victory of the seventeenth-century fighting noble's way of life. That way of life was already moribund as an absolute standard for aristocratic living, and for the upper nobility at least, another was taking shape, one in which the high robe was to contribute almost as much as it absorbed.

Did the high robe think as other nobles thought? Again a question which perhaps suggests too much solidarity among the rest of the noblesse. In 1715, however, there were certain marked differences between the magistral mind, as it is revealed in letters, memoirs and judicial minutes, and that of such articulate nobles de race as Saint-Simon, Dangeau, and Boulainvilliers. Both groups had a keen sense of privilege and the desire to protect it. Both were resentful of ground lost under Louis XIV and eager to make the most of the opportunity offered by his death. But in the case of the robe the bourgeois roots were too deep not to call forth a strong *rentier's,* businessman's reaction to the fiscal crisis confronting the new government, while the nobles d'épée with only a few exceptions favored sacrificing investors by declaring the crown bankrupt. The seventeenth-century strain of Jansenism was still strong in the magistracy—probably stronger than it was by the 1730's when it became a major political issue for the sovereign courts. Hence the religious and moral tenets of the robe could not fail to be considerably different, more austere, self-conscious, personalized, than those of a Jesuit-trained noble de race. Of differences in mental outlook enough evidence will emerge for the years just after 1715 to make the subsequent drawing together a truly striking development.

Taken as a whole, the names, titles, dress, habits and daily pursuits of the sovereign court officers in 1715 combined to form a pattern quite different from that of a non-robe noble living nobly. Some magistrates still worked hard, albeit at a profession which carried no reflection on their nobility. Even a marquis or count with several seigneuries and a good pack of hounds for his vacations in the country was not apt to be confused with retired colonels or the ruffled heirs of territorial houses as long as he was also called "Monsieur le Conseiller," was named Marc-Achille or Jean-Baptiste, wore a rabat and flat dark hat in town, and during several months of the year went early each morning to his duties at the palais. Only when these characteristics become less clear-cut, in the course of the eighteenth century, can one speak of increasing social assimilation.

The heightened social standing of the magistrates could scarcely fail to be reflected in their own attitudes and manner of living. First of all, by the 1740's they no longer poured forth those elaborate polemics against the noblesse d'épée which had appeared in abundance under Louis XIV and until the prestige conflicts of the Regency had subsided. Gone from public debate were the bombastic claims of robe superiority and the heavy scorn which once had sought to conceal the defensive insecurity beneath an aggressive surface.

Not that the hauteur of the robe had become any less pronounced. Professional pretensions had in some instances reached ridiculous heights, as revealed in the Portail correspondence of 1731 to 1740 concerning the claims of the first presidents to be styled "Monseigneur," even by princes of the blood. And the parlementaires of Brittany modestly described themselves as the "chevaliers de Malte de la robe." This pride, however, was no longer the by-product of resistance to pretensions of the sword. The high robe was more and more inclined to take for granted its own nobility and to direct its aspersions at groups below itself.

In this respect, the general attitude of the magistrates had come to coincide with First President Brulart's reference to the town officers of Dijon, "ces bourgeois . . . sans autorité et sans considération."[1] I have already noted that sovereign court remonstrances embodied aristocratic attacks on newly risen financiers. When the Parlement of Languedoc lashed out in 1720 at "cette abondance chez des hommes que nous avons vu s'elever parmi nous et qui nous etoient jusqu'a lors inconnus,"[2] it was speaking for an established nobility against a pressure which was as menacing in the social sphere as was royal policy

[1] These bourgeois . . . without authority and unrespected.

[2] This affluence among men whom we have seen rising among us and who were unknown to us until then.

in the political. Common enmities were doing their work of strengthening common interests.

Hand in hand with this shift in class outlook went changes in the magistracy's way of life which stemmed partly from the desire to conform to older aristocratic standards, especially in seigneurial living, but which also reflected the robe's assimilation of and reciprocal influence upon the rules of a more elegant urban society. Bastard d'Estang has left an admiring account of a typical sovereign court officer's daily routine: early audiences at the palais, mass by the company's chaplain, commission meetings, study of evidence and precedents relating to cases on the docket, editing of arrêts, visits to prisons, distribution of alms, and perhaps a quiet supper at home, followed by an evening spent in sober contemplation of the Roman law or some classic author. This Spartan regime, however, though it may still have applied to a few of the most conscientious among early eighteenth-century presidents and councilors, is hardly the norm revealed in contemporary documents.

Considering the rise in the standards of pleasant living since the crude days of a century earlier, one would scarcely expect the parlementaires to have denied themselves the creature comforts which their economic position made possible. The households described above, in connection with the robe fortune, were designed for something more than the routine Bastard d'Estang portrays. It did not require a cook and two helpers to give the master breakfast before a pre-dawn departure to his chores, nor a maître d'hôtel and several lackeys to set out a volume of Livy for fireside reading when he returned home.

The officers of the Parlement of Paris spent their five months' exile at Pontoise in 1720 amid banquets, gaming, and entertainments both musical and dramatic. The magistrates' chamber music group consisted of the two La Landes (violins), President de Lubert (clavecin), and Councilor Roujault (bass viol), abetted by several hired performers. In the house loaned to him by the Duc d'Albret, First President de Mesmes gave daily feasts for forty or more of his colleagues, with the aid of seafood and creamery products supplied by wagons which were diverted from their normal route to Paris. In this society the premier's hospitality set a standard for emulation; it was unique only in degree.

The bottle and the baize-covered table had a share in more than one eighteenth-century robe nobleman's existence which must have tortured the shades of his Jansenist forebears. In a satirical account of the Dijon parlementaires' adoration of the Christ Child one reads numerous verses such as the following:

> Courtivron comme un arlequin
> Y vint en habit tout de pièces
> Mais n'ayant point trouvé de vin
> Soudain il tomba en faiblesse.[3]

Some of the old frugality lingered in the habits of many cooler magistrates, who now would spend for luxuries but would not join in that wild bravado of

---

[3] Courtivron like a harlequin
Arrived in clothes all in pieces
But having found no wine
Suddenly he collapsed from weakness.

risk which sought to bring battlefield virtues to the baccarat game. "It is said," noted Pöllnitz in the 1730's, "that the jurists are less subject to this contagion." Yet the robe noblemen who had gained admission to salon society could not wholly escape its fads, including that of gambling; and some, including President Hénault, did not even attempt to do so.

Standards of sexual conduct, of course, played a large part in the era's definition of elegant living; and in this department of polite existence the eighteenth-century magistrate showed himself the equal, mistress for mistress, of any other nobleman. The Dijon satire quoted at the top of this page specifies, in execrable rhyme, some professional implications of non-professional appetites:

> Lantenay dit pour mes amis
> Je renverse Loix et Coutumes,
> Mais c'est bien pire, quand il s'agit
> De servir la Blonde ou la Brune.[4]

The judge might, of course, be victim rather than exploiter, as a Bordeaux versifier suggests in warning Président de Pommiers that he is playing the cuckold in favor of his own brother; and in 1726 Président aux Requêtes Lambert de Torigny at Paris, avowed lover of Madame la Première Présidente Portail, had the misfortune to catch from her a fatal case of smallpox. (His ignominious death in the house of her husband made him the object of considerable posthumous sympathy.) In general, however, the robe nobleman seems to have abided by the canons of aristocratic love without suffering any more than its other devotees: Councilor de Brégis could feel honored to see his daughter, Madame d'Averne, become one of the Regent's long series of mistresses; and Councilor Antoine-Nicolas Nicolay de Goussainville, who had "wit, good sense, and a probity which seems ferocious in this century," lived contentedly with Madame Pinon for ten years before his death in 1731.

The evolution of physical appearance is not easy to document; but the various collections of magistral portraits are nonetheless interesting for what they show of the high robe's conception of itself. I have already mentioned the series of Secondats who line the walls of Montesquieu's salon at La Brède. The same gradual change in expression, in pose, and above all in what the subjects wanted shown of their characters impresses the beholder of the long row of paintings in the gallery of first presidents in the Palais de Justice at Toulouse.

Among the manuscripts in the Bibliothèque Méjanes at Aix, one may study a volume showing Jacques Cundier's engravings of first presidents of the Provencal Parlement: Riccio, Beaumont, Chassannée of the early sixteenth century, with their broad, clean-shaven faces and close-cropped hair; Maynier and Foresta, with the pointed, Italianate beards of the 1550's to 1580's; du Vair, glowering from behind his square "Navarre whiskers" in 1600; the two For-

---

[4] Lantenay says, "For my friends
  I upset Laws and Customs,
  But it's much worse, when it's a matter
  Of bringing out the Blond or the Brunette."
  [This last line is a pun on the colors of the ladies' hair and the colors of ale.]

bins, L'Aisné, and Bernet, stubborn countenances adorned with mustachios and goatees of the Richelieu era; Marin, with the small Ludovican mustache and hair in long, soft curls; and finally the Le Brets, father and son, with calm yet haughty faces, clean-shaven, wigged with heavy perukes of the early eighteenth century. Had Cundier gone beyond the Regency period, he would have shown a final stage which is to be seen elsewhere: the less formidable, more refined features of Louis XV portraiture, with smooth powdered hair and perhaps an artificial mole at one corner of the mouth. The older professional virtues of equity, sternness, and somewhat ponderous honesty had yielded to other qualities which the eighteenth-century magistrate preferred to see looking down from his own likeness: haughty poise, refinement of taste, and sensitivity to forms of expression beyond the reach of roturier comprehension. Cato could scarcely remain as idol where Ovid was enthroned.

After all this discussion of mutations, there still remains the question: what was left of the robe-épée line by mid-century? I have suggested that in the urban society of Paris and the provincial centers having sovereign courts it had become socially blurred and politically all but meaningless. In published writings of nobles de race—admittedly, these literate ones were the most likely to be on cordial terms with magistrates—it survived in only a handful of atypical passages reminiscent of Saint-Simon's diatribes. In rural areas, where jealousy and a desperate clinging to remembered honors combined to keep the hobereaux hostile, it still produced bad feeling, but bad feeling directed primarily against the officers of the scattered lower courts. So far as the high robe was concerned, in other words, within what I have called the politically significant aristocracy, its external marks were scarcely visible save at Versailles.

There, in the king's immediate surroundings, were still to be found special honors reserved to the oldest noblesse de race or the greatest among nobles d'épée, regardless of lineage. Sovereign court officers, it is true, now appeared in those surroundings with growing frequency. The first president of the Parlement of Paris had New Year's dinner with Louis XV and the princes of the blood in 1725, for example; and he was one of the 120 noblemen who had places on the official roster of "Logement du Château de Marly" that year and again in 1731. Such magistrate-diplomats as Claude-Antoine Boquet de Courbouzon (councilor at Besançon) or Councilor de Chateauneuf of the Paris Parlement (ambassador successively to Portugal, the Sublime Porte, and Holland) came and went in the royal establishments with perfect ease.

Nevertheless, they suffered from certain disabilities which survived as long as the old monarchy itself. For example, they might hold administrative offices attached to the royal Ordre du Saint-Esprit and in such cases were authorized to wear a distinctive variant of the cordon bleu; but in the rolls of regular Chevaliers du Saint-Esprit there was not one high robe officer inscribed in the eighteenth century. Similarly, the 323 persons listed by the Petite Écurie at one time or another between 1715 and 1748 as eligible to ride with the king in his own carriage included the princes and princesses of the blood, most of the peers, marshals, the highest ministers, and numerous army officers, but no regular member of a sovereign court. D'Aguesseau and Chauvelin had their "entrées de carrosse" as ministers, not as former magistrates. Carré points out that in the 1780's the wives of robe officials were still staying away from the court because they could not be honored with the king's (ceremonial) kiss—only with a "simple greeting."

These, however, were gauzy barriers indeed. The condescension of courtiers, like the resentment of hobereaux, counted for little in the position of the high robe as dramatized in the various settings which had real importance for the class: in public ceremonies, in the salons and academies, in the provincial estates, and in the sovereign courts themselves. The line which still existed between the robe and the sword in the mid-eighteenth century can never be understood purely in terms of ceremonial rules and verbal niceties. It lay much more in the residual margin of difference in ways of life. For as marked as had been the magistracy's assimilation of seigneurial interests and salon manners, there remained certain characteristics peculiar to the parlementaires.

Most obvious of the surviving distinctions were those growing out of the high robe's professional status and organization. No matter how lax a president, councilor or maître des comptes might be about his judicial functions, no matter how inclined to recognize only their prestige value, he was still a titular judge in one of the high courts of French justice. He might never appear except at great ceremonies and might never be seen outside the palais in a robe; but he still wore the rabat above his brocaded waistcoat, still took pride in his official title as well as in his landed one, still jealously guarded his right to sit in a secret assembly which was forbidden ground to the haughtiest non-robe marquis or count. Finally, he had one further attribute which set him apart from most other noblemen: his education.

It would be all too easy to let one's view of magistral education remain fixed on some of its most imposing products: Montesquieu, for example, or Jean Bouhier, président à mortier in the Parlement of Burgundy, student of Greek literature, author of the authoritative *Coutume de Bourgogne,* and predecessor of Voltaire in the Académie Française. One is tempted perhaps to overweight the cases of President de Brosses, Bouhier's younger colleague in Dijon (he entered the Parlement in 1730), historian, geographer, friend of Buffon; President de Valbonnais of the Grenoble Chambre des Comptes, author of the *Histoire du Dauphiné,* member of the Académie Royale des Inscriptions et Belles-Lettres; and Jean II de Castellan, conseiller clerc in the Parlement of Languedoc, son of an old Toulouse robe family, author of *Les antiquités de l'Église de Valence* in 1724, as well as works on jurisprudence.

Even if the above examples must be treated as atypical, however, it is impossible not to be struck by a literary circle such as that which met at Dijon in the 1730's and 1740's: Bouhier and de Brosses, President Legouz de Saint-Seine, Councilors Loppin, Bernard de Blancey, de Migieu, Fevret de Fontette, and Procureur-général Quarré de Quintin (all of the Parlement), Presidents Rigoley de Migeon and Richard de Ruffey of the Chambre des Comptes. In the public library of Dijon, itself founded by the bequest of a Fevret in 1701, one may read Councilor Devoyo's translations from Erasmus and Councilor Jehannin's from Shaftesbury, Councilor Fleutelot's *Voyage en Provence,* and Councilor Bazin's *Remarques sur les auteurs latins.*

These and similar examples elsewhere illustrate the dual nature of robe writing under Louis XV: on the one hand, a faithful continuation of seventeenth-century emphasis on classical commentaries or scholarly histories; on the other hand, a growing admixture of favorite eighteenth-century subjects, such as travel, science, new political ideas, belles-lettres. The same combination is to be seen in the catalogues of robe libraries, some of them huge collections: Valbonnais' at Grenoble, Councilor de La Mare's, Councilor de Chevigny's or President Bouhier's at Dijon, and Montesquieu's, much of it still on its original shelves at La Brède. The transmission of such libraries forms an important chapter in the history of modern French collections, as one realizes when reading the names of principal donors inscribed in the foyer of the Bibliothèque Municipale of Bordeaux: eleven in all, including for this period Jean Jacques Bel (the founder in 1720), Godefroye de Baritault, François de La Montaigne—all councilors in the Parlement of Guienne—President Jean Barbot of the Cour des Aides, and Montesquieu himself. Burgundian Councilor Fevret de Fontette's huge accumulation of prints is one of the richest *fonds* in the Bibliothèque Nationale's Cabinet des Estampes, and Jourdain's *Journal* of eighteenth-century additions to the Bibliothèque Royale is filled with references to acquisitions from such libraries as President Lambert's.

The characteristic subject matter of the new era emerges most clearly, however, from the robe scholars' correspondence. There, in the thick, yellowed bundles, are displayed the omnivorous interest and amazing epistolary productivity which we associate with the Enlightenment. Science and religion, politics and painting, society gossip and literary criticism, all were grist for the letter-writer's mill. Here is Justus Fontanini writing to Valbonnais from Rome, there, Bouhier to the Abbé d'Olivet or to Mathieu Marais (to the latter at least once every fortnight for five years), and there, La Mare to Du Cange, Heinsius or Pierre Gassendi.

The mere citation of *érudits,* though it could be spun out to great length, would still not make clear the whole contrast between robe and sword in terms of literacy. Some members of the noblesse d'épée also wrote, with the learning of Boulainvilliers or the subtlety of Vauvenargues. Boulainvilliers' library too contained thousands of volumes, chiefly history and astrology, while that left by the Marquise de Vielbourg had to be catalogued under 306 subject headings, including theology, Italian history, diplomatic history, geometry, astronomy, and parlementary remonstrances. It is rather in the education of an average noble d'épée in the 1740's, as opposed to that of a typical noble de robe, that evidence emerges of the latter's superiority in this important aspect of both social and political life.

In the Archives Nationales there is a memorandum addressed to the king in 1750 and largely devoted to an appeal to rescue the old aristocracy from a system of education "so neglected, so defective, one can even say so evil, that to it alone must be attributed the paucity of outstanding servants which the state has a right to expect from [the nobility]." In the anonymous writer's view, "the education of youth among us still shows the effects of the grossness of barbarous ages." For a large part of the gentry this gloomy diagnosis was all too accurate. Tutors who would come to remote and perhaps dilapidated manors, there to labor for little beyond board and room, were apt to be at best incompetent and at worst corrupting. The Marquis de Franclieu, having just expelled a tutor for having seduced a chambermaid while completely neglecting his pupils, wrote sadly:

I think things would be different if we could keep our children in the good colleges at Paris, but how can a father of such a family as mine [ten children] arrange to have his children educated far from home?

Even in the wealthier noble families education was apt to be viewed as little more than training in social accomplishments; and a young aristocrat could pass through one of the many Jesuit colleges with nothing to show for it but improved manners, the ability to dance, perhaps the knack of writing bad poetry, and in any case a set of success values considered appropriate to a career at court and in the army. The Marquis de Valfons has left an account of his father had sent him up from Languedoc to the Collège des Jésuites at Paris in 1719. Less than a year-and-a-half later "one of my uncles, major in the cavalry and a friend of the Comte d'Evreux, secured me a lieutenancy in the Regency Horse"—his formal education was at an end.

Boulainvilliers was one of those nobles d'épée who had made the most of his schooling, in his case at the Oratorian College of Juilly. The note inserted by the publisher in his *Essais sur la noblesse de France* (1732), however, speaks volumes concerning the class as a whole:

M. de Boulainvilliers takes for granted in his readers a more profound knowledge of our History than is generally to be found among the rank and file [*commun*] of the Nobility, especially in the Provinces & the Country. Their responsibilities, the care of their property, often just the earning of a livelihood, and finally, their differing talents do not permit us to picture them as normally devoted to study & reading.

To find any large group of noblemen who could read Boulainvilliers with interest and appreciation, it would be necessary to go not to his beloved gentry but to the magistracy.

No doubt the decline of sovereign court standards in the eighteenth century had its effect on the seriousness of robe education. The new generation of magistrates no longer had the careful grounding which Oratorian, Jesuit, but most of all, Jansenist teachers had given so many of their fathers. Against the cases of scholars such as de Brosses and Valbonnais must be set those of indolent sons of secure robe houses, young men who went through the motions of a legal education with no intention of putting its substance to any real use. The schooling which had once been a priceless means of social and political advancement had become for many a professional adornment.

Nevertheless, the robe as a class never lost its tradition of interest in and close connection with the universities, each of which was a corporation responsible solely to the king *and* to the parlement of its province. On occasion a court might assert its authority over a university, as when the Parlement of Franche-Comté denounced the rector at Besançon for having claimed criminal jurisdiction over his students. But just as frequently it was as the protector of higher learning that a sovereign company took the field. Had the Parlement of Burgundy not successfully fought those of Paris and Franche-Comté (defending their own schools) all the way to the royal council, the University of Dijon could not have made its modest beginning with a faculty of law in 1722.

In the 1740's a future robe officer was still expected to complete at least two years' work in law at a university after finishing college-level preparation in philosophy and the classics. Even the dullest or laziest could scarcely emerge without having picked up some advantages over the needy sons of the gentry. The young magistrates' performances might differ widely, but it is impossible to deny the opportunities provided them by the wealth of their fathers and the traditions of their caste.

I have permitted myself this digression on learning, at the end of a chapter on social assimilation, because it is essential to bear in mind this fundamental factor in the robe-épée distinction as it survived in the late 1740's. The noble de robe had gained admission to salon circles; he suffered far less than had his forefathers from the slurs of other aristocrats, who now joined him in ridiculing the hobereaux and despising the anoblis. But he was still officially a guardian of the law, a member of a tightly-knit professional corporation; and he was better educated than any but a handful of non-magistral noblemen; in that combination of remaining peculiarities lay the key both to the political importance of the robe and its special role in the intellectual development of the aristocratic position.

5.

On the surface the rhythmic life of prayer, fasting, and masses made the daily life of the clergy of Angers appear changeless and serene. The petty quarrels among canons, occasional scandals, and interminable rivalries between chapters and bishops changed little from century to century. Obsessed with precedents, some of which went back to Carolingian times, the upper clergy of Angers lived on believing that little had changed in a thousand years.

Beneath the surface, however, a "class consciousness" was developing on the parish level. Professor John McManners (1916–   ), of the University of Tasmania, re-creates the inner world of canons and *curés* in the eighteenth century and discovers just how precarious its survival had become by 1750. From what social group were the canons? The parish priests? A cleavage between these groups had doubtlessly existed for centuries, and even in medieval times, but new tensions developed over this cleavage in the eighteenth century. Why?

The fabric of law, custom, institutions, and psychology which bound the Church together had been influenced by feudal institutions. What was changing to make the society held together by this fabric unstable? What was the *curé primitif?*

JOHN MC MANNERS: **Canons and Curés: Angers** *

The cathedral church of Saint-Maurice claimed Charlemagne as its founder, in an age before fiefs were invented and two centuries before the counts of Anjou had graduated from "simple officers of the crown" to feudatories of the *comté*. Forty proud and pious generations had laboured to build up its territories and form its traditions. Within the walls of Angers the cathedral chapter was the wealthiest proprietor and the greatest corporation. In the "old city" (*cité*) its full feudal superiority was attested by the payment of *cens,* a small imprescriptible due which indicated feudal dependence. Here, tradesmen still asked permission to put up signs on the street and the property of individuals dying without heirs was confiscated; here too, by converse obligations, the canons paid for public utilities like the installation of new street lighting, or for the maintenance of children abandoned in the area of the fief. When aldermen were elected, two deputies of the chapter were invited to the municipal assembly and were given places of honour, while at any official service in another church of the town, the officers of justice, who normally would be entitled to stalls on the right of the choir, had to yield precedence and take the left when the cathedral chapter attended. The bishop himself had no domination in his own episcopal church. From a canon to a sub-cantor, all clerics of the cathedral were exempt from the jurisdiction of the see of Angers, rights of visitation being vested in the metropolitan, the archbishop of Tours. In the parishes of Saint-Maurice and Saint-Evroul in the *cité* and in four capitular fiefs in the countryside the chapter itself exercised full episcopal authority, these parishes being subject to its *loi diocésaine.* Thus the canons of Saint-Maurice were entitled to convoke their six curés to a private synod on the Friday after Pentecost, the day after the allotted time for a diocesan synod; they gave letters demissory to ordinands, approved confessors, permitted the publication of indulgences and jubilees and laid down the stations to be performed, made visitations of churches and reviewed audits of parish accounts, authorized schoolmasters, sent round instructive booklets on artificial respiration, gave marriage dispensations in cases of spiritual affinity and in some cases of consanguinity, granted dispensation from banns or "fixation of domicile." Year after year they sent round to their curés a solemn declaration "permitting the use of eggs in the coming Lent, from Ash Wednesday inclusive up to Palm Sunday exclusive, and the use of meat on Sundays, Mondays, Tuesdays and Thursdays of each week, from the first Sunday inclusive, up to the Thursday of Passion week, also inclusive, to be by them published at the sermon time of their parish masses, and to be put into execution." In diocesan affairs generally, the cathedral claimed to be associated with the bishop on terms of high dignity. Any legal document which the officers of that church might require had to be furnished free of sealing fees by the diocesan registry. On great national occasions, when royal injunctions prescribed festivities or mourning, the bishop was not entitled to issue instructions to his diocese on his own au-

* From John McManners, *French Ecclesiastical Society under the Ancien Regime; a Study of Angers in the Eighteenth Century* (Manchester: Manchester University Press, 1960), pp. 57–63, 163–73.

thority. The canons of Saint-Maurice insisted that all royal letters be passed on to them and that any directions concerning ceremonial which were subsequently circulated should contain a statement showing that they were drawn up "in accord" with the chapter. The vicars-general, having inadvertently omitted this formula in their orders for the tolling of bells when Louis XV died, were compelled to apologize, and bishop de Grasse faced strong protests, tantamount, he complained, to "threats," when he withheld the royal letters announcing the birth of a daughter to Louis XVI and victories in the war against England.

This proud-cathedral chapter did not enjoy the scandalous affluence which characterized some ecclesiastical establishments of the old régime; nevertheless, its canons were very comfortably off. A canonry was worth rather more than 3,000*l*. in the first instance, which would be augmented, as time went on, by provision to various chapels of the foundation, or to similar benefices without cure of souls in the gift of other patrons. Thus Brossier, after being a canon for ten years, possessed six such additional benefices, and Nioche de la Brosse, after sixteen years, held four. Canon Boulnoy, who had been prevented by gout and other infirmities from rendering a complete return of his benefices earlier, in June 1790 informed the Ecclesiastical Committee of the Constituent Assembly that he held, in addition to his canonry, five chapels in the diocese of Angers, three having been bestowed on him by lay patrons. In addition, he held five priories of the Benedictines of Saint-Maur, scattered in the dioceses of Poitiers, La Rochelle, Nantes and Chartres, one being worth 1,000*l*. a year, one 800, another 400, and another, thanks to the beauty of its situation, was farmed to a rich individual for a substantial rent in kind. This considerable accumulation of benefices was not, however, all profit; indeed, the abbé Boulnoy argued that he had consumed his patrimony of 30,000*l*. in repairs, re-building and lawsuits. One chapel brought in 100*l*. income and had cost him 3,600*l*. in repairs; the priory farmed for 1,000*l*. had swallowed up more than a year's income in repairs and had been saddled with a pension and a lawsuit costing 8,000*l*.—"jamais liste de bénéfices plus imposante n'a moins fait le bien être de quelqu'un."[1] Pluralities, indeed, were speculative investments, rather than assured increments to income. However, ignoring all additional benefices other than those in the direct gift of the chapter itself, it is clear that canons of Saint-Maurice were enjoying considerable incomes. This is so on their own showing, for while they no doubt erred on the side of caution, it is significant that in the abortive negotiations of 1784 for the union of two other chapters of the town to the cathedral, their terms envisaged arrangements which would ensure new revenue in the proportion of over 5,700*l*. for each new prebend created. As canon Brossier's personal accounts reveal, it was possible, in the early sixties, to live in Angers at a basic expense—on wine, bread, meat, coal, lodging and the wages of a servant —of 515*l*. a year. Prices had risen since then, but even so, when all necessities were paid for, the surplus remaining was enough to enable a canon to furnish agreeably one of those dignified capitular houses on the cathedral square, the place du château or the rue des Jacobins, to entertain and move in society, and, perhaps, maintain a small estate in the country as a retreat in the summer.

---

[1] Never did a more imposing list of benefices do less good for someone.

Canonries of Saint-Maurice were distributed with the injustice which was common form in the disposal of all well-endowed benefices in France. It is true that, of the canons of 1789, one was the son of a tanner, and another had risen to the priesthood after a five years' apprenticeship as schoolmaster to the choir-boys, but these were exceptions and the chapter was very largely a preserve for younger sons of distinguished families, who could hope to crown an ecclesiastical career with dignity and modest affluence before reaching the age of thirty. Dutertre des Roches, son of a royal officer at Saumur, became a canon at the age of nineteen, Charles de Creny, descended from a noble family of Normandy of six centuries' standing, was appointed at the age of twenty-three, when still only a sub-deacon, and four years later became archdeacon of Outre-Maine as well. These were unusually youthful appointments, but even those who decently took a theological doctorate before promotion to a stall had not long to wait: Pou-laine de la Forestrie, whose family accepted municipal office in Angers only on condition that its claims to *ancienne noblesse* were not thereby impugned, was a canon at twenty-eight; Louet, son of a *conseiller* of the *Présidial* at Angers, whose line went back to a fifteenth-century treasurer of the Dukes of Anjou, joined the chapter, which a hundred and fifty years ago had had a Louet for its dean, at the age of twenty-seven; while Lenoir de la Cochetière, of a noble family of Lude, took his doctorate a year younger than Louet and was a canon at twenty-five. At the same age, Waillant received both his doctorate and his canonical stall, a rapid promotion which was no doubt connected with the fact that canon Wiot was his uncle. The dean himself, César-Scipion de Villeneuve, had not come to the cathedral until the age of thirty-four, but this comparative hold-up in his career was due to the fact that he had at first been a Jesuit, and the delay was compensated by his appointment as dean only two months after taking up his canonry. A profitable alternation between Church and Army was the standard method of providing for younger sons of the nobility, and a stall at Saint-Maurice took its place in the economy of various families. Dean de Villeneuve was a second son, with an elder brother who inherited the manor of Tourettes-lès-Vence, and a younger brother who became a dashing major of cavalry. Another second son was Charles de Creny, whose three brothers were all Army officers. Dary d'Ernemont, who, but for an accident to his family archives, could have proved descent from a companion of William the Con-queror, was a third son; his elder brother had inherited Ernemont, another brother was a canon of Saint-Waas at Arras, and the other three took up mili-tary careers. One of the canons of Angers was himself an ex-soldier, for Le Perrochel, son of a general, had originally followed his elder brothers into the Army, where he had been an officer in the dragoons of *Monsieur,* before turning to the Church and becoming abbot of Toussaint and a canon of Saint-Maurice. Every noble family had its network of ecclesiastical connexions. Tugal-François Hullin de la Maillardière had had a second cousin a canon of the cathedral be-fore him, his sister was a nun at Beaufort, more distant relatives had taken the veil at Le Calvaire and the Ursulines of Angers, and a half-cousin was a canon of Saint-Martin. A brother of Lucien-François de la Corbière had been chaplain to the princess Adélaïde and another relative dean of the cathedral of Verdun, which no doubt accounted for his elevation to a prebend at Verdun at the age of twenty-three, before returning to Angers, the place of his university studies, as a canon eleven years later. But while appointments at Saint-Maurice were regarded as rightful perquisites by noble families of Anjou in particular, and, in a widening circle, by those of Normandy, Brittany and the Vendée, they were not rich enough to attract solicitations by the greatest courtiers, and at the beginning of 1789 only two stalls were affording supplements to the salaries of clerics at Versailles.

One of these had fallen to Fayon, a priest in the royal chapel, who was appointed a canon in 1784. The other was held by one Chaussard, who in twenty-six years of office had never graced a service in his cathedral. He was in minor orders only, and was, perhaps, adequately punished by his task of tutor to the most riotous and refractory pupils in France, the pages of the *grande écurie du Roi*. A third canonry fell into the hands of an absentee sinecurist in January 1789, being appropriated by Dumouchel, rector of the University of Paris, to the despair of the senior graduate of the diocese, who at seventy-five years of age had still not given up hopes of ultimate recognition, and the anger of Dumouchel's enemies in the capital, who regarded the affair as a shameless piece of jobbery. With these exceptions, the chapter consisted of canons subject to normal obligations, and residence was enforced strictly, without favour to the great. Le Perrochel, holding his prebend in virtue of his position as abbot of Toussaint, indulged in his hobby of foreign travel, and, being absent from chapters-general at St. John Baptist-tide, was deprived of the fruits of his benefice. Supplies were cut off during Waillant's illegal and suspicious absence in Paris and the dean was instructed at one time to summon Poulain de la Guerche back to town. Le Noir de la Cochetière lost his turn for a canonical residence which fell vacant during his absence in Rome, even though his journey was authorized, his application for the house received, and his delay in returning fully explained by "a feverish cold on the chest," attested by a medical certificate endorsed by cardinal Bernis in person.

Residence was enforced, and discipline was strict in minor matters too. Registers of attendance at services were kept, the bald needed capitular permission to wear wigs, as the gouty did to remain seated, during the offices. Standards of morality, in the narrower sense of that word, were high. In the last years of the old chapter, there was but one serious offender, canon Waillant, who, ten years after his appointment, decamped to Paris and refused to come back. His eventual return revealed his reason for staying in the capital and gave his colleagues cause to regret their complaints of his absence. His uncle Wiot and the grave Louet were sent to urge him to send away the woman he had installed in his house. They persuaded him to send her to a nunnery in town, but this proved to be only a staging point on the way to Waillant's country retreat; finally, however, after asking for three days to think over his position, he sent the lady back to Paris, and the chapter decided to pursue the offender no further. In the light of this major scandal, it is not surprising to find Waillant failing to fulfil his preaching duties, so that the chapter now had cause to complain of unauthorized preachers turning up on the first Sunday of the month to fill his place in the pulpit, and of one Sunday without any sermon at all. But Waillant's adventures are a startling exception, and his colleagues' groping efforts to deal with the crisis reveal their confusion and consternation in face of untoward circumstances.

Free from the grosser vices, canons of Saint-Maurice seem also to have been —through lack of opportunity—but little tempted by promptings of ambition. Dean d'Autichamp moved off to become bishop of Tulle in 1741, and eleven years later Joseph de Saint-André Marnay de Vercel, newly consecrated, toured Anjou "to enjoy the sweet satisfaction of showing himself in cross and mitre in this Diocese where he had formerly been Grand Vicar and canon." But these were unusual cases, the result of unusual influence. Fate perhaps left a loophole for Le Noir de la Cochetière, who happened to be in Rome in 1786-7 at a time when the Clergy of France were anxious to settle an affair of dispensations with the Papal Curia. For a time, the pilgrim became a diplomat, and cherished hopes of "a flattering recompense." But outmanœuvred by cardinal Bernis, the French ambassador, who wished to smother the matter, he received nothing more than a bishopric *in partibus*, a Roman reward which the Crown refused to recognize, and was reproached by bishop de Lorry for "foolishly missing the only chance that I might hope for, to come, in my state of life, to the office which marks the term of ambition." Such opportunities were rare. A canon of Angers at the end of the old régime seemed certain to remain where he was for life. His office was not a spring-board for promotion: it was a dignified *cul-de-sac* in the ecclesiastical hierarchy. Idleness was, no doubt, the greatest temptation. Even so, many canons were more active than their critics supposed. Six were vicars-general of the bishop, seven were doctors of theology (including Dutertre des Roches, who redeemed his youthful appointment somewhat by taking his doctorate seven years later), their ermine stoles bearing witness that the theological tradition of the cathedral created by Babin and de la Chalinière in the first half of the century was not defunct. Much time was lavished on the management of property, care of the fabric and supervision of fine music and magnificent ceremonial. After all, the life of a canon was what the individual chose to make it. Some drifted along in their agreeable sinecures; Le Perrochel took possession of his prebend and departed for England, Germany and the bracing north; some found scope for literary or social activities at the Academy or in free-masonry; Brossier plunged into the archives. Canon Louet was a scholar, an administrator and a divine. Four years after his induction he became one of the two professors at the Faculty of Theology of the University, after holding this post for six years he became *maître-école*, an office corresponding to that of Chancellor of the University, in 1782, a senior canon of thirty years' standing, he was appointed Vicar-General, and as *official* was in charge of the legal and disciplinary business of the diocese. He was much in demand as a preacher. The municipality sought him for public occasions (unavailingly when the virtues of Louis XV were to be extolled), the comtess de Brionne presented him with a handsome snuff-box as a token of gratitude for his funeral oration on her husband, and Fleury's *Histoire Ecclésiastique* on his shelves and presentation silver at his table bore witness to the admiration of his colleagues for his Lent and Advent courses at the cathedral. Leisure which Louet devoted to administration and preaching was very differently but no less worthily employed by canon Cassin, whose death in 1783 was shortly followed by the opening of an instance of canonization. Urbain-Elie Cassin, son of a wealthy merchant of Angers, had obtained his stall at Saint-Maurice at the age of twenty-five, and lived a comfortable worldly life, until a chance remark of his friend Tourny, *intendant* of Bordeaux, made in casual conversation at a country house party, led to a fit of remorse and a startling conversion. Conscience-stricken by his facile promotion, he resigned his canonry and, when the bishop immediately re-appointed him, gave away his furniture, sent his tapestries to the hospital, and thenceforward lived a ruthlessly ascetic life, wearing a hair shirt, abjuring meat and fish in his diet, refusing fires even in the depths of winter. Instead of taking the fashionable summer vacation in the country, he remained at the cathedral until All Souls day every year and then went off on foot to his rural property for a fifteen days' retreat. Since ecstatic seizures obliged him to renounce preaching, his entire work in his later years was that of a director of souls, being confessor to the Carmelites, the hospital of the Incurables, and the nuns of Ronceray. On the 3rd of September 1783, knowing all the while that his last illness was upon him, canon Cassin was at the cathedral at 4.30 in the morning, half an hour before mattins, said his mass, heard confessions, attended chapter, took several interviews afterwards, returned to his house, where he received the mother superior of the Incurables, said his own vespers alone as he did not feel well enough to sit in choir, then set off for the abbey of Ronceray to hear confessions, down the short steep hill to the bridge where the dark river flowed between the crowded quays in the shadow of the cathedral towers, and there, on the bridge, he collapsed and died. Which is very far from the traditional picture one forms of a day in the life of a canon of the old régime. . . .

Generally speaking, parish priests of eighteenth-century France fell into two distinct categories. There were beneficed curés, named by a bishop or lay patron and holding their tithes in their own hands; some of these were very comfortably off, and even those who were not, were at least independent. On the other hand, there was a whole class of curés who were nominated by abbeys, chapters, congregations of canons-regular or the Order of Malta. These corporations and communities retained the title of *curé primitif*—to use English terminology for this phenomenon, they were "rectors" in their parishes, while the actual parish priests were their "vicars." Royal declarations had given security of tenure to a curé in this position, but the galling honorific superiority of his *curé primitif* remained, most usually demonstrated by the right of celebrating divine service in his parish church on the four solemn feasts of each year and the day of the patronal festival. A monastery or chapter would also, like as not, have impropriated the tithe and revenues of the living, paying its priest a mere "portionem congruentem," which, though congruous with law, certainly bore small relation to the cost of living. Hence, such curés were described as "curés à portion congrue," though it is important to notice that the *congrue* did not automatically accompany dependence on a *curé primitif*. The latter's rights might be honorific only, though, as such, a blow to the pride of both priest and parish, or, they might extend to possession of revenues which ought more properly to have constituted an endowment for the living, and thus be doubly hated.

At the beginning of 1768, that is, before the royal edict of May of that year, we find all seventeen parishes of our town of Angers dependent on monasteries or chapters. The tiny parish of Saint-'Aignan, which had the status of *prieuré-cure,* is an exception, but only technically so, for the canons-regular always turned it over to a secular priest on account of its miserable income. Six parishes had a monastery as *curé primitif:* Saint-Michel du Tertre and Saint-Samson depended on the abbey of Saint-Serge, Saint-Michel de la Palud on Saint-Aubin, Saint-Jacques and La Trinité on Ronceray, and Saint-Nicholas on the Benedictine house of that name. Three parishes, Sainte-Croix, Saint-Maurice and Saint-Evroul, came under the cathedral, while Saint-Pierre, Saint-Maurille, Saint-Laud and Saint-Martin were dependent on the other four collegiate churches whose names they bore. When the moribund chapters of Saint-Julien and Saint-Maimbeuf had been suppressed at the end of the seventeenth and the beginning of the eighteenth centuries, their privileges, including the status of *curé primitif* in their respective parishes, had fallen to the Seminary, though actual appointment to these benefices was from henceforward vested in the bishop.

Financial provisions were heterogeneous. Saint-Nicolas and Saint-Samson were, quite simply, on the *congrue,* which had been fixed, by a royal declaration in 1686, at 300*l.* for a curé and 150*l.* for a vicaire. One says "quite simply," but no arrangement in eighteenth-century France was ever very simple. While the abbeys of Saint-Nicolas and Saint-Serge were responsible for finding most of the money, small contributions towards each *congrue* were made by other ecclesiastical institutions; the abbot of Saint-Aubin gave 15*l.* towards that of Saint-Nicolas, and the canons of Saint-Maurille, the Seminary (on behalf of the defunct chapter of Saint-Julien), and the treasurer of the cathedral were obliged to assist in paying the parish priest of Saint-Samson. In addition to this complication of composite payments, the curé of Saint-Nicolas was entitled to free salt from his abbey, and both he and his colleague on the other side of town enjoyed *novales,* that is, tithes on any new crops cultivated within their boundaries. The other four parishes dependent on monastic houses had their own revenues. Such miserable tithes as there were in the parish of Saint-Jacques were collected by its curé, and the priest of La Trinité drew his income from the property of his benefice, thus neither received a subvention from the abbess of Ronceray. Saint-Michel de la Palud and Saint-Michel du Tertre were also, in the main, financially independent of the abbeys of Saint-Aubin and Saint-Serge. When parishes had been split off from their chapters, varying agreements on finance had originally been made. Thus the canons of Saint-Laud had left their curé in full possession of his temporal, reserving only a share in parochial oblations to themselves. On the other hand, the chapter of Saint-Pierre had undertaken to pay a *congrue* of 300*l.,* without prejudice to surplice fees, which were very large; this it had exchanged, early in the century, for the usufruct of a farm and tithes from certain lands, and when this income proved inadequate, it had been compelled to make an additional money payment.

As prices steadily rose, some revision of the edict of 1686 became an obvious necessity, and in the seventeen-sixties, the *curés congruistes* of France began to league together to press their demands. Finally, in May 1768, a new edict raised the *congrue* to 500*l*. A parish priest could opt for this payment if he wished, though to obtain it, he would have to surrender, not only any rents and normal tithes which his benefice might still hold, but also any *novales,* or new tithes, which he might be enjoying. In spite of these qualifications, this was joyful news in the vicarages of Saint-Nicolas and Saint-Samson. In the former parish, the *novales* consisted of a mere composition of 50*s.* from the Hôpital Général for new cultivation in a single paddock; a greater income was drawn from tithe on the fields of Saint-Samson, but it was uncertain and variable. Thus an exchange for an extra 200*l*. in perpetuity was a welcome one. More especially, our curé of Saint-Nicolas was jubilant. Earlier in the century, his parish registers had taken envious note of the abbey's ostentatious building programme: now they record this triumph of the *congrue,* with a special note for posterity telling how monkish machinations to withdraw the yearly gift of salt were also defeated. His neighbour of Saint-Jacques, seeing this new opulence of some of his colleagues, decided to follow their example and abandon the land and tithes of his benefice to Ronceray, in exchange for this newly augmented *congrue.* By 19 December 1770, he had plucked up courage to make his request to the abbess. That great lady, however, was a shrewd woman of business, not anxious to give away any of her revenues as a Christmas present. She therefore abandoned her rights as *curé primitif,* retaining only her patronage and her curé's obligations in the church of Ronceray. These legal formalities went through, as her lawyers said, "without discussion of the question as to whether it is a fact that the revenue of the cure of Saint-Jacques, in fixed income, surplice fees and foundation masses, is not adequate to provide the curé with a reasonable amount to live on." In resorting to this mean shift and abandoning privileges which were transforming themselves into obligations, the abbess was but imitating the action of the cathedral with respect to its parish of Saint-Evroul, whose curé had applied for the augmented *congrue* two years earlier. When the chapter of Saint-Maurice had heard of the edict of May 1768, it had hastened to consult its lawyers, and to put up various subtle objections to the agents-general of the Clergy of France. On the whole, these evasive suggestions had been rejected, but a legal right to abandon the title of *curé primitif* (while retaining all rights derived from other sources) had been established, and this was enough to outmanœuvre the parish priest of Saint-Evroul. The canons probably quietened their consciences by arguing that article 16 of the edict of 1768, which ordered the union of small and poor benefices, was a more reasonable remedy for penury than sacrifices on their part. Whether this is so or not, a diocesan project to unite Saint-Evroul to Sainte-Croix, Saint-Maurice, or Saint-Aignan was brought forward in the following April. The parishioners of Saint-Evroul gave this design a bitter reception. Angers, they pointed out, needed more parish priests, not fewer.

There are in this diocese an infinite number of benefices without cure of souls, many chapters and monasteries, and the unions of these would be more than sufficient to augment the temporal of the cures of this town, which are already too few in number. His highness has just united forty-five chapels to his chapter of the cathedral of Angers, a proof of the multiplicity of benefices without cure of souls, and they (the parishioners) hope that his love for the Church and for his co-operators of the second order of clergy will produce a proportionate beneficence to satisfy the intentions of his Majesty indicated in the edict cited.

It is true that, in their zeal to preserve their parish, they went on to use arguments which contradicted their pastor's claim for a higher income. He was, they said, satisfied with what he got, and managed to save enough to give handsomely to the poor—"Bel exemple à suivre." Even so, these modest requirements which they ascribed to their parish priest only served to sharpen their criticism of rich benefice holders. The living of Saint-Evroul, they darkly admit, would never satisfy "a priest who might be drawn to the ministry by ambition rather than by the holiness of that state of life." Saint-Evroul remained an independent parish, but its curé failed to obtain the *congrue*. He did, however, get something from this crisis of the early months of 1769. In alliance with his colleague of Saint-Maurice, he had formed an opposition at law to the union of forty-five chapels to the cathedral which had so angered the parish, and in February 1769, the chapter of Saint-Maurice agreed to buy off this opposition by promising 200*l*. a year to each of these parish priests once the proposed union of benefices had been accomplished.

While the edict of 1768 had evoked speculation on the maldistribution of ecclesiastical revenues, it had benefited only three of our seventeen curés of Angers. History repeated itself when the *congrue* was raised to 700*l*. in 1786. Once again, a welcome augmentation was presented to Saint-Nicolas and Saint-Samson, while the parish priest of Saint-Michel de la Palud, who now decided that it was worth his while to apply for this revised income scale, found that his abbey of Saint-Aubin preferred to renounce its rights as *curé primitif* to escape its obligations. In Angers, the steady success of the dependent parochial clergy of France in their demands for increased salaries was exasperatingly irrelevant. Three peripheral parishes of minor importance were rising in income at the expense of three monastic houses, while all other livings, holding their own property or tangled up in complicated arrangements with their chapters, were stationary. Every increase in the *congrue,* in fact, made it more unlikely that this increased *congrue* would ever be granted, and merely served to underline the rising cost of living as well as illustrating the need for parochial reorganization and for the redistribution of monastic and capitular wealth. And then, concerning honorific precedences and monopolies—what claim had they to respect if a monastery or chapter was willing, in the last resort, to abandon some of them rather than pay two or three hundred *livres* a year to a struggling priest?

Indeed, it was these distinctions of dignity, rather than financial disputes, which aroused the parochial clergy of Angers to ire against dominant ecclesiastical corporations. This was a fantastically litigious age, when courts resounded continually with expostulations of claimants to precedence and empty formal honours. Eighteenth-century France was too civilized: the term of an introverted existence had been reached. Society had settled into an infinitely complex hierarchy of caste and privilege, whilst passions and aspirations of a new age, so long as they continued to grow within traditional cadres, found expression in the law courts. Legal subtleties manifested society's attempts to sublimate revolutionary tendencies into the labyrinthine complexities of accepted forms. It was in this context of chicanery, and under a disguise of argument from precedent, that a battle against privilege was being waged within the clerical order, which itself was divided by a steadily developing rivalry of nobility and *Tiers Etat*. We have seen that this rift between aristocrat and commoner within the Church does not strictly coincide with a frontier drawn between monks and canons on one hand and curés on the other, but that, in so far as monasteries and chapters afforded well-paid sinecures, they had become aristocratic preserves. Here, no doubt, is an important factor in the growing class-consciousness of our parish clergy of Angers, and yet it would seem that their stirrings of common interest and resentment were really more of an ecclesiastical phenomenon than a social and economic one. It was less a question of hatred of privilege on logical and egalitarian grounds, than of a pride in their own office, and a desire to rescue its rightful dignity from eclipse or belittlement. Curés did not wish to be able to rise out of their station so much as to receive proper recognition in the place to which they had been called. They were men accustomed to command in their parishes, they performed innumerable social functions, and every day of their lives made them conscious of the importance of matters ceremonial. Naturally, they resented a system whose absurdities served no purpose beyond that of guaranteeing an artificial superiority to corporations whose privileges now greatly exceeded their social and religious usefulness. "The title of *curé primitif*," said the canons of La Trinité in 1781, unconscious of the beam in their own eye, "is foreign to pastoral direction, and to the care of souls. It is a vain and meaningless rank in the Church." How vain and meaningless it was, a survey of the complicated pattern of capitular and monastic domination over parishes will serve to show.

The most remarkable example of this domination is seen in two parishes of the old city, where the cathedral enjoyed unprecedented powers, extending far beyond any normal rights of patron and *curé primitif*. It is true that Saint-Maurice and Saint-Evroul had their own churches, and that the chapter had not absorbed such meagre possessions as formed the endowments of these livings. Yet in all other respects, the church of Angers was supreme, being patron, rector, feudal overlord and diocesan superior all rolled into one. The curé of Saint-Maurice was held in complete tutelage; he was, said the canons (replying to a circular of the chapter of Perpignan, which was experiencing some difficulties with its dependent parish), merely a chaplain. He was obliged to take an oath of obedience, and could be fined for negligence, he was forbidden to have his cross or banner carried aloft before him, he had to ask permission before he could expose the Holy Sacrament or stage new ceremonies or processions—indeed, the cathedral registers contain twenty pages of orders and prohibitions issued at one time or another by the chapter to its curé of Saint-Maurice.

This peculiar enclave of interlocking jurisdictions was a remarkable anomaly. In all other parishes of Angers, the powers of monasteries and chapters were simply those of *curé primitif* overlaid and embellished by local variations and idiosyncrasies. Generally, a parish priest, whether he were the pastor of poor

Lesvière or of the rich official parish of Saint-Michel du Tertre, was excluded from his own altar at the High Mass of Christmas, Easter, Pentecost, All Saints and the patronal festival. Saint-Laud was an exception. Here, a succession of watchful incumbents had contrived to restrict their canons to minor usurpations —blessing the fonts on Easter Saturday and the eve of Whit-Sunday: which, said an ecclesiastical annalist earlier in the century, proved the value of constant vigilance, "for against a chapter one cannot be too careful . . . O happy, happy curé!" When an abbess of Ronceray was installed, ceremonies in the church of La Trinité were calculated to leave no possible doubt as to her supremacy. She sat with her nuns in the principal stalls of the choir, her parochial clergy presented incense and holy water and brought the gospel book for her to kiss, and finally, she moved off in procession back to Ronceray under a canopy held by the four senior churchwardens. Excluded by her sex from exercising sacerdotal functions, the abbess nevertheless demonstrated her domination when the sacrament was administered, for a parish priest had to receive the key of his tabernacle from her hand. A double servitude weighed upon this curé who ruled the largest parish in Angers. The canons of his church took their toll where the abbess left off. They celebrated mass on great festivals, they blessed ashes and palms and fonts according to season, they gave absolution on Maundy Thursday, they claimed a right to bury nuns and canons and other persons of distinction, they had first voice in the nomination of a precentor and choir-men and even of preachers. In parishes dependent on monasteries, a curé who suffered some usurpation of honourable functions in his own church might find himself obliged, by an unequal exchange of courtesies, to render humble services in the church of his *curé primitif*. The incumbent of Saint-Jacques had to say an early mass once a month in the choir of Ronceray, his colleague of Saint-Michel de la Palud was obliged to attend high mass on feast days at Saint-Aubin. When the Benedictines of Saint-Serge processed in town, the prior was escorted by the curés of Saint-Michel du Tertre and Saint-Samson, and preceded by the crosses and banners of these two dependent churches. At all major processions of the cathedral, the parish priests of Saint-Aignan, Saint-Evroul and Sainte-Croix had to take their turn in carrying a reliquary which held the bones of Saint-Séréné. Every parish had its tariff of such ceremonial obligations, thoroughly codified by the decisions of law courts.

As the liturgical year rolled on, its lofty festivals revived memories of rivalries, precedences, feuds and litigation. In some churches, too, every daily service was held in the shadow of tutelage. At Saint-Maurille, Saint-Pierre, Saint-Laud, Saint-Martin and La Trinité, high altar and choir were a canonical fortress, while curés said their masses in bleak naves or in humble side-chapels. The parishioners of Saint-Nicolas crowded into the chapel of Saint-André of their abbey church, and had to decamp to Saint-Jacques for their Easter communion, those of Lesvière used the monastic nave until its tottering roof became too dangerous, and then were allowed, under due restrictions, to borrow the high altar of the monks. In the church of the extinct chapter of Saint-Julien, monopoly achieved its crowning absurdity. Dust gathered on derelict choir stalls, while the parish worshipped in the nave; once or twice a year, the Seminary staff came down in hoods and surplices and copes of violet velvet to say a minimum of offices and preserve their prescriptive rights. Bells reverberated eternally to the glory of chapters and monasteries, rather than calling the faithful to their parochial duties. At Saint-Pierre and Saint-Maurille, the parish bell was banished to an obscure gable-end belfry, while the cathedral would not grant even this minor privilege to Saint-Maurice, lest a plebeian tintinnabulation detract from the ordered beauty of the mightiest peals of Angers. Parishes which had obtained a right to share the main bell-tower had still not achieved equality of status, for a sacristan would have instructions to distinguish between capitular and parish offices by his method of ringing. However, while the faithful laity envied the bells, choirs, high altars and sacristies of monks and canons, as things were, they certainly did not wish to take them over. Financial apprehensions overwhelmed their pride and their interest in the splendour of liturgical worship. Saint-Samson and La Trinité, parishes with their own churches, never ceased to bewail the ill-fortune which had left their monastic patrons free from responsibility for repairs to their bell-towers, and where buildings were shared with chapters and monasteries the chief concern of ratepayers was to avoid any action which might furnish an excuse for a transfer of financial burdens. Those who used a church were, in the end, likely to have to pay for its upkeep. "Subtle and crafty politicians," the directors of the Seminary had watched all the century for the inhabitants of Saint-Julien to make a false step. Every crack in the paving stones or wormhole in the beams was a warning to thrifty churchwardens of the parishes of Angers.

Desultory warfare between parish priest and *curé primitif* took place along a well-surveyed battle-front, which traditional rulings and old litigation had very largely stabilized. At one point, at least, all strategic features were held by the curé. It was his exclusive prerogative, within his parish boundaries, to administer sacraments and bury the dead. Lawyers cited Angers as a town which provided the clearest case law to justify this contention, and a secret consultation of the legal experts of the Clergy of France in 1759 admitted that these precedents were conclusive. In 1737, the crucial victory had been won. It was then that the united curés of Angers, backed by their bishop, had obtained a decision of the Parlement of Paris against the royal chapters of Saint-Martin and Saint-Laud. By this ruling, parish priests were confirmed in their rights of administering the sacraments to all parishioners, and of saying the last suffrages over all who died within their boundaries, even if the dead man were a canon, or a chaplain or a benefice-holder of a chapter. This case would not be valid, perhaps, against the powerful cathedral, but it seems clear enough as regards all other chapters. Lawsuits still continued, however—curé Robin was sued by the canons of Saint-Pierre, the canons of La Trinité began an action against the abbess of Ronceray —for every general rule in the eighteenth century was subject to qualifications of privilege or tradition. A dispute of 1774 between the Seminary and curé Huchelou des Roches of Saint-Julien illustrates one of these manifold contingencies which baffled human foresight. Huchelou des Roches claimed his simple legal right—to bury a parishioner, the deceased abbé Blouin. However, until 1768, Blouin had been curé of the parish himself, and the Seminary, as heir to the privileges of the chapter of Saint-Julien, was entitled to preside at the interment of its own parish priest. Furthermore, Blouin had been an honorary canon of Saint-Julien, and in his will had asked to be buried by representatives of that chapter. There was, inevitably, a scene. Just as Huchelou des Roches was singing a *subvenite* over his predecessor, the clergy of the Seminary arrived, and drowned his chant with their own; he replied by taking the names of witnesses of the scandal with a view to prosecution. By way of corporate protest, all other parish priests of the town refused to be present at the actual burial. From the first, it had been a shabby comedy. This is how the registers of the Seminary recorded the receipt of news that the abbé Blouin had died—"The differences which have arisen during many years between chapters and curés made us in no hurry to ring the big bell, as the custom is."

Another class of disputes, less macabre, but no less unedifying, concerned the joint use of churches by chapters and parishes, and here, the law was more likely to favour the former. We have seen how the Seminary lay in wait for an opportunity to unload its repairing obligations upon the parish of Saint-Julien, insisting meanwhile upon all obsolete rights in a strategy of patient provocation. A curé was not allowed to "take possession" of font and sacristy—he merely had permission to use them. Similarly, while he could borrow the plate and chalices of Saint-Julien for his celebrations, it was always made clear that this loan was of favour and not of obligation. Indeed, on one occasion, a sacrist of the Seminary established his point by depriving curé Blouin of communion plate altogether, an incident which caused a dispute of twenty-four years' duration, ending only in 1783, when the parish was granted a sacristy of its own and at last admitted that the altar silver was loaned out of "pure goodwill." A chapter might also be under an obligation to make loans of a very different sort, and send some of its chaplains or inferior clergy to assist at a parish mass as deacons, subdeacons or precentors. Each Sunday, for example, the Seminary had to send six ecclesiastics to high mass at Saint-Denis, and, up to 1723, the cathedral had been under a similar obligation towards its parish of Saint-Maurice. In that year, however, various stray benefices were suppressed and their income annexed to general capitular revenues, a reform which had logic on its side, but which ignored the interests of curés of Saint-Maurice, and deprived them of their accustomed assistance. As late as 1768, memories of this injustice were still green in the mind of the abbé Lepron. The chapters of Saint-Laud, Saint-Martin and Saint-Maurille still continued to send minor ecclesiastics to grace parochial masses, and up to 1763 all went smoothly. Indeed, the chapter of Saint-Maurille had just congratulated itself upon "the concord and good relations which have always reigned between the canons and their parishioners," when a difficulty about precedence, hitherto unsuspected, was suddenly discovered. Chaplains of chapters claimed priority over vicaires of parishes. Although both the diocesan bishop and the lawyers of the Clergy of France decided in favour of the parochial clergy, our canons still took up the cause of their subordinates; the three chapters leagued themselves together by "concordats" and "procurations" to fight a law-suit to a final conclusion, and representatives were sent off to initiate litigation before the Parlement of Paris. This apparently trivial dispute had wide repercussions: so much so, that two chapters, Saint-Laud and Saint-Martin, were very glad to fade out of a debate which was receiving dangerous publicity. There were those in high places who sought occasion to confiscate the revenues of useless benefices, and at Court they were suggesting that these two royal chapters, incurably quarrelsome and litigious, should be "reformed" and united into a single and more economical institution. As soon as this rumour became current, we find the chapter of Saint-Laud very anxious to prove that it had always aided its curé in his functions, and had striven "to forestall any possible complaint by showing politeness and avoiding everything which might have the appearance of resentment." But the chapter of Saint-Maurille, which ran no such risks, made no attempt to be genial. Curé Roussel lost his income from capitular distributions, anniversaries and foundations, and as late as 1768 he was still complaining that the ecclesiastics of the chapter were absent from his parish mass, with the connivance of their canons.

While this dispute was laying up a fund of ill-will between parish and chapter at Saint-Maurille, other minor vexations were accumulating. The canons built a new rood-screen which deprived the parish of pew space worth 18*l.* a year. They refused to pass on any of the fee paid by M. de Tremblay for a plot of land in their main cemetery, and when the "little" cemetery was levelled and cleared and handed over as a public square, none of the indemnity paid by the city found its way into the churchwarden's accounts. There was some controversy, too, concerning a right to appoint two choir-boys, and to remunerate them by selling off candle ends remaining after high masses and funerals. Royal officials, lawyers and notaries predominated in this parish assembly and they were worldly-wise, legalistic and uncompromising. "There is no further hope of agreement," they minuted in August 1765, "nothing remains but a resort to the courts." A conference with canons Péan and Guillot failed to clear the air— "It is henceforward impossible to rely on any of the promises of the gentlemen of the chapter, they break them all." Already, thanks to the feud of vicaires and chaplains, curé Roussel was an angry man, and he now volunteered to prosecute a parochial law-suit in person, at his own costs and charges. His parishioners accepted this offer, and promised to recompense him with the yearly interest on any sum of damages to which the chapter might be condemned.

Sixteen years later this furious litigant was senior parish priest of Angers and a pillar of sobriety, even somewhat suspect by his more advanced colleagues as a weak collaborator in canonical dominion. Law-suits were expensive, lay support was fickle and, after all, Christian charity counted for something. Age and the passage of time soothed and mellowed the discontented. And so it would have gone on, had not the curés become more conscious of their identity and interests as a class and developed a common set of arguments to defend their rights. Once this was the case, natural leaders could arise and clerical revolt could be organized.

14

THE FATE OF MONARCHY

POLITICAL SITUATIONS arise where, no matter how dramatic and forceful he is, a king fails as a statesman. His policies are repudiated and he is scorned, perhaps even ridiculed, disgraced, or assassinated. Following his failure there may be a revolution, bankruptcy, rioting, or some drastic solution to the problems which he faced before his political demise.

A king's policies may therefore be excellent; he may have the best of intentions; but he may fail nevertheless. Reforms may be indispensable to the very survival of the state; and though a king may perceive this, he may fail to effect them. His ministers may be intelligent, astute, and filled with integrity, and in theory the king may have absolute power to make his will law for his subjects, but he may still be repudiated or overthrown.

Dynamic kings, like other men of power, sometimes meet overwhelming opposition to their policies. That opposition may arise within the king's own government: there may be administrative sabotage by his subordinates, bureaucratic inertia, or opposition to his aims by members of his own family. More dangerous is a king's failure to find a basis of support for his policies among his subjects. When his policies are scorned, his success is limited unless he relies on military support and police-state methods to suppress opposition to his rule.

It is important to distinguish between the monarch as an individual and monarchy as an institution. There is a fundamental distinction between them. Monarchy contributes to and sustains the power of the individual who, as king, makes his will into law. The distinction between monarch and monarchy has enabled historians to study and, in some cases, to discern the success or failure of government in a given reign. The old refrain "given the conditions under which he ruled" referred in part to the relationship between institutions and individuals, and how each affected the other.

A king's power is determined not only by his own abilities but by the strength or weaknesses of the institutions which uphold his power. In the seventeenth century some monarchs, though not strong themselves, exercised great power because the institution of monarchy was strong. Louis XIII's reign is a case in point. In other instances, though a king might be very effective personally, his power was weak because the monarchical institutions in his realm limited his power. Such was the reign of John Sobieski of Poland.

All the major powers in the eighteenth century were monarchies, yet each one differed considerably from the others. English kings, for example, did not constitutionally have at their disposal the power of their Prussian counterparts. A strong, personally effective king invariably left monarchical institutions stronger, whereas weaker kings often passed on shaky thrones. Though in theory Louis XVI had as much power as Louis XIV, the institution which made his will law had in fact been undermined. Public support for absolute monarchy had declined.

As you study these selections bear in mind the relationships between monarchical institutions and the monarchs themselves. Each affects the other. Would a strong, effective ruler in Louis XVI's place have made much of a difference?

1.

M. S. Anderson (1922–   ) is Reader in International History at the London School of Economics and Political Science. Examining the impact of the Enlightenment on the monarchs of Europe, he finds it very uneven. How does he define enlightened despotism?

Some rulers changed their notion of their duties and even their conceptions of sovereignty because of the Enlightenment, but did this alter their aims? In what instances did the Enlightenment provide merely a new rhetoric for carrying out already established policies?

M. S. ANDERSON: Monarchs and Despots*

It is often claimed that the government of many European States in the generation or more before the French Revolution is distinguished from the practice of the first half of the century by the existence of something called "Enlightened Despotism." How far is this claim justified? Undoubtedly some rulers and governments were being influenced from the 1760s onwards by the intellectual movement usually known as the Enlightenment. In particular Physiocratic ideas of a natural social order which could be easily discovered and which all intelligent men would support, of a natural harmony of interests which could be given practical expression by an enlightened government, were now being fairly widely diffused outside France, their country of origin. The widespread assumption that the principles of good government were absolute and unchanging, and could be applied virtually anywhere with little modification, also helped to create among the ruling classes of much of Europe a certain community of political outlook. Even a Khan of the Crim Tatars is said to have wished to govern according to "enlightened" ideas.

Most European rulers, however, could not afford the luxury of close adherence to an ideology, even one so loosely defined as that of the Enlightenment. All of them were inevitably the prisoners of history, in that their actions were for the most part determined by economic, political and military forces which were the product of past events. Completely "enlightened" government was a goal which, even had they wished to attain it, the internal complexities of their own countries and the external pressure of others placed beyond their reach. Only small States, freed from the burden of playing a leading rôle in international affairs and often more homogeneous economically and socially than their more pow-

* From M. S. Anderson, *Europe in the Eighteenth Century, 1713–1789* (London: Longmans, 1961), pp. 121–29.

erful neighbours, could afford to apply the political panaceas of the Enlighten-ment with some approach to thoroughness. Thus the only European ruler to introduce, even on a restricted scale, the *impôt unique* (a single tax on land) which was perhaps the most important practical innovation advocated by the Physiocrats, was the Margrave Charles Frederick of Baden. (The experiment was a failure.) With the great exception of Joseph II the rulers of the major States in the later eighteenth century were not prepared to face the problems involved in really radical changes of this kind. Louis XV and his successor clearly had neither the desire nor the ability to become enlightened despots. In Britain government of this type was always out of the question. Neither Freder-ick II nor Catherine II was deeply influenced in practice by the ideas of the Enlightenment.

The last statement may appear to need some justification. Did not the reigns of both see many reforms achieved and others attempted—the efforts of Fred-erick to increase the efficiency of the Prussian administration, of Catherine to develop education, of both to produce legislative codes? They did: but these reforms were in part the mere continuation of policies already well-established which owed nothing to the ideas of the Enlightenment, and in part a pretentious façade covering policies which were selfish and even frivolous.

Frederick II, during most of his reign, was treading where internal adminis-tration was concerned in paths marked out for him by his predecessors. In spite of his superficial unlikeness to his father and the personal conflicts between them, he remained throughout his life in many ways the political executor of Frederick William I. He was more conscious than his father of the State as an entity distinct from the person of the ruler, but his only important addition to the system of government he inherited was a series of judicial reforms which were mainly the work of one of his ministers, Samuel von Cocceji. His flute-playing, the reams of bad French poetry he wrote, his friendship with Voltaire, which have so impressed many historians, are no index to his attitude to matters of real importance. This is seen rather in his snobbish preference for aristocratic ministers and officials, in his unyieldingly mercantilist ideas on economic affairs, and in his lack of any real interest in education. It is no accident that so many contemporary German writers and scholars—Wieland, Winckelmann, Lessing, Gottsched—disliked both him and Prussia; and it is hard to point to any aspect of his activities which would have been very different if the ideas of the En-lightenment had never existed.

Much the same criticisms can be made of Catherine II. Like Frederick she was to a large extent executing policies suggested or initiated in the past. Her local government reforms of 1775 had been anticipated in proposals made during the reign of the Empress Elizabeth, as had the great survey of landownership which she set in motion in 1765 and even the Legislative Commission which she as-sembled two years later. The idea of limiting by law the obligations of the Rus-sian serfs to their masters, which she half-heartedly attempted to apply in the early years of her reign, had been put forward as early as the 1730s. Her secu-larization of Church lands in 1764 was the completion of a process begun by Peter I. The governmental system she eventually constructed, an autocracy based on the support of the landowning class, was completely Russian. It owed little to French or other foreign influences. It is true that she attempted, more systematically than Frederick II, to pose as a patron of progressive ideas and to disseminate in Western Europe the idea that she alone was a truly enlightened despot. These efforts had considerable success. A chorus of writers, hardly any of whom had even set foot in Russia, were soon singing her praises. In fact however she, at least as much as any of her contemporaries, was the captive of the historical situation in which she found herself, a situation which forbade her to introduce any radical changes in the internal organization of Russia. She was far less adventurous, less bold and far-seeing, than Peter I; she lacked the sincerity, intellectual honesty and even humility which did so much to counter-balance his cruelty and ruthlessness.

All this is not to deny that there were in the later eighteenth century a certain number of monarchs and ministers who were prepared to break quite violently with the past, to override vested interests and long-standing traditions in the interests of the States they ruled. Such was the Marques de Pombal, who for over a quarter of a century (1750–77) was virtual ruler of Portugal. His efforts to revive the country's economic life and to challenge the dominance which British merchants had established over its foreign trade, his ferocious repression of noble opposition, above all his expulsion of the Jesuits marked a far more dis- tinct breach with the past than any of the domestic legislation of Frederick II or Catherine II (and for that reason had less enduring effect.) Whether he can be considered an "enlightened" minister is nevertheless doubtful. His policies were essentially empirical; although he had lived as a diplomat in both Vienna and London he does not seem to have owed much, at least directly, to the ideas of the Enlightenment. His contemporary Bernardo Tanucci, chief minister of the Kingdom of the Two Sicilies for seventeen years (1759–76) is in some ways a more satisfactory example of the species, in spite of his pedantry and dislike of Voltaire. Naples and Sicily produced during the eighteenth century a greater number of original and often radical writers on political, legal and economic questions than any other part of Europe except France and Great Britain—the anti-clerical historian Giannone, the political theorist Filangieri, the economist Galiani—and of Tanucci's sympathy with many of the ideas of the Enlighten- ment there can be no doubt. His attempts to restrict the power of the nobility, to improve the judicial system, and above all to curb the power of the Church, show his willingness to apply these ideas in practice even in the face of great difficulties and intense opposition. He was not merely a reformer but a reformer on principle, acting under the influence of some of the most progressive politi-- cal theorists of the period.

The Grand Duke Leopold of Tuscany (1765–90) was in many ways the most remarkable of the "enlightened despots." The Grand Duchy at the begin- ning of his reign was still what it had been under its Medici rulers in the early decades of the century, a personal union of a number of medieval City-States, above all Florence and Siena. These remained distinct in their administration, their laws and their economic institutions. From this accumulation of the debris of the past Leopold had created by the end of his reign one of the best-governed

States in Europe. The administration had been unified and rationalized, the taxation system simplified and tax-farming abolished, internal tariffs swept away. These reforms moreover were inspired by the most progressive ideas of the period, particularly by those of the Physiocrats, and by a desire for the welfare of his subjects whose sincerity is almost without parallel among the rulers of this period.

Unlike those of so many of his contemporaries, Leopold's reforms were not influenced by a desire to increase the military power or international influence of the State he ruled. On the contrary he hoped to establish the perpetual neutrality of the Grand Duchy as a tradition of European diplomacy, to give it more or less the status which Switzerland was to enjoy in the following century. Also, again unlike almost all contemporary rulers, he made consistent efforts to decentralize power. He attempted to create a system of local government which would be at least in part representative, and to give his subjects some control even over the central administration. In a Charter of 1782, perhaps the most remarkable constitutional document of the generation before the French Revolution, he envisaged the sending by the communal assemblies which already existed in the Tuscan towns of representatives to provincial assemblies. These would in turn be represented in a central assembly for the whole State. Without the consent of the latter neither the succession to the throne nor the territorial limits of the Grand Duchy were to be changed, nor was war to be declared nor existing legislation altered. The finances of the State were to be separated from those of its ruler, while the judicial system was to be free from government interference. These proposals remained only a paper project, but they illustrate strikingly the extent to which the most radical political ideas of the period could be adopted by an energetic and open-minded ruler.

Simultaneously Leopold's brother, the Emperor Joseph II, was struggling to impose some at least of the political ideas of the Enlightenment on the Habsburg lands. The brothers differed both in character and in the position in which they found themselves. Joseph had none of the mental flexibility which characterized Leopold: the whole idea of compromise was repugnant to him. In the rigidity and dogmatism which made him, as one writer has put it, "the Ignatius Loyola of the idea of the absolute State," he contrasts not merely with his brother but also with his mother, the Empress Maria Theresa. She, though endowed with courage, a high sense of duty, and a profound though narrow religious faith, was innocent of political ideas, at least in any sophisticated sense of the term. Nor was he attracted by his brother's near-pacifism: one of his earliest surviving letters is a protest against proposals to reduce the Austrian army for financial reasons and throughout his reign he played with schemes for the conquest of new provinces.

His political ideas were for the most part those current in enlightened circles all over Europe. He thought of his authority as originating in a "social contract," and of himself as the personification and in a certain sense the mandatory of his people. The power delegated to him by his subjects to be used on their behalf was absolute, however: no subordinate authority in his dominions could be valid unless it emanated from or was confirmed by him. He tended always to think in highly unrealistic terms of his peoples as a mere aggregate of individuals face to face with an absolute State. To him the institutions intermediate between ruler and people, still in fact so powerful, appeared completely unimportant. His reign thus witnessed a series of efforts, sincere, tactless and sometimes ruthless, to put into effect the programme of reform which he had imbibed from theorists of "enlightened despotism" such as Martini and Sonnenfels. It saw a fierce and partially successful attack on the powers and position of the Catholic Church in his territories. It saw a series of efforts, not altogether without effect, to improve the position of the peasant. These were embodied mainly in the *Unterthanspatent* of 1781 which abolished personal serfdom though not labour services, in the *Strafpatent* of the same year which limited the lord's right to punish the peasant, and in the abolition of the *corvée* and the introduction in 1789 of a very ambitious though short-lived scheme of taxation reform. They won him peasant gratitude of a kind no other eighteenth-century ruler received or deserved. Joseph's reign also saw a continual movement, largely unsuccessful in the long run, towards greater administrative centralization and uniformity in the areas under his rule. This is visible above all in the extension of conscription to Hungary in 1784 and in the abolition of the exemption from taxation which the Hungarian Church and nobility had hitherto enjoyed. Efforts were also made, on a larger scale than hitherto, to increase the prosperity of the Habsburg lands by policies such as the exemption of skilled workers from conscription and the ennoblement of wealthy bourgeois, though Joseph's economic ideas remained throughout his reign conservative and mercantilist.

A man of this stamp, ruling what was still in essentials a mere group of provinces, a random aggregation of territories, was certain to encounter opposition. Of the great established interests in his dominions—Church, nobility, estates, privileged towns—none were on his side. Active and intelligent support Joseph could expect only from a small number of officials. Far from leading him to abandon or modify his policies, opposition incited him to more drastic methods. If his subjects, the victims of generations of oppression and obscurantism, were unwilling to accept the progress and enlightenment he offered, so much the worse for them. If they could not be enlightened by persuasion it must be done by force. We thus find a ruler who had spent his life in efforts to make his subjects prosperous and happy compelled in his last years to create a system of secret police (the ancestor of that of the Metternich era), to abolish the limited degree of freedom which he had previously granted to the Press, and to hold down considerable parts of his territories by armed force. A Lombard observer, commenting on his methods, remarked that "the time seems to have returned in which Mahomet, sabre in hand, was the most eloquent teacher in the world." Events were to show that the persuasive power of force was not lasting and that some parts of the Habsburg lands were still able to defend their privileges effectively against the pressure of the central government. The Emperor's reforming policies in the Austrian Netherlands, in particular his efforts to reduce the power of the Catholic Church there and to override provincial traditions and institutions, meant that from 1787 onwards much of the area was in open opposition to him. This, coupled with an almost equally difficult situation in Hungary, seemed to threaten the break-up of the fragile unity of the Habsburg dominions. Even before his death in 1790 Joseph, ill and discouraged, had been driven to revoke some of his most unpopular measures: his successor Leopold II, skilfully mingling force and concessions, was able to restore stability in the disturbed areas. It can be argued, however, that the abandonment of many of the radical policies of the earlier part of Joseph's reign paved the way for the political stagnation of the first half of the nineteenth century, and thus for the complete governmental collapse which overwhelmed all the Habsburg lands in 1848.

The three generations before the French Revolution therefore saw in government and administration, as in many other respects, a process of change which tended to accelerate from about 1760 onwards. The main lines of development remained the same throughout this period. Almost everywhere there was a tendency for bureaucracies to become larger and more elaborate. Almost everywhere the organs of central administration tended to become more effective and more flexible. Almost everywhere except in Britain and some of the smaller States the demands of the armed forces . . . were the ultimate reason for most of these improvements. Almost everywhere, again with the partial exception of Britain, efforts were made with varying success to strengthen central governments and to make administrative systems more uniform and more rational. Almost everywhere the increasing wealth of Europe was reflected in a tendency for the yield of taxation to rise, sometimes very sharply. Almost everywhere the exertions of powerful monarchs and their ministers played an essential part in improving methods of administration.

Changes of what may be called a qualitative kind, changes of temper and objectives, were less marked in the decades before 1789 in government than in economic, social or intellectual life. They nevertheless took place. Sales of offices tended, as the century progressed, to be increasingly frowned upon by the governments of the more advanced States. This was an essential prerequisite of the growth of a modern administrative system and was, as might be expected, most noticeable in Prussia. There Frederick II restricted sales of government offices, in 1743, to the Rhenish–Westphalian provinces, and abolished them completely soon afterwards. In their economic policies, again, many governments were increasingly influenced during the generation before the French Revolution by ideas making for greater freedom, above all greater commercial freedom. The more extreme forms of mercantilism were now losing many of their attractions, at least in Western Europe. This can be seen in the belated liberalization of trade between Spain and her colonies from 1776 onwards, in the growth of the system of "free ports" in the British and French West Indies, and in the important Anglo-French commercial treaty of 1786. The legal and administrative restrictions which had been imposed in past generations on trade in certain vital commodities were now being lifted. Thus the grain trade was freed temporarily in France in 1763 and 1774, while similar developments were seen in Tuscany in 1781, in Milan in 1785, and later in Naples and even in ultra-conservative Venice. More significant still, the belief that rulers and governments might benefit by having available the advice of some body which could claim to represent the politically significant part of their subjects was slowly gaining ground. Catherine II's Legislative Commission of 1767 was a striking though unsuccessful and half-hearted experiment in this direction. Later ideas of this kind were to find more serious and systematic expression in the suggestions of Dupont de Nemours and the innovations of Necker in France, and in the remarkable constitutional proposals of the Grand Duke Leopold in Tuscany.

Most important of all, the levelling and rationalizing tendencies of most European governments in the later eighteenth century, the increasingly wide diffusion of the idea that the ruler, however absolute, was ultimately no more than the supreme representative and first servant of his people, helped to lay the foundations of the epoch of revolutions which opened in the 1780s. A heavier emphasis than ever before came to be laid, in many cases by monarchs themselves, on a ruler's duties to his subjects. These duties were now increasingly defined in terms of progress towards a better, or even an ideal, form of society and government. The frequent acceptance of ideas of this kind by absolute monarchs and their ministers helps to explain the lack of hostility, sometimes even enthusiasm, with which the French Revolution in its early stages was received in many royal families. In St. Petersburg in 1789 the French ambassador was publicly congratulated by the Grand Duke Alexander (later Alexander I) on the fall of the Bastille, while the Grand Duke Constantine, later an extreme reactionary, was also at first an enthusiastic partisan of the Revolution. In the same way the Emperor Leopold II approved of much of the work of the Constituent Assembly. Even when the more violent and disruptive aspects of events in France had become clearly visible, it was often the methods as much as the objectives of the revolutionaries which aroused opposition. Increasingly in the later eighteenth century it was felt that monarchy was on trial, that kings must now justify their existence by efforts to increase the welfare and happiness of their peoples, that they must now provide not merely good government but progressive government. The careers of Louis XV and Louis XVI showed that rulers unwilling or unable to meet this test could not, at least in the more advanced States, rely implicitly upon the loyalty of their subjects. Even in the 1760s or 1770s there were very few European monarchs who could feel quite the same unquestioning self-assurance as Louis XIV a century earlier.

2.

Brief and disarming because of its boldness and clarity, Hajo Holborn's (1902–   ) analysis of Frederick the Great is overwhelmingly convincing. One senses after reading it that though further research might add to our knowledge of details, this knowledge would not undermine Holborn's interpretation of the reign. His debt to previous great historians, notably Otto Hintze, is considerable, but Holborn refines and stamps his own definitive interpretation on the whole complex of personal and institutional developments during a crucial reign in German history.

For Holborn, who is Sterling Professor of History at Yale, Frederick II did not successfully establish the administration of the Prussian state. Though the King's knowledge of Enlightenment thought was very great, this knowledge never spurred him to recast the royal administration. Why? Did this dynamic leader leave the Prussian state stronger or weaker at his death?

HAJO HOLBORN: Frederick the Great*

Frederick was more a man of action than of organization. On the whole, he kept the government structure as his father had left it. The additions and changes he made were not altogether improvements. The creation of functional departments besides the old regional ones in the General Directory, which began in 1740 with the department of commerce, produced some friction in the central administration. But the overlapping organization could hardly be avoided at a time not yet ripe for a fully centralized administration. Most dubious, however, was the establishment of separate treasuries, especially the chest at the exclusive disposal of the king (*Dispositionskasse*), into which the great expansion of revenue was flowing. Frederick instituted the system after the Seven Years' War, when he wished to have greater flexibility in employing funds than a rigid budget would have allowed him. The multiplicity of state chests made it finally impossible for anyone except the king to know the general state of public finance. Had Frederick not been an unusually shrewd and conscientious financial administrator, this would have created the most serious dangers.

Great complications of the existing administrative organization developed as a consequence of the introduction of the so-called *Regie* in 1766. Frederick believed that the yield of the excise tax could be raised considerably by using the refined methods the French had perfected. The excise and customs administration was set up as a separate administration on the local, provincial, and central levels, and about two hundred French professionals were appointed for its direction. The French techniques brought good financial results, but it may be questionable whether they were worth the resentment that the *Regie* and the subsequently instituted tobacco and coffee monopolies caused. The establishment of the French *Regie* was a clear declaration of lack of confidence in the ability of the Prussian bureaucracy, and the public tended to ascribe the guilt for the heavy and exacting taxation to the foreigners whom the king had imported.

The institutional changes that Frederick made in the Prussian administrative system necessitated an even greater centralization of all supervision and decision in the hands of the autocratic monarch. Frederick's regime was the utmost realization of the *Kabinettsregierung,* that is, government from the king's study, on the basis of reports, usually in writing, of government agencies and ministers. But the king's decisions were based also on opinions which he formed by regular inspections on the spot and through conversations with local people of various classes. Regular travels brought him to all of the provinces, where he inspected

* From Hajo Holborn, *A History of Modern Germany* (New York: Knopf, 1964), II, pp. 262–77.

both his troops and civil administration. He also encouraged the presentation of complaints, which gave the lower classes the impression that the king was on their side against the bureaucracy. On the other hand, the relative omniscience and omnipresence of the king drew him into the settlement of details which might more usefully have been left to the local official. His autocratic manner did not encourage initiative among his subordinates.

The Great Elector and Frederick William had built the structure of the new despotic state over and above the old dualistic state. Though they tore down many of the old institutions, they bent some of them as well as they could to their own purposes, while leaving others intact. Among the latter was not only the old class division as such but also the very special social privileges of the nobility. Frederick William might have gone still further in demolishing the exemptions of the *Junkers* if he had lived longer. He felt the tension between the new royal power and the old feudal traditions acutely. For Frederick this was a thing of the past, especially since, much more distinctly than his father, he felt himself an aristocrat, and his modern education rather confirmed this attitude. In Frederick's opinion, the interest of the state justified the privileged caste character of the Prussian nobility. It provided the state with its military officers and high civilian officials, and for this reason it deserved to be protected in its social and political rights. Frederick was most careful to preserve and even fortify the *Junkers'* existing position. He never contemplated extending taxation of the nobility to all Prussian provinces, a practice which had been customary in East Prussia and Silesia. He was most anxious to keep the *Junkers* owners of their landed estates. The best way seemed to him the creation of entailed estates, but meanwhile he disapproved the purchase of land by burghers and took steps to enhance the credit of the landowning nobility.

What endeared the *Junkers* to him, though he was not blind to some of their foibles, was their sense of honor, which he could not discover in most burghers, who had "low minds" and made for poor and useless officers. The fairly large numbers of nonnoble officers whom the king used in the last years of the Seven Years' War were dismissed after the war or transferred to the second-rate fortress troops. On the other hand, he realized that there were not enough Prussian *Junkers* for a greatly enlarged army and advised his successor to draw foreign noblemen into the Prussian army. Among the burghers, he found it worthwhile to give the sons of managers of royal domains commissions in fortress battalions, to knight them after ten years of satisfactory performance, and to allow them to serve with regular regiments thereafter. No doubt, Frederick's pragmatic justification of noble privileges was greatly tempered by his personal social prejudices.

In Frederick's view the burghers had the duty of producing the wherewithal for the army. Although there were among them some people of extraordinary intellectual gifts and even some people of noble honor and virtue, whom Frederick proposed to treat with special recognition, the burghers formed the class that by its industry contributed most to the maintenance of the government. For this reason they received their special privileges, which consisted chiefly in the exemption from military service and special assistance to new economic enterprises. Below the class of noblemen and burghers, lived the vast majority of the population, the peasants. To maintain and increase this class was of vital interest to the state. The livelihood and a substantial part of the income of the state depended on them, but even more important were their military services. In order to preserve the peasant population, at least one limitation had to be imposed on the *Junkers'* freedom. They were not allowed to add the acreage of peasants to their land, and the government saw to it that every peasant's place that fell vacant was filled again. Otherwise the state did very little for the peasants on the estates of the noblemen. Frederick wanted to limit the forced labor services of peasants to three to four days, but did not dare impose such a rule on the *Junkers.* Not even with regard to the peasants on the royal domains was he fully successful in this respect. The domain peasants at least received their land as hereditary holdings.

While these policies were entirely conservative, one could find a slightly different tone in Frederick's colonization of the state. This is one of the finest pages of his government's record. Over 57,000 families were settled during his reign. It is assumed that at the time of his death every fifth Prussian belonged to a family of colonists. One of the greatest achievements was the drainage and amelioration of the large marshes of the Oder valley in the years 1747–53, a work that was repeated in the Netze district after 1772. In these new lands, his peaceful conquests, Frederick settled free peasants, and the feudal structure of eastern Germany was avoided.

Frederick's economic policy remained mercantilistic throughout. What distinguished his policy from his father's was the greater emphasis on the development of manufacturing and commerce, although agriculture, still by far the most important part of the economy, was not neglected. Every effort was made to attract foreign capitalists, manufacturers, and skilled workers to Prussia. Berlin, Potsdam, and Brandenburg, which were singled out by the king as centers of manufacturing, were for this reason entirely exempted from the canton system. Special attention was given to transportation. The Oder river in its entirety was in Prussian hands after the acquisition of Silesia, and it was made safe for navigation by the building of dikes and the dredging of the estuary, at the entrance of which the port of Swinemünde was founded. Whereas the Great Elector was satisfied with linking up the central Oder with the Elbe and Hamburg through an Oder-Spree canal, Frederick wished to deflect some of the Elbe traffic to the Oder and Stettin. The Finow canal between the Havel and the Oder north of Berlin, built after 1746, served at the same time as a convenient connection between the Prussian capital and the Baltic.

Among the manufactures, the textile industries were the most important. The woolen cloth manufacture, relying on domestic wool production, was economically the most profitable industry, but the linen industries of Silesia and Westphalia were also of great significance. Frederick endeavored to develop the Prussian silk industry. But the stimulation of manufacturing was extended to practically every field that promised profit or at least the exclusion of the need for imports. In the years after the Seven Years' War, Frederick played temporarily with the idea of a completely centralized economy, steered and planned by the government, in whose hands capital and credit was to be fully concentrated. Little remained of this project for a complete state socialism or state capitalism. A royal bank was founded, as were a number of foreign trade companies and certain state factories. Besides some arsenals, the best-known of these factories was the Berlin royal porcelain factory. But the activities of the state as a rule did not take the form of ownership. In addition to exercising the close supervision over productive labor, the government promoted industries by grants of initial capital and credit, very often as a free gift. A frequently used method was the gift of buildings. Through the exclusion of competitive production, either by limiting the numbers of producers or the grant of exclusive market rights, governmental protection was quite common.

In these conditions, the growth of an entrepreneurial group was slow and devious. Frederick complained about the lack of enterprising spirit among the Prussian merchants. Most of them were satisfied to act as traders on a commission basis. The dependence on state capital and credit, as well as on state protection and guidance, did not permit the development of independent entrepreneurs either in the commercial or industrial field. A great number of eighteenth-century industries in Prussia were closely connected with agriculture. The *Junker* estates produced grain, wool, and flax for the market. At least in Silesia, linen manufacture was closely connected with the landed estates. Other industries, such as mills, sawmills, distilleries, and brick factories, were found on many estates. In the last years of Frederick's reign, the development of mining was given particular care. It was the work of Baron von Heinitz, a native of Saxony, whom Frederick brought to Prussia in 1777, and to whom he left more freedom than to any of his ministers. Under him, Count Reden devoted himself with great success to the opening of the large mineral resources of Upper Silesia, while the young Baron Stein was active in Westphalia. But here again the part played by the nobility was remarkable. In 1785, one year before the first coke-heated steel furnace was started in Germany, only 2 out of 243 mining enterprises in Upper Silesia were owned by merchants, while 20 were owned by the king, and the rest by the nobility.

At the end of Frederick's reign, Prussia had become the fourth largest industrial state, after England, France, and Holland, but actually she was so far behind the three others that the statement is not very meaningful. Foreign trade was small, too, though no longer insignificant. In 1781–82, imports and exports amounted to 26 to 27 million thaler, with a favorable balance of about 3 million. As industrial production was steadily rising, so was foreign trade. Yet the full benefit of Frederick's economic policies was reaped by the country only after his death. Some extraordinary circumstances contributed to this, for example, the lesser production of France during the years of the French Revolution and new opportunities for grain export. But by then Prussia had become capable of taking advantage of such conditions. In the five years after 1769, 200 to 300 Prussian ships annually passed through the Danish Sound; in 1798: 1,621; in 1804: 2,012. All this proved that Frederick's mercantilistic policies had laid foundations for a growing economic life, though a good many of their special measures and individual creations had to be discarded.

The whole system was violently criticized in Prussia and abroad as early as the 1780's. Excluding the criticism that stemmed from an absolute hostility to mercantilism—for how could small Prussia have turned liberal in a mercantilistic world?—it was obvious that internal trade barriers and customs, as well as the excessive concern with immediate tax revenue, albeit less pronounced than under Frederick William I, acted as brakes on the economic development. Frederick took deep satisfaction when he looked at the results of the *rétablissement* of his devastated provinces after 1763 and noticed the progress in the Prussian peoples' well-being. Nevertheless, his chief goal was the power of the state. The growth of the population and economy was to feed the expanding army and war treasury. Frederick had managed to conduct twelve years of war without running up more than a negligible public debt. In 1740, the state revenues had been 7 million thaler, and 10 million had been in the war chest left by Frederick's father. In 1786, Prussia collected 23 million in revenues and maintained a war chest of 54 million. It was as amazing as some of his most brilliant military victories that Frederick proved able to finance the Seven Years' War, although at times income from taxes dwindled to almost nothing owing to the occupation of most provinces by the enemy. To the actual war cost of around 100 million thaler English subsidies contributed 16 million. The major part of the funds was extracted from occupied Saxony and Mecklenburg. Out of these unhappy states, 50 million and 8 million were exacted, respectively. Meanwhile, internal payments were cut to a minimum. The Prussian state officials were paid in promissory notes to be cashed after the war. Internal loans could not produce much, and Frederick was finally driven to coin bad money and pass it off not only on his own subjects but also on Poland and on neighboring German states. It was a rather desperate means of war financing, but it gave Frederick sufficient cash just at a time when he resisted the importunities of Lord Bute for political concessions to Austria. Although the consequences of these malpractices in coinage were not easily overcome after peace had been made, Frederick had money left in 1763 to begin at once the restoration of Prussia. It was understandable that on the basis of his experiences Frederick considered the accumulation of a war chest imperative, although he was not unaware of the deflationary impact that the hoarding and sterilization of money was bound to have on the economy. However, it is true that the chances for capital investment were limited so long as rigid mercantilistic laws prevailed.

The power of the state was the lodestar of all of Frederick's policies and autocratic management the method for the realization of his aims. This autocracy extended to every corner of the government and was exercised in a most personal manner. The king, who seemingly moved simply and easily among all classes of the people, actually was a world apart from them. The sensitive man had maintained his own courage and determination under the enormous strain of the Seven Years' War, which also demanded great physical endurance. The tragic emotions of his beloved Racine, the Stoic philosophers, and Lucretius comforted him in hours of defeat as well as victory. But he grew more skeptical and contemptuous with regard to man. In his testament, he expressed the wish to be buried on the garden terrace of Sans Souci close to the graves of his little French greyhounds, which he liked to spoil. His relationship with the French Enlightenment became more distant in his later years. The materialism of a Helvétius or a Holbach was to him the recrudescence of a particularly ugly metaphysics, and the signs of democratic thought that appeared among the young French writers annoyed him.

"Old Fritz," as the Prussians named him, was a lonely person among his people. He did not wish to make personal friends among his officers and officials. Rather, he wanted them to obey and do their assigned duty meticulously and with dispatch. Frederick was distrustful not only of their intelligence and industry but also of their integrity. In general, he believed that the members of this *maudite race* were moved chiefly by their desire for personal advantage and that a system of penalties interspersed with occasional premiums was the best way of keeping them on their toes. Frederick no longer knocked out the teeth of his officials nor beat them up, as his father had done. But his acid vituperations were equally wounding, and he was as quick as his father in sending officials to the Spandau prison. No doubt, there were cases of corruption. The days of feudal spoils were still in living memory, and officials served for starvation wages. But it is questionable whether abuses were really widespread. There is plenty of evidence that the number of officials and officers who took their duties with a deep sense of moral responsibility was great, and this sense of responsibility was much more than outward conformity with higher orders. Religion, whether of the orthodox-pietistic or enlightened variety, was a potent force in Germany, and Frederick knew little about such sources of loyalty.

Planting fear and trembling into the hearts of all subordinates produced automatons galore but not men of strong character and self-reliance. This was true even with the king's officer corps, which enjoyed more royal respect and attention than any other group in the state. But Frederick failed to replace Field Marshals Schwerin, Winterfeldt, and Keith, who met death in battle in the early years of the Seven Years' War, by officers of his own training. In Seydlitz and Ziethen, the Prussian army possessed cavalry generals of the highest talent and bravura. What was missing, however, was a group of generals fit for high command. There was nothing Frederick's generals feared more than being selected as leaders of detached armies. As a matter of fact, none of them ever did well in such a position, and, at least in some cases, this was due to Frederick's interference. Only one general was a born captain of war like Frederick; that was his younger brother Prince Henry (1726–1802), who resembled the king in education and thought as well as in the desire for recognition. This highly gifted, unhappy prince, who was obsessed by a consuming jealousy of his elder brother, was in a position to gain more independence, or at least distance, from Frederick than men of lesser birth.

Frederick was not unmindful of the necessity for training officers who were experienced in higher tactics. In the years after 1763, he attached a group of young staff officers to the quartermaster-general's staff and he himself taught them tactics. One of these officers, Baron von Steuben, was to become one of the chief organizers of the American army. But this training was discontinued after a few years. The king also attempted to raise the very low general educational level of the officer corps. Courses were introduced for junior officers. A small number of gifted cadets were brought together in an elite school, the "academy of nobles," in Berlin. But at best these efforts could have borne fruit only after a long period of time. Moreover, technical education was not the real answer to the weaknesses of the Prussian army, which were caused by the mechanical enforcement of rules and the suppression of the initiative of the individual. Frederick was greatly dissatisfied with the showing of the Prussian army during the war of 1778–79, but his dissatisfaction only served to make him an even tougher taskmaster in the subsequent years.

Frederick did not consider it a structural infirmity of the monarchy that it demanded a king able to rule by himself as he had done. In view of Frederick's judgment of his prospective successor's character it is perhaps hard to understand why he tried to impress upon him the imperative need for royal autocracy and to warn him even against a chief minister or council of ministers. There was no intimation that the shortcomings of the heir to the throne might call for adjustments in government. He also was fully unaware of the changeability of social forces. They were to him timeless, and although he did not deny that they could get out of hand, he felt certain that a good government could hold them in their natural place. It was surprising that he did not see the conflict between the old feudal order and the new conception of equal service to the state, while as an enlightened *philosophe* he believed in the possibility of doing away with old prejudices and institutions. But a more conscious attack on the social order would have jeopardized the immediate use of the state's ready resources in the foreign field. Frederick's preoccupation with power politics dictated his social conservatism, which stands in contrast to his intellectual and religious radicalism.

Much of the steel frame which Frederick constructed for the Prussian state remained standing in the nineteenth and even twentieth centuries. This was partly the result of the incomplete character of all subsequent social reforms. But it was also due to the fact that Frederick's regime created certain institutions that were only loosely connected with the military objectives of the Prussian state and acted as channels through which the warmer air of humane ideals could eventually flow into the cold atmosphere of the northern Sparta.

In the administration of justice and education, Frederick reached most clearly beyond power politics. In describing the *ancien régime* in Prussia, Friedrich Meinecke has referred to the saying of an ancient Sassanide king: "There is no kingdom without soldiers, no soldier without money, no money without population, no population without justice." This is an apt description, and it is true that Frederick's reforms of justice and education intended to improve the economy on which the military state was built. But the scope of his reforms was broad enough to carry them beyond their original objectives. Frederick devoted himself to an improvement of the administration of justice in the years between 1746 and 1756. In Samuel von Cocceji (1679–1755), whom Frederick William I had appointed Minister of Justice in his last years, Frederick found the man who combined a belief in natural law with practical knowledge of state administration. Cocceji made short shrift of thousands of law cases, which had been piling up in all the provinces, and created a unified and centralized state court system on the local, provincial, and central levels. The judges became salaried state officials, and judges' personal fees were abolished. The procedure, for which the rules were laid down in the *Codex Fredericianus Marchicus* of 1748, was greatly simplified and expedited. The whole judiciary, which so far had retained much of the guild character, was made a branch of state government by Cocceji. At the same time, he gave it greater dignity by providing personal security and solid legal training. In the course of the reorganization of the courts, many incompetent judges were removed. Judgeships no longer could be purchased but required the passing of an examination and years of preparatory service with the courts.

Cocceji argued that the king, though supreme judge, should not interfere with the course of justice by personal rulings or decisions. Frederick agreed to this principle, for "in the courts the laws must speak and the sovereign must remain silent." But the king remained supervisor of the judges, whom he reprimanded or dismissed at his discretion. The independence of judges was by no means guaranteed. Another limitation of the courts' power resulted from the continuation of broad judicial authority in the war and domain chambers. They retained jurisdiction in all matters concerning the state's police, domain, and tax administration. On the other hand, the ecclesiastical consistories ceased to have judiciary functions, which formerly had been rather extensive in family law.

Cocceji did not accomplish the unification and modernization of the laws themselves. A new generation of jurists grew up, trained in the school of Thomasius and Wolff. From the Roman and German legal tradition, alive in the greatly diversified laws of the various provinces, these jurists tried to single out the norms which could express the practice of both an enlightened state and of natural law. After 1779, the work was taken up under Minister J. H. von Carmer (1721–1801). His closest associate Karl Gottlieb Suarez (1746–98) was the chief author of the Prussian Law Code (*Preussisches Landrecht*). Suarez, a student of Christian Wolff, attempted in this book of statutes to define and carry forward the moral principles that the monarchy of Frederick had developed. The *Code* was intended to give every citizen a clear conception of the state's purpose, and for that reason was not confined to private civil and criminal law but treated constitutional questions as well. The authors of the *Code* hoped to implant a public spirit that would make the enforcement of laws by the government an easy task. The sovereignty of the monarch was formulated in all its absolutist consequences. For the first time, the *Code* clearly defined as a right what so far had been only the practice of the Prussian rulers, namely to levy taxes without popular consent. But on the other hand, even the rights of the king were defined as duties as well. It was the king's obligation to act for the welfare of the people and respect those moral purposes that the human individual had a duty to realize in his life. "The general rights of man are founded on the natural freedom to seek and advance his own welfare without interfering with the rights of others." These rights were to be protected by reasonable laws administered by judges who were secure against the disturbing intervention of arbitrary government.

Carmer and his collaborators were believers in Montesquieu's division of powers and wanted to establish the judiciary as an intermediary power between the executive and the people. But they were not allowed to write this theory into the *Code,* which was not promulgated under Frederick but only under his successor. In vain did Suarez argue that a paragraph protecting the citizen against the arbitrary decisions of the crown merely meant the spelling out of the existing difference between the Prussian monarchy and oriental despotism. Frederick William II did not wish to see his absolute royal sovereignty committed in this manner, and the paragraph was dropped before the *Code* became law in 1794. Even the statement "mutual promises and contracts must be holy to the state and its citizens alike" had to go. Still the general tenor of the *Code* pointed in the direction of contractual rights. Alexis de Tocqueville later on described the *Prussian Code* as a constitution as well as a code of civil and criminal law. This is going too far. But it is true that the *Code* marked the beginning of a tendency for authoritarian government to limit its absolute powers by the rule of law or, in German terminology, that the *Obrigkeitsstaat* was supplemented by the *Rechtsstaat.* Then and later, it was easily forgotten in Germany that this rule of law depended on the absolute will of the sovereign and had no guarantee of stability without representative institutions or, in other words, without a popular constitution.

But neither was absolutism ready to abdicate, and the distinctions between classes were not abandoned. The *Code* defined the rights of the citizens according to the three social "estates"—peasants, burghers, and noblemen. It is characteristic that the peasants were now called an estate, and that in the opinion of the lawgivers an estate was constituted not only by "birth" but also by "main occupation."

The peasants had the right to remain on their land, while the nobility, still called the "first estate," enjoyed protection of its landholdings and had the first right to state positions. The latter, however, presupposed that the *Junker* had acquired the necessary skills for the job and was selected by the king from among a group of candidates. Thus the social distinctions were preserved in a scale of political and social rights that corresponded to the functions that the individual class performed for the community. General rights were recognized only in religion and, to a lesser extent, education. "Every inhabitant of the state must be granted complete freedom of religion and conscience," was the conclusion the *Code* drew from almost two centuries of denominational conflict.

The state did not relinquish its authority to decide what religions should be admitted, but the criteria applied were no longer theological but entirely practical ones. Obedience to the laws, loyalty to the state, and the inculcation of morally good attitudes toward fellow-citizens were expected from all religious groups. But Frederick followed a liberal practice even here. The Moravian Brethren gained exemption from military service in exchange for the payment of a tax. Antitrinitarians were allowed to have church buildings, and Hussites were admitted into Prussia. Frederick even invited Tartars to settle in West Prussia and promised to build mosques for them if they came. Still, the supervision of the churches remained strict. In particular, the churches were prevented from engaging in controversies with each other. The assertion of exclusive sovereignty, which tolerated no independent church government at its side, was naturally simple in the case of the Protestant churches, since the king retained the episcopal authority. This authority was exercised, through the control of church appointments, in molding the teachings of the Protestant churches. Differences between Reformed and Lutheran doctrine were played down, and the representatives of the Enlightenment given preference.

Protestantism continued to be the favored religion. Catholics were not chosen for higher state positions. Frederick showed great fairness in his dealings with the Prussian Catholics, most of whom were in Silesia. But he did not tolerate papal interference with the exercise of his royal control over the Catholic church in Prussia. This exclusion of papal authority might have led to conflicts between Prussia and the papal see had the Vatican not been pressed even harder by Spain, France, and Austria.

Closely connected with the policy toward religion were censorship questions. The state manifested its interest in the spread and expansion of knowledge by the maintenance of the academy and universities. With the division of labor prevailing in Frederick's state, however, the members of academy and universities were the only people who were free from censorship. Private persons had only limited rights of public communication. The *Code* contained severe penalties against the critical discussion of many subjects, particularly criticism of political conditions, derogatory statements about the laws, and the diffusion of ideas likely to endanger order. Beyond such penalties, censorship did its work. It could be fairly liberal, because the state authority was safely anchored and because German writers showed no revolutionary spirit.

In these circumstances of the age, the criminal law was also relatively liberal. Through the abolition of torture and many of the ugly penalties of life and limb, a great step was taken beyond the *Carolina* of the sixteenth century, which was still the predominant code of criminal penalties. The protection of the community's security, peace, and welfare was the supreme principle that defined crimes. Not so much vengeance for committed crimes as deterrence from future crimes was sought. The absolute state could be lenient compared to practices of the past, since it could hope to be more effective in the prevention of crime. Through its officialdom, it felt itself to have the capacity to control the everyday life of the people and thus keep them on the right path. The bureaucracy had its eyes not only on all aspects of economic life but also on all private movements. They believed themselves able to direct everything through reputedly wise ordinances for the welfare of both the state and individual. But while the omnipresence and omniscience of the government was stifling, government was no longer justified in theological terms as punishment for human sin, but rather as an institution for the realization of the moral qualities of man. Government claimed to be the leader in the moral progress possible in this world and asserted an identity of objectives, if not of functions, between itself and its subjects. All this was still conceived in a crudely mechanistic spirit and largely concealed by practices which did not jibe with lofty ideal aims. But these ideas formed powerful incentives for the future reform of governmental practices and, more than this, for an attempt at finding true unity between people and government.

The development of education added another element to this process. Frederick did not consider education an integral part of state policy, but his personal interest in it was lively, especially after 1763. The notion that education would make absolute government more difficult seemed to him ridiculous. Education for him had a largely practical aim. It was to make people better fit for the performance of their work and was not designed to carry them beyond their station in life. To Frederick it was undesirable to give a peasant a schooling that might make him wish to become a secretary in a town. It was enough to teach him "a little reading and writing" and the moral commandments of Christian religion, which Frederick thought could be summed up in the single sentence: "Do not anything to others that you do not want to have done to yourself."

Not too much was accomplished in elementary education during Frederick's lifetime. A good many schools were established in villages and towns, but adequate teachers were lacking. Tailors and other artisans, finally even disabled sergeants, were widely used. Conditions were better in Catholic districts because of the Catholic orders. But at least the schools were drawn into the scope of state activities. Methods of inspection were devised, and schools for the training of teachers supported. In Karl Abraham von Zedlitz (1731–93), who was responsible for all cultural affairs in Prussia after 1770, education received a director of high talent and enlightened convictions. But utilitarian motives and a strong emphasis on socially divided education characterized Zedlitz's administration, and full contact with the new German literature was not established.

Frederick saw no need for rooting the life of the state deeply in a common civilization. Education was to provide the individual with a set of moral rules and equip him with the practical knowledge necessary in his occupation. Only a small group of the most eminent men was to be free to devote itself to the critical enjoyment of philosophy, literature, and art. A real understanding that civilization is largely a search for new ideals was alien to him. Without denying the expansion of knowledge over the ages, he conceived of truth and the ideals of beauty as essentially identical throughout the ages. The culture of the Augustan age was submerged by medieval superstition and stupidity, but had revived with the able men who lived under Louis XIV. French civilization was for Frederick the resurrection of the eternal beauty and truth of the ancients. He was greatly displeased to see new ideas presented by the post-Voltairean writers of France. He most emphatically rejected that "obsessed cynic" Rousseau, although he did not deny him a refuge in the Prussian Neufchâtel in 1762. But his rigid cultural concepts deprived him of any access to the ideas of the French thinker who had an infinitely greater influence on the thought and art of Germany than Voltaire. Even if Frederick had followed the growth of German literature in his later life, he would have pronounced the same negative judgment as the one expressed in his article *On German Literature,* of 1780. Klopstock, Lessing, or Wieland were not mentioned by the king. Goethe's *Goetz* he called an "abominable imitation" of Shakespeare's "bizarre aberrations." Although he held out some hope for the future, he found German literature without an educated language and sense of taste.

Frederick clung to the type of French thought that corresponded to his own aristocratic style. For his state, a utilitarian moral culture appeared to be the healthiest form of education. As a cement for the cohesion of the political community, cultural ideals were not considered of great importance. The authority of the government was firmly anchored. As Kant put it, a monarch "who enlightened himself has no fear of shadows and, in addition, has a well-disciplined and numerous army as guarantor of public peace, can say what a republic could not dare: 'Argue as much as you please and about anything you please, but obey.'" With the significant exception of politics itself, this definition was correct. The existing freedom at least stimulated intellectual growth, which, as Kant also predicted, was bound eventually to build a public spirit.

When Frederick died, on August 17, 1786, he left a state that he had raised to European stature by his military genius and by a government that mobilized every ounce of strength for the increase of Prussia's armed might. Frederick was fully aware of Prussia's precarious position among the European powers owing to her weak physical and material resources, but he had no idea of the tremendous forces which were hidden in the unawakened political energies of the peoples themselves. Frederick warned that an indolent ruler on the Prussian throne could ruin the state within thirty years. Actually it took only twenty years until Frederick the Great's monarchy crashed to the ground for reasons much more complex than he had foreseen. It is not surprising that Frederick's successors never mastered his method of government. They must be called his inferiors chiefly because they failed to remodel the state in accordance with the needs of a new historic age. Only after the disaster of Jena did a new generation of statesmen breathe a new spirit into the Prussian monarchy, though even nineteenth-century Prussia was built on the foundations which Frederick had laid.

3.

In a classic essay Sir Lewis Namier (1888–1960) examines the old assertion that George III tried to overthrow the English Constitution in order that he might rule autocratically. According to Namier, this assertion is a legend. But that it may be a legend has not kept it from being considered historical fact.

By studying George III's thought and actions, Namier finds the King free from heady ambitions and makes it abundantly clear that the King merely wanted to be a good and successful ruler. But George failed even by his own standards. Namier demonstrates how the King himself sensed his failure.

The institutions of monarchy in the United Kingdom, however, were such that George's failure did not bring about as grave a crisis as did Louis XVI's failures in France. But George and Louis resembled one another in strange ways: their sense of inadequacy, their social conservatism, and their inability to seize and hold the initiative in government. Namier intimates that, at least for George III, the power was there, but the King could not make the most of it.

His genius as a historical psychoanalyst permits Namier to see that George III's own attempts to reduce his sense of failure by blaming things that went wrong on his ministers, subjects, and even on his "wicked age" suggests that the divorce from reality so prevalent among monarchs came from their own neuroses rather than from life at court. Namier's essay recalls to historians the persistent need to study every aspect of the behavior of men in power. George III's failure as a monarch seems to have been of his own making, derived from that "concentration camp" of a nursery, rather than from general institutions and social forces present in his age.

SIR LEWIS NAMIER: George III*

There were three large pictures of George III at the exhibition of Royal Portraits arranged by the Academy of Arts in the Spring of 1953. Looking at the first, by Reynolds, painted when the King was 41, I was struck by the immaturity of expression. The second, by Lawrence, painted in 1792 at the age of 54, depicts him in Garter robes; face and posture seem to attempt in a naive, ineffective, and almost engaging manner to live up to a grandeur which the sitter feels incumbent on him. The third, by Stroehling, painted in November 1807, at the age of nearly 70, shows a sad old man, looking dimly at a world in which he has no pleasure, and which he soon will not be able to see or comprehend.

A picture in a different medium of the King and his story presents itself to the student when in the Royal Archives at Windsor he surveys the papers of George III. They stand on the shelves in boxes, each marked on a white label with the year or years which it covers. The eye runs over that array, and crucial dates recall events: 1760, '65 and '67, '74 and '75, '82 and '83, 1789, '93, '96, 1802, 1805—the series breaks off in 1810; and brown-backed volumes follow, unlabelled: they contain the medical reports on a man shut off from time, which means the world and its life.

Fate had made George III ruler when kings were still expected to govern; and his active reign covered half a century during which the American conflict posed the problem of Imperial relations, while at home political practice constantly ran up against the contradiction inherent in the then much belauded "mixed form of government": personal monarchy served by Ministers whose tenure of office was contested in Parliament. Neither the Imperial nor the constitutional problem could have been solved in the terms in which the overwhelming majority of the politically minded public in this country considered them at the time; but George III has been blamed ever since for not having thought of Dominion status and parliamentary government when constitutional theory and the facts of the situation as yet admitted of neither.

* From Sir Lewis Namier, "King George III: A Study of Personality," *Crossroads of Power, Essays on Eighteenth-Century England* (New York: Macmillan, 1962), pp. 124–40.

In the catalogue, *Kings and Queens,* on sale at the exhibition, the introduction dealing with the reign of George III gave the traditional view of his reign:

Conscientious and ambitious, he tried to restore the political influence of the Crown, but his intervention ended with the humiliating American War of Independence.

Conscientious he certainly was, painstakingly, almost painfully, conscientious. But was he ambitious? Did he try to exercise powers which his predecessors had relinquished, or claim an influence which was not universally conceded to him? And was it the assertion of Royal, and not of Parliamentary, authority over America which brought on the conflict and disrupted the First British Empire?

Let us place ourselves in March 1782. Dismal, humiliating failure has turned public opinion, and the House of Commons is resolved to cut losses and abandon the struggle; it is all over; Lord North's government has fallen; and the King is contemplating abdication. He has drafted a message to Parliament (which was never sent); here are its first two paragraphs:

His Majesty during the twenty-one years he has sate on the throne of Great Britain, has had no object so much at heart as the maintainance of the British Constitution, of which the difficulties he has at times met with from his scrupulous attachment to the rights of Parliament are sufficient proofs.

His Majesty is convinced that the sudden change of sentiments of one branch of the legislature has totally incapacitated him from either conducting the war with effect, or from obtaining any peace but on conditions which would prove destructive to the commerce as well as essential rights of the British nation.

In the first paragraph the King declares his unswerving devotion to the British Constitution, and shows himself conscious of his difficulties in America having arisen through "his scrupulous attachment to the rights of Parliament"; the second paragraph pointedly refers to the Commons as "one branch of the legislature," and gives the King's view of the American war: he is defending there the vital interests and essential rights of the British nation.

A year later, in March 1783, when faced by the necessity of accepting a Government formed by the Fox-North coalition, George III once more contemplated abdication; and in a letter (which again was never sent) he wrote to the Prince of Wales:

The situation of the times are such that I must, if I attempt to carry on the business of the nation, give up every political principle on which I have acted, which I should think very unjustifiable, as I have always attempted to act agreeable to my duty; and must form a Ministry from among men who know I cannot trust them and therefore who will not accept office without making me a kind of slave; this undoubtedly is a cruel dilemma, and leaves me but one step to take without the destruction of my principles and honour; the resigning my Crown, my dear Son to you, quitting this my native country for ever and returning to the dominions of my forefathers.

Your difficulties will not be the same. You have never been in a situation to form any political system, therefore, are open to addopt what the times may make necessary; and no set of men can ever have offended you or made it impossible for you to employ them.

Alongside this consider the following passage from a letter which George III wrote on 26 December 1783, after having dismissed the Coalition and while he was trying to rally support for the newly formed Administration of the younger Pitt:

The times are of the most serious nature, the political struggle is not as formerly between two factions for power; but it is no less than whether a desperate faction shall not reduce the Sovereign to a mere tool in its hands: though I have too much principle ever to infringe the rights of others, yet that must ever equaly prevent my submitting to the Executive power being in any other hands, than where the Constitution has placed it. I therefore must call on the assistance of every honest man . . . to support Government on the present most critical occasion.

Note in these two passages the King's honest conviction that he has always attempted to do his duty; that he has been mindful not to infringe the rights of others; but that it would be equally wrong in him to submit "to the Executive power being in any other hands, than where the Constitution has placed it." And while I do not for a moment suggest that these things could not have been done in a happier manner, I contend that the King's statements quoted above are substantially correct.

In the eighteenth century, a proper balance between King, Lords, and Commons, that is, the monarchical, aristocratic, and representative elements of the Constitution acting as checks on each other, was supposed to safeguard the property and privileges, the lives and liberty of the subjects. Single-Chamber government would have been no less abhorrent to the century than Royal autocracy. The Executive was the King's as truly as it is now of the President in the United States; he, too, had to choose his Ministers: but from among Parliamentary leaders. And while aspirants to office swore by the "independency" of the Crown and disclaimed all wish to force themselves on the King, if left out they did their level best to embarrass and upset their successful rivals. The technique of Parliamentary opposition was fully established long before its most essential aim, which is to force a change of government, was recognized as legitimate; and because that aim could not be avowed in its innocent purity, deadly dangers threatening the Constitution, nay the life of the country, had to be alleged for justification. Robert Walpole as "sole Minister" was accused of arrogating to himself the powers of both King and Parliament; the very tame Pelhams, of keeping George II "in fetters"; Bute, who bore the name of Stuart, of "raising the standard of Royal prerogative"; and George III of ruling not through the Ministers of his own choice whom he avowed in public, but through a hidden gang of obscure and sinister "King's friends." It is obviously impossible here to trace the origin and growth of that story, or to disprove it by establishing the true facts of the transactions to which it has become attached—it was a figment so beautifully elaborated by Burke's fertile imagination that the Rockinghams themselves finished by believing it, and it grew into an obsession with them. In reality the constitutional practice of George III differed little from that of George I and George II. William Wyndham was proscribed by the first two Georges as a dangerous Jacobite, and C. J. Fox by the third as a dangerous Jacobin; while the elder Pitt was long kept out by both George II and George III on personal grounds. But for some the Royal veto and Royal influence in politics lose their sting if exercised in favour of successful monopolists in Whiggery.

I go one step further: in the eighteenth century the King had to intervene in politics and was bound to exercise his political influence, for the party system, which is the basis of Parliamentary government, did not exist. Of the House of Commons itself probably less than half thought and acted in party terms. About one-third of the House consisted of Members who looked to the King for guidance and for permanency of employment: epigoni of earlier Courts or forerunners of the modern Civil Service; and if they thus pursued their own interest, there is no reason to treat them as more corrupt than if they had done so by attaching themselves to a group of politicians. Another one-fifth of the House consisted of independent country gentlemen, ready to support the King's Government so long as this was compatible with their conscience, but averse to tying themselves up with political groups: they did not desire office, honours, or profits, but prided themselves on the disinterested and independent line they were pursuing; and they rightly claimed to be the authentic voice of the nation. In the centre of the arena stood the politicians, their orators and leaders fighting for the highest prizes of Parliamentary life. They alone could supply the facade of governments: the front benches in Parliament. But to achieve stability a Government required the active support of the Crown and the good opinion of the country. On matters about which public opinion felt strongly, its will would prevail; but with the House constituted as it was, with the electoral structure of the unreformed Parliament, and an electorate which neither thought nor voted on party lines, it is idle to assume that modern Parliamentary government was possible.

I pass to the next point: was George III correct in saying that it was "his scrupulous attachment to the rights of Parliament" which caused him the difficulties in America? Undoubtedly yes. It was not Royal claims that the Americans objected to, but the claims of "subjects in one part of the King's dominions to be sovereigns over their fellow-subjects in another part of his dominions." "The sovereignty of the Crown I understand," wrote Benjamin Franklin; "the sovereignty of Britain I do not understand. . . . We have the same King, but not the same legislature." Had George III aspired to independent Royal Power nothing could have suited him better than to be Sovereign in America, the West Indies, and possibly in Ireland, independent of the British Parliament; and the foremost champions of the rights of Parliament, recalling the way in which the Stuarts had played off Ireland and Scotland against England, would have been the first to protest. But in fact it would be difficult to imagine a King simultaneously exercising in several independent countries executive powers in conjunction with Parliamentary leaders. It will suffice to remember the difficulties and jealousies which Hanover caused although itself politically inert. The two problems which George III is unjustly accused of having mismanaged, those of Imperial and constitutional relations, were interconnected: only after responsible government had arisen did Dominion status within the Commonwealth become possible. Lastly, of the measures which brought on the American conflict none was of the King's making: neither George Grenville's Stamp Act, nor the Declaratory Act of the Rockinghams, nor the Townshend Duties. All that can be said against him is that once the struggle had started, he, completely identifying himself with this country, obstinately persevered in it. He wrote on 14 November 1778:

If Lord North can see with the same degree of enthusiasm I do, the beauty, excellence, and perfection of the British Constitution as by law established, and consider that if any one branch of the Empire is alowed to cast off its dependency, that the others will infalably follow the example . . . he . . . will resolve with vigour to meet every obstacle . . . or the State will be ruined.

And again on 11 June 1779, expecting that the West Indies and Ireland would follow:

Then this island would be reduced to itself, and soon would be a poor island indeed.

On 7 March 1780:

I can never suppose this country so far lost to all ideas of self importance as to be willing to grant America independence, if that could ever be universally adopted, I shall despair of this country being ever preserved from a state of inferiority and consequently falling into a very low class among the European States . . .

And on 26 September 1780:

. . . giving up the game would be total ruin, a small State may certainly subsist, but a great one mouldering cannot get into an inferior situation but must be annihilated.

When all was over, Lord North wrote to the King on 18 March 1782:

Your Majesty is well apprized that, in this country, the Prince on the Throne, cannot, with prudence, oppose the deliberate resolution of the House of Commons . . . Your Majesty has graciously and steadily supported the servants you approve, as long as they could be supported: Your Majesty has firmly and resolutely maintained what appeared to you essential to the welfare and dignity of this country, as long as this country itself thought proper to maintain it. The Parliament have altered their sentiments, and as their sentiments whether just or erroneous, must ultimately prevail, Your Majesty . . . can lose no honour if you yield at length . . .

Your Majesty's goodness encourages me . . . to submit whether it will not be for Your Majesty's welfare, and even glory, to sacrifice, at this moment, former opinions, displeasures and apprehensions (though never so well-founded) to . . . the public safety.

The King replied:

I could not but be hurt at your letter of last night. Every man must be the sole judge of his feelings, therefore whatever you or any man can say on that subject has no avail with me.

What George III had never learnt was to give in with grace: but this was at the most a defect of character.

Lord Waldegrave, who had been Governor to the Prince of Wales 1752–6, wrote in 1758 a character sketch of him so penetrating and just that it deserves quoting almost in full.

The Prince of Wales is entering into his 21st year, and it would be unfair to decide upon his character in the early stages of life, when there is so much time for improvement.

A wise preamble: yet a long and eventful life was to change him very little. Every feature singled out by Waldegrave finds copious illustration in the fifty years that followed (in one case in a superficially inverted form).

His parts, though not excellent, will be found very tolerable, if ever they are properly exercised.

He is strictly honest, but wants that frank and open behaviour which makes honesty appear amiable. . . .

His religion is free from all hypocrisy, but is not of the most charitable sort; he has rather too much attention to the sins of his neighbour.

He has spirit, but not of the active kind; and does not want resolution, but it is mixed with too much obstinacy.

He has great command of his passions, and will seldom do wrong, except when he mistakes wrong for right; but as often as this shall happen, it will be difficult to undeceive him, because he is uncommonly indolent, and has strong prejudices.

His want of application and aversion to business would be far less dangerous, was he eager in the pursuit of pleasure; for the transition from pleasure to business is both shorter and easier than from a state of total inaction.

He has a kind of unhappiness in his temper, which, if it be not conquered before it has taken too deep a root, will be a source of frequent anxiety. Whenever he is displeased, his anger does not break out with heat and violence; but he becomes sullen and silent, and retires to his closet; not to compose his mind by study or contemplation, but merely to indulge the melancholy enjoyment of his own ill humour. Even when the fit is ended, unfavourable symptoms very frequently return, which indicate that on certain occasions his Royal Highness has too correct a memory.

Waldegrave's own endeavour was to give the Prince "true notions of common things." But these he never acquired: which is perhaps the deepest cause of his tragedy.

The defect Waldegrave dwells upon most is the Prince's "uncommon indolence," his "want of application and aversion to business." This is borne out by other evidence, best of all by the Prince's own letters to Bute:

July 1st, 1756: I will throw off that indolence which if I don't soon get the better of will be my ruin.

March 25th, 1757: I am conscious of my own indolence . . . I do here in the most solemn manner declare, that I will throw aside this my greatest enemy . . .

September 25th, 1758: . . . . that incomprehensible indolence, inattention and heedlessness that reigns within me . . .

And he says of his good resolutions: "as many as I have made I have regularly broke"; but adds a new one: "I mean to attempt to regain the many years I have fruitlessly spent."

December 19*th,* 1758: . . . through the negligence, if not the wickedness of those around me in my earlier days, and since perhaps through my own indolence of temper, I have not that degree of knowledge and experience in business, one of my age might reasonably have acquir'd . . .

March 1760: . . . my natural indolence . . . has been encreas'd by a kind of indifference to the world, owing to the number of bad characters I daily see . . .

By shifting the blame on to others, he tries to relieve the bitter consciousness of failure: which is one source of that excessive "attention to the sins of his neighbour" mentioned by Waldegrave. Indeed, George III's letters, both before and after his accession are full of it: "the great depravity of the age," "the wickedest age that ever was seen," "a degenerate age," "probity and every other virtue absorb'd into vice, and dissipation"; etc. "An ungrateful, wicked people" and individual statesmen alike receive castigation (*in absentia*) from this very young Old Testament prophet. Pitt "is the blackest of hearts," "the most dishonourable of men," and plays "an infamous and ungrateful part"; Lord Temple, an "ungrateful arrogant and self-sufficient man"; Charles Townshend is "a man void of every quality," "the worst man that lives," "vermin"; Henry Fox, a man of "bad character," "void of principles"; Lord Mansfield is "but half a man"; the Duke of Bedford's character "contains nothing but passion and absurdity"; etc. As for George II, the Prince felt ashamed of being his grandson. And on 23 April 1760, half a year before his accession, aged twenty-two he wrote to Bute: ". . . as to honesty, I have already lived long enough to know you are the only man who possesses that quality . . ."

In Bute he thought he had found the tutelary spirit who would enable him to live up to his future high vocation. Here are further excerpts from the Prince's letters to him:

July 1*st,* 1756: My friend is . . . attack'd in the most cruel and horrid manner . . . because he is my friend . . . and because he is a friend to the bless'd liberties of his country and not to arbitary notions . . .

By . . . your friendship . . . I have reap'd great advantage, but not the improvement I should if I had follow'd your advice . . . I will exactly follow your advice, without which I shall inevitably sink.

March 25*th,* 1757: I am resolved . . . to act the man in everything, to repeat whatever I am to say with spirit and not blushing and afraid as I have hitherto . . . my conduct shall convince you that I am mortified at what I have done and that I despise myself . . . I hope this will persuade you not to leave me when all is at stake, when nobody but you can stear me through this difficult, though glorious path.

In June 1757 Leicester House were alarmed by rumours of an alliance between the Duke of Newcastle and Henry Fox, and were ascribing fantastic schemes to the Duke of Cumberland. The Prince already saw himself compelled to meet force by force or to "yield up the Crown,"

for I would only accept it with the hopes of restoring my much beloved country to her antient state of liberty; of seeing her . . . again famous for being the residence of true piety and virtue, I say if these hopes were lost, I should with an eye of pleasure look on retiring to some uninhabited cavern as this would prevent me from seeing the sufferings of my countrymen, and the total destruction of this Monarchy . . .

August 20*th,* 1758: . . . by . . . attempting with vigour to restore religion and virtue when I mount the throne this great country will probably regain her antient state of lustre.

Was this a Prince nurtured in "arbitrary notions," ambitious to make his own will prevail? or a man with a "mission," striving after naively visionary aims? No doubt, since early childhood it must have been rammed into him, especially when he was being reproved, to what high station he was born; and disparaging comparisons are said to have been drawn between him and his younger brother. He grew up with a painful consciousness of his inadequacy: "though I act wrong perhaps in most things," he wrote on one occasion. Excessive demands on a child, complete with wholesome exhortations, are fit to reduce it to a state of hebetude from which it is not easy to recover. A great deal of the pattern of George III's behaviour throughout life can be traced back to his up-bringing.

He spent his young years cut off from intercourse with boys of his own age, till he himself ceased to desire it. Bubb Dodington notes in his *Diary* on 15 October 1752, that the Princess Dowager of Wales

did not observe the Prince to take very particularly to anybody about him, but to his brother Edward, and she was glad of it, for the young people of quality were so ill-educated and so vicious, that they frightened her.

And so they did him for the rest of his life. Isolation by itself would be apt to suggest to a child that there was something wrong with those he had to shun; but this he was probably told in so many words. On 18 December 1753, Dodington records another talk with the Princess:

I said, it was to be wished he could have more company. She seemed averse to the young people, from the excessive bad education they had, and from the bad examples they gave.

So the boy spent joyless years in a well-regulated nursery, the nearest approach to a concentration camp: lonely but never alone, constantly watched and discussed, never safe from the wisdom and goodness of the grown-ups; never with anyone on terms of equality, exalted yet oppressed by deferential adults. The silent, sullen anger noted by Waldegrave, was natural to one who could not hit back or speak freely his mind, as a child would among children: he could merely retire, and nurture his griefs and grievances—and this again he continued through life. On 3 May 1766, during a political crisis, he wrote to Bute: "I can neither eat nor sleep, nothing pleases me but musing on my cruel situation." Nor could he, always with adults, develop self-reliance: at nineteen he dreamt of reforming the nation, but his idea of acting the man was to repeat without blushing or fear what he had to say.

For the pious works which were "to make this great nation happy" Bute's "sagacious councils" were therefore indispensable. When in December 1758 Bute expressed doubts whether he should take office in the future reign, the Prince in a panic searched his own conscience:

Perhaps it is the fear you have I shall not speak firmly enough to my Ministers, or that I shall be stagger'd if they say anything unexpected; as to the former I can with great certainty assure that they, nor no one else shall see a want of steadiness either in my manner of acting or speaking, and as to the latter, I may give fifty sort of puts off, till I have with you thoroughly consider'd what part will be proper to be taken . . .

George III adhered to this programme. On his grandfather's death he waited to hear from Bute what "must be done." When expecting Pitt at a critical juncture: "I would wish to know what I had best say. . . ." With regard to measures or appointments: "I have put that off till I hear my Dear Friend's opinion"; "If this [is] agreeable to my D. Friend I will order it to day . . ."; "I desire my D. Friend to consider what I have here wrote, if he is of a contrary opinion, I will with pleasure embrace it." And when in November 1762 Bute declared he would retire on conclusion of peace:

I had flattered myself [wrote the King] when peace was once established that my D. Friend would have assisted me in purging out corruption . . .; . . . now . . . the Ministry remains compos'd of the most abandon'd men that ever had those offices; thus instead of reformation the Ministers being vicious this country will grow if possible worse; let me attack the irreligious, the covetous &c. as much as I please, that will be of no effect . . . Ministers being of that stamp . . .

Two years on the throne had worked little if any change in his ideas and language; nor did the next twenty. The same high claims on himself, and the same incapacity to meet real situations he was faced with: hence his continued dependence on others. By 1765 he saw that Bute could not help him, by the summer of 1766 he had written off Bute altogether. In the spring of 1765 he turned to the Duke of Cumberland, the bugbear of his young years: "Dear Uncle, the very friendly and warm part you have taken has given me real satisfaction. . . ." And to Pitt, "the blackest of hearts": "My friend for so the part you have acted deserves of me. . . ." In July 1765 Cumberland formed for him the Rockingham Administration and presided over it a quasi-Viceroy; but a few months later Cumberland was dead. In July 1766 Chatham formed his Administration; but a few months later his health broke down completely. Still George III clung to him like a molusc (a molusc who never found his rock). "Under a health so broken," wrote Chatham, "as renders at present application of mind totally impossible. . . ." After nearly two years of waiting for his recovery, the King still wrote: "I think I have a right to insist on your remaining in my service." Next he clung to the ineffective Grafton who longed to be relieved of office; and when Grafton resigned, the King wrote to him on 27 January 1770:

My heart is so full at the thought of your retiring from your situation that I think it best not to say more as I know the expressing it would give you pain.

Then came North. Totally unequal to the difficulties of the American crisis, in letter after letter he begged the King to let him resign. Thus in March 1778:

Lord North cannot conceive what can induce His Majesty, after so many proofs of Lord North's unfitness for his situation to determine at all events to keep him at the head of the Administration, though the almost certain consequences of His Majesty's resolution will be the ruin of his affairs, and though it can not ward off for a month that arrangement which His Majesty seems to apprehend.

But the King would not hear of it. July 2nd, 1779: "no man has a right to talk of leaving me at this hour. . . ." October 25th, 1780: he expects North "will show that zeal for which he has been conspicuous from the hour of the Duke of Grafton's desertion."

George III's attitude to North conformed to the regular pattern of his behaviour. So did also the way in which after a while he turned against North in bitter disappointment. By the '70s the King spoke disparagingly of Bute and Chatham; and in time his imagination enabled him to remember how on the day of his accession he had given the slip to them both. A month after Grafton had resigned, George III wrote to him: "I . . . see anew that the sincere regard and friendship I have for you is properly placed. . . ." Somewhat later his resignation changed into "desertion." When North resigned: "I ever did and ever shall look on you as a friend as well as a faithful servant. . . ." But incensed at the new situation he soon started attacking North, and treated him niggardly and unfairly over his secret service accounts. George III's attachment was never deep: it was that of a drunken man to railings—mechanical rather than emotional. Egocentric and rigid, stunted in feelings, unable to adjust himself to events, flustered by sudden change, he could meet situations only in a negative manner, clinging to men and measures with disastrous obstinacy. But he himself mistook that defensive apparatus for courage, drive, and vigour, from which it was as far removed as anything could be. Of his own mental processes he sometimes gave discerning though embellished accounts. Thus to Bute in 1762: "I . . . am apt to despise what I am not accustom'd to . . ." And on 2 March 1797, to the younger Pitt when criticizing the way measures were weakened in passing through Parliament:

My nature is quite different I never assent till I am convinced what is proposed is right, and then . . . I never allow that to be destroyed by after-thoughts which on all subjects tend to weaken never to strengthen the original proposal.

In short: no after-thoughts, no reconsideration—only desperate, clinging perseverance.

Still it might be said: at least he broke through his indolence. Yes, indeed: from pathologically indolent he turned pathologically industrious—and never again could let off working; but there was little sense of values, no perspective, no detachment. There is a legend about a homunculus whose maker not knowing what to do with him, bid him count poppy-seed in a bag. That George III was doing with his own busy self. His innumerable letters which he copied in his own hand, or the long documents transcribed by him (he never employed an amanuensis till his eye-sight began to fail) contain some shrewd perceptions or remarks, evidence of "very tolerable parts if . . . properly exercised." But most of his letters merely repeat approvingly what some Minister, big or small, has suggested. "Lord A. is very right . . ."; "General B. has acted very prop-

erly . . ."; "the minute of Cabinet meets with my fullest concurrence . . .";
"Nothing can more deserve my approbation than"—whatever it was. But if a
basic change is suggested, his obstinacy and prejudices appear. On 15 March
1778, in a letter to Lord North, he makes an unusual and startling admission:

I will only add to put before your eyes my most inmost thoughts, that no advantage
to this country nor personal danger can ever make me address myself for assistance
either to Lord Chatham or any other branch of the Opposition. . . .

As a rule he would sincerely assert, perhaps with somewhat excessive ostenta-
tion, that first and foremost he considered the good of the country. When told
by Bute that it would be improper for him to marry Lady Sarah Lennox, he
replied: "the interest of my country ever shall be my first care, my own inclina-
tions shall ever submit to it" (and he added: "I should wish we could next
summer . . . get some account of the various Princesses in Germany"—and he
settled down to "looking in the New Berlin Almanack for Princesses"). When
considering withdrawal from the German War, he wrote (with a sidelong
glance at the late King) about the superiority of his love "to this my native
country over any private interest of my own. . . ." He was "a King of a free
people"; "I rely on the hearts of my subjects, the only true support of the
Crown," he wrote in November 1760. They will not desert him—

if they could be so ungrateful to me who love them beyond anything else in life,
I should then I realy believe fall into the deepest melancholy which would soon
deprive me of the vexations of this life.

The same note, of love for this country and trust that his subjects would
therefore stand by him, continues for almost twenty years. But gradually other
overtones begin to mix with it. He had become the target of virulent attacks
and unjust suspicions which he deeply resented. Thus to Lord North on 7 March
1780: ". . . however I am treated I must love this country." And to the Prince
of Wales on 14 August 1780:

The numberless trials and constant torments I meet with in public life, must certainly affect any man, and more poignantly me, as I have no other wish but to fulfill
my various duties; the experience of now twenty years has convinced me that however long it may please the Almighty to extend my days, yet I have no reason to
expect any diminution of my public anxiety; where am I therefore to turn for comfort, but into the bosom of my own family?

And he appealed to his son, the future George IV, to connect himself only
with young men of respectable character, and by his example help "to restore
this country to its former lustre"—the old tune once more. And, in another
letter:

From your childhood I have ever said that I can only try to save my country, but it
must be by the co-operation of my children only that I can effect it.

In the 1780s there is a more than usually heavy crop of bitter complaints
about the age by one "righteous overmuch": "it has been my lot to reign in the

most profligate age," "depravity of such times as we live in," "knavery and indolence perhaps I might add the timidity of the times. . . ." And then:

I thank Heaven my morals and course of life have but little resembled those too prevalent in the present age, and certainly of all objects in this life the one I have most at heart, is to form my children that they may be useful examples and worthy of imitation . . .

With the King's disappointments in country and son another note enters his letters. He warns the Prince—

in other countries national pride makes the inhabitants wish to paint their Princes in the most favourable light, and consequently be silent on any indiscretion; but here most persons if not concerned in laying ungrounded blame, are ready to trumpet any speck they can find out.

And he writes of the "unalterable attachment" which his Electoral subjects have shown to their Princes. When George III went mad in 1788, he wanted to go back to Hanover. Deep down there was a good deal of the Hanoverian in him.

His insanity was a form of manic-depression. The first recorded fit in March 1765 was of short duration, though there may have been a slight relapse in May; and a year later he wrote to Bute—

if I am to continue the life of agitation I have these three years, the next year there will be a Council [of] Regency to assist in that undertaking.

During the next twenty-three years he preserved his normal personality. The attack in 1788 lasted about half a year: the King was over fifty, and age rendered complete recovery more difficult. His self-control weakened and his irritability increased. He was conscious of a growing weakness. Yet there was something about him which more and more endeared him to the people. He was never popular with London society or the London mob; he was much beloved in the provinces—perhaps it was his deeper kindness, his real piety, and sincere wish to do good which evoked those feelings. These appear strikingly, for instance, in his own account of his journey to Portsmouth in 1788, and in Fanny Burney's account of his progress through Wiltshire in 1789. He was not a politician, and certainly not a statesman. But in things which he could judge without passion or preconceived ideas, there appears basic honesty and the will to do the right thing. I shall limit myself to two examples. When in 1781 a new Provost was to be appointed at Eton, George III insisted on choosing a man "whose literary tallents might make the appointment respectable . . . for Eton should not be bestowed by favour, but merit." And when in 1787 a new Lord Lieutenant had to be chosen for Ireland, the King wrote to the younger Pitt about the necessity

of looking out for the person most likely to conduct himself with temper, judgement, and an avowed resolution to avoid partiality and employ the favours he has to recommend to with the justice due to my service and to the public. . . . When

I have stated this Mr. Pitt must understand that I do not lean to any particular person . . . when I state that a Lord Lieutenant should have no predelection but to advance the public good I should be ashamed to act in a contrary manner.

I have given here a picture of George III as seen in his letters, "warts and all." What I have never been able to find is the man arrogating power to himself, the ambitious schemer out to dominate, the intriguer dealing in an underhand fashion with his Ministers; in short, any evidence for the stories circulated about him by very clever and eloquent contemporaries. He had a high, indeed an exaggerated, notion of royalty but in terms of mission and duties rather than of power; and trying to live up to this idealized concept, he made unreasonable demands on himself. Setting himself unattainable standards, he could never truly come to grips with reality: which condemned him to remain immature, permanency of inner conflict precluding growth. Aware of his inadequacy, he turned to others and expected them to enable him to realize his visionary program (this appears clearest in his relations with Bute); and he bitterly reproached them in his own mind, and blamed the age in which he lived, for his own inevitable failure. The tension between his notions and reality, and the resulting frustration, account to a high degree for his irritability, his deep-seated resentments, and his suppressed anger—for situations intolerable and disastrous for himself and others; and it may have been a contributory factor in his mental breakdowns. The desire to escape from that unbearable conflict repeatedly shows itself in thoughts of abdication which must not be deemed insincere because never acted upon (men of his type cannot renounce their treadmill). He himself did not understand the nature and depth of his tragedy; still less could others. There was therefore room for the growth of an injurious legend which made that heavy-burdened man a much maligned ruler; and which has long been accepted as history.

4.

Louis XV possessed a high sense of duty to the best interests of his state and of his subjects. At times he could be courageous in the face of strong opposition. But the support for his policies and for the monarchy itself withered away. Why?

R. R. Palmer (1909–   ), Dean of the Faculty of Princeton University, describes the quasi-revolution in France, 1763–74. Despite the lofty claims to absolute government and despite a sound program, Louis XV failed as a king. Here we see Louis at his best and recognize the limits of his power as his subjects confidently attack their king.

R. R. PALMER: The Quasi-Revolution of 1763–1774*

Before we launch into a narrative of what happened in France it is well to make a few observations to set the story in perspective. It must be remembered that the reader of history is in a position to understand these events much better

* From R. R. Palmer, *The Age of the Democratic Revolution, a Political History of Europe and America, 1760–1800* (Princeton: Princeton University Press, 1959), I, pp. 86–99.

than contemporaries could. Or rather, contemporary observers were exposed to a one-sided presentation of the issues. The French parlements after the death of Louis XIV, and increasingly as the eighteenth century went on, adopted the practice of publishing their remonstrances, or formal protests, against actions taken by the royal government. These published remonstrances were of great importance in the formation of a public opinion. For the first time, the interested person could now obtain some kind of information on matters of current practical politics. He could see something of the conflict of interests behind decisions not yet made. The government, however, insisted on the maintenance of administrative privacy, or secrecy, in its affairs. Often it tried to silence the parlements, either by prohibiting publication of their remonstrances, or by temporarily "exiling" or rusticating their members. Such measures were never successfully carried through. The parlements and their allies always managed to express their views. But no one in authority within the government ever tried to explain its policies to the public. At most, certain officials in an indirect way might tolerate the printing of unorthodox opinions, as when Malesherbes in the 1750's and 1760's let the royal censorship go almost unenforced. Or other officials might engage pamphleteers to respond to tracts made public by the parlements. But at bottom the government supplied no information.

This was generally true of all countries. In England it was only in the 1760's that the substance of parliamentary debates came to be known "out of doors," or outside the two parliamentary houses; here, however, since the dominant group in Parliament was the governing group, led by the ministers themselves, the views and purposes of government came to be known. Thus in England a public opinion could take form around practical issues and concrete decisions, whereas in France, where public opinion was beginning to grow as it did everywhere in the Atlantic world, it took rather the form of what Tocqueville called literary politics. There was no public discussion by men in executive office or hoping to be so, or by writers associated with them and informed of their intentions. Discussion was carried on rather by intellectuals, *philosophes* and *hommes de lettres,* or by pamphleteers dependent on their sponsors. It tended either to be abstract on the one hand or to reflect mere intrigue on the other. Writers at their best under these conditions might be searching or even profound; at worst, they were merely voluble, polemical, or shallow; in either case they were uninformed.

Since the actual though unknown policies of the French government were often perfectly justifiable, and could have been made to appeal to important segments of the French population, it may be said that the main victim of the withholding of public information was the French monarchy itself, and that its failure was a failure of public relations. Or, in a more general sense, the unfortunate consequence was to favor ideology at the expense of realism in French political consciousness at an important stage in its early growth. The voice of opposition to government could be heard, but not that of government itself. The irresponsible talked, where the responsible kept silent.

Even within what must be called the government it was the most irresponsible parts that were the most public. The most visible aspects of the Bourbon

monarchy were the worst. The kings had in fact devised a form of public relations aimed at impressing fellow monarchs, potent feudatories, and lesser people
of an earlier day when they had been more naïve. Versailles symbolized this
program. The royal court at Versailles was a monument to everything grandiose,
lavish, magnificent, and openly displayed. It seethed also with the trivial and
the petty. It represented, in the highest'degree, the influence upon government
of the non-governmental, the private, the "social." Composed of the king, his
wife, brothers, sisters, and relatives, his intimates and confidants and those
aspiring to such position, high churchmen and princes of the blood, together
with the households, retinues, and functionaries attendant upon such personages,
reinforced by great noblemen and their clienteles, along with the mistresses,
business agents, dependents, and servants of all and sundry, the court created an
irresponsible and frothy environment in which the functioning officers of
government had to work, when, indeed, they did not emanate from it in themselves. The Marquis d'Argenson, a firm upholder of monarchy against aristocracy, though inclined to be petulant after his own removal from office, described
it very well, writing in 1750, privately in his diary:

"The court, the court, the court! There is the whole evil.

"The court has become the only senate of the nation. The lowest lackey at
Versailles is a senator, the chambermaids have a part in government. . . .

"The court prevents every reform of finances . . .

"The court corrupts the army and navy by promotions due to favoritism . . .

"The court gives us ministers without merit, authority or permanence . . .

"The court corrupts morals by teaching intrigue and venality to young men
entering upon a career, instead of emulation by character and work. . . ."

It must be noted, and probably d'Argenson would admit, that these evils were
due not to the court alone, but to certain oligarchic and entrenched hereditary
interests in French society, of which the parlements came to be the spokesmen.
But the court at Versailles was easier to see.

With its most shameful parts thus paraded before the public, and its most
creditable efforts studiously concealed, the French government was an easy
target for all who had a mind to be critical. The charges against it, made with
increasing openness from the middle of the century until the Revolution—that
it was extravagant, wasteful, despotic, and arbitrary—were all true. The parlements enunciated many liberal principles in making these charges. It was also
true that the government undertook many serious reforms, but of this part of
the truth much less was heard, because it was the parlements, as much as the
court, that brought these reforms down in failure. And public opinion, until
late in 1788, generally supported the parlements. To the modern observer today
nothing is clearer than that the Bourbon monarchy, in the generation before the
Revolution, seriously attempted to solve the basic problem of French society,
the existence of special privileges based on legal stratification or hierarchy; and
nothing is more remarkable than that the French public, bourgeois and intellectuals, seldom saw this to be the issue, took so long to develop any sense of
hostility to the nobility as a class, and so widely supported the Grand Whiggery
of France, the noble-aristocratic-parliamentary opposition to despotism. The

government was blamed by all classes for its faults, and received credit from none for its merits.

The Parlement of Paris, together with its sister magistracies in the provinces, had had numerous clashes with the royal government for half a century, when new royal enactments in 1763 opened the way to a quasi-revolution. It was the fate of the parlements that in launching a quasi-revolution in the 1760's they opened the way for the King, who crushed them in 1770 in order to drive through certain reforms, just as in launching a real revolution in 1787 the same parlements opened the way for persons acting in the name of the nation, and bent on a program of reforms not wholly unlike the King's in 1770. Between 1774 and 1787 a kind of parliamentary-aristocratic counterrevolution was at work, as again after 1789.

Before 1770, however, as again before 1789, the parlements contributed significantly to the political education of the French people. Their repeated resistance to the crown gave a respectable precedent for more flagrant disobedience. To force the recognition of a constitutional monarchy, they formed an unauthorized and extra-legal union—what Louis XV called an "association," a word that was to take on revolutionary implications in England and America also. They emphasized "law" as the basis of authority, and they declared that certain fundamental laws, or a certain constitution by which the royal and other powers were defined, already existed in France. They forced a definition and justification of sovereign power. They brought such key words as "citizen," "nation," "country," and "natural and imprescriptible rights" into the vocabulary of official debate. Increasingly they claimed, hereditary and closed bodies though they were, to "represent" the French people, and so raised the whole problem of the nature of political representation.

The royal enactments of 1763 were tax decrees. One called for an indefinite continuation of the *vingtième,* which had been expected to expire at the end of the war. The *vingtième* was the most recent and modern tax of the French monarchy, in principle a levy of a twentieth, or of one *sou* in the *livre,* of income, theoretically paid on income from all property, in practice on income from ownership of land. It was payable by nobles and commoners alike. The decree of 1763 also announced a reassessment to ascertain real income as opposed to valuations currently on the tax rolls. In France in the eighteenth century, as in the United States today, assessments tended to become frozen or stereotyped, the difference being that the mighty Bourbon monarchy lacked the flexibility in raising the rate that the smallest American municipality enjoys. Another decree laid a one per cent tax on *immeubles fictifs,* "fictitious real property," a legal term which included property in office. The *parlementaires* held their seats by virtue of property in office; as landowners they benefited from low and obsolete assessments. The controller-general, Bertin, justified the tax on offices by observing (like George Grenville explaining the Stamp Act to the American colonies) that owing to the costs of the late war it was necessary "to make sources that had not yet participated contribute to the public burdens."

The Parlements of Paris, Grenoble, Toulouse, and Rouen remonstrated strenuously. Paris insisted that the *vingtième* be levied "on the now existing rolls, without increase of valuation," under penalty of prosecution by the courts. Besides urging the King to pay his debts without new taxes, and observing that half of what the taxpayer paid never reached the treasury because of faulty administration, the Parlement of Paris added a long disquisition on the French constitution. It claimed that in France there were fundamental laws, immutable by nature. By these laws the parlement had the right to "verify" legislation, i.e., authenticate it before it could take effect. By these same laws the King himself received his throne. To deny these laws, the parlement ominously declared, "would be to shake the solidity of the throne itself." These "laws of the State" could not be violated without bringing in doubt the very "power and authority of the said Lord King." May it please God that no one suppose "that the king is king by force, for such are the signs of robbers and pirates." The parlement took care to publish all this against the royal will.

In the provinces matters went even further. The governors having received orders to force through the tax edicts, the Parlement of Toulouse put the governor of Languedoc, the duc de Fitz-James, under arrest, and the Parlement of Grenoble ordered the arrest of the lieutenant-general of Dauphiny, Dumesnil. Dumesnil, who managed to remain at large under the protection of his troops, was ostracized socially by the combined parliamentary and territorial nobility of the province; Mme. la marquise de Virieu, who was related to him, joined in the refusal to enter his house, announcing that she was "a citizen before a kinsman." Regicide scrawlings appeared on the walls of buildings.

The Parlement of Paris enflamed the general agitation, and set up a three-way dispute between itself, the King, and the Parlement of Toulouse, by asserting jurisdiction in the case of Fitz-James, on the ground that as a peer he could be tried only by the peers, and that the peers sat only in the Parlement of Paris, not in any parlement of the provinces. The Fitz-James case led the Paris bench to further sweeping constitutional affirmations: that if Fitz-James had *pensé en citoyen* he would realize that he had "contracted engagements with the Nation and the laws" (that is, was not responsible to the King alone); that the essence of government was to assure the "liberty, honor and rights" of its subjects; and that the parlement was "responsible for bringing these important truths before the sacred person of the king." The parlement drew a distinction between the royal sovereignty in external and internal affairs. (The reader may be reminded of attempts sometimes made by Americans, at this time, to distinguish between parliamentary sovereignty in the internal and external affairs of the colonies.) In foreign affairs, according to this remonstrance of January 1764, the King's authority is "without limits," and "blind obedience is a duty." "But civil government, while its fulness resides entirely in the hands of the sovereign, is regulated by entirely different principles. Its object being to maintain the citizens in the enjoyment of rights which the laws assure them, with respect either to the sovereign or to one another, it is the law that commands, or, more precisely, the sovereign commands by the law." The history of France was reviewed to support this proposition; and, it was added, anyone telling the King the contrary offended against "the sovereign, the law and the Nation."

No King of France had ever admitted to being a despot, and before this barrage of argument, collective hostility, and outright arrest of his agents, the "despot" yielded. The controller-general, Bertin, and the three provincial administrators most offensive to the parlements, Fitz-James, Dumesnil, and Harcourt in Normandy, were all replaced. The project for a tax on offices was given up. The plan for reassessment remained, but came to nothing. The year 1764 saw a striking parliamentary victory.

Matters were soon complicated again. The Assembly of the Clergy, the quinquennial convocation of the French church, met in 1765. It denounced the rising wave of anticlerical, antireligious, and general *philosophe* literature. It also, as often in the past, took action against Jansenism. The importance of Jansenism in France and Italy at this time has perhaps never been properly understood in the English-speaking world. Jansenists, as they were called by their orthodox enemies, were Catholics who inclined to a severe theology, and criticized the opulence and worldliness of the upper clergy. They had come into conflict with Rome, and been declared heretics; hence they became critical of the centralization in Rome of power in the Catholic church. The French parlements for centuries had also opposed the growth of Roman jurisdiction in France; they were hence Jansenist in a popular or sloganizing sense. They were certainly anti-Jesuit, and in 1762 had won a great victory with the expulsion of the Jesuits from France.

The Assembly of the Clergy, in 1765, in its continuing attempt to suppress Jansenism, renewed its rule that no one might receive the sacraments unless he presented a certificate—the famous *billet de confession*—stating that he had been confessed by a priest in good standing with the church. The Parlement of Paris thereupon declared all the acts of the assembly null and void. The clergy ran to the King, and the King quashed the action of the parlement. Few incidents better illustrate the role of royal absolutism as arbiter between irreconcilables—or explain the continuing popularity of absolutism in many quarters. As Voltaire put it: "There were 50,000 madmen in Paris who did not know what country the Danube or Elbe was in, who believed the universe to be shaken at its foundations by certificates of confession." For the King, he went on, to command his subjects to stop calling each other "innovators, Jansenists and semi-Pelagians was to command fools to be wise." The matter is important, for Jansenism driven underground was to have an influence during the Revolution, and because the church, by the measures it used to repress it, lost the sympathy of many people who cared nothing for Jansenism.

In any case, the provincial parlements, which had been irked by the highhandedness of the Parlement of Paris in taking the Fitz-James case away from Toulouse, now all rallied to its support. All disliked clerical influence, and all objected to the abrupt annulment of an act of the Paris Parlement by the King.

Then came the *affaire de Bretagne*. Here as elsewhere the royal governor, the duc d'Aiguillon, had run afoul of the local constituted bodies. An active administrator, he had launched a great program to develop this still wild and backward province. He projected a great system of roads to join Brest and the interior of the peninsula to the main body of France. He therefore sought to conscript the peasants, who were more dependent on their local *seigneurs* in Brittany than in other parts of France, for labor in construction of roads and bridges. He wished to introduce the *corvée royale,* by which, in other parts of France, peasants were required to spend a certain number of days a year on the building or maintenance of highways. The Estates of Brittany considered road-building to be under their own jurisdiction, and were in any case dominated, as has been seen, by a swarm of ancient gentry with little interest in internal improvements. The Estates resisted d'Aiguillon, and were strongly supported by the Parlement of Rennes. Both vigorously affirmed the historic autonomy of the province. The Parlement of Rennes, instead of arresting the governor, like the parlements of Grenoble and Toulouse, declared a suspension of the courts of justice as a means of bringing pressure on the King. The King thereupon created a special tribunal to carry on judicial business at Rennes. The leader of the troublesome Breton parlement was La Chalotais. The King, to discipline La Chalotais and enforce royal authority in the province, arraigned La Chalotais and a few others before another special tribunal, set up for the purpose at Saint-Malo. The Parlement of Paris and all the other parlements of the country rushed to the defense of La Chalotais, and of the regular court system against such special administrative tribunals.

The Brittany affair thus brought to a head a movement that had gathered strength for several years. The parlements of Paris, Rennes, Grenoble, Rouen, Dijon, Toulouse, Bordeaux, and others (there were about a dozen with varying degrees of regional importance) had formed the habit of corresponding, exchanging documents, and supporting one another in altercations with the crown. They now claimed that they were parts of a general or super-parlement, a parlement of all France, of which the several actual parlements were simply subdivisions, or what they called "classes" in the older or Latin sense of the word. This parlement-in-general, they held, represented the "nation," by which they meant the people or the governed, whether of France as a whole or of Brittany and such sub-nations in particular. No law could be valid, or tax properly authorized, they asserted, without the consent of the nation as shown by its representative, the parlement.

This position assumed by the parlements was revolutionary in its implications, not only because the King rejected it, but because the law and constitutional practice of France gave it no support. Kings in the past had acknowledged the right of the several parlements to "register" legislation or remonstrate against it; but no King had ever agreed, nor parlement until recently claimed, that parlements had an actual share in the process of legislation. Nor was there any lawful ground for parlementary unity. The several parlements had not arisen by devolution from the Parlement of Paris or from the King, as they now claimed. They were coordinate with the Parlement of Paris; that of Brittany, for example, was simply the modern form of the old high court of the duke of Brittany before the incorporation of Brittany into France. France had taken form by a gradual coming together of previously separate parts, not by delegation of authority to branch offices of an original central power. The claim of the parlements to be really one parlement was in line with historic development; it showed the growth of interests, contacts, communication, and joint action on the scale of France as a whole. But constitutionally, it was without foundation. The *union des classes* was as much the assertion of new and hitherto unknown power as the Continental Congress to which a dozen British-American provinces sent delegates in 1774.

That the parlements sought to turn themselves into a true national and representative body could be abundantly documented, but one quotation from a decree of the Parlement of Rouen may suffice: "By the fundamental laws of the Monarchy the Parlement of France, the one and only public, legal and necessary council of the Sovereign, is essentially ONE, like the Sovereign whose council and organ it is, and like the political constitution of the State, of which it is the custodian and depository. . . . The Parlement is in each of its said classes [i.e. actual parlements] the plenary, universal, capital, metropolitan, and sovereign court of France." And in the name of this alleged national institution the various actual parlements persisted in telling the King that he owed his position to law, that he had taken an "oath to the Nation," that a true country, or *patrie,* was one where "Law, Sovereign and State formed an indissoluble whole," that the law existed only by consent of the Nation, that Parlement alone expressed the "cry of the Nation" to the King, and watched over, for the Nation, the maintenance of its rights, its interests, and its freedom. In short, the Nation and the Law were set up, not yet expressly in opposition to the King, but as his coequal.

After ten years of such legal harangues the indolent Louis XV was goaded by the Brittany affair into a rebuttal. Early in the morning of March 3, 1766, he rode at full speed with a few companies of soldiers from Versailles to Paris. Held up at the Pont Neuf, where he knelt in the street as the Holy Sacrament was carried by, he found himself in such a traffic congestion, it is said, that he simply walked the remaining steps to the Palais de Justice. While soldiers occupied the building, a few of the magistrates received him at the steps facing the Sainte-Chapelle. It was all too sudden to constitute a formal *lit de justice.* The King had not even brought his chancellor with him, but only a few gentlemen of his court. He sat in an ordinary armchair, in his ordinary attire; the hastily assembled members of the parlement wore their usual black robes. The royal speech was then read. The session is known in French annals as the *séance de la flagellation.*

"I will not allow, [said Louis XV] an association to be formed in my kingdom that would pervert the natural ties of duty and obligation into a confederation of resistance, nor an imaginary body to be introduced into the Monarchy to disturb its harmony. The magistracy does not form a body, nor an order separate from the three orders of the kingdom. The magistrates are my officers, charged with the truly royal duty of rendering justice to my subjects . . ."

He flatly denied that: "all the parlements form a single body divided into classes; that this body, necessarily indivisible, is essential to the Monarchy and serves as its base; . . . that it is the protector and depository of the Nation's liberty, interests and rights. . . ; that it is responsible for the public good not only to the King, but to the Nation; that it is the judge between the King and his people; that it maintains the balance of government . . . ; that the parlements cooperate with the sovereign power in the establishment of the laws . . ."

He affirmed: "In my person only does the sovereign power rest, of which the distinctive character is the spirit of counsel, justice and reason. From me alone do my courts derive their existence and their authority, but the plenitude of this authority, which they exercise in my name, remains always in me. . . . To me alone belongs legislative power without dependence or division. . . . By my authority alone do the officers of my courts proceed, not to the formation of law, but to its registration, publication and execution. . . . Public order in its entirety emanates from me, and the rights and interests of the Nation, which some dare to set up as a body distinct from the Monarch, are necessarily joined with mine, and rest only in my hands."

Respectful remonstrance, made privately and decently, he would continue to allow; but he would not allow the parlements to proclaim to all France that submission to his will was a crime, or that "the whole Nation is groaning to see its rights, liberty and security perish under a terrible power"; for in that direction lay anarchy and confusion, and he would use all the authority he had received from God to save his people from such a fate.

Never had a French King made so strong an official statement of absolutism. One might be excused for believing, in the enlightened France of 1766, that if any sovereign power existed so enormous as the King described it, and from which all law and lawful authorities derived their existence, it was too much to be located in a single man. On the other hand, one could agree with the King that the parlements, as they really were, did not represent the French people any better than he did, and that officers of justice must draw their authority from some source outside their own hereditary positions. As events were later to have it, it was the new "body," the Nation, so passively argued over by King and parlements in 1766, to which sovereign power and the source of lawful authority were to be imputed.

The parlements were not intimidated by the King's blast against them. They continued their protests, remonstrances, and obstruction. The Brittany affair dragged on; the parlements of Paris and Rennes, while both opposing the use of administrative or prerogative courts, and upholding "law" against "circumstance," disputed with each other for jurisdiction over the hapless La Chalotais. In 1768 the royal government, moving toward economic liberalism and freedom of the market, attempted to abolish regulations on the grain trade. The parlements of Grenoble, Aix, and Toulouse favored such free trade in grain, but those of Paris and Rouen declared against it. There was also the usual opposition to taxes. In 1768 the King reactivated the *Grand Conseil,* a kind of supreme court operating directly under the King, and empowered to decide cases arising from government, or those involving conflicts of jurisdiction between the parlements. The parlements, fearing the "evocation" or transfer of their own lawsuits to this council, naturally protested, and fortified their protests by again urging the rights of the usual judiciary against administrative and presumably unfree courts.

In 1770 Louis XV decided to make an end of parlementary opposition. He put into office a reform administration composed of Maupeou as chancellor, with his aide the young lawyer, C. F. Lebrun, and the Abbé Terray as controller-general of finance.

Maupeou simply abolished the parlements, putting their members on permanent vacation, and set up a new system of law-courts in their place. He did away with property in judicial office. Judges no longer received fees from litigants for their decisions. The new judges, drawn in part from men experienced in the Grand Conseil, received a fixed salary, with assurances of secure tenure. They had no personal or proprietary right to their position. They were appointed by the crown, which, according to the edict, could now select men according to professional qualifications, without regard to financial or family considerations. The overgrown area within which the Parlement of Paris had had jurisdiction, embracing most of the interior of France, was broken up among a number of high courts, so that less travel was necessary to obtain judicial settlements. At the same time overlapping jurisdictions among courts in the city of Paris, the source of infinite confusion, expense, and delay, were clarified and redefined. The new system answered to demands that had been made sporadically for generations, and anticipated the definitive reforms carried out a generation later.

With the old parlements and their obstructive tactics done away with, the Abbé Terray launched a systematic and carefully thought out fiscal reform, aimed at a more equitable distribution of the tax burden, without regard to social class, and levied in proportion to real income. He thus resumed the program of the tax decrees of 1763 which parlementary resistance had rendered abortive. He made progress in getting modern and realistic valuations of landed income, and increased the yield of the *vingtième* by about one-half in those parts of the country where he could get reassessments made. He met with furious opposition, and though his private instructions to the intendants were full of wise and moderate counsels, he was denounced publicly all over France as a robber, an extortionist, and a minion of despotism. So great was the outburst from parlementary pamphleteers, and later from outraged authors of memoirs (it was mostly the upper classes who wrote memoirs), that Terray has in fact enjoyed a rather poor historical press ever since, though he is a hero for M. Marion, the great authority on the financial history of France.

The reforming efforts of Louis XV, coming at the end of a long and unrespected reign, failed to capture the public imagination. The new courts were derisively called Maupeou parlements, and the tax reforms were considered no better than banditry. Not only were the few hundred families that had monopolized the old parlements now relegated, and hence disgruntled. The legal profession as a whole disapproved. It was hard to find men for the new positions. Public opinion, such as it was, opposed the change. It was in vain that a few writers, like the aging Voltaire, exposed the pretensions of the old parlements and heartily endorsed the new. It was in vain that a pamphleteer, perhaps hired by the government, declared that only despots or feudal lords combined judicial and legislative powers, which enlightened monarchs separated and balanced, and that if the old parlements were to triumph France would become a "republic" under "a monstrous hereditary aristocracy."

The very limits of noble loyalty were strained. One excited aristocrat declared that France must be "de-Bourbonized." The self-interest of the nobility in the matter is apparent. Why the country as a whole should have agreed with the aristocracy is not so clear, yet is after all understandable. The old Louis XV had lost all prestige. He was even widely hated. The government simply was not trusted. And at best it had nothing better than enlightened despotism to offer—reform without consultation of anyone outside the bureaucracy, reform at the cost of the suppression of liberty.

When Louis XV died in 1774, Maupeou and Terray were dismissed. There had been a quasi-revolution in France, but only a quasi-revolution. The nobility, through the parlements and a lesser extent the Provincial Estates, had led an attack on the monarchy. The monarchy had replied with a counterattack on the aristocracy entrenched in these constituted bodies. The parlements had laid down a broad program of constitutional liberalism. The King and Maupeou had led an assault upon privilege. But no power had changed hands. The old parlements, restored by Louis XVI, led a kind of quasi-counterrevolution, an "aristocratic resurgence," after 1774. But the last word was not spoken. Maupeou's aide, the young Lebrun, who is said to have written Maupeou's speeches to the Parlement of Paris, became a busy man in the committees of the Revolutionary assemblies, turned up as Third Consul in 1799, and was one of the chief reorganizers of France under Napoleon.

5.

Douglas Dakin (1907–   ) of Birkbeck College, London, recounts Turgot's desperate effort to reform the grain trade under Louis XVI. Though Dakin is too hard on Terray, his narrative account of the politics behind the "Flour War" is thoroughly convincing. Every element of outstanding political history is here; the influence of ideas, the personalities of the participants, and the drama of failure for Turgot are all connected in sustained narrative form.

Turgot recognized the enormous political consequences of the grain trade, not only in the countryside but also at Versailles and in Paris. At this early stage in his reign Louis XVI also seemed to grasp what Turgot was trying to do and supported him through the worst of the crisis. Did Louis's other ministers support Turgot? What accounts for Turgot's disgrace—Louis XVI's weakness or the institution of monarchy? How do you explain the lack of support in the populace for Turgot's program?

DOUGLAS DAKIN: The Flour War*

Shortly after Turgot had written the seven letters on the grains, the Abbé Terray, having virtually rescinded free trade, renewed Chaumont's commission to purchase corn supplies for Paris. About the same time he organized a grain administration, which he placed under the charge of Sorin de Bonne and Doumerck, it being arranged that these two men should receive a commission of 2 percent upon all transactions and also interest upon their advances. Under their supervision were placed also the King's mills at Corbeil, and later other mills at Lamothe and Chiessat, both of which were Terray's own property. Against these measures Albert, the intendant of commerce, whose department supervised commerce in grain, vigorously protested; but he was dismissed from

* From Douglas Dakin, *Turgot and the "Ancien Régime" in France* (London: Methuen, 1939), pp. 177–93, 254–63.

office, and in his place Terray installed the notorious Brochet de Saint-Prest. And, even when a governmental commission reported unfavourably upon this new administration, the Abbé Terray refused to mend his ways and defiantly continued his sinister operations. Actually the purchases of grain made in the provinces were never considerable; but Sorin and Doumerck, working first in one locality and then in another, caused rapid fluctuations in prices, which invariably resulted in much speculation. An outcry arose, and the shortage of bread that was really the result of failing harvests was usually ascribed to the manoeuvres of Terray's agents. Véri, who toured the provinces in 1773, found that every one was convinced that a monopoly existed and that enormous profits went to enrich the King, the Du Barry, and the Abbé Terray. Riots broke out in several places. But Terray, having persuaded the Ministers that these were engineered by his political enemies, ordered the intendants to seek out disaffected persons and to take criminal proceedings against them. He never succeeded, however, in imposing silence upon his detractors, and when, at the accession of Louis XVI, the mediocre harvest was becoming slowly exhausted, it was openly said, though there was no truth in the statement, that the corn company was meeting at Brochet's house. And Louis XVI, in spite of his gesture of distributing corn freely at the beginning of his reign, was now accused of stealing his people's sustenance; and Sartine, who as lieutenant of the police had been universally respected, suddenly became the subject of the vilest calumnies.

Louis, thus taken by surprise, was most anxious indeed to remove the cause of popular suspicion. Marie-Antoinette, with whom he discussed the matter, was also, as Mercy has revealed, of a like opinion; and Maurepas, called upon to shield his charge from such base accusations, could not remain indifferent. All three were disposed, therefore, to listen to Turgot's economic doctrines. On 13 September he submitted to the King an *arrêt du conseil,* which received immediately the royal sanction. But the measure gave rise to Ministerial wranglings; for the preamble had not only denounced previous governmental policy, but it had also departed from the usual forms. In it Turgot had appealed to public opinion. "You will find it platitudinous and long-winded," he told Véri with a laugh, "but I wished to make it so clear that every village lawyer can explain it to the peasants." In other words, he wanted to avoid a repetition of those misconceptions that prevailed in 1763, when no one seemed to grasp the real intention of the law. In the end he had his way, and the legislation was promulgated in the form that he had cast it.

But the measure itself, which re-enacted the Declaration of May 1763, was certainly moderate. It established the freedom of the grain trade within the kingdom only, and it left in their entirety the restrictions obtaining in Paris. Upon second thoughts after consideration of Bertin's words of warning, Turgot had abandoned his original intention to establish complete freedom of export, and he contented himself with reserving to the King the right to declare such freedom when times were more propitious. At the moment little was to be gained from facilitating export. As he told Stormont at Compiègne, if it were a matter of setting an example, then it was England which ought to take the lead. What France needed at the time was an import of grain to supplement her dwindling supplies. To meet this requirement Turgot was even prepared to offer bounties upon incoming corn, and, as yet another precaution until such time as a flourishing trade would render the measure superfluous, he retained a corn depot at Corbeil, which he placed under the control of the lieutenant of the police. Here, having recourse to the expedient that had proved successful at Limoges, he provided for the making of bread, which was to be sold at a price determined strictly by costs of production. So cautious, indeed, was Turgot's corn policy that Galiani, the author of the *Dialogues sur le commerce des blés* and an accomplished critic of the *économistes,* received congratulations from all parts of Europe on having gained such a convert.

But it was only in thus restricting his programme that Turgot was able to obtain sufficient ministerial support to reverse the Abbé Terray's régime; and it was that same moderation of his legislation that led that Parlement of Paris to accept it with very little comment. Turgot, as Stormont discovered, thought it advisable to wait until the magistrates returned before actually promulgating his measure in the form of letters patent. At first sight this must appear a concession which asked for trouble, for the last act of the old Parlement before its exile had been the registration of Terray's decrees destroying the liberty of the grain trade. But it seems that Turgot was well aware that during their exile in the provinces the magistrates had learned that a growing body of opinion favoured the removal of restrictions. His information proved to be correct. Although in registering his legislation the Parlement added a *retentum* (which had no legal force), that the King should take all steps within his power to see that the markets were well supplied with grain, the motive, as Stormont learned from conversation with a number of magistrates, was primarily to satisfy the more disgruntled members, who claimed that the provisions for feeding Paris were most inadequate. Perhaps, moreover, the magistrates as a body wished to keep a door open in the event of a skirmish with the Crown; and no doubt it was policy to pay lip-service at least to the popular prejudices that they had voiced so long. In contrast, however, to those of Paris, the magistrates of Rouen were staunchly opposed to Turgot's legislation and, upheld by Miromesnil, who had once been their colleague, issued a ruling which violated its very principles. But in the end Turgot carried the day and quashed the ruling in an *arrêt de cassation.*

Turgot was now free to liquidate Terray's administration of the King's grains. Already a very strange incident had made a full inquiry an urgent necessity. On 17 September fishermen at Boulogne had found in the River Seine a number of sacks full of documents, and these, when taken to the *contrôle général,* were found to be the records of the dealings of Terray's agents. A judicial inquiry, which was opened on 29 September and the findings of which Turgot summed up in a *Mémoire* to the King, resulted in a damning case against Sorin and Doumerck. These two agents, instead of employing the 12,000,000 *livres* advanced to them from the Treasury to reward the merchants whose services they engaged, had kept the money for their private use; they had purchased grain on credit: to pay one merchant they had borrowed from another, to pay him they had borrowed from a third, to pay the third they had borrowed from a fourth, and so on. They had also drawn interest upon fictitious advances, and they had fraudulently obtained commission upon sales and purchases of supplies, many of which they had exported to America and some of which were not composed of grain but of sugar and other commodities. These men were not alone in perpetuating such frauds, but had been aided and abetted by the officials Brochet and Leclerc. The former had received a large share of the spoils. A poor man before he acquired his office, he had built a palatial dwelling, where he entertained lavishly and gambled adventurously. When he was dismissed, a wit chalked on the wall of his house *L'Hôtel de la Farine*. For long Brochet protested his innocence in vague and general terms; but he never succeeded in answering the specific charges of dishonesty that Turgot brought against him.

Sorin and Doumerck were ordered to refund the money advanced by the Treasury. But at the time no further action was taken against them, and it was not until the days that followed the corn riots of 1775, when the Government was attempting to discover the organizers, that Sorin and Doumerck were cast into the Bastille and subjected to a cross-examination by Albert, who had become the lieutenant of the police. The further inquiry merely confirmed Turgot's original indictment; but there was no evidence forthcoming that they had been subsequently engaged in stirring up sedition, and they were given their freedom on 20 June 1775. Both had been extremely fortunate, for the original charges might have led to heavy penalties. But Turgot, probably wishing to avoid a sensational law-case which would undoubtedly have given rise to a bitter conflict, was content to ask for their dismissal, and did not probe the matter further. Métra, who makes a running commentary on these events, and Du Pont, in his correspondence with the Margrave of Baden, both aver that Terray was implicated; but Véri, who was usually well informed, contends that the fallen Comptroller-General was not so much a rogue as a fool and the dupe of his prodigal and intriguing hirelings. At any rate, Turgot was not disposed to rake up Terray's past: once begun, there was simply no knowing where the affair might end.

The legislation freeing the grain trade was well received. The industrial interests for the most part pronounced in its favour, the merchants of Bordeaux going so far as to address to Turgot a congratulatory message, and the grain-producers, too, looked forward once more to times of prosperity. Turgot therefore had every hope that in time other interests would come to recognize the value of free trade in grain. Nevertheless, his measures soon gave rise to a renewal of the pamphlet war between the mercantilist and the free-trade schools, Turgot's own supporters tending to cast caution aside in a literary onslaught against their enemies. It was Véri's opinion that the physiocrat journalists only succeeded in making the grain trade the subject of quite unnecessary controversy. What is more, they created the impression that the Comptroller would systematically carry into effect the whole range of his doctrines within a short space of time, with the result that many people who were prepared to tolerate a small measure of reform now became unduly alarmed. Opponents were quick to seize upon the opening thus afforded and, if it was invective that won over opinion, the Physiocrats were fighting a losing battle. In Linguet, the most scurrilous and most poisonous of all the pamphlet-writers of the age, they certainly met their match. But of even greater concern than the literary attacks upon free trade were the popular outcries that arose towards the end of the winter. The harvest of 1774 had been mediocre, and prices soon began to rise. There was a repetition of the events that had followed the free-trade laws of 1763 and 1764. The police officials of the towns, ignoring Turgot's edict, began to revive the old regulations, in La Rochelle, for example, a house-to-house search being organized in March 1775. Turgot acted as he had done at Limoges: he quashed the rulings of the local officials and reissued printed copies of his edict; he ordered the intendant of Caen to have troops in readiness and to arrest the ringleaders of a grain mob at Cherbourg; and he advised other intendants to offer bounties to merchants who undertook to bring in supplies by sea. On 24 April he gave this last measure application throughout the kingdom. "All merchants, French and foreigners alike, who bring in grain between 15 May and 1 August," so runs his preamble, "shall be paid 18 *sols* on every quintal of wheat and 12 *sols* on every quintal of rye . . . and to those who during this same period transport grain to Paris and Lyon shall be paid, over and above the bounties awarded at the ports, at Paris 20 *sols* on every quintal of wheat and 12 *sols* on every quintal of rye; at Lyon 25 *sols* on every quintal of wheat and 15 *sols* on every quintal of rye." Nor was this all. As at Limoges, so now at Paris, he persuaded a number of merchants that it was in the long run to their advantage to uphold the cause of free trade by tiding over the period of shortage. Finally, where the dearth was exceptional—for example, at Dijon, Beaunne, Saint-Jean-de-Losne, Montbard, and Pontoise—he abolished various local duties on grain which caused supplies to "avoid the markets." Upon all these measures Maurepas commented flippantly to Véri: "It is the high price of bread that occupies us now, or to put it better, causes us anxiety without wasting our time; for we have no remedy to suggest when even M. Turgot changes his principles."

The situation was becoming really serious. In March revolts had taken place at Evry and Metz, and early in April there was a riot at Rheims. On 18 April an ugly demonstration took place at Dijon. Here the insurgents, 400 to 500 strong, drawn mainly from the countryside around, plundered houses, demolished a mill, and tore up the streets. Then, attacking the house of one of the Maupeou magistrates, whom they accused of causing the shortage of grain, they drank dry his wine-cellar and, becoming extremely violent, next went off to find the Governor to put him to death. It was not until the Bishop, who, risking his life, remonstrated with them that they finally dispersed. This "little Bartholomew of Dijon," as Voltaire termed the riot, was merely a prelude to what was to follow. It was not the spontaneous violence of hungry wretches, or a natural reaction to rising prices which were only 30 percent above the normal, but an organized looting, the insurgents destroying the grain whenever they found it. Turgot was quick to realize that political enemies were at work. It had been reported to him that more peasants than usual were loitering round the markets in the towns north of Paris, their general demeanour showing that they meant no good. In Brie, Soissonais, Vexin, and Haute Normandie bands of disaffected persons were exciting the poorer classes to rebel. There were occasional lootings in the markets, and the merchants, taking alarm, sometimes sold their grains at a loss. Granaries and farmhouses, and vessels on their way to Paris were being pillaged, and on 29 April two whole boatloads of grain at Pontoise were thrown into the river.

Turgot's plans for bringing relief to Paris were seriously jeopardized. He had already planned *bureaux de charité* somewhat similar to those he had established at Limoges, in order to furnish the poor with money with which to buy the incoming flour and bread; and among the indigent for whom no work could be found he had arranged to distribute alms. But now there was the danger that supplies would be destroyed in transit. No sooner had he sent out the circulars to the *curés* organizing relief than further riots broke out at Beaumont-sur-Oise. The revolt spread like wildfire southwards. On 30 April the depots at Brie, Meaux, Saint-Maur, and Saint-Germain were raided, and on 1 May the army of Jean Farine reached Versailles. It was late in the evening when they arrived. Next morning they stormed the flour-stores and the market, and later they invaded the courts of the palace, demanding loudly a reduction of the price of bread and displaying specimens of a green and mouldy aliment upon which they claimed to be subsisting.

Turgot was in Paris at the time, making ready for the defence of the capital; for Versailles was safe enough, there being 10,000 troops in attendance on the King. Louis, in his own obstinate way, remained quite firm; he had refused to listen to the courtiers who advised him to abolish free trade, and in the morning he had ordered the Prince de Beauvau to protect the markets. To Turgot he hastily penned two letters—one at 11 a.m., the other at 2 p.m. In the first he wrote: "Versailles is being assailed, and they are the same men of Saint-Germain. I am going to confer with M. du Muy and M. d'Affy (Colonel of the Swiss Guards) to see what can be done; you can count upon my firmness. I have just ordered a guard for the market. I am very pleased with the precautions you have taken in Paris; it was for there I was most afraid. . . . You will be doing the right thing in arresting those people of whom you speak; but remember when you have got them—no haste and many questions. . . ." Three hours later Louis wrote his second letter, which refutes the often-repeated story (taken from Métra) that, having failed to harangue the crowd from the balcony, and being full of pity and fear, he commanded the police to sell bread at 2 *sols* the *livre*. Actually it was the Prince de Beauvau who gave this order. While guarding the market he had been covered from head to foot in flour; he had weakly asked the rioters what they wanted; and, on being told, had granted their demand. Louis heard of this as he was writing to Turgot. Having first of all described the further precautions he had taken to defend the markets and the highways, Louis went on to say: "I am not going out to-day—not from fear, but just to let everything settle down. M. de Beauvau interrupts me to tell me of the foolish manoeuvre that was made, which was to let the insurgents have bread at 2 *sols*. He contends that there is no middle course between this and obliging them at the point of the sword to buy it at its present price. This particular bargain is an accomplished fact; but it must not be repeated, and precautions must be taken to prevent their coming back to dictate the law; let me know what these measures should be, for this situation is very awkward." Such was Louis's letter. It is somewhat strange that an apocryphal version from the *Mémoires de l'Abbé Terray* was the only one to be known until the original was found. At the time Véri knew the truth; but, then, there was little which he did not know. And it is interesting to note that St. Paul, who was deputizing for Lord Stormont, also knew, for he had acquired a copy of the King's letter, and this he sent to England on 10 May. St. Paul had watched the riot at Versailles (he had gone there to discuss the debts of the French East India Company), and his account agrees substantially with Louis's own. The apocryphal version maintains that Louis confessed to an "error of policy," which he was "anxious to repair," and that he summoned Turgot to return "without delay." As a fact Turgot did return (as a normal course) that very day. But in Foncin's somewhat vague suggestion that he tried without success to persuade Louis to command the troops to fire upon the mob there is no truth. Actually the insurgents had already gone. Véri tells us that they had been led away "like a flock of sheep." Neither Louis nor Turgot, who seem to have planned carefully all their moves, was anxious merely to disperse the rabble. They wanted to find out the organizers. "Remember," Louis had said, "no haste and many questions."

All night the troops patrolled Paris and the countryside around. Next morning the rioters, 400 to 500 strong, and armed with batons, drew near Paris. The bakers outside the gates were emptying their ovens and arranging their loaves for sale. A police ordinance posted by Lenoir after consultation with Turgot on the previous day required them to carry on their business and to sell bread at current rates, compensation being promised to those whose shops were looted. But a number of the bakers, considering the risk too great, had hidden their bread in neighbouring houses. These were the first to have their supplies stolen. About seven o'clock the insurgents rushed through the gates on the northern boundary. The populace locked their doors and gazed from the windows calmly as upon a procession, watching the rioters systematically demolish the bakers' shops. By midday not a loaf was to be bought. All this while the troops did nothing. The *Gardes françaises* were attending Notre Dame for the blessing of their banners, the Duc de Biron, acting upon Maurepas's advice, having refused to postpone the ceremony. Some of the other troops fraternized with the rioters, and even when the Musketeers arrested a dozen rebels, the police released them, saying their orders were merely to disperse, and not to apprehend those who got out of hand. But, if these were really the orders, the police had not obeyed them. The Chief, Lenoir, making the excuse that he was waiting for a written command, did nothing at all. Turgot, upon hearing of the fiasco, made haste from Versailles, and arrived in Paris at ten o'clock to find that the mob, having pillaged the Abbaye Saint-Victor and having first contemplated an attack on the Bastille, were swarming round the *contrôle général,* displaying their specimens of mouldy barley bread and shouting, "This is what we have to eat." While Turgot was talking to Lenoir, the mob moved off to the Halls and Markets, and again destroyed supplies. About eleven o'clock the rioters calmed down from sheer exhaustion, while the huge crowds of citizens, who later in the morning had unlocked their doors and ventured into the streets, gradually dispersed to take a midday meal. Throughout the afternoon all was relatively quiet. Biron had now posted his men at all important places, and the Dragoons and the Suisses patrolled the streets.

Turgot returned to Versailles in the evening and prevailed upon Louis to call a Council, which sat until the early hours of the morning of 4 May. Maurepas was not consulted. According to the *Relation historique,* he went that night to the opera, but Véri holds that he had gone on the previous evening— the day of the revolt at Versailles. At all events, he kept constantly clear of the whole business and, when reprimanded by the Abbé de Véri for this neglect, his only excuse was that as he had found Turgot giving orders to everybody, he therefore let him carry on. But he could not explain—and this was his real folly —his advice to Biron to take the troops to Notre Dame. If he was at the Council he took a back seat and said nothing at all. Turgot did all the talking. He spoke vehemently against Lenoir, and had him dismissed along with two of his commissioners and the commandant of the watch. Véri seems to think that Lenoir's insubordination was due not to design (not, as was rumoured, to a plan concerted with his friend Sartine), but to lack of experience in a new office. And that seems to have been Turgot's own opinion: he could "not risk a second day like yesterday"—these were his words in informing Lenoir of his master's wishes.

Another result of the Council was that Turgot was given a *blanc-seing* to employ the military authority as he thought best. The generalissimo, as he was called, drew up immediately a plan of campaign. An army of 25,000 was organized. Biron took charge of Paris; the Marquis de Poyanne, the Haute Seine; the Comte de Vaux, the Basse Seine; and the Musketeers patrolled the Marne. Throughout the morning of 4 May, Paris was relatively calm. Two or three men were posted at each bakery; the markets and public squares were guarded; and pickets continually went the rounds. There were a few instances of disorder. One or two people were robbed; sentinels were occasionally insulted; here and there insurgents began to tear up the streets; and the bolder spirits posted placards with the words: "If the price of bread does not diminish we shall exterminate the King and all the race of Bourbons." Later the cry went up for an attack on the Bicêtre to free the prisoners; but the soldiers intervened and arrested nearly 200.

By this time the Parlement of Paris had begun to interfere. Louis had kept the magistrates informed of his actions and he had warned them that they were not in any circumstances to take a line different from his own. These instructions had been received in silence. But on 4 May the Parlement assembled to discuss the events of the previous day. The outcome was a ruling which, while forbidding the populace to assemble, affirmed that the King ought "to take measures . . . to reduce the price of bread to a rate proportionate to the needs of the people." The next day the magistrates protested against the *commission prévôtale* that had been set up to try the insurgents who had been arrested, a function which they claimed for the *Grand' Chambre.* Already the magisterial ruling of 4 May was being posted in the streets. At Turgot's instigation the Musketeers were ordered to smash the printing-blocks and to cover over the notices with the King's ordinance of 3 May forbidding crowds to gather or to demand grain and bread below the current prices. This done, Turgot hurried back to Versailles, wakened the King at midnight, and persuaded him to hold a *lit de justice* for the registration of the letters patent establishing the extraordinary tribunal. Next morning the magistrates were ordered to present themselves at Versailles wearing their black robes. But before they set out they defiantly demanded that bread should be sold in Paris at 2 *sols* the *livre.*

At the Palace the magistrates were sumptuously entertained. Later Miromesnil spoke on behalf of the King. He described briefly the disorders that had taken place, and ascribed them to a foul conspiracy: "It seemed that a plot was hatched to lay desolate the countryside, to impede navigation, to hinder the transport of grain on the highways, and to starve the large towns, above all Paris." And he went on to explain the necessity of taking summary proceedings against the malefactors in an extraordinary tribunal, thus avoiding the serious delays of the usual legal procedure. Neither d'Aligre, the First President, nor Seguier, the *avocat général,* opposed the King and, among the peers only the Prince de Conti voiced a dissenting opinion. Then Louis himself, with force and firmness, closed the session: "Sirs, you have heard my intentions. I forbid you to make remonstrances which will impede the execution of my commands." Afterwards he wrote to Turgot: "I have just carried out that upon which we agreed. . . . A few demanded the restoration of the old regulations, but the majority had modified its impertinent tone and was in great fear. I hope all this will give tranquillity. . . ." Later he wrote again and, having described the instructions he had given to the military, added: "It will be seen from all this that I am not so feeble as is believed, and that I know how to carry out that upon which I am resolved. . . . The truth is that I am more afraid of one man alone than of fifty. . . . The news from Paris is good. . . . All is quiet here." Louis was revelling in his strength. As Véri says, he showed a spirit of courage and a *sang-froid* which could hardly be expected at his age and with his peaceful frame of mind. After the Council at Versailles he had said to Turgot: "We ourselves have a good conscience, and in this we are very strong."

In his second letter of 6 May he had gone on to refer vaguely to the sinister organization behind the revolt. All sources are agreed that the rioters had moved with military precision, and that much time and money had been spent in planning their movements. None of them was hungry; they were not pitiful specimens of humanity, not winged raggedness, as Carlyle calls them, crying out for bread, but healthy ruffians singing as they marched. The mouldy bread they carried had been specially prepared: plenty of corn was obtainable, but none of them seemed to want it except to destroy it. They all had money in their pockets; the rank and file received twelve francs a day and the leaders of each band a golden *louis.* One man who was arrested (he was probably a paymaster) had 500 *louis.* When Poumeuze, a magistrate, offered a woman rioter a coin, she threw it away and jingling her pockets said she had money enough. What is more, they carried printed copies of a false *arrêt du conseil* purporting to authorize the pillage and the sale of grain at 12 *livres* the *setier.* All this Louis knew, and from the beginning had his own suspicions of the master-hand behind the scenes. But already bewildering and conflicting rumours were reaching his ears. The factions had begun the attempt to reap where others had sown. Louis wrote to Turgot: "It is a very dreadful thing—the suspicions that we have already and the embarrassing course it will be necessary to take; unfortunately these are not the only ones who are spoken of; I hope for my good name that these rumours are only the work of calumniators. . . ."

There were few people of importance who were not at some time or other accused of having engineered the flour war. The Prince de Conti, the Abbé Terray and his grain officials, the clergy, Maupeou and his magistrates, the Choiseulistes, Sartine and Lenoir, the Queen, Maurepas, the English, even Turgot himself—all in turn were said to have been behind the plot. Du Pont holds that Louis finally penetrated the secrets of the conspiracy, but took no action and destroyed the evidence. Weber, a brother of Marie-Antoinette's nurse, suggests that the King, being afraid to strike at some high personage, decided that clemency was the best means of restoring tranquillity. Conclusive proof as to the origin of the plot will never be forthcoming. All the same, there is much evidence, vague and circumstantial though it is, which makes it possible to narrow down the issue. What is more, in itself the evidence is interesting. It gives a glimpse of those tortuous political manoeuvres of the age.

The charge against Turgot (it is not known who made it) was that he organized the revolt so that he could put it down, and thus make himself indispensable to the King. A slightly different version of this calumny, one which was held by Mirabeau and later by Maurepas, was that there had been no plot at all, but that Turgot had misrepresented to Louis a trivial grain riot for the same political reasons. Such wild accusations require no comment. Nor do the vague rumours that English agents were behind the affair. And as for the fantastic suggestion—again a base calumny—that Maurepas was the culprit, there is not a scrap of evidence. The revolt, as Véri shows, took him by surprise. At the time, though far from happy about the outcome of free trade, he had simply no motive, and certainly no wish to bring about, the Comptroller's dismissal. It was the flour war itself that produced their estrangement, for, in giving Turgot the complete confidence of the King and in leading to intrigues against the Ministry, it excited in Maurepas a jealous resentment for his colleague. Turgot wrote on 13 May to Véri, who was then at Toulouse: ". . . Never has your presence been more necessary for me. The King is as firm as I am . . . but . . . the dismissal of M. Lenoir is not approved by one of your friends (Maurepas). He does not appreciate the services I have rendered him. If M. Lenoir had remained, I could have answered for nothing. I would have been dismissed and, in consequence, M. de Maurepas. Come without delay. I have courage, but come and help me." Véri loved the fields of early summer far too dearly to take alarm at the Ministerial crisis. He replied: "Be steadfast in your measures and, above all, keep your master firm."

Upon the eve of the grain riots the Queen, too, was perfectly satisfied with Turgot. She had, of course, begun to visit the *salon* Guéménée, the meeting-place of the young Choiseulistes, and the intrigue to employ her to dislodge Maurepas had already begun. But Mercy still wrote hopefully to Vienna that her interest was really in the keeping of Turgot and the Abbé Vermond. She was much affected, says Mercy, by the troubles; and Métra has it that during the days of the riots she would not eat her food. She, too, had her own suspicions, as she told her mother without mentioning names, and Marie-Thérèse agreed that there was "something underneath." Any suggestion that the Queen knew of the plot is patently absurd. The rumour, like so many other calumnies, was spread by her enemies. Nor is it even likely that the party with which she was associated had any share in preparing the revolt. Mme du Deffand, the hostess to the chief Choiseulistes, writing to Mme de Choiseul on 13 May, seems to be a bewildered yet delighted spectator. No doubt the party hoped that the events would lead to the dismissal of Turgot and Maurepas, and that the Queen would then be able to bring about the return of Choiseul. But there is nothing to suggest that the Choiseulistes themselves prepared the riot.

Nevertheless Sartine, a friend of the Queen and an associate of the Choiseulistes, was later accused of being the culprit by Baudeau, who, however, disclaimed ability to produce absolute proof owing to the death of his witness. Mairobert and Métra contend that Turgot subsequently compelled Baudeau to retract his remarks and to make apologies to Sartine. "I abandon the economist to you"—so runs Métra's version of Turgot's reply to Sartine—"and if he is culpable may he be put in the Bastille." A sensational lawsuit was daily expected, but for some reason or other Sartine decided not to take action against the querulous Baudeau. But Baudeau was not the only one to accuse Sartine. Turgot's friend, Saint-Sauveur, also denounced him and pointed to Lenoir as his accomplice. Certainly Lenoir took his cue from his friend and predecessor when he disobeyed instructions on 3 May. But it is most unlikely that Sartine had a hand in preparing the mischief. In all probability he, like Maurepas, welcomed the embarrassment that the affair gave Turgot, yet strongly resented the difficulties created for the Ministry and also the credit that the Comptroller obtained.

What, then, of the clergy? Of the thirty-one persons thrown into the Bastille, eight were parish priests. Several others had been arrested, but were finally acquitted. Their offence was that they had exhorted their parishioners to join the revolt and to demand bread below the market price. But as a body the clergy had restrained their parishioners, and Turgot later commended them for their behaviour, in some instances giving them considerable rewards. And what is true of the clergy—that a number of wilder spirits joined in when the trouble had begun—holds good of the lawyers, who were little men chiefly without a reputation to stake. There were simply no signs of concerted activity upon the part of Maupeou's fallen magistrates, or, for that matter, upon the part of those who had recently returned to power.

There remain the Prince de Conti and Terray's monopolists. Gustave Bord has maintained that the riot was the work of the corn speculators, whose calculations had been upset when Turgot, in liquidating Terray's administration, flooded the market with grain to the value of 6,400,000 *livres*. If that is so, then their motive was to create a shortage in order that they might get rid of their stocks at a good price before the next harvest, and also to prevent the influx of corn brought in by bounties. That corn speculators sometimes adopted such tactics is evident from a letter which Turgot wrote to Condorcet in 1771 describing an organized riot at Clermont. It is highly significant that the Government promptly arrested Sorin de Bonne and his partner Doumerck. But nothing, as we have seen, was proved against them. It is possible, of course, that other speculators organized the riot in a frantic attempt to raise the price of corn. Yet at the time suspicions of people usually well informed fell almost without exception upon the Prince de Conti. Véri (who on this point is somewhat vague, though he may have dealt more fully with it in the parts of his diary which are lost), Turgot himself (though the assertion rests on the unreliable word of Marmontel), and also Louis—all seem to have believed that it was Conti's that was the master-mind of the plot. Du Pont, in his correspondence with the Margrave of Baden, states that Conti, Cardinal Laroche-Aymon (the Grant Almoner), and Souche (the Grand Provost) were incensed with Turgot because they believed that he was about to abolish the guilds, from which they drew considerable revenues, Morellet and Baudeau having imprudently announced that an edict suppressing the communities had been prepared. Du Pont adds that these conspirators were joined by members of the clergy and magistracy, by courtiers and financiers, and (he hints) also by grain speculators.

No man was more capable than Conti of carrying out such a bold adventure. Possessed of much courage of a wild and romantic kind, of good looks and fine bearing, all of which gained him many daring friends, yet he was arrogant, intolerant, and quick to take revenge on those who crossed his path; and a staunch upholder of feudal privilege, he was greatly attached to his high prerogatives. He had quarrelled, for instance, with Marie-Antoinette on the occasion of the Archduke Maximilian's stay in France, his complaint being that the Austrian prince had not visited him. For years he had nursed other grievances against the Court. Falling from favour in 1757, he had formed the Court of the Temple, and from there had directed a constant opposition to the King and Ministers. It was from the Temple Press that the *Correspondance secrète de Maupeou et de Sorhouet* had been issued, while the *Mémoires de Beaumarchais* had been paid for with his money. From first to last he was a *frondeur*. He had now conceived a hatred for Turgot and his policy. It is therefore possible that it was he who organized the riots, and all the more likely because the insurgents first began to move in the region of his estate, L'Isle d'Adam. By what means did he recruit his army? It may be (though this is highly conjectural) that he utilized the services of the *Illuminés,* a freemasonry organization founded in 1762, or perhaps the Order of the Grand Orient, which had been established in 1772 with the future Philip Egalité as Grand Master. Danican's *Le Fléau des Tyrans* (1797) definitely attributes the corn riots of 1775 to the Templar Jacobins.

But if Louis had any evidence against the Prince de Conti, he never acted upon it. Perhaps he thought that Conti's waiting grave would soon render punishment superfluous; or perhaps he feared to stir into greater activity Conti's subversive movement. Neither Louis nor Turgot struck boldly. Two wretches were hanged, as Carlyle tells us three times over, on "a new gallows forty feet high," one a master wig-maker, the other a gauze-maker, and they cried that they were dying for the people. The assassins of Lally, Calas, and La Barre protested. Turgot and Louis, it appears, had no share in this butchery, which was simply a matter of police routine. On that same day, 11 May, they issued an amnesty to those who would return peacefully to their homes, and they threatened to treat as vagabonds all people wandering without a licence. As the news of the flour war had gone round, the peasants, led by agitators who said that they brought instructions from the King, began to riot and to burn the barns. But order was restored by the intendants employing the troops, and the amnesty soon produced a salutary effect. The situation was well in hand (though the precaution of guarding the markets was continued in Paris throughout the summer) and Turgot began the laborious and costly task of granting the indemnities that he had promised.

He now proceeded to increase the liberty of the grain trade, issuing in all no less than twenty-three separate regulations towards this end, some of general application and some designed to meet local circumstances. On 2 June, as a result of numerous petitions from the towns, he abolished the *octrois* on grain, flour, and bread in all parts of the kingdom excepting Paris and Marseilles. That same month he suppressed the privileged companies of porters and grain merchants at Rouen, who, enjoying also a monopoly in neighbouring towns of Normandy, impeded the movement of corn to Paris. Later, in conjunction with the Minister for War, he attempted, and in part succeeded in, reducing the monopolist purchases of the army contractors. Again, in collaboration with Vergennes he was planning reciprocity treaties with European Powers. In October 1775 he permitted a coastal trade in corn and flour so that supplies might more easily pass by water from one region to another. Next year he drew up a project for the suppression of feudal dues on grain. Already the provincial Estates of Burgundy had abolished these charges and had provided indemnities for the owners; but elsewhere there had been an increasing number of sheer defaults, and in July 1775 he found it necessary to make it known that the grain rents had not been abolished by the King. The next month he caused all owners of these dues to present within half a year their titles to these rights and he established a commission to hold an inquiry. It was as a result of the information thus collected that he drew up the project of suppression. But he fell from power before executing this reform, having previously failed to persuade the Estates of Languedoc to undertake a similar reform. He had also hoped to abolish the *banalités* (or restrictions and levies upon milling) throughout the kingdom; but he allowed his project to remain a dead letter, finding that the burden of indemnities would be greater than the existing obligations. More serious actually than the *banalités* were the monopolies of the guilds of bakers. Hence he encouraged the intendants to establish a just ratio between the price of grain and that of bread—in fact, to do what he himself had done while at Limoges. "If the Guilds of Bakers," he wrote, "are an obstruction to the fixing of a just proportion, then there will be another reason for hastening the day when this profession will be thrown open to all. . . ." Yet, except for establishing freedom of the bread trade in Lyon, he did not follow up this threat—not until he abolished the guilds of Paris.

The grain riots, while increasing Turgot's credit with the King, led to many attempts to undermine his power. Libels poured forth in great profusion. One caricature, which was widely distributed, depicted Turgot driving with Mme d'Enville in a coach drawn by Baudeau, Roubaud, Vaines, Du Pont and other economists. One of the scenes showed the coach capsized by a heap of grain, with Turgot and the Duchess in a most indecent posture and the words "Freedom, freedom, complete freedom."

But of all the writings that appeared none caused greater stir than Necker's *La Legislation et le commerce des grains*. In some measure the *Nechromanie* of later years was now anticipated. Taciturn, cold, silent, and aloof, Necker loved humanity in the mass rather than as individuals. His life had been spent in an impersonal and narrow world of commercial speculation; he had that arrogance that comes from success in early ventures, and all the assurance of men of little minds. He was one of those people whose ideas were so shallow that he was practised, and even eloquent, in what he had to say. His glib patter brought him many friends among an aristocracy which never thoroughly despised wealth of plebeian origin; and that same confidence and ease of manner were to captivate and deceive even Louis himself. For Necker, Geneva's hell was sufficiently real, and commercial prudence such an adequate buttress to conscience, that he was disarmingly honest; he had come by money fairly, even as a corn speculator; and he quickly acquired an influential following. His wife had opened her own *salon,* but this, dedicated not to culture, but to Necker himself, was merely the door through which he passed from the counting-house to the world of letters; and Necker won admirers not because he defended mercantilist theories with any degree of skill, but merely because he, a successful man from the world of finance, had chosen to defend them.

About the time that Turgot was preparing the free-trade law of September 1774, Necker was writing a defence of Galiani. According to Morellet, a mutual friend, Necker offered to read Turgot his work in manuscript so that it might be decided whether it was suitable for publication. Turgot replied drily and hastily that, speaking for himself, Necker might publish what he pleased and the public would judge his work upon its merits. Bachaumont's legend that Turgot tried to suppress the book is entirely without foundation. He could easily have done so, but, as Morellet shows, he upheld always the freedom of the Press, providing opinions were honestly and academically expressed. As a matter of course the royal censor examined Necker's work and deleted several passages, but Turgot insisted that it should be published as it stood.

It was not until 19 April 1775 that Necker applied for a licence to sell his book. Sales began on 20 April, and the first edition was soon sold out. On 23 April Turgot was presented with a copy. He wrote to Necker: ". . . I should have waited for a more peaceful moment, when the matter would have interested only those people who can judge it without passion." Necker replied that he had sent his book to the printers on 12 March, when there was no shortage of grain, and that he would gladly have withheld its publication had he been asked to do so. Morellet holds that Necker was in the right, and there is no obvious cause to disagree with this opinion. But some of Turgot's partisans accused Necker of being one of Conti's agents. If he were, then it is reasonable to suppose that, in view of his career and character, he was the dupe rather than an active accomplice. Necker was a vain man. Did Conti, then, and his agents lay their plans so deeply that they provided an "independent authority" to justify the revolt in the eyes of the world? It is possible. Necker's work was completed in September 1774. Publication was delayed for over six months; and there is no evidence that Necker revised his work or that any opponent obstructed him. It is obvious that Turgot himself suspected some design. Yet he remained always true to his principles. . . .

With him [Turgot] there was now no real danger that a utopian zeal would lead him to embark on schemes which were administratively impossible. He was merely moving too fast for those who did not want to move at all. The pace that he wished to set was determined by his own abilities and by the administrative machine that he handled. There is no evidence that in this respect he was guilty of any grave miscalculations. The accusation, made by his enemies and frequently repeated by historians, that he failed to prepare men's minds for his reforms is quite beside the point. Actually there was really no question of preparing men's minds in the sense of coaxing them gradually to discern the light of reason. There was no question, because those very minds that were hostile to him would have resented the preparation which would have appeared, and indeed did appear to them, more revolutionary than his moderate measures of reform. Ideas do not triumph by their mere quality according to a law of gradual dissemination which it is dangerous to violate. Nor can constant reiteration of these ideas in a rational form gain for them acceptance in a world moved by forces of a different kind—though Turgot himself at times seemed to think that it could. In reality the only minds that could be prepared were those that needed no anterior appeal, but were already receptive—receptive, that is to say, not of the abstract principles upon which reforms were based, but of the particular benefits flowing from them. It was only by supplying the demand for reforms that Turgot could prepare men's minds. Yet to do this was also to create a determined opposition. His two most popular reforms, the suppression of the guilds and the abolition of the *corvées,* were precisely those that heightened the conflict. That these reforms were applauded by the masses there is not the slightest doubt. On the night of the *lit de justice* Paris was illuminated and there were great rejoicings and demonstrations among the working population. For once the magistrates were unpopular. In the provinces the peasants sang:

> Je n'irons plus aux chemins,
> Comme à la galère,
> Travailler soir et matin,
> Sans aucun salaire.[1]

And soon they were demanding the abolition of the feudal dues. "The provinces," wrote Véri, "felt that Turgot was their support; but," he adds, "their voices did not reach the King who believed that every one without exception hated the Comptroller-General."

Turgot's opponents renewed their efforts to bring about his downfall. The day after the *lit de justice* the magistrates reiterated their protests, and made

[1] I will no longer go to the roads,
  As to the galley,
  Working evening and morning,
  Without pay.

much of two incidents which seemed to justify their forebodings, the first the *jacquerie* upon the Marquis de Vibray's estates, which they attributed to a reading of Boncerf's brochure, the second, the brutal attack upon one of the Duc de Mortemart's relatives while he was hunting. Shortly afterwards the Parlement denounced a work, *Le Parfait Monarque,* which, having eulogized Joseph II, went on to advocate a popular rebellion against the vested interests at the Court. Seguier, in leading the attack, associated these doctrines with Turgot's policy and, when the Comptroller wrote to him vehemently answering the insinuation, the magistrates complained of effrontery to one of their officials.

Meanwhile a whole crop of libels made an appearance. One of the most scurrilous, *Les Mannéquins du gouvernement français,* which came from the pen of Monsieur, portrayed Louis and his adviser as the dupes of the charlatan, Turgot. Another, *Les Étonnements des Chartreux,* ridiculed the Ministers. A third, the *Prophétie Turgotine,* written by the Chevalier de Lisle, singled out Turgot as a visionary and an encyclopaedist who would overthrow the monarchy, the aristocracy, and the Church. A fourth, *Les Trois Maries,* libelled Mme d'Enville, Mme Blondel, and Mme Du Marchai. All these, and many more besides, circulated freely, and the composition of scurrilous literature became more than ordinarily the occupation of the Court. Whether Louis himself read these libels we do not know, but Maurepas certainly did, and now began to work in earnest for Turgot's disgrace. His task was made all the easier by the efforts of two intriguers, the one, Pezay, who was still plying Louis with his secret correspondence, the other d'Oigny, the *intendant général des postes.* It was to Pezay that Maurepas gave the copies of Turgot's budget for 1776, on the understanding that he should obtain the advice of experts and pass on the information to the King. As we have seen, one of the "auditors" was Necker, who seriously questioned the claims that Turgot was making. Mme Marmontel believed that Necker's report had brought about Turgot's downfall; and so did Morellet, who for several years refused to visit the Necker's house, but Du Pont holds that since Louis suspected an intrigue, the move produced no immediate effect. Probably it was d'Oigny's machinations that first shook Louis's faith in the Comptroller-General. A forged correspondence between Turgot and a friend was brought to his notice. At first the letters contained no offensive matter, but later, when it was felt that Louis was convinced of their authenticity, the forgers began to attribute to Turgot bitter comments upon the King and Queen. Louis consulted Maurepas, who gave as his opinion that the correspondence was genuine. At the same time other letters were intercepted in the post, and any containing accusations against Turgot were also placed before the King.

Yet these intrigues alone were not sufficient to bring about Turgot's dismissal. It had taken Louis some little time to decide to part with Abbé Terray, and it was most unlikely that he would make up his mind immediately to send Turgot a-packing. And much as Maurepas might want to be rid of his colleague, it was not his intention to appear too eager, for he was always sensitive to the danger that were he to come out into the open, he himself might be the victim of a sudden reaction upon the part of Louis. He preferred to retain his wonted pose of remaining aloofly and non-committally wise, and, by gentle insinuations, to help events to turn Louis's mind in a direction in which it would have been difficult to force it by argument. Merely by refraining from defending Turgot, and merely by confirming Louis's growing suspicions with a word here and there, he was bound in the long run to achieve his object. For everything that came to Louis's ears—facts endlessly distorted, fortuitous happenings which in normal times would have had little significance, the fatuous lies concocted by Turgot's detractors—all came to assume a unity and to take on the character of incontrovertible evidence, some of which, it must be admitted, deceived even Maurepas. One incident in particular gave plausibility to the growing case against the Comptroller. Delacroix, one of his nominees in the Finances, was discovered to be guilty of corruption. Louis said to Turgot: "Your departmental chief, Delacroix, is a rogue. He employs your name . . . to sell offices for his own profit." Turgot, who was taken by surprise, and who believed that here was yet another malicious invention, defended his subordinate with great fervour and appealed to the King to punish Delacroix's calumniators. But Louis pulled from his pocket a bundle of papers which the accusers had lodged with the Queen and, turning his back upon Turgot said, "I love neither rogues nor those who uphold them."

Another scandal, the *affaire Chanvallon,* was even more serious, for it concerned the Chevalier Turgot. The Chevalier had been appointed Governor of Guyane, a French colony which in 1763 Choiseul had attempted to transform into a centre for the defence of French America, in order to compensate the strategic weakness incurred by the loss of Canada. The emigrants who had been poured into this pestilential and famine-stricken region had died like flies, and the intendant Chanvallon was made the scapegoat of the disaster. In 1764 the Chevalier Turgot had been sent out to arrest Chanvallon. But while he was in Guyane he disembarked other emigrants who, contrary to his advice, had been sent out by the Government. In turn he, too, was made the scapegoat of Choiseul's ill-planned measures and was dismissed from office. Chanvallon was even less fortunate: he was forced to pay out of his own pocket for Masses for the souls of the deceased emigrants, to found a hospital in the colony, and to undergo detention at Mont-Saint-Michel. In 1775 he appealed against the sentence upon the technical point that evidence favourable to him had not been heard. Sartine and Turgot examined the affair, and their finding was that the trial had been legally conducted. Exactly one year later Sartine, without informing Turgot, lodged with Louis a dossier of papers, asking that the case should be heard in secret before fresh commissioners. Louis informed Turgot, who immediately suspected, and this time quite rightly, that here was yet another intrigue to diminish his credit.

Véri, before leaving for the country, had advised him to write frequently to the King in defence of his policy, and thus to discredit his enemies. He took this counsel, and it is in one of these letters, one dated 30 April, which Soulavie found among the King's papers at the Tuileries, that we may read of his efforts to expose his calumniators. Having first of all denounced d'Oigny's vile plot and having warned the King of the dangers of trusting to information obtained from the *cabinet noir,* he went on to discuss the *affaire Chanvallon.* He explained that evidence could not possibly have been suppressed, and then proceeded to inquire into the motives that had led Sartine to reopen the inquiry. "Last year," he wrote, "the arrival of M. de Malesherbes at the Ministry and the favours Your Majesty bestowed upon me, gave no hope of my being overthrown. . . . This year the (impending) retreat of M. Malesherbes, the more decided union of all parties against me, my absolute isolation, the enmity of M. Miromesnil, which is common knowledge, and his influence over M. de Maurepas—all show that I hang by a thread only. It is necessary (for them) to break that strand by arranging secretly a new plot which revives an old affair long forgotten. . . . These are the reasons why the conduct of M. Sartine in 1776 is so different from his conduct in 1775. Your Majesty has done me the honour to tell me that it is neither a question of my own behaviour nor even of my brother's. Admittedly! These gentlemen are too adroit to announce at first their project in its entirety. They know their trade too well." Turgot went on to describe the plot in detail, and to show that it was neither for the love of justice, nor for the peace of mind of the unhappy Chanvallon that the matter had been raised, but out of hatred for himself; and he concluded: "As for the rest, Sire, I have been able very easily to explain clearly this intrigue, which will serve to let you know these men a little. . . . I shall inform M. de Maurepas and I shall make him feel the indecency of this subterfuge. I shall demand from M. de Sartine that M. Chanvallon's request shall be taken before the original commissioners to see if there is any ground for action. I am sure that M. de Sartine seeing himself exposed will return to the right path."

But by this time yet another protracted affair was taking a course which was dangerous to Turgot. On 22 January the decision had been taken in the Council to recall the Comte de Guines, who, contrary to instructions, had informed the English Court that France would give neither direct nor even indirect assistance to the English colonies. Malesherbes had convinced the Queen of the urgency of this move, but Vergennes had been afraid to carry out instructions for fear he should displease her. Turgot and Malesherbes exhorted their Sovereign to act upon the decision, but, when a week passed by and nothing happened, they feared that some intrigue had caused Louis and Marie-Antoinette to change their minds. Turgot wrote a letter to the King imploring him to act at once and, on going to learn the answer, found that Louis stood by his original intention. But the Queen, evidently under the influence of the Choiseulistes, was making difficulties. She had insisted—and Louis had agreed—that no successor to Guines should be appointed, on the ground that the Ambassador would justify his conduct publicly on his return. This challenge upon the part of the Choiseulistes placed the Ministry in a quandary, because to take it up meant the disclosure of diplomatic secrets. Turgot's suggestion was that the matter should be thrashed out and Guines's dispatches read in the hearing of the King, the Queen, Malesherbes, Vergennes, and himself. In no way did he resent the Queen's share in political affairs. All that he wished to do was to save her from becoming the dupe of political adventurers. But on 9 February the Queen talked for an hour with Choiseul at the Opera, and later declared against Turgot's plan, being convinced, it seems, that the recall of the Ambassador was a plot engineered by him and his accessory, Malesherbes, to regain the favour of the Comte de Maurepas.

When Guines returned from London on 25 February he received a warm reception from the Choiseulistes, who continued to clamour for a public inquiry, in hopes of embarrassing Maurepas's Ministry. This demand met with no success, and it is probable that the Queen could not bring herself to favour it wholeheartedly. It is even likely that at this point she bore no real grudge against Turgot and Malesherbes. Véri, in his entry for 4 March, where he is obviously citing information received from Abbé de Vermond, states that Marie-Antoinette admired Turgot's courage and honesty and despised thoroughly the crafty Maurepas, who once again had been attempting to bargain with her. But a few days later, just before leaving to spend the spring-time in the provinces, Véri heard that the Queen had been saying in public that she gave Turgot only a fortnight more in office. Véri suspected that Maurepas had been busy, and sounded him upon the matter, but receiving an evasive answer, left at once for his abbaye Saint-Satur. What had probably happened in the meantime is that which Mercy relates to Marie-Thérèse in a letter of 13 April, in which he announces his intention of doing his utmost to keep Marie-Antoinette clear of intrigue. "I have discovered," he wrote, "and have made it known to the Queen, that the Comtesse de Polignac is obviously won over by the Comte de Maurepas and is acting with him. My evidence with regard to this goes so far as to prove that the Comtesse de Polignac has attempted . . . to persuade the Queen that it would be in her interest to prevail upon the King to appoint the Comte de Maurepas prime minister." Mercy's efforts, however, were unavailing, and it is without doubt that the Choiseulistes and their allies at the Court succeeded ultimately in turning the Queen against the Comptroller. Mairobert's account of Marie-Antoinette's words to Louis after her cold reception at the Opera is probably true: "I would like to see you there, Sire, with your Saint-Germain and your Turgot. I believe that you would be rudely hooted." Nevertheless it is most unlikely that she played a decisive part in bringing about Turgot's downfall. Though she had become in some measure the agent of the Choiseulistes, she was never a party to the whole of their design, but merely to the lesser aim of obtaining satisfaction for the Comte de Guines. Nor did she fall easily into the snare set by Maurepas, who wanted her assistance in order that he himself remaining in the background might later throw upon her the blame for Turgot's dismissal. She had learned to be wary of Maurepas's movements; and he, finding the Queen an unwilling accomplice, in the end dispensed with her aid.

Events, it must be admitted, did not run altogether in Maurepas's favour. His wife, whose wishes he always respected, was not at all anxious to see Turgot overthrown, and was inopportunely demanding the recall of d'Aiguillon. Again, even though the Comptroller might be disgraced, a satisfactory successor must be found, or else the fruits of victory might be lost. It was with the greatest caution that Maurepas made his final moves. Rather than attempt openly to dislodge Turgot, he thought it advisable first to expedite Malesherbes's departure, thinking that Turgot might then resign. In the King's presence he assumed an air of injured innocence. "Here are two men," he said, "whom I have given to you. . . . The one, Malesherbes, leaves you in time of difficulty; the other, Turgot, threatens to resign if you do not follow his advice on all occasions." For a long while Malesherbes had talked of going and, much to Turgot's consternation, after the *lit de justice* wanted to retire immediately. His departure had been fixed for Whitsuntide, all promises to relieve him of administrative detail and all Turgot's entreaties having failed to make him change his mind. As early as the end of April, Maurepas was trying to persuade Louis to appoint a successor at once. Already he had made an agreement with Marie-Antoinette that together they would secure the Household for Sartine. But some time later Maurepas endeavoured to revise the bargain, and proposed Amelot, his own nephew, for the office, believing that Marie-Antoinette would be satisfied if a dukedom were given to the Comte de Guines. The Queen was angry. She accused Maurepas of breaking faith, and told him that she would have no haggling in having justice done to Guines. She soon gave proof of her assertion. She caused Louis, who consulted no Minister on the matter, to give the Ambassador a dukedom and to write to him an honourable letter, which she herself revised three times, expressing the greatest satisfaction with his conduct.

Maurepas's manoeuvre to advance Amelot meant that Turgot would be isolated in the Ministry and that his plans for the reform of the Household—to say nothing of other schemes he was preparing—could not possibly be carried out. Upon hearing what Maurepas was doing (he was not informed officially but learned of it from the public), he wrote straightway, on 30 April, to Véri, imploring him to return. "Oh, if you were only here, at least you would prevail upon them (M. and Mme de Maurepas) to make a reasonable choice—as would be that of M. Fourqueux. I dare not tell you all. Change your plans for your journey and return. But I can tell you that it concerns the honour of your friends, the peace and glory of the King, and the welfare of more than twenty million men during all his reign and perhaps for centuries, for we know what roots evil pushes down into this unfortunate land and what it takes to pull them up. . . ." Yet perhaps, he added playfully, the Abbé Véri, like a true rustic, only wanted rain for his fields. Véri did not return. He hated more than ever being the focus of ministerial intrigues; but, he subsequently confessed, he would have returned immediately had he foreseen that Maurepas, in working for Turgot's downfall, would make such headway. Turgot, who would have liked him as a successor to Malesherbes, later rebuked him for showing no enthusiasm to enter the Ministry. Yet while he would have accepted responsibilities had he been invited, he was not disposed to intrigue his own way into office. Nor at this stage could he have done so, for Maurepas was beginning to regard him as Turgot's disciple and political agent.

On 30 April, Turgot wrote another letter, his second of that date to the King. He first complains of the cruel silence with which Louis had received him on the previous Sunday and also of Louis's failure to reply to earlier letters, in which he had intimated that he could no longer carry on unless he were given full support. "I cannot conceive, Sire," he continued, "that from levity of heart you will consent to sacrifice all your reign and the welfare of your people: it would be necessary to think that Your Majesty had not believed a single word I had said or written. . . . Sire, it was my opinion that Your Majesty, having a love of justice and goodness graven in his heart, merited to be served with affection. I gave myself up to such service; and I have seen my recompense in your happiness and in that of your people. . . . What is my reward to-day? Your Majesty surely sees how impossible it is for me to resist those who hinder me . . . and yet Your Majesty gives me neither help nor consolation. Sire, I have not merited this treatment. . . ." At this point Turgot warns Louis of the dangers to the royal authority, contending that "the Parlements are already more impassioned, more audacious, more linked with cabals of the Court," than in 1770. This done, he denounces Maurepas for listening to Miromesnil, who, fearing that Véri might succeed Malesherbes, had suggested that the incapable Amelot should have the Household. Nor is this all. He openly accuses Maurepas of attempting to bring about his dismissal. "I would not be astonished," he writes, "to learn that your confidence had changed, since M. de Maurepas, who tells every one he fears my systems, will undoubtedly have told Your Majesty. He has certainly informed M. de Malesherbes . . . that, if he had kept the Abbé Terray, receipts at present would balance expenditure, which would be true if the Abbé Terray had imposed 20 millions of taxes or had defaulted to the extent of that sum. I wish for your sake, Sire, that he has not communicated to you this way of thinking." Turgot now goes on to attribute Maurepas's manoeuvres to weakness of character—his inability to keep a course, his deference to his wife's opinions, his petty fears, and his susceptibility to the murmurs at the Court. "My own character," he continues, "which is firmer than his, must naturally place him in the shade. My external timidity perhaps gave him, especially at first, some consolation; but I have reason to believe that quite soon he came to fear that I would obtain Your Majesty's confidence independently of him." Then, having explained that he would not have spoken thus of Maurepas were he not convinced that the King and his authority were imperilled, he again implores Louis to be firm and unflinching; and it is here that occurs a famous passage which, until the discovery of Véri's diary, was the only part of the letter to be known. "Do not forget, Sire,"—so the passage runs—"that it was weakness that placed the head of Charles I on the block; it was weakness that made Charles IX cruel; it was weakness that led to the formation of the League under Henry III, that made Louis XIII and makes the King of Portugal today crowned slaves; it was weakness that led to all the unhappiness of the last reign." Turgot finally answers his accusers: "You have been told that I am hotheaded and flighty: it hardly seems to me that all I tell you resembles the words of a fool; to me it seems that even the measures I have introduced, in spite of the outcries and resistance to which they have led, have succeeded precisely as I announced."

Véri, while admitting that Turgot's habit of speaking the truth, even when it was unpleasant, was in itself highly laudable and usually efficacious, holds that Maurepas would have been perfectly justified in pressing for the dismissal of a Minister who thus denounced his colleagues to their master. But Véri has no wish to make out a case for Maurepas. On the contrary, he explains that, as Maurepas was determined to dismiss Turgot before the letters were written, Turgot had no other course than to make this frantic effort to enlighten the King.

Louis maintained a disconcerting silence. On 10 May he interviewed Clugny, the intendant of Bordeaux. That same day Turgot wrote to Véri: "Well, my friend, all is said and done. Your old friend has used such energy and such art to come by his object that he decided the King this morning. He has just announced to Malesherbes that the King will send for him this evening or to-morrow to resign, and he has announced to him Amelot as his successor. I have reason to believe that he has been working for a long time in a masterly fashion to ruin your two friends. He is counting with reason upon my resignation, and I know . . . he has spoken to M. de Clugny. In a few days' time I was to have placed before the King a plan of reform for the Royal Household: it will surely not be adopted, and I will ask for my liberty. I shall part with the regret of seeing a good dream disappear, of seeing a young King, who deserves a better fate, and a kingdom lost entirely by one who ought to have saved it. But I shall depart without shame and without remorse, and I shall see how I can make my leisure useful."

It was Mme Blondel who had advised Turgot to resign. But later Mme d'Enville implored him to remain to the bitter end. Much earlier—actually in March—he had told Véri that he would never give in, because he believed that truth was always likely to triumph over lies and intrigue. So, after writing to Véri, he journeyed to Versailles to see the King. "What do you want?" said Louis. "I have not the time to see you." The next day, Saturday 11 May, he went again to Versailles. Louis was hunting. He called later, but Louis was dressing. He left intending to return the following day. But on 12 May the old Minister Bertin carried to him the King's demand to resign his office. That same day Malesherbes handed in his resignation. "You are a happy man," said Louis; "would that I could also leave my post." In December 1792 Louis was on trial before the Convention. Malesherbes had volunteered to defend him. One wonders, did they remember and did they regret their failure to uphold Turgot sixteen years before? Did they reflect upon what might have happened had they chosen to do so?

"What you, my friend, might have foreseen has happened," wrote Turgot to Véri on 14 May. Then, having denounced Maurepas for leaving the young King to the flux and reflux of the cabals, he gently reprimands Véri for failing to return and to strive for office. "Good-bye, my friend," he added. "I will pardon you if you come to see me." Four days later, on 18 May, he wrote his farewell letter to the King, having received permission through the intercession of the Comte d'Angivillers. It is a dignified and noble letter. It contains no petulant accusations against Maurepas and the Ministers, for these were now certainly uncalled for. All that he complained of was that Louis had dismissed him in such a cruel fashion and had denied him a hearing; and once again he asked that he should be given the chance to answer any charges that might be made against him. Then for the future he wished the King well. "All I wish, Sire, is that you may always believe that my vision was wrong, and that I pointed out to you chimerical dangers. I hope that time will not justify me, that your reign will be as happy and as tranquil for you and your people as your principles of justice and your concern for the public good once promised." To these words Louis made no reply. Yet again, one wonders, did he ever reflect upon them at a later time?